Formal Analysis for Natural Language Processing:
A Handbook

Zhiwei Feng

Formal Analysis for Natural Language Processing: A Handbook

UNIVERSITY OF SCIENCE AND TECHNOLOGY OF CHINA PRESS

Zhiwei Feng
Institute of Applied Linguistics
Ministry of Education of the People's
Republic of China
Beijing, China

Translated by
Lan Sun
Xiaowei He
Bo Sun

ISBN 978-981-16-5174-8   ISBN 978-981-16-5172-4 (eBook)
https://doi.org/10.1007/978-981-16-5172-4

Funded by Chinese Fund for the Humanities and Social Sciences
Jointly published with University of Science and Technology of China Press
The print edition is not for sale in China (Mainland). Customers from China (Mainland) please order the
print book from: University of Science and Technology of China Press.
ISBN of the Co-Publisher's edition: 978-7-312-04130-3

This Springer imprint is published by the registered company Springer Nature Singapore Pte Ltd.
The registered company address is: 152 Beach Road, #21-01/04 Gateway East, Singapore 189721,
Singapore

Preface

The use of computer technology to study and process the natural language started in the late 1940s and 1950s. Over the past 60 years, this research termed the natural language processing (NLP) has made considerable progress, becoming an important emerging subject in contemporary computer science. In the age of information network, NLP has attracted an increasing attention from scholars, including computer experts and linguists, and has become a typical interdisciplinary subject, which is closely integrated with liberal arts and sciences. Now that we have entered the era of artificial intelligence (AI), NLP, an important part of artificial intelligence, has become a bright pearl on the crown of AI.

Due to the complexity of the natural language, it is incredibly hard to handle it straightly by computer. To render the natural language to be directly processed by computer, we need to abstract "problems" from NLP in relation to its processing requirements in various NLP applications. The problems abstracted then have to be formalized in terms of linguistics so as to establish a "formal model" of the natural language, which can be further expressed in a certain mathematical form in a strict and regular manner, known as algorithm. Finally, to be realized on computer, a computational model of NLP should be established. In NLP, the algorithm, a means to implement a formal model, depends on the formal model whereas the formal model is the essence of the natural language computer processing. Therefore, to establish formal models of the natural language is very important, as it is essentially the basic theoretical research in NLP.

This book, a handbook on the formal analysis of NLP, systematically summarizes and discreetly sorts out various NLP theories and methods. The handbook is composed of two parts, History Review and Forma Models, with 12 chapters in all. In Part I, a brief historical retrospect of NLP has been presented and pioneering studies of the language computing have been introduced. Part II has been largely devoted to a description of formal models, including the ones based on phrase structure grammar, on unification operation, on dependency and valence, and on lexicalism as well. Formal models for automatic semantic processing, for contextual and pragmatic automatic processing, discourse analysis, probabilistic grammar, neural networks and deep learning, and knowledge graph have also been accounted for. Finally, concluding remarks discuss the pros and cons of both the rationalist approach and the empirical one in the study of NLP and explores, tentatively, the ways to combine these two approaches.

I have been engaged in the research on NLP for more than 60 years. Over 60 years ago, I was still a young man who knew little of the world. Now, I am already an old man in my aging eighties. However, NLP that has fascinated our generation all the time is still an emerging discipline, young and full of youthful vitality. Although she is still in her adolescence, infantile and immature, she has undoubtedly a brilliant and promising prospect. Although a man's life is limited, the exploration and research of scientific knowledge is unlimited. Compared with the evergreen towering tree of science, our lives are so insignificant, just like drops of water in the ocean. Every time I think of it, I find myself constantly pondering over what life should be. To live a fulfilling life, I believe we should love reading, as books are our best friends and that we should work hard, as it is diligence that leads us to the top. All of us should make the best use of our limited time to explore the unknown.

This handbook can be used as a reference and guide for the analysis of NLP. Anyone interested in NLP, researchers, engineering technicians, teachers, under-graduates, or graduate students, can learn from it something captivating about it. It can also be used as a self-study material, or as a textbook for learners of NLP and of computational linguistics in colleges and universities, or as teaching aids for those taking artificial intelligence courses.

In writing this handbook, I have consulted many works by domestic and foreign scholars, especially the first and second editions of *Speech and Language Processing* by D. Jurafsky and J. Martin. Without their work, the publication of mine would not have been possible. Herein, I express my sincere gratitude to all of them.

This handbook covers knowledge from linguistics, computer science, mathematics, and some other fields. I am alone responsible for the mistakes and errors that might occur in the handbook. All comments and criticisms are highly appreciated.

Beijing, China   Zhiwei Feng
February 2020

Contents

About the Author

Zhiwei Feng is a computational linguist and senior research fellow at the Institute of Applied Linguistics, Ministry of Education, China. He has a broad and extensive background in linguistics, mathematics and computer science, and has been engaged in interdisciplinary research in linguistics, mathematics and computer science for more than 50 years. One of the first natural language processing and computational linguistics scholars in China, he has published more than 30 books and more than 400 papers in China and abroad. He is the winner of the NLPCC (Natural Language Processing & Chinese Computing) Distinguished Achievement Award of the CCF (China Computer Federation) in 2018.

Acronyms

Preface

AI   Artificial intelligence
NLP   Natural language processing

Chapter 1

AAC   Augmentative and alternative communication
ALPAC   Automatic Language Processing Advisory Committee
ARPA   Advanced Research Project Agency
BDI   Belief-desire-intention
CFG   Context-free grammar
CNN   Convolutional neural network
DARPA   Defense Advanced Research Projects Agency
DL   Deep learning
DOC   Dictionary on computer
DSP   Digital signal processing
FAHQMT Fully automatic, high-quality machine translation
FUG   Functional unification grammar
HLT   Human language technique
HMM   Hidden Markov model
HPSG   Head-driven phrase structure grammar
HTML   HyperText Makeup Language
HTTP   Hypertext Transfer Protocol
IBM   International Business Machines Corporation
IP   Internet protocol
LFG   Lexical functional grammar
LSTM   Long-short-time memory
LW   Language weaver
ML   Machine learning

MT	Machine translation
NIST	National Institute of Standards and Technology
NLU	Natural language understanding
NMT	Neural machine translation
NN	Neural network
OCR	Optical character recognition
PBMT	Phrase-based machine translation
PCFG	Probabilistic context-free grammar
PCR	Printed character recognition
RNN	Recurrent neural network model
SMT	Statistical machine translation
SMTS	Statistical machine translation software
SRC	Science Research Committee
TCP	Transmission control protocol
TDAP	Transformation and discourse analysis project
TTS	Transformation and text interpretation for text-to-speech
URL	Universal Resource Locator
W3C	World Wide Web Consortium

Chapter 2

CCG	Combinatory categorial grammar
LSP	Linguistic string parser
MIT	Massachusetts Institute of Technology
TTP	Tagged text parser

Chapter 3

ATN	Augmented transition network
CYK	Cocke-Younger-Kasami algorithm
DAG	Directed acyclic graph
DBS	Database semantics
FSTD	Finite state transition diagram
GSP	General syntactic processor
LTAG	Lexicalized tree adjoining grammar
NAG	Numbered arc graph
PSG	Phrase structure grammar
RTN	Recursive transition network
SLIM	Surface compositional linear internal matching
SRG	Semantic relations graph
TAG	Tree adjoining grammar
TAL	Tree adjoining language
UG	Universal grammar

Chapter 4

CAP	Control agreement principle
DCG	Definite clause grammar
DSP	Di-State Principle
FCR	Feature co-occurrence restriction
FD	Functional description
FFP	Foot feature principle
FSD	Feature specification default
GPSG	Generalized phrase structure grammar
HFC	Head feature convention
LMT	Lexical mapping theory
LPS	Linear precedence statement

Chapter 5

DUG	Dependency unification grammar
FGD	Functional generative description
IMAG	Institute of Applied Mathematics
PVP	Probabilistic valency pattern

Chapter 6

BSO	Brandeis Semantic Ontology
GLML	Generative Lexicon Markup Language
GLT	Generative lexicon theory
LADL	Laboratoire Automatique de Documentation Linguistique
LCP	Lexical conceptual paradigm
POS	Part of speech
WSD	Word sense disambiguation

Chapter 7

AP	Associated Press
AVP	Attribute-value pairs
B	Basic expression
BNC	British National Corpus
CD	Conceptual dependency
CNI	Construct null instantiated
DNI	Definite null instantiated
ELI	English language interpreter
EPROM	Erasable programmable read-only memory
FE	Frame element
FRUMP	Fast reading understanding and memory program
INI	Indefinite null instantiated
IPP	Integrated partial parser
KDG	Kernel dependency graph
MARGIE	Meaning analysis, response generation and inference of English

ME   Meaningful expressions
MOP   Memory organization packet
MTM   Meaning-text model
MTT   Meaning-text theory
NSF   National Scientific Foundation
OUP   Oxford University Press
PAM   Plan applier mechanism
PTQ   Proper treatment of quantification
RDF   Resource description framework
SAM   Script applier mechanism

Chapter 8
DAMSL   Dialogue act markup in several layers
PDA   Personal data assistant

Chapter 9
CP   Cue phrase
HCI   Human-computer interaction
N-S   Nucleus-satellite
RRC   Restrictive relative clause
RST   Rhetorical structure theory

Chapter 10
SCFG   Stochastic context-free grammar

Chapter 11
BERT   Bidirectional Encoder Representations from Transformers
BLEU   Bi-Lingual Evaluation Understudy
BP   Backpropagation
CAM   Content-addressable memory
CAP   Credit assignment problem
CBOW   Continuous-bag-of-word
DA   Direct assessment
DS   Source domain
DT   Target domain
FCNN   Fully connected neural network
FNN   Feed-forward neural network
FSA   Finite state automaton
GNMT   Google Neural Machine Translation
LSA   Latent semantic analysis
LSI   Latent semantic indexing
MANN   Memory augmented neural network
MLM   Masked language model
MN   Memory network

MSRA	Microsoft Research Asia
NLG	Natural language generation
NLI	Natural language inference
PCA	Principal components analysis
PDP	Parallel distributed processing
PMI	Pointwise mutual information
PPMI	Positive-pointwise-mutual information
QA	Question answering
RAM	Random access memory
SIFT	Scale-invariant feature transform
SRN	Simple recurrent network
SVD	Singular value decomposition
XNLI	Cross-lingual natural language inference

Chapter 12

CVT	Compound value type
NBA	National Basketball Association
RDFs	RDF schema
SQL	Structure query language
URI	Universal resource identifier

Chapter 13

ACL	Association of computational linguistics
DNN	Deep neural network
EACL	European association of computational linguistics
LDC	Linguistic data consortium
SIGDAT	Special interest group for data

Part I
History Review

Chapter 1
Past and Present of Natural Language Processing

The use of computer technology to study and process the natural language started in the late 1940s and the early 1950s. Over the past 60 years, this research has made considerable progress and has become an important emerging discipline in the contemporary computer science. In the network information age, NLP has attracted an increasing attention, becoming a globally significant learning. Various theories and methods have been proposed. This handbook is a manual on formal analyses of NLP, being devoted to a systematic summary of NLP theories and methods developed so far with emphasis on its formal models.

In the era of the Industrial Revolution, humans needed to explore the physical world. Therefore, the study of atoms and basic particles became a very important discipline, as the physical world is composed of them. However, in the information network era, NLP that studies the structure of languages is bound to become a very important subject, like physics, in the near future, for the information network is mainly composed of languages. Physics studies laws of physical movements in the world, while NLP studies rules of languages, information carriers, in the world of information networks. I believe that NLP is completely comparable to physics in terms of its significance and that both of them will become two pillars in the scientific world. Although it is my intuitive estimate, I believe it will become a reality.

This chapter first introduces the basic concepts of NLP, then reviews its historical development, and finally discusses its current characteristic features.

1.1 What Is Natural Language Processing?

The research and processing of the natural language by computer should generally include four aspects, formalization, algorithmization, programming, and practicalization.

© Springer Nature Singapore Pte Ltd. 2023
Z. Feng, *Formal Analysis for Natural Language Processing: A Handbook*,
https://doi.org/10.1007/978-981-16-5172-4_1

First, we should formalize the problems to be studied in terms of linguistics and establish a formal model of the language so that it can be expressed strictly and regularly in a certain mathematical form. This process can be called formalization.

Second, we should express this strict and regular mathematical form in terms of an algorithm. This process can be called algorithmization.

Third, we need to write a computer program based on the algorithm and implement it on computer to formulate a variety of practical NLP systems. This process can be called programming.

Fourth, we should evaluate the established NLP system to continuously improve the quality and performance to meet its users' requirements. This process can be called practicalization.

Bill Manaris, an American computer scientist, defines NLP in his article entitled "Natural language processing: A human-computer interaction perspective" (vol. 47, in *Advances in Computers*, 1999) as what follows:

> NLP could be defined as the discipline that studies the linguistic aspects of human-human and human-machine communication, develops models of linguistic competence and performance, employs computational frameworks to implement process incorporating such models, identifies methodologies for iterative refinement of such processes/models, and investigates techniques for evaluating the result systems.[1]

Bill Manaris' definition of NLP fairly comprehensively expresses the above four aspects involved in the research and processing of the natural language by computer. We totally agree with his definition.

We believe that the establishment of NLP models requires nine specifications of linguistic knowledge:

1. Acoustics and prosody: knowledge needed to describe the rhythm, intonation, and tone of the language and to explain how speech forms phonemes.
2. Phonology: knowledge needed to describe the combination of phonemes and how phonemes form morphemes.
3. Morphology: knowledge needed to describe the combination of morphemes and to explain how morphemes form words.
4. Lexicology: knowledge needed to describe the rules of the lexical system and to explain the inherent semantic and grammatical properties of words.
5. Syntax: knowledge needed to describe the rules of structure between words (or phrases) and to explain how words (or phrases) form sentences.
6. Semantics: knowledge needed to describe semantic relationships between components of a sentence and to explain how to derive the meaning of the whole sentence from the components that make up the sentence.
7. Discourse analysis: knowledge needed to describe syntactic rules between sentences and to explain how sentences form discourse or dialogue.

---

[1] Bill Manaris: Natural language processing: A human-computer interaction perspective, *Advances in Computers*, Vol. 47, 1999.

8. Pragmatics: knowledge needed to describe the meaning of an utterance in relation to its context and to explain how to derive various meanings of the speech act related to the context in which it occurs.
9. Common sense encyclopedia knowledge: general knowledge needed to describe language users and the context of language use.

Of course, there are different views on the aspects of linguistic knowledge involved in NLP. Generally speaking, most NLP researchers believe that linguistic knowledge involved in NLP should, at least, include lexical, syntactic, semantic, and pragmatic specifications. And each specification conveys linguistic information in ways different from one another. For example, a lexical specification may cover knowledge of basic constituents at the word level (e.g., morphemes) and of its inflectional forms; a syntactic specification may involve knowledge of how words or phrases are combined to form sentences in a given language; a semantic one may involve knowledge of how to assign meanings to specific words or sentences; the pragmatic specification may involve knowledge of how to interpret a shift in the focus of discourse in a conversation and how to interpret the meaning of sentences in a given context.

We now explain in detail how these aspects of linguistic knowledge work in NLP. For instance, if we issue a verbal command to the computer, "Delete File X," we need to let the computer understand the meaning of this command through the NLP system, and to execute this command generally needs to go through the following processing processes (Fig. 1.1).

As can be seen from Fig. 1.1, the NLP system first converts the verbal demand, "Delete File X," into a phonemic string "dilet' # fail # eks" with its stored phonemic knowledge. Then, by using its morphological knowledge, the phoneme string is transformed into a morpheme series, "delete," "file," and "X," which is further converted into a word series with their corresponding parts of speech having been marked ("delete" VERB) ("file" NOUN) ("X" ID). After that, the NLP system goes on performing a syntactic analysis to get the syntactic structure of this word series represented by a tree diagram. The semantic interpretation of the syntactic structure, delete-file ("X"), and the final pragmatic interpretation of this verbal demand, "rm –i x," are secured before the verbal demand is finally executed by computer.

This example is taken from a speech understanding interface called UNIX Consultant designed for UNIX by Wilensky, an American NLP scholar. This speech understanding interface uses linguistic knowledge (Specifications 1 to 6 out of the 9 mentioned above) to get the semantic interpretation of the verbal command "Delete File X" and then uses pragmatic knowledge (Specification 8) to translate this semantic interpretation into a computer's language instruction "rm–I x," which allows the computer to execute the given verbal demand. This is how verbal instructions can be used to direct the operation of the computer.

Different NLP systems may require different specifications of linguistic knowledge than those of UNIX Consultant. Depending on actual applications, many NLP systems only need to use some specifications of linguistic knowledge out of the nine. For example, the machine translation (MT) system of the written language only

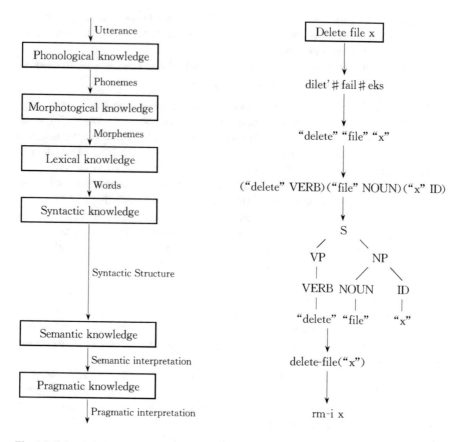

Fig. 1.1 Linguistic knowledge involved in NLP

needs Specifications 3 to 7 of linguistic knowledge; other MT systems also need Specification 8; and the speech recognition system needs Specifications 1 to 5.

The nine specifications introduced above mainly involve linguistic knowledge, as we believe that NLP is, in principle, a linguistic problem. However, in addition to linguistic knowledge, NLP might also involve other knowledge from such areas as follows:

- Computer science: techniques needed for the model representation, algorithm design, and computer implementation of NLP.
- Mathematics: knowledge needed to provide formal mathematical models and methods for NLP.
- Psychology: knowledge needed to provide NLP with psychological models and theories of the human speech behavior.
- Philosophy: knowledge needed to provide NLP with the underpinning theories about human thought and language.

- Statistics: knowledge needed to provide statistical means for NLP to predict future events based on sample data.
- Electronic engineering: knowledge needed to provide the theoretical basis of information theory and the processing technology of language signals for NLP.
- Biology: knowledge needed to provide NLP with the mechanism for the human language behavior in the brain.

Therefore, the research on NLP, an interdisciplinary subject, should combine knowledge of these disciplines. Everyone engaged in NLP should strive to be both literate and knowledgeable.

The scope of NLP ranges from automatic recognition and synthesis of speech, MT, natural language understanding, human-computer dialogue, information retrieval, and text classification to automatic abstracting and so on, all of which, in our view, can be boiled down to the following four areas:

- Linguistics: As a branch of linguistics, NLP only studies those aspects of language in relation to language processing and computing, regardless of the specific implementation on computer. The most important issue in this area is the development of the formal grammar theory and of the mathematical theory of NLP.
- Data processing: NLP is viewed as a subject that develops programs for language data processing. Early research in this area includes the construction of terminology databases and the development of various machine-readable electronic dictionaries. In recent years, with the emergence of large-scale corpora, research in this area has become increasingly important.
- Artificial intelligence and cognitive science: NLP is also viewed as a discipline that realizes natural language capabilities on computer and explores the intelligent and cognitive mechanisms of natural language understanding. Research along this line is closely related to artificial intelligence and cognitive science.
- Language engineering: NLP can be viewed as a subject that studies the practical, engineering language software development, called "human language technique (HLT)" or "language engineering."

In 2004, a book called *Computerlinguistik und Sprachtechnologie* was published in Germany, which also categorizes, in roughly the same way as we do, the current research of NLP into four different areas (Carstensen 2004). This broad categorization includes almost all the issues in the current research of NLP, which can be further subdivided into the following 14 subareas:

1. Spoken Language Input

   - Speech Recognition.
   - Signal Representation (voice signal analysis).
   - Robust Speech Recognition.
   - Hidden Markov Model (HMM) Methods in Speech Recognition.

- Language Representation (Language Model).
- Speaker Recognition.
- Spoken Language Understanding.

2. Written Language Input

- Document Image (format) Analysis.
- Optical Character Recognition (OCR): Printed Character Recognition (PCR).
- OCR: Handwriting.
- Handwriting as Computer Interface (e.g., pen computer).
- Handwriting Analysis (e.g., signature verification).

3. Language Analysis and Understanding

- Sub-sentential Processing (morphological analysis, morphological disambiguation).
- Grammar Formalisms (e.g., context-free grammar (CFG), lexical functional grammar (LFG), functional unification grammar (FUG), head-driven phrase structure grammar (HPSG)).
- Lexicons for Constraint-Based Grammars.
- Computational Semantics.
- Sentence Modeling and Parsing.
- Robust Parsing.

4. Language Generation

- Syntactic Generation.
- Deep Generation.

5. Spoken Output Technologies

- Synthetic Speech Generation.
- Text Interpretation for Text-to-Speech (TTS) Synthesis.
- Spoken Language Generation (conception to speech).

6. Discourse and Dialogue

- Discourse Modeling.
- Dialogue Modeling.
- Spoken Language Dialogue.

7. Document Processing

- Document Retrieval.
- Text Interpretation: Extracting Information.
- Summarization (e.g., text abstraction).
- Computer Assistance in Text Creation and Editing.
- Controlled Languages in Industry and Company.

8. Multilinguality

   - Phrase-Based Machine Translation (PBMT).
   - Statistical Machine Translation (SMT).
   - Neural Machine Translation (NMT).
   - Human-Aided Machine Translation.
   - Machine-Aided Human Translation.
   - Multilingual Information Retrieval.
   - Multilingual Speech Processing.
   - Automatic Language Identification.

9. Multimodality

   - Representations of Space and Time (automatic abstraction of space and time from text).
   - Text and Image Processing.
   - Modality Integration: Speech and Gesture (using data gloves).
   - Modality Integration: Facial Movement and Speech Recognition.
   - Modality Integration: Facial Movement and Speech Synthesis.

10. Information Transmission and Storage

   - Speech Coding (speech compression).
   - Speech Enhancement (speech quality improvement).

11. Mathematical Methods in NLP

   - Statistical Modeling and Classification.
   - Digital Signal Processing (DSP) Techniques.
   - Parsing Techniques.
   - Connectionist Techniques.
   - Finite State Technology.
   - Optimization and Search in Speech and Language Processing.

12. Language Resources

   - Written Language Corpora.
   - Spoken Language Corpora.
   - Lexicons and WordNet.
   - Terminology and Terminological Databank.
   - Data Mining and Information Extract in Web.
   - Knowledge Graph.

13. Neural Network (NN) and Deep Learning (DL)

   - Perception.
   - Free-Forward NN.
   - Convolutional NN.
   - Recurrent NN.
   - Attention Mechanism.

- External Memory.
- Multitask Learning and Transfer Learning.
- Sequence Generative Model.
- Pre-training Model.

14. NLP System Evaluation

- Task-Oriented Text Analysis Evaluation.
- Evaluation of MT and Translation Tools.
- Evaluation of Broad-Coverage Natural Language Parsers.
- Human Factors and User Acceptability.
- Speech Input: Assessment and Evaluation.
- Speech Synthesis Evaluation.
- Usability and Interface Design Evaluation.
- Speech Communication Quality Evaluation.
- Character Recognition Evaluation.

All these 14 subareas of NLP are related to issues in the natural language, which, of course, all involve linguistic knowledge. These studies must formally describe the language, establish appropriate algorithms, and implement these algorithms on computer. Therefore, mathematics and computer science are required in NLP. In addition, issues as spoken language input, written language input, spoken language output, information transmission, and information storage all demand knowledge from electronic engineering technology. Similarly, issues such as multimodal computer processing and discourse analysis and the evaluation of natural language systems involve psychology. Furthermore, representation of space and time involves philosophy, whereas the construction of machine dictionaries and the WordNet requires knowledge from ontology and philosophy to classify knowledge. And the processing of written and spoken corpora requires the use of statistical methods, which involves statistics. Finally, NNs and DL techniques are related to biology and psychology. Obviously, NLP involves such fields as linguistics, computer science, mathematics, psychology, philosophy, statistics, electronic engineering, and biology.

1.2 History Review of Natural Language Processing

The development of NLP can be divided into three stages: its embryo, growth, and boom.

1.2.1 Embryo

The British mathematician, A. M. Turing (1912–1954), had foreseen that computers would raise new questions about research on the natural language long before there were computers.

He points out, in his article entitled "Can Machines Think" published in 1950, that one day in the future machines will be expected to compete with people in all realm of intelligence, but it is hard to decide which point will be the starting point for competition. Many people think that extremely abstract activities such as playing chess can be used as the best starting point, but I tend to support the claim that the best starting point is to create an intelligent machine that people can pay to get it. This intelligent machine can then be taught to understand English and to speak English, the process of which is similar to the way in which we teach kids to learn the language. Turing proposes that the best way to test the computer's intelligence is to let the computer understand English and speak English. He has a genius foresight that the computer and the natural language will form an indissoluble bond.

The period from the 1940s to the late 1950s is the beginning of NLP. The earliest roots of the NLP study can be traced back to the age full of reason at the end of World War I when the computer was just invented. In its budding period, the following three basic studies are particularly noteworthy:

The first is the study of A. M. Turing's algorithmic calculation model.
The second is the study of N. Chomsky's formal language theory.
The third is the study of C. E. Shannon's probability and information theory model.

In the 1950s, the theory of automata was derived from the algorithmic calculation model proposed by A. M. Turing in 1936, which is regarded as the basis of modern computer science.

Turing's work first contributed to the development of McCulloch-Pitts' theory of neurons, in which a simple neuron is a calculation unit described by propositional logic. His work also promoted Kleene's research on finite automata and regular expressions. As A. M. Turing is a mathematician, his algorithmic calculation model has a close relationship with mathematics.

In 1948, C. E. Shannon applied the probability model of discrete Markov processes to the automata of language description. In 1956, having taken the idea of finite state Markov processes from Shannon's work, N. Chomsky describes the grammar of the language using the finite state automata and defines the finite state language as one that is generated by finite state grammar. These early attempts led to the emergence of research fields such as the formal language theory, which uses algebra and the set theory to define language forms as sequences of signs. Chomsky first proposed context-free grammar when studying the natural language. Similarly, Backus and Naur also discovered this context-free grammar when describing the ALGOL programming language in 1959 and 1960, respectively. These studies have intricately combined mathematics, computer science, and linguistics.

With a unified viewpoint, N. Chomsky, in his research, took into equal account of both the computer programming language and the natural language while conducting research.

Chomsky, in his paper entitled "Introduction to the formal analysis of natural languages," put forth a new definition of the language from the perspective of mathematics, believing "the definition applies both to natural languages and the artificial language in logic and in the computer programming theory."[2] In the article "On certain formal properties of grammar," he devoted a section to the programming language and discussed the compiler problems related to the programming languages. These issues arising from the perspective of mathematics are regarded as the formal research on "the grammar of the component structure"[3] from the perspective of computer science. In his article "The algebraic theory of context-free languages," he claimed "what we have to consider here are various devices for generating sentences, which, in a variety of ways, are closely related both to the grammar of natural languages and to the grammar of various artificial languages. We can think of a language as a set of symbol strings in a certain limited set of symbols V, and V is called the vocabulary of the language... We view the syntax as a specification of the programming language, and strings as programs."[4] Here, with a unified view, Chomsky investigated such basic concepts as language and vocabulary in linguistics and has obtained a highly abstract understanding from the perspective of mathematics and computer science, giving the same weight to both the natural language and the programming language.

Another basic research during this period was the development of probabilistic algorithms for speech processing and language processing, which is another contribution of C. E. Shannon. Shannon likened the behavior of transmitting a language through a medium such as a communication channel or an acoustic speech to a noisy channel or decoding. Besides, he used the thermodynamic term "entropy" to measure the information capacity of channels or the amount of information transmitted in the language. In addition, he manually counted the probability of English letters, determining the entropy of English to be 4.03 bits for the first time through probabilistic techniques.

These studies, the basic research of information theory, are closely related to mathematics and statistics.

The study of the automatic speech processing is an important aspect of NLP, which has a long history.

As early as 1780, von Kempelen (1734–1804, Fig. 1.2) invented the Kempelen machine (Fig. 1.3) to simulate human pronunciation.

The Kempelen machine is actually a resonance box made of leather.

The image at the top simulates the lungs, and the air flow can be generated by controlling the blower as is shown in Fig. 1.3.

The image in the middle simulates the mouth and the nasal cavity. The machine makes a nasal sound with two fingers pressing the nasal cavity.

---

[2]N. Chomsky and G. A. Miller. *Introduction to the formal analysis of natural languages.* New York: Wiley, 1963.

[3]N. Chomsky. *Formal properties of grammar.* New York: Wiley, 1963.

[4]N. Chomsky and M. P. Schützenberger. The algebraic theory of context-free grammars in *Computer Programming and Formal Systems.* Amsterdam: North-Holland Publishing Company, 1963.

Fig. 1.2 von Kempelen

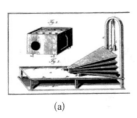
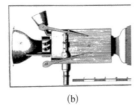
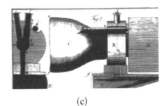

(a)   (b)   (c)

Fig. 1.3 Kempelen machine

The image at the bottom simulates the mechanism underlying unvoiced consonants, by which different unvoiced consonants are emitted by air vibration when the
back of the mouth is closed.

Riezs designed a mechanical acoustic cavity in 1937 (Fig. 1.4).

The front end simulates the lips and the mouth, whereas the back end simulates
the pharynx and the velum.

In the early twentieth century, Homer Dudley (Fig. 1.5) invented the Dudley
machine, which is also called Voder speech synthesizer (Fig. 1.6).

The Dudley machine exhibited at the New York International Fair in 1939 can
synthesize English.

In 1936, the British designed the speaking clock as is shown in Fig. 1.7.

The voice signal is stored on four glass discs, which emit "hour, minute, second,"
respectively.

A technician is adjusting the amplifier of the speaking clock (Fig. 1.8).

Copper at the Hopkins Laboratory developed a pattern playback device (Fig. 1.9).
The light beam is projected onto the spectrogram through a prism and a 45° plane

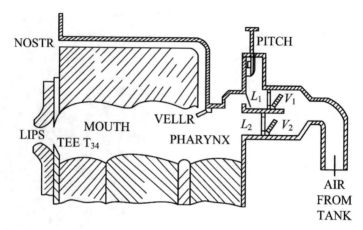

Fig. 1.4 Simulation of the acoustic cavity

Fig. 1.5 Homer Dudley

mirror. The spectrogram representing the speech mode is converted into a speech signal, output by the loudspeaker through an amplifier.

In 1946, König and others studied sound spectrum. Basic research on the sound spectrum and the experimental phonetics laid the foundation for the subsequent research on speech recognition, leading to the successful development of the first machine speech recognizer in the 1950s. In 1952, researchers at Bell Labs established a statistical system to recognize ten arbitrary numbers spoken by a single speaker. The system stores ten speaker-dependent models, which roughly represent the formants of the first two vowels of a numeral. Researchers there achieved an accuracy of 97–99% using the method of selecting the mode with the highest correlation coefficient with the input. These studies are closely related to electronic engineering.

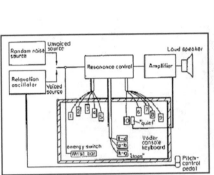

Fig. 1.6 Voder speech synthesizer

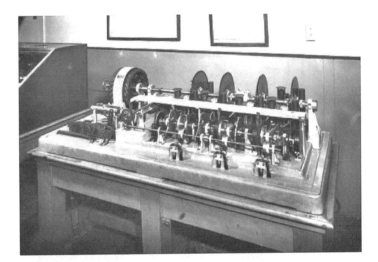

Fig. 1.7 Speaking clock

In 1968, Umeda developed the first text-to-speech converter.

In 1977, Joe Oliver developed a commercial speech synthesizer, Speak & Spell (Fig. 1.10), which can read out the spelled words.

Another important area of NLP is MT.

In 1946, J. P. Eckert and J. W. Mauchly at the University of Pennsylvania designed and manufactured the world's first electronic computer, ENIAC. The amazing computing speed of electronic computers inspired people to consider the

Fig. 1.8 A technician is adjusting the amplifier of the speaking clock

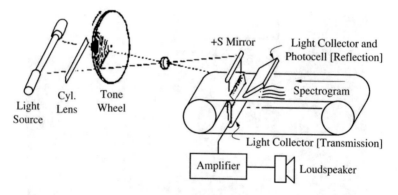

Fig. 1.9 Pattern playback device

innovation of translation technology. In the same year when the electronic computer came out, A.D. Booth, a British engineer, and W. Weaver, director of Natural Science Section of the US Rockefeller Foundation (Fig. 1.11), proposed the idea of using electronic computers for automatic language translation while discussing the scope of its application.

On March 6, 1947, Booth and Weaver met at the Rockefeller Center in New York. Weaver suggested that "it should be more promising to use computers in non-numeric calculations." Before they met, Weaver wrote a letter to N. Wiener, a cybernetician, on March 4, 1947, discussing the issue of MT. In his letter, Weaver wrote "I wonder whether a translating computer could be built. I think it is worth a try even if it can only translate scientific articles (less semantically problematic), or if the translated version is not very elegant (but understandable)." Wiener, however,

Fig. 1.10 Speak & Spell

Fig. 1.11 W. Weaver

threw cold water on Weaver, writing in his April 30's reply, "Honestly, I'm afraid that the range of words in every language is rather vague; it's probably not very optimistic that the feeling and the implied meaning could be dealt with in a machine-like way." But Weaver still stood by his opinion. In 1949, Weaver published a memo entitled "Translation," officially raising the issue of MT. In this memo, in addition to his claim that various languages share many common features, there are two points worth noting.

First, he sees translation as akin to the process of deciphering a code. He said, "I have a text in front of me written in Chinese but I am going to pretend that it is really written in English and that it has been coded in some strange symbols. All I need to do is to strip off the code in order to retrieve the information contained in the text."

Here, Weaver first proposed the idea of MT by means of deciphering codes, which became the origin of the later noisy channel theory. The memo also tells another interesting story about R. E. Gilman in Mathematics Department of Brown University who interpreted a cipher of about 100 words in Turkish that he neither understood nor knew that it was written in Turkish. Weaver believes that skills and ability to interpret a cipher are not influenced by the language, as is exemplified by Gilman's success, and that MT can be performed by means of decoding the code.

Second, he thinks the original text and the translated version "mean the same thing." Therefore, when Language A is translated to Language B, it means that Language A is converted to Language B through a "universal language" or the "interlingua," which is assumed to be common to all mankind.

It can be seen that Weaver regards MT only as a mechanical process of decoding codes. He is far from seeing the complexity of MT in terms of lexical, syntactic, and semantic analyses.

The development of early MT systems was greatly influenced by Weaver's ideas mentioned above. Many researchers on MT have compared the process of MT with that of decoding codes, trying to implement a word-to-word MT by consulting the dictionary. Therefore, it is hard to put it into practical use, for the translation is of poor readability.

Due to the enthusiastic advocacy of scholars and the strong support from the industry, research on MT in the United States flourished. In 1954, Georgetown University in the United States conducted the first MT experiment in the world using the IBM-701 computer in collaboration with the International Business Machines Corporation (IBM) and translated several simple Russian sentences into English. Then, the Soviet Union, the United Kingdom, and Japan also conducted MT experiments, and a boom in the study of MT followed.

What follows are some pictures related to the first MT experiment:

1. The designers of the first MT experiment, Hurd, Dostert, and Watson (Fig. 1.12)

2. The Linguist, Garvin (Fig. 1.13), who proposed the fulcrum analysis

3. The IBM-701 computer used for the first MT (Fig. 1.14)

4. Punched card input on the keyboard used in the first MT (Fig. 1.15)

5. Sentence input on punch cards: cards with 72 lines, which can be transferred to 150 binary codes in 1 min (Fig. 1.16)

Fig. 1.12 Hurd, Dostert and Watson

Fig. 1.13 Garvin

Fig. 1.14 The IBM-701 computer

Fig. 1.15 Punched card input

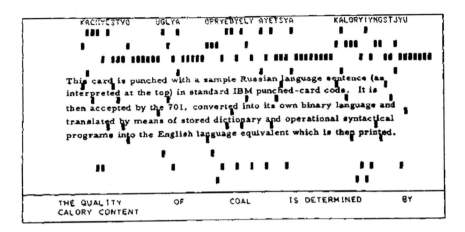

Fig. 1.16 Punch card

Fig. 1.17 Photocells used to read data

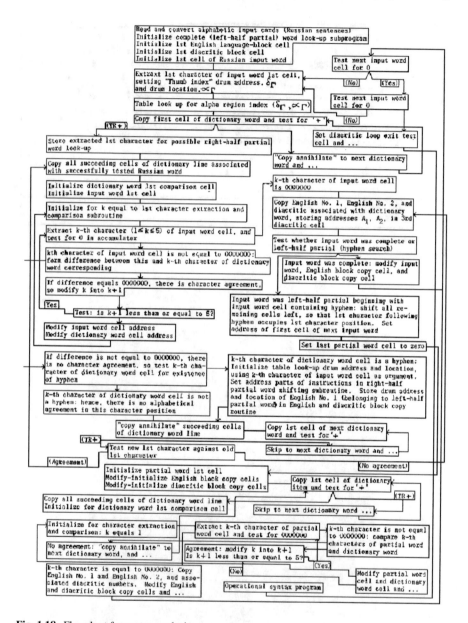

Fig. 1.18 Flowchart for syntax analysis

Dictionary output for example sentence

| Russian input | English equivalents | | 1st code | 2nd code | 3rd code |
	Eng$_1$	Eng$_2$	(PID)	(CDD$_1$)	(CDD$_2$)
vyelyichyina	magnitude	---	***	***	**
ugl-	coal	angle	121	***	25
-a	of	---	131	222	25
opryedyelyayetsya	is determined	---	***	***	**
otnoshyenyi-	relation	the relation	151	***	**
-yem	by	---	131	***	**
dlyin-	length	---	***	***	**
-i	of	---	131	***	25
dug-	arc	---	***	***	**
-i	of	---	131	***	25
k	to	for	121	***	23
radyius-	radius	---	***	221	**
-u	to	---	131	***	**

Fig. 1.19 Dictionary output for example sentence of the machine translation

6. Photocells used to read data in the first MT (Fig. 1.17)

7. The program flowchart of the first MT (Fig. 1.18)

8. Dictionary output for example sentence of the first MT (Fig. 1.19)

9. Output in English on a wide-line printer of the first MT (Fig. 1.20)

On January 7, 1954, when performing to the public, they transcribed Russian sentences into English letters and used punch cards to read data, making it easier for operators who do not understand Russian.

We copied the report in English by *the New York Times* (January 8, 1954) titled "701 translator" the following day as follows:

In the demonstration, a girl operator typed out on a keyboard the following Russian text in English characters: "Mi pyeryedayem mislyi posryedstvom ryechi"(Мы передаем мысли посрество речи). The machine printed a translation almost simultaneously: "We transmit thoughts by means of speech." The operator did not know Russian. Again she typed out the meaningless (to her) Russian words "Vyelyichyina ugla opryedyelyayatsya otnoshyenyiyem dlyini dugi k radyiusu" (величина угла определяется отношением длины дуги к радиусу). And the machine translated it as "Magnitude of angle is determined by the relation of length of arc to radius" (*The New York Times*, January 8, 1954).

Fig. 1.20 Output in English
on a wide-line printer

The first MT was a great success. However, it was soon attacked by conservatives.

In 1962, *Harper's Magazine*, in its August issue, published John A. Kouwenhoven's article entitled "The trouble with translation," which makes up the following story.

Several electronic engineers have designed an automatic translator. The machine contains a dictionary with 1500 basic English words and their Russian counterparts. These engineers claim that this machine can translate right away without making mistakes committed in human translation. During the first experiment, the audience asked for the translation of the sentence "Out of sight, out of mind." After a flash of light, the Russian sentence turned out to be "invisible idiot." As they found such proverbial sentences were more difficult to translate, they tried another sentence from the Bible, "The spirit is willing, but the flesh is weak," to the MT system. The machine-translated Russian sentence means "The liquor is holding out all right, but the meat has spoiled."

Obviously, such stories are fabricated out of thin air. We know that at that time, the United States had only developed MT systems for translating Russian into English. MT systems for translating English into Russian had not been studied at all. This shows that the author, Kouwenhoven, knows little about the history of American MT. Although this is a false story fabricated out of nothing, we can get a sense of the strong dissatisfaction of many people in the United States toward MT at that time.

In the summer of 1956, John McCarthy, an assistant professor at Dartmouth College, Marvin Minsky of Harvard University, Claude Shannon at Bell Labs, Nathaniel Rochester at IBM Information Research Center, Alan Newell and Herbert Simon in Carnegie Mellon University, Oliver Selfridge and Ray Solomonoff of MIT, Arthur Samuel of IBM company, and Trenchard More of Preston University, all in ten (Fig. 1.21), held a 2-month seminar at Dartmouth College in the United

1956 Dartmouth Conference:
The Founding Fathers of AI

John MacCarthy   Marvin Minsky   Claude Shannon   Ray Solomonoff   Alan Newell

Herbert Simon   Arthur Samuel   Oliver Selfridge   Nathaniel Rochester   Trenchard More

Fig. 1.21 The founding fathers of AI

States. They, young and energetic, explored the basis of various human learning and its other functional characteristics from different disciplines, studied how to accurately describe it in principle, and discussed the problems of simulating human intelligence with machines. At the meeting, they also discussed the issue of natural language understanding (NLU), and John McCarthy proposed the term *artificial intelligence* (AI) for the first time. It can be seen that ever since the very beginning of the research on AI, it has been closely related to NLP.

In 1959, back in the early days when MT came out, Y. Bar-Hillel, a famous American mathematical logician, claimed that the fully automatic, high-quality MT (FAHQMT) was impossible.

Bar-Hillel explained that FAHQMT was not only impossible at the technical level at the time, but it was also theoretically impossible.

He cited the following simple English string to illustrate that it is very difficult to find the correct translation of the polysemy *pen* in the context.

John was looking for his toy box. Finally he found it. The box was in the pen. John was very happy.

His reasons are as follows:

1. Here, the word *pen* can only be translated as a playpen, but not as a pen, a writing tool.
2. The key to translating this string is to determine the meaning of the word *pen*.
3. The determination of a correct translation depends on the computer's general knowledge store.
4. But there is no way to feed a computer with this knowledge.

In the early days of MT, Bar-Hillel showed his foresight by scientifically anticipating the difficulties that MT would encounter. At that time, most scholars realized that knowledge and information required by NLP were more abundant and complex

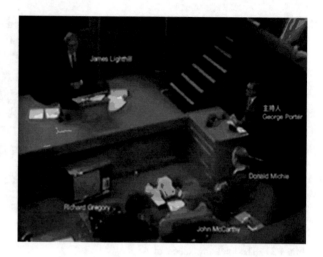

than those required by decoding ciphers although it is already a challenging task. Research on MT was much more difficult than decoding ciphers!

In 1964, the American Academy of Arts and Sciences established the Automatic Language Processing Advisory Committee (ALPAC) to evaluate the research on MT and released a report entitled "Language and Machines" in November 1966. It reads, with a negative tone, that "There are not many reasons for giving strong support to MT at present, for its study has encountered an insurmountable semantic barrier".

Influenced by the ALPAC report, MT studies in many countries came almost to a standstill. In addition, many established MT research units also witnessed administrative and financial difficulties. All over the world, the boom in MT suddenly disappeared, and there was an unprecedented depression.

At the same time, the study of AI also raised doubts from scholars. In 1973, the British Science Research Committee (SRC) submitted a report by the famous applied mathematician James Lighthill to the British government, which questioned the actual AI progress. Pessimistic about the prospects of the AI technology, Lighthill noted that AI for tasks such as speech recognition is difficult to scale up to be useful for governments or the military (Fig. 1.22).

Under such circumstances, research on NLP and on AI was brought to a complete standstill. Both the US and the UK government began to cut funding for the AI research in universities. Defense Advanced Research Projects Agency (DARPA) of the US Department of Defense, which had generously funded AI, also started to require that AI research plans with a clear timetable and the possible results of the project be formulated.

In this period, although NLP reduced its investment in MT, it still made notable progress in its basic theoretical research.

Basic theoretical research of NLP during this period was clearly divided into two schools, symbolic and stochastic.

The work of the symbolic school can be boiled down into two aspects.

On the one hand, the late 1950s and the early and middle 1960s saw Chomsky and others' research on the formal language theory and generative syntax, linguists and computer scientists' research on the analysis algorithm and the research on top-down and bottom-up algorithms in the early stage, and the research on dynamic programming in the later stage as well. Transformation and Discourse Analysis Project (TDAP) by Zellig Harris is the earliest complete analytical system, which was successfully developed at the University of Pennsylvania from June 1958 to July 1959. These studies are jointly conducted by both linguists and computer scientists.

On the other hand, there were studies on AI. After the Dartmouth conference in the summer of 1956, most of AI researchers focus on issues as inference and logic, although a few remain focused on stochastic and statistical algorithms (including probabilistic models and NNs). Newell and Simon's research on "Logic Theorist" and "General Problem Solver" are typical examples. Almost all early NLU systems have been established based on this view. These simple systems combine pattern matching and keyword search with simple heuristic methods for reasoning and automatic Q&A, although they can only be used in a given field. In the late 1960s, scholars developed more formal logic systems. Obviously, the research on AI is a joint effort among computer science, philosophy, biology, psychology, and linguistics.

The stochastic school is mainly composed of researchers in statistics and electronics. In the late 1950s, the Bayesian method was used to solve the optimal character recognition. In 1959, Bledsoe and Browning established a Bayesian system for text recognition, in which a large dictionary was used to calculate the likelihood of the letter series observed in the words of the dictionary. By multiplying the likelihood of each letter in the word, one can find the likelihood of the letter series. In 1964, Mosteller and Wallace used this Bayesian method to solve the distribution problem of the authors encountered in *The Federalist*. These studies are closely related to statistics and electrical engineering.

The 1950s also saw the emergence of the first rigorously measurable mental models of computer processing of the human language based on transformational grammar and that of the first online corpus called the Brown Corpus of American English. The Brown Corpus contains a corpus of one million words, with samples from more than 500 written texts in different styles, including news, novellas, realistic fiction, and scientific and technological articles. The data in the corpus were collected by Brown University in 1963–1964. In 1976, William S. Y. Wang, a Chinese scientist at the University of California in the United States, compiled Dictionary on Computer (DOC), an online Chinese dialect dictionary. These results are products of the combination of linguistics and computer science.

After the ALPAC report was released, researchers of MT calmly reflected from the hard times they had experienced. They all realized that in order to improve the quality of MT, the machine-translation-oriented language research should be strengthened. In MT, differences between the source language and the target language are reflected not only in terms of vocabulary but also in terms of the syntactic structure. In order to get a readable translation, more efforts must be made in the automatic syntactic analysis.

As early as 1957, V. Yngve, an American scholar, points out in his paper "A framework for syntactic translation" that a good MT system should properly depict both the source language and the target language, independently of each other. He argues that MT can be carried out in three stages:

Stage 1: Use coded structural signs to represent the structure of the original text.
Stage 2: Convert the structural signs of the original text into those of the target text.
Stage 3: Generate the output sentence of the translated text.

The first stage involves only the source language unaffected by the target language, whereas the third stage involves the target language unaffected by the source language. It is in the second stage that both the source language and the target language are involved. In the first stage, the syntactic analysis of the source language should be carried out in addition to its lexical analysis, so that the structure of the source language can be represented as coded structural symbols. In the second stage, the structural transformation between the source language and the target language should be carried out after the lexical conversion from the source language to the target language, so as to transform the structural signs of the source language into those of the target language. In the third stage, in addition to the lexical generation of the target language, the syntactic generation of the target language should be performed to correctly output the translated text.

V. Yngve's views widely spread in this period and were generally accepted by developers of MT systems. Therefore, almost all the MT systems in this period put syntactic analysis in the first place and made great achievements in syntactic analysis, which promoted the study of the syntactic formalization.

Another feature of MT studies in this period was the separation of grammar from algorithm. As early as 1957, V. Yngve proposed the idea of separating grammar from the "mechanism," essentially an algorithm in his mind. The separation of grammar from algorithm is to separate language analysis from programming. Programmers propose a method of describing rules to be used by linguists to describe the rules of a language. The separation of grammar and algorithm is a major advancement in the MT technology, which is very conducive to the cooperation between programmers and linguists, leading the computer-oriented language research.

These excellent basic researches in the budding period of NLP have laid a solid foundation for its theory and technology. From its very beginning, NLP had the characteristics of the marked interdisciplinarity. It grew out of the integration and collaboration of various related disciplines.

1.2.2   Growth

From the mid-1960s to the late 1980s was the growth period of NLP, in which researchers in various related disciplines collaborated with one another, achieving some encouraging results with joint efforts.

Since the 1960s, the Centre d'Etude de Traduction Automatique (CETA) at the Institut Mathematique Appliquèe de Grenoble (IMAG) has been developing MT systems. The director of CETA is the famous French mathematician, Professor B. Vauquois (1929–1985), who is also the founder and the first chairman of the International Committee on Computational Linguistics (COLING).

Prof. B. Vauquois clearly stated that a complete MT process can be divided into the following six steps:

1. Lexical analysis of the source language.
2. Syntactic analysis of the source language.
3. Lexical conversion of the source language to the target language.
4. Syntactic conversion of the source language to the target language.
5. Syntactic generation of the target language.
6. Lexical generation of the target language.

These six steps form an "MT pyramid" (Fig. 1.23). Among them, the first and second steps are related only to the source language; the fifth and sixth steps are related only to the target language, and only the third and fourth steps involve both the original and the translated languages. This is called the independent analysis, independent generation, and correlation conversion method in MT. The Russian-French MT system developed by this method is close to the practical level.

They also designed a set of MT software, ARIANE-78, based on the idea of syntax and algorithm independent of each other. This software is divided into four levels, ATEF, ROBRA, TRANSF, and SYGMOR, which can be used to describe various rules of the natural language by language research fellows. Among them, ATEF, a nondeterministic finite state converter, is for the lexical analysis of the

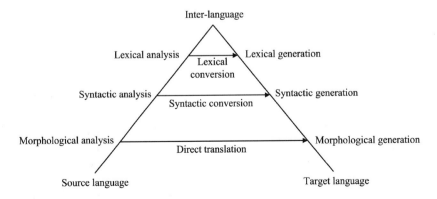

Fig. 1.23 MT pyramid

source language. It receives the source text as input and provides the morphological interpretation of each word as output. ROBRA, a tree graph converter, receives the output of the lexical analysis as input and outputs a tree graph that represents the structure of the source text with the help of grammatical rules. ROBRA can also implement structural conversion and syntactic generation in the same way. TRANSF can achieve lexical conversion with the help of a bilingual dictionary. SYGMOR, a deterministic tree chain converter, receives the output of the syntactic generation of the target text as input and provides the target text in the form of character chains.

Through a lot of scientific experimentation, MT researchers have realized that the semantics of the original language and the translated one must be kept consistent in MT. In other words, a good MT system should accurately interpret the semantics of the original language to be unmistakably expressed in the target language. Therefore, the semantic analysis is getting more and more attention in MT.

Preference semantics was proposed by Y.A. Wilks at Stanford University.

Y. A. Wilks designed an English-French MT system based on preference semantics, emphasizing that the semantic issues should be put in the first place in the generation stage of both the source language and the target language. The English input is first converted into a general universal semantic representation, and then the French output is generated by this semantic representation. Due to its detailed semantic representations, this system can solve such difficult problems as ambiguity or pronoun reference, which could not be otherwise handled by the syntactic analysis, leading to a higher quality of translation. These excellent works have laid a foundation for a formal study of semantics.

In 1976, the University of Montreal, Canada, and the Canadian Federal Government's Translation Bureau jointly developed a practical MT system, TAUM-METEO, providing official weather forecast services. When put into practical use, the system can translate 60,000 to 300,000 words per hour and 1500 to 2000 weather forecasts per day, which can be immediately televised or published in newspapers. The TAUM-METEO system is a milestone in the history of MT.

In 1978, the European Community (now the "European Union") proposed EUROTRA, a multilingual MT program that translates multidirectionally among seven (later eleven) languages within the European Community. Implemented in 1982, the program lasted for more than 10 years, failing to achieve the expected results.

From 1982 to 1986, the Japanese government carried out research on the development of an English-Japanese and Japanese-English MT system, Mu, at the same time when Japan proposed the fifth-generation computer plan. Then Japan's four neighboring Asian countries, China, Indonesia, Malaysia, and Thailand, organized by the Ministry of International Trade and Industry cooperated in the development of an MT system called ODA, lunched a program for the multi-language MT in five languages (Japanese, Chinese, Indonesian, Malay, and Thai). Originally scheduled to be completed between 1987 and 1992, the plan was finally completed in 1995. However, the results fail to live up to what was expected.

In 1982, while the European Community began implementing the EUROTRA program, it also supported the feasibility study of the multilingual MT system called

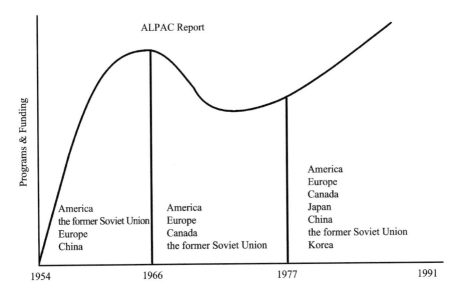

Fig. 1.24   A saddle-shaped MT development

DLT. Since 1984, the Dutch government and a Dutch software company, BSO, have provided a long-term support for the development of this system with each funding 50%. From 1984 to 1992, the annual investment was around US $ one million. The DLT system was originally intended for application in practice in the mid-1990s, but no satisfactory results have been obtained so far.

MT has gone through a saddle-shaped development shown in Fig. 1.24.

During this period, statistical methods succeeded in the development of speech recognition algorithms, of which the hidden Markov model and the noisy channel model and the decoding model are of top importance. These models were independently developed by two teams, one with Jelinek, Bahl, and Mercer, researchers at IBM's Watson research center, and the other with Baker and others in Carnegie Mellon University. Baker was influenced by the work of Baum and his colleagues at the institute for defensive analysis in Princeton. Bell Laboratories of AT & T are also among centers of speech recognition and speech synthesis. These are the results of the application of statistical methods in NLP.

Logic methods have achieved good results in NLP as well. In 1970, A. Colmerauer and his colleagues developed the Q-system and metamorphosis grammar using logic methods and applied them in MT. Colmerauer, pioneer in Prolog language, designed the Prolog language using the logic programming. Definite clause grammar proposed by Pereira and Warren in 1980 is also one of the successful examples of using logic methods in NLP. M. Kay's research on functional grammar in 1979 and Bresnan and Kaplan's work on lexical function grammar (LFG) in 1982 are notable results in the feature structure unification research, important achievements of the combination of mathematics, logic, and linguistics.

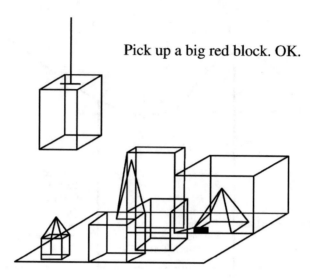

Pick up a big red block. OK.

Fig. 1.25 World of toy blocks

Research on NLU has also achieved remarkable results.

The study on NLU in this period began with the SHRDLU system developed by Terry Winograd in 1972, which simulates the behavior of a robot embedded in a world of toy blocks (Fig. 1.25). The system is programmed to take written instructions in the natural language, such as "Pick up a big block" or "Move the red block on top of the smaller green one," directing the robot to play with the toy blocks with a complex and delicate NLU system. The system also made the first attempt to establish a comprehensive (as it seemed to be at the time) English grammar based on systemic grammar by Halliday. The SHRDLU system also clearly shows the importance of the syntactic analysis in relation to the development of semantic and discourse formal models.

In 1977, R. Schank with his colleagues and his students at Yale University established a series of language understanding programs that focus on human conceptual knowledge such as scripting, planning, and intention, as well as human memory mechanisms. They introduced the network-based semantic theory to their systems and the concept of case roles proposed by Fillmore in 1968 in their expressions. Their works, results of a clever combination of linguistics, computer science, and mathematics, are called the "Yale School" of NLP.

Logic methods have also been used in the study of NLU. For example, in 1967, Woods used the predicate logic in his LUNAR Q&A system to deal with the semantic interpretation.

Discourse analysis focuses on four key areas in discourse research, including discourse structure, discourse focus, automatic reference resolution, and logic-based verbal behavior. In 1977, Crosz with her colleagues studied the substructure and focus of discourse; in 1972, Hobbs began to study automatic reference resolution. In the study of logic-based verbal behavior, Perrault and Allen established the framework of "belief-desire-intention" (BDI) in 1980. Such research is closely related to psychology, logic, and philosophy.

In 10 years from 1983 to 1993, NLP researchers reflected on the past and found that the finite state model and empirical methods previously held negative were reasonable to some extent. In this decade, research on NLP has returned to finite state models and empirical methods, which were almost denied in the late 1950s and early 1960s. The reason for this recovery is partly due to the fact that Chomsky's critical comments on Skinner's *Verbal Behavior* in 1959 were theoretically opposed to at the turn of the 1980s and 1990s.

This reflection first led to a re-evaluation of the finite state model. The model was found to be powerful as a result of Kaplan and Kay's work on the finite state phonology and morphology and of Church's work on the syntactic finite state model. Accordingly, the finite state model regained the attention of the NLP community.

In addition, this reflection resulted in a so-called return to empiricism. Of particular interest here is the development of probabilistic models of speech and language processing, which are strongly influenced by those of speech recognition developed at IBM's Watson research center. These probabilistic models and other data-driven methods have also been adopted in the study of the part-of-speech tagging, syntactic analysis, resolution of the ambiguity of noun phrase attachment, and of the connectionist methods for issues ranging from speech recognition to semantics.

During this period, the research on the generation of the natural language also made remarkable achievements.

1.2.3 Boom

Since the 1990s, NLP has been booming. In July 1993, J. Hutchins, a famous British scholar, pointed out in his special report at the 4th MT Summit held in Tobei (Japan) that the MT development entered a new era in 1989. The hallmark of this era is the introduction of corpus-based methods to rule-based technologies, including statistical methods, example-based methods, methods of transforming corpora into language knowledge bases by means of corpus processing, etc. MT based on large-scale authentic text processing is a revolution in the history of the MT research, which would move NLP onto a new stage. The beginning of the new era of MT suggests that NLP has entered its boom.

Especially in the last 5 years of the 1990s (1994–1999) and the early years of the twenty-first century, research on NLP underwent great changes and achieved unprecedented prosperity in the following three aspects:

First, probabilistic and data-driven approaches have almost become standard methods in NLP. Probabilistic approaches have been introduced to research on syntactic parsing, part-of-speech tagging, reference resolution, and speech processing algorithms, and evaluation methods borrowed from speech recognition and information retrieval have also been adopted.

Fig. 1.26 Tim Berners-Lee

Second, the increasing speed and memory of computers make possible the commercial development of speech and language processing, especially in those subareas of speech recognition, spelling check, and grammar checking. Algorithms for speech and language processing began to be used to enhance augmentative and alternative communication (AAC).

Third, network technology has given a great impetus to NLP. The development of the World Wide Web (WWW) has made the need for information retrieval and information extraction on the network more prominent, and the data mining technology is becoming more and more mature. Therefore, the study of NLP becomes more and more important with the development of WWW, as it is mainly composed of the natural language. The study of NLP is closely related to the development of WWW.

Here, in particular, we will talk about the development of WWW.

WWW is an Internet-based computer network. Users using WWW can access massive information stored on the Internet worldwide through the Internet. WWW works in a client-server mode with clients connecting to a "server" that stores data remotely through a program called "client." Web browsing is performed through a client program called "browser" (e.g., Navigator, Internet Explorer, etc.), which sends the user's request to the remote server to search for relevant information, then returns the searched files written in HyperText Makeup Language (HTML), and displays them on the user's computer screen.

The operation of the Web depends on the structure of hypertext files. The hypertext allows the authors of the Web page to hyperlink their files to other files on the Web to read the relevant files.

The concept of the Web was first proposed by Tim Berners-Lee (Fig. 1.26) in 1989.

At that time, Tim Berners-Lee was working at the Centre Europeen pour la Recherche Nucleaire (CERN) in Switzerland. He wrote the first WWW server-client program called the World Wide Web. In March 1989, Tim Berners-Lee submitted a proposal to CERN's senior leadership. In this proposal, he analyzed the shortcomings of the hierarchical organization of information used at the time and also pointed out the advantages of the programs based on the hypertext system, proposing tentatively a set of basic rules to establish a "distributed hypertext system." Unfortunately, his suggestion did not receive support needed from CERN's top management.

In 1990, Berners-Lee submitted to CERN again his proposal, which was then supported by the organization. As a result, Berners-Lee and his colleagues at CERN immediately adopted the idea of a distributed hypertext system to study the Web, laying the foundation for its future development. To this end, they developed a Web server and a browser and developed a communication mode between the client and the server, Hypertext Transfer Protocol (HTTP), HTML, and Universal Resource Locator (URL).

In February 1993, Marc Andreessen of the National Center for Supercomputing Applications at Illinois University and his research team designed a graphical user interface using Mosaic Technology and used it as a Unix Web browser. Within a few months, Macintosh and Windows operating systems used the Mosaic user graphical interface technology, successively. The user could perform various operations on computer, if he clicks the graphics on the computer screen. In 1994, Jim Clark, together with Marc Andreessen, founded the Mosaic Communication, which was later renamed the Netscape Communication. They successfully developed the Netscape browser only after a few months and popularized it among Web users. In August 1995, Microsoft announced its Web browser, the Internet Explorer, a challenge to the Netscape. Since then, users can roam freely on the Web through the browser.

WWW created by Tim Berners-Lee and the Mosaic browser are the two most important events in the history of the development of the Web. They enable the Web to be quickly promoted and popularized among users.

The Internet is a communication network of the Web. Without the Internet, the Web would not have functioned at all. The predecessor of the Internet was the computer network ARPANET built in 1969 with the support from the Advanced Research Project Agency (ARPA) of the US Department of Defense. In 1972, ARPANET put on a show at the first International Conference on Computers and Communications. Scientists at ARPA used ARPANET to connect together computers in more than 40 different places. Later, ARPANET was further developed into today's Internet.

In 1973, Vinton Cerf and Bob Kahn began to study the Internet Protocol. In 1974, they published an article entitled "Transmission Control Protocol," in which they officially name it Transmission Control Protocol/Internet Protocol (TCP/IP). TCP/IP enables computer networks to connect and communicate with one another. However, it was not until 1982 that the TCP/IP protocol was officially adopted and used by the Internet to connect different networks.

In order to effectively obtain information on networks all over the world, a "search engine" needs to be developed. The search system, Excite, was developed in 1993 by six students of Stanford University in the United States; in 1994, the University of Texas in the United States developed the EINet Calaxy; and in the same year, the famous search engine, Yahoo, came out. In 1998, Sergey Brim and Larry Page of Stanford University launched a search engine called Google, and in 2005, Microsoft launched another search engine, MSN.

To promote the spread and use of the Web worldwide, the Massachusetts Institute of Technology (MIT) and CERN in Switzerland established the World Wide Web Consortium (W3C) in 1994. It is an international organization of WWW, the establishment of which has made the Web rapidly gain popularity internationally. Almost every person's life and work in modern times are closely related to the Web. Since the first W3C meeting held in 1994, the international W3C meeting has been held every year.

Of all the network information, more than 90% is text information, information that uses the natural language as a carrier. With the rapid development of the Web, how to effectively obtain the vast amount of information on the Web has become a key issue in the current research on NLP. It is foreseeable that the further development of the Web will definitely push NLP research onto a new stage.

Since 2007, introduced into NLP has been the NN technology, which uses the method of DL and the large-scale bilingual aligned spoken language corpus as the source of language knowledge. For example, in MT, a multilayer neural network is used to acquire translation knowledge from the bilingual aligned spoken corpus. The statistical MT is further developed into the neural MT, whose accuracy rate of the spoken neural MT has exceeded 90%. The neural MT of the spoken language is already comparable to human translation. MT, originally a dream of scholars, has finally become a living reality.

As can be seen from the above discussion, NLP has integrated the disciplines of linguistics, computer science, mathematics, psychology, philosophy, logic, statistics, electronic engineering, and biology in the course of its more than 60 years' development, forming an interdisciplinary subject. NLP, spanning three major areas of knowledge, liberal arts, science, and engineering, is such positioned in the entire human knowledge system.

With the further development of the network technology in the information network era, research on NLP will become more and more important, since the Web is mainly composed of the natural language. In the near future, NLP will be as important as physics.

With the advancement of the NLP technology, we will be able to translate voice messages in news broadcasts in various languages on the Web into texts by using the speech recognition technology. Using the MT technology, we will be able to translate these texts into English or Chinese stored as a document that can be retrieved at any time, so that we can have access to them from around the world in a timely manner at any time and in any place. We are no longer restricted by the "language barrier," becoming well-informed men with a remote viewing, who can

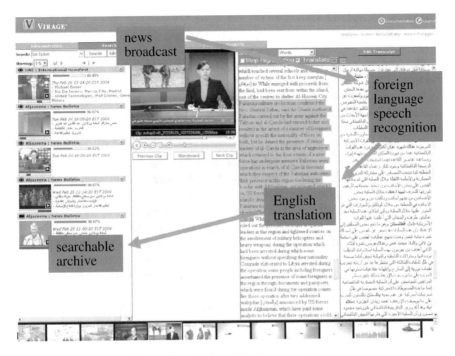

Fig. 1.27 The NLP technology will greatly benefit the human society

hear voices a long way off and who has the faculty of foreseeing distant future events as clairvoyants claim to do.

As is shown in Fig. 1.27, using the foreign language speech recognition technology, we can first translate Arabic news broadcasts into Arabic texts, and then through the MT technology, we can translate them into English stored in a searchable archive for us to retrieve and query at any time. As the technology can be applied to all other languages, we will be away from the "language barrier" forever. What an exciting thing this is! Such a moment is no longer a distant future, and it is gradually becoming a living reality close at hand. The NLP technology will greatly benefit the human society, and its future applications are very promising.

1.3   Characteristics of Current Trends in Natural Language Processing

Since the twenty-first century, computer processing of the natural language has become an important means to acquire knowledge from the Web due to its popularity. Living in the information network era, almost all modern people have to deal with the Web, and all of them have to use more or less the research results of NLP to acquire or mine all kinds of knowledge and information on the boundless Web.

Therefore, all countries in the world attach great importance to the NLP research, into which a great deal of manpower, material, and financial resources has been invested.

The current research on NLP, we think, has the following four characteristic features:

First, the rationalist approach based on syntactic-semantic rules has been questioned. With the construction of corpora and the rise of corpus linguistics and with the increasing popularity of the Web, the large-scale processing of authentic texts has become the main strategic goal of NLP.

In the past 40 years, most scholars engaged in the development of the NLP systems have basically adopted the rule-based rationalist method, whose philosophical underpinning is logical positivism. They believe that the basic unit of intelligence is the symbol and that the cognitive process is a symbolic operation under the representation of symbols, so thinking is a symbolic operation.

J. A. Fodor, a famous linguist, states in his book *Representations* (MIT Press, 1980) that "if we believe that the mental process is a computational one, a formal operation defined by representational forms, the mind could naturally be thought of as a kind of computer, in addition to thinking of it as something else. In other words, we would assume that the mind would perform the symbolic operations involved in the hypothetical calculation, which we believe to be very similar to the operations of a Turing machine." This statement represents a rule-based (symbolic manipulation) rationalist view of NLP.

However, this view has been challenged by other scholars. In the paper entitled *Minds, Brains and Programs* published in *Behavioral and Brain Sciences* (1980, Vol. 3), J. R. Searle raised the question of the so-called Chinese house. He proposed that assuming that a person who knew English but not Chinese was confined in a room with a set of English instructions explaining the correspondence and operation relationship between English and Chinese symbols; he was supposed to answer several questions written in Chinese. To do this, he must first handle the Chinese symbols in the questions according to the instruction rules, understand their meaning, and then use the instruction rules to write his answers in Chinese one by one. For example, he must write A1 in Chinese to Q1 in Chinese, A2 in Chinese to Q2 in Chinese, and so on. This is obviously a very challenging thing almost impossible to achieve. And even if this person could do this, he couldn't prove that he understands Chinese, which might only suggest that he was good at doing mechanical operations according to the rules. Searle's criticism led to a widespread skepticism of the rule-based rationalist view.

The rationalist approach is also quite limited in practice. Rationalists in NLP have limited their practices to a very narrow field of its expertise. Although their dominant techniques, the rule-based syntactical and semantic analysis, have had some success in some given "sub-languages," it is still very difficult to further expand the coverage of their applications to process large-scale authentic texts, for the NLP systems should be equipped with linguistic knowledge of a magnitude and granularity far beyond that of any previous systems. Moreover, with the tremendous changes in the size and degree of knowledge involved in the system, it has to find a new way in how to acquire, express, and manage such knowledge. Thus, the question on how to process large-scale authentic texts is raised. In August 1990, the 13th International Conference on Computational Linguistics (COLING'90) was held in Helsinki, Finland, with its theme being "Theories, Methods and Tools for Processing Large-Scale Authentic Texts," suggesting that the processing of large-scale authentic texts will be the strategic goal of NLP for a considerably long time in the future. To achieve the strategic objectives, major innovations in terms of the theory, methods, and tools are expected. In Montreal, Canada, in June 1992, the fourth International Conference on Theory and Methods of Machine Translation (TMI-92) was held, with the theme being "Empirical and Rationalist Methods in Machine Translation." Here, the word *rationalist* refers to methods based on generative linguistics, whereas the word *empirical* refers to methods based on large-scale corpus analysis, which clearly reveals the current focus of NLP. The construction of corpora and the rise of corpus linguistics at that time are precisely important indicators of the shift in the strategic goals of NLP. As the large-scale authentic text processing attracts an increasing attention, more and more scholars realize that the corpus-based analysis (empiricism) is at least an important complement to the rule-based analysis (rationalism), because the corpus is the most ideal language knowledge resource in terms of both being "large-scale" and "authentic."

This large-scale authentic corpus also provides a powerful means for the modernization of the research on languages. Zhiwei Feng, the author of this handbook, manually calculated the entropy of the Chinese character more than 40 years ago, a basic research in Chinese information processing. In order to calculate the entropy of Chinese characters, Feng first needed to count the occurrence frequency of Chinese characters in the text. In the 1970s, he manually looked up the frequency according to the written texts, as there was no such a machine-readable Chinese corpus; even a small Chinese corpus was not available then. It took him nearly 10 years to manually check the frequency of millions of words of modern Chinese texts (70%) and ancient Chinese texts (30%), gradually expanding the size of statistics and establishing six frequency tables of Chinese characters with different capacities. Finally, according to these different Chinese character frequency tables, the capacity of the Chinese characters is gradually expanded and the entropy of the Chinese characters calculated to be 9.65 bits at last. This is an extremely difficult and cumbersome job. Now that we have a machine-readable Chinese corpus, there is no need to manually check the frequency. And the frequency statistics can be performed on computer. Now a very simple program can easily count the frequency of Chinese characters from the corpus and further calculate the entropy of Chinese characters, which greatly improves the efficiency of the language research, hundreds and thousands of times faster than before! Manual frequency check is like driving an old ox to pull a broken car on a rugged mountain road, whereas frequency check by using the corpus is like taking a spaceship to soar in the vast space, which was far beyond our wild imagination in the past.

The construction and use of large-scale machine-readable corpora have emancipated linguists from the arduous manual labor and allowed them to concentrate on those more important issues, which has played an immeasurable role in promoting the modernization of linguistic research.

Second, ML (machine learning) is increasingly used in NLP to acquire language knowledge.

Traditional linguistics basically obtains linguistic knowledge through the manual method of linguists summarizing language phenomena. Due to the limited memory capacity of human beings, any linguist, even leading authorities in the field, cannot memorize and process vast numbers of words. Therefore, using traditional manual methods to acquire language knowledge is like peeping at the leopard with a pipe or measuring the sea with a ladle. Using the manual method to acquire language knowledge is not only extremely inefficient but also highly subjective. In the traditional linguistics, the basic philosophy that rules cannot be established without ten positive examples or that a rule cannot be broken without ten negative examples seems to be strict. In fact, in a sea of linguistic data, ten positive or negative examples can easily determine the choice of linguistic rules. Is it a safe bet that these rules are reliable? This is highly doubtful.

The data source of the early research on the natural language mainly relied on the subjective "introspection" of linguists, the one supported by the basic philosophy that rules cannot be established without ten positive examples or that a rule cannot be broken without ten negative examples. These ten positive or negative examples, small data, obviously, are highly unreliable.

Another source of data for the early natural language research is "elicitation," which is to induce relevant data from second-hand materials such as books or dictionaries or through questionnaires, dialect surveys, etc. to deduce the conclusion. As the data the method relies on is, of course, small data again, it is inevitable that they might be one-sided or imperfect.

Now we have entered the era of big data. The concept of big data was proposed by Michael Cox and David Ellsworth of NASA Research Institute in 1997. They believe that big data are a huge amount of scientific data that can be visualized.

American IBM believes that big data has a 3-V feature: volume, variety, and velocity.

We also advocate relying on big data to obtain information from large-scale authentic texts. Big data characterized by being large-scale and authentic are also objective without subjectivity.

Having entered the era of big data, we no longer rely on introspection or induction to get data; we rely on observation and verification, instead.

Using big data to study the natural language makes it possible for us to acquire objective knowledge through observation and examination, avoiding subjectivity and one-sidedness to a large extent.

Therefore, the study of NLP driven by big data is a significant change in our approach to understanding and studying the objective world, which means a lot in methodology.

At present, research on NLP advocates the establishment of large-scale corpora. Computers can automatically acquire accurate language knowledge from vast corpora by using NNs and ML methods. The construction of machine dictionaries and large-scale corpora has become a hot issue in NLP. With the rapid development of the Web, there are extremely rich text language data on the Web, including both structured and unstructured language ones. We can also automatically acquire language knowledge from the language data on the Web, a big change in the way linguists acquire language knowledge. Linguists in the twenty-first century should be aware of this change and gradually change their means of acquiring language knowledge.

With the rapid development of the Web, data mining, the process of discovering useful knowledge from data sources on the Web, has become an important research field in computer science. The data to be mined is mainly text data, as most of the data exist in the form of text, which is exactly the object of study in NLP. Therefore, the method of the automatic ML in data mining is of great value to NLP.

Currently, there are three main types of automatic learning methods, including the supervised learning, the unsupervised learning, and the semi-supervised learning.

The supervised learning is, in fact, about the classification of data. First, instances of data are annotated with predefined category or category tags as training data. The machine learns automatically from these labeled training data and then classifies the new data according to the acquired knowledge. Since the training data used for learning are labeled with predefined tags, the process of ML is guided by these training data. Therefore, it is called the supervised learning.

In the unsupervised learning, the data used for learning are not marked with predefined category or category tags. Instead, ML algorithms are used to automatically discover structures or patterns hidden in the data. A key technique for such learning is clustering, which automatically clusters data instances into different groups based on their similarities or differences. For example, we can cluster the Web pages into different combinations, each of which represents a specific topic, or we can cluster files into different levels, each of which represents a specific topic level. DL is basically a kind of the unsupervised learning. As it adopts a multilevel NN to automatically learn language features from large-scale authentic corpus, it significantly improves the performance of NLP.

As the supervised learning requires a huge amount of predefined manual labeling of data instances, it is laborious and time-consuming. Labeling language features is no easy job at all. To reduce the labor of manual labeling, machines can learn simultaneously from both labeled and unlabeled data instances. The set of labeled data instances can be relatively small, while the set of unlabeled data instances can be large. Such a model is called the semi-supervised learning. Using DL methods, the computer directly obtains language features from a large-scale corpus, liberating people from the arduous task of linguistic characterization.

At present, these three methods of the automatic ML have been very mature and widely used in the research of NLP, which fundamentally changes the traditional means of acquiring language knowledge and has a revolutionary significance for the NLP development.

In 2000, issues of the statistical-based MT were discussed at the Summer Vacation Machine Translation Workshop at the Johns Hopkins University among scholars from the University of Southern California, the University of Rochester, the Johns Hopkins University, Xerox, the Pennsylvania State University, the Stanford

University, and other universities. A final report on "syntax for statistical machine translation" was completed by 13 scientists led by Franz Josef Och, a young doctoral candidate at the Aachen University, Germany. This report proposed an effective way to combine rule-based methods with statistical-based methods. In 2002, Och published a paper entitled "Discriminative Training and Maximum Entropy Models for Statistical Machine Translation" at the International Conference on Computational Linguistics (ACL 2002), in which a systematic method of the statistical MT was further proposed, which won him the best paper award of ACL 2002.

In January 2002, Language Weaver (LW), a company that specializes in the development of the statistical machine translation software (SMTS), was established in the United States with Och being its consultant. LW is the first company in the world to commercialize SMTS. Researchers at LW used the ML technology to obtain large amounts of language data from translation memories, translated archives, dictionaries and glossaries, the Internet, and human translators. In this process, they preprocessed the language data in various ways, including format filtering, optical character recognition and scanning (Scan+OCR), text transcription, and document alignment, segment alignment, etc. Then, the preprocessed language data were aligned at the sentence level with the source language and the target language to form a bilingual parallel corpus. After that, with the automatic learning method, the Language Weaver Learner (LW Learner) developed by LW was used to process a bilingual parallel corpus, from which language information, such as probability translation dictionaries, probability translation templates, and probability translation rules, has been extracted. The extracted language information was collectively called translation parameters, actually probabilistic language knowledge. After the above processing, the language data became probabilistic language knowledge. Translation parameters are an important part of LW's translation software. In order to deal with these translation parameters, LW has also developed a statistical translator called Decoder, another important part of the translation software of the company. The decoder and translation parameters have become core components of LW's translation software. The decoder uses translation parameters obtained through the statistical learning to perform MT of the new text, automatically translating the new source language documents into new target language translations for its users.

The workflow of LW's translation system is shown in Fig. 1.28.

At present, the Chinese-English MT system and the English-Spanish bidirectional MT system developed by LW are about to come out. The same method will be used to develop a two-way MT system for English-French, a one-way MT system for Hindi-English and Somali-English.

In July 2003, Och came out top in the MT competition hosted by the National Institute of Standards and Technology (NIST) of the United States' Department of Commerce in Baltimore, Maryland. Using statistical methods to automatically acquire language knowledge from a bilingual corpus, Och has established statistically a set of MT rules and constructed several MT systems for Arabic and Chinese to English in a short time. Archimedes, the great Greek scientist, once said: "Give me a place to stand on, and I will move the world." Similar to what Archimedes has

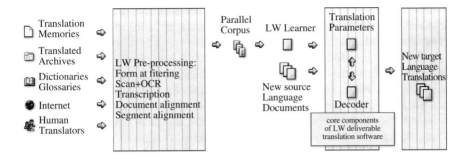

Fig. 1.28   Workflow of language weaver's translation system

claimed, Och now said: "Give me enough parallel data, and I can have a translation system for any two languages in a matter of hours," which indicates the energetic spirit of exploration and the ambition of a new generation of NLP researchers. Och, it seems, has found an effective method for MT. At the very least, in his way, the automate learning might open up a new world of the MT research and shine a bright light on our tortuous quest for truth. In the past, it took years to build an MT system by the method of manually formulating language rules. Now Och's ML approach has greatly improved the speed, by which an MT system can be built in hours.

Since 2007, the statistical MT has been further developed into the neural MT, in which DL methods are used to directly extract natural features from large-scale corpora. As a result, the level and performance of MT have been greatly improved, gradually and excitingly approaching to those of human translation.

Third, mathematical methods are getting more and more attention.

In NLP, methods of mathematical statistics are increasingly used to analyze language data, as it is obviously impossible to obtain accurate and reliable language knowledge from vast corpora and the Web by observation or introspection.

The core of NLP is to construct language models, which are mathematical models that describe the inherent laws of the natural language. Language models can be divided into rule-based models and statistics-based ones. The rules that the language models are based on are the ones prescribed by linguists in relation to their linguistic knowledge, which might be subjective or one-sided. It is, therefore, hard to use such models to process large-scale authentic texts. Statistics-based language models are usually probabilistic models, the probabilistic parameters of which help computers estimate the possibility of the appearance of language components in the natural language, instead of simply judging whether such language components conform to linguistic rules.

At present, statistics-based language models in NLP, such as the hidden Markov model (HMM), probabilistic context-free grammar (PCFG), the decision tree-based model, and the maximum entropy model, are quite mature.

The study of such statistics-based language models requires knowledge of statistical mathematics. Therefore, we should strive to update our knowledge and learn statistical mathematics. The knowledge of statistical mathematics learnt seriously and mastered skillfully makes us even more powerful in the process of acquiring language knowledge.

DL in NLP is a kind of ML modeled on complex NNs. Artificial NN inspired by biological NNs is a network composed of artificial neuron connections, which is essentially a mathematical model. A neuron is a nonlinear function, and an NN is a compound function composed of many neurons. NN has a large number of parameters, which can be estimated by optimizing the objective function on the data. Parameter learning uses back propagation algorithm. As long as the function of NN can be differentiated, such functions as MT and the image recognition can be realized. A two-layer NN can approximate an arbitrary continuous function with arbitrary precision due to its powerful function approximation capability. If there is an ideal function to achieve a certain function, there may be an NN that is a sufficient approximation of this function. Deep NNs have more streamlined expression capabilities and higher sample complexity than those of shallow NNs. A deep and narrow NN is equivalent to a shallow and wide NN. However, the parameters of a deep and narrow NN are fewer than those of a shallow and wide NN, and to learn them, only a few samples are needed. In extreme cases, the width of the shallow and wide NN is exponential, which is hard to realize in reality. Therefore, in NLP, deep and narrow NNs are used for DL, which has a strong generalization ability. Models with small errors learned from the training set also only have small errors on the test set. Therefore, DL has a powerful ability to learn complex patterns. The word embedding model, the recurrent neural network (RNN) model, the long short-time memory (LSTM) model, the convolutional neural network (CNN) model, and the pre-training model used in NLP are all language models based on DL. With the development of the NN technology, we should strive to master the mathematical knowledge of DL and study the mathematical principles of these models.

Fourth, there appears a strong tendency of lexicalism, as more and more attention is paid to the role of vocabulary in NLP.

The resolution of syntactic ambiguity is related not only to the probability or the structure but also to the characteristics of vocabulary. The importance of lexical features has also been observed in solving the prepositional phrase attachment in English automatic analysis and the ambiguity of parallel structures.

In theoretical linguistics, N. Chomsky recently proposed "the minimalist program," within which all important grammatical principles are directly applied to the surface layer, reducing specific rules to a minimum. Differences between different languages are handled by vocabulary, the role of which has been attached great importance to, suggesting a tendency of lexicalism in linguistics. In NLP, the construction of the lexical knowledge base has become a common concern. The construction of the WordNet and the FrameNet in the United States, and of various grammatical and semantic knowledge bases in China and the word embedding technology adopted in NNs all have reflected this strong tendency of lexicalism.

Under such new circumstances, the interdisciplinary and marginal nature of NLP becomes more prominent. If our NLP researchers are confined to a narrow field of our original professions and do not learn from other related disciplines to enrich our

Table 1.1 Top 20 countries with the highest number of the Internet users

#	Country or Region	Population 2019 Est.	Population 2000 Est.	Internet Users 31 Mar 2019	Internet Users 31 Dec 2000	Internet Growth 2000–2019
1	China	1,420,062,022	1,283,198,970	829,000,000	22,500,000	3,584 %
2	India	1,368,737,513	1,053,050,912	560,000,000	5,000,000	11,100 %
3	United States	329,093,110	281,982,778	292,892,868	95,354,000	207 %
4	Brazil	212,392,717	175,287,587	149,057,635	5,000,000	2,881 %
5	Indonesia	269,536,482	211,540,429	143,260,000	2,000,000	7,063 %
6	Japan	126,854,745	127,533,934	118,626,672	47,080,000	152 %
7	Nigeria	200,962,417	122,352,009	111,632,516	200,000	55,716 %
8	Russia	143,964,709	146,396,514	109,552,842	3,100,000	3,434 %
9	Bangladesh	168,065,920	131,581,243	92,061,000	100,000	91,961 %
10	Mexico	132,328,035	101,719,673	85,000,000	2,712,400	3,033 %
11	Germany	82,438,639	81,487,757	79,127,551	24,000,000	229 %
12	Turkey	82,961,805	63,240,121	69,107,183	2,000,000	3,355 %
13	Philippines	108,106,310	77,991,569	67,000,000	2,000,000	3,250 %
14	Vietnam	97,429,061	80,285,562	64,000,000	200,000	31,900 %
15	United Kingdom	66,959,016	58,950,848	63,061,419	15,400,000	309 %
16	Iran	82,503,583	66,131,854	62,702,731	250,000	24,981 %
17	France	65,480,710	59,608,201	60,421,689	8,500,000	610 %
18	Thailand	69,306,160	62,958,021	57,000,000	2,300,000	2,378 %
19	Italy	59,216,525	57,293,721	54,798,299	13,200,000	315 %
20	Egypt	101,168,745	69,905,988	49,231,493	450,000	10,613 %
	TOP 20 Countries	5,187,499,066	4,312,497,691	3,117,533,898	261,346,400	1,140 %
	Rest of the World	2,565,984,143	1,832,509,298	1,229,027,955	109,639,092	1,021 %
	Total World	7,753,483,209	6,145,006,989	4,346,561,853	360,985,492	1,104 %

knowledge, we will find no way out in the NLP research. What should we do in face of such situation? Is it better to keep ourselves confined to a narrow field of study or to catch up with the times, striving to learn new knowledge to meet the requirements of the interdisciplinary and marginal discipline? This is a big issue that all of the NLP practitioners must consider.

According to a survey by Miniwatts Marketing Group in 2019, top 20 countries with the highest number of the Internet users are listed in Table 1.1.

As can be seen from Table 1.1, in 2019, the number of the Internet users in China exceeded 827 million. From 2000 to 2019, the growth of the Internet users in China was 3584%. In addition to using English on the Internet, as can also be seen from Table 1.1, Chinese, Arabic, Spanish, Russian, German, French, Japanese, Korean, and Vietnamese are increasingly used. From 2000 to 2019, the number of the Internet users in the United States increased by only 207%, while the number of the Internet users in Bangladesh, Nigeria, Vietnam, Iran, Russia, and Brazil increased by 91,961%, 55,716%, 31,900%, 24,981%, 3434%, and 2881%, respectively. It can be seen that the number of people using languages other than English on the Internet is also increasing, as many of the abovementioned countries use languages other than English. English no longer dominates the Internet.

According to a survey by Miniwatts Marketing Group in 2019, top ten languages used in the Web are as follows (Table 1.2).

It can be seen from Table 1.2 that from 2000 to 2019, the growth of the Internet users in English was only 685.7%, while the growth of the Internet users in Arabic, Russian, Indonesian/Malay, Chinese, Portuguese, and Spanish was 8917.3%, 3434.0%, 2861.4%, 2572.3%, 2164.8%, and 1425.9%, respectively. The growth

Table 1.2   Top ten languages used in the Web in 2019

Top Ten Languages Used in the Web - April 30, 2019 (Number of Internet Users by Language)					
TOP TEN LANGUAGES IN THE INTERNET	World Population for this Language (2019 Estimate)	Internet Users by Language	Internet Penetration (% Population)	Internet Users Growth (2000 - 2019)	Internet Users % of World (Participation)
English	1,485,300,217	1,105,919,154	74.5 %	685.7 %	25.2 %
Chinese	1,457,821,239	863,230,794	59.2 %	2,572.3 %	19.3 %
Spanish	520,777,464	344,448,932	66.1 %	1,425.8 %	7.9 %
Arabic	444,016,517	226,595,470	51.0 %	8,917.3 %	5.2 %
Portuguese	289,923,583	171,583,004	59.2 %	2,164.8 %	3.9 %
Indonesian / Malaysian	302,430,273	169,685,798	56.1 %	2,861.4 %	3.9 %
French	422,308,112	144,695,288	34.3 %	1,106.0 %	3.3 %
Japanese	126,854,745	118,626,672	93.5 %	152.0 %	2.7 %
Russian	143,895,551	109,552,842	76.1 %	3,434.0 %	2.5 %
German	97,025,201	92,304,792	95.1 %	235.4 %	2.1 %
TOP 10 LANGUAGES	5,193,327,701	3,346,642,747	64.4 %	1,123.0 %	76.3 %
Rest of the Languages	2,522,895,508	1,039,842,794	41.2 %	1,090.4 %	23.7 %
WORLD TOTAL	7,716,223,209	4,386,485,541	56.8 %	1,115.1 %	100.0 %

of the Internet users using English is slower than that of the Internet users using other languages. The Internet has indeed become a multilingual online world. As a result, translation between different languages on the Internet is of course becoming more and more urgent. In addition to studying the single language NLP, we should also vigorously study the multilingual NLP.

In recent years, NLP has developed rapidly, and more and more papers on NLP have been published. Here is the ACL Anthology (AA) for the number of NLP papers published from 1965 to 2018. In 1965, there were only 24 NLP papers, but since 1990, the number of the NLP papers has increased dramatically, and in 2018, the number has reached 4173 (Fig. 1.29).

NLP has clear application goals. Speech synthesis, speech recognition, information retrieval, information extraction, and MT that we have listed are all important NLP application fields. Since the natural language is extremely complex, we should study formal models of NLP, its basic theoretical research.

Due to the complexity of NLP, the study of such formal models is often a strongly ill-posed problem. That is to say, when using formal models to establish algorithms to solve an NLP problem, it is often difficult to meet the requirements of the existence, uniqueness, and stability of the solution to the problem. Sometimes one of them cannot be met, and sometimes even three of them cannot be met. Therefore, for solving such a strongly ill-posed problem, appropriate constraint conditions should be put in place to make a part of the strongly ill-posed problem into a well-posed one within a certain range, solving the problem smoothly in the end.

As NLP is a multi-edge interdisciplinary subject, the power of human knowledge should be combined with the computational power of computers through a multidisciplinary effort that includes computer science, linguistics, psychology, cognitive science, and artificial intelligence to provide a large number of constraints

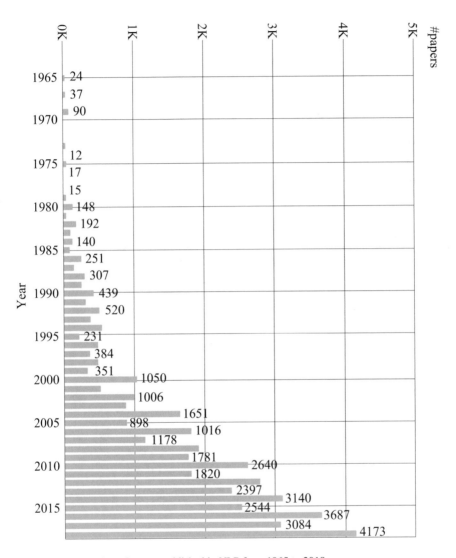

Fig. 1.29 The number of papers published in NLP from 1965 to 2018

to NLP formal models, solving various tough issues of NLP. The marginal and interdisciplinary nature of NLP provides a powerful means for solving such strongly ill-posed problems. In the study of NLP formal models, we may turn the strongly ill-posed problem into a well-posed one, which is something we are particularly fortunate to do and something that is worthy of our special attention.

This handbook focuses on the formal analysis of NLP, which is its basic theoretical research. When introducing these basic theoretical issues, we will inevitably involve some practical applications. A practice without theory is a blind practice; a theory without practice is an empty one. We should closely combine the basic theoretical research with practical application to promote the NLP development.

Bibliography

1. Bakushinsky, A., and A. Goncharsky. 1994. *Ill-Posed Problems: Theory and Application*. Dordrecht/Boston/London: Kluwer Academic.
2. Bo, Zhang. 2007. Computational Models of Natural Language Processing. *Chinese Journal of Information Technology* 3: 3–7.
3. Jurafsky, D., and J.H. Martin. 2000. *Speech and Language Processing: An Introduction to Natural Language Processing, Computational Linguistics and Speech Recognition*. Upper Saddle River, NJ: Prentice Hall. (in Chinese): Zhiwei Feng, Le Sun. *A Review of Natural Language Processing*. Beijing: Electronic Industry Press, 2005.
4. Kai-Uwe, Carstensen, et al. 2004. *Computerlinguistik und Sprachtechnologie—Eine Einführung*. Spektrum Akademischer Verlag: Heidelberg/Berlin.
5. Manaris, B. 1999. Natural Language Processing: A Human-Computer Interaction Perspective. *Advances in Computers* 47: 1–66.
6. Zhiwei, Feng. 1996. *Computer Processing of Natural Languages*. Shanghai: Shanghai Foreign Language Education Press.
7. ———. 2004. *Machine Translation*. Beijing: China Translation and Publishing Company.
8. ———. 2007. *On Machine Translation Now and Then*. Beijing: Language and Culture Press.

Chapter 2
Pioneers in the Study of Language Computing

Before the advent of electronic computers, there were some farsighted scholars who studied computational issues of the language. They studied this linguistic phenomenon from the perspective of computation, revealing the mathematical nature of the language.

In 1847, Russian mathematician B. Buljakovski suggested that the probabilistic method could be used for the comparative study of grammar, etymology, and language history.

In 1851, British mathematician A. De Morgen used the word length as a feature of article style to conduct statistical research.

In 1894, Swiss linguist De Saussure stated that in terms of basic properties, the relationship between the quantity and quantity of a language can be expressed regularly using mathematical formulas. In his *Course in General Linguistics* published in 1916, he also pointed out that the language is like a geometric system, which can be reduced to theorems to be proved.

In 1898, German scholar F. W. Kaeding counted the frequency of German words in the text and compiled *German Frequency Dictionary*, the first frequency dictionary in the world.

In 1904, Polish linguist Baudouin de Courtenay claimed that linguists should master not only elementary mathematics but also advanced mathematics. He expressed his firm belief that linguistics will be increasingly close to a precision science and that linguistics will expand the concept of quantity and develop new methods of deductive thinking based on the mathematical model.

In 1933, American linguist L. Bloomfield advanced a famous argument: "Mathematics is nothing but the highest state that the language can reach."

In 1935, E. Varder Beke, a Canadian scholar, put forward the concept of the distribution rate of words and took it as the main criterion for selecting words in dictionaries.

In 1944, British mathematician G. U. Yule published his book *The Statistical Study of Literary Vocabulary*, in which he used probability and statistical methods to study vocabulary on a large scale.

© Springer Nature Singapore Pte Ltd. 2023
Z. Feng, *Formal Analysis for Natural Language Processing: A Handbook*,
https://doi.org/10.1007/978-981-16-5172-4_2

Fig. 2.1 A. A. Markov

These facts show that the thoughts and research on language computation have a long history.

In this chapter, we focus on six of the most important pioneering studies on linguistic computation. They are Russian mathematician A. A. Markov's study on Markov chain, American scholar G. K. Zipf's study on Zipf's law, American scientist Shannon's study on entropy, American mathematical logician Y. Bar-Hillel's research on category grammar, American linguist Z. Harris's study on the language string analysis, and Russian mathematician О. С. Кулагина's study on linguistic set theory models. These pioneering studies have laid a preliminary foundation for the subsequent study of formal models of NLP.

2.1   Markov Chains

As early as 1913, the famous Russian mathematician A. A. Markov (1856–1922, Fig. 2.1) noticed the interplay between occurrence probabilities of linguistic symbols. He tried to study the mathematical theory of stochastic processes by taking the occurrence probability of linguistic symbols as an example.

Markov was born in Ryazan, Russia, the son of a mid-ranking official who later moved his family to St. Petersburg. In 1874, Markov was enrolled at the University of St. Petersburg, where he remained to teach after graduation. He was elected a member of the St. Petersburg Academy of Sciences in 1886. Markov's main research areas are probability and statistics, whose work initiated a new field of stochastic processes. The Markov chain named after him has a wide range of applications in modern engineering, natural sciences, and social sciences.

To study the mathematical problem of stochastic processes, he chose, among many literary works, the famous Russian poet А. ПУШКИН's popular narrative

Fig. 2.2 A. ПУШКИН's
popular narrative poem
Eugen Onegin

poem *Eugen Onegin* (Fig. 2.2) as the object for his research on mathematical problems.

Markov classified consecutive letters in *Eugen Onegin*, recorded vowels as V and consonants as C, and then used consecutive letters as a statistical unit to study the mutual influence between the probability of vowel and consonant letters. Since there were neither computers nor large-scale corpora at that time, Markov had to use the manual frequency search method to count the number of occurrences of the three-letter sequence consisting of vowels and consonants in *Eugen Onegin* and obtained the following vowel and consonant sequence table (Table 2.1).

As can be seen from this table, the total occurrences of all the letters (including vowels and consonants) in the texts are 20,000 times, of which 8638 are vowels and 11,362 are consonants. When vowels are followed by vowels, the letter sequence VV appears 1104 times; when consonants appear after vowels, the letter sequence VC appears 7534 times; when the letter sequence VV is followed by a vowel, the letter sequence VVV appears 115 times; when the letter sequence VV is followed by a consonant letter, the letter sequence VVC appears 989 times; and so on.

The probability of the occurrence of vowels and consonants can be calculated based on the data in the above table.

For example, the occurrence probability of vowels is

Table 2.1 Vowel and consonant sequence table observed in *Eugen Onegin*

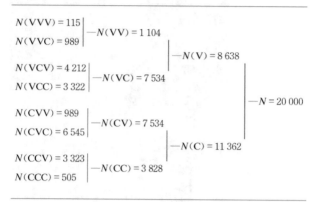

N represents the number of letter sequences, namely, count number

$$P(V) = \frac{N(V)}{N} = \frac{8638}{20,000} = 0.432$$

The occurrence probability of vowels after consonants is

$$P(V|C) = \frac{N(CV)}{N(C)} = \frac{7534}{11,362} = 0.663$$

The occurrence probability of vowels after vowel letters is

$$P(V|V) = \frac{N(VV)}{N(V)} = \frac{1104}{8638} = 0.128$$

Obviously, in Russian, the occurrence probability of vowels after consonants is greater than that of vowels after vowels. Markov's table clearly illustrates how the occurrence probability of vowels and consonants affects each other.

The above phenomena can be summarized as stochastic processes.

Stochastic processes have two meanings:

First, it is a function of time, and it changes over time.

Second, the function value at each moment is indeterminate and random, that is, the value of the function at each moment is distributed according to a certain probability.

When we write or speak, the appearance of each letter (or phoneme) changes with the change of time, a function of time. However, what letter (or phoneme) appears at each moment has a certain probability and is random. Therefore, we can regard the use of language as a stochastic process.

In this stochastic process, the language symbol appears as the outcome of a random trial, and the language is a series of chains with different outcomes of random trials.

If, in a randomized trial, the linguistic symbols appear independently of each other and do not affect each other, then the chain is an independent chain.

If the occurrence probability of each linguistic symbol in an independent chain is equal, then this chain is called an equal probability independent chain.

If in an independent chain the appearance probability of linguistic symbols is not equal with some being high and others being low in probability, this chain is called an unequal probability independent chain.

In the independent chain, the preceding linguistic symbol has no effect on the following linguistic symbol and is memoryless. Therefore, the independent chain is sent by a memoryless source, and it is a random process with no aftereffect. Given the known current state, the future state of the process is independent of its past state, which is a primitive form of Markov process.

Markov's study on vowels and consonants in *Eugen Onegin* breaks through the original form of Markov process. The future state of the process is found to be related to its past state, which moves the research of Markov process a step forward.

In random experiments, such as the vowel and consonant strings in *Eugen Onegin*, the appearance probability of each linguistic symbol is not independent of each other, and the individual outcome of each random experiment depends on the results of the previous random experiment. This kind of chain is called "Markov chain."

The previous linguistic symbol has an influence on the following one in the Markov chain, which is sent by a memory source. This is exactly what Markov faced when studying the sequence of letters in *Eugen Onegin*. As Markov pointed out, the language is a Markov chain issued by this kind of memory source.

If we consider only the influence of the previous linguistic symbol on the appearance probability of the following linguistic symbol, the resulting chain of language components is called the onefold Markov chain or binary grammar.

If we consider the influence of the first two linguistic symbols on the appearance probability of the next linguistic symbol, the resulting chain of symbol signs is called the double-fold Markov chain or ternary grammar.

If we consider the influence of the first three linguistic symbols on the appearance probability of the next linguistic symbol, the chain of linguistic symbols thus obtained is called the triple-fold Markov chain or quaternary grammar.

Similarly, if we can also consider the influence of the first four linguistic symbols or the first five linguistic symbols... on the appearance probability of the following linguistic symbols, the chain of linguistic symbols thus obtained is called fourfold Markov chain (5-gram syntax) or fivefold Markov (6-gram syntax), respectively, etc.

As the weight of Markov chains increases, the chain of linguistic symbols obtained from random experiments is getting closer to meaningful natural language texts.

American linguist N. Chomsky and psychologist G. Miller pointed out that the multiplicative number of such Markov chains does not increase infinitely and that its limit is the collection of grammatically and semantically valid natural language sentences. Thus, it is reasonable to think of sentences in the natural language as Markov chains with large multiplications. Markov chain mathematically describes the generation process of natural language sentences, which is an early formal model of the natural language. Many subsequent studies (e.g., the study of "N-gram") are based on the Markov model.

2.2 Zipf's Law

At the beginning of the twentieth century, with the massive accumulation of information about words in different languages and the compilation of frequency dictionaries, scholars tried to theoretically summarize the facts in these primary linguistic data from the perspective of mathematics.

In the frequency dictionary, the occurrence frequency of words and the ordinal rank of words are the two most basic data, which describe the properties of a word in the word list. Therefore, scholars focus on the study of the interrelationship between the two basic data in the glossary, putting forward the frequency distribution law of words.

Scholars, such as J. Estoup, E. Condon, G. K. Zipf, M. Joos, and B. B. Mandelbrot, have explored this issue successively.

In 1916, French stenographer J. Estoup observed the following pattern in his research on the improvement of the shorthand writing system.

If there is a text containing N words (N should be sufficiently large), the words in it are arranged in the order of decreasing n in their absolute frequency of occurrence in the text and are numbered in the order of natural numbers from 1 (absolute frequency is the largest word) to L (words with the smallest absolute frequency) to create a vocabulary list of this text. The frequency of words is denoted by n, and the number of words is denoted by r, which takes the value of all natural numbers in the $1 \leq r \leq L$ interval. The frequency vocabulary is as follows (Fig. 2.3).

J. Estoup found that the product of r between the absolute frequency of the word n_r and its corresponding serial number is generally stable at a constant k. That is

$$n_r \cdot r = k \qquad (2.1)$$

In 1928, E. Condon, a physicist at Bell Telephone Company in the United States, discovered an interesting pattern in his work to improve the communication capabilities of telephone lines.

The serial number of a word	1	2	$\cdots$	r	$\cdots$	L
Frequency of words	n_1	n_2	$\cdots$	n_r	$\cdots$	n_L

Fig. 2.3 The frequency vocabulary

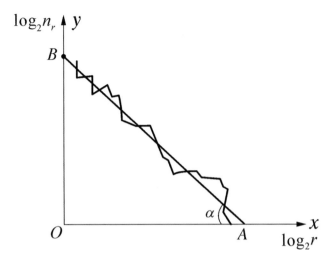

Fig. 2.4 Function chart by E. Condon

According to the frequency statistics of words, he made the function chart (Fig. 2.4).

The abscissa records the logarithm of the number of the word log r; the ordinate records the logarithm of the absolute frequency of the word log n_r. The reason for using logarithm is to make the ratio appropriate. For example, when $r = 1, n = 104$, and when $r = L$ (L is very large), $n_r = 1$, it is inconvenient to draw on the coordinate chart, but if you write it logarithmically, the difference between the two is not so great that you can draw it on the chart.

E. Condon found that the distribution relationship between log r and log n_r is close to a straight line AB.

Let $x = \log r$, $y = \log n_r$.

Let OB $= \log k$ (k is a constant).

The angle between the straight line and the x axis in the opposite direction is α. If $tg\alpha = \gamma$, then there is

$$\mathrm{OA} = \frac{\mathrm{OB}}{tg\alpha} = \frac{\log k}{\gamma}$$

According to the intercept equation of a straight line, obviously there is

$$\frac{x}{\mathrm{OA}} + \frac{y}{\mathrm{OB}} = 1$$

namely

$$\frac{\log r}{\frac{\log k}{\gamma}} + \frac{\log n_r}{\log k} = 1$$

$$\frac{\gamma \cdot \log r}{\log k} + \frac{\log n_r}{\log k} = 1$$

$$\gamma \cdot \log r + \log n_r = \log k$$

$$\log r^\gamma + \log n_r = \log k$$

Thus, there is

$$n_r = kr^{-\gamma}$$

After many tests, it was found that $\alpha = 45°$, namely

$$\gamma = tg\alpha = tg\ 45° = 1$$

So the above formula becomes $n_r = kr^{-1}$.

Divide the total length N of the text under consideration by both sides of the equation. Then we obtain

$$\frac{n_r}{N} = \frac{k}{N}r^{-1}$$

where $\frac{n_r}{N} = f_r$ and $\frac{k}{N}$ is a constant. Let $\frac{k}{N} = c$.

Then we get

$$f_r = cr^{-1} \qquad\qquad (2.2)$$

E. Condon states that c in Formula (2.2) is treated as a constant, but more tests are needed to test whether c is a constant.

In 1935, G. K. Zipf (1902–1950, Fig. 2.5), a professor and linguist at Harvard University, first examined the results obtained by E. Condon. Based on the frequency dictionary compiled by M. Hanley for J. Joyce's novella *Ulysses*, which contains 260,432 words and 29,899 different words, he tested E. Condon's findings on a much larger text scale than that of E. Condon.

Based on relevant data, G. K. Zipf made a function chart (Fig. 2.6) similar to that drawn by E. Condon.

The result obtained by G. K. Zipf is the same as that of E. Condon, namely

$$f_r = cr^{-1}$$

When the number of trials is $t \to \infty$ $t \to \infty$, the frequency f_r becomes the probability p_r. Thus we get

Fig.2.5 G. K. Zipf

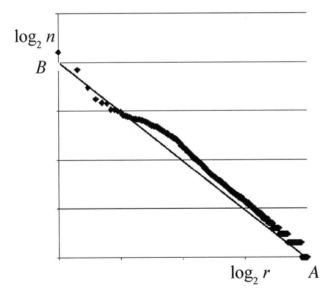

Fig. 2.6 Function chart by G. K. Zipf

$$p_r = cr^{-1}$$

Next, G. K. Zipf measures the value of c. At the beginning, he pointed out that in the above formula, when $r = 1$,

$$p_r = cr^{-1}$$
$$= c \times 1^{-1}$$
$$= c$$

It can be seen that c is the probability of the word whose serial number is 1, that is, the probability of the word with the highest frequency in the text. G. K. Zipf measured $c = 0.1$ and considered c to be a constant. In this way, his conclusion is almost exactly the same as that of E. Condon, who also thought that c is a constant. He differs from E. Condon in that he uses a larger corpus than that of E. Condon, and he specifically calculates the value of c, which should be equal to 0.1.

However, a large number of facts later showed that in most European languages, the relative frequency of words with the serial number 1 is generally less than 0.1 and that there is hardly a European language with a relative frequency of words with the serial number 1 being 0.1. Therefore, Zipf later revised his original statement. He pointed out that c is not a constant, but a parameter, and its value range is

$$0 < c < 0.1$$

For $r = 1, \ldots, n$, this parameter c makes

$$\sum_{r=1}^{n} p_r = 1$$

This one-parameter frequency distribution law is called "Zipf's law" in most of the literature on computational linguistics and NLP.

In 1936, shortly after G. K. Zipf published his results, American linguist M. Joos revised Zipf's formula.

M. Joos pointed out that in the Zipf's formula

$$p_r = cr^{-1}$$

not only is c a parameter, but 1 in the negative exponent -1 of r is also a parameter γ. This is because γ will increase when there are many words in the dictionary, that is, the angle α in the image will increase. When there are a few words in the dictionary, γ will decrease, that is, the angle α in the image will become smaller. It can be seen that γ is not always equal to 1 and that the angle α is not always 45°. In other words, γ is not a constant but a parameter. If this parameter is made to be $\gamma = b$, then we get

$$p_r = cr^{-b} \tag{2.3}$$

where $b > 0$, $c > 0$, for $r = 1, \ldots, n$, the parameters b and c should be

$$\sum_{r=1}^{n} p_r = 1$$

This is M. Joos' two-parameter frequency distribution law.

In the formula of M. Joos, when $b = 1$, the formula becomes

$$p_r = cr^{-1}$$

This is the Zipf's formula in that the Zipf's formula is just a special case of the Joos' formula when $b = 1$. Therefore, the Joos' formula can also be called the two-parameter Zipf's law.

In the early 1950s, B. B. Mandelbrot, a French British mathematician, used probability and information theory to study the frequency distribution of words. He regarded words as the random sequence of letters ending in blank and sentences as the random sequence of words encoded by words and treated articles as the random sequence of sentences formed by the increasing or decreasing process of the sentences. From this point of view, B. B. Mandelbrot, through a strict mathematical derivation, theoretically put forward the three-parameter frequency distribution law, whose form is as follows:

$$P_r = c(r + a)^{-b} \tag{2.4}$$

where $0 \leq a < 1$, $b > 0$, $c > 0$, $r = 1..., n$, the parameters a, b, and c have to be

$$\sum_{r=1}^{n} p_r = 1$$

The meaning of the three parameters a, b, and c are as follows:

Parameter c is related to the probability of the word with the highest occurrence probability.

Parameter b is related to the number of high-probability words. For high-probability words with $r < 50$, b is a non-subtractive function. As r increases, parameter b does not decrease.

Parameter a is related to the number of words N. Since a has more freedom of choice, the formula is more flexible and can better adapt to the measured data under various conditions.

In B. B. Mandelbrot's formula,
when $a = 0$, the formula is

$$p_r = cr^{-b}$$

This is Joos' formula, a two-parameter Zipf's law.

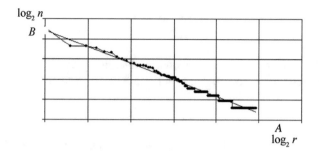

Fig. 2.7 AB is actually a broken line

When $a = 0$ and $b = 1$, the formula is

$$p_r = cr^{-1}$$

This is Zipf's formula, a one-parameter Zipf's law.

It can be seen that Joos' formula and Zipf's formula are just special forms of Mandelbrot's formula. Mandelbrot's formula is a three-parameter Zipf law.

Of course, the frequency distribution of words is a complicated issue. The above formulas cannot fully reflect their distributions. For example, from the formulas, the value of r can only correspond to the value of p_r. Therefore, the nature of the formulas determines that words with the same frequency cannot exist in the text, which is obviously inconsistent with the objective facts in the language. Tests show that when $15 < r < 1500$, the capacity of word groups with the same frequency is not large, but when $r > 1500$, that is, when the frequency of words is relatively small, the capacity of word groups with the same frequency is greatly increased. At this point, issues of sparse data occur. It can be seen that none of the above formulas can be used to describe the frequency distribution of low-frequency words. In fact, the function graph previously shown should be in the form shown in Fig. 2.7.

In fact, AB is not a straight line, but a broken line in the stepped form. As can be seen from the figure, the low-frequency words with high serial numbers are likely to have the same low frequency with different serial numbers. Therefore, these low-frequency words have many different serial numbers and the same frequency, while high-frequency words with low serial numbers have more and more words with the same frequency as the serial number increases. The less frequent the word, the more the same number, and the more frequent the word, the fewer the same number. This fact cannot be well described by any of the above formulas. It can be seen that although the frequency distribution of words helps establish a preliminary formal model for the structure of frequency dictionaries, this formal model is not yet perfect, and further research is necessary.

In Mandelbrot's formula

$$P_r = c(r+a)^{-b}$$

if $a = 0$, $b = 1$, and $c = 0.1$ in a given language are experimentally measured, then

$$
\begin{aligned}
p_r &= 0.1(r+0)^{-1} \\
&= 0.1r^{-1} \\
&= \frac{0.1}{r}
\end{aligned}
$$

Let's calculate the percentage of the first 1000 words with the highest frequency in the total number of words in the language text:

$$
\begin{aligned}
\sum_{r=1}^{1000} p_r &= \sum_{r=1}^{1000} \frac{0.1}{r} \\
&= 0.1 \sum_{r=1}^{1000} \frac{1}{r} \\
&= 0.1 \times \left(\frac{1}{1} + \frac{1}{2} + \frac{1}{3} + \ldots + \frac{1}{1000} \right) \\
&= 0.748 \\
&= 74.8\%
\end{aligned}
$$

It can be seen that for a given language, the first 1000 words with the highest frequency account for 74.8% of the total number of words in the texts of the language. In other words, as long as you recognize the 1000 words used most frequently in the language, you can understand most of the content in this language text. This conclusion based on Zipf's law is of great reference value for language learning and foreign language teaching.

Of course, to truly understand an article, you also need to have grammar, semantics, pragmatics, and other background knowledge, in addition to lexical knowledge. A language is not easy to learn, and it requires painstaking efforts.

Having learnt Zipf's law in the 1980s, Zhiwei Feng wrote an article introducing Zipf's law[1] in 1983. This is the earliest paper on Zipf's law by a Chinese scholar.

2.3 Shannon's Work on Entropy

In 1948, American scientist C. E. Shannon (1916–2001, Fig. 2.8) published an article entitled "A Mathematical Theory of Communication" in *The Bell System Technical Journal* (27: pp. 379–423, 1948), which laid the theoretical foundation of information theory. Shannon is regarded as "the father of information theory."

---

[1]Zhiwei Feng. The ins and outs of the Zipf's law. *Information Science*. 1983, (2).

Fig. 2.8 C. E. Shannon

Shannon was born in Petoskey, Michigan, USA, on April 30, 1916. He graduated from the University of Michigan with a bachelor's degree in mathematics and electrical engineering in 1936 and received a doctorate in mathematics and a master's degree in electrical engineering from the Massachusetts Institute of Technology (MIT) in 1940. He joined the Mathematics Department of Bell Labs in 1941 and worked there until 1972. He became a visiting professor in 1956, a lifelong professor in 1958, and an honorary professor in 1978 at MIT. Shannon died on February 26, 2001, at the age of 84.

Information theory is a science that studies general laws in information transmission and information processing systems. Before the emergence of information theory, people's understanding of information systems was relatively superficial, and information carrying messages was generally regarded as transient periodic signals. Later, people applied important concepts in modern statistical mechanics, Markov stochastic process theory, and generalized harmonic analysis and other mathematical methods to the study of information systems, only to see that information in the communication system is essentially a probabilistic stochastic process, from which some general conclusions are drawn, leading to the establishment of the discipline of information theory.

The research object of information theory is information transmission and information processing system in a broad sense. Telegraph, telephone, fax, radar, sonar and the perception system of various organisms, all can be described with the same information theory and can be summarized as random processes of one kind or another and studied in depth.

From the perspective of information theory, the process of communication with the natural language is the process of information transmission from the message sender to the message receiver through a communication medium. The schematic diagram of the communication process is as follows (Fig. 2.9).

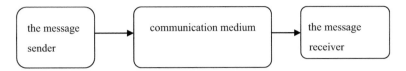

Fig. 2.9 Schematic diagram of the communication process

The sender (i.e., the source) sends out language symbols one by one sequentially over time, and the receiver receives language symbols one by one sequentially over time. Obviously, the process is a random process, as the process is a function of time, and the values at each moment (i.e., what signs appear) are random.

In this random process, if we make an experiment to determine what language signs appear in a given language, such an experiment is called a random test, and the language sign that appears is the outcome of the random test. The language can be viewed as a series of chains with different outcomes of the random trials. In this way, we can use the Markov chain theory described in Sect. 2.1 to study the generation process of language signs.

If in a random experiment, the appearance of each language symbol is independent of each other and does not affect each other; this chain is an independent chain.

If in an independent chain the occurrence probability of each language symbol is equal, this chain is called the equal probability independent chain. If the language symbols are English letters (including 26 letters and blanks), the independent chain of the equal probability of English letters is as follows:

XFOML   RXKHRJFFJUJ   ZLPWCFWKCYJ   FFJEYVKCQ   SDHYD QPAAMKBZAACIBZLHJQD

If the occurrence probability of each language symbol in the independent chain is not equal with some having a high probability and some a low probability, this chain is called an unequal probability independent chain. The unequal probability independent chain of English letters is as follows:

OCRO   HLIRGWR   NMIELWIS   EU   LLNBNESEBYA   TH   EEI ALHENHTTPA   OOBTTVA   NAH   BRL

In the above independent chain source, the preceding language symbol has no effect on the following language symbol. As it is memoryless, it is emitted from a memoryless source.

If in a random trial the occurrence probability of each language symbol is not independent of each other and if the individual outcome of each random trial depends on the outcome of the previous random trial, this chain is a Markov chain. In the Markov chain, if the preceding language symbol has an effect on the following language symbol, it is emitted by a memorized source.

The language is obviously a Markov chain sent from a memorized source. In English, for example, the occurrence probability of vowels increases when the preceding letter is a series of interconnected consonants. This chain is obviously a Markov chain.

If we only consider the effect of the preceding language symbol on the occurrence probability of the following language symbol, the resulting chain of language symbols is onefold Markov chain. The onefold Markov chain of English letters is as follows:

ON   IE   ANTSOUTINYS   ARE   TINCTORE   BE   S   DEAMY
ACHIND   ILONASINE   TUCDOWE   AT   TEASONARE   FUSO
TIZIN   ANDY   TOBE   SEACE   CTIBE

If we consider the effect of the first two language symbols on the occurrence probability of the language symbol that follows, the resulting chain of language symbols is a double-fold Markov chain. The double-fold Markov chain of English letters is as follows:

IN   NO   IST   LAT   WHEY   CRATICT   FROUREBIRS   CROCID
PONDENOME   OF   DEMONSTURES   OF   THE   REPTAGIN   IS
REGOAQCTIONA   OF   CRE

If we consider the effect of the first three language symbols on the occurrence probability of the next language symbol, the resulting chain of language symbols is a triple-fold Markov chain. Similarly, if we consider the first four language symbols, the first five language symbols, etc. on the effect of the occurrence probability of the following language symbol, respectively, we can get fourfold Markov chains, fivefold Markov chains, and so on.

As the weight of Markov chains increases, each chain of English language symbols with a larger weight is closer to meaningful English texts than those with smaller weights. When the language symbol is a word, we can see this more clearly.

For example, if the language symbol is an English word, the independent chain of unequal probabilities for English words is as follows:

REPRESENTING   AN   SPEEDILY   IS   AN   GOOD   APT   OR
CAME   CAN   DIFFERENT   NATURAL   HERE   HE   THE   A   IN
CAME   THE   TOOF   TO   EXPERT   GRAY   COME   TO   FUR-
NISHES   THE   MESSAGE   HAD   BE   THESE

The following is the onefold Markov chain of English words:

THE   HEAD   AND   IN   FRONTAL   ATTACK   ON   AN   ENGLISH
WRITER   THAT   THE   CHARACTER   OF   THIS   POINT   IS
THEREFORE   ANOTHER   METHOD   FOR   THE   LETTERS
THAT   THE   TIME   OF   WHO   EVER   TOLD   THE   PROBLEM
FOR   AN   UNEXPECTED

What follows is the double-fold Markov chain of English words:

FAMILY   WAS   LARGE   DARK   ANIMAL   CAME   ROARING
DOWN   THE   MIDDLE   OF   MY   FRIENDS   LOVE   BOOKS   PAS-
SIONATELY   EVERY   KISS   IS   FINE

The following chain is the fourfold Markov chain of English words:

ROAD IN THE COUNTRY WAS INSANE ESPECCIALLY
INDREARY ROOMS WHERE THEY HAVE SOME BOOKS
TO BUY FOR STUDYING GREEK

It is not difficult to see that this chain already looks a lot like English. Although it's still a meaningless word chain, it is easier to remember than other word chains.

So, what should the multiplicity of a Markov chain be to produce a satisfactory English sentence? Let's consider the following English sentences:

The *people* who called and wanted to rent your house when you go away next year *are* from California.

In this sentence, the grammatical correlation extends from the second word *people* to the seventeenth word *are*. To reflect this correlation, a minimum of 15 Markov chains is required. In some cases, Markov chains may have even greater weights.

An important feature of stochastic processes is the correlation between signs and symbols, which predicts the future of a language text from the history of its production. As the multiplicity of Markov chain increases, we can better predict the occurrence of the next language symbol based on the previous one. In other words, as Markov chain multiplicity increases, the uncertainty of the random trial in which we predict the occurrence of the next language symbol based on the previous one gets smaller. For those independent chains, which are not Markov chains, the occurrence of language symbols is the most difficult to predict. That is to say, every language symbol appears with great uncertainty.

In information theory, the amount of information is precisely measured by the uncertainty of the random trial before the message is received. The magnitude of the uncertainty in a random test is called entropy. Entropy varies with the number and probability of language symbols before they are received. After receiving language symbols, the uncertainty is eliminated, and entropy is reduced to zero. It is thus clear that the amount of information is equal to the entropy of being eliminated. Therefore, as long as we measure the entropy of the language symbol, we can learn how much information the language symbol is loaded with.

As early as 1928, L. Hartley raised the question of how to measure the size of information. He argued that if a device has D possible locations or physical states, two such devices working together would have D^2 states. When three such devices work together, there are D^3 states, and as the number of devices increases, so does the number of possible states of the system. In order to measure its information capacity, the capacity of two devices ($2D$) should be exactly twice that of the D device. Therefore, Hartley defines the information capability of a device as $\log D$, where D is the number of different states that the entire system can enter.

In information theory, Shannon adopted Hartley's method to determine entropy.

Shannon proposes that if we carry out a random experiment with n possible equal probability outcomes (e.g., roll a dice, $n = 6$), the entropy of this random experiment is measured by $\log_2 n$. This method of measuring entropy is reasonable. The reasons are as follows:

First, the greater the possible outcome n of the random experiment, the greater the uncertainty of the random experiment, and the greater its entropy.

Second, if we do a compound test containing two random trials at the same time, each random trial has n possible outcomes (e.g., throwing two dice simultaneously). This compound test has n^2 outcomes, and its entropy is equal to $\log_2 n^2 = 2\log_2 n$. This is equal to twice the time when only one dice is rolled. This is completely consistent with Hartley's view.

Third, if we do a compound test with two random trials at the same time, with one random trial having m possible outcomes and the other random trial n possible outcomes (e.g., when a coin is thrown, $m = 2$; when a dice is rolled, $n = 6$), this compound test has $m \cdot n$ possible equal probability outcomes. In other words, the entropy of this compound experiment should be equal to $\log_2 mn$. Again, we can also think that the entropy of this compound experiment should be equal to the sum of the entropies of the outcomes of the two random trials that constitute this compound experiment, which is equal to $\log_2 m + \log_2 n$. However, we know that

$$\log_2 mn = \log_2 m + \log_2 n$$

It can be seen that the entropy of the compound test is the same whether it is viewed as a unified test or as the sum of two random tests.

All of these facts justify the rationality of using $\log_2 n$ to measure the entropy.

We record the entropy of a random experiment with n possible equal probability outcomes as H_0,

$$H_0 = \log_2 n \tag{2.5}$$

In this formula, when $n = 2$,

$$H_0 = \log_2 2 = 1$$

The entropy then is called 1 bit.

This means that if a message consists of two equal probability language components, the entropy contained in each language component is 1 bit.

If the random experiment has n outcomes with unequal probabilities, the probability of the ith outcome is p_i. The entropy H_1 of this random experiment is calculated by the following formula:

$$H_1 = -\sum_{i=1}^{n} p_i \log_2 p_i \tag{2.6}$$

In 1951, Shannon first calculated the entropy H_1 of an unequal probability independent chain of English letters to be 4.03 bits.

The unequal probability of the random experiment outcome reduces the uncertainty of this random experiment. Therefore, there are

Fig. 2.10 Prior probability
of each horse

Horse 1	1/2	Horse 5	1/64
Horse 2	1/4	Horse 6	1/64
Horse 3	1/8	Horse 7	1/64
Horse 4	1/16	Horse 8	1/64

$$\log_2 n \geq -\sum_{i=1}^{n} p_i \log_2 p_i \tag{2.7}$$

$$H_0 \geq H_1$$

When $p_1 = p_2 = \ldots = p_n = 1/n$,

$$H_0 = H_1$$

For computer scientists, the most intuitive way to define the entropy is to deem it the lower bound on the number of bits in a certain judgment or information encoding in the optimal encoding.

Suppose we want to place a bet on a horse at the racetrack in the place where we live, but the racetrack is too far away from where we live. Instead of going to the racetrack ourselves, we send a short message to the bookkeeper at the racetrack, telling him which horse we are betting on.

Suppose there are eight horses in the race. One way to code this message is to use a binary code to represent the horse's number. Thus, the binary code for a horse of number 1 is 001, the binary code for a horse of number 2 is 010, the binary code for a horse of number 3 is 011, and so on. The binary code for a horse of number 8 is 000. If it takes a day for us to place a bet and if each horse is coded in bits, we will send out 3 bits of information per race.

Can't we do something better? Yes. We can transmit the message according to the actual distribution of bets, assuming that the prior probability of each horse is shown in Fig. 2.10.

The entropy of the random variable X of these horses can let us know the lower bound of the number of bits, which is calculated as follows:

$$
\begin{aligned}
H(X) = & -\sum_{i=1}^{i=8} p(i) \log p(i) \\
= & -\frac{1}{2}\log\frac{1}{2} - \frac{1}{4}\log\frac{1}{4} - \frac{1}{8}\log\frac{1}{8} - \frac{1}{16}\log\frac{1}{16} - 4\left(\frac{1}{64}\log\frac{1}{64}\right) \\
= & -\frac{1}{2}(\log 1 - \log 2) - \frac{1}{4}(\log 1 - \log 2^2) - \frac{1}{8}(\log 1 - \log 2^3) \\
& -\frac{1}{16}(\log 1 - \log 2^4) - 4\left(\frac{1}{64}\right)(\log 1 - \log 2^6)
\end{aligned}
$$

$$= \frac{1}{2} + \frac{1}{2} + \frac{3}{8} + \frac{4}{16} + \frac{6}{16} = 2 \text{ bits}$$

The code with an average of 2 bits per game can be encoded as follows: The shortest code is used to represent the horse with the highest probability we estimate. The smaller the estimated probability is, the longer the code. For example, we can use 0 to encode the horse with the highest estimated probability and arrange them according to the estimated probability in a decreasing order. The codes of the remaining horses are 10, 110, 1110, 111,100, 111,101, 111,110, and 111,111, respectively.

What if we estimate the probability of each horse to be the same? We have seen earlier that if we use the equal length binary encoding for each horse and if each horse is encoded with 3 bits, the average number of bits is 3. Is the entropy the same then? Yes, in this case, the estimated probability of each horse is 1/8. The entropy of our choice of the horse is calculated as follows:

$$H(X) = -\sum_{i=1}^{i=S} \frac{1}{S} \log \frac{1}{S} = -\log \frac{1}{8} = 3 \text{ bits.}$$

From this example, we can understand why

$$H_0 \geq H_1$$

Closely related to the entropy is the concept of perplexity. If we take the entropy H as the index of 2, the value of 2^H is called the degree of perplexity. Intuitively, we can understand the degree of perplexity as the weighted average of random variables selected in random trials. Therefore, if we choose among 8 horses with equal probability estimates (in this case, the entropy $H = 3$ bits), the perplexity is 2^3, that is, 8. If we choose among 8 horses with different probabilities (in this case, the entropy $H = 2$ bits), the perplexity is 2^2, that is, 4. Obviously, the greater the entropy of a random experiment is, the greater is its perplexity.

In NLP, the entropy and perplexity are the most common measurement methods used to evaluate N-gram models.

If we consider the effect of the preceding language sign on the occurrence probability of the following language sign, we can get the conditional entropy. The entropy of Markov chain is the conditional entropy. More specifically, its calculation formula can be concisely written as

$$H = -\sum_{i,j}^{n} p[b_i(n-1),j] \log_2 p_{b_i(n-1)}(j)$$

where $b_i(n-1)$ is a combination of $n-1$ outcomes, followed by the jth outcome. $P[b_i(n-1), j]$ is the probability of the occurrence of this combination, and $P_{bi(n-1)}(j)$ is the conditional probability of the jth outcome after the combination of $n-1$ outcomes.

According to this formula, we can calculate the first-order conditional entropy (H_2) for the onefold Markov chain (binary grammar), the double-fold Markov chain (ternary grammar), the triple-fold Markov chain (quaternary grammar)..., respectively, and the second-order conditional entropy (H_3), third-order conditional entropy (H_4)..., and so on.

The first-order conditional entropy is calculated according to the following formula:

$$H_2 = -\sum_{i,j}^{n} P_{i,j} \log_2 p_i(j) \tag{2.8}$$

where P_{ij} represents the occurrence probability of all possible bilingual symbol combinations in the text and where $P_i(j)$ represents the conditional occurrence probability of language symbol j under the condition that the preceding language symbol is i.

The second-order conditional entropy is calculated according to Formula (2.9):

$$H_3 = -\sum_{i,j}^{n} P_{i,j,k} \log_2 p_{i,j}(k) \tag{2.9}$$

where P_{ijk} represents the occurrence probability of all possible trilingual symbol combinations and where $P_{ij}(k)$ represents the conditional occurrence probability of language symbol k after language symbols i and j.

As the multiplicity of Markov chain increases, the conditional entropy becomes smaller and smaller. We always have

$$H_0 \geq H_1 \geq H_2 \geq H_3 \geq \ldots \geq H_{k-1} \geq H_k \ldots \geq \ldots H_\infty \tag{2.10}$$

This shows that every time a language symbol is added to the preceding language symbol, the entropy of a language symbol contained in the text will not increase. On the other hand, because the entropy contained in a language symbol of the text is always positive in any case, there is

$$\lim_{k \to \infty} H_k = H_\infty \tag{2.11}$$

In other words, the entropy has a lower limit. When k gradually increases, the entropy gradually stabilizes and no longer decreases. The entropy that no longer decreases is the amount of the real information contained in a symbol of the natural language, which is called the limit entropy.

From the entropy of the equal probability independent chain to that of the unequal probability independent chain, from the entropy of the unequal probability independent chain to the first-order conditional entropy, from the first-order conditional entropy to the second-order, third-order, ... to the limit entropy is the embodiment of language information structure, which suggests the restriction of language structures on language information. The concept of the limit entropy scientifically reflects this restriction of language structures in the entropy of language symbols, and it is of great significance to the study of NLP.

In many cases, we need to calculate the entropy of a word sequence. For example, for a grammar, we need to calculate the entropy of the word sequence $W = \{w_0, w_1, w_2, ..., w_n\}$, where $w_0, w_1, w_2, ..., w_n$ means different words. One of the methods is to allow variables to cover the sequence of words. For example, we can calculate the entropy of all finite sequences of random variables of words with length n in language L in the same way as suggested above. The calculation formula is as follows:

$$H(w_1, w_2, \ldots, w_n) = -\sum_{w_1^n \in L} p(W_1^n) \log (W_1^n) \qquad (2.12)$$

We can define the entropy rate as the value obtained by dividing the entropy of this sequence by the number of words n (we can also think of the entropy rate as the entropy of each word):

$$\frac{1}{n} H(W_1^n) = -\frac{1}{n} \sum_{w_1^n \in L} p(W_1^n) \log (W_1^n) \qquad (2.13)$$

But to calculate the limit entropy of a language, we need to consider sequences of the infinite length. If we think of language L as a random process of generating word sequences, its entropy rate $H(L)$ can be defined as

$$\begin{aligned}
H(L) &= \lim_{n \to \infty} \frac{1}{n} H(w_1, w_2, \cdots, w_n) \\
&= \lim_{n \to \infty} \frac{1}{n} \sum_{w \in L} p(w_1, \cdots, w_n) \log p(w_1, \cdots, w_n)
\end{aligned} \qquad (2.14)$$

The Shannon-McMillan-Breiman theorem states that if a language is regular in a sense (to be precise, if a language is both stationary and ergodic), there is

$$H(L) = \lim_{n \to \infty} -\frac{1}{n} \log p(w_1, w_2, \ldots, w_n) \qquad (2.15)$$

This means that we can take a sufficiently long sequence in a language to replace the sum of all possible sequences in the language. The intuitive interpretation of the Shannon-McMillan-Breiman theorem is that a sufficiently long word sequence can contain many other shorter sequences, each of which can appear repeatedly in the longer ones according to their respective probabilities.

If the probability assigned to a sequence by the random process is constant over time, the random process is said to be stationary. In other words, in a stationary random process, the probability distribution of words at time t is the same as the probability distribution at time $t + 1$. The probability distribution of both the Markov model and N-grams is stable as well. For example, in binary grammar, P_i depends only on P_{i-1}. If we move the index of time to x, P_{i+x} still depends on P_{i+x-1}. However, the natural language is not stationary. In a natural language, the probability of the next word may depend on events at any distance and on time. Therefore, our statistical model is approximate to the correct distribution of the natural language and the description of its entropy.

Finally, following this simple and convenient assumption, which is incorrect, we can take a very long output sample to calculate the limit entropy of a random process and to calculate its average logarithmic probability.

The cross entropy of a model can be used as an upper bound on the limit entropy of a random process. We can use this method to estimate the limit entropy of English.

Why should we care for the English limit entropy?

One reason is that the limit entropy of English will provide a reliable lower bound for our experiments with probabilistic grammar. Another reason is that we can use English limit entropy to help us understand which parts of the language provide the most information. For example, does the ability to predict English mainly depend on word order, or semantic, or morphological, or compositional, or pragmatic clues? This can greatly help us understand what our language models should focus on.

There are usually two ways to calculate the limit entropy in English.

The first method is the one used by Shannon, which is part of his pioneering work in the field of information theory. His idea is to use subjects to construct an experiment on information, requiring the subjects to guess letters with researchers observing how many of their guessed letters are correct to estimate the probability of letters, and estimating the entropy of the sequence.

The design of the actual experiment is as follows: In the experiment, we show the subjects an English text and ask them to guess what might be the next letter. Participants use their knowledge of the language to guess the most likely letter that might follow, then the next most likely letter, and so on. We record the number of times the subjects guess right. Shannon pointed out that the entropy of guessing sequences is the same as the limit entropy of English letters. Shannon's intuitive interpretation of this view is that if the subjects make n guesses, given a sequence of guesses, we can reconstruct the original text by selecting the nth most likely letter. This method requires guessing letters rather than guessing words, and the subjects sometimes have to do exhaustive searches for all the letters. Therefore, Shannon calculates the limit entropy of each letter in English, not the limit entropy of each word in English. He reports that the limit entropy of English letters is 1.3 bits (for 27 letters [26 letters with a space]). Shannon's estimate is a bit too low, because he is experimenting with a single text (Dumas Malone's *Jefferson the Virginian*). Shannon also noticed that for other texts (news reports, scientific works, poems), the entropy is relatively high, as his subjects often guessed wrong.

The second method of calculating the entropy in English can help to avoid the single text problem that leads to the error in Shannon results. This method uses a smart random model to be trained on a large corpus, assigns a logarithmic probability to a very long English sequence, and uses Shannon-McMillan-Breiman theorem for calculation:

$$H(\text{English}) \leq \lim_{n \to \infty} -\frac{1}{n} \log m(w_1 w_2 \cdots w_n)$$

For example, Brown et al. trained a ternary grammar model on 583 million words of English text (293,181 types) to calculate the probability of the entire Brown corpus (1,014,312 tokens). Training data include news, encyclopedias, novels, official correspondence, proceedings of the Canadian Parliament, and a variety of other resources.

They then used ternary grammar of words to assign probabilities to the Brown corpus, treating the corpus as a sequence of letters and thus calculating the entropy of the characters in the Brown corpus. The result obtained is that the limit entropy of each character is 1.75 bits (the character set here contains all 95 printable ASCII characters). This is the conditional entropy of English letters in terms of ternary grammar. Obviously, this conditional entropy is larger than the limit entropy of 1.3 bits measured by Shannon. In addition, the character set used by Brown is the ASCII character set, which contains 95 characters, many of which exceed the English limit of 26 letters.

Most literature reports that the limit entropy contained in an English letter is between 0.9296 bits and 1.5604 bits, with an average value being 1.245 bits, which is close to the result measured by Shannon (1.3 bits). Generally speaking, we use this calculation result.

For urgent practical reasons, people started to measure the entropy of some Indo-European languages after Shannon measured the entropy H_1 of the unequal probability independent chain of English letters. So far, the nine-order conditional entropy of English has already been measured, and the fourteenth-order conditional entropy of Russian has been measured as well. What follows is a comparison of the entropy H_1 list of independent chains with unequal probability in French, Italian, Spanish, English, German, Romanian, and Russian (Table 2.2).

In the 1970s, Chinese scholar called Zhiwei Feng, imitating Shannon's study on the entropy of English letters, first estimated the entropy H_1 of Chinese characters to be 9.65 bits by means of the manual frequency search, and he proposed the limit theorem of Chinese character capacity. Following Zipf's law and using mathematical methods, he proved that the entropy H_1 contained in a Chinese character increases with the increase of the capacity of Chinese characters, when the capacity of Chinese characters in the statistical sample is not large. When the capacity of Chinese characters in the statistical sample reaches 12,366 characters, the entropy H_1 contained in a Chinese character no longer increases, which means that there is a limit to the capacity of the Chinese character in the statistical sample when determining the entropy H_1 of a Chinese character. The limit value is 12,366 characters. Beyond this limit value, the measured entropy of Chinese characters will never increase. Among the 12,366 Chinese characters, more than 4000 are frequently used

Table 2.2   The entropy H_1 of some languages

Language	Number of symbols	Entropy H_1	Note
French	27 (with a space)	3.98	Latin alphabet
Italian	22 (with a space)	4.00	Latin alphabet
Spanish	27 (with a space)	4.01	Latin alphabet
English	27 (with a space)	4.03	Latin alphabet
German	27 (with a space)	4.10	Latin alphabet
Romanian	27 (with a space)	4.12	Latin alphabet
Russian	32 (with a space)	4.35	Cyrillic alphabet

characters, another more than 4000 are less frequently used characters, and still another more than 4000 are least frequently used characters. He believes that these 12,366 Chinese characters can represent the basic features of Chinese characters in ancient and modern documents. From this, he concludes that in the context of written Chinese as a whole, the entropy H_1 contained in a character is 9.65 bits across all written Chinese (both modern and ancient), which, of course, is just a premature guess of Zhiwei Feng.

In 1988, Yuan Liu from the Department of Computer Science, Beijing University of Aeronautics and Astronautics, calculated the entropy H_1 of Chinese characters to be 9.71 bits by the automatic frequency search method. In 1994, Kim Teng Lua from the Department of Computer Science, National University of Singapore, calculated the entropy H_1 of Chinese characters as 9.59 bits by computer. Their results are very close to that obtained by Zhiwei Feng through a former manual frequency search method.

In 1996, Zhiwei Feng also estimated the limit entropy of Chinese characters to be 4.0462 bits based on the comparison between Chinese and English texts. In 2006, on the basis of a large-scale corpus (10^6–10^7 Chinese characters), Maosong Sun and Fan Sun from the Department of Computer Science, Tsinghua University, used Brown's method to estimate the limit entropy of Chinese characters to be 5.31 bits. This value is more accurate.

According to the channel coding theorem proposed by Shannon, the length of the code word cannot be less than the entropy H_1 of the symbol when coding. The entropy H_1 of Chinese characters is 9.65 bits, which is greater than 1 byte (1 byte = 8 bits). Therefore, Chinese characters cannot be coded with a single byte like English characters, but it must be coded with 2 bytes (2 bytes = 16 bits) or 3 bytes. Zhiwei Feng's work of measuring Chinese character entropy provides a theoretical basis for the establishment of a double-byte encoding for the character set of the Chinese character encoding for information processing in the 1980s.

Zhiwei Feng also found that there is an inverse relationship between the text reading speed V and the character entropy H_1. In the text reading with different characters, the smaller the entropy of the character, the faster the reading speed; the greater the entropy of the character, the slower the reading speed. The product of the reading speed V and the character entropy H_1 is a constant, and this constant k reflects people's ability to read text characters. The ability to read texts with different characters is roughly the same among all people, although the characters are different. Therefore, there should be the following formula:

$$V \cdot H_1 = k$$

This formula reflects a universal law that people who use different characters to read texts follow. Of course, this is just a bold yet-to-be-tested hypothesis by Zhiwei Feng.

Entropy is a measure of the amount of information. In NLP, entropy, very valuable information, is used to portray the mathematical feature of a language. It can also be used to measure the amount of information in a particular grammar, to measure how well a given grammar matches a given language, and to predict what the next word in a given N-gram is. If there are two given grammars and a corpus, we can use the entropy to estimate which grammar matches the corpus better. In addition, we can use the entropy to compare the difficulty of two speech recognition tasks, to measure how well a given probabilistic grammar matches human grammar, and to estimate people's ability to read text characters.

2.4 Bar-Hillel's Categorial Grammar

Categorial grammar was proposed by Mathematical logic specialists Kazimierz Ajukievicz (1890–1963) and Yehoshua Bar-Hillel (1915–1975, Fig. 2.11).

As early as 1935, a mathematical logician called Kazimierz Ajukievicz came up with the basic concepts of categorial grammar. In 1958, mathematician J. Joachim Lambek in his article entitled "The mathematics of sentence structure" published in *The American Mathematical Monthly* (Vol. 65, p. 154–170) put forward the theory of syntactic type calculus, according to which it is possible to identify whether a string of symbols is a valid sentence in a given language. In 1959, Y. Bar-Hillel further developed the theory of syntactic type calculus in his paper entitled "Decision procedures for structure in natural languages" published in *Logique et analyse* (2-e annee, No 5), discussing in detail the decision procedure for structure in the natural language. Since syntactic types are categorial, in 1960, Y. Bar-Hillel et al. in their article entitled "On categorial and phrase structure grammars" published in *Bull. Res. Council Israel* (Sec. F. 9, 1–16) named this grammar categorial grammar. For decades, categorial grammar has been a focus of NLP research and has always maintained its vitality.

Born in Wien, Austria, in 1915, Y. Bar-Hillel served in the British Army's Jewish Brigade during World War II and lost an eye during Israel War of Independence. After the war, Y. Bar-Hillel received his Ph.D. at Hebrew University in Israel and in 1950 did postdoctoral research at the University of Chicago under the distinguished mathematical logician Carnap and later worked at MIT. He was one of the pioneers of MT, who organized the first conference on MT in 1952. In 1953, he left MIT for the Philosophy Department in Hebrew University and died in 1975 in Jerusalem.

In this handbook, we discuss categorial grammar based on Bar-Hillel's theory.

We first introduce the concept of syntactic types.

Any word can be classified into certain syntactic types according to its function in a sentence. If n is used for the syntactic type of a noun and S for a sentence, other

Fig. 2.11 Y. Bar-Hillel

syntactic types can be revealed by combining *n* and *S* in different ways. The rules are as follows:

1. If there is a word B, the syntax type of the following word C is γ, and if the function of the word sequence BC is the same as β, the syntax type of this word B is recorded as β/γ.
2. If there is a word B, the syntax type of the preceding word A is α, and if the function of the word sequence AB is the same as β, the syntax type of this word B is recorded as α\β.
3. If there is a word B, the syntax type of the preceding word A is α, and the syntax type of the following words is γ, and if the function of the word sequence ABC is the same as β, the syntax of the word B is α\β/γ.

According to these rules, the syntactic type of words in the natural language can be written.

For example, in English, the syntactic type of the word *John* is n.

As the word *poor* in "Poor John" is followed by the noun "John," "Poor John" has the same function as the noun. Its syntax type is n/n.

The word *works* is preceded by the noun "John" and constitutes "John works," which has the same function as a sentence. Its syntactic type is n\S.

The word *likes* is preceded by the noun *John* and followed by the noun *Jane*, constituting "John likes Jane," which has the same function as the sentence. Its syntactic type is n\S/n.

The word *soundly* in "John slept soundly" is preceded by the "slept" (n\S), constituting "slept soundly," which has the same function as the sentence. Its syntactic type is (n\S)\n\S.

Table 2.3 Table of English syntax types

	Words	Syntax types	Parts of speech
(1)	John	n	n.
(2)	poor	n/n	adj.
(3)	works	n/S	vi.
(4)	likes	n\S/n	vt.
(5)	soundly	(n\S)\n\S	adv.
(6)	here	S\S	adv.
(7)	never	n\S/(n\S)	adv.
(8)	for	S\S/n	pre.
(9)	and	S\S/S	con.

In "John never works," the syntactic type of the word *John* is n, so the syntactic type of "never works" is n\S. It can be seen that the word *never* precedes the word *works* with a syntax type of n\S to form "never works," and that the syntax type of the word *works* is still n\S, so the syntax type of the word *never* is n\S/(n\S).

In "John works for Jane," the function of the word *for* is similar to that of the word *here* in "John works here," but there is a noun *Jane* after it. The syntax type of the word *for* is S\S/n.

In "John works and Jane rests," the word *and* is a connective, which connects the two sentences both before and after it to form a new sentence, so its syntax type is S\S/S.

So we get the English syntax type table (Table 2.3).

It can be seen from Table 2.3 that syntax types are roughly equivalent to parts of speech in traditional grammar. We can see that the word *John* in (1) is a noun; the word *poor* in (2) is an adjective; the word *works* in (3) is an intransitive verb; the word *likes* in (4) is a transitive verb; the word *soundly* in (5), the word *here* in (6), and the word *never* in (7) are adverbs with different functions; the word *for* in (8) is a preposition; and the word *and* in (9) is a connective. In this way, categorial grammar expresses the English parts of speech in terms of the two most basic categories, S and n. S and n are atomic categories, and other parts of speech represented by them can be regarded as compound categories. In terms of logical semantics, S represents the proposition represented by the declarative sentence, and n represents the argument in the proposition, which is a very simple way of expressing sentences. In mathematics, if we regard the language units other than S and n in the sentence as functions and that the language units that combine them into a new structure as arguments of the function, the value of the function is the new structure obtained by combining the two. In this way, the grammatical characteristics of any word can be expressed through these atomic and compound categories. This is a typical lexicalism approach. It can be said that in the language information processing, categorial grammar is a typical representative of lexicalism.

After a complete list of syntactic types for words in the language has been made, syntactic calculus can be performed according to the following rules:

If there is a symbol sequence like α, $\alpha\backslash\beta/\gamma$, and γ, then use β to replace it.

This rule also includes the following two rules:

Rule 1 Replace the symbol sequence of α,α\β with β, namely, (α)(α\β) → β.
Rule 2 Replace the symbol sequence of β/γ, γ with β, namely, (β/γ)(γ) → β.

If the words in the language are marked with syntactic types, so that the sequence of the words can be converted to S through finite calculation steps, then the sequence of the words is a qualified sentence in the language. In this way, the syntactic behavior of various components in the language can be described through the calculation of atomic and compound categories.

Example 1. John works.

```
n    n\S
└────┘

     S
```

Example 2. Poor John works.

```
n/n   n    n\S
└────┘      │
     n      │
     └──────┘
         S
```

Example 3. John works here.

```
n    n\S   S\S
└────┘      │
     S      │
     └──────┘
         S
```

Example 4. John never works.

```
n    n\S/(n\S)   n\S
│    └───────────┘
│            n\S
└────────────┘
         S
```

Example 5. John works for Jane.

```
n    n\S   S\S/n   n
└────┘     └───────┘
     S         S\S
     └─────────┘
          S
```

Example 6. John likes Jane.

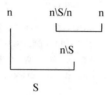

Example 7. John slept soundly.

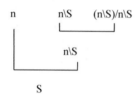

Example 8. John works and Jane rests.

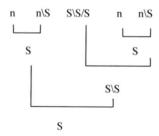

A word can belong to several syntactic types. For example, the word *knows* in "John knows" belongs to n\S; the word *knows* in "John knows Jane" belongs to n\S/n. In actual calculations, we should list all possible syntactic types for each word and make a list of syntactic types for it.

For example, we have a sequence of words:

Paul   thought   that   John   slept   soundly

We make a list of syntax types for each word in the sequence and mark all the symbols of the syntax types below the corresponding words. Ellipsis indicates that the list also includes some other syntax types, but for the sake of simplicity, we will not consider it here.

Paul	thought	that	John	slept	soundly
n	n	n	n	n\S	(n\S)\n\S
	n\S	n\n			(n\S/n)\n\S/n
	n\S/n	n/S			⋮
	n\S/S				
	⋮				

Assuming that the syntax types of the word *thought* are the 4 types listed above only and that the syntax types of the word *soundly* are the 2 ones listed above only, from the listed syntax types, we can get 24 initial symbol sequences ($1 \times 4 \times 3 \times 1 \times 1 \times 2 = 24$).

Now, we apply the above rules to calculate these initial symbol sequences.

In the initial symbol sequence "n n n n n\S (n\S)\n\S," applying Rule 1 to the fourth syntax type n and the fifth syntax type n\S, we get the symbol sequence "n n n S (n\S)\n\S." For this sequence, we can no longer apply our rules to the calculus.

In the same initial symbol sequence, if Rule 1 is applied to the fifth syntax type n \S and the sixth syntax type (n\S)\n\S, the symbol sequence "n n n n n\S" can be obtained. For this sequence, we can no longer apply our rules to the calculus.

Applying our calculation rules to the 24 initial symbol sequences, we can draw two conclusions:

The first conclusion

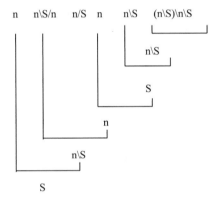

The second conclusion

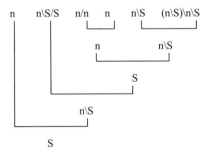

The calculation rules can turn the sequence "Paul thought that John slept soundly" into S. It can be seen that this sequence is a qualified sentence in English. However, what we can get here are two different meanings, which shows that this sentence has a homomorphic structure with two different meanings in syntax. One means "Paul thinks; John is asleep" (the word *that* in the initial sequence is a conjunction), and the other means "Paul thinks; that John sleeps soundly" (the word *that* in the initial sequence is a demonstrative pronoun. The conjunction *that* in the object clause is omitted after the verb *thought*.)

In order to distinguish the different forms of the verb *works* and the verb *work*, we stipulate that n* is used to represent the syntactic types of all plural nouns such as *men* (people) and *chair* (some chairs). Thus, in "men work," we mark *men* as n* and *work* as n*\S; in "poor men work," we mark *poor* as n*/n*, *men* as n*, and *work* as n*\S; in "John works for men," we mark *John* as n, *works* as n\S, *for* as S\S/n*, and *men* as n*; in "John likes girls," we mark *John* as n, *likes* as n\S/n*, and *girls* as n*; in "men like Jane," we mark *men* as n*, *like* as n*\S/n, *Jane* as n, and so on.

Using this notation, we can use the calculation rules to judge sentences that contain plural nouns.

In Example 5 "John works for Jane," difficulty arises if we first perform the calculus for "works for." The reason is that the syntactic type of "John works for Jane" is "n n\S S\S/n n" in sequence, in which the second and third syntactic types cannot be combined by using the calculation rules discussed earlier. To this end, Lambeck added the following calculation rules:

Rule 3 $(\alpha\backslash\beta)(\beta\backslash\gamma) \rightarrow \alpha\backslash\gamma$
Rule 4 $(\alpha/\beta)(\beta/\gamma) \rightarrow \alpha/\gamma$

Using these rules, we can first merge the second and third syntax types in Example 5. The calculations are as follows:

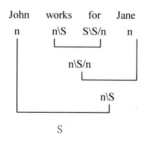

Thus, rules of the syntactic type calculus in categorial grammar are as follows:

1. $(\alpha)(\alpha\backslash\beta) \rightarrow \beta$
2. $(\beta/\gamma)(\gamma) \rightarrow \beta$
3. $(\alpha\backslash\beta)(\beta\backslash\gamma) \rightarrow \alpha\backslash\gamma$
4. $(\alpha/\beta)(\beta/\gamma) \rightarrow \alpha/\gamma$

It is easy for a discerning eye to see that categorial grammar takes into account the semantics when determining these rules, but semantics in categorial grammar is implicitly expressed through syntactic types and the rules that reflect the semantic linkage of those syntactic types. This unique expression makes categorial grammar significantly different from that of phrase structure grammar, which tries to slice sentences with an analytic pattern, while categorial grammar tries to reflect the semantic linkage of syntactic types with a constructive pattern. As categorial grammar tries to express semantics directly in syntax, it is, therefore, much appreciated by researchers of the language information processing. Its mathematical thoroughness and model simplicity have maintained its vigorous vitality for the past 40 years.

Categorial grammar has made a careful study of the syntactic calculus of English phrasal verbs. Here is a brief overview.

The calculation of English phrasal verbs is rather complicated. Therefore, in addition to the n and S syntax symbols mentioned above, the following syntax symbols should be added in the calculation:

Symbol i is used for the syntactic type of an infinitive for intransitive verbs.
Symbol p is used for the syntactic type of the present participle of intransitive verbs.
Symbol q is used for the syntactic type of the past participle of intransitive verbs.

Now we explain how these syntactic type symbols are used.

In "John must work," the word *work* is an infinitive of an intransitive verb, so its syntax type is i. The word preceding *must* is n, which is followed by i. As the function of "John must work" is the same as that of a sentence, its syntax type is n\S/i.

In "John is working," the word *working* is the present participle of an intransitive verb, so its syntax type is p. The word preceding *is* is n, which is followed by p. As the function of "John is working" is the same as that of a sentence, its syntax type is n\S/p.

In "John has worked," the word *worked* is the past participle of an intransitive verb, so its syntax type is q. The word preceding *has* is n, which is followed by q. As the function of "John has worked" is the same as that of a sentence, its syntax type is n\S/q.

Obviously, the reason why we choose these syntax types for *must*, *is*, and *has* is to ensure the syntactic types n\S for *must work*, *is working*, and *has worked*, making them work like the bare verb *work*.

In "John must be working," the word *working* is the present participle of an intransitive verb, so its syntax type is p. As the word *working* is preceded by the word *be*, the function of *be working* is equivalent to that of an infinitive verb. Its syntax type is i/p.

In "John has been working," the word *working* is the present participle of an intransitive verb, so its syntax type is p. As the word *working* is preceded by the word *been*, the function of *been working* is equivalent to that of a past participle of the intransitive verb, and its syntax type is q/p.

Now we illustrate the calculation of these syntactic types with examples:

Example 1. John must work.

Example 2. John is working.

Example 3. John has worked.

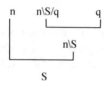

Example 4. John must be working.

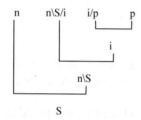

Example 5. John has been working.

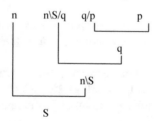

Now let us look at the calculation of sentences containing transitive verbs.

In "John calls Jane," the words both preceded and followed by the word *calls* are n. As the function of "John calls Jane" is equivalent to that of a sentence S, the syntax type of the word *calls* is n\S/n.

In "John must call Jane," the word *call* is followed by n. The function of *call Jane* is equivalent to that of an intransitive verb infinitive i, so its syntax type is i/n.

In "John is calling Jane," the word *calling* is followed by n. As the function of *calling Jane* is equivalent to that of a present participle p of an intransitive verb, its syntax type is p/n.

In "John has called Jane," the word *called* is followed by n. As the function of *called Jane* is equivalent to that of a past participle q of an intransitive verb, its syntax type is q/n.

The following examples are provided to illustrate the calculation of syntactic types of transitive verbs:

Example 6. John calls Jane.

Here, the syntactic type of the word *calls* is the same as that of the word *likes* above. They are both the forms of the present tense and the third person singular of transitive verbs.

Example 7. John must call Jane.

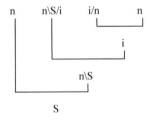

Example 8. John is calling Jane.

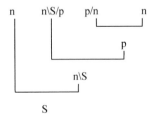

Example 9. John has called Jane.

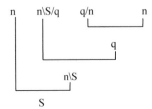

The syntactic types of components in English verb phrases can be summarized in Table 2.4.

It is more convenient to calculate the syntactic types of verb phrases with Table 2.4.

Below, we use categorial grammar to determine whether a more complex string of symbols is a valid sentence in English:

Example 10. John must have been calling Jane.

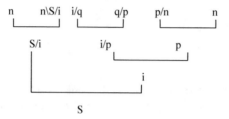

The meaning of this sentence is that "John must still be calling Jane." As the outcome of the syntactic type calculation is S, we know that this is a valid sentence.

Example 11. John is being calling.

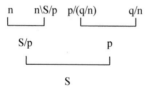

This sentence means "Someone is calling John on the phone." This is a valid

Table 2.4 Syntactic types of components in English verb phrases

	Modal verbs	Intransitive verbs	Transitive verbs	Auxiliary verbs	Auxiliary verbs forming continuous tense	Auxiliary verbs forming passive voice
Infinitive		work i	call i/n	have i/q	be i/p	be i/(q/n)
Present participle		working p	calling p/n			being p/(q/n)
Past participle		worked q	called q/n		been q/p	been q/(q/n)
Third person singular	must n\S/i	works n\S	calls n\S/n	has n\S/q	is n\S/p	is n\S/(q/n)

sentence based on S, the outcome of the syntactic type calculation.

However, the above table of syntactic types of components in English verb phrases is not complete, as some important verb types are not listed there. For example, not included in the table are verbs that require double objects, such as verbs *give* and *appoint*, and verbs that associate nouns with adjectives, such as the verb *tastes* in "lunch tastes good," the first-person form of verbs like *am*, and the plural form of verbs like *are*.

The verbs listed in the table are actually representative of certain types of verbs. For example, the verb *work* represents all intransitive verbs, the verb *call* represents all transitive verbs, and the modal verb *must* represents all modal auxiliary verbs, including *will, shall, can, may, would, should, could,* and *might*.

Some verbs in the table can also have other syntax types. For example, the verb *call* can also be a noun; verbs *have* and *be* can also be principle verbs. In the sentences "John must have lunch" and "John must be good," *have* and *be* are principle verbs.

There are blank slots in the first column of the table because there is no infinitive for *must*, and there are no such forms as *musting* (p/i) and *musted* (q/i). There are also blanks in the fourth and fifth columns because the auxiliary verb *have* has no present participle and no past participle forms. In addition, the progressive auxiliary verb *be* has no present participle form. However, the notional verb *have*, the passive auxiliary verb *be*, and the notional verb *be* have present participle forms. For example,

John is having lunch.
John has had lunch.
John is being called.

Among them, the syntax type of *having* is p/n, the syntax type of *had* is q/n, and the syntax type of *being* is p/(q/n).

According to calculation Rules 1–4, we can summarize the calculation results of each syntax type in the table into the following multiplication table (Table 2.5).

For example, when the current item is p/i and the next item is i,

$$(p/i)i \rightarrow p.$$

Therefore, the intersection of p/i and i is p.
When the current item is q/i and the next item is i/p,

$$(q/i)(i/p) \rightarrow q/p$$

Therefore, the intersection of q/i and i/p is q/p.

The intersecting values in the multiplication table can be reversed. For example, since there is (p/i)i → p in the multiplication table, p can be reversed to (p/i)i. As there is (q/i)(i/p) → q/ p in the multiplication table, q/p can be reversed to (q/i)(i/p).

If we expand the values at the intersections in the multiplication table in this way, we may gain some new understanding of the language phenomena.

Table 2.5 Multiplication table of syntactic type calculus

Next item \ Preceding item	i/i	i	i/n	i/q	i/p	i/(q/n)
i/i	i/i	i	i/n	i/q	i/p	i/(q/n)
p/i	p/i	p	p/n	p/q	p/p	p/(q/n)
q/i	q/i	q	q/n	q/q	q/p	q/(q/n)
n\S/i	n\S/i	n\S	n\S/n	n\S/q	n\S/p	n\S/(q/n)

For example, the syntax type of the word *works* is n\S, and n\S is reversely expanded to (n\S/i)i according to the multiplication table, which means that *works* can be regarded as having two syntax types n\S/ i and i. In "does work," the syntax type of the word *does* is n\S/i, and the syntax type of the word *work* is i. Therefore, we can interpret *does work* as a variant of *works*. In fact, when the word "works" is in an interrogative sentence, it becomes "does work."

Compare the following two sentences:

Declarative sentence: John works.
Interrogative sentence: Does John work?

For another example, the syntactic type of the adverb *today* is S/S. In "John works today," the syntactic types of each word are n, n\S, and S/S, respectively. According to the calculation rules, there are n(n\S) → S and S(S/S) → S, so this is a valid sentence. However, we can also write the syntax type of the word *today* as i/i. If we reverse the syntax type of the word *works* n\S to (n\S/i)i, the syntax type of the word *today* is i/i, so i(i/i) → i, and (n\S/i)i → n\S. Therefore, ((n\S/i)i)(i/i) → n\S and n(n \S) → S. In this way, we can also determine that "John works today" is a valid sentence. It means John works today. The calculation of this sentence is shown as follows:

```
John    works    today
  n       n\S      S\S
           └────────┘

                n\S
  └──────────────┘

          S
```

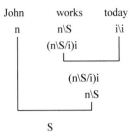

By reverse expansion, it is also possible to distinguish the coordinating conjunction from the subordinating one. For example, in the sentence "John works and Jane sleeps," the word *and* is a coordinating conjunction, and its syntax type is S\S/S. the calculation process is as follows:

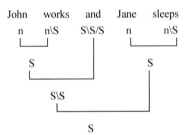

However, the syntactic type of the word *works* n\S can also be reversely expanded to (n\S/i)i, so in the sentence "John works while Jane sleeps," the syntactic type of the subordinating conjunction *while* is now i\i /S. After the reverse expansion of the word *works*, the calculation process of this sentence is shown below:

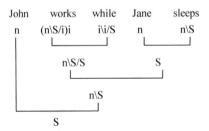

In this way, we can determine that it is a valid sentence.
Here, $((n\backslash S/ i) i)(i \backslash i /S) \to n\backslash S/S$ is because

$$i(i\backslash i/S) \to i/S$$

$$(n\backslash S/i)(i/S) \to n\backslash S/S$$

It can be seen that an alternative interpretation of the language phenomena can be made from a new perspective by means of the reverse expansion of syntactic types.

As early as 1974, Zhiwei Feng published an article in *Computer Application &
Applied Mathematics*, introducing categorial grammar to China, which did not
attract its due attention from the linguistic circle and computer circle at that time.
Due to the increasing popularity of lexicalism in NLP in recent years, some Chinese
NLP scholars started to pay attention to categorial grammar.

Categorial grammar proposed many years ago is an early formal model in NLP
and has been widely valued by logic and linguistics circles. It has a unique style in
NLP and has a far-reaching influence.

In the 1990s, M. Steedman and J. Baldridge proposed combinatory categorial
grammar (CCG), which has extended categorial grammar. The essence of the
expansion lies in being combinatory. On the basis of categorial grammar, combinatory operation of the operator category is added, which is similar to the composition
of functions in mathematics. In recent years, combinatory categorial grammar has
been widely used in NLP and has become an important NLP formal model.

2.5 Harris's Approach of Linguistic String Analysis

Zellig S. Harris (1909–1992, Fig. 2.12), representative of American structural
linguistics, was Noam Chomsky's teacher. In his "String Analysis of Sentence
Structure" published in 1962, he proposed the linguistic string theory. Based on
this theory, he put forward the linguistic string analysis, an approach to parsing
English by computer. This is one of the first formal models of NLP implemented by
computer.

In Harris's work, the term "string" is used to denote both the word sequence and
string formula in a way that leads to no misunderstanding.

The word sequence refers to one or more words in any sentence or its constituent
parts arranged in a linear order. For example,

Fig. 2.12 Zellig S. Harris

客厅	里	坐	着	两	位	客人	(1)
/Ke ting	li	zuo	zhe	liang	wei	ke ren/	(1)
living room	li	sit	zhe	two	wei	guest	(1)

(Two guests sit in the living room)

This Chinese sentence is a string of seven words arranged in sequence. Among them, "living room," "li," "sit," "zhe," "two," "wei," and "guest" are respectively the constituents of the sentence, therefore, forming a word sequence.

The string formula refers to a string of symbols formed by replacing specific words in a word sequence with parts of speech or its subcategories. For example, the string formula of sentence (1) is.

$$<N> \quad <FN> \quad <V> \quad <PART> \quad <NUM> \quad <MEA> \quad <N> \qquad (2)$$

where <N>means nouns, <FN> means location words, <V>means verbs, <PART> means auxiliary particles, <NUM> means numerals, and <MEA> means quantifiers.

The word sequence "living room," "li," "sit," "zhe," "two," "wei," and "guest" corresponds to <N>, <FN>, <V>, <PART>, <NUM>, <MEA>, and <N> in the string formula, respectively.

The word sequence and the string formula are actually symbol strings formed by a linear arrangement of symbols. The only difference between them is that these symbols are words in the word sequence and parts of speech in the string formula. When using linguistic string analysis to analyze sentences, we will use terms such as the word sequence or the string formula to analyze the sentence or some of their components.

In terms of linguistic string analysis, each sentence can be seen as a combination of several basic strings through addition, connection, and replacement. At least one of the basic strings that make up a sentence is the center string, which represents the backbone of the sentence. For example, the center string in sentence (1) is.

客厅	坐	客人	(3)
/Ke ting	zuo	ke ren/	
living room	sit	guest	
<N>	<V>	<N>	(4)

Generally speaking, the center string represents the basic sentence pattern in a language. In addition to the center string, the basic string also includes the adjunct string, the conjunct string, and the replacement string. Each sentence is composed of a center string and a zero or more elementary adjuncts. These elementary adjuncts are word sequences with a special structure, which are not sentences themselves. Instead, they are directly adjacent either before or after the center string or an adjunct, or they are adjacent either before or after a given constituent within a center string or an adjunct, generating arbitrarily complex sentences. For example, sentence (1) can be regarded as the center string (3) based on the following operations:

The noun "living room" within the center string is followed by the localizer "li."

The verb "sit" within the center string is followed by the auxiliary particle "zhe."

The noun "guest" in the center string is adjacent to a numeral and a quantifier "liang" and "wei," modifiers of the noun "guest".

In this way, infinite sentences in the language can be generated by gradually expanding from the center string.

Syntactic rules can be summarized in terms of linguistic string analysis. The steps are as follows:

1. Replace the word sequence with the string formula by way of the corresponding parts of speech symbols. For example, the word sequence in (1)

客厅	里	坐	着	两	位	客人
/Ke ting	li	zuo	zhe	liang	wei	ke ren/
living room	li	sit	zhe	two	wei	guest

should be replaced with the following string formula:

<N>   <FN>   <V>   <PART>   <NUM> <MEA>   <N>   (2)

2. The adjuncts in the word sequence are gradually removed to obtain the center string. For example, for sentence (1), do the following:

   – Cut off the adjunct "li" behind "living room."
   – Cut off the adjunct "zhe" after "sit."
   – Cut off the adjuncts, the numeral and quantifier, "two" and "wei" in front of the "guest."

   In this way, the center string and its string formula are obtained:

客厅	坐	客人	
/Ke ting	zuo	ke ren/	
living room	sit	guest	(3)
<N>	<V>	<N>	(4)

3. The syntactic rules for the above analysis can be specified. For example, for (1), (2), (3), and (4), the following syntax rules can be obtained:

   – R1. <center string> → <N> <V> <N>.
   – R2. <N> → <N> <FN>.
   – R3. <V> → <V> <PART>.
   – R4. <N> → <NUM> <MEA> <N>.

The above four rules are based on the analysis of just one example. However, these syntactic rules are already abstract enough to describe not only this sentence but also a class of sentences similar in structure to this sentence. For example, each of the following sentences can be described using the four rules above:

桌子	上	放	着	五	个	苹果
/Zhuo zi	shang	fang	zhe	wu	ge	ping guo/
desk	shang	put	zhe	five	ge	apple

(There are five apples on the desk)

天空	中	出现	了	一	朵朵	云彩
/Tian kong	zhong	chu xian	le	yi	duo duo	yun cai/
sky	zhong	appear	le	one	duo duo	cloud

(The clouds appear in the sky)

墙	上	挂	着	一	幅	山水画
/Qiang	shang	gua	zhe	yi	fu	shan shui hua/
wall	shang	hang	zhe	one	fu	landscape painting

(A landscape painting hangs on the wall)

招待所	里	来	了	三	位	旅客
/Zhao dai suo	li	lai	le	san	wei	lü ke/
guest house	li	come	le	three	wei	passenger

(Three passengers came to the guest house)

花瓶	里	插	着	一	束	鲜花
/Hua ping	li	cha	zhe	yi	shu	xian hua/
vase	li	insert	zhe	one	shu	flower

(A bunch of flowers inserts in the vase)

广场	上	耸立	着	一	座	纪念碑
/Guang chang	shang	song li	zhe	yi	zuo	ji nian bei/
square	shang	stand	zhe	one	zuo	monument

(A monument stands on the square)

The string formula corresponding to these sentences is

<N> <FN> <V> <PART> <NUM> <MEA> <N>

If we slightly expand the above syntactic rules based on more language facts, we can get more syntactic rules. If we use the method of linguistic string analysis to systematically analyze various types of sentences in modern Chinese, it is possible to generalize Chinese grammatical rules with a wider coverage.

Harris used this method to analyze all kinds of sentences in English. Later, researchers at the State University of New York in the United States successfully developed some practical English syntactic analysis programs using the method of linguistic string analysis. There are two well-known programs. One is the linguistic string parser (LSP) developed by N. Sager in the 1980s, which includes about 250 context-free syntactic rules and 200 restrictions with nearly 10,000 words in its dictionary. LSP has been applied to the medical information management system of the United States and has achieved considerable success in the language information processing of hospital medical records and medical literature. The other is the tagged text parser (TTP) developed by T. Strzalkowski. The machine dictionary of TTP is developed based on the *Oxford Modern Advanced English Dictionary*. Linguistic string analysis is adopted to perform grammatical analysis. TTP, which can analyze two sentences per second, parses English sentences with part-of-speech tags and has completed a fast syntactic analysis of an English corpus of 50 million words.

2.6   O. C. Кулагина's Linguistic Set Theory Model

In 1958, Russian mathematician O. C. Кулагина published an article entitled "A Method of Defining Grammatical Concespts Based on Set Theory" (Об одном способе определения грамматических понятий на базе теории множеств) in the first volume of *Cybernetic Problems* (*Проблемы Кибернетики*). She set up a mathematical model of the natural language using the set theory, and she used this model to simulate a hierarchical process of reducing words to phrases and of reducing phrases to sentences in MT.

O. C. Кулагина pointed out that in a given natural language, all combinations of words formed by the adjacent operations can be divided into two subsets: one is a subset of valid sentences, and the other is a subset of invalid sentences.

Any sentence that is formally correct is called a valid sentence. A formally correct sentence means a sentence that is grammatically correct, but it is not semantically correct. Therefore, in Russian, Стол стоит на полу (the table stands on the floor) and Тупой куст врсзалку хихикнул (literally, the sentence means "the dull bush lurches and laughs," which is only grammatically correct) are both valid sentences. And Он пошел в школа is an invalid sentence, because школа has not changed to its fourth case, школу, which is grammatically incorrect.

A set of valid sentences is denoted as θ.

If we have a set of words W and a set of valid sentences formed by W, we have language L. In other words, L = {W, θ} is called a language formed by the lexical set W.

The complete formal system of a word, the set of all the forms of a word's inflection, is called the domain of the word. For example, for the word *стол* (table), there are стол, стола, столу, столом, столе, столы, столов, столами, столах, etc., which form the domain of the word *стол*. The domain of the word x is denoted as $\Gamma(x)$.

$\Gamma(x)$ can divide the set W into a collection of disjoint subsets, so the division of the domain can be obtained, which is denoted as "Γ."

For words x or y in a given language, if

i. any sentence with the form of A_1xA_2 is valid, the sentence A_1yA_2 is also valid;
ii. any sentence with the form of B_1yB_2 is valid, the sentence B_1xB_2 is also valid.

In these sentences, A_1, A_2, B_1, and B_2 are arbitrary word strings, which can also be empty word strings that do not contain any word. Then, we can say that the word x is equivalent to the word y, denoted as x ~ y.

Such equivalence has reflexivity, symmetry, and transitivity. It can divide the set W into a series of disjoint subsets, which are called families. Two equivalent elements enter the same family, while two unequal elements enter a different family. The family of word x is S(x).

We take Russian sentences, for example:

1. Я пошёл к окну.

   (I walk to the window)
2. прямоугольник, равный окну, очень красиво.

   (The rectangular frame, which is the same size as the window, is beautiful)

In sentence 1, the word *окну* uses two word strings as its context. One is "Я пошёл к" and the other is an empty word string. In this context, the words *столу, человеку*, etc. still form a valid sentence. In sentence 2, the word *окну* uses the word string "прямоугольник, равный" and the word string "очень красиво" as its context. In this context, the words *столу, человеку*, etc. still form a valid a sentence. Therefore, the words *окну, столу*, and *человеку* are equivalent and belong to one family.

The family S(x) divides the set W into a collection of disjoint subsets, so the division of the family can be obtained, which is denoted as "S." In this way, we have obtained two methods of representing the entire set of words in the form of a disjoint subset system, the Γ partition and the S partition. In this case, regardless of the criteria for dividing the subsets, we use the form of the union of disjoint subsets to represent the set W, that is,

$$W_i = B_1 \cup B_2 \cdots \cup B_i \cdots \cup B_n$$
$$= \overset{n}{\underset{i-1}{\cup}} B$$

Then, we call it the B partition of the set W. If $X \in B_i$, B_i sometimes can be written as B(x).

If a subset consists of only one word, we call this division E partition. Obviously, E division is a special case of B partition.

Now we introduce the concept of the B structure of Sentence A.

If we take any sentence $A = x_1 x_2 ... x_i ... x_n$, we put the sequence of subsets $B(x_1)B(x_2)...B(x_i)...B(x_n)$ in the given B partition. The word x_i enters the sequence of the subset, which is called the B structure of Sentence A, denoted as B(A).

We take the same sentence

A = раздался звонок (bell rang)

as an example to see what the B structure of this sentence looks like under different partitions:

1. Under E partition, the B structure has the form.

   E(A) = {раздался} {звонок}

   This B structure is called E structure.
2. Under S partition, the B structure has the form (Fig. 2.13).

   This B structure is called S structure.

$$S(A) = \left\{ \begin{array}{l} \text{р а з д а л с я} \\ \text{з а з в о н и л} \\ \text{у е х а л} \\ \text{ш ё л} \\ \text{п л а к а л} \\ \text{...} \end{array} \right\} \left\{ \begin{array}{l} \text{з в о н о к} \\ \text{н о ш} \\ \text{к л у б} \\ \text{т р а м в а й} \\ \text{...} \\ \text{...} \end{array} \right\}$$

Fig. 2.13 S structure

$$(A) = \left\{ \begin{array}{l} \text{р а з д а т ь с я} \\ \text{р а з д а л о с ь} \\ \text{р а з д а л и с ь} \\ \text{р а з д а ю т с я} \\ \text{...} \end{array} \right\} \left\{ \begin{array}{l} \text{з в о н к у} \\ \text{з в о н к а} \\ \text{з в о н к а м и} \\ \text{з в о н к и} \\ \text{...} \end{array} \right\}$$

Fig. 2.14 Γ structure

3. Under Γ partition, the B structure takes the form (Fig. 2.14)
   This B structure is called Γ structure.

If at least one valid sentence has a certain B structure, the B structure is valid.
   Taking any B partition of set W, we call such a B structure the first-level B format, denoted as $\widetilde{B}_{(1)}$, if

1. $\widetilde{B}_{(1)}$ contains at least two elements, and
2. there is an element $B_{\alpha 1}$ in B partition, leaving the $B(A_1)$ $\widetilde{B}_{(1)}$ $B(A_2)$ and $B(A_1)$ $B_{\alpha 1}B(A_2)$ of the B structure in any word strings A_1 and A_2 valid or invalid at the same time.

The element $B_{\alpha 1}$ can replace $\widetilde{B}_{(1)}$ while maintaining the validity of the structure. We call it the result element, which may not be unique. In fact, if $B_{\alpha 1}$ is the result element of $\widetilde{B}_{(1)}$, any $B_i\left(B_i\widetilde{B}B_{\alpha 1}\right)$ equivalent to $B_{\alpha 1}$ in B partition can also be the result element of $\widetilde{B}_{(1)}$.

If we replace the first-level B format with the result element $B_{\alpha 1}$, we get the first-level B structure, denoted as $B_{(1)}$.

Generally speaking, we call such a B structure an n-level B format, denoted as $\widetilde{B}_{(n)}$, if

1. $\widetilde{B}_{(n)}$ contains at least two elements, and
2. there is an element $B_{\alpha n}$, leaving the $(n-1)$ level B structure $B(A_1)$ $B(A_2)$ and B structure $B(A_1)$ $B_{\alpha n}$ $B(A_2)$ in any word strings A_1 and A_2 valid or invalid simultaneously.

Among them, the B structure $B(A_1)$ $B_{\alpha n}$ $B(A_2)$ of the n-level B format is not included, which is called the n-level B structure.

It can be seen that the definition of the B format is recursive. The n-level B format is defined by the $(n - 1)$ level B structure, and the $(n - 1)$ level B format is defined by the $(n - 2)$ level B structure and so on. In this way, the B structure of the same level is obtained after each B format is replaced with the result element.

Following this point of view, we now analyze the B structure in the following sentence:

B (маленькая) B (девочка) B (долго) B (ласкала) B (кошку).

This is the B structure of the Russian sentence:

маленькая девочка долго ласкала кошку.
(The little girl strokes the kitten for a long time)

If we replace B (маленькая) B (девочка) with B (девочка), we get.

B (девочка) B (долго) B (ласкала) B (кошку).

This is also a valid B structure. However, at this time, we have no reason to think that the B structure of B (маленькая) B (девочка) is the first-level B format, because we have not checked all the contexts that can perform this kind of replacement.

We then take the same context:

B (весьма) B (маленькая) B (девочка) B (стояла).

This is the B structure of the sentence:

весьма маленькая девочка стояла.
(The very little girl is standing)

If we replace B (маленькая) B (девочка) with B (девочка) in the valid B structure, we will get.

B (весьма) B (девочка) B (стояла).

This B structure is obviously invalid. It can be seen that B (маленькая) B (девочка) is not a first-level B format.

It is easy to find out whether B (весьма) B (маленькая) is the first-level B format, because B (весьма) B (маленькая) can be replaced by B (маленькая) in all contexts. At this time, the result element of this first-level B format is $B_{\alpha2} = B$ (маленькая).

If we only study the first-level B structure (i.e., there is no first-level B format B structure), B (маленькая) B (девочка) can be replaced by B (девочка) in any context. It can be seen that B (маленькая) B (девочка) is the second-level B format, whose result element $B_{\alpha2} = B$ (девочка).

We will continue to analyze the B structure. B (долго) B (ласкала) is the second-level B format, whose result element is B (ласкала). In this way, the secondary B structure can be obtained from the original B structure:

B (девочка) B (долго) B (ласкала) B (кошку).

If we only study this secondary B structure, B (ласкала) can be used to replace B (ласкала) B (кошку) in any context. In other words, intransitive verbs are used to replace predicate-object phrases. In this way, we get the three-level B structure:

B (девочка) B (ласкала).

As can be seen from this example, the theory of format transformation is actually an induction process, which reduces complex structures step-by-step according to their hierarchy to simple structures that cannot be reduced again. The reduction process, in fact, is the process of syntactic analysis in MT. Therefore, the formal model of the language proposed by О.С. Кулагина can be regarded as a mathematical simulation of the syntactic analysis process of MT.

О. С. Кулагина applies this formal model to the French-Russian MT system, so that this system can be built on a relatively complete theoretical basis. This provides a good tool in theory for further research on MT and on other natural language information processing.

Bibliography

1. Bar-Hillel, Y. 1959. Decision Procedure for Structure in Natural Language. *Logique et Analyse* 2-e annee: 5.
2. ———. 1960. On Categorial and Phrase Structure Grammars. *Bulletin of the Research Council of Israel* 9: 1–16.
3. Brown, P.L., et al. 1992. An Estimate of an Upper Bound for the Entropy of English. *Computational Linguistics* 1: 31–40.
4. Fan, Sun, and Maosong Sun. 2006. Estimation of the Limit Entropy of Chinese Characters Based on Statistics. In *Chinese Information Society of China. Frontiers of Chinese Information Processing*, 542–551. Beijing: Tsinghua University Press.
5. Harris, Z.S. 1962. *String Analysis of Sentence Structure*. The Hague: Mouton.
6. Кулагина, О.С. 1958. Об одном способе определения грамматических понятий на базе теории множеств. In *Проблемы Кибернетики*. том-I.
7. Lambek, J. 1958. The Mathematics of Sentence Structure. *American Mathematical Monthly* 65: 154–170.
8. Markov, A.A. 1913. Essai d'une recherche statistique Sur le texte du roman "Eugene Onegin" illustrant la liaisong des epreuve en chain (Example of a Statistical Investigation of the Text of "Eugene Onegin" Illustrating the Dependence Between Sample in Chain). *Bulletin de l'Academie Impériale des Sciences de St.-Petersbourg* 7: 153–162.
9. Shannon, C.E. 1948. A Mathematical Theory of Communication. *Bell System Technical Journal* 27: 379–423.
10. Zhiwei, Feng. 1983. The Ins and Outs of Zipf's Law. *Information Sciences* 2.
11. ———. 1984. Entropy of Chinese Characters. *Character Reform* 4: 12–17.
12. ———. 1986. The Limit Entropy of Chinese Characters. *Chinese Information* 1: 53–56.
13. ———. 1991. *Mathematics and Language*. Changsha: Hunan Education Press.
14. ———. 2001. Categorial Grammar. *Application of Language and Writing* 3.
15. ———. 2002. Mathematical Linguistics. In *Multidisciplinary Research and Application of Linguistics*, ed. Zijian Yang, 399–431. Nanning, Guangxi Education Press.
16. ———. 2011. *Language and Mathematics*. Beijing: World Book Publishing.
17. Zhiwei, Feng, and Fengguo, Hu. 2012. *Mathematical Linguistics (Updated Edition)*. Beijing: The Commercial Press.

Part II
Formal Models

Chapter 3
Formal Models Based on Phrase Structure Grammar

In most rule-based NLP systems, phrase structure grammar (PSG), which is also called context-free grammar (CFG), is currently most widely used. This is a very important formal model in NLP.

Chomsky used mathematical methods to describe the language formally and proposed the concept of formal grammar. Such formal grammar can describe both the natural language and the computer programming language. Phrase structure grammar (i.e., context-free grammar) is the most suitable formal grammar for describing the natural language.

In this chapter, we will discuss Chomsky hierarchy of grammar, finite state grammar, and phrase structure grammar, respectively, and introduce phrase structure grammar-based augmented transition network, recursive transfer network, bottom-up analysis, top-down analysis, general syntactic processor, chart parsing, Earley algorithm, left-corner analysis, CYK algorithm, Tomita algorithm, government and binding theory, the minimalist program, tree adjoining grammar, and lexicalized tree adjoining grammar. Finally, we will give a formal description of the structure of Chinese characters using context-free grammar, and left-associative grammar will also be introduced.

3.1 Chomsky's Hierarchy of Grammar

W. Wundt (Fig. 3.1, who is the founder of experimental psychology, first put forward the idea of dividing sentences into the component hierarchy in *popular psychology* (Voelkerpsychologie, 1900). However, from the classical period, traditional European grammar focused on how to determine the relationship between specific words, rather than studying the hierarchical relationship between the components represented by the words.

Wundt's thoughts on constituency were introduced into linguistics by Leonard Bloomfield (Bloomfield, Fig. 3.2) in his early work *An Introduction to the Study of*

© Springer Nature Singapore Pte Ltd. 2023
Z. Feng, *Formal Analysis for Natural Language Processing: A Handbook*,
https://doi.org/10.1007/978-981-16-5172-4_3

Fig. 3.1 W. Wundt

Fig. 3.2 Leonard Bloomfield

Language published in 1914. When his work *Language* was published in 1933, "immediate constituent analysis" had become a quite established method in American linguistic research. On the contrary, European syntacticians still emphasized word-based grammar or dependency grammar. Component-based grammar and word-based grammar have their own merits, and they form two representative formal models in NLP. First, we will discuss formal models based on components (such as

Fig. 3.3 N. Chomsky

"phrase structure grammar"), and later we will discuss formal models based on words (such as "dependency grammar").

American structuralism put forward some definitions of immediate constituents, describing their research as a "discovery procedure." This is a methodological algorithm for describing language syntax. Generally speaking, these studies tried to confirm the intuition that "the primary criterion of immediate constituents is the degree to which a combination functions as a simple unit"[1] (Bazell 1952). The most famous definition is Z. Harris's idea of using the "substitutability" test to test the "distributional similarity" of individual units. In essence, this method is to decompose a structure into several constituents and replace it with a simple structure of possible constituents. If a simple form (e.g., *man*) can be used to replace a more complex structure (e.g., an *intense young man*), then this more complex structure "intense young man" may be a possible constituent. Harris's experiment became the beginning of the intuition that takes constituents as an equivalent class.

The earliest formal description of this hierarchical constituent was found in his definition of phrase structure grammar by American linguist N. Chomsky (1928–, Fig. 3.3) in 1956. Later Chomsky further expanded it in 1957 and 1975 and put forward the reasons to argue against it. Since then, most generative grammar theories have been based on phrase structure grammar, at least in part.

Chomsky was born in Philadelphia, USA, on December 7, 1928. In 1947, he met the famous linguist Z.Harris. After studying some parts of Harris's *Methods in Structural Linguistics*, he was deeply attracted by Harris's rigorous methods. From then on, he decided to make linguistics his life's work and went to the University of Pennsylvania, where Harris taught, to specialize in linguistics. He decided to make appropriate changes to Harris's method to establish a formal language theory using recursive rules to describe the formal structure of sentences so that grammar can gain

---

[1] C. E. Bazel, The correspondence fallacy in structural linguistics, 1952, *Studies by members of the English department*, Istanbul University (3), pp. 284. Reprinted in *Reading in Linguistics II* pp 271–298, University of Chicago Press, Chicago, 1966.

a strong explanatory power. To complete the meaningful research topic of formal language theory, with the suggestion of Harris, Chomsky began to study philosophy, logic, and modern mathematics from 1953. In 1954, Chomsky began to write the book *The Logical Structure of Linguistic Theory*. In this book, he sketched out the theoretical viewpoint and methods of thinking of generative grammar. In the autumn of 1955, Chomsky went to Electronics Research Department to do research at the Massachusetts Institute of Technology (MIT) and worked in the Department of Modern Linguistics, teaching linguistics, logic, and philosophy of language to graduate students. In addition to his professorship in linguistics at the Massachusetts Institute of Technology, Chomsky is the John Locke lecturer at Oxford University and a visiting professor at the University of California, Berkeley. He is also a senior fellow at the Princeton College of Advanced Studies and the Harvard Cognitive Research Center in London. He also chaired the Sherman Memorial Lecture at London University. Chomsky is an academician of the American Academy of Arts and Sciences, a correspondent academician of The British Academy of Sciences, and a director of the world alliance for disarmament and peace. He received honorary doctorate degrees from the University of Chicago, Loyola University of Chicago, and the University of London.

In his "Three models for the description of language" (1956), *Syntactic Structure* (1957), "Finite state language" (1958), "On certain formal properties of grammars" (1959), "Formal properties of grammars" (1963), and other works, Chomsky established a complete system of formal language theory basically from the perspective of language generation. Phrase structure grammar is the major element of formal language theory and the most important formal model in NLP.

In formal language theory, Chomsky proposed a definition of "formal grammar" that is different from traditional grammar. Consequently, to understand phrase structure grammar, we must first understand what formal grammar of Chomsky is.

Chomsky took formal grammar as a collection of a limited number of rules that can generate qualified sentences and exclude unqualified ones in language. The symbol of formal grammar is represented by G, and the formal language generated by the grammar G is represented by L(G). Formal language is a language with a very wide extension. It can refer to both the natural language and various languages composed of symbols (e.g., the programming language used by computers). Chomsky studies the natural language and various symbolic languages on a unified plane, so his theory is more general.

Chomsky defines formal grammar G as a quaternion:

$$G = (Vn, Vt, S, P)$$

where Vn is a non-terminal symbol and cannot be at the end of the generation process, Vt is the terminal symbol and can only be at the end of the generation process, Vn and Vt do not intersect and have no common elements, S is the initial symbol in Vn, and P is the rewriting rule. Its general form is

$$\varphi \rightarrow \psi$$

Here, φ and ψ are both strings.

If the symbol # is used to represent the boundary in a string, then from the initial string #S#, the rewriting rule #S# $\rightarrow$ #φ_1# can be applied to form a new string, #φ_1#. Using the rewriting rule #φ_1# $\rightarrow$ #φ_2#, the new string #φ_2# is formed from #φ_1# and so on until the string #φ_n# that can no longer be rewritten is obtained and then the terminal string #φ_n# is obtained. Obviously, this is a qualified sentence in the formal language L(G).

This formal grammar can be used to generate a natural language. For example, we write the simplest formal grammar for Chinese as follows:

```
G= (Vn, Vt, S, P)
Vn={NP,VP,N}
Vt ={编写(/bian xie/; compile), 研究(/yan jiu/; study), 大学(/da xue/;
university), 教授(/jiao shou/; professor), 物理(/wu li/; physics), 教材
(/jiao cai/; textbook) ...}
S=S
P:
    ① S →NP VP
    ② NP→N  N
    ③ VP→V  NP
    ④ N → { 大学(/da xue/; university), 教授(/jiao shou/; professor),
物理(/wu li/; physics), 教材(/jiao cai/; textbook) ...}
    ⑤ V → { 编写(/bian xie/; compile), 研究(/yan jiu/; study) ...}
```

Here, the initial symbol S indicates a sentence. NP indicates a noun phrase. VP indicates a verb phrase. And N indicates a noun. Using these rewriting rules, we can start from the initial symbol S to generate Chinese sentences:

大学教授编写物理教材 (/Da xue jiao shou bian xie wu li jiao cai/; University professor compile physics textbook) "University professor compile physics textbooks".

大学教授研究物理教材 (/Da xue jiao shou yan jiu wu li jiao cai/; University professor study physics textbook) "University professor study physics textbooks".

The generation process of the sentence "大学教授编写物理教材" (/Da xue jiao shou bian xie wu li jiao cai/; University professors compile physics textbooks) can be written as follows (the number of the rules applied is indicated at the end of each line):

```
            S                 rule number

        NP   VP                  ①

        NP   V   NP              ③
```

N   N   V   NP   ②

N   N   V   N   N   ②

大学(/da xue/; university)   N   V   N   N   ④

大学(/da xue/; university) 教授(/jiao shou/; professor)   V   N   N   ④

大学(/da xue/; university) 教授(/jiao shou/; professor) 编写(/bian xie/; compile)   N   N   ⑤

大学(/da xue/; university) 教授(/jiao shou/; professor) 编写(/bian xie/; compile) 物理(/wu li/; physics)   N   ④

大学(/da xue/; university) 教授(/jiao shou/; professor) 编写(/bian xie/; compile) 物理(/wu li/; physics) 教材(/jiao cai/; textbook)   ④

The generation process written in this way is called "derivation history" or "derivation process."

Chomsky divides formal grammar into four categories according to the form of rewriting rules:

1. Type 0 grammar: The rewriting rule is $\varphi \rightarrow \psi$ and requires that φ cannot be an empty string.
2. Context-sensitive grammar: The rewriting rule is $\varphi_1 A\varphi_2 \rightarrow \varphi_1\omega\varphi_2$. In the context φ_1–φ_2, a single non-terminal symbol A is rewritten as the string ω. Therefore, this grammar is context-sensitive and context-related. It is also called type 1 grammar.
3. Context-free grammar: The rewriting rule is $A \rightarrow \omega$. When A is rewritten to ω, there is no context constraint. Therefore, this grammar is context-free and not context-related. Context-free grammar is also called type 2 grammar. Applying context-free grammar to the formal analysis of natural language forms "phrase structure grammar."
4. Finite state grammar: Rewriting the rule as $A \rightarrow aQ$ or $A \rightarrow a$. A and Q are non-terminal symbols, a is the terminal symbol, while $A \rightarrow a$ is just a special case in the rewriting rule of $A \rightarrow aQ$ when Q is an empty symbol. If A and Q are regarded as different states, then from the rewriting rules, it can be seen that when the state A goes to the state Q, a terminal symbol a can be generated. Therefore, this grammar is called finite state grammar. Finite state grammar is also called type 3 grammar.

Every finite state grammar is context-free. Every context-free grammar is context-sensitive. And every context-sensitive grammar is type 0. Chomsky calls the language generated by type 0 grammar type 0 language. The languages generated by context-sensitive grammar, context-free grammar, and finite state grammar are called context-sensitive languages, context-free languages, and finite state languages, respectively. The finite state language is included in the context-free languages. The context-free language is included in the context-sensitive languages. And the context-sensitive language is included in the type 0 language. This forms the

Fig. 3.4 W. V. Humboldt

"Chomsky hierarchy" of grammar. In NLP, we are most interested in context-free grammar and context-free language, which are the main research objects of phrase structure grammar theory.

Chomsky believes that according to such formal language theory, finite rules can be used to describe potentially infinite sentences that are potentially infinite in form, to achieve the purpose of simplifying the complexity. He said in the preface of the book *A Brief Introduction to Chomsky's Linguistic Theory* published by Heilongjiang University in China: "A person's language knowledge is embodied in the finite body of the human brain in some way. Therefore, language knowledge is a limited system composed of certain rules and principles. But a person capable of speaking can understand sentences that he has never heard and sentences that are not very similar to what we have heard. Moreover, this ability is unlimited. If it is not limited by time and memory, then the knowledge system acquired by a person stipulates the number of sentences of a specific form, structure, and meaning will also be unlimited. It is not difficult to see that this ability is used freely in normal human life. The range of sentences we use and understand in our daily life is enormous. It is entirely reasonable to assume that the range of sentences we use and understand is infinite, both in practical terms and for the sake of theoretical description. We have every reason to believe that the range of sentences people use and understand is unlimited."[2] As early as the beginning of the nineteenth century, W. V. Humboldt (Humboldt, 1767–1835, Fig. 3.4), an outstanding German linguist and humanist, observed that "language is the infinite use of finite means." W. V. Humboldt said in Chap. 12 "Detailed Analysis of Language Methods" in the book *On Language: On the Diversity of Human Language Construction and Its Influence on the Mental Development of the Human Species* (published separately in 1836), "Language faces an infinite and boundless realm, i.e., the sum of all thinkable objects. Therefore,

---

[2] Chomsky, Preface in *A Brief Introduction to Chomsky's Linguistic Theory* published by Heilongjiang University," 1984

Fig. 3.5 State diagram 1

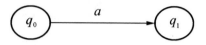

language must use infinitely limited means, and the identity of thinking power and language creation power ensures that language can do this."[3] However, since the technical tools and methods that revealed the essential content of this understanding had not been found at the time, W. V. Humboldt's assertion was immature.

Chomsky developed W. V. Humboldt's theory and made a rigorous mathematical demonstration. In this way, we can reveal the essence of the assertion that "language is the infinite use of finite means" according to the theory of formal language.

Chomsky's formal language theory is one of the basic theories of contemporary computer science. It is widely used in algorithm analysis, compilation technology, image recognition, artificial intelligence, and other fields. It is an important formal language model in NLP.

To get an overview of the formal language theory, we will further explain these four types of grammar.

3.2   Finite State Grammar and Its Limitations

According to the rewriting rule of finite state grammar, when state A is transferred to state Q, a terminal symbol can be generated. Thus, we can think of finite state grammar as a generating device that can generate a terminal symbol at a time, and each terminal symbol is related to a certain state.

We use the lowercase letter q to represent the state. If this generation device is originally in the state q_i, then after generating a terminal symbol, it will go to state q_j. In the state q_j, after generating another terminal symbol, it goes to state q_k and so on. A state diagram can be used to represent this case.

For example, if such a generating device is originally in a certain state q_0, after generating a terminal symbol a, it goes to state q_1. Then, the state diagram is shown in Fig. 3.5.

The language that it generates is "a."

If this generation device is originally in state q_0, after the terminal symbol is generated, it goes to state q_1. In the state q_1, after generating the terminal symbol b, it goes to state q_2. Then, the state diagram is shown in Fig. 3.6.

The language that it generates is "ab."

If this generation device is in state q_0, after generating the terminal symbol a, it returns to state q_0, and then the state diagram is shown in Fig. 3.7.

---

[3] Humboldt, *On Language: On the Diversity of Human Language Construction and Its Influence on the Mental Development of the Human Species*, p114. The Commercial Press, 1997.

Fig. 3.6 State diagram 2

Fig. 3.7 State diagram 3

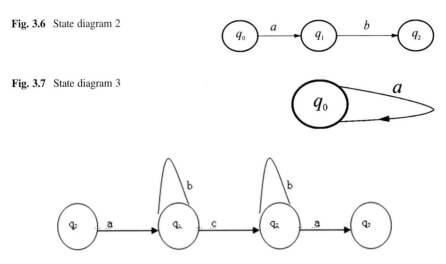

Fig. 3.8 State diagram 4

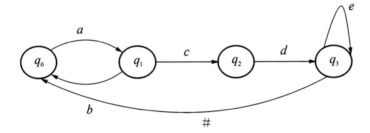

Fig. 3.9 State diagram 5

This kind of the state diagram is called a loop, and the language it generates is "a, aa, aaa, aaaa. . . ." It can be abbreviated as $\{a^n\}$, where $a \geq 0$.

If the generating device is in state q_0, it will turn to state q_1 after generating the terminal symbol a. In the state q_1, either it returns to state q_1 after generating the terminal symbol b, or it turns to state q_2 after generating the terminal symbol c. In the state q_2, it returns to q_2 after generating the terminal symbol b, or it turns to state q_3 after generating the terminal symbol a. Then its state diagram is shown in Fig. 3.8.

The languages it generates are "aca, abca, abcba, abbcba, abcbba," and so on. It can be abbreviated as $\{ab^n cb^m a\}$, where $n \geq 0$, $m \geq 0$.

After generating several terminal symbols, this generating device can also return to the previous state to form a large closed loop, as is shown in the following state diagram (Fig. 3.9).

It can generate such terminal symbol strings as "acde#, abacdee#, ababacdeee#," and so on. Here, "#" indicates the end of the symbol string. However, it can also enter the initial state q_0 and continue to generate new symbol strings. In this case, q_0

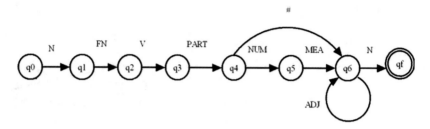

Fig. 3.10 The state diagram of Chinese sentence analysis

is both the initial state and the final state. The language generated by this state diagram can be abbreviated as $\{a(ba)^n cde^m\}$, where $n \geq 0$, $m \geq 0$.

It can be seen that given a state diagram, we can start from the initial state and follow the path in the state diagram and always follow the direction indicated by the arrow to generate a language. When a state in the diagram is reached, it can proceed along any path leading from this state, regardless of whether this path has been traversed in the previous generation process. When going from one state to another, it allows a number of different paths. The state diagram also allows any finite length and any finite number of loops. Such a generating device is mathematically called the finite state Markov process.

The state diagram is the vivid representation of finite state grammar. Therefore, according to the state diagram, we can easily write its corresponding finite state grammar.

For example, finite state grammar corresponding to the above state diagram is as follows:

```
G = (Vn, Vt, S, P)
   Vn = {q₀, q₁, q₂, q₃}
   Vt = {a, b, c, d, e, #}
   S = q₀
   P:
      q₀ → aq₁
      q₁ → bq₀
      q₁ → cq₂
      q₂ → dq₃
      q₃ → eq₃
      q₃ → #q₀
```

In this grammar, q_0, q_1, q_2, and q_3 represent the states. They are all non-terminal symbols. It is not difficult to see that each rule in the grammar rewriting rule P conforms to the form of finite state grammar rewriting rules.

Using this finite state grammar, we can also draw the state diagram (Fig. 3.10) of the following Chinese sentences in Sect. 2.4, Chap. 2:

(a) 客厅里坐着两位客人 (/Ke ting li zuo zhe liang wei ke ren/; There are two guests sitting in the living room).

(b) 桌子上放着五个苹果 (/Zhuo zi shang fang zhe wu ge ping guo/; There are five apples on the table).
(c) 天空中出现了一朵朵云彩 (/Tian kong zhong chu xian le yi duo duo yun cai/; There are clouds in the sky).

Where q_0 is the initial state, q_f is the final state.

Because the state diagram uses lexical category labels, N, FN, V, etc., such finite state grammar can not only describe a sentence but also describe a class of sentences. This kind of sentence is the existential sentence in Chinese. Its basic format is as follows:

"Words or phrases that indicate location and time—verbs that indicate the existence, such as, appear, or disappear—auxiliaries that represent someone or something that exists."

This shows that finite state grammar can describe sentences in the natural language. However, since authentic natural language sentences often have structures such as nesting and recursion, the ability of finite state grammar to deal with these structures is not strong. Therefore, in NLP, people like to use finite state grammar for morphological analysis of agglutinative and inflectional languages.

There are additional components that specifically express the grammatical meaning in the words of agglutinative languages. An additional component expresses a grammatical meaning, which basically can only be expressed by this additional component. The combination of the root and the stem is not close. Japanese is an agglutinative language, whose words can be divided into two major categories, independent and auxiliary. Words in the independent category can be used alone in sentences, such as nouns, pronouns, numerals, verbs, adjectives, adjective verbs, adverbs, conjunctions, interjections, etc. However, words in the auxiliary category cannot be used alone in a sentence. They can only be appended to independent words to play a certain grammatical role, such as auxiliaries and auxiliary verbs. In addition to interjections and conjunctions, the position and grammatical function of independent words in sentences are represented by auxiliaries or auxiliary verbs. Therefore, auxiliaries and auxiliary verbs play a particularly important role in Japanese. Verbs, adjectives, and adjective verbs have inflectional changes, which depend on the adhesive component behind. If we regard the inflectional words in Japanese and the auxiliaries or auxiliary verbs attached to them as a string of symbols connected by several different morphemes, we can use finite state grammar to segment them. In the process of segmentation, we can record the lexical meaning of the stem and the grammatical meaning of various additional components on the inflected words. The lexical and grammatical information of this inflectional word can achieve the purpose of morphological analysis. To this end, we can build a machine dictionary. In the machine dictionary, for each word, its form information, morphological information, syntactic information, semantic information, possible adjuncts, and so on are labeled. In the process of using finite state grammar to segment inflectional words, we can transfer the relevant information recorded for each morpheme in the machine dictionary to the inflectional morpheme, to obtain all kinds of information about the inflectional change and realize the morphological analysis of Japanese. For

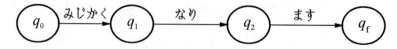

Fig. 3.11 The state diagram for analyzing a Japanese phrase

example, we can build the following state diagram (Fig. 3.11) to analyze the Japanese phrase "みじかくなります" (shortened):

We build the following dictionary:

みじかく :conjunctive form of the adjective
なり :conjunctive form of the verb なる
ます :verbal form of ます in the polite termination form.

In the above state diagram, starting from the initial state, it traverses the state diagram in the direction of the arrow and records the relevant information in the dictionary on "みじかくなります," completing the morphological analysis of this phrase.

Inflectional languages use inflectional endings to indicate grammatical meanings. Words can be composed of roots, affixes, and suffixes. Roots and affixes can form stems. Roots can also become stems on their own. Therefore, we use state diagrams to express the morphological analysis process of inflectional words.

In a language, the number of affixes is limited. According to the position of affixes relative to the root (or stem), they can be divided into three categories: prefix, suffix, and infix.

The prefix is added before the root (or stem). For example, un- in English often turns the meaning of the original word into the opposite, *lucky – unlucky*.

A suffix is attached to the root (or stem). For example, −ness in English often changes adjectives into nouns, *straight – straightness*.

An infix is attached to the root (or stem), such as -um- in Tagalog, which tends to express the past tense: *sulat* (write) – *sumulat* (written).

There are generally no infixes in inflectional languages. Therefore, when designing a state diagram for inflectional morphological analysis, we only consider prefixes and suffixes.

In a word of an inflectional language, the relations among the prefix, stem, suffix, and ending are as follows:

- Words which only have stems, for example, *form* in English.
- Words which are composed of prefixes and stems, for example, *reform* in English (*re-* is the prefix, and *form* is the stem).
- Words which are composed of roots and suffixes, for example, *formation* in English (*form* is the root, and *-ation* is the suffix).
- Words which consist of prefixes, roots, and suffixes, for example, *reformation* in English (*re-* is the prefix, *form* is the root, and *-ation* is the suffix).
- Words which are composed of stems and endings, for example, *forms* in English (the plural of the word *form*, *form* is the stem, and *-s* is the ending).

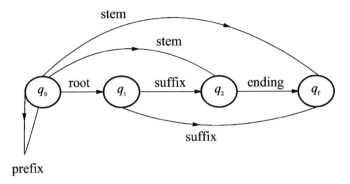

Fig. 3.12 The state diagram for analyzing English morphology

- Words which are composed of roots, suffixes, and endings, for example, *forma-tions* in English (the plural of the word *formation*, *form* is the root, *−ation* is the suffix, and *-s* is the ending).
- Words which consist of prefixes, roots, suffixes, and endings, for example, *reformations* in English (the plural of *reformation*, *re-* is the prefix, *form* is the root, *−ation* is the suffix, and *-s* is the ending).

Therefore, we design the following state diagram (Fig. 3.12) to perform morphological analysis of various forms of English nouns:

It can be seen that the state diagram can describe the process of the morphological analysis of inflectional words very clearly.

When the root is connected with a suffix, the sound sometimes changes. For example, when the English word root *decide* is connected with the suffix *-ion* to form *decision*, *−de-* becomes *-s-*, the vowel letter *i* in *decide* is read as [ai], and in *decision*, it becomes [i]. To handle such sound changes, we should establish rules that correspond to them. Therefore, finite state grammar is a powerful tool for morphological analysis.

However, finite state grammar has the following defects due to its strict restrictions on the form of the rewriting rules:

First, some formal languages composed of very simple symbol strings cannot be generated by finite state grammar. Chomsky cited the following three types of languages:

1. *ab, aabb, aaabbb*, and so on: All the sentences are composed of several *a* followed by the same number of *b*. This formal language can be expressed as $L_1 = \{a^n b^n\}$, where $n \geq 1$.
2. *aa, bb, abba, ba, aaaa, bbbb, aabbaa, abbbba*, and so on: This formal language is a mirror structure language without a central element. If α is used to represent any non-empty symbol string in the set $\{a,b\}$, α^* is used to represent the mirror image of α. This language can be expressed as $L_2 = \{\alpha\alpha^*\}$.
3. *aa, bb, abab, aaaa, bbbb, aabaab, abbabb*, and so on: All the sentences are composed of symbol strings α either with several *a* or several *b* only followed by

the same symbol string α. If α represents any non-empty symbol on the set $\{a, b\}$ string, then this language can be expressed as $L_3 = \{\alpha\alpha\}$.

L_1, L_2, and L_3 cannot be generated by finite state grammar. It can be seen that the generation ability of this grammar is not strong.

Second, in English, there are sentences in the following forms:

1. If S_1, then S_2.
2. Either S_3 or S_4.
3. The man who said S_5 is arriving today.

In these sentences, there is an interdependency relationship among *if*, *then*; *either*, *or*; and *man*, *is*. This kind of sentence is similar to the formal language L_2 specified by Chomsky, which has a mirror structure and which cannot be generated by finite state grammar.

There are also mirror structure sentences in other languages. For example, you can see this kind of sentence in French:

> Chez <u>la maitresse</u> d'<u>un member</u> d'<u>une societe</u>   <u>linguistique</u>   <u>enrhume</u>   <u>envoyee</u> à Paris.
>   a   b   c   c   b   a

(A member of the Paris Linguistic Society who had a cold visited a female teacher in Paris when the person was in Paris on business.)

We can see that in this sentence, *societe* matches *linguistique* (both feminine), *member* matches *enrhume* (both masculine), and *maitresse* matches *envoyee* (both feminine), thus forming a mirror structure like *abccba*. As we said earlier, such sentences cannot be generated by finite state grammar.

Third, American linguist P. Poster pointed out in *Limitation of Phrase Structure Grammar* (1964) that in Indian Mohawk language, the object of a verb should be repeated both before and after the verb in the same order.

For example,

The sentence "I read books" is expressed in Mohawk as

"I books read books", the symbol string of which is *aa*.
      a   a

The sentence "I like reading" is expressed in Mohawk as

"I books read books like books read books", the symbol string of which is *babbab*.
   b   a   b   b   a   b

"I have tasted the sweetness of reading" in Mohawk:

The sentence "I have benefited a lot from reading" in English is expressed in Mohawk as

"I books read books the taste of sweet things books read books the taste of sweet things",
   b   a   b   c   d   b   a   b   c   d

the symbol string of which is *babcdbabcd*.

This kind of structure in Mohawk is similar to the structure of L_3. Obviously, such a structure cannot be generated by finite state grammar.

Fourth, finite state grammar is not suitable for describing the syntactic structure of natural languages. Take the Chinese sentence that we mentioned earlier for example:

"客厅里坐着两位客人" (/Ke ting li zuo zhe liang wei ke ren/; There are two guests sitting in the living room).

It is an existential sentence, the structure of which is very complicated. It would be more complicated if we describe structures like nesting and recursion in Chinese. It can be seen that finite state grammar is unqualified as a model to describe the syntactic structure of natural languages.

Fifth, finite state grammar can only explain the order in which symbols are arranged in a language, but not the hierarchical levels of language symbols. Therefore, it cannot explain many ambiguities in natural languages.

For example, the English sentence "They are flying planes" has two different meanings, one of which means "They are planes that are flying" [try to compare with the following sentence: "Those specks on the horizon are flying planes."]. The other meaning is "They are piloting the planes" [try to compare with the sentence that follows: "Those pilots are flying planes."]. This difference in meaning cannot be explained by finite state grammar.

It can be seen that finite state grammar is not strong in explaining the language phenomenon.

3.3 Phrase Structure Grammar

To overcome the shortcomings of finite state grammar, Chomsky proposed context-free grammar.

The form of rewriting rules for context-free grammar is

$$A \rightarrow \omega$$

where A is a single non-terminal symbol and ω is a symbol string that is not empty, that is,

$$|A| = 1 \leq |\omega$$

It should be noted that the term "context-free" refers to the form of rewriting rules in the grammar, not the fact that the language it generates is not related to the context.

For example, we propose the following context-free grammar:

```
G = (Vn, Vt, S, P)
Vn = {S}
Vt = {a, b}
S = S
P: S → aSb
   S → ab
```

The left side of this grammar rewriting rule is a single non-terminal symbol S, and the right side is a symbol string aSb and ab composed of a terminal or non-terminal symbol, which meets the requirements of context-free grammar rewriting rule.

Such grammar can generate language $L_1 = \{a^n b^n\}$.

The derivation process is as follows: starting from S, using the first rewriting rule (n-1) times and then using the second rewriting rule 1 time, we can get

$$S => aSb => aaSbb => aaaSbbb => \ldots\ldots => a^{n-1}Sb^{n-1} => a^n b^n$$

As mentioned above, L_1 cannot be generated by finite state grammar.

We can also propose the following context-free grammar to generate $L_2 = (\alpha\alpha^*\}$:

```
G = {Vn, Vt, S, P}
Vn = {S}
Vt = {a, b}
S = S
P:
   S → aa
   S → bb
   S → aSa
   S → bSb
```

The form of this grammar rewriting rule also meets the requirements of context-free grammar rewriting rule. The left is the single terminal symbol S, and the right is the symbol string aa, bb, aSa, and bSb.

If we want to generate the symbol string $babbbbab$, the derivation is as follows:

$$S => bSb => baSab => babSbab => babbbbab.$$

However, $L_3 = \{\alpha\alpha\}$ cannot be generated with context-free grammar. It can be seen that the ability to generate context-free grammar is also limited.

The derivation of context-free grammar can be described by a derivation tree.

Let $G = (Vn, Vt, S, P)$ be context-free grammar. If there is a component structure tree that meets the following conditions, it is a derivation tree of context-free grammar:

1. Each node has a label, and this label stands for the symbol in Vn ∪ Vt.
2. The label of the root is S.

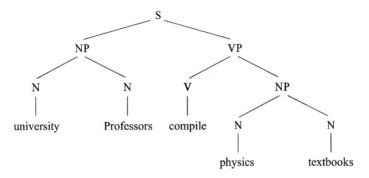

Fig. 3.13 A tree diagram

3. If a node n has at least one descendant different from itself and has the label A, then A must be a symbol in the non-terminal symbol set V.
4. If the nodes n_1, n_2. . ., n_k are direct descendants of the node n arranged from left to right, whose labels are A_1, A_2. . ., A_k, then, $A \rightarrow A_1 A . . . A_k$ must be the rewriting rule in P.

The derivation tree is a tree diagram, which also represents the syntactic structure of the sentence.

For example, the generating rules of the Chinese sentence "大学教授编写物理教材" (/Da xue jiao shou bian xie wu li jiao cai/; University professors compile physics textbooks) that we cited earlier also satisfy the form of rewriting rules of context-free grammar, which are also generated using context-free grammar. The derivation process can be expressed as a tree diagram in Fig. 3.13. This tree diagram illustrates its syntactic structure.

A tree diagram is composed of nodes and branches that connect the nodes, and the labels indicate the relevant information on the nodes. Between the nodes in the tree diagram, there are two relationships worth noting: one is dominance, and the other is precedence.

In the tree diagram, if there is a series of branches connecting node X to node Y and all the branches are in the same direction, then it is said that node X dominates node Y. In the tree diagram above, the node labeled S dominates the node labeled VP, because the branches connecting node S and node VP all sequentially drop from the higher node to the lower node: $S \rightarrow VP \rightarrow V$. When X dominates Y, Y is called the descendant of X.

If node X and node Y are different, X dominates Y, and there is no other node between X and Y; this is called direct dominance. In the above tree diagram, the node S directly dominates the node VP, and the node VP directly dominates the node V, while the node S only dominates the node V, and does not directly dominate the node V. If the node is not dominated by any other node in the dominant relationship, it is called the root. The node labeled S in the figure is the root. A node that is dominated by other nodes but does not dominate any other node is called a leaf. As shown in the figure, nodes labeled "大学" (/da xue/; university), "教授"

(/jiao shou/; professors), "编写" (/bian xie/; compile), "物理" (/wu li/; physics), and "教材"(/jiao cai/; textbooks) are all leaves.

The two nodes in the tree diagram can only be sorted from left to right when there is no dominant relationship between them. At this time, there exists a precedence relationship between the two nodes, and the left node precedes the right node. In the diagram above, the node labeled "大学" (/da xue/; university) precedes the node labeled VP and the nodes dominated by the VP node, because there is no dominant relationship between the VP node and the node labeled "university," but the node labeled "大学" (/da xue/; university) cannot dominate the nodes such as NP and N. Therefore, the dominant relationship and the precedence relationship are mutually exclusive. In a tree diagram, if there is a precedence relationship between the nodes X and Y, then there must not be a dominant relationship between X and Y, and if X precedes Y, then all the nodes dominated by X precede the nodes dominated by Y.

Generally speaking, the tree diagram can provide the following three aspects of language information for automatic analysis of language:

1. Word order in sentences: The leaves in the tree diagram are arranged from left to right in a precedence relationship, which is the word order of the sentence it represents. There must be no dominant relationship between these leaves.
2. Sentence hierarchy: The direct descendant of a node must be the direct component of this node. According to the direct dominant relationship between nodes, the hierarchical relationship of sentences can be seen.
3. Part-of-speech information, phrase type information, syntactic function information, and semantic and logic relationship information between words and phrases:

   For example, the tree diagram above provides the word order information in the Chinese sentence "大学教授编写物理教材" (/Da xue jiao shou bian xie wu li jiao cai/; University professors compile physics textbooks), indicating that the linear order of the words in the sentence from left to right is: "大学" (/da xue/; university) → "教授" (/jiao shou/; professors) → "编写" (/bian xie/; compile) → "物理" (/wu li/; physics) → "教材" (/jiao cai/; textbooks), which also illustrates this sentence S is composed of NP and VP. NP is composed of N and N. VP is composed of V and NP. The latter NP is composed of N and N. It also shows that "大学", "教授", "物理", "教材" (/da xue/, /jiao shou/, /wu li/, /jiao cai/; university, professors, physics, textbooks) are all nouns, "编写" (/bian xie/; compile) is a verb. "大学" (/da xue/; university) and "教授" (/jiao shou/; professors) constitute the noun phrase "大学教授" (/da xue jiao shou/; university professors). "物理" (/wu li/; physics) and "教材" (/jiao cai/; textbooks) constitute the noun phrase "物理教材" (/wu li jiao cai/; physics textbooks). This information is very important for automatic syntactic analysis.

To describe and generate a natural language with context-free grammar, Chomsky proposed the Chomsky normal form. Chomsky proved that any language generated by context-free grammar can be generated by the grammar with rewriting rules of A → BC or A → a, where A, B, and C are non-terminal symbols and a is the terminal symbol. Context-free grammar with such rewriting rules can be reduced to a binary form so that the dichotomy can be used to analyze natural languages and the

Fig. 3.14 Hierarchical analysis

				A			
		$A1$				$A2$	
	$A11$		$A12$		$A21$		$A22$
			$A121$ $A122$	$A211$ $A212$	$A221$ $A222$		

binary tree can be used to represent sentence structures of natural languages. Therefore, context-free rewriting rule A → BC or A → a is called the Chomsky normal form.

In the Chomsky normal form, both the rewriting rules and the derivation trees have a binary form, which provides a mathematical model for the formal description of natural languages.

As we know, syntactic structures of natural languages are generally dichotomous, so it generally has a binary form. Take Chinese for example. In addition to the joint structure and the pivotal structure, the syntactic structure with binary form accounts for the majority:

Predicate-object structure: 思考问题 (/si kao wen ti/; think problem).
Subject-predicate structure: "张三咳嗽" (/Zhang San ke sou/; San Zhang cough).
Modifier-head structure: 大学教授 (/da xue jiao shou/; university professor).
Predicate-complement structure: 打扫干净 (/da sao gan jing/; sweep clean).

In the history of linguistics, many linguists have recognized this dichotomy in natural languages in their description of natural languages.

Chinese linguist Jianzhong Ma put forward the idea of "two elements" in his *Ma's Grammar*. He pointed out that "A sentence must be made up of the subject and predicate, otherwise it is not clear and complete in meaning and structure." American linguist E.A. Nida pointed out in his work *Morphology* that "according to experience, we find that language structure tends to be dichotomous." In his book *English Structures*, American linguist C. C. Fries put forward the idea of dichotomy. He pointed out that there are usually only two immediate constituents in one structural level in English. Of course, each constituent can be composed of several units, but the number of the immediate constituent of the structure at the same level is usually two.

Hierarchical analysis in linguistics embodies the idea of the dichotomy of the Chomsky normal form. The theoretical basis of this method should be context-free grammar.

According to the hierarchical analysis, a complex language form cannot be directly analyzed into several words but must be analyzed layer by layer. For example, the language constituent A should be analyzed according to the following steps (Fig. 3.14).

Instead of dividing A at once into A11, A121, A122, A211, A212, A221, and A222, we first divide A into A1 and A2, then divide A1 into A11 and A12, divide A2 into A21 and A22, then divide A12 into A121 and A122, and so on. This analysis continues until the word is analyzed. Usually, A1 and A2 are called immediate constituents of A. A11 and A12 are called immediate constituents of A1, and A121 and A122 are called immediate constituents of A12. This method of finding out the immediate constituents of a language in the sequence is the hierarchical analysis, which can also be called immediate constituent analysis.

Context-free grammar uses this dichotomous hierarchical analysis to reveal the rules of the internal syntactic structure of languages. It shows that to judge whether the two language fragments are identical, it depends on not only whether the word forms and word order of the two language fragments are the same but also whether their hierarchical structures are the same. However, finite state grammar is difficult to reflect the differences in the hierarchical structure of language fragments. It can be seen that the explanatory power of context-free grammar is much stronger and deeper than that of finite state grammar.

So, what is the relationship between context-free grammar and finite state grammar? Chomsky pointed out the following:

First, every language generated by finite state grammar can be generated by context-free grammar.

In rewriting rule $A \rightarrow \omega$ of context-free grammar, when ω is aQ or a, we can get

$$A \rightarrow aQ \quad \text{or} \quad A \rightarrow a$$

This is the rewriting rule of finite state grammar. This shows that finite state grammar is included in context-free grammar.

Second, there is a non-terminal symbol A in context-free grammar, which has the property

$$A => \varphi A \psi$$

Here, φ and ψ are non-empty symbol strings, G represents context-free grammar, and $=>$ represents derivation relationship, and then this grammar is "self-embedding grammar." Chomsky pointed out that if G is a nonself-embedding context-free grammar, then the language L(G) generated by G is a finite state language. If L(G) is a context-free language, then L(G) is not a finite state language if and only if the grammar G is context-free grammar with self-embedding properties.

For the context-free languages, such as $\{a^n b^n\}, \{\alpha \alpha^*\}$ which we discussed earlier, not only in the rewriting rules of their grammar but also in the process of generating symbol strings, the following will appear:

$$A => \varphi A \psi$$

Such a derivation has the property of self-embedding. Therefore, such languages are not finite state languages, but context-free languages with self-embedding properties. This is the reason why such a language cannot be generated by finite state grammar.

In the following, we will discuss context-sensitive grammar.

The rewriting rule P of context-sensitive grammar has the form

$$\varphi \to \psi,$$

where φ and ψ are symbol strings and $|\varphi| \le |\psi|$, that is, the length of ψ is not less than the length of φ. Now there is a formal language $L = \{a^n b^n c^n\}$, which is a symbol string formed by $a^n b^n c^n$ adjacent to each other and requires $n \ge 1$. The grammar G that generates this language is.

```
G = {Vn, Vt, S, P}
    Vn = {S, B, C}
    Vt = {a, b, c}
    S = S
    P :
        S → aSBC        ①
        S → aBC         ②
        CB → BC         ③
        aB → ab         ④
        bB → bb         ⑤
        bC → bc         ⑥
        cC → cc         ⑦
```

Starting from S, using rule (1) $n - 1$ times, we get

$$S \Longrightarrow a^{n-1} S (BC)^{n-1}$$

Then, use rule (2) once to get

$$S \Longrightarrow a^n (BC)^n$$

Rule (3) can transform $(BC)^n$ into $B^n C^n$.
For example, if $n = 3$, then,

$$aaaBCBCBC \Longrightarrow aaaBBCCBC \Longrightarrow aaaBBCBCC \Longrightarrow aaaBBBCCC,$$

In this way, there will be

$$S \Longrightarrow a^n B^n C^n$$

Then, use rule (4) once to get

$$S \Longrightarrow a^n b B^{n-1} C^n$$

Then, using rule (5) $n - 1$ times to get

$$S \Longrightarrow a^n b^n C^n$$

Then, use rule (6) once to get

$$S => a^n b^n c C^{n-1}$$

Finally, use rule (7) $n - 1$ times, to get

$$S => a^n b^n c^n$$

This is the formal language we want to generate.

In each rewriting rule of this grammar, the number of symbols on the right is always greater than or equal to the number of symbols on the left, to satisfy the condition

$$|\varphi| \leq |\psi|$$

Therefore, this grammar is context-sensitive.

Chomsky pointed out that there is the following relationship between context-sensitive grammar and context-free grammar:

First, every context-free grammar is included in context-sensitive grammar.

In the context-sensitive grammar rewriting rule $\varphi \rightarrow \psi$, both φ and ψ are symbol strings. When the symbol string on the left of the rewriting rule degenerates into a single non-terminal symbol A, there is A $\rightarrow \psi$. Because ψ is a symbol string, it can therefore be replaced by ω, and we get A $\rightarrow \omega$. This is the rewriting rule of context-free grammar.

Second, there exist context-sensitive languages that are not context-free languages. For example, as Chomsky pointed out, the language $L_3 = \{\alpha\alpha\}$ cannot be generated using finite state grammar, nor can it be generated using context-free grammar. However, it can be generated with context-sensitive grammar. The grammar that generates language L_3 is as follows:

```
G = {Vn, Vt, S, P}
   Vn = {S}
   Vt = {a, b}
   S = S
   P:
       S → aS              ①
       S → bS              ②
       αS → αα             ③
```

In rule (3), α is any non-empty symbol string on the set $\{a, b\}$. Since the length of αS is not greater than the length of $\alpha\alpha$ and αS is not a single non-terminal symbol, but a symbol string, this grammar may not be context-free grammar, but context-sensitive grammar.

For example, formal language *abbabb* can be generated in this way. Starting with S, use rule (1) once to get S=> aS. Use rule (2) twice to get S=> abbS, and use rule (3) once to get S=> abbabb.

It can be seen that the generative power of context-sensitive grammar is better than that of finite state grammar and context-free grammar. However, because context-free grammar can use the Chomsky normal form to realize hierarchical analysis, people are still willing to adopt context-free grammar in the computer processing of the natural language.

Finally, let us discuss type 0 grammar.

The rewriting rule of type 0 syntax is $\varphi \rightarrow \psi$, which has no other restrictions except for the requirement of $\varphi \neq \psi$. Chomsky proved that every type 0 language is a recursively enumerable set of symbol strings, that any context-sensitive language is also a type 0 language, and that there exist type 0 languages that are not context-sensitive languages. Therefore, context-sensitive languages should be included in type 0 languages, and they are subsets of type 0 languages. However, because there are almost no restrictions on the rewriting rules of type 0 grammar, it is quite difficult to describe natural languages. Its generative power is too strong, so it can generate countless unqualified sentences. Therefore, among the four types of Chomsky's grammar, context-free grammar is the most suitable one to describe natural languages. This kind of grammar is used to be called phrase structure grammar by Chinese scholars in NLP.

Chomsky's formal linguistic theory has a great influence on computer science. Chomsky associated his four types of grammars with Turing machines, linear bounded automata, last-in-first-out automata, and finite automata (automata are abstract machines used to recognize languages). He also proved four important results of equivalence between the generative power of grammar and the recognition power of language automata:

1. If a language can be recognized by a Turing machine, it can be generated by using type 0 grammar, and vice versa.
2. If a language can be recognized by a linear bounded automaton, it can be generated with context-sensitive grammar, and vice versa.
3. If a language can be recognized by a last-in-first-out automaton, it can be generated with context-free grammar, and vice versa.
4. If a language can be recognized by finite automata, it can be generated with finite state grammar, and vice versa.

The above conclusions drawn by Chomsky provide great insights into the process of language generation and the process of language recognition, which are very useful for the design of computer programming languages, algorithm analysis, compilation techniques, image recognition, artificial intelligence, etc. They also play a great role in NLP.

3.4   Recursive Transition Networks and Augmented Transition Networks

In his "Transition network grammars for natural language analysis" (Communication of the ACM, 13) in 1970, American artificial intelligence expert W. Woods proposed the idea of an augmented transition network (ATN).

ATN is based on finite state grammar and has been developed after important extensions.

We know that finite state grammar can be represented by state diagrams, but its function is only to generate. From the perspective of syntactic analysis, we can also use the state diagram to represent the analysis process of a sentence vividly. Such a state diagram is called the finite state transition diagram (FSTD). An FSTD is composed of a group of states (nodes) and several arcs, including one or more start states and final states. The arcs lead from one state to another, and there are labels on the arcs. These labels can be non-terminal symbols of grammar, for example, the part-of-speech symbols in a language, such as <Verb>, <Adj>, <Noun>, etc. The analysis process begins from the start state, moves one by one along the direction of the arc in FSTD (indicated by arrows), scans the input sentence at the same time, and matches the words in the sentence with the labels on the arc. If there exists such a case, that is, scanning to the end of the input sentence and entering the final state of FSTD, the sentence is accepted by FSTD, and the analysis is completed.

FSTD can only recognize finite state languages. We know that the rewriting rules of finite state grammar are $A \rightarrow aQ$ and $A \rightarrow a$. This kind of grammar is relatively simple. FSTD has enough power to recognize the language generated by finite state grammar.

For example, we can input such a noun phrase for FSTD to analyze. This noun phrase begins with <Det> and ends with <N > (Noun), and there can be any number < A > (adjective) in between. For example,

the pretty girl
the handsome boy
the excellent success

FSTD is shown in Fig. 3.15.

If the input noun phrase is *the pretty girl*, scan along the arc labeled with Det from the state q_0. Because *the* is the leftmost word in the input symbol string and its part of

Fig. 3.15   A finite state
transition diagram

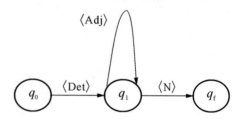

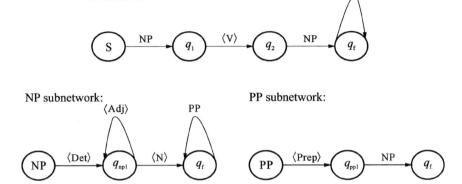

Fig. 3.16 Recursive transfer network

speech is Det, the two match, and then enter the state q_1. The rest of the input string that should be analyzed is *pretty girl*. After passing through the circle arc labeled with $< adj >$, the two match, since *pretty* is Adj. Then enter the state q_1. At this time, the remaining part in the input symbol string is *girl*. Since this word is N, which matches the label on the arc $< N >$, the analysis enters the final state q_f. At this point, all the words in the input string are checked, and the noun phrase is accepted by FSTD.

FSTD has sufficient ability to recognize the language generated by finite state grammar. Due to the limitations of finite state grammar, it is difficult to recognize complex sentences. Therefore, FSTD needs to be expanded by adding a recursive mechanism to make it capable of dealing with context-free languages.

After the expansion, FSTD becomes recursive transition networks (RTN). In RTN, the label of the arc is not only the part of the speech symbol but also the phrase type symbol, such as NP, VP, etc. These phrase type symbols also represent the name of the subnetwork of corresponding phrases. Each type of phrase can be represented by a single FSTD. With such subnetworks, RTN gains recursive capability. When the arc label is not a phrase type symbol in the process of sentence analysis and processing, RTN operates in the same way as FSTD. When a phrase type symbol is encountered, the current analysis state is stored in the stack, and the control is transferred to the subnetwork corresponding to the symbol. The sentence is processed continuously until the processing in the subnetwork is completed or fails. Then it returns to the original place again and continues to operate according to the previous state. For example, we can propose the RTN shown in Fig. 3.16. This RTN is made up of a network named S and two subnetworks named NP and PP, respectively.

Here, NP represents a noun phrase and PP represents a prepositional phrase. When the input sentence is "the little boy in swimsuit kicked the red ball," the above RTN will analyze the sentence in the following steps:

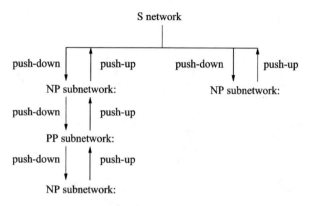

Fig. 3.17 Pushdown and push-up in the recursive transfer network

NP: the little boy in the swimsuit
PP: in the swimsuit
NP: the swimsuit
<V>: kicked
NP: the red ball

In the S network, starting from S, scan to NP, and push down to the NP subnet to deal with NP *the little boy in the swimsuit*. In the NP subnet, after scanning *the little boy*, the PP *in the swimsuit* is encountered. Further push down to the PP subnet to process the PP. In the PP subnet, after scanning <Prep> (*in*), the NP *the swimsuit* should be scanned. Then pushdown to the NP subnet handles the NP *the swimsuit*. After scanning *the swimsuit*, enter the final state of the NP subnet. In this way, the noun phrase *the little boy in the swimsuit* is processed. Then, go to the PP subnet first, and enter the final state of the PP subnet, and then continue to push up to the NP subnetwork, and enter the final state of the NP subnetwork. Then continue to push up to the state of the S network q_1. In the state q_1, scan the verb *kicked*, and enter the state q_2. In the state q_2, scan the NP *the red ball*. Then push down to the NP subnetwork again to process *the red ball*. After processing the noun phrase, push up to the final state of the S network q_f. At this time, the input sentence has been scanned, and RTN has entered the final state. This sentence is accepted by RTN. The above process can be illustrated in Fig. 3.17.

RTN can process context-free languages, but it is still not good enough for NLP. In the process of analysis, if there is more than one path at the same time, the mechanism of RTN cannot make a choice and make the analysis go on smoothly. Take the string *the building blocks* for example. Because *blocks* can be either a noun or a verb, whether the word string is NP or NP + V depends on what the following word is. However, RTN does not have such a mechanism. Therefore, RTN should be expanded to have such a processing mechanism. For more than one optional line, either parallel processing or first try on a path, backtracking is needed in the case of failure, and then analysis continues on another path. After W. Woods improved and expanded RTN, he proposed the augmented transition network (ATN). Compared with RTN, ATN mainly improves and expands in the following three aspects:

1. A set of registers is added to store information. Some derivation trees formed locally in each subnet can be temporarily stored in these registers, and other necessary information in the analysis process can also be stored in the registers; the backtracking operation should be based on the previous background information. For example, the string *the building blocks* may be regarded as an NP at first. But later when it is found that the following string is *the sun*, the system will return to one of the previous transfer points for reanalysis and choose another path. The phrase *the building* is judged as NP, and *blocks* is judged as V. So the correct result is obtained: the structure of "the building blocks the sun" is NP + V + NP, which means "the building blocks the sun."

2. In addition to the terminal symbol and non-terminal symbol, the label of the arc in the network can also be attached to some conditions. Before entering the arc, it is necessary to test whether the current state meets the condition required.

3. Some actions can also be attached to the arc. To go through an arc, the specified operations are performed. Usually, the data structure generated by sentence analysis is rearranged. For example, in the English sentence "the red ball was kicked by the little boy," the first NP (the red ball) is first stored in the register as a possible logical subject of the sentence. Later, when the verb is found to be passive, an action is performed to store *the little boy* in the register to replace the previous NP. As a result, the structure of the analysis result is adjusted appropriately.

The operation mode of ATN is similar to that of RTN. The difference is that before and after passing through an arc, it is necessary to test conditions and execute corresponding actions. Based on RTN, ATN is expanded by adding registers, conditions, and actions on the arc. The recognition function can be improved to the level of the Turing machine. In theory, ATN is capable of recognizing any language that the computer can recognize, and it is more natural and has higher expressive power than the Turing machine. Due to its overdependence on syntactic analysis, ATN still has limitations in dealing with some words which have clear semantics but are not fully grammatical. And because ATN is procedural rather than descriptive, static data and dynamic analysis are often confused and do not fully comply with the general principles of knowledge organization in the computational sense. Modifying a large ATN often leads to an unexpected side effect. However, despite these deficiencies, ATN is still a kind of very effective tool for analyzing natural languages. ATN has been widely used in the field of NLP, such as machine translation, text generation, discourse understanding, human-machine dialogue, etc., and has achieved remarkable results.

3.5   Bottom-Up and Top-Down Analysis

The recursive transition network (RTN) and the augmented transition network (ATN) discussed in Sect. 3.4 are all based on finite state grammar. In this section, we discuss natural language analysis methods based on context-free grammar: top-down analysis and bottom-up analysis. First, we discuss the top-down parsing method.

When using the top-down parsing method, follow the rewriting rules of context-free grammar, search top-down from the initial symbol, and construct the derivation tree until the end of the sentence, as shown in Fig. 3.18.

For example, we propose the following context-free grammar:

```
            G = {Vn, Vt, S, P}
      Vn = {S, NP, VP, Det, N, V, Prep}
      Vt = {the, boy, rod, dog, hits, with, a}
      S = S
      P: S → NP VP        (a)
         NP → Det N        (b)
         VP → V NP         (c)
         VP → VP PP        (d)
         PP → Prep NP      (e)
         Det → [the]       (f)
         Det → [a]         (g)
         N → [boy]         (h)
         N → [dog]         (i)
         N → [rod]         (j)
         V → [hits]        (k)
         Prep → [with]     (l)
```

When searching, the first target is the initial symbol S. Starting from S, select the applicable rules in the grammar to replace the search target, and use the right part of the grammar rules to match the words in the sentence. If the match is successful, erase the word, record the relevant rules in the search target, and then continue to search in the remaining part of the input sentence. If the analysis comes to the end of the sentence and the search target is empty, the analysis is successful.

The analysis process of the English sentence "the boy hits the dog with a rod" is as follows (the number of the rule is indicated next to the down arrow "↓," and the

Fig. 3.18 Top-down parsing method

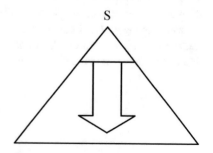

underlined symbol in the search target indicates it is the left part of the rule that is used):

	search target	**input the remaining part of the sentence.**
(1)	<u>S</u>	the boy hits the dog with a rod
	↓(a)	
(2)	<u>NP</u> VP	the boy hits the dog with a rod
	↓(b)	
(3)	<u>Det</u> N VP	the boy hits the dog with a rod
	↓(f)	
(4)	<u>N</u> VP	boy hits the dog with a rod
	↓(h)	
(5)	<u>VP</u>	hits the dog with a rod
	↓(c)	
(6)	<u>V</u> NP	hits the dog with a rod
	↓(k)	
(7)	<u>NP</u>	the dog with a rod
	↓(b)	
(8)	<u>Det</u> N	the dog with a rod
	↓(f)	
(9)	<u>N</u>	dog with a rod
	↓(i)	

If *dog* is erased according to rule (i), *with a rod* remains in the sentence. The search target has become empty at this time; consequently, the analysis cannot continue. Next, back to step (5) to see if other rules can be used for analysis:

(5')	<u>VP</u>	hits the dog with a rod
	↓(d)	
(10)	<u>VP</u> PP	hit the dog with a rod
	↓Repeat the search process from (5) to (9), at this time, the search target is PP	
(11)	<u>PP</u>	with a rod
	↓(e)	
(12)	<u>Prep</u> NP	with a rod
	↓(l)	
(13)	<u>NP</u>	a rod
	↓(b)	
(14)	<u>Det</u> N	a rod
	↓(g)	
(15)	<u>N</u>	rod
	↓(j)	
(16)	End. Analysis succeeded	

In the search process, when the analysis comes to step (5), the analysis cannot continue due to the use of rule (c). And then we adopt the backtracking method and return to step (5). Instead of using rule (c), we use rule (d), and the search is successful.

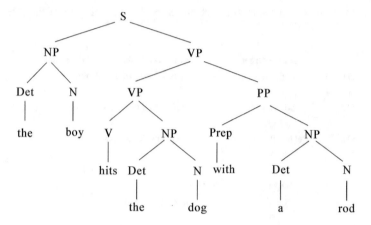

Fig. 3.19 Derivation tree 1 of the English sentence

Fig. 3.20 Bottom-up
analysis

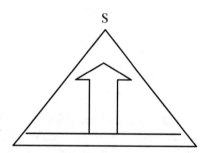

Based on such a search process, we can express the derivation tree of the English sentence "the boy hits the dog with a rod" is shown in Fig. 3.19.

Now let us discuss the bottom-top parsing method.

When the bottom-top parsing method is used to analyze sentences, words are taken from the beginning of the input sentence to shift forward and reduce step-by-step upward according to the rewriting rules of the grammar until the entire derivation tree representing the sentence structure is constructed, as shown in Fig. 3.20.

The bottom-top parsing method is a kind of shift-reduce algorithm, which takes words from the sentence to shift in sequence and uses rewriting rules in grammar to reduce according to certain conditions. This algorithm is similar to the LR algorithm in the compilation technology (L represents left to right [the direction of analysis is from left to right]; R represents rightmost production [the rightmost node is expanded in each derivation]). The information storage method of the shift-reduce algorithm is mainly the stack, and the information operation mode mainly includes shift, reduction, rejection, and acceptance. This algorithm uses a stack to store the "historical" information (i.e., information about the processes that have been traversed) in the analysis and determines whether to shift or reduce based on this historical information and the symbol string currently being processed. The so-called shift is to move a symbol that has not been processed to the top of the stack and wait for more information to arrive before making a decision. The so-called reduction is to replace some symbols at the top of the stack with the symbols on the left of a certain rewriting rule of grammar. At this time, the right part of the rewriting rule must match those symbols at the top of the stack. Use this method to process symbols and input symbol strings in the stack in shift and reduce operations. The operation continues until the input symbol string is processed and only the initial symbol S is left in the stack and then the input symbol string is accepted. In the current state, if neither shift nor reduction operation can be performed, and the stack does not have the only initial symbol S, or there are still symbols in the input symbol string which have not been processed, then the input symbol string is rejected.

It is often possible to perform both a shift operation and a reduction operation at a certain moment. This is called a shift-reduction conflict. It is often possible that several rules satisfy the reduction condition at a certain moment. In this case, it is called a reduction-reduction conflict. Issues such as when to perform the shift operation, when to perform the reduction operation, and how to define the conditions for the reduction are the central ones of the shift-reduce algorithm.

Next, we take "the boy hits the dog with a rod" as an example to illustrate the bottom-top parsing method of sentence analysis by using this shift-reduce algorithm:

	stack	operation	The remaining part of the input sentence
(1)			the boy hits the dog with a rod
(2)	the	shift	boy hits the dog with a rod
(3)	Det	use rule (f) to reduce	boy hits the dog with a rod
(4)	Det boy	shift	hits the dog with a rod
(5)	Det N	use rule (h) to reduce	hits the dog with a rod
(6)	NP	use rule (b) to reduce	hits the dog with a rod
(7)	NP hits	shift	the dog with a rod
(8)	NP V	use rule (k) to reduce	the dog with a rod
(9)	NP V the	shift	dog with a rod
(10)	NP V Det	use rule (f) to reduce	dog with a rod
(11)	NP V Det dog	shift	with a rod
(12)	NP V Det N	use rule (i) to reduce	with a rod
(13)	NP V NP	use rule (b) to reduce	with a rod
(14)	NP VP	use rule (c) to reduce	with a rod
(15)	S	use rule (a) to reduce	with a rod
(16)	S with	shift	a rod
(17)	S Prep	use rule (l) to reduce	a rod
(18)	S Prep a	shift	rod
(19)	S Prep Det	use rule (g)to reduce	rod
(20)	S Prep Det rod	shift	
(21)	S Prep Det N	use rule (j) to reduce	
(22)	S Prep NP	use rule (b) to reduce	
(23)	S PP	use rule (e) to reduce	

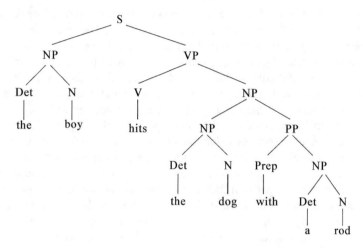

Fig. 3.21 Derivation tree 2 of the English sentence

At this time, there are no suitable rules in grammar, and the analysis cannot continue. Therefore, we return to (14). Instead of using rule (a) to reduce, we move forward to the next word *with* and then use rule (l) to reduce:

(14')	NP VP	backtrack	with a rod
(24)	NP VP with	shift	a rod
(25)	NP VP Prep	use rule (l) to reduce	a rod
(26)	NP VP Prep a	shift	rod
(27)	NP VP Prep Det	use rule (g) to reduce	rod
(28)	NP VP Prep Det rod	shift	
(29)	NP VP Prep NP	use rule (b) to reduce	
(30)	NP VP PP	use rule (e) to reduce	
(31)	NP VP	use rule (d) to reduce	
(32)	S	use rule (a) to reduce	

At this time, only the initial symbol S is left in the stack, and the input symbol string is empty. The sentence is accepted, and the analysis is successful.

In English, the prepositional phrase (PP) can be used to modify not only verbs but also nouns. The above grammar only considers the case where PP modifies the verb, not the case where PP modifies the noun. If we add a new rule to the grammar rewriting rules, NP → NP PP, then in addition to the above result, we can also get another result from other analysis processes. The tree diagram is shown in Fig. 3.21.

Although this result is not very semantically satisfactory ("the boy hit the dog with a stick," which means "the dog carries with a stick in its body"; such case is rare), it is qualified syntactically.

If we change the words into "the man saw a boy with a telescope" according to the structure of the above sentence, the new sentence has two different meanings: one meaning "the man saw a boy who had a telescope" and the other meaning "the man using a telescope saw a boy." The ambiguity arises. If we add a prepositional phrase "in the park" before the prepositional phrase "with a telescope," we have a new sentence "the man saw the boy in the park with a telescope." In this case, these two PPs can modify the noun *boy* and the verb *saw* at the same time. It is also possible that the first PP modifies the noun *boy* and the second PP modifies the verb *saw* or the first PP modifies the verb *saw* and the second PP modifies the noun *boy*. As a result, four different structures are obtained, corresponding to four different meanings:

"The man saw a boy in the park who had a telescope."
"In the park, the man with a telescope saw a boy."
"The man with a telescope saw a boy who was in the park."
"The man in the park saw a boy who had a telescope."

From a purely syntactic point of view, the noun *park* in the first PP can also be modified by the second PP "with a telescope," which means "the park equipped with a telescope."

If we take this situation into account, we can get the fifth structure and correspondingly get a fifth different meaning:

"In the park equipped with a telescope the man saw a boy."

In this way, the results of the analysis will be ambiguous. Ambiguity is a common phenomenon in natural languages. We will discuss the resolution of ambiguity in natural languages in the following chapters.

The shift-reduce algorithm is essentially a left-to-right (LR) algorithm. The standard LR algorithm was originally designed for programming languages. Although the efficiency is high, it is in a dilemma when dealing with the ambiguity of natural languages. Therefore, it is difficult to deal with ambiguity in natural languages by using the common shift-reduce analysis technology based on the LR algorithm.

3.6   General Syntactic Processor and Chart Parsing

In 1973, American scholar R. M. Kaplan proposed the general syntactic processor (GSP).

GSP is a very good system for analyzing and generating natural language symbol strings. Its data structure is intuitive, its control structure is concise, and its operation is easy to handle. If some control parameters are adjusted, GSP can directly simulate ATN.

GSP seeks to integrate the formal characteristics of various analysis methods to establish a unified framework to compare these methods. In this sense, GSP is a

Fig. 3.22 Dominance
relationship represented by
the tree diagram

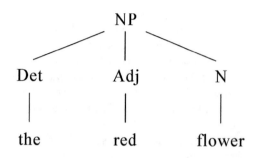

meta-system, which is not only a processing method but also a system that can formally describe various methods.

The basic data structure of GSP is the chart, which is a kind of graph formed by modifying the tree diagram.

We know that there are two kinds of relationships between the nodes in the tree diagram. One is precedence, and the other is dominance. The dominance relationship is fairly intuitive in the tree diagram, where we can see at a glance the dominance relationship between the nodes, while the precedence relationship is not very intuitive in the tree diagram, and it is not easy to see such a relationship at a glance. For example, a tree diagram for "the red flower" can be shown in Fig. 3.22.

In this tree diagram, the node NP directly dominates nodes Det, Adj, and N and also dominates *the*, *red*, and *flower*. The node Det directly dominates *the*, the node Adj directly dominates *red*, and the node N directly dominates *flower*, which is very intuitive. However, the precedence relationship between Det, Adj, and N and the precedence relationship between *the*, *red*, and *flower* are not very intuitive.

To visualize the precedence relationship, Kaplan made some modifications to the tree diagram. The modification is as follows: for each node in the tree diagram, add an edge with an arrow. The direction of the arrow is from left to right. Label the node on this edge and then connect the dominating nodes with a straight line. If a node directly dominates several nodes, only a straight line is needed to connect this node with the first node directly dominated by it. If a node only directly dominates another node, use a straight line to connect these two nodes.

After such a modification of the tree diagram, we get a new diagram, which is called a chart.

For example, after such modification, the above tree diagram becomes a chart as shown in Fig. 3.23.

In the tree diagram, there is no direct connection between DET and Adj, but in the corresponding chart, the connection between DET and Adj is expressed. This is very beneficial to NLP, because in natural languages, especially in analytical languages such as Chinese and English, the relationship between one language unit and the one that follows is the most basic one. The chart is more intuitive than the tree diagram in expressing the precedence relationship. Of course, a chart can also represent a dominant relationship. In addition to showing the precedence relationship intuitively, the chart has two other obvious advantages:

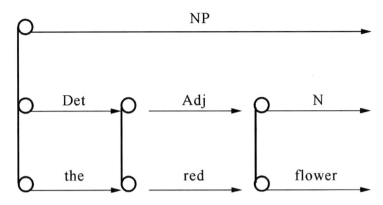

Fig. 3.23 The precedence relationship represented by a chart

A chart can represent unconnected subtrees. In the analysis of natural languages, sometimes the structural analysis is successful locally, but not so good globally, which makes it difficult to form a complete tree in the end. Consequently, the analyzed structure cannot be represented by a tree diagram, resulting in the failure of analysis. Since a complete tree has not been formed, the overall analysis failed. Even if the original partial analysis results are correct, they cannot be shown on the tree diagram. As a result, these partial correct structures are also abandoned, which is a pity. The chart can represent unconnected subtrees. It does not necessarily require that a complete tree must be formed at the end. Therefore, the correct structure of the local analysis can be saved in the form of a subtree, so that the analysis will not be abandoned.

For example, the English sentence "the nurses book her travel" can be represented by the following three disconnected subtrees (Fig. 3.24), one with NP (for *the nurses*), one with N (for *book*), and another which begins with NP (for *her travel*). Because the node *book* in the subtree N can be both a noun (meaning "book") and a verb (meaning "reserve"), here *book* is misclassified as the noun N. Therefore, it is difficult for the three subtrees to form a complete tree. The ancestor nodes of NP and N and the next NP are unclear. We will temporarily label it with a question mark "?."

Such unconnected subtrees do not form a complete tree, which leads to the failure of the analysis. However, if we convert this unconnected subtree into a chart as shown in Fig. 3.25, each subtree can be saved. Although the analysis of *book* is wrong, the two partial correct analysis results of *the nurses* and *her travel* are preserved. In this way, although the global analysis fails, the partial correct analysis results are saved without losing all.

First, charts can represent words with multiple interpretations. In a chart, if a word has multiple interpretations (a word might be polysemous), the multiple interpretations can be expressed as multiple edges so that the ambiguity can be clearly expressed. For example, in the English sentence "I saw the log," the word *saw* can be interpreted as the past tense form of the verb *see* or the present tense form of the verb *saw*. Therefore, the sentence has two meanings: one is "I saw (see) the log," and

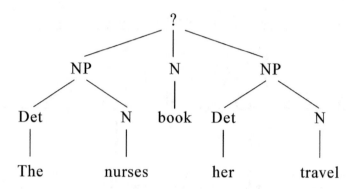

Fig. 3.24 An incomplete structure

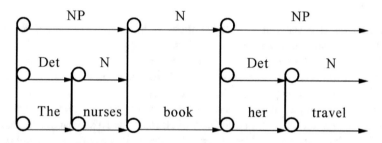

Fig. 3.25 A chart to represent an incomplete structure

the other is "I saw the log (with a saw)." In such a case, it is difficult to represent it with a tree diagram, but it is very clear if it is represented with the following chart (Fig. 3.26).

In the chart, Pro represents a pronoun, and other symbols have the same meaning as before.

To deal with various complex grammatical phenomena, GSP has the following control mechanisms:

1. Register: Its function is the same as the register in ATN.
2. Hierarchical stack: This hierarchical stack has a recursive function. It first stores the chart and some syntactic information in the stack for the recursive call.
3. Nondeterministic table: This is an instruction table for selecting grammar. When making a selection, the user can store the current format in the table at will for backtracking processing.
4. Process stack: This is a pause processing table, which has functions such as pause and restart.

R. M. Kaplan used GSP and successfully implemented Martin Kay's MIND system (a context-free bottom-up parsing system) and J. Friedman's transformational grammar text generation system.

Fig. 3.26 A chart showing polysemy

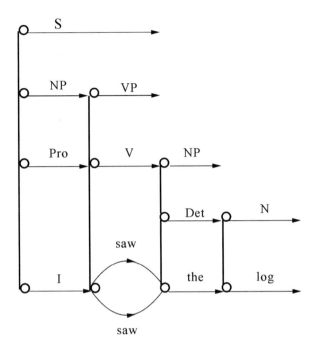

Zhiwei Feng first noticed M. Kaplan's research on GSP. In his book *Mathematical Linguistics* published in 1985, he introduced GSP in detail in a separate section, thinking that this theory is very vital.

J. Earley published his doctoral thesis "An Efficient Context-Free Parsing Algorithm" in 1968. He proposed the concepts of Earley algorithm and dotted rules, which laid a theoretical foundation for chart analysis.

Based on GSP and Earley algorithm, Martin Kay proposed a chart parser in 1980 in *Algorithm Schemata and Data Structures in Syntactic Processing*. He called the chart algorithm schemata at the beginning and later adopted the term chart proposed by R. M. Kaplan.

For the convenience of expression, the above three charts can be changed to the forms shown in Figs. 3.27, 3.28, and 3.29.

Although such a chart can help us to save some correct intermediate results of analysis and avoid doing repeated useless work when the analysis fails, it cannot help us to remember the assumptions and conjectures made before, nor can we understand the objective of the analysis. In other words, such a chart can only represent some facts of the structure. It cannot represent assumptions, conjectures, and goals of the structure. Therefore, Martin Kay proposed the method of adding partial analysis trees (local trees) to the edge of a chart, the concepts of active edge, and the inactive edge.

Let us study the following English sentence:

Failing students looked hard.

Fig. 3.27 Chart 1

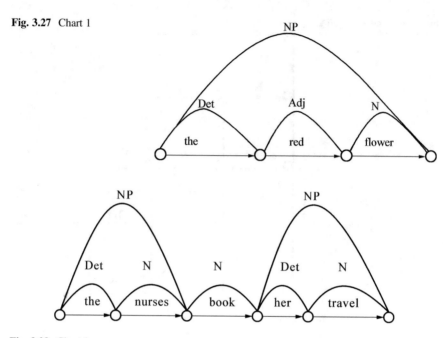

Fig. 3.28 Chart 2

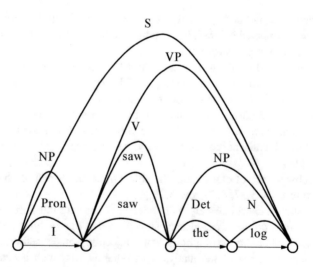

Fig. 3.29 Chart 3

The phrase *failing student* in this sentence has two meanings: one meaning is "let the student fail the list." Here *failing* is a gerund, and we use Grd to represent it. The other meaning is "failing student," and we label it as Adj here. The phrase *looked hard* also has two meanings: One meaning is "it looks difficult." Here, *hard* is an

Fig. 3.30 A local tree

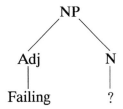

adjective and is labeled as Adj. The other meaning is "seems to work hard"; here, *hard* is an adverb, and it is labeled as Adv. This means that the sentence has four meanings:

To fail the students is difficult.
They seem to have worked hard to fail the student.
It seems hard for the failed students.
Failed students seem to work hard.

We propose the following grammatical rules to analyze this sentence:

1. S → NP VP.
2. NP → Adj N.
3. NP → Grd N.
4. VP → V Adj.
5. VP → V Adv.
6. Adj → failing | hard.
7. GRD → failing.
8. N → student.
9. V → looked.
10. Adv → hard.

Using these rules to analyze the sentence, we can get a local tree as shown in Fig. 3.30 before analyzing the second word.

Because the second word has not been analyzed,? is used in the local tree.

In the chart, the data structure representing the local tree is called "term." The term of this local tree is:

[[failing]Adj [?]N]NP

where "[?] N" refers to the noun whose contents have not been determined. "?" is called an empty place. The meaning of this term is it has been found that *failing* is Adj, but the content of noun N has not been determined, and the whole phrase is NP.

Using the bottom-up method, the initial state of the chart at the beginning of the analysis is as follows:

Number	Location of the local tree in the chart	The length of local tree	Term
1	0	1	[failing]Adj
2	0	1	[failing]Grd
3	1	1	[student]N
4	2	1	[looked]V
5	3	1	[hard]Adj
6	3	1	[hard]Adv

In the chart, the starting position (the position of the first word) is counted as 0, and the order is arranged as position 1, position 2, position 3, etc. In order not to be confused with the term number, in the following chart, the location number is self-evident, so we do not label it anymore. We only label the term number. The length of the local tree refers to the number of words contained in the local tree. The meaning of the term has been described above. For example, the term numbered 1 is at the starting position of 0 in the chart, its length is 1, and the term is shown as [failing] Adj. The chart at the beginning of the analysis is shown in Fig. 3.31.

The edge of the chart is labeled with the number of the term. Since *failing* can be either Adj or Grd at position 0, there are two edges, which are labeled as 1 and 2, respectively. Their terms are [failing]Adj and [failing]Grd, respectively, and so on and so forth. The edge of the chart is labeled ith the number of the item. At position 0, because the word *failing* can be Adj or Grd, there are two sides, which are denoted as 1 and 2, and their terms are [failing]Adj and [failing]Grd, and so on and so forth.

There are two kinds of terms represented on the edge of the chart: One is the term like [failing]Adj and [failing]Grd, and there is no empty space. The other is the term like [[failing]Adj [?]N]NP, which contains empty space. The edge which has no empty space is called the inactive edge. There is no empty space in the inactive edge. Such an edge no longer needs to be confirmed. Therefore, it is inactive. The edge representing the term which contains empty space is called the active edge. The empty space in the active edge needs further confirmation, so it is active. For example, on the active edge [[failing]Adj[?]N]NP, [failing]Adj is the confirmed part, and the empty space [?]N is the part that needs to be confirmed. It needs to guess whether it is the noun (N) after *failing*, which makes the analysis move

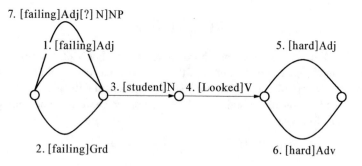

Fig. 3.31 Chart at the beginning of the analysis

forward. If the empty space of the active edge is confirmed by the relevant rules, then fill the empty space, change the active edge to an inactive edge, and advance the process. This operation turns the active edge into an inactive edge. It is the basic operation of the chart analysis, which makes the chart analysis run step-by-step.

The chart can be used for both bottom-up analysis and top-down analysis. We use an example to further illustrate the process of chart analysis.

The bottom-up analysis process of the above sentence is as follows (for simplicity, "local tree position in the chart" is abbreviated as "position"; "local tree length" is abbreviated as "length"; in "rules used and the number of the term," the term number is labeled as #, both are connected with &):

Number	Position	Length	Term	Number of rules and items used
1	0	1	[failing]Adj	6
2	0	1	[failing]Adj	7
3	1	1	[student]N	8
4	2	1	[looked]V	9
5	3	1	[hard]Adj	6
6	3	1	[hard]Adv	10
7	0	1	[[failing]Adj[?]N]NP	2&#1

When all the words in the sentence have been labeled with part of speech, the phrase is analyzed from position 0. According to rule (2) NP → Adj N and #1, Adj is *failing*, but the content of N is unknown. The whole phrase is NP, so the term is labeled as [[failing]Adj[?]N]NP, and the number of the rules used and term number is 2&#1. Next, let us look at the case when *failing* is Grd.

8	0	1	[[failing]Grd[?]N]NP	3&#2
9	0	2	[[failing]Adj[student]N]NP	#3&#7

Get to know [student]N from #3, and substitute #7 to get [[failing]Adj[student]N] NP; at this time, the length of NP is 2.

10	0	2	[[failing]Grd[student]N]NP]	#3&#8
11	0	2	[[failing]Adj[student]N]NP[?]VP]S	1&#9

After analyzing the NP according to #9, continue to analyze the VP that is empty place according to rule (1).

12	0	2	[[failing]Grd[student]N]NP[?]VP]S	1&#10

After analyzing NP according to #10, continue to analyze the VP that is empty place according to rule (1).

13	2	1	[[looked]V[?]Adj]VP	4&#4

At position 2, analyze *looked*, using rule (4) and number #4. Adj is an empty place.

14	2	1	[[looked]V[?]Adv]VP	5&#4

Use rule (5) and number #4; Adv is empty.

15	2	2	[[looked]V[hard]Adj]VP		#5&#13

Fill the empty space Adj in an active edge #13 with inactive edge #5. At this time, the length of the analyzed field is 2.

16	2	2	[[looked]V[hard]Adv]VP	#6&#14

Fill the empty space Adv in an active edge #14 with inactive edge #6.

17	0	4	[[[failing]Adj[student]N]NP[[looked]V[hard]Adj]VP]S	#11&#15

Use the inactive edge #15 to fill the empty space VP in the active edge #11, and get the first analysis result: "It seems hard for the failed students."

18	0	4	[[[failing]Grd[student]N]NP[[looked]V[hard]Adj]VP]S	12&#15

Use the inactive edge #15 to fill the empty space in active edge #12, and get the second analysis result: "To fail the students is difficult."

19	0	4	[[[failing]Adj[student]N]NP[[looked]V[hard]Adv]VP]S	#11&#16

Fill the empty space in an active edge #11 with inactive edge #16, and get the third analysis result: "The failed students seem to work hard."

20	0	4	[[[failing]Grd[student]N]NP[[looked]V[hard]Adv]VP]S	#12&#16

Use the inactive edge #16 to fill the empty space in an active edge #12, and get the fourth analysis result: "They seem to have worked hard to fail the student."

The top-down analysis of this sentence is similar to the bottom-up analysis. We write it down below and suggest that the reader patiently goes through the whole process in numbered order.

Number	Position	Length	Term	Number of rules and items used
1	0	0	[?]S	1
2	0	1	[failing]Adj	6
3	0	1	[failing]Grd	7
4	1	1	[student]N	8
5	2	1	[looked]V	9
6	3	1	[hard]Adj	6
7	3	1	[hard]Adv	10
8	0	0	[[?]NP[?]VP]S	1&#1

According to rule (1), the active edge [?]S in #1 is replaced by the active edge [?] NP [?] VP] S.

| 9 | 0 | 0 | [[?]Adj[?]N]NP | 2&#8 |

According to rule (2), transform NP in #8 into active edge [[?]Adj[?]N]NP.

| 10 | 0 | 0 | [[?]Grd[?]N]NP | 3&#8 |

According to rule (3), transform NP in #8 into active edge [[?]Grd[?]N]NP.

| 11 | 0 | 1 | [[failing]Adj[?]N]NP | #2&#9 |

Fill inactive edge #2 into active edge #9.

| 12 | 0 | 1 | [[failing]Grd[?]N]NP | #3&#10 |

Fill inactive edge #3 into active edge #10.

| 13 | 0 | 2 | [[failing]Adj[student]N]NP | #4&#11 |

Fill inactive edge #4 into active edge #11 to form an inactive edge.

| 14 | 0 | 2 | [[failing]Grd[student]N]NP | #4&#12 |

Fill inactive edge #4 into active edge #12 to form an inactive edge.

| 15 | 0 | 2 | [[[failing]Adj[student]N]NP[?]VP]S | #8&#13 |

Fill inactive edge #13 into active edge #8, and continue to search for VP.

| 16 | 0 | 2 | [[[failing]Grd[student]N]NP[?]VP]S | #8&#14 |

Fill inactive edge #14 into active edge #8, and continue to search for VP.

| 17 | 2 | 0 | [[?]V[?]Adj]VP | 4&#15 |

According to rule (4), at position 2, further analyze the empty space [?]VP in an active edge #15.

| 18 | 2 | 0 | [[?]V[?]Adv]VP | 5&#15 |

According to rule (5), at position 2, further analyze the empty space [?]VP in an active edge #15.

| 19 | 2 | 1 | [[looked]V[?]Adj]VP | #5&#17 |

Fill the inactive edge #5 into the empty space [?]V in an active edge #17.

| 20 | 2 | 1 | [[looked]V[?]Adv]VP | #5&#18 |

Fill inactive edge #5 into the empty space [?]V in an active edge #18.

| 21 | 2 | 2 | [[looked]V[hard]Adj]VP | #6&#19 |

Fill the inactive edge #6 into the empty space [?]Adj in an active edge #19, to form an inactive edge.

| 22 | 2 | 2 | [[looked]V[hard]Adv]VP | #7&#20 |

Fill the inactive edge #7 into the empty space [?]Adv in an active edge #20, to form an inactive edge.

| 23 | 0 | 4 | [[[failing]Adj[student]N]NP[[looked]V[hard]Adj]VP]S | #15&#21 |

Fill the empty space in active edge #15 with inactive edge #21 [?]VP, to get the first analysis result.

| 24 | 0 | 4 | [[[failing]Grd[student]N]NP[[looked]V[hard]Adj]VP]S | #16&#21 |

Fill the empty space in active edge #16 with inactive edge #21 [?]VP, to get the second analysis result.

| 25 | 0 | 4 | [[[failing]Adj[student]N]NP[[looked]V[hard]Adv]VP]S | #15#22 |

Fill the empty space in active edge #15 with inactive edge #22 [?]VP, to get the third analysis result.

| 26 | 0 | 4 | [[[failing]Grd[student]N]NP[[looked]V[hard]Adv]VP]S | #16&#22 |

Fill the empty space in active edge #16 with inactive edge #22 [?]VP, to get the fourth analysis result.

Later, R. M. Kaplan also proposed dotted rules to express the active edge and the inactive edge more intuitively. Let us look at the chart in Fig. 3.32.

This chart intends to show certain conditions in the analysis, mainly including the following:

- This symbol string consists of the sequences NP and VP.
- The analysis program is trying to analyze S into the sequence NP VP and confirm this assumption.
- The analysis program has confirmed that the NP on the edge from the starting point to the second point is equivalent to the NP in the sequence NP VP.
- The analysis program also needs to verify that the sequence V NP can be reduced to VP.

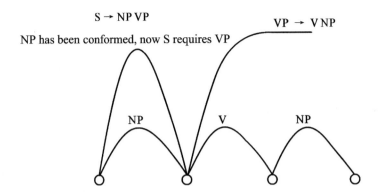

Fig. 3.32 Situation represented by the chart

It is not difficult to see that such a chart can show some of the analysis statuses. However, to fully represent the above analysis, it is necessary to show some assumptions in the analysis. Therefore, Kay made the following modifications to the data structure of the above chart:

First, in a chart, it is allowed to start from a node and return to this node again without passing through other nodes in the middle. However, it is not allowed to start from a node and pass through other nodes in the middle before returning to this node.

Second, the labeler on the edge of a chart can be not only a simple category but also a grammatical rule. The dot can be added to the symbol string on the right of such a rule, which is called the dotted rule. For example, if S → NP VP is a rule in grammar, then the following dotted rules with dots can be labeled on the edge of the chart:

$$S \rightarrow .NP\ VP$$

$$S \rightarrow NP.VP$$

$$S \rightarrow NP\ VP.$$

In these dotted rules, the dots are used to represent the range of hypothesis extension involved in the current rules that have been verified by the analysis program at a certain point in the analysis. Such dotted rules tell us what has been tested in the rules and what has not been tested in the rules and needs to be further tested.

Under the edge labeled by the dotted rule "S → NP.VP," it should be able to cover another edge labeled NP → <category>, which shows that the first part of the hypothesis (i.e., the part of NP in front of the dot) has been confirmed. The second part of the hypothesis (i.e., the part of VP behind the dot) has yet to be tested and confirmed.

The dotted rule "S → NP VP." indicates that it is assumed that S → NP VP has been tested and confirmed. The dotted rule "S → .NP VP" is labeled on the edge that starts from a certain point and returns to that point. This edge happens to form a self-closed loop, which means that the hypothesis S → NP VP has not been tested, nor has it been confirmed.

It is easy to see that the part behind the dot in the dotted rule is equivalent to the "empty place" part of our previous "term." If it is not empty behind the dot, this means that there is an empty place in the term, and the edge of such a term must be active; if it is empty behind the dot, this means there is no empty space in the item, and such an edge must be an inactive edge. Therefore, it is not difficult to rewrite all the previous "term" into the form of corresponding dotted rules and write them on the edge of the chart.

Based on this understanding of the active chart, it is necessary for us to slightly modify the previous definitions of "active edge" and "inactive edge." In such an active chart, the edge representing the hypothesis that has not been verified is called the "active edge," and the edge representing the hypothesis that has been verified is called the "inactive edge."

The dotted rule S → .NP VP and S → NP.VP are active edges, and the part after the dot is an unproven hypothesis; and the edge of the dotted rule S → NP VP. is the inactive edge, where it is empty after the dot, indicating that there is no unproven hypothesis.

It is more convenient and intuitionistic to use dotted rules to represent the active edge and inactive edge than the former "term."

Next, from the dotted rule, we will give a general definition of the active chart.

The active chart is a graph composed of edges with the following properties:

1. Starting point: represented by <START>, which is an integer.
2. Endpoint: expressed as <FINISH>, which is also an integer.
3. Label: represented by <LABEL>, which is a category.
4. The part that has been confirmed in the analysis is indicated by <FOUND>, which is a category series.
5. The part of the analysis that has yet to be confirmed is indicated by <TOFIND>, which is also a category series.

In such a way, an edge of the active chart can be recorded with a quintuple as shown below:

(<START>, <FINISH>, <LABEL>→<FOUND>.<TOFIND>)

Here, in the dotted rule <LABEL>→<FOUND>.<TOFIND>, <FOUND> is the confirmed part, and <TOFIND> is the part to be confirmed. Using dotted rules can better express guesses and assumptions.

For example, (0,2, NP → Det N.) represents an edge in the active chart, its starting point is node 0, and its endpoint is node 2. Label the part that NP has been confirmed in the analysis as Det and N. The unconfirmed part is empty. It is recorded in the form of quintuple:

<START> = 0
<FINISH> = 2

<LABEL> = NP
<FOUND> = Det N
<TOFIND> = Empty

Since the right part of the rule is all confirmed, this is an inactive edge.

For another example, (0,2, S → NP.VP) represents an edge in the active chart. Its starting point is node 0, and its endpoint is node 2. The label S has been confirmed to be NP in the analysis. The part to be confirmed is the VP. It is recorded in the form of quintuple as follows:

<START> = 0
<FINISH> = 2
<LABEL> = S
<FOUND> = NP
<TOFIND> = VP

Obviously, this is an active edge, where the part to be confirmed after the dot "." is VP, indicating that this edge has not been fully confirmed, and it needs further confirmation.

For another example, (2,3, VP → V.NP) represents another edge in the active chart, its starting point is node 2, and the endpoint is node 3. The labeled part of VP has been confirmed as V in the analysis. The part of VP that has been confirmed in the analysis is NP. It is recorded in the form of quintuple:

<START> = 2
<FINISH> = 3
<LABEL> = VP
<FOUND> = V
<TOFIND> = NP

This is also an active edge.

For another example, (3,5, NP → Det N) represents another edge in the active chart, its starting point is node 3, and its ending point is node 5. The part of NP that has been confirmed in the analysis is Det N, and there is no part yet to be confirmed. It is recorded in the form of quintuple:

<START> = 3
<FINISH> = 5
<LABEL> = NP
<FOUND> = Det N
<TOFIND> = Empty

This is an inactive edge, where the part to be confirmed after the dot "." is empty, indicating that this edge has been confirmed.

It can be seen that it is very convenient to distinguish the active edge from the inactive edge according to the position of the dot in the dotted rule.

The chart with the above active edges and inactive edges is shown in Fig. 3.33.

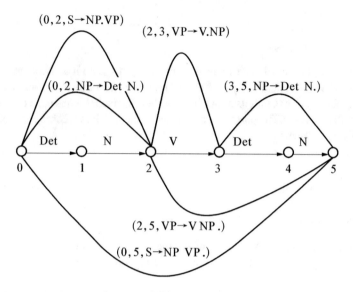

Fig. 3.33 Active and inactive edges in the chart

In the inactive edge (0,2, NP → Det N.) whose starting point is 0 and endpoint is 2, the left part of the dotted rule is NP, and in the active edge (0,2, S → NP.VP) whose starting point is 0 and endpoint is 2, the part that has been confirmed before the dot on the right of the dotted rule is also NP, and the two match exactly. This shows that part of the analysis process before node 2 has been successful. In the active edge (0,2, S → NP.VP), the part that needs to be confirmed after the dot on the right of the dotted rule is VP. If we can find an inactive edge with the dotted rule with VP on the left, then the assumption can be satisfied. But we have not found such an inactive edge at this time. In this case, we have to turn our attention to the active edge (2,3, VP → V.NP) starting from 2. In the dotted rule VP → V.NP, since the part after the dot is NP, we need to find an inactive edge with NP as the left part. The left category of the dotted rule "NP → Det N." on the inactive edge (3,5, NP → Det N.) whose starting point is 3 and endpoint is 5 happens to be NP, which just satisfies our condition since it is an inactive edge with starting point 3 and endpoint 5. After the dot in the right part of the dotted rule, it is already empty, so there is no need to consider the part after the dot. Therefore, you can directly use the dotted rule "VP → V.NP" of the active edge and move the dot forward to get the new dotted rule "VP → V NP." and a new edge (3,5, VP → V NP.), which is also an inactive edge. Because the part after the dot in the dotted rule of the active edge (0,2, S → NP. VP) is VP and the left part of the dotted rule in the new inactive edge (3,5, VP → V NP.) happens to be VP, so we can get a new edge (0,5, S → NP VP.).

At this time, the new edge is above the active edge (0,2, S → NP.VP) and the inactive edge (2,5, VP → V NP.) and is between nodes 0 and 5. As the part after the dot on the right of the dotted rule "S → NP VP." in the new edge is empty, this

Fig. 3.34 Illustration of the
basic rules of chart analysis

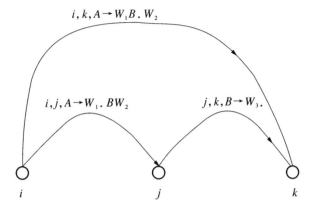

indicates that this edge is inactive. At this point, the analysis has reached the end of
the sentence, and the sentence analysis is completed.

In the above chart analysis, we have combined the active edge and the inactive
edge twice and directly moved the dot in the active edge to the category that matches
the category in the inactive edge label. After that, a new edge was created to advance
the analysis. Such operations are the most basic operations in chart analysis. If the
active edge temporarily does not meet the inactive edge that satisfies the condition
during the analysis, the analysis continues; you move your attention to other active
edges, try to find the inactive edge that meets the condition, and create a new inactive
edge to see if this new inactive edge can meet the conditions of the original active
edge. In a word, in the analysis, we must try to find the inactive edge that can meet
the active edge conditions, to promote the analysis. This is essential for chart
analysis.

We can summarize this approach as the following rule: if an active edge meets an
inactive edge and the category of the label of the inactive edge meets the requirements of the active edge, then a new edge can be added to the chart, which spans the
active edge and the inactive edge.

Martin Kay called this rule "fundamental rule for chart analysis."

The basic rules of chart analysis can be expressed more strictly as follows:

If a chart contains active edges (i, j, A $\rightarrow$ W_1. BW_2) and inactive edges (j, k,
B $\rightarrow$ W_3.), where A and B are categories and W_1, W_2, and W_3 (may be empty) are
category sequence or words, then add a new edge (i, k, A $\rightarrow$ $W_1B.W_2$) in the chart as
shown in Fig. 3.34.

The basic rules of chart analysis do not specify whether the new edge is active or
inactive because it depends entirely on W_2. If W_2 is not empty, the new edge is the
active edge; if W_2 is empty, then the new edge is inactive. In the analysis of the
above example, we use the basic rules of chart analysis to combine the active edge
(2,3, VP $\rightarrow$ V.NP) with the inactive edge (3,5, NP $\rightarrow$ Det N.) to form a new edge
(2,5, VP $\rightarrow$ V NP.). At this time, i = 2, j = 3, A = VP, W_1 = V, B=NP, W_2 = empty,
k = 5, and W_3 = Det N. Since W_2 = empty, the new edge is an inactive edge. We

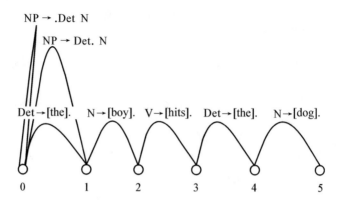

Fig. 3.35 Chart analysis

then combine the active edge (0,2, S → NP.VP) with this new inactive edge (2,5, VP → V NP.) to form a new edge (0,5, S → NP VP.). At this time, i = 0, j = 2, A = S, W_1 = NP, B = VP, W_2 = empty, and W_3 = V NP. Since W_2 = empty, the new edge is also inactive. If there is a prepositional phrase (PP) after VP, then W_2 is not empty. At this time, the new edge formed is the active edge.

Another important issue in chart analysis is the chart startup.

From the basic rules of chart analysis, we can know that there must be at least one active edge and one inactive edge in chart analysis. Only in this way can we find a way to combine the inactive edge with the related active edge according to the requirements of the basic rules, so that the analysis of the chart can run. According to the basic rules of chart analysis, if there is an inactive edge and a related active edge when the chart starts to run according to basic rules, the chart can be started. Therefore, to start a chart, we can look up the dictionary to record the relevant category information of the word in the dictionary on the edge of the chart, thereby forming an inactive edge. For example, when analyzing the English sentence "the boy hits the dog," we have the following rules:

(a) S → NP VP
(b) NP → Det N
(c) VP → V NP
(d) Det → [the]
(e) N → [boy]
(f) N → [dog]
(g) V → [hits]

Rules (d), (e), (f), and (g) are equivalent to a dictionary, so we can record the relevant information on the chart (Fig. 3.35).

In this way, we can create the following inactive edges:

(0, 1, Det → [the].)
(1, 2, N → [boy].)
(2, 3, V → [hit].)

(3, 4, Det → [the].)
(4, 5, N → [dog].)

According to rule (b), we can also create an active edge starting at node 0 and ending at node 0:

$$(0, 0, NP \rightarrow .Det\ N)$$

Combine this active edge with the inactive edge (0, 1, Det → [the].); since the first part after the dot of the active edge is Det, which is the same as the left part of the inactive edge rule, the conditions of the basic rules are met, so we can create a new edge:

$$(0, 1, NP \rightarrow Det.N)$$

In the new edge, the dot has moved forward one position, and the analysis has also advanced one step, thus starting the chart.

At this time, we can see that the left part of the point rule of the inactive edge (1, 2, N → [boy].) between node 1 and node 2 is exactly N, which matches the part after the dot in the new edge rule, so we can make a new edge by using the basic rule and then continue to use the basic rule to advance the analysis step-by-step to complete the analysis of this sentence.

We described the basic rules of chart analysis and the method of chart startup above. Obviously, as long as we combine the two, we can have the chart analysis step-by-step.

In the Earley algorithm proposed by J. Earley in his doctoral dissertation in 1968, the rule representation is similar to the chart analysis method. If the rule of chart analysis is expressed as (i, j, A→α·β), then in the early formulation of Earley algorithm, the rule of the term j is expressed as (A→α·β,i); such a rule representation method in Earley algorithm embodies the basic spirit of the dotted rule and is essentially consistent with the rule of chart analysis.

3.7 Earley Algorithm

In this section, we will further discuss the Earley algorithm. For the convenience of expression, we still use the method of dotted rules in chart analysis and write the dotted rule as "A→α · β, [i, j]."

The core of the Earley algorithm is the chart. For the words in a sentence, the chart contains a state table to represent the parts that have been generated before. At the end of the sentence, the chart provides all possible analysis results of the sentence.

The state in the chart contains three kinds of information:

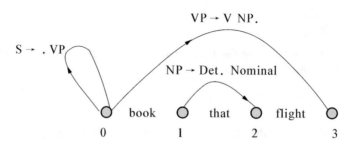

Fig. 3.36 The state of the chart

- Information about the subtree corresponding to a rule of the grammar.
- Information about the processes that have passed to complete this subtree.
- Information about the position of this subtree relative to the input.

Let us study the following three examples of states, which are generated during the analysis of the sentence "Book that flight" using the Earley algorithm.

The rules we use are

S → VP.
NP → Det Nominal.
VP → V NP.

The three states produced are

S → ·VP, [0,0].
NP → Det·Nominal, [1, 2].
VP → V NP·, [0,3].

In the first state, the dot is on the left side of the component, indicating that the specific start node S is predicted as top-down. The first 0 indicates that the predicted component of this state begins at the beginning of the input symbol string. The second 0 indicates that the dot is also at the beginning. The second state is generated in the next stage of processing this sentence, which indicates that NP begins at position 1. At this time, Det has been successfully analyzed, and the next step is to process Nominal. In the third state, the dot is on the right of the two components in the rule, indicating that the tree corresponding to the VP has been successfully found, and this VP spans the entire input string. These states can also be represented by graphs, where the analyzed state is edge or arc and the chart is a directed acyclic graph (DAG), as shown in Fig. 3.36.

Earley proposed three different basic operations in his algorithm: Predictor, Scanner, and Completer. Their functions are as follows:

- Predictor: Its function is to predict. In the top-down search process, the role of the Predictor is to generate a new state – to predict what can be done next. A Predictor is used for those states in the dotted rule where the right side of the dot is a non-terminal symbol. For each such non-terminal symbol, further extensions are made according to the grammatical rules. These newly generated states can be added to the chart. The Predictor starts from the position of the generated new state and returns to the same position. For example, by applying Predictor to state "S→. VP, [0,0]," the new states "VP→. V, [0,0]" and "VP→. V NP, [0,0]" can be generated, and they added to the chart.

- Scanner: Its function is to scan. When a part-of-speech category symbol in a state is on the right of the dot, Scanner checks the input sentence to judge whether the part of speech of the word to be analyzed matches this part-of-speech category. If it matches, it moves the dot one position to the right and adds the new state to the chart. For example, in the state "VP→.V NP, [0,0]," on the right of the dot is the category V, while in the input sentence, the word *book* is being analyzed, and according to the rule "V→**book**., [0,1]," the part-of-speech category of *book* is also V, and the two match each other. At this time, the dot is moved one position to the right, and the state is changed to "VP→V. NP, [0,1]" and added this new state to the chart.

- Completer: Its function is to complete a certain kind of analysis. When the right side of the dot in the state is a non-terminal symbol and in the input sentence the input symbol string spanned by the non-terminal symbol has been analyzed, then the position of the dot in the state is moved to the right of the non-terminal symbol and added the new state to the chart. For example, if the computer is in the state "VP→Verb.NP, [0,1]" through Scanner, at this time, the symbol string that has spanned between nodes 1 and 3 has been processed in the input sentence, and the state is "NP→Det Nom., [1, 3]," where the non-terminal symbol NP and the state "VP→Verb.NP, [0,1]" match the NP on the right of the dot. At this time, move the dot in the state "VP → Verb. NP, [0,1]" to the right to the position of node 3, and get the new state "VP→Verb NP., [0,3]," thus completing the analysis of VP.

Obviously, the Earley algorithm is completely consistent with the basic rules of chart analysis.

Next, we use the Earley algorithm to analyze sentences to further understand the technical content of the Earley algorithm.

We have the following context-free grammar:

1. S → NP VP.
2. S → AUX NP VP.
3. S → VP.
4. NP → Det Nominal.
5. Nominal → Noun.
6. Nominal → Noun Nominal.
7. Nominal → Nominal PP.
8. NP → Proper-Noun.
9. VP → Verb.
10. VP → Verb NP.
11. Det → that I this I a.
12. Noun → book I flight I meat I money.

13. Verb → book | include | prefer.
14. Aux → does.
15. Prep → from | to | on.
16. Proper Noun → CA937 | ASIANA | KA852
    (Note: CA937, ASIANA, and KA852 are flight names.)

If we use our context-free grammar rules to analyze the sentence "book that flight," then the state sequence in the chart can be expressed as follows:

Chart [0]

γ → .S	[0,0]	γ indicates that the starting state is a dummy state
S → .NP VP	[0,0]	Predictor
NP → .Det Nominal	[0,0]	Predictor
NP → .Proper-Noun	[0,0]	Predictor
S → .Aux NP VP	[0,0]	Predictor
S → .VP	[0,0]	Predictor
VP → .Verb	[0,0]	Predictor
VP → .Verb NP	[0,0]	Predictor

Chart [1]

Verb → book.	[0.1]	Scanner
VP → Verb.	[0,1]	Completer
S → VP.	[0,1]	Completer
VP → Verb. NP	[0,1]	Completer
NP → .Det Nominal	[1]	Predictor
NP → .Proper-Noun	[1]	Predictor

Chart [2]

Det → that.	[1, 2]	Scanner
NP → Det. Nominal	[1, 2]	Completer
Nominal → .Noun	[2]	Predictor
Nominal → .Noun Nominal	[2]	Predictor

Chart [3]

Noun → flight.	[2, 3]	Scanner
Nominal → Noun.	[2, 3]	Completer
Nominal → Noun. Nominal	[2, 3]	Completer
NP → Det Nominal.	[1, 3]	Completer
VP → Verb NP.	[0,3]	Completer
S → VP.	[0,3]	Completer
Nominal → .Noun	[3]	Predictor
Nominal → .Noun Nominal	[3]	Predictor

We have listed above the state sequence created during the analysis of the sentence "book that flight." In the beginning, the algorithm sows a seed chart to predict S from top to bottom. The planting of this chart graph is achieved by adding a dummy state γ→·S, [0,0] to Chart [0]. When processing this state, the algorithm turns to Predictor and creates three states to represent the prediction of each possible type of S and creates all the left-corner states of these trees one by one. When processing the state VP→·Verb, [0,0], Scanner is called to find the first word. At this time, the state representing the meaning of the verb *book* is added to the chart item Chart [1]. Note that when processing the state VP→·Verb NP, [0,0], Scanner must be called again. However, this time there is no need to add a new state because there is already an equivalent state in the chart. It should also be noted that since our grammar is indeed very imperfect, it cannot predict the meaning of the noun *book*, so there is no need to create a chart item in the chart.

When all the states in Chart [0] are processed, the algorithm moves to Chart [1], where it finds the state that represents the verb meaning of *book*. Since the dot of the dotted rule in this state is on the right side of its component, obviously this is a completed state, so the Completer is called. Then, Completer finds the two previous VP states, predicts verb at this position in the input, copies these states and advances their dots, and then adds them to Chart [1]. The completed state corresponds to an intransitive verb VP, which will result in a state representing the imperative sentence S. Besides, there is NP after the dot in the transitive verb phrase, which will result in two states to predict NP. Finally, the state NP→· Det Nominal, [1] causes the Scanner to find the word *that* and add the corresponding state to Chart [2].

When moving to Chart [2], the algorithm finds the state of the determiner meaning representing *that*. This completed state leads to pushing the dot forward in the NP state predicted by Chart [1] and predicting various types of Nominal. The first Nominal causes the last call to Scanner to process the word *flight*.

When moving to Chart [3], a state representing *flight* appears, which leads to a series of fast Completer operations, completing an NP, a transitive VP, and an S, respectively. The state S → VP·, [0,3] appears in this last chart, which means that the algorithm has found a successful analysis result.

The version of Earley algorithm that we just described is a recognizer, not an analyzer. After the processing is completed, the correct sentence will leave the state S→ α·, [0,N] in the chart. Unfortunately, at this time, we have not been able to retrieve the structure of sentence S. To turn this algorithm into an analyzer, we must be able to extract all the analysis one by one from the chart. To do this, the representation of each state must add an area to store information about the completed state of each component in the sentence.

This kind of information can be collected by simply modifying the Completer. We know that when the component after the dot in the state is found, the Completer creates a new state by advancing the old unfinished state. The only thing that needs to be modified is to let the Completer add a pointer to the state preceding the new state. When the algorithm retrieves the analysis tree from the chart, as long as it starts from the state (or some states) that represents a complete S in the last chart item, and recursively searches, the analysis tree can be retrieved from the chart. Below we write the process of constructing a chart using the modified Completer:

Chart [0]

S0 γ → .S	[0,0]	[]	Start from a dummy state
S1 S → .NP VP	[0,0]	[]	Predictor
S2 NP → .Det Nominal	[0,0]	[]	Predictor
S3 NP → .Proper-Noun	[0,0]	[]	Predictor
S4 S → .Aux NP VP	[0,0]	[]	Predictor
S5 S → .VP	[0,0]	[]	Predictor
S6 VP → .Verb	[0,0]	[]	Predictor
S7 VP → .Verb NP	[0,0]	[]	Predictor

Chart [1]

S8 Verb → book.	[0.1]	[]	Scanner
S9 VP → Verb.	[0,1]	[S8]	Completer
S10 S → VP.	[0,1]	[S9]	Completer
S11 VP → Verb. NP	[0,1]	[S8]	Completer
S12 NP → .Det Nominal	[1]	[]	Predictor
S13 NP → .Proper-Noun	[1]	[]	Predictor

Chart [2]

S14 Det → that.	[1, 2]	[]	Scanner
S15 NP → Det. Nominal	[1, 2]	[S14]	Completer
S16 Nominal → .Noun	[2]	[]	Predictor
S17 Nominal → .Noun Nominal	[2]	[]	Predictor

Chart [3]

S18 Noun → flight.	[2, 3]	[]	Scanner
S19 Nominal → Noun.	[2, 3]	[S18]	Completer
S20 Nominal → Noun. Nominal	[2, 3]	[S18]	Completer
S21 NP → Det Nominal	[1, 3]]	[S14, S19]	Completer
S22 VP → Verb NP.	[0,3]	[S8, S21]	Completer
S23 S → VP.	[0,3]	[S22]	Completer
S24 Nominal → .Noun	[3]	[]	Predictor
S25 Nominal → .Noun Nominal	[3]	[]	Predictor

It can be seen that in the whole process of using the Earley algorithm to analyze the sentence "book that flight," the predictor is only used for prediction and does not participate in the actual analysis. After the Predictor operation is deleted in the process of constructing the chart, the entire analysis can be summarized as follows:

S8 Verb → book.	[0.1]	[]	Scanner
S9 VP → Verb.	[0,1]	[S8]	Completer
S10 S → VP.	[0,1]	[S9]	Completer
S11 VP → Verb. NP	[0,1]	[S8]	Completer
S14 Det → that.	[1, 2]	[]	Scanner
S15 NP → Det. Nominal	[1, 2]	[S14]	Completer
S18 Noun → flight.	[2, 3]	[]	Scanner
S19 Nominal → Noun.	[2, 3]	[S18]	Completer
S20 Nominal → Noun. Nominal	[2, 3]	[S18]	Completer
S21 NP → Det Nominal.	[1, 3]]	[S14, S19]	Completer
S22 VP → Verb NP.	[0,3]	[S8, S21]	Completer
S23 S → VP.	[0,3]	[S22]	Completer

The above analysis results can be represented by DAG in Fig. 3.37.

Here are a few more complicated examples:

Example 1: Use the Earley algorithm to analyze the sentence "Does KA852 have a first-class section?"

In this sentence, *first* is an ordinal numeral, for which we use "Ord" to express and add rules to our grammar NP → Ord Nom.

The state of this sentence is.

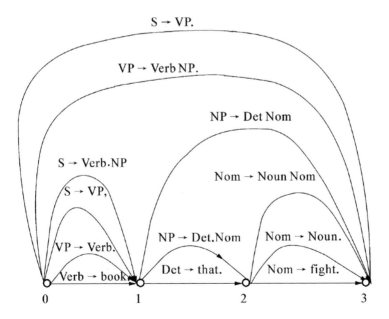

Fig. 3.37 DAG representation of analysis result (1)

• Does	• KA 852	• have	•first	• class	• section	•
0	1	2	3	4	5	6

The state sequence of the chart is as follows:

Chart [0]		
$\gamma \rightarrow$ .S	[0,0]	Start from a dummy state
S $\rightarrow$ .NP VP	[0,0]	Predictor
NP $\rightarrow$ .Ord Nom	[0,0]	Predictor
NP $\rightarrow$ .PrN	[0,0]	Predictor
S $\rightarrow$ .Aux NP VP	[0,0]	Predictor
S $\rightarrow$ .VP	[0,0]	Predictor
VP $\rightarrow$ .V	[0,0]	Predictor
VP $\rightarrow$ .V NP	[0,0]	Predictor

Chart [1]		
Aux $\rightarrow$ does.	[0,1]	Scanner
S $\rightarrow$ Aux. NP VP	[0,1]	Completer
NP $\rightarrow$ .Ord Nom	[1]	Predictor
NP $\rightarrow$ .PrN	[1]	Predictor

Chart [2]		
PrN $\rightarrow$ KA852.	[1, 2]	Scanner
NP $\rightarrow$ PrN.	[1, 2]	Completer
S $\rightarrow$ Aux NP. VP	[0,2]	Completer
VP $\rightarrow$ .V	[2]	Predictor
VP $\rightarrow$ .V NP	[2]	Predictor

Chart [3]		
V $\rightarrow$ have.	[2, 3]	Scanner
VP $\rightarrow$ V.	[2, 3]	Completer
VP $\rightarrow$ V. NP	[2, 3]	Completer
NP $\rightarrow$ .Ord Nom	[3]	Predictor

Chart [4]		
Ord $\rightarrow$ first.	[3, 4]	Scanner
NP $\rightarrow$ Ord. Nom	[3, 4]	Completer
Nom $\rightarrow$ .N Nom	[4]	Predictor
Nom $\rightarrow$ .N.	[4]	Predictor
Nom $\rightarrow$ .N PP	[4]	Predictor

Chart [5]

N → class.	[4, 5]	Scanner
Nom → N.	[4, 5]	Completer
NP → Ord Nom.	[3, 5]	Completer
VP → V NP.	[2, 5]	Completer
S → Aux NP VP.	[0,5]	Completer (the span of S is 5, 5 < 6)
Nom → N. Nom	[4, 5]	Completer
Nom → .N	[5]	Predictor

Chart [6]

N → section.	[5, 6]	Scanner
Nom → N.	[5, 6]	Completer
Nom→ N Nom.	[4, 6]	Completer
NP → Ord Nom.	[3, 6]	Completer
VP → V NP.	[2, 6]	Completer
S → Aux NP VP.	[0,6]	Completer

[Analysis succeeded!]
The analysis process is as follows:

Aux → does.	[0,1]	Scanner
S → Aux. NP VP	[0,1]	Completer
PrN → KA 852.	[1, 2]	Scanner
NP → PrN.	[1, 2]	Completer
S → Aux NP. VP	[0,2]	Completer
V → have.	[2, 3]	Scanner
VP → V.	[2, 3]	Completer
VP → V. NP	[2, 3]	Completer
Ord → first.	[3, 4]	Scanner
NP → Ord. Nom	[3, 4]	Completer
N → class.	[4, 5]	Scanner
N → section.	[5, 6]	Scanner
Nom → N.	[5, 6]	Completer
Nom→ N Nom.	[4, 6]	Completer
NP → Ord Nom.	[3, 6]	Completer
VP → V NP.	[2, 6]	Completer
S → Aux NP VP.	[0,6]	Completer

[Successful analysis!].
The DAG of the analysis result is as follows (Fig. 3.38).

Example 2: Use the Earley algorithm to analyze the sentence "It is a flight from Beijing to Seoul on ASIANA.".

The state of this sentence is.

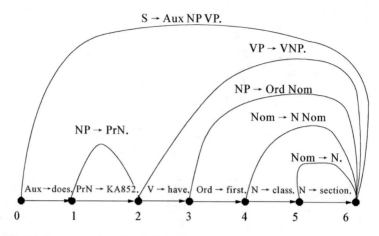

Fig. 3.38 DAG representation of analysis result (2)

it • is • a • flight • from • Beijing • to • Seoul • on • ASIANA•
0   1   2   3   4   5   6   7   8   9   10

It is a pronoun, and there is a prepositional phrase (PP) in the sentence, so we need to add two new rules to the grammar:

NP → Pron.
    and
PP → Prep NP.

The state sequence of the chart is as follows:

Chart [0]		
γ → .S	[0,0]	Start from a dummy state
S → .NP VP	[0,0]	Predictor
NP → .Pron	[0,0]	Predictor
NP → .PrN	[0,0]	Predictor
S → .Aux NP VP	[0,0]	Predictor
S → .VP	[0,0]	Predictor
VP → .V	[0,0]	Predictor
VP → .V NP	[0,0]	Predictor

Chart [1]			
Pron → it	[0,1]		Scanner
NP → Pron.	[0,1,]		Completer
S → NP. VP	[0,1]		Completer
VP → .V	[1]		Predictor
VP → .V NP	[1]		Predictor

Chart [2]

V → is.	[1, 2]	Scanner
VP → V.	[1, 2]	Completer
S → NP VP.	[0,2]	Completer (the span of S is 2 < 10)
VP → V. NP	[1, 2]	Completer
NP → .Det Nom	[2]	Predictor

Chart [3]

Det → a.	[2, 3]	Scanner
NP → Det. Nom	[2, 3]	Completer
Nom → .N	[3]	Predictor
Nom → .N Nom	[3]	Predictor
Nom → .Nom PP	[3]	Predictor

Chart [4]

N → flight.	[3, 4]	Scanner
Nom → N.	[3, 4]	Completer
NP → Det Nom.	[2, 4]	Completer
VP → V NP.	[1, 4]	Completer
S → NP VP.	[0,4]	Completer (the span of S is 4 < 10)
Nom → N. Nom	[3, 4]	Completer

Note: There is no Nom after N, so the process goes to the following state

Nom → Nom. PP	[3, 4]	Completer
PP → .Prep NP	[4]	Predictor

Chart [5]

Prep → from.	[4, 5]	Scanner
PP → Prep. NP	[4, 5]	Completer
NP → .PrN	[5]	Predictor

Chart [6]

PrN → Beijing.	[5, 6]	Scanner
NP → PrN.	[5, 6]	Completer
PP → Prep NP.	[4, 6]	Completer
Nom → Nom PP.	[3, 6]	Completer

Note: PP is followed by a dot (this PP = "from Beijing"), so this is an inactive edge

| Nom → Nom. PP | [3, 6] | Completer |

Note: The dot is before PP (this PP = "to Seoul"), so this is an active edge

| PP → .Prep NP | [6] | Predictor |

Chart [7]		
Prep → to.	[6, 7]	Scanner
PP → Prep. NP	[6, 7]	Completer
NP → .PrN	[7]	Predictor

Chart [8]		
PrN → Seoul.	[7, 8]	Scanner
NP → PrN.	[7, 8]	Completer
PP → Prep NP.	[6, 8]	Completer
Nom → Nom PP.	[3, 8]	Completer

Note: After PP, there is a dot (this PP = "to Seoul"), so this is an inactive edge

| Nom → Nom. PP | [3, 8] | Completer |

Note: The dot is before PP (this PP = "on ASIANA"), so this is an active edge

| PP → .Prep NP | [8] | Predictor |

Chart [9]		
Prep → on.	[8, 9]	Scanner
PP → Prep. NP	[8, 9]	Completer
NP → .PrN	[9]	Predictor

Chart [10]		
PrN → ASIANA.	[9, 10]	Scanner
NP→PrN.	[9, 10]	Completer
PP → Prep NP.	[8, 10]	Completer
Nom → Nom PP.	[3, 10]	Completer
NP → Det Nom.	[2, 10]	Completer
VP → V NP.	[1, 10]	Completer
S → NP VP.	[0,10]	Completer

[Successful analysis!].

The analysis process is as follows:

Pron → it	[0,1]	Scanner
NP → Pron.	[0,1,]	Completer
S → NP. VP	[0,1]	Completer
V → is.	[1, 2]	Scanner
VP → V. NP	[1, 2]	Completer
Det → a.	[2, 3]	Scanner
NP → Det. Nom	[2, 3]	Completer
N → flight.	[3, 4]	Scanner
Nom → N.	[3, 4]	Completer
NP → Det Nom.	[2, 4]	Completer
Nom → Nom. PP	[3, 4]	Completer
Prep → from.	[4, 5]	Scanner
PP → Prep. NP	[4, 5]	Completer
PrN → Beijing.	[5, 6]	Scanner
NP → PrN.	[5, 6]	Completer
PP → Prep NP	[4, 6]	Completer
Nom → Nom PP.	[3, 6]	Completer

Note: PP is followed by a dot (this PP = "from Beijing"), so this is an inactive edge

Nom → Nom. PP	[3, 6]	Completer

Note: The dot is before PP (this PP = "to Seoul"), so this is an active edge

Prep → to.	[6, 7]	Scanner
PP → Prep. NP	[6, 7]	Completer
PrN → Seoul.	[7, 8]	Scanner
NP → PrN.	[7, 8]	Completer
PP → Prep NP.	[6, 8]	Completer
Nom → Nom PP.	[3, 8]	Completer

Note: After PP, there is a dot (this PP = "to Seoul"), so this is an inactive edge

Nom → Nom. PP	[3, 8]	Completer

Note: The dot is before PP (this PP = "on ASIANA"), so this is an active edge

Prep → on.	[8, 9]	Scanner
PP → Prep. NP	[8, 9]	Completer
PrN → ASIANA.	[9, 10]	Scanner
NP→PrN	[9, 10]	Completer
PP → Prep NP	[8, 10]	Completer
Nom → Nom PP.	[3, 10]	Completer
NP → Det Nom.	[2, 10]	Completer
VP → V NP	[1, 10]	Completer
S → NP VP.	[0,10]	Completer

[Analysis succeeded!].

DAG representation of the analysis result is shown in Fig. 3.39.

There is no backtracking in the analysis of the above sentence, which significantly improves the effect of top-down parsing. There is no backtracking in the analysis process of the above sentence, which obviously improves the effect of top-down analysis and shows the superiority of Earley algorithm.

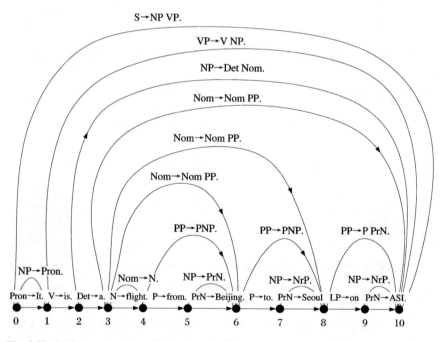

Fig. 3.39 DAG representation of analysis result (3)

Fig. 3.40 Tree representation of the rewriting rule

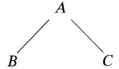

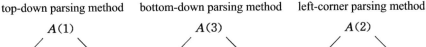
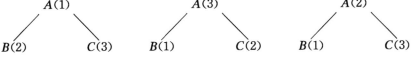

top-down parsing method   bottom-down parsing method   left-corner parsing method

Fig. 3.41 The comparison of three analysis methods

3.8   Left-Corner Analysis

The left-corner parsing method is an analysis method that combines top-down analysis and bottom-up analysis. The so-called left corner refers to the symbol in the lower left corner of any subtree of the tree diagram representing the sentence syntactic structure. For example, in the tree diagram representing the sentence "the boy hits the dog with a rod," *the* is the left corner of Det, Det is the left corner of NP, NP is the left corner of S, *hits* is the left corner of V, V is the left corner of VP, *with* is the left corner of Prep, and Prep is the left corner of PP. From the perspective of rewriting rules, the "left corner" is the first symbol on the right side of the rewriting rule. If the form of the rewriting rule is A → BC, then B is the left corner.

The rewriting rule A → BC can be expressed as the following tree diagram (Fig. 3.40).

If the top-down parsing method is used, the analysis should be A → B → C, which is from the top to the bottom; if the bottom-up parsing method is used, the analysis should be B → C → A, which is from the bottom to the top; if the left-corner parsing method is used, the analysis should be B → A → C, which is up and down. Write the number on the corresponding node. The analysis sequence of the three methods is shown in Fig. 3.41.

The analysis of the left-corner parsing method starts from the left corner B, then derives A from bottom to top according to the rewriting rule A → BC, and finally derives C from top to bottom.

Next, we use the left-corner parsing method to analyze the sentence "the boy hits the dog with a rod":

1. First of all, start from *the* at the beginning of the sentence. According to the grammatical rule (f), from the left corner of rule (f), make Det (Fig. 3.42).

2. Since the left corner of rule (b) is Det, select grammar (b) from Det, and predict N which is after Det (Fig. 3.43).

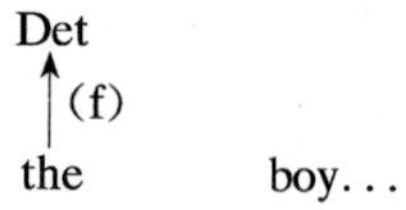

Fig. 3.42 The left-corner
parsing method (1)

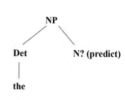

Fig. 3.43 The left-corner
parsing method (2)

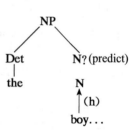

Fig. 3.44 The left-corner
parsing method (3)

Fig. 3.45 The left-corner
parsing method (4)

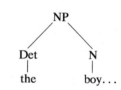

Fig. 3.46 The left-corner
parsing method (5)

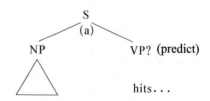

3. According to rule (h), N is made from "boy" (Fig. 3.44).

4. Since the father node of *boy* happens to be N, we can see that our prediction of N
   is correct, so we make a subtree NP (Fig. 3.45).

5. NP is the left corner of rule (a). NP selects rule (a) and predicts VP (Fig. 3.46).

6. According to rule (k), V is made from *hits* (Fig. 3.47).

7. Since V is the left corner of rule (c), select rule (c) and predict NP (Fig. 3.48).

8. Make NP from *the dog*, and the prediction of NP is confirmed. Since NP is
   confirmed, the prediction of VP can be confirmed (Fig. 3.49).

Fig. 3.47 The left-corner
parsing method (6)

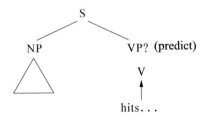

Fig. 3.48 The left-corner
parsing method (7)

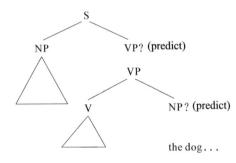

Fig. 3.49 The left-corner
parsing method (8)

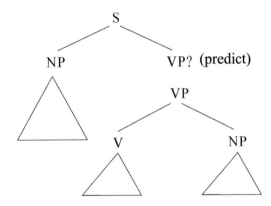

9. Since VP can also be the left corner of rule (d) and there are words such as *with* after *the dog*, it indicates that the reduction cannot be too early and backtracking is required. Take VP as the left corner of rule (d), and select rule (d) to predict PP (Fig. 3.50).

10. The prediction of VP is confirmed, so sentence (S) is completed (Fig. 3.51).

Backtracking is used in the above analysis methods. When the input symbol string belongs to the language described by this kind of grammar, to add a backtracking mechanism can ensure that the input symbol string is accepted. However, if the input string does not belong to the language described in this kind of grammar and there is no new choice to backtrack through multiple backtracking, the

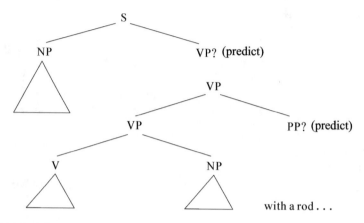

Fig. 3.50 The left-corner parsing method (9)

Fig. 3.51 The left-corner
parsing method (10)

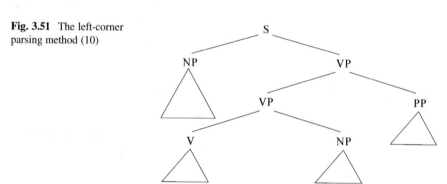

input string will be rejected. Systematic backtracking can ensure the correctness of
the algorithm, but backtracking also involves a lot of repetition and redundant
calculations.

In 1980, the American computational linguist M. Marcus proposed to control the
condition of reduction manually, to avoid backtracking. This is the "Marcus deterministic analysis algorithm." Marcus' deterministic algorithm consists of two parts:
the mode part and the behavior part. The mode part describes the circumstances
under which the stack and buffer contents can be executed by the analysis algorithm.
The buffer introduced by Marcus is a promotion of the input concept. It stores some
of the built sentence components in order from left to right. The content in the buffer
that is allowed to be viewed is limited, which avoids the complexity of the rules. In
the behavior part, some operations which are allowed are similar to reduction and
shift in. Some operations move the top element of the stack to the buffer, some move
the component of the buffer out and hang under the node of the component placed on
the top of the stack, and so on.

American scholar J. Earley proposed the Earley algorithm in his doctoral dissertation in 1968. Based on the left corner analysis method, this algorithm combines the top-down parsing method with bottom-up analysis and alternately uses the two methods in the analysis. First, the starting point of a language component is predicted from top to bottom, and then a subtree is formed from bottom to top. Earley algorithm proposed "the dotted rule." This kind of dotted rule uses dots in the rules to systematically represent the structural parts that have been built and the structural parts that need to be further analyzed, to analyze the sentences step-by-step from left to right, which improves the efficiency of the analysis. Martin Kay's chart analysis method is based on the Earley algorithm. From this, we can see that the scholars engaged in NLP have made arduous efforts in the study of the analysis algorithms of phrase structure grammar.

3.9 Cocke-Younger-Kasami Algorithm

The CYK algorithm is the abbreviation of the "Cocke-Younger-Kasami algorithm." It is a parallel syntax analysis algorithm and takes the Chomsky normal form as its descriptive object. The form of the rewriting rules of the Chomsky normal form is as follows:

$$A \rightarrow BC$$

where all A, B, and C are non-terminal symbols. The Chomsky normal form rewrites the single non-terminal symbol A into two non-terminal symbols B and C, which reflects the dichotomy of natural languages. It is convenient to use binary trees to represent the data structure of natural languages in language information processing, which is more suitable for describing natural languages. Obviously, the rewriting rule of Chomsky normal form is a special case when $\omega = BC$ in the rewriting rule $A \rightarrow \omega$ of context-free phrase structure grammar. Since any Chomsky normal form is equivalent to context-free phrase structure grammar, such restrictions are not without generality.

For the English sentence "the boy hits a dog," we can get the following table by using the CYK algorithm (Fig. 3.52).

In this table, the numbers in the row direction (horizontal) indicate the position of the word in the sentence, and the numbers in the column direction (vertical) indicate the number of words contained in the language component. The language components are all contained in a box. We use b_{ij} to indicate the position of the box in the ith column and the jth row. In this way, the location of each language component can be determined. For example,

$Det \in b_{1\ 1}$ indicates that Det is in the first column and the first row.
$N \in b_{2\ 1}$ indicates that N is in the second column and the first row.
$V \in b_{3\ 1}$ indicates that V is in the third column and the first row.

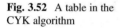

Fig. 3.52 A table in the
CYK algorithm

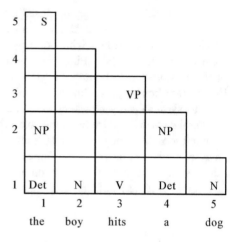

$Det \in b_{4\ 1}$ indicates that Det is in the fourth column and the first row.
$N \in b_{5\ 1}$ indicates that N is in the fifth column and the first row.

In this way, the position of the NP in the first column and the second row can be represented by $b_{1\ 2}$ (NP $\in b_{1\ 2}$). This notation shows that the NP is at the beginning of the sentence and contains two words ("the" and "boy"). In other words, the NP is composed of Det and N. The position of the NP in the fourth column and the second row can be represented by $b_{4\ 2}$ (NP $\in b_{4\ 2}$). This notation shows that it is in the position of the fourth word, which contains two words ("a" and "dog"). That is to say, this NP is composed of Det and N. The position of VP in the third column and third row can be represented by $b_{3\ 3}$ (VP $\in b_{3\ 3}$). The notation shows that the VP is in the position of the third word and contains three words ("hits," "a," and "dog"). That is to say, the VP is composed of V (containing one word) and NP (containing two words). The position of S in the first column and the fifth row can be represented by $b_{1\ 5}$ (S $\in b_{1\ 5}$). This notation shows that the S is at the beginning of the sentence and contains five words ("the," "boy," "hits," "a," and "dog"). That is to say, the S is composed of NP (containing two words) and VP (containing three words). The notations in these boxes clearly illustrate the syntactic structure relationship of the sentence. Therefore, if we can construct such a table through a limited number of steps, it is equivalent to completing the syntactic structure analysis of the sentence.

Since the grammar rules are expressed by the Chomsky normal form, b_{ij} must contain A if $b_{i\ k}$ contains B and $b_{i+k\ j-k}$ contains C for k ($1 \le k < j$) in the grammar rule A → BC. That is to say, if starting from the ith word in the input sentence, a subtree representing the component B which is composed of k number of words is created (at this time, the length of B is k, and its initial label is the ith column, and the label of its final word is $i + k - 1$-th column. For example, if the length of B is 4 and the label of the initial word is 3, then the label of its final word is $i+k-1 = 3+4-1 = 6$, namely, the labels of the four words are 3, 4, 5, and 6, respectively). Starting from the $i + k$th word, generate the subtree-of component C which is composed of j–k words

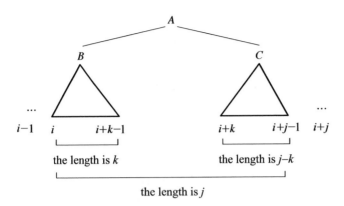

Fig. 3.53 The labels in the CYK algorithm

(at this time, the length of C is $j-k$, the label of its initial word is the $i + k$th column, and the label of its final word is the $i + j - 1$-th column. For example, if the length of A is $j = 6$ and the length of C is $j-k = 6-4 = 2$, then the label of the initial word is $i + k = 3 + 4 = 7$, and the label of its final word is $i + j - 1 = 3 + 6-1 = 8$). Then the following tree diagram representing A can be made (Fig. 3.53).

In the above figure, for instance, $b_{1\ 2}$ contains NP, $b_{1\ 1}$ contains Det, and $b_{2\ 1}$ contains N, which reflect the grammar rule NP $\rightarrow$ Det N. At this time, $k = 1$, $i = 1$, and $j = 2$.

The CYK algorithm is an algorithm that sequentially constructs the above table. When the length of the input sentence is n, the CYK algorithm can be divided into the following two steps:

Step 1: Starting from $i = 1$, for each word Wi in the input sentence of length n, there is obviously a rewriting rule A $\rightarrow$ Wi. Therefore, the corresponding non-terminal symbol A for each word Wi is recorded in sequence in box $b_{i\ 1}$. In the example sentence, "the boy hits a dog," we record Det in $b_{1\ 1}$, N in $b_{2\ 1}$, V in $b_{3\ 1}$, Det in $b_{4\ 1}$, and N in $b_{5\ 1}$ sequentially according to the corresponding rewriting rules.

The first step is equivalent to determining the part of speech of each word in the input sentence. If a word belongs to several different categories, each category should be recorded in the table.

Step 2: For $1 \leq h < j$ and all i, create $b_{i\ h}$. At this time, the set of non-terminal symbols containing b_{ij} is defined as follows:

$b_{ij} = \{$A| For $1 \leq k < j$, B is contained in $b_{i\ k}$, C is contained in $b_{i\ +\ k\ j-k}$, and there is a grammar rule A $\rightarrow$ BC$\}$.

The second step is equivalent to constructing the syntactic structure of the sentence. According to the rewriting rules of the grammar, start from the beginning of the sentence, and take words from 1 to n in sequence to construct the box b_{ij}. If the box S$\in b_{1\ n}$ contains the start symbol S, that is, S $\in b_{1\ n}$, then the input sentence is acceptable.

For example, according to the rule NP $\rightarrow$ Det N and Det$\in b_{1\ 1}$ and N$\in b_{2\ 1}$, we can see at this time that $i = 1$, $k = 1$, and $j = 2$, so the number of the NP's box should be numbered as $b_{1\ 2}$. We can see that $i = 4$, $k = 1$, and $j = 2$ at this time according to the rule NP $\rightarrow$ Det N and Det$\in b_{4\ 1}$和N$\in b_{5\ 1}$, so the box number of this NP should be b_4 $_2$. We can see that $i = 3$, $k = 1$, and $j = 3$ at this time according to the rules VP $\rightarrow$ V NP and V$\in b_{3\ 1}$ and NP$\in b_{4\ 2}$. Therefore, the number of the VP box should be $b_{3\ 3}$. We can also see at this time that $i = 1$, $k = 2$, and $j = 5$ according to the rule S $\rightarrow$ NP VP and NP$\in b_{1\ 2}$ and VP$\in b_{3\ 3}$, so the number of S box should be $b_{5\ 1}$. Since the sentence length is $n = 5$, there is S$\in b_{n\ 1}$. So the input sentence is accepted and the analysis is successful.

Next, let us apply the CYK algorithm to analyze a more complicated sentence.

If context-free grammar has the following rules:

S $\rightarrow$ NP VP.
NP $\rightarrow$ PrN.
NP $\rightarrow$ DET N.
NP $\rightarrow$ N WH VP.
NP $\rightarrow$ DET N WH VP.
VP $\rightarrow$ V.
VP $\rightarrow$ V NP.
VP $\rightarrow$ V that S.

We use this grammar to analyze the English sentence "the table that lacks a leg hits Jack":

- Convert the rewriting rules to the Chomsky normal form:

    S $\rightarrow$ NP VP.
    NP $\rightarrow$ PrN
        Since this rule is not the Chomsky normal form, it is converted to
    NP $\rightarrow$ Jack | John | Maria.
    NP $\rightarrow$ DET N
    NP $\rightarrow$ N WH VP This rule is not the Chomsky normal form, so it is converted to
    NP $\rightarrow$ N CL.
    CL $\rightarrow$ WH VP.
    NP $\rightarrow$ DET N WH VP This rule is not the Chomsky normal form, so it is converted to.
    NP $\rightarrow$ NP CL.
    NP $\rightarrow$ DET N.
    CL $\rightarrow$ WH VP.
    Here, CL is a WH clause, which is composed of "that" and VP.
    VP $\rightarrow$ V This rule is not the Chomsky normal form, so it is converted to
    VP $\rightarrow$ cough | walk | . . .
    VP$\rightarrow$V NP
    VP $\rightarrow$ V that S This rule is not the Chomsky normal form, so it is converted to.
    VP $\rightarrow$ V TH.

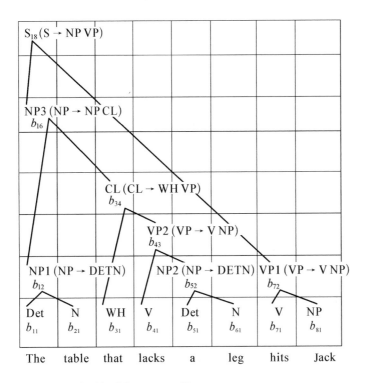

Fig. 3.54 The boxes and grids of the sentence (1)

TH → WH S.
Here, TH is a "that clause," which consists of "that" and "S."

- Calculate the column number and row number of the non-terminal symbol b_{ij}:

    Arrange the non-terminal symbol bij that represents the part of speech (POS) according to the order of words in the sentence, and calculate their column numbers and row numbers:

"The	table	that	lacks	a	leg	hits	Jack"
DET	N	WH	V	DET	N	V	NP
b_{11}	b_{21}	b_{31}	b_{41}	b_{51}	b_{61}	b_{71}	b_{81}

    Calculate the column and row numbers of the non-terminal symbol bij that represents a phrase, so we get the following boxes and grids in Fig. 3.54.

    where the calculation details in each box$_{ij}$ are as follows:

b_{ij} (NP1): $i = 1. j = 1 + 1 = 2,$
b_{ij} (NP2): $i = 5, j = 1 + 1 = 2,$
b_{ij} (VP1): $i = 7, j = 1 + 1 = 2,$

b_{ij} (VP2): $i = 4, j = 1 + 2 = 3$,
b_{ij} (CL): $i = 3, j = 1 + 3 = 4$,
b_{ij} (NP3): $i = 1, j = 2 + 4 = 6$,
b_{ij} (S): $i = 1, j = 2 + 6 = 8$.

The sentence length is8, and the column number in the box of S is also8, so the analysis of the sentence is successful.

We use the CYK algorithm to construct the nodes in the table above. These nodes can be connected to form a pyramid. The pyramid is a tree diagram that can represent the structure of the sentence.

Now, we analyze the sentence "book that flight" with the CYK algorithm.

The rules of context-free grammar are the same as those used previously; they are

1. S → VP.
2. VP → Verb NP.
3. NP → Det Nominal.
4. Nominal → Noun.

Since the right side of rule 1 contains only a single non-terminal symbol VP, this is not the Chomsky normal form, but rule 2 is. Therefore we combine rule 1 and rule 2 to form the following rule, which meets the requirement of the Chomsky normal form:

$$S \rightarrow Verb\ NP$$

The right side of rule 4 also contains only a single non-terminal symbol that is not the Chomsky normal form, and rule 3 is the Chomsky normal form, so we combine rule 4 and rule 3 to form the following rule, which meets the requirements of the Chomsky normal form:

$$NP \rightarrow Det\ Noun$$

Now, the rules of this context-free grammar are as follows:

$$S \rightarrow Verb\ NP$$

$$NP \rightarrow Det\ Noun$$

These rules meet the requirements of the Chomsky normal form. According to such rules, the results of using the CYK algorithm to analyze the above sentence are as follows (Fig. 3.55).

where the details of calculating the b_{ij} in each box are displayed as follows:

b_{ij} (NP): $i = 2,. j = 1 + 1 = 2$.
b_{ij} (S): $i = 1, j = 1 + 2 = 3$.

Fig. 3.55 The boxes and grids of the sentence (2)

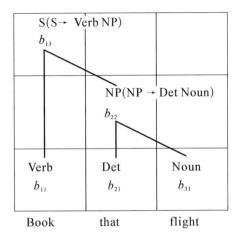

The pyramid generated by the CYK algorithm is the tree diagram representing the sentence structure. It can be seen that the CYK algorithm is easy and effective.

The CYK algorithm expands gradually from a small analysis tree. The same analysis tree never repeats operations and does not require backtracking. All the rules adopt the Chomsky normal form, which is its advantage.

Phrase structure grammar has the advantages of clear structure, conciseness, easy operation, etc., which bring many conveniences to the computer processing of natural languages. Therefore, the abovementioned automatic syntactic analysis approach based on phrase structure grammar is widely applied in computational linguistics, and it still has a strong vitality at present.

3.10 Tomita Algorithm

M. Tomita, a computational linguist at Carnegie Mellon University in the United States, proposed the Tomita algorithm in 1985. The algorithm is an extended LR algorithm and an efficient natural language analysis algorithm based on context-free phrase structure grammar. In this algorithm, M. Tomita introduced technologies such as graph structure stack, subtree sharing, and local ambiguity reduction, which improved the efficiency of the algorithm.

When using a standard LR analyzer to analyze natural languages, the primary task is to construct all the analysis states and transfer the relationship between these analysis states. When all the analysis states and the transfer relationship between them are determined, it will be very clear what kind of analysis action is made in what kind of state. The LR analysis method organizes the corresponding relationship between the analysis state and the analysis action in an analysis table. In a certain analysis state, the LR analyzer only needs to check the analysis table to know what kind of analysis action should be performed. There is a unified method for constructing the analysis table, and it can be performed automatically. For any

Table 3.1 The LR analysis table

STATE	ACTION					GOTO			
	a_1	a_2	$\cdots$	a_k	$	N_1	N_2	$\cdots$	N_m
0			$\cdots$					$\cdots$	
1			$\cdots$					$\cdots$	
$\vdots$			$\cdots$					$\cdots$	
N			$\cdots$					$\cdots$	

context-free grammar, an analysis table can be constructed. The LR analysis table is composed of two parts: One is the ACTION, which describes the analysis actions that the analyzer should take when encountering a certain prospect symbol in a certain state, and the other part is the GOTO, which describes how the analysis state should transfer after the reduction action occurs, as shown in Table 3.1.

Each row in the LR analysis table corresponds to a state that the analyzer may encounter during analysis, and each column of ACTION corresponds to an terminal symbol in the grammar (represented as a_1, a_2, ..., ak, and $). If the current state of the analyzer is i and the first input symbol in the current input buffer is a_j, then the next analysis action of the analyzer can be obtained from the cell at the intersection of row i column a_j. That is, it is obtained from ACTION (i, aj). Therefore, the analysis action is recorded in ACTION. Each column of GOTO corresponds to a non-terminal symbol in the grammar (represented as N_1, ..., Nm). When a reduction occurs, the GOTO is used to determine the state of analysis that the analyzer should turn to after the reduction occurs. If the analyzer reduces several grammatical symbols at the top of the stack to non-terminal symbols and the state number before the reduced symbol string in the analysis stack is i, then the initial state of the analyzer after the reduction can be obtained from the cell at the intersection of row i and the column N_j. That is, it is obtained from GOTO (i, Nj). It can be seen that the number of analysis states to be turned is recorded in GOTO.

For a certain context-free grammar, if we express the state transition relationship of this grammar with a finite state transition network, then such an LR analysis table can be automatically constructed from this finite state transition network.

The LR algorithm is proposed to analyze programming languages. It can successfully turn an uncertain analysis process into a certain one. However, the LR algorithm does not apply to all context-free grammars. Because the LR algorithm is a bottom-up analysis algorithm that is driven by the analysis table, its certainty depends on the certainty of the LR analysis table. If there is at most one analysis action or state in each cell of the analysis table, it can ensure that each analysis action of the analyzer is determined; otherwise, it is uncertain. In fact, not every context-free grammar can construct a deterministic analysis table. This means that the LR analyzer can only deal with context-free grammar that can construct deterministic analysis tables. This kind of grammar is called "LR grammar" in formal languages. The LR analyzer cannot handle non-LR grammar. Besides, if the grammar is ambiguous, it is not LR grammar.

Since natural languages are full of structural ambiguity, the grammar corresponding to natural languages is generally ambiguous and is non-LR grammar.

Therefore, the standard LR analyzer is not appropriate to analyze natural languages. If we construct an analysis table for the grammar of natural languages, there will be more than one analysis action in some cells of the analysis table, and there will be multiple entries in the analysis table. Due to the ambiguity, many of the analysis actions may be correct. Therefore, the analyzer for NLP has to provide multiple analysis results for a sentence. Such an analyzer cannot analyze by only following one path; in some analysis stages, it needs to analyze along multiple paths.

For multiple entries in the LR analysis table, the analysis action is performed along multiple analysis paths at the same time because the corresponding analysis actions are multiple. For this reason, Tomita introduced the graph structure stack technology.

The graph structure stack is developed from stack table technology and tree structure stack technology.

When the LR algorithm uses the stack table technology, the operations on the processes are performed in parallel. Each process corresponds to a stack, and the actions of each process are the same as the standard LR analysis. The disadvantages of stack table technology are that there is no relationship between each process and no one process can use the analysis results that other processes have done. Moreover, the number of stack tables will increase exponentially when there is ambiguity.

To overcome the shortcomings of stack table technology, a tree structure stack technology is introduced. The specific method of the tree structure stack technology is as follows: if several processes are in the same state, then the work of these stacks will be the same until a certain point in time, and the top vertex of the stack is ejected by a reduction action. To eliminate redundancy, these processes can be reduced to one process. As long as the corresponding top vertex of the stack has the same state among several processes, these processes will be merged. At this time, these stacks become a tree structure, and the root node of the tree is the top of the stack. So it is called "tree structure stack." The tree structure stack will be decomposed into several original stacks when the top of the stack is ejected. In fact, the system may have several sets of tree structure stacks in parallel. Therefore, the stacks in the system constitute a forest as a whole.

Although the tree structure stack technology can reduce the amount of calculation significantly, the number of branches of the tree structure stack will increase exponentially with the increase of ambiguity. To solve this problem, Tomita put forward a "graph structure stack" based on the tree structure stack.

By using the tree structure stack technology, when the stack splits, several copies of the entire stack are needed. But in practice, the entire stack may not be copied, as long as some parts of the stack can be split. When a stack splits, it is represented as a tree, and the bottom of the stack corresponds to the root of the tree. By using stack merging technology, stacks can be represented as directed acyclic graphs (DAG), thus forming a "graph-structured stack." Using graph stack technology, the Tomita algorithm does not analyze any part of the input sentence twice or more in the same way. This is because if two processes analyze a certain part of a sentence in the same way, then the two processes will be in the same state, and they will be combined into one process.

In this way, in the analysis process, whenever the analysis process encounters multiple actions that can be carried out at the same time, the analysis process is split into corresponding sub-processes, and the top of the stack is also split into several stack tops, which are analyzed according to the different actions specified in the analysis table. If two processes handle the same state, the top of the stack is merged into a stack top, and the two processes are merged into a process to form a graph structure analysis stack. Therefore, Tomita calls this stack a graph-structured stack.

Due to the application of the graph structure stack, the space complexity and time complexity of the analysis algorithm are greatly reduced.

Non-LR grammar is ambiguous, and the number of ambiguities in natural language sentences increases exponentially with the increase of sentence length. At this time, even if we use the LR algorithm, the cost of the analyzer will increase exponentially, and to store all possible analysis, trees require storage space that will also increase exponentially accordingly.

A natural language automatic analysis system should be able to find all the analysis results of an ambiguous sentence, and the results should be presented and stored reasonably, to deal with ambiguity resolution in the later stage. However, since the total number of ambiguous sentences (which form the "analysis forest") may increase exponentially with the increase of sentence length, even if all the analysis results are output, it will cost exponential time. Therefore, the results of syntactic analysis have to be represented effectively to avoid the exponential increase of the analysis forest. To solve the problem, Tomita proposed the "subtree sharing" and "local ambiguity compaction" techniques to ensure that the size of the analysis forest does not increase too quickly.

The so-called subtree sharing means that if several trees have a common subtree, then such subtrees can only be expressed once to form a "shared forest."

To realize the technology of "subtree sharing," the specific grammatical category symbols are no longer put on the stack, but only the pointer to a node of the shared forest is stored in the stack. When the analyzer moves in a word, it will produce a leaf node, which is labeled by the word and its part of speech. At this time, instead of directly pushing the word and its part of speech into the stack, it only pushes a pointer to this newly created node. If an identical leaf node already exists, a pointer to the existing node is pushed into the stack, and no new node is created for it. When the analyzer reduces in the stack, it only needs to pop up the pointer of the related node from the stack to create a new node. The successor node of the new node is the node pointed to by these pop-up pointers and then pushes a pointer to the newly created node into the stack. This is repeated until the corresponding shared forest structure is constructed.

For example, when using the Tomita algorithm to analyze the ambiguous sentence "I saw a boy with a telescope" (which means "I saw a boy who had a telescope with him" or "With a telescope, I saw a boy"), the constructed shared forest can be presented in Fig. 3.56.

As can be seen from this shared forest, the noun phrase (NP) "a boy" forms a subtree NP (Det(a)N(boy)) rooted at the node NP. This subtree has two parent nodes, one is the VP at the upper left, and the other is the NP at the upper right. It indicates

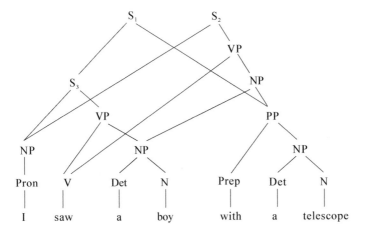

Fig. 3.56 The shared forest

that the subtree rooted at the node NP is a shared subtree, which is simultaneously shared by two different parent nodes. There are other shared subtrees in this shared forest. For example, the subtree PP (Prep(with)NP(Det(a)N(telescope))) formed by "with a telescope" is shared by the two parent nodes S1 and S_2 above it, the subtree NP (Pron(I)) formed by "I" is shared by the two parent nodes S_3 and S_2 above it, etc.

When two or more subtrees have the same leaf node and the roots of these subtrees have the same non-terminal symbol, that is to say, a certain part of the sentence can be reduced into one non-terminal symbol in two or more ways. At this time, these several subtrees constitute a "local ambiguity." For example, in the shared forest above, "with a telescope" can form the subtree PP (Prep(with)NP (Det(a)N(telescope))), and the non-terminal symbols of the two parent nodes S_1 and S_2 which share this subtree are both S. At this time, the two parent nodes can be reduced to a non-terminal symbol S and constitutes a local ambiguity. It is not difficult to see that there are other local ambiguities in the shared forest in Fig. 3.57. If there are too many local ambiguities in a sentence, the total number of ambiguities in the sentence will increase exponentially. Therefore, it is necessary to combine several tops of the subtree with local ambiguity into a whole to carry out "local ambiguity compaction."

The working mode of "local ambiguity compaction" is as follows: When a local ambiguity occurs, the root of the subtree expressing the local ambiguity is merged into a node. The new node is called the "compaction node," while the root node of the subtrees before the merge is called the subordinate node of the compaction node. In the graph structure stack, if the tops of two or more symbols have the same state top on their left and the same state top on their right, this means that these symbols have "local ambiguity." Therefore, the nodes pointed by the tops of these symbols should be compacted into one node. For example, in the sentence "I saw a boy in the park with a telescope," the shared forest before and after local ambiguity compaction is as follows (Fig. 3.57 and Fig. 3.58):

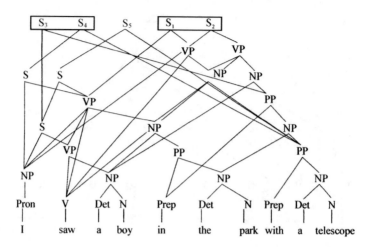

Fig. 3.57 The shared forest before local ambiguity compaction

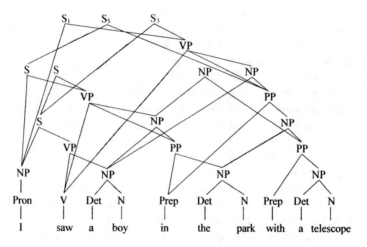

Fig. 3.58 The shared forest after local ambiguity compaction

The shared forest before local ambiguity compaction is shown in Fig. 3.57.

The shared forest after local ambiguity compaction is shown in Fig. 3.58.

It can be seen that the number of nodes is greatly reduced after the local ambiguity compaction. For example, the nodes S_1 and S_2 in the shared forest before compaction become node S_1 after compaction; the nodes S_3 and S_4 in the shared forest before compaction become node S_3 after compaction. This improves the analysis efficiency of the algorithm. Because the Tomita algorithm is quite efficient for natural language analysis, it is very popular among researchers in the field of computer processing of natural languages.

3.11 Government and Binding Theory and Minimalist Program

In this section, we will introduce the new development of Chomsky's linguistic theory after phrase structure grammar. These new developments are Chomsky's new exploration of language formal models in linguistic theory and are also valuable for the study of formal models of NLP.

Chomsky made a series of speeches at the Symposium in Pisa, Italy, in 1979. After returning to the United States, he published "On Binding" in *Linguistic Inquiry* Volume 2 Issue 1 in 1980, and in 1981, he published *Lectures on Government and Binding: The Pisa Lectures* studying language issues from the perspective of universal grammar. In 1993, the Chinese Social Sciences Press published a Chinese version of Pisa's academic speeches, titled *The Collection of Government and Binding Theory (Pisa Academic Speeches)*. In this Chinese version, "government" is translated into "支配" (/zhi pei/; domination). This book still uses the term "government." For the sake of brevity, we refer to the "government and binding theory" as "GB."

Chomsky believes that universal grammar belongs to the commonality of human languages. For any linguistic phenomenon that can be explained by universal grammar principles, there is no need to make specific provisions in the grammar of individual languages. Universal grammar is suitable for every language, and at the same time, it is flexible, allowing different languages to be somewhat different within a certain range. Chomsky pointed out what we hope to find is a highly structured universal grammar theory based on a few basic principles. These principles strictly limit the types of grammar that can be acquired, and strongly restrict their form, but have the necessary experience to determine many parameters. If these parameters are included in universal grammar that is structurally rich enough, then the languages determined by determining the values of these parameters in one way or another will show considerable differences, because the consequences of a set of choices can be very different from the consequences of another set of choices. Nonetheless, only limited materials sufficient to determine the parameters of universal grammar will determine a grammar, which may be complex and generally lack empirical (inductive) grounds. Each such grammar will become the basis for judgment and understanding and will enter behavior. However, as a kind of knowledge system, grammar is only indirectly related to the experience acquired. Universal grammar is the medium of this connection.

GB is Chomsky's effort in this direction. The core of GB is a series of basic principles that are interrelated and mutually restricted. These principles are universal, applicable to every language, and flexible at the same time, allowing different languages to have certain differences. The difference lies in Chomsky's so-called "parameter." The difference is learned after birth. Therefore, Chomsky said that it is "determined by experience."

The core of GB is a series of universal principles, called "principle subsystem." Chomsky put forward the following principle subsystems: X-bar theory, thematic theory, Case theory, government theory, binding theory, bounding theory, and control theory, which are independent and interconnected, forming an intricate system, which restricts human language. Below we explain them one by one:

1. X-bar theory: In 1970, Chomsky proposed the "X-bar theory". This theory holds that:

First, the phrase category should be analyzed as the bar projection of the lexical category. The bar can be divided into several levels. The word X at the lowest level is the head, and the head has several complements and it governs the complement.

Second, the lexical category should be analyzed as a set of features.

In the X-bar theory, Chomsky compares English noun phrases with verb phrases. He points out that there are some common features in the internal structure of noun phrases and verb phrases. Let us look at the comparison:

1. John proved the theorem.
2. John's proof of the theorem.

(1) is a verb phrase (denoted as VP), the head of which is the verb (denoted as V) *prove*, and *the theorem* is the complement of the verb, noted as Comp. (2) is a noun phrase (denoted as NP), the head of which is a noun (denoted as N) *proof*, and the complement of the noun is *the theorem*. The rewriting rules of phrase structure grammar can be expressed as

$$VP \rightarrow V\ Comp \quad NP \rightarrow N\ Comp$$

Not only verb phrases and noun phrases can be expressed in this way, adjective phrases (denoted as AP) and prepositional phrases (denoted as PP) can also be expressed as adjectives (denoted as A) plus complement and preposition (denoted as P plus complement):

$$AP \rightarrow A\ Comp$$

$$PP \rightarrow P\ Comp$$

It is not difficult to see that the rewriting rules for verb phrases, noun phrases, adjective phrases, and prepositional phrases are very similar and can be summarized in the following format:

$$XP \rightarrow X\ Comp$$

In this rule, X is equivalent to the variable in mathematics. You can use any of V, N, A, and P to get the above rules. This rule can be represented by a tree diagram in Fig. 3.59.

If we write XP as X' (you can also add a dash on X), then the rewriting rule becomes

Fig. 3.59 The tree representation of an XP rule

Fig. 3.60 The tree representation of an X′ rule

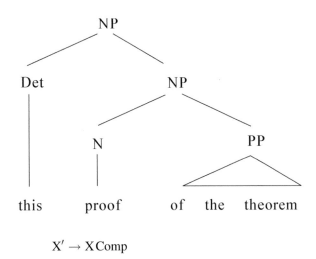

Fig. 3.61 A tree diagram of phrase structure grammar

$$X' \rightarrow X \, Comp$$

The tree diagram becomes (Fig. 3.60).

In this way, the entire presentation method becomes very concise.

From the tree diagram, we can see that X′ represents a category one level higher than X and a category higher than X′ can be represented by adding another' above X′, represented as X″ (or two short bars on X).

In the following, we take the sentence "this proof of the theorem" as an example to compare the similarities and differences between the tree diagram of phrase structure grammar and the tree diagram of X-bar grammar.

The tree diagram of phrase structure grammar of this sentence is shown in Fig. 3.61.

The tree diagram of X-bar grammar for this sentence is shown in Fig. 3.62.

The above is an example of a noun phrase. Verb phrases also have corresponding levels of V′ and V″, and adjective phrases also have corresponding levels of A′ and A″. The general form of various categories is X, X′, and X″ and the hierarchical relationship can be expressed as a tree diagram as is shown in the following (Fig. 3.63).

Fig. 3.62 A tree diagram of X-bar grammar

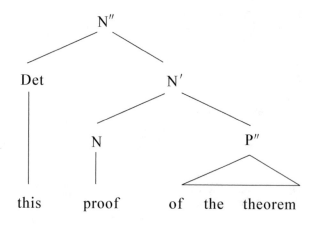

Fig. 3.63 Hierarchical relationship in X-bar grammar

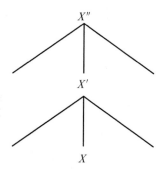

Scholars have different opinions on whether there is any X''' above X''. Some think that there is, and others think that there is not. Since we can't determine how many layers there are in total, for the time being, we can write the lowest layer as X and the top layer as XP and add several layers as needed in the middle. In this way, the whole tree under XP is the "maximum projection" to which XP belongs. X-bar grammar is more expressive than phrase structure grammar. Phrase structure grammar has only two categories, lexical category and phrasal category, lacking an intermediate level. For example, "This proof of the theorem" and "Proof of the theorem" can only be called NP if phrase structure grammar is used, and the two phrases cannot be distinguished, but X-bar grammar can call the former X'' and the later X', so that the two phrases can be distinguished.

X-bar grammar is more rigorous than phrase structure grammar. In X-bar grammar, V' must be under V'', and V is not allowed to appear, let alone N or A. However, there is no such restriction in phrase structural grammar. For unreasonable structures such as VP $\rightarrow$ A PP, phrase structural grammar cannot prevent its appearance.

2. *θ-Theory*: Chomsky expresses the relationship between the predicate and individual word in logic propositions as θ, which is called "thematic relation." For example,

1. John ran quickly.
2. John likes Mary.

In (1), "ran quickly" is a predicate, and "John" is a Nominal word. Example sentence (1) is a unary proposition, in which *John* is "agent." In example sentence (2), *likes* is a predicate, and *John* and *Mary* are Nominal words. Example sentence (2) is a binary proposition, in which *John* serves as "agent" and *Mary* serves as "patient." Chomsky refers to the words that bear θ-roles as "arguments." For example, *John* and *Mary* in the above examples are both arguments. Those which do not serve as arguments are called nonarguments. For example, in the following sentence, *it* and *there* are nonarguments:

3. It is certain that John will win.
4. There are believed to be unicorns in the garden.

Chomsky put forward the following "thematic criteria":

1. Each argument is assigned one and only one θ-role.
2. Each θ-role is assigned to one and only one argument.

For example, according to the first criterion, the argument John in example sentence (2) is assigned the θ-role *agent*, so it cannot be assigned θ-role *patient*, and the argument Mary is assigned the θ-role *patient*, which can no longer be assigned the θ-role *agent*. According to the second criterion, the θ-role *agent* is assigned to the argument John, so it cannot be assigned to the argument "Mary" anymore, and the θ-role *patient* is assigned to the argument Mary; therefore, it can no longer be assigned to the argument John. With the two θ-role criteria, the conditions for transformation can be restricted.

The argument position must be filled with an invisible word if there is no visible word in that position. These invisible words are empty categories called "proforms," which are abbreviated as PRO. For example, although *see* is a two-place predicate in the sentence "It is unclear to see who." There is the only *patient who* and no visible *agent* in the sentence. As a result, the *agent* position in the sentence is filled with PRO, and the sentence is written in the following form:

It is unclear [COMP [PRO to see who]].

In the sentence above, COMP is for complementizer which can introduce a clause after it. All the letters in the "COMP" are capitalized, and it is different from the "Comp" used in the "X-bar theory" which refers to the word "complement." In the clause "to see who" introduced by COMP, the *agent* position is filled with the empty category PRO.

3. *Case Theory*: "Case" is a traditional grammatical concept. Nouns in Russian and German have different morphological forms which refer to different "case." The

word "Case" in "Case theory" is an abstract concept. As long as nouns are in a certain syntactic relationship, whether there are morphological changes or not, they have Case. Case in "Case theory" is not necessarily represented by different phonetic forms (morphological changes). Therefore, although nouns in Chinese, English, and French have no morphological changes and no phonetic forms, they all have Case in this sense. Chomsky proposed that the first letter of "case" should be capitalized as "Case" to distinguish it from the "case" in traditional grammar.

In the X-bar theory, all verbs, nouns, adjectives, and prepositions have complements. However, the ways to express complements are not the same for different classes of words. Verbs and prepositions can be directly followed by a noun phrase which serves as a complement, such as "John proved the theorem," while nouns and adjectives cannot be directly followed by a complement, and a preposition must be inserted between a noun (or an adjective) and its complement, such as "John's proof of the theory." The reason is that the complements of verbs and prepositions have Case, while the complements of nouns and adjectives have no Case. That is to say, verbs and prepositions can assign Case, while nouns and adjectives cannot. The categories in the X-bar theory are divided according to the presence or absence of the two features, "Nominal (N)" and "predicate (V)":

Noun: [+N, −V] (with the Nominal feature, no predicate feature).
Verb: [−N, +V] (no Nominal feature, with predicate feature).
Adjectives: [+N, +V] (with the Nominal feature, with predicate feature).
Preposition: [−N, −V] (no Nominal feature, no predicate feature).

In English, only categories with the feature [−N] can assign Case. Since nouns and adjectives do not have the feature [−N], a preposition must be inserted between nouns (or adjectives) and the complements, and Case is assigned by the preposition. With the Case theory, different properties of categories can be explained.

4. *Government Theory*: The so-called "government" refers to the dominance relationship between the components in a sentence. It indicates whether each component in a phrase is within the same governing category, and which component is the dominance and which component is governed in the governing category

Take the following three English sentences, for example:

1. John likes him.
2. John says Bill likes him.
3. John likes himself.

The tree diagram of sentence (1) is shown in Fig. 3.64.

In the tree diagram in Fig. 3.64, *John* and *him* are in the same governing category S, *John* is the dominant component, and *him* is the governed component. Therefore, *John* governs *him* in sentence (1).

The tree diagram of sentence (2) is shown in Fig. 3.65.

In the tree diagram in Fig. 3.65, it can be seen that *Bill* and *him* are in the same governing category S1. *Bill* is the dominant component, *him* is the governed

Fig. 3.64 The tree diagram of sentence (1)

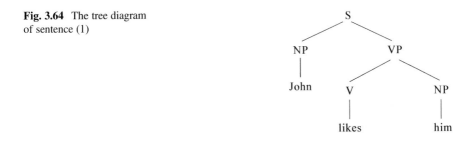

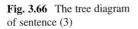

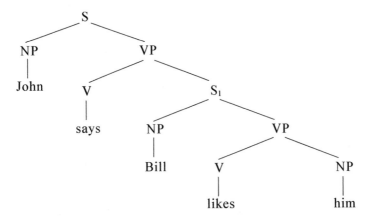

Fig. 3.65 The tree diagram of sentence (2)

Fig. 3.66 The tree diagram of sentence (3)

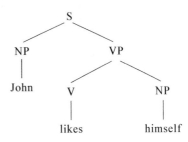

component, and *Bill* governs *him*. However, *him* and *John* are not in the same governing category because there is S1 layer between *John* and *him*. *John* is not in the governing category of S1 and is not within the maximum projection of S1.

The tree diagram of sentence (3) is shown in Fig. 3.66.

In the tree diagram Fig. 3.66, *John* and *himself* are in the same governing category S, *John* is the dominant component, *himself* is the governed component, and *John* governs *himself*.

From the perspective of the X-bar theory, the dominant component is the lowest level X in the X-bar structure, and the governed component is the Comp of X's complement.

5. *Binding Theory*: The so-called binding is the anaphoric relationship of semantic interpretation. "Binding" intends to indicate under what circumstances the constituent in a governing category is free and under what circumstances it is bound.

Chomsky proposed three binding principles:

Principle A: An anaphor must be bound in its governing category.
Principle B: A pronoun must be free in its governing category.
Principle C: A referential expression must be free everywhere.

Here, anaphors refer to words like reflexive pronoun *himself*. Pronouns refer to the words like *him* and *her*. And referential expression refers to words like *John* and *Bill*.

Both "bind" and "free" are terms in logic. In logic, quantifiers bind variables. Any variable that is bound by a quantifier is called a "bound variable." The variables that are not bound by quantifiers are called "free variables." If a noun phrase is "bound," this means that the noun phrase and another noun phrase refer to the same object. If a noun phrase is "free," this means that the noun phrase and another noun phrase refer to different objects. "The governing category" refers to the lowest S and NP.

According to Principle C, *John* and *Bill* in sentences (1), (2), and (3) are all referential expressions that are free everywhere. They cannot be bound by other words under any circumstances. However, they can bind other words.

According to Principle B, the pronoun *him* in sentence (1) is free in its governing category S. It is not bound by the dominant component *John* in the same governing category. Therefore, *John* and *him* in sentence (1) do not refer to the same person.

Similarly, according to Principle B, the pronoun *him* in sentence (2) is also free in its governing category S1, and it is not bound by the dominant component *Bill* in S1. Therefore, *Bill* and *him* do not refer to the same person. However, Principle B does not constrain *him* and *John* to refer to the same person, because *John* is out of the governing category of *him*. Hence, *him* in sentence (2) cannot refer to *Bill*, but it can refer to *John* or anyone else.

According to Principle C, the anaphor *himself* in sentence (3) is bound by its dominant component *John* in the governing category S. Therefore, *himself* and *John* refer to the same person.

The explanation of the above linguistic phenomenon is consistent with our language intuition about English. Furthermore, the same explanation can be applied to the corresponding Chinese sentences (1), (2), and (3). It can be seen that the three binding principles are universal in language. Such principles as binding principles have attracted the attention of linguists because they are based on a correct understanding of the general nature and characteristics of human languages and such issues have special research value.

6. *Bounding Theory*: the bounding theory studies the constraints of the scope of transformation, focusing on the range of wh-movement.

In English, interrogative words should be moved when they constitute special questions. For example, in the English sentence "who does the book criticize?", *who* is the patient object of *criticize* and has been moved to the beginning of the sentence when it turns into an interrogative sentence. It can be expressed as.

who$_i$ [$_s$ does this book criticize t$_i$].

where t$_i$ represents the trace of *who*, namely, the position of *who* in the declarative sentence. From this position, *who* moves to the beginning of the sentence, only passing an S.

However, when the wh word is in a relative clause, it cannot be moved to the beginning of a sentence. For example, "Who are you reading the book that criticize?" in English is an incorrect sentence. Its structure can be presented as the following:

who$_i$ [$_s$ are you reading [$_{NP}$ the book [that [$_s$ criticize t$_i$]]]].

The movement of "who" from its original position in the declarative sentence to the beginning of the interrogative sentence crosses two S and one NP.

Why can *who* sometimes move to the beginning of a sentence and sometimes cannot? This is due to the regional limitation of wh movement. In English, both S and NP are bounding nodes. They specify certain regional boundaries and cannot be crossed arbitrarily. The subjacency condition stipulates that in the case of wh movement, a wh word cannot cross more than one bounding node in one step. In the first sentence, the movement of *who* only crosses one bounding node, which meets the requirements of the subjacency condition, so the qualified sentence is obtained. In the second sentence "Who are you reading the book that criticize?", the movement of *who* crosses three bounding nodes. As a result, the movement violates the subjacency condition and the sentence is unqualified.

7. *Control Theory*: The control theory proposed by Chomsky mainly concerns the empty category PRO which is silent in speech. Let us look at the following English sentences first:

1. John promised Bill to leave.
2. John persuaded Bill to leave.

The difference between the two sentences is that *John* in sentence (1) is the logical subject of *leave* and *Bill* in sentence (2) is the logical subject of *leave*. However, in both sentences, there is no movement of any constituent, no traces. The actual structure of these two sentences should be.

John promised Bill [PRO to leave].
John persuaded Bill [PRO to leave].

Obviously, the nature of PRO is determined by the verbs *promised* and *persuaded*. Therefore, the characteristics of the verbs should be specified in their lexical items to ensure that the PRO and the subject of the verb *promised* have the same referent in sentence (1), and in sentence (2), PRO refers to the same referent as the object of the verb *persuaded*. This can be expressed by subscripts as follows:

John$_i$ promised Bill [PRO$_i$ to leave].
John persuaded Bill$_i$ [PRO$_i$ to leave].

This means that the verb *promise* assigns "subject control" and the verb *persuade* assigns "nonsubject control." In this way, verbs can be divided into control verbs and non-control verbs.

The basic principle of the control theory is the "minimum distance principle." That is to say, if the control has an object, then the object is the controlling element; if there is no object, the subject is the controlling element. Most verbs take the object as the control element. Only a few verbs such as *promise* take the subject as the control element. Verbs like *promise* should be labeled with [+ SC] to indicate subject control.

In some cases, PRO has arbitrary references. For example,

It is unclear [what PRO to do].
It is difficult [PRO to see the point of this].

In this kind of structure, PRO can be interpreted as "someone, everyone."

The principles put forward from the perspective of universal grammar in "government and binding theory" can guide NLP. The theory has become one of the important foundations for the theories and methods of language information processing. In the 1990s, Chomsky put forward the principle-parameter approach and the minimalist program, which promoted the study of generative grammar to a new stage. During this period, generative grammar focused on universal grammar (UG). Such a study is of great theoretical value to the development of computational linguistics.

In the past 60 years after its foundation, generative grammar has undergone several significant changes in its theoretical model. It keeps developing toward a new direction. In the process of its development, generative grammar was endowed with vitality by its philosophical theory. The most important questions are about the nature, source, and use of human knowledge.

Chomsky calls the essential problem of language knowledge "Humboldt's problem."

Humboldt once proposed that "language is by no means a product (Ergon), but a creative activity (Energeria)." Language is the repeated activities of the human mind, and it enables syllables to become expressions of ideas. The essence of human linguistic knowledge is the question of how linguistic knowledge is constituted, the core of which is "the infinite use of finite means" pointed out by Humboldt. The essence of language knowledge lies in the existence of a language cognitive system in the mind/brain of human members. Such a cognitive system manifests itself as a system of a limited number of principles and rules. Highly abstract grammatical rules constitute the language knowledge required for language applications. Because people cannot consciously realize these abstract grammatical rules, Chomsky maintains that it is self-evident or unconscious knowledge. We should distinguish language knowledge from language ability. Two people have the same knowledge of the same language. They are the same in pronunciation, vocabulary knowledge, the mastery of sentence structures, and so on. However, two people may behave very differently in terms of language use. Therefore, language knowledge and language ability are two different concepts. Language ability can be improved, while language knowledge remains unchanged. Language ability can be damaged or disappeared, but people will not lose language knowledge. Therefore, language knowledge is the characteristic and expression of the inner mind, and language ability is the expression of external behavior. Generative grammar studies the mental knowledge of the language, not the behavioral ability of language. Language knowledge is embodied in the cognitive system of the mind/brain.

The origin of language knowledge is a special case of "Plato problem" in Western philosophy. The so-called Plato problem is the following: the empirical evidence we can get is so poor, but how do we obtain such rich and specific knowledge, such a complex belief and rational system? The contact between a man and the world is so short, narrow, and limited. Why can we know so many things? Why is there such a huge difference between the poverty of stimulus and the knowledge we acquired? Corresponding to the "Plato problem," the origin of human language knowledge is why the children can acquire a language quickly and consistently with less direct language experience? Chomsky believes that in the mind/brain of human members, there is a cognitive mechanism system determined by biological inheritance. Under the appropriate experience or certain experience environment, these cognitive systems can grow and mature normally. These cognitive systems are called "mental organs." It is a system in the mental organs that determines the composition of human language knowledge, called "language faculty." The growth and maturity of this language faculty triggered by the experience environment determine the acquisition of human language knowledge. The language faculty has an initial state and attained state. The initial state is common and universal among human beings, while the attained state is specific and individual. The initial state of the language faculty is called "universal grammar" (UG). The attained state of the language faculty is called "particular grammar." The research and determination of the essential characteristics of UG and its relationship with PG are the key to solving the "Plato problem" of language knowledge.

Chomsky calls the use of language knowledge the "Cartesian problem."

Based on the concept of matter in mechanistic philosophy, French philosopher and mathematician Descartes believed that all phenomena in the nonliving material world, the physiology and behavior of animals, and most human organ activities can be incorporated into the category of the science of the body. However, Descartes also pointed out that certain phenomena cannot be within the scope of materials science, among which the most significant is human language, especially the "creative aspect of language use," which is beyond the scope of the mechanistic material concept. Therefore, the normal use of language is the real difference between human beings and other animals or machines. To find an explanation for such a phenomenon as language, Descartes set up the existence of a "second entity," which is the "thinking substance." "Thinking substance" is different from a material entity. It is separated from the material entity and interacts with the material entity in some way. This kind of "thinking substance" is the mind. The use of language knowledge is inherent in the mind/brain, so it is difficult to solve and answer such questions. The problem of language use is mysterious to Descartes at that time, and it is also mysterious to us at present. Chomsky believes that we should first solve the problem of the essence of language knowledge and the origin of language knowledge. On this basis, it is possible to make meaningful explorations on the use of language.

Chomsky insists that the language faculty is internalized in the mind/brain. The study of language is the study of the mind and terminally the study of brain structure at an abstract level. Therefore, generative grammar belongs to "cognitive psychology" and terminally to "human biology." It should be called "biolinguistics." This is the fundamental difference between generative grammar and any other traditional language research. The goal of generative grammar is to construct the theory of language and the mind under the conditions of idealization and abstraction. It expects to be unified with the natural sciences. The abstract research of generative grammar on universal grammar, language acquisition mechanism, acquired state, and relationship between language and other cognitive systems is one part of natural sciences, whether it is good or bad, right or wrong. This is the "methodological naturalism" of generative grammar. This naturalistic study of generative grammar is essentially identical to that of natural sciences. Chomsky strives to unify the study of language, the mind, and the brain under a common theoretical principle and finally brought it into the overall study of natural sciences.

Chomsky proposes that language is the state presented by the language faculty or language organ. To say that someone has language (L) means that his language faculty is in the state L. The state obtained by the language faculty can generate an infinite number of linguistic expressions, and each expression is some arrangement and combination of phonetic, structural, and semantic features. The state obtained by this language faculty is a generating system or an operating system. To distinguish it from the external language understood by ordinary people, Chomsky calls such a computational system "I language." Here, the letter I stands for concepts of internal, individual, intensional, and so on. This means that I language is an integral part of the mind and terminally manifested in the neural mechanism of the brain. Therefore, I language is "internal"; I language is directly related to the individual, and it has an indirect connection with the language community. The existence of a language community depends on the members of the community who have similar I language. Therefore, I language is "individual"; I language is a function or generating program that generates a series of structural descriptions that are inherent in the mind/brain. Therefore, I language is "intensional."

Based on this understanding of I language, Chomsky points out that the general concepts of language based on sociopolitical and normative teleological factors have nothing to do with scientific linguistic research, and these concepts are not suitable for scientific language research. The scientific understanding of language in generative grammar is internalist, while that of structuralism is externalist. The research method of structural grammar is to summarize the grammatical rules of language through the procedures of segmentation, classification, and substitution based on the extensive collection of language materials. These structural rules exist in the external world, outside the human mind/brain. The research method of structuralist grammar is that of empiricism, which is based on the externalist view of language. According to Chomsky, the externalist view of language held by structuralist cannot correctly understand and reveal the essential characteristics of human language, and cannot explain the process of human language knowledge acquisition. Only the internalist view of language can correctly and comprehensively understand and explain the nature, origin, and use of human language knowledge.

"Minimalism" is an important principle of generative grammar, which can be divided into "methodological minimalism" and "substantive minimalism." Methodological minimalism is based on the views and concepts of general scientific methodology, while substantive minimalism is about the research object itself.

Methodological minimalism requires people to create the best theory in scientific research, and the main criterion of a good theory is simplicity. The principle of simplicity is displayed as follows: use the minimum number of theoretical principles and theoretical components in scientific research, minimize complexity, eliminate redundancy, increase the abstraction and generality of theoretical principles, construct the simplest theoretical model and the most explanatory theory, and seek the symmetry and perfection of theory.

Substantial minimalism requires that the scientific research object itself has simplicity, optimization, and perfection in the design and structure.

Under the principle of minimalism, the theoretical construction of generative grammar is a process of gradual abstraction, generalization, and simplification.

In the early stage of generative grammar construction, Chomsky pointed out that although Humboldt recognized the nature of language as "the infinite use of finite means," due to the lack of corresponding technical means at that time, it was difficult to develop Humboldt's excellent insight. With the development of modern mathematics and logic, generative grammar has provided powerful means of formal description, which makes the study of generative grammar consistent with other natural scientific research in terms of expression.

Chomsky pointed out in the early stage of generative grammar that the generative power of phrase structure grammar is too strong and it often generates ungrammatical sentences, which violates the requirements of minimalism. Therefore, he put forward the transformation approach and focused on the transformation rule system. The result did not achieve the goal of simplicity, but it made the rule system more complicated. In his pursuit of minimalism, he took various ways to limit and reduce the number of rules, changing the study of generative grammar from the theory of rules to the conditional theory of restricting rules and then from the study of conditional theory to the study of principles and parameter approach.

In the principles and parameters stage of generative grammar, Chomsky proposed a grammatical rule system. The grammatical rule system is composed of lexicon, syntax, PF component, and LF component. Corresponding to the grammatical rule system, Chomsky also proposed the principle subsystems of UG, which include the X-bar theory, θ-theory, Case theory, government theory, binding theory, bounding theory, and control theory in GB. There exists a relationship of interdependence and interaction among the various theories of the principle subsystems.

In addition to these rule systems and principle subsystems, there are some general principles in universal grammar model studied and described by the principle and parameter approach. The most important principles are the projection principle, licensing principle, and full interpretation principle. These general principles are

Fig. 3.67 Y model of
principle and parameter
approach

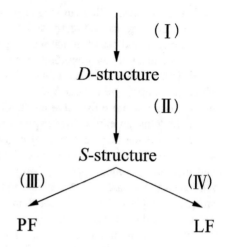

more abstract and theoretical than the principle subsystem. The study of the principle-parameter approach is further restricted so that the grammar rules with specific language features are eliminated. The necessary rules are abstracted and reduced to a minimum, and the characteristics and meanings of universal grammar are endowed to them. The application of specific rules is explained by general principles.

These principles are universal and contain some parameters whose values are not determined. The values of parameters are selected and determined by individual languages.

Chomsky presented the following "Y model" schema to illustrate the rules of grammar and the representation of operations (Fig. 3.67).

Since this model looks like an inverted letter Y, so it is called the "Y model." In the Y model, (I) represents the phrase structure rule of the basic part of grammar. (II) represents the transformation rule move–α. (III) is the phonological rule. (IV) is the logical rule. Application rule (I) generates D-structure. The application rule (II) transforms D-structure into S-structure. Application rule (III) transforms S-structure directly into phonetic form PF. Application rule (IV) transforms S-structure into logical representation LF. The operation of the four sub-rule systems generates four different levels of representation: rule (I) generates D-structure, rule (II) generates S-structure, rule (III) generates phonetic PF, and rule (IV) generates logical LF. D-structure and S-structure are completely internal to the language faculty. PF and LF form interface relations with other cognitive systems and belief systems, respectively. On the one hand, they produce direct voice expressions. On the other hand, they produce meaning expression in the interaction with other systems. Here, there is no problem with the order between D-structure and S-structure. The letters D and S do not mean any deep and shallow meaning. They are only theoretical components of the internal function of language. Grammar rules assign each linguistic expression a structure with four levels of representation, which can be expressed by the formula $\Sigma = (D, S, P, L)$, where Σ is the description of the language structure, D represents D-structure, S represents the S-structure, P represents the phonetic form, and L represents the logical form.

For example, the operation of the sentence "What is easy to do today?" is as follows:

First, the following D-structure is generated according to phrase structure rules:

[s [NP it] [VP is [AP easy [s NP[VP to do [NP what]]]] today]]

After using the move rule, the following S-structure is obtained:

[NP what] [s [NP it] [VP is [AP easy [s NP[VP to do [NP e]]]] today]]

Apply the logic rules, the interpretation of the logical form of the S-structure is as follows:

For which x, it is easy [s NP[VP to do [NP e]]] today

Here, "what" is regarded as a quasi-quantifier and transformed into the form of "for which" to constrain the variable x.

Apply phoneme rules; the phonetic representation of the S-structure is interpreted as follows: What is easy to do today?

In this way, the result of the calculation based on the Y pattern is the surface sentence "What is easy to do today?"

In the four representations(D-structure, S-structure, PF, and LF), PF and LF have external interface relationships with other cognitive systems, and D-structure has an internal interface relationship with the lexicon. S-structure acts as a central hub during the operation. In the development of generative grammar, Chomsky gradually eliminated the redundant parts of the theoretical model of grammar and minimized the rule system. Finally, Chomsky canceled the rule system in theory. After entering the stage of the "principles and parameters" and with the establishment of the internalist view of language, Chomsky began to follow the principle of substantive minimalism, to analyze and explore the simplicity and perfection of the internal language itself. Generative grammar entered the stage of the minimalism. At that stage, from the design features of the language itself and the relationship between language and other cognitive systems, generative grammar eliminates all the theoretical components which only serve the internal language faculty, making the overall model of generative grammar achieve unprecedented simplicity and perfection.

In his book *A Minimalist Program for Linguistic Theory*, Chomsky expounded some of the most basic viewpoints on the minimalist for linguistics and raised some questions that need to be further considered and explored.

Chomsky believes that the following two questions are related to the reasons and motivations for the formation of the minimalist program for linguistic theory:

First, what are the general conditions that the human language faculty should be expected to satisfy?

Second, to what extent is the language faculty determined by these conditions without a special structure that lies beyond them?

The first question in turn has two aspects:

(a) What is the place of the language faculty within the array of cognitive systems of the mind/brain?
(b) What are general considerations of conceptual naturalness that have some independent plausibility, namely, simplicity, economy, symmetry, nonredundancy, and the like?

Chomsky's answer to the first question is the following:

(a) The place of the language faculty in the sequential cognitive system of the mind/brain is the interface condition imposed by the other cognitive systems in the mind/brain for the language faculty.
(b) The general conditions imposed by scientific research on objects belong to the category of methodological minimalism.

Starting from the substantive minimalism, Chomsky's answer to the second question is the language faculty can meet these external constraints well. In this sense, language is a "perfect system."

The minimalist program for linguistic theory seeks to explore the possibilities expressed by these answers. Out of his unremitting pursuit of minimalism, Chomsky's discussion on these issues has become more internalized and abstract in general.

In his book *A Minimalist Program for Linguistic Theory*, Chomsky once again explains his internalist view of language. Language is the state presented by the language faculty determined by biological inheritance in the mind. One of the components of the language faculty is a generative program, namely, the internal language (I language). The generative program is called computational derivation. I language generates the structure description, i.e., the representation of language. The process of generating structure description (SD) is the computational derivation. I language is embedded in the performance system which applies the representation generated by the language to language-related activities. The structure description (SD) can be regarded as the "instructions" issued to these performance systems.

Regarding the overall consideration of the minimalist program, Chomsky discussed the following issues:

1. In the minimalist program, there are two performance systems related to the I language in general: one is the articulatory-perceptual (A-P) system, and the other is the conceptual-intentional (C-I) system. Each linguistic expression generated by computational operations contains the instructions given to the two application systems. The interfaces between language and the two systems are A-P and C-I, respectively. The two interfaces issue instructions respectively to the articulatory-perceptual system and the conceptual-intentional system. The A-P interface is generally taken to be PF, and the C-I interface is generally regarded as LF. Considering the necessity of the construction of language theory, the

language design in the simplest scheme only needs A-P and C-I interfaces. This idea is in line with our understanding that the form of language is mainly composed of voices and meanings, which is also the thinking of ancient Greek philosopher Aristotle 2000 years ago about the nature of language. This shows that the internal levels of D-structure and S-structure in the Y model of the "principle and parameter" approach are not necessary for the design of the language itself. They are internal components of the linguistic theory set artificially by the linguists for their study. The reduction and even elimination of the number of the levels for internal language expressions are exactly the objectives of the minimalist program.

2. In the minimalist program, language consists of two components: a lexicon and a computational system. The lexicon specifies the items that enter into the computational system, with their idiosyncratic properties. The computational system uses these elements to generate derivations and SDs. The derivation is the process of computation, and the structural description is the result of the computation. On this assumption, each language will determine a set of pairs (π, λ) (π drawn from PF and λ from LF) as its formal representations of sound and meaning, insofar as these are determined by the language itself. Parts of the computational system are relevant only to π, not λ: the *PF component*. Other parts are relevant only to λ, not π: the *LF component*. The parts of the computational system that are relevant to both are the *"overt syntax."* Since the arbitrary combinations of phonetic components and meanings exist inevitably, there are language variations in the phonetic form. Besides, vocabulary is also arbitrary. As a result, language variations also exist in lexical items. However, variations in the overt syntax or LF component would be more problematic, since evidence could only be quite indirect. We can even speculate that there is no variation in the "overt syntax" and LF. The minimalist program assumes that in addition to the choice of PF and the arbitrariness of vocabulary, the language variation is limited to those non-substantial parts in the lexicon and general features of lexical items. In this way, for all human languages, there are only two things besides the limited variations: one is the general computational system, and the other is the lexicon. As far as the operating system is concerned, the initial state of language is composed of universal principles, and the options related to the principles are limited to the general features of functional elements and the lexicon. A selection Σ among these options determines a language. The process of language acquisition is the process of determining Σ, and the description of a certain language is the statement made for Σ. In this way, the problem of language acquisition has been substantially revised in the minimalist program.

3. In the minimalist program, binding theory, Case theory, θ-theory, and so on can only work on the interface, and the reason and motivation of their existence can be obtained through the interface. In this way, the work previously done on the D-structure and S-structure levels must be completed on the A-P and C-I interfaces now. The conditions related to the computation can only be the interface conditions. The linguistic expressions are the ideal satisfaction and realization of the interfaces and reflect the ideality and optimization of language computation.

4. In the minimalist program, the computational derivation of UG can produce two results: "converge" and "crash." A derivation converges if it yields a legitimate SD and crashes if it does not. Specifically, if the structure description π is legitimate, the derivation will converge at PF; otherwise, it will crash at the PF. And if the structure description λ is legitimate, the derivation will converge at LF; otherwise, it will crash at LF. These conditions are relatively loose because the structure descriptions π and λ might be legitimate, respectively, but they cannot be combined into a legitimate pair of PF and LF. Therefore, a more stringent condition should be as follows: if a derivation converges at the PF and LF levels at the same time, it can be considered as true convergence.

Based on these minimalist ideas, the theoretical model of generative grammar has undergone great changes.

The minimalist program advocates that language consists of two parts, namely, the lexicon and the computation system. This idea is very close to the understanding of NLP. We know that in the machine translation system, we rely on the word bank and operation rules to organize the whole system. Therefore, Chomsky's profound theoretical discussion on the minimalist program will inevitably have a huge impact on the study of formal models of NLP.

3.12   Joshi's Tree Adjoining Grammar

In 1975, A. K. Joshi (1929–2017, Fig. 3.68), L. S. Levy, M. Takahashi, and others proposed "tree adjoining grammar" (TAG), which can identify and generate "tree adjoining language" (TAL).

Tree adjoining grammar is developed based on phrase structure grammar. It uses the syntactic structure tree as the core operation object to organize language knowledge based on the tree. Its production rules also correspond to the tree structure. It expresses the two-dimensional tree structures in a linear one-dimensional form.

The difference between tree adjoining grammar and phrase structure grammar is that the rules of tree adjoining grammar are more detailed than those of phrase structure grammar. For example,

The rule of tree adjoining grammar of Chinese double object can be written as

$$VP \rightarrow VP(V\ NP)\ NP$$

This rule contains two rules of phrase structure grammar:

$$VP \rightarrow VP\ NP \quad VP \rightarrow V\ NP$$

If we use the two phrase structure grammar rules to generate Chinese, since the first rule VP→VP NP is a self-embedded rule, the VP on the right of the rule can be

Fig. 3.68 A. K. Joshi

used continuously to rewriting the VP on the left of the rule in the derivation, resulting in

$$VP \cdot NP \cdot NP \cdot NP \cdot NP \cdot NP \ldots NP$$

Such a symbol string which contains several NPs will not appear in Chinese, and it is an ungrammatical Chinese sentence.

However, if we use tree adjoining grammar, only VP→VP(V NP) NP, which contains the rules of the tree structure, can be generated

$$VP(V \cdot NP)NP$$

Such a tree structure, which contains only two NPs as double objects, is in accordance with Chinese grammar. In this way, the excessively strong generative ability of phrase structure grammar is restricted, and the accuracy of the rules is guaranteed.

It can be seen that phrase structure grammar is a generation system based on symbol strings, while tree adjoining grammar is a tree-based generation system. Of course, tree adjoining grammar language generated by tree adjoining grammar is still a symbol string language, and the generated result does not include the tree structure. Tree adjoining grammar is an important improvement to phrase structure grammar. It can reflect the true appearance of the natural language better than phrase structure grammar.

Below we discuss the basic components and operation modes of tree adjoining grammar from a formal perspective:

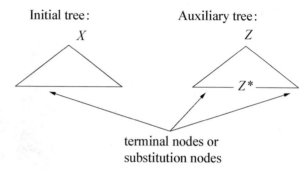

Tree adjoining grammar is a 5-tuple ($\sum$, NT, I, A, S), where

1. $\sum$ is a finite set of terminal symbols.
2. NT is a finite set of non-terminal symbols[4], $\sum \cap NT = \varphi$.
3. S is the initial symbol, and it is a special non-terminal symbol, S∈NT.
4. I is the initial tree[5] (refer to Fig. 3.69) and has two characteristics:

   (a) All non-leaf nodes are labeled with non-terminal symbols.
   (b) All leaf nodes are either labeled with the terminal symbol or non-terminal
   symbol label with a down arrow ($\downarrow$). The down arrow ($\downarrow$) is the label of the
   initial tree. Its meaning is "substitution," which means that the node can be
   replaced by other tree structures.

   If the root node of an initial tree is X, then this initial tree is called an initial tree
   of type X in the TAG system.
5. A is the auxiliary tree[6] (refer to Fig. 3.69), it also has two characteristics:

   (a) All non-leaf nodes are labeled with non-terminal symbols.
   (b) The nodes on the leaves of the auxiliary tree are labeled with terminal
   symbols or non-terminal symbols. The non-terminal symbol nodes on the
   leaves of the A tree have an adjunction symbol, and the node to be connected
   is labeled with an asterisk (*). This node is called a "foot node." The
   non-terminal symbol (phrase-like symbol) of the foot node must be the
   same as the root node of the tree structure in which it is located.

None of the trees in the initial tree set I and the auxiliary tree set A has been
operated on. They are originally stored in the set. Such trees are called elementary
trees and are mainly used for some operations in TAG.

---

[4]In tree adjoining grammar, lowercase letters are used to represent the terminal symbol, and large
and small letters are used to represent non-terminal symbols.

[5]The initial tree is the initial tree on the left of Fig. 3.69, referred to as I tree for short.

[6]The tree is the auxiliary tree on the right side of Fig. 3.69, referred to as A tree for short.

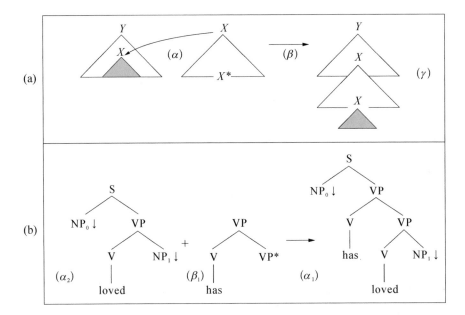

Fig. 3.70 Adjoining operation

All trees in the set I∪A are called elementary trees. If the root of an elementary tree is labeled with a non-terminal symbol X, we call it an X-type elementary tree. In TAG, the elementary tree is the tree stored in I or A without any operations.

TAG is a tree generation system rather than a string generation system, but the tree finally generated by TAG can be used to analyze and interpret the string language of the target language.

In TAG, the tree in the target language is generated through the derivation of the tree. The following describes the "tree" in the target language and the generation process of these "trees."

If a tree is composed of any two trees in the set of I∪A, then this tree is called a derived tree.

The process of obtaining a derived tree is called the derivation process. There are two operations used in this process: one is adjoining, and the other is the substitution.

Adjoining is the process of inserting the auxiliary tree β into any tree α[7] to build a new tree.

Let α be a tree that includes a non-replacement node n, where n is a non-replacement node, and there is a label X on the non-replacement node of tree α. Let β be an auxiliary tree, and the label on the root node of β is also X. A result tree can be obtained by inserting β and α at node n. This process is illustrated in Fig. 3.70 (a), and its specific steps are as follows:

---

[7] α can be an initial tree, an auxiliary tree, or a derivation tree.

1. Let the subtree of α be t, which is dominated by node n, and the label on n is X. After cutting off t, save a copy of n.
2. The root node of β is the same as X, so the auxiliary tree β can be connected to the copy of node n.
3. The root node of t is the same as the end node of β. Connect the root node of subtree t to the foot node labeled with * in the β tree to get the result tree γ.

Let us take a specific look at an example of the adjoining operation in tree adjoining grammar (refer to Fig. 3.70, bottom B). In the tree a_2, the auxiliary tree β_1 is adjoined to the VP node, and α_1 is the final result tree (refer to Fig. 3.70 bottom b). Its specific operation process is as follows:

1. Let the subtree of α_2 be t and the root node of t be n; the label on n is VP, save a copy of n after cutting out t, and the label is still VP.
2. The label of the root node of the auxiliary tree β_1 is the same as the label of n, both are VPs, and the auxiliary tree β_1 is inserted into the copy VP.
3. The root node of subtree t is the same as the foot node labeled with * on β_1, and both are VPs. Connect the root node of subtree t to the foot node with * on β_1 to get the result tree α_2.

There are three kinds of adjunction in TAG. After the label is adjoined, it can be determined that a certain auxiliary tree can be adjoined on a specified node in the initial tree. This label can make the adjoining operation more convenient.

Assuming that G is TAG, $G = (\sum, NT, I, A, S)$, one of the following adjoining operations can be specified for each node on the basic tree in I and A:

1. Selective Adjunction (referred to as SA (T)): The auxiliary tree can be adjoined to the specified node, but the adjunction on this auxiliary tree is not mandatory, so this insertion is called selective insertion.
2. Null Adjunction (NA): No adjacent components are allowed on the specified node.
3. Obligatory Adjunction (OA (T)): Let T be the set of auxiliary trees; when $T \subseteq A$, the tree in T must be adjoined at the specified node. In this case, the adjoining component of the auxiliary tree is mandatory, so this adjunction is called obligatory adjunction.

Let us look at another operation in the derivation – substitution.

Substitution is the process of establishing a new tree by substituting the initial tree α with a derivation tree β.

Substitution only occurs on the non-terminal nodes of tree leaves (refer to Fig. 3.71 top A). All nodes that will be substituted in TAG are labeled with a down arrow ($\downarrow$).

Let us look at an example of a specific substitution operation in TAG. In the lower part B of Fig. 3.71, the root node NP of the tree α_3 is the same as the NP_1 node under the VP subtree in the initial tree α_2. NP_1 is labeled with down arrow ($\downarrow$), so you can substitute the NP_1 in the initial tree α_2 with the NP in the tree α_3, so you get the result tree α_4.

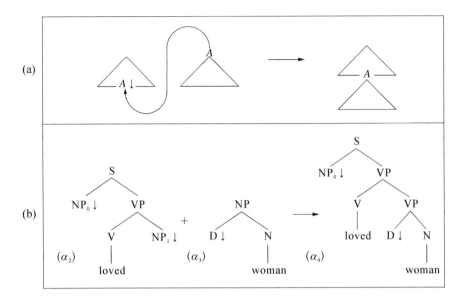

Fig. 3.71 Substitution operation

When a substitution occurs on a node n, this node is substituted by the tree to be substituted. When the node is labeled to be substituted, only the derivation tree can replace it. No adjoining operation is allowed on the node labeled with substitution. For example, in the tree α_2 in the lower part of Fig. 3.70 and Fig. 3.71, no adjoining operation is allowed on the two nodes: NP_0 and NP_1.

In a TAG derivation tree, not enough information is given to determine how this tree is formed, but this information is given in the TAG derivation tree.

What is a derivation tree?

A derivation tree is a tree that determines the formation process of the tree. Both adjunction and substitution operations are included in the derivation of TAG. For example, the derivation tree α_5 can produce the following sentence (Fig. 3.72).

1. Yesterday a man saw Mary.

Figure 3.72 is the derivation tree of the sentence (1), which shows the internal composition of the sentence (1), but it does not tell us the process of obtaining the sentence. In Fig. 3.73, sentence (1) is decomposed into several local elementary trees. Fig. 3.74 is the derivation tree of the sentence (1), which shows how the tree in Fig. 3.72 is acquired.

In the derivation tree of TAG, in addition to the root node, the address of the tree is associated with each node. With reference to the local elementary tree in sentence (1) in Fig. 3.74, the derivation tree in Fig. 3.74 will be explained as follows: α_a is in the tree α_{man}, and it is substituted at address 1 which is associated with node D in Fig. 3.73. α_{man} is in the tree α_{saw} and is substituted at address 2.2 which is associated with node NP_0 in Fig. 3.73. α_{Mary} is in the tree α_{saw} and is substituted at address

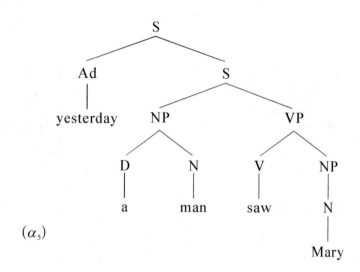

Fig. 3.72 Derivation tree of the sentence (1)

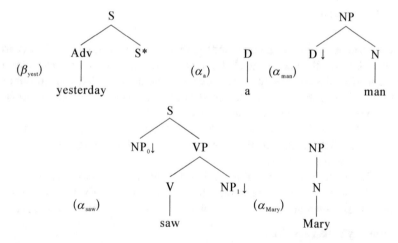

Fig. 3.73 Partial elementary tree of the sentence (1)

1 which is associated with node NP_1 in Fig. 3.73. The tree β_{yest} is adjacent to the address O which is associated with the node S in Fig. 3.73.[8]

In the derivation tree of TAG, if the two trees have an adjunction relationship, they are connected by solid lines; if they have substitution relationships, they are connected by dotted lines. For example, in Fig. 3.74, β_{yest}, and α_{saw} are connected by a solid line, and they have an adjunction relationship. In Fig. 3.73, S^* is above the

---

[8] In TAG, which order is used to explain the derivation tree has no effect on the final derivation tree.

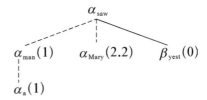

Fig. 3.74 Derivation tree of
sentence (1)

tree β_{yest}, and the root node of α_{saw} is S. Therefore, S^* in the tree β_{yest} should be adjoined by α_{saw}. Next, let us look at the dotted line in Fig. 3.74. In Fig. 3.73, the leaf node D in α_{man} is labeled with a down arrow, the root node of α_a is D, so α_a can be substituted by D↓, and the relationship between other trees can be analogized.

Since adjunction can only happen once at a node, the addresses of all child nodes of a parent node are different in the derivation tree, that is, the addresses of sibling nodes at the same level cannot be the same. For example, in the derivation tree of a sentence (1), all the child nodes of α_{saw} have different addresses. α_{saw} and α_a are parent-child relationships, so the addresses can be the same.

As mentioned earlier, tree adjoining grammar is a tree generation system, and the trees generated by it can be combined to form a tree set. The following describes the definition and attributes of the tree set generated by TAG.

The tree sets in TAG refer to the set of completed initial trees derived from an initial tree rooted at S. Here, the completed initial tree refers to the initial tree without substitution nodes on the leaves. It has the following properties:

1. Recognizable tree sets[9] are strictly included in the tree sets of tree adjoining grammar.[10]
2. In a given TAG tree set, the set of path P(T(G)) of all trees in the tree set is a context-free language.
3. For each grammar G in TAG, the tree set T(G) of G can be identified multiple times.

The language that tree adjoining grammar can recognize and finally generate is the tree adjoining language (TAL). The tree adjoining language no longer contains any form of trees; it is a string language. The tree generated by tree adjoining grammar is terminally to identify and generate such a string language. The definition and properties of the string language in TAG are introduced below:

Let TG = {tlt be the derivation result from some initial tree rooted at S}.

Assuming that L(G) is the string language of TAG, then L(G) is the set of generated results of all trees in the tree set. The definition is as follows:

LG = {wlw is the generated result of a tree t in TG}.

The string language in TAG has the following properties:

---

[9] The set of recognizable trees is also called regular tree sets.
[10] The formal formula:recognizable tree sets ⊂T(G)

1. Tree adjoining languages include the context-free languages; if CFL is used to represent the context-free languages and TAL is used to represent the tree adjoining languages, there will be CFL $\subset$ TAL.
2. Tree adjoining languages are semi-linear.
3. Tree adjoining languages are a full family of languages (full AFLs).
4. The TAG automaton is an embedded pushdown automaton (EPDA), which accurately summarizes the characteristics of the tree adjacent language set.
5. All tree adjoining languages have a pumping lemma.
6. Tree adjoining languages can be analyzed multiple times.

In general, TAG includes a limited set of initial trees and auxiliary trees. Using TAG to generate sentences in natural languages is to start from the S-type initial tree and continue to perform substitution and adjunction operations until all the nodes with the substitution labels have been substituted and all the nodes with adjunction labels have been adjoined. Finally, the leaf nodes of the obtained tree are listed in order; you get the set of sentences generated by TAG.

TAG can also be used to analyze natural language sentences. In the analysis, starting from the tree structure containing the words in the tree, through substitution and adjunction operations, a tree structure with S as the root node is formed.

Above, we introduced and discussed the basic definitions and operations of tree adjoining grammar. Under the joint effect of these definitions and operations, tree adjoining grammar can eventually generate tree sets in the target language, and these trees can in turn analyze string languages in the target language. Although tree adjoining grammar was established in the field of linguistics, it has become a theory of interest in mathematics and computer science. The study of TAG has produced important mathematical results, which will in turn be beneficial to linguistics. Therefore, it can be said that TAG is a kind of grammar, a formal language theory, and an automaton theory. Therefore, TAG is a formal model of NLP, which embodies the interaction among formal linguistics, mathematics, and computer science.

Since the establishment of TAG, its appearance has changed a lot, and its description of natural languages has become more and more refined. Lexicalized TAG (LTAG) is recently proposed to introduce lexical information into the rules of TAG.

The extension of LTAG for TAG is mainly to associate each initial tree and auxiliary tree with one or some specific words. The node with the word in the LTAG tree structure is called the "anchor" of this tree. The following is an example of an LTAG tree (Fig. 3.75).

Tree A is an initial tree, which anchors on the verb *walked*, and Tree B is an auxiliary tree of a VP type, which anchors on the preposition *to*. In Tree A, since *walked* on the anchor point is an intransitive verb, it cannot take an object, and Tree A can't participate in the generation of ungrammatical sentences like "John walked Beijing." However, if Tree B and Tree A perform the adjoining operation, the grammatical sentences like "John walked to Beijing" can be obtained. The tree structure is shown in Fig. 3.76.

Fig. 3.75 Tree with anchor

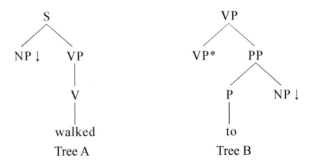

Tree A   Tree B

Fig. 3.76 Tree generated
by adjoining of Tree B and
Tree A

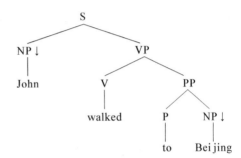

Obviously, due to the introduction of word information to the tree structure, lexicalized tree adjoining grammar (LTAG) further limits the strong generation power of phrase structure grammar, which improves the accuracy and efficiency of NLP. Adjoining grammar and lexicalized tree adjoining grammar are better formal models of NLP than phrase structure grammar.

3.13   Formal Description of the Structure of Chinese Characters

Computer processing of written language is an important aspect of NLP. The analysis of Chinese character structures is an issue that should be paid special attention to in NLP.

Chinese characters can be divided into two types: single characters and compound characters. The single character cannot be decomposed into several separated components in the character structure, but can only be decomposed into strokes, for example, "甘" (/gan/; sweet, pleasant), "手" (/shou/; hand), and "亦" (/yi/; also, too). A compound character is a character composed of two or more components. For example, the word "休" (/xiu/; rest, stop) is composed of two components "亻"(/dan ren pang/) and "木" (/mu/; wood). "霜" (/shuang/; frost) is composed of three components: "雨" (/yu/; rain), "木" (/mu/; wood), and "目" (/mu/; eye). The structure of the compound character can be divided into three levels: the first level is the compound Chinese character itself, the second level is the components that make up the compound character, and the third level is the stroke of the component.

Among the three levels of the Chinese character structures, the component is a pivotal link and the core of the Chinese character structure.

From the perspective of the development of Chinese characters, ancients had the saying that "One single component is Wen (文/wen/), and two or more components combined together is Zi (字/zi/)." In the 15th chapter of *Shuowen Jiezi* (《说文解字》 /Shuo Wen Jie Zi/; a kind of dictionary), Shen Xu (许慎/Xu Shen/) of the Eastern Han Dynasty said: "At the beginning of Cangjie's writing, he wrote pictographs only, so it was called Wen (文/wen/). Later, pictographs which represent images in nature combined with components which represent the sound, then we had Zi (字/zi/)."[11] Here, Shen Xu clearly distinguishes the Wen (文/wen/) from the Zi (字/zi/) and believes that Zi (字/zi/) are derived from Wen (文/wen/). It can be seen that the development of Chinese character creation is not to create strokes first, then components, and then the entire Chinese character, but to create some Wen (文/wen/), which are reproduced as components to form a large number of compounds Zi (字/zi/). For example, from the two components "日" (/ri/; the sun) and "月" (/yue/; the moon), the compound character "明" (/ming/; bright) is synthesized. As for the formation of the stroke system, it was only after the transition into a clerk script (隶书 /li shu/; an ancient style of calligraphy current in the Han Dynasty). The evolution of the Chinese characters is a change in stroke style instead of the structure itself, except for cursive hand script (草书 /cao shu/; a style of Chinese calligraphy) and simplified characters. It can be seen from single Wen to the compound Zi is in line with the development rules of Chinese characters. Therefore, to study the shape and structure of Chinese characters, we should start with the components of characters, so that we can grasp the key to the problem.

From the current state of Chinese characters, since the Chinese characters formed a straight stroke and a square block system, components have a connecting role. On the one hand, they are composed of several simple strokes. On the other hand, they further constitute thousands of Chinese characters. The component is in the pivotal position, which links the strokes with the Chinese characters and becomes the core of the structure of Chinese characters. The total number of components is only a few hundred. When a Chinese character is synthesized, only a few components are needed. If the components are decomposed into strokes, the number of strokes is not large. If we do not use components as the connecting link and directly decompose Chinese characters into strokes, the number of strokes will be very large, and they will be arranged like a long "snake array," making it difficult to explain the sequence relationship among them. Besides, the components have fixed forms, most of which have certain meanings and many of which have their pronunciation. They are close to Chinese characters in nature. Some components are also single Chinese characters, which are far superior to strokes.

---

[11] Shen Xu, *Shuowen Jiezi*, published by Zhonghua Book Company in 1963

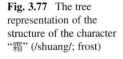

Fig. 3.77 The tree representation of the structure of the character "霜" (/shuang/; frost)

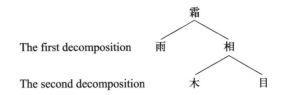

The first decomposition

The second decomposition

Therefore, components should be the central content of the study on the form and structure of Chinese characters. When we study the formal description of Chinese character structures, we must pay full attention to the pivotal role of components.

If a component is further decomposed into strokes, then it means that the component can no longer be decomposed into smaller parts. Such a component is called a primitive component. The further decomposition of the single character results in strokes. Therefore, a single character can also be regarded as a Chinese character composed of primitive components. In this sense, all Chinese characters (including single characters and compound characters) are composed of primitive components.

For example, the character "霜" (/shuang/; frost) can first be decomposed into two parts, "雨" (/yu/; rain) and "相" (/xiang/; looks, posture), where "雨" (/yu/; rain) is a single character, which belongs to the primitive component. Its further decomposition results in strokes. "相" (/xiang/; looks, posture), on the other hand, is a compound character. It can be further decomposed into primitive components "木" (/mu/; wood) and "目" (/mu/; eye). This can be illustrated by the following tree diagram (Fig. 3.77).

We noticed that in Fig. 3.77, "雨" (/yu/; rain), "木" (/mu/; wood), and "目" (/mu/; eye), which are primitive components, appear on the leaf nodes of the tree diagram, while "霜" (/shuang/; frost) and "相" (/xiang/; looks, posture) do not.

For each compound Chinese character, we can use this method to decompose it into a tree diagram to reveal its structure. This is very beneficial for Chinese character information processing and teaching Chinese as a foreign language.

According to the results of computer statistics, modern Chinese characters are composed of 648 primitive components, among which 327 are single characters, such as "口, 木, 土, 十, 又" (/kou, mu, tu, shi, you/; mouth, wood, soil, ten, again), etc. The remaining 321 are not single characters. They are just the constituent units of the compound characters, such as "纟" (/jiao si pang/), "犭" (/fan quan pang/), "扌" (/ti shou pang/), "辶" (/zou zhi di/), "忄" (/shu xin pang/), "亻" (/dan ren pang/), "钅" (/jin zi pang/) and so on. If we have mastered these 648 primitive components and the decomposition method of compound characters, then we can be very efficient in Chinese character information processing and teaching Chinese as a foreign language.[12]

---

[12] Zhiwei Feng, *Modern Chinese Characters and computers*, Peking University Press, 1989

Chomsky's context-free grammar (CFG) is one of the most widely used formal grammars in NLP. This grammar is mathematically concise and clear, with good linguistic explanatory power, and is a relatively mature algorithm in program implementation.

Can we also use context-free grammar to describe the structure of Chinese characters? In the book in German *Die chinesischen schriftzeichen in Vergangenheit und Gegenwart*[13] (The History and Current State of Chinese Characters), Zhiwei Feng gives a positive answer to this question. After a comprehensive analysis of the structure of 6763 Chinese characters in the national standard of China GB2313–80, he concluded that the structure of Chinese characters can be described by context-free grammar.

According to Chomsky's formal linguistic theory, context-free grammar G can be represented by a four-tuple. This quadruple can be defined as follows:

$$G = (Vn, Vt, S, P)$$

where Vn is the set of non-terminal symbols, Vt is the set of terminal symbols, S is the initial symbol, and P is the rewriting rule, and the form is

$$A \rightarrow \omega$$

Here, A is a single non-terminal symbol, and ω is a symbol string, which can be composed of a terminal symbol or a non-terminal symbol.

In Fig. 3.77, "雨" (/yu/; rain), "木" (/mu/; wood), and "目" (/mu/; eye) which appear on the leaf node of the tree diagram are equivalent to the terminal nodes in context-free grammar, and "霜" (/shuang/; frost) and "相" (/xiang/; looks, posture) which do not appear on the leaf nodes of the tree diagram are equivalent to the non-terminal nodes in context-free grammar. "霜" (/shuang/; frost) appears on the root node of the tree diagram, and the root is also the non-terminal node. Because "霜" (/shuang/; frost) and "相" (/xiang/; looks, posture) do not appear on the leaf nodes of the tree diagram, their structures express some kind of information. "霜" (/shuang/; frost) is composed of "雨" (/yu/; rain) and "相" (/xiang/; looks, posture), which are connected in up and down order, and represents the information of the construction pattern of up and down order. "相" (/xiang/; looks, posture) is composed of "木" (/mu/; wood) and "目" (/mu/; eye) connected in left and right order and represents the information of the construction pattern of left and right order.

Therefore, we can write the following rewriting rules:

"霜" (/shuang/; frost) (upper and lower structure)→ "雨" (/yu/; rain) + "相" (/xiang/; looks, posture) (left and right structure)

"相" (/xiang/; looks, posture) (left and right structure)→ "木" (/mu/; wood) + "目" (/mu/; eye).

---

[13]Zhiwei Feng, Die chinesiscnen Schriftzeichen in vergangenheit und Gegenwart(German), Wissenschaftlicher Verlag Trier, Germany, 1994.

Since "霜" (/shuang/; frost) and "相" (/xiang/; looks, posture) do not appear on the leaf nodes of the tree diagram, in rewriting rules, we only need to write the information of the construction pattern they represent. In this way, the above rewriting rules can be rewritten as follows:

Upper and lower structure→"雨" (/yu/; rain) + left and right structure.
Left and right structure→"木" (/mu/; wood) + "目" (/mu/; eye).

The left part of these two rules is "up and down structure" and "left and right structure." They are independent non-terminal symbols, corresponding to the left part A in the rewriting rule A → ω of context-free grammar. The right part of the first rule is "雨 (/yu/; rain) + left and right structure," and "雨" (/yu/; rain) is a primitive component, which belongs to the terminal symbol. "相" (/xiang/; looks, posture) is the non-terminal symbol, which is a string composed of the terminal symbol and the non-terminal symbol, corresponding to the right part ω in the rewriting rule A → ω of context-free grammar.

In this way, we can use context-free grammar to describe the structure of the character "霜" (/shuang/; frost).

This context-free grammar can be written as follows:

$$G = (Vn, Vt, S, P).$$

where.

Vn = {upper and lower structure, left and right structure}.
Vt = {雨, 木, 目 (/yu, mu, mu/; rain, wood, eye)}.
S = {upper and lower structure}.
P:

Upper and lower structure →雨 (/yu/; rain) + left and right structure.
Left and right structure→木 (/mu/; wood) + 目 (/mu/; eye).

"Upper and lower structure" and "left and right structure" are concepts that represent categories, and we can use symbols to represent them. For example, we can use symbol A for "upper and lower structure" and symbol C for "left and right structure," and then the above context-free grammar can be written more concisely:

$$G = (Vn, Vt, S, P)$$

where.

Vn = {A, C}.
Vt = {雨, 木, 目 (/yu, mu, mu/; rain, wood, eye)}.
S = {A}.
P:

1. A → 雨 (/yu/; rain) + C.
2. C → 木 + 目 (/mu/; eye).

Obviously, from the perspective of context-free grammar, Vn is the construction pattern of Chinese characters, Vt is the primitive component that constitutes Chinese characters, S is the top-level structure of a Chinese character that needs to be decomposed, and P is the rule of decomposition. The left part of P is a single non-terminal symbol, and the right part is a string. Therefore, such a grammar fully conforms to Chomsky's definition of context-free grammar.

How many construction patterns are there in Chinese characters? Confirmed by statistical analysis, Vn of Chinese characters is limited, and there are 11 types as follows[14]:

1. The upper and lower structure denoted as A:

    for example, 志 (/zhi/; will, aspiration, ideal), 呆 (/dai/; dull, wooden, stupid), 苗 (/miao/; seeding, young plant), 字 (/zi/; character, style of handwriting).

2. Upper, middle, and lower structure, denoted as B:

    for example, 曼 (/man/; graceful, prolonged), 禀 (/bing/; report, receive), 复 (/fu/; complex, turn over), 享 (/xiang/; enjoy).

3. Left and right structure denoted as C:

    for example, 伟 (/wei/; great, magnificent), 亿 (/yi/; a hundred million), 课 (/ke/; course, lesson), 化 (/hua/; change, transform).

4. Left-center-right structure denoted as D:

    for example, 衍 (/yan/; spread out, redundant), 棚 (/peng/; booth, shed), 树 (/shu/; tree, cultivate), 狱 (/yu/; prison, jail).

5. Upper left surrounding structure denoted as E:

    for example, 庙 (/miao/; temple, shrine), 病 (/bing/; illness, be ill), 房 (/fang/; house, room), 尾 (/wei/; tail, end).

6. Upper right surrounding structure denoted as F:

    for example, 句 (/ju/; sentence), 氧 (/yang/; oxygen), 可 (/ke/; may), 习 (/xi/; practice, habit).

7. Lower left surrounding structure denoted as G:

    for example, 达 (/da/; reach, amount to), 旭 (/xu/; brilliant of the rising sun), 连 (/lian/; link, connect, repeatedly), 爬 (/pa/; crawl, climb).

8. Left, upper, and right surrounding structure denoted as H:

    for example, 同 (/tong/; same, with), 问 (/wen/; ask, inquire after), 闹 (/nao/; noisy, make a noise), 风 (/feng/; wind, style).

9. Upper, left, and lower surrounding structure denoted as I:

    for example, 区 (/qu/; area, region), 医 (/yi/; doctor, medical service, cure), 匿 (/ni/; hide, conceal), 匣 (/xia/; small box).

10. Left, lower, and right surrounding structure denoted as J:

    for example, 凶 (/xiong/; inauspicious, fierce), 画 (/hua/; paint, picture), 击 (/ji/; beat, strike, attack), 函 (/han/; envelope, letter).

11. Fully surrounding structure denoted as K:

    for example, 困 (/kun/; be hard pressed, surround), 国 (/guo/; country, nation), 回 (/hui/; circle, return), 团 (/tuan/; round, group).

---

[14] Some scholars think that there are 13 kinds of Chinese character structures, and their classification method is slightly different from this.

Besides, there is a kind of special symmetrical structure, such as 米 (/mi/; rice), 韭 (/jiu/; fragrant-flowered garlic, chives), 隶 (/li/; be subordinate to), and 垂 (/chui/; hang down, let fall). Such structures cannot be further decomposed. From structural analysis, their properties are the same as those of single characters and primitive components. They belong to structures that cannot be further decomposed. It is denoted as O. Since they cannot be further decomposed, they should belong to the terminal symbol Vt. In the tree diagram, they are all in the position of the leaves and are represented by the symbol ■.

According to this analysis, in context-free grammar that represents the structure of Chinese characters, the non-terminal symbols Vn are 11 symbols: A, B, C, D, E, F, G, H, I, J, and K. They represent the construction pattern types of Chinese characters. The terminal symbols Vt are 648 primitive components, including single characters (such as "□ (/kou/; mouth), 木 (/mu/; wood), 土 (/tu/; soil), 十 (/shi/; ten), 又 (/you/; again)," etc.), component parts (such as "纟 (/jiao si pang/), 犭 (/fan quan pang/), 扌 (/ti shou pang/), 澶 (/chan/; still, still water), 忻 (/xin/; happy, lucky), 钅 (/jin zi pang/)," etc.) and characters with symmetric structures (such as "米 (/mi/; rice), 韭 (/jiu/; fragrant-flowered garlic, chives), 隶 (/li/; be subordinate to), 垂 (/chui/; hang down, let fall)," etc.).

In this way, we can redefine context-free grammar representing the structure of Chinese characters as follows:

$$G = (Vn, Vt, S, P)$$

where

$$Vn = \{A, B, C, D, E, F, G, H, I, J, K\}$$

$$Vt = \{O\}$$

O can be a different kind of terminal symbols, such as □ (/kou/; mouth), 木 (/mu/; wood), 土 (/tu/; soil), 十 (/shi/; ten), 又 (/you/; again), 纟 (/jiao si pang/), 犭 (/fan quan pang/), 扌 (/ti shou pang/), 辶 (/zou zhi di/), 忄 (/shu xin pang/), 亻 (/dan ren pang/) , 钅 (/jin zi pang/), 米 (/mi/; rice), 韭 (/jiu/; fragrant-flowered garlic, chives), 隶 (/li/; be subordinate to), 垂 (/chui/; hang down, let fall), etc.

The initial symbol S is the Chinese character itself whose structure is to be analyzed, and it can take the value of the symbol in Vn as its value. When we use context-free grammar to analyze a sentence in a natural language, there is only one initial symbol S, which represents a sentence. When describing Chinese characters in context-free grammar, the value of initial symbol S can be taken from the symbols in Vn. There are 11 different choices, which means that for the description of Chinese characters, we always have $S \in Vn$, and S can take different values from Vn. However, when describing a sentence in context-free grammar, S can only take one value in Vn (i.e., the abbreviation S which is a non-terminal symbol itself), and there is only one choice. This is the difference between describing the structure of Chinese characters with context-free grammar and describing syntactic structures.

The rewriting rule P has the form of the context-free grammar rule. Its left part must be a single non-terminal symbol, and the right part is a symbol string.

Its form is

$$A \rightarrow \omega$$

For example,

1. A → 雨 (/yu/; rain) + C
2. C → 木 (/mu/; wood) + 目 (/mu/; eye)

Using rewriting rules (1) and (2), we can write the derivational history of the character "霜" (/shuang/; frost) as follows:

A (initial symbol)
雨 (/yu/; rain) + C (use rule 1)
雨 (/yu/; rain) + 木 (/mu/; wood) + 目 (/mu/; eye) (use rule 2)

In this way, we can also regard a Chinese character as being generated step-by-step starting from the initial symbol, using the rewriting rules of context-free grammar. That is to say, we can regard a Chinese character as a result of the generation of context-free grammar.

In the tree diagram shown in Fig. 3.77, "霜" (/shuang/; frost) is the upper and lower structure, and "相" (/xiang/; look, posture) is the left and right structure. We can add "upper and lower structure" and "left and right structure" to the corresponding nodes in the tree diagram. "雨, 木, and 目 (/yu/; rain), (/mu/; wood), and (/mu/; eye)" are all primitive components; no other labels are needed. In this way, the tree diagram in Fig. 3.77 can be rewritten as the tree diagram in Fig. 3.78.

This tree diagram can be further abstracted as follows (Fig. 3.79).

Using the terminal and non-terminal symbols in context-free grammar, the tree diagram can be represented as shown in Fig. 3.80.

Fig. 3.78 The labeled tree diagram

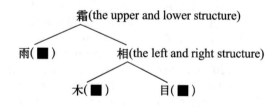

Fig. 3.79 Further abstraction of the tree diagram

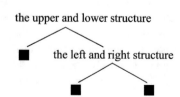

Fig. 3.80 Nodes represented by terminal and non-terminal symbols

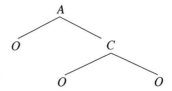

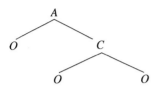

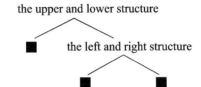

Fig. 3.81 The tree diagram corresponding to bracket formula A(O,C(O,O))

This tree diagram can be written into an equivalent bracket formula:

$$A(O, C(O, O))$$

This means that the compound character "霜" (/shuang/; frost) can be expressed as a bracket formula A(O,C(O,O)).

Any compound character can be expressed as such a bracket formula. In this way, we have found a formal representation of the structure of Chinese characters – bracket representation. This is a representation method based on context-free grammar.

Many commonly used Chinese characters contain more than two or three components. Therefore, we must decompose them step-by-step. Next, we will explain the structural decomposition of compound characters containing three or more components. Such structural decomposition is a formal description of them.

1. A formal description of compound characters containing three components

Compound characters that contain three components can be divided into 15 subcategories according to their forms:

1. A(O,C(O,O))

The tree diagram corresponding to this bracket formula is shown in Fig. 3.81.
For example, "花" (/hua/; flower) can be represented as the following tree diagram (Fig. 3.82).
The structure of "花" (/hua/; flower) and "霜" (/shuang/; frost) belong to the same subcategory; both are A(O,C(O,O)).
In addition, there are subcategories with the bracket formula as follows:

2. C(O,A(O,O)): for example, "陪" (/pei/; accompany).
3. C (O, E (O, O)): for example, "缠" (/chan/; twine, tangle).

Fig. 3.82 Tree diagram of "花" (/hua/; flower)

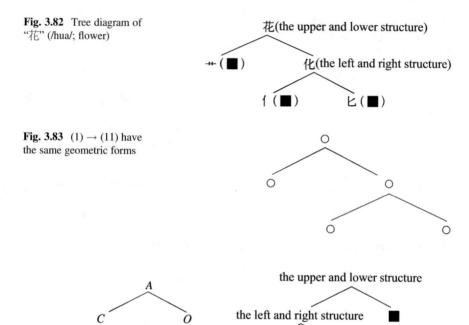

Fig. 3.83 (1) → (11) have the same geometric forms

Fig. 3.84 The tree diagram corresponding to bracket formula A(C(O,O),O)

4. C(O,G(O,O)): for example, "挺" (/ting/; straight, straighten up).
5. C(O,H(O,O)): for example, "润" (/run/; smooth, moist).
6. C(O,I(O,O)): for example, "抠" (/kou/; dig out with a finger).
7. C(O,K(O,O)): for example, "捆" (/kun/; tie, bundle up).
8. E(O,A(O,O)): for example, "庶" (/shu/; numerous, multitudinous, rich, populous).
9. E(O,C(O,O)): for example, "厢" (/xiang/; wing room, compartment).
10. H(O,A(O,O)): for example, "闾" (/lü/; village and town).
11. K(O,A(O,O)): for example, "圄" (/yu/; prison, jail).

The structure of (1) to (11) can be summarized in the following geometric form (Fig. 3.83).

12. A(C(O,O),O)

The corresponding tree diagram is shown in Fig. 3.84.

For example, the structure of the compound character "型" (/xing/; type, mode, model, pattern) is as follows (Fig. 3.85).

13. C(A(O,O),O): for example, "部" (/bu/; part, section).
14. G(A(O,O),O): for example, "逞" (/cheng/; show off, flaunt).
15. G(C(O,O),O): for example, "逊" (/xun/; abdicate, modest).

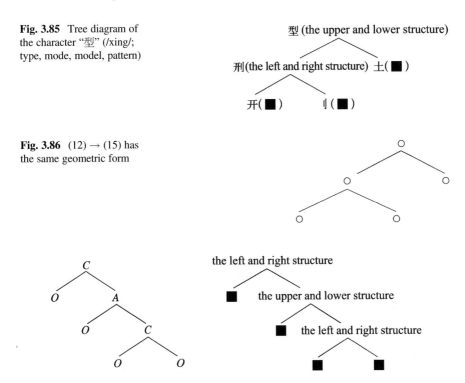

Fig. 3.85 Tree diagram of the character "型" (/xing/; type, mode, model, pattern)

Fig. 3.86 (12) → (15) has the same geometric form

Fig. 3.87 The tree diagram corresponding to the bracket formula C(O,A(O,C(O,O)))

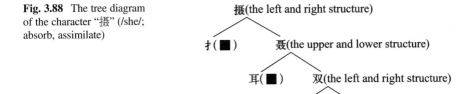

Fig. 3.88 The tree diagram of the character "摄" (/she/; absorb, assimilate)

The structure of (12) → (15) can be summarized into the following geometric form (Fig. 3.86).

2. A formal description of compound characters containing four components

This type can be divided into 19 subcategories:

1. C(O,A(O,C(O,O)))

The tree diagram is shown in Fig. 3.87.

For example, "摄" (/she/; absorb, assimilate) can be represented as the following tree diagram (Fig. 3.88).

Fig. 3.89 A geometric form
of the structure (1) to (6)

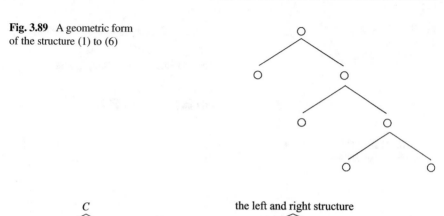

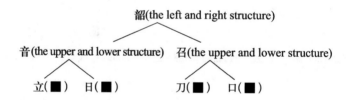

Fig. 3.90 The tree diagram corresponding to the bracket formula C(A(O,O),A(O,O))

韶(the left and right structure)

音(the upper and lower structure)   召(the upper and lower structure)

立(■)   日(■)   刀(■)   口(■)

Fig. 3.91 The tree diagram of "韶" (/shao/; splendid, beautiful)

Besides, there are subcategories, as shown in the following bracket formula:

2. A(O,C(O,A(O,O))): for example, "寤" (/wu/; wake up).
3. A (O, A (O, C (O, O))): for example, "蕊" (/rui/; stamen, pistil).
4. C(O,I(O,C(O,O))): for example, "榧" (/fei/; Chinese torreya).
5. H(O,C(O,A(O,O))): for example, "阔" (/kuo/; wide, extensive).
6. I(O,A(O,E(O,O))): for example, "匿" (/ni/; hide, conceal).

The structure of (1) to (6) can be summarized in the following geometric form (Fig. 3.89).

7. C(A(O,O),A(O,O))

The tree diagram is shown in Fig. 3.90.

For example, "韶" (/shao/; splendid, beautiful) can be represented as the following tree diagram (Fig. 3.91).

Fig. 3.92 Geometric form
of (7) → (10)

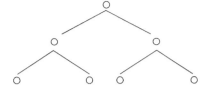

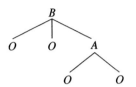

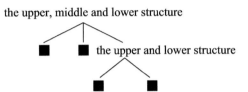

Fig. 3.93 The tree diagram corresponding to bracket formula B (O, O, A (O, O))

Fig. 3.94 The tree diagram
of "营" (/ying/; seek,
manage)

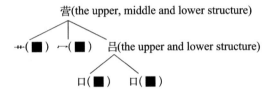

Besides, there are subcategories, as shown in the following bracket formula:

8. A(C(O,O),I(O,O)): for example, "筐" (/kuang/; basket, crate).
9. A(C(O,O),E(O,O)): for example, "嫠" (/li/; widow).
10. C (I (O, O), A (O, O)): for example, "欧" (/ou/; short for Europe).

The structure of (7) → (10) can be reduced to the following geometric form
(Fig. 3.92).

11. B(O,O,A(O,O))

The tree diagram is shown in Fig. 3.93.
For example, the character "营" (/ying/; seek, manage) can be represented as the
following tree diagram (Fig. 3.94).
Besides, there are other subcategories, as shown in the following bracket formula:

12. D(O,O,A(O,O)): for example, "游" (/you/; swim, travel).

The structure of (11) → (12) can be reduced to the following geometric forms
(Fig. 3.95).

13. C(B(O,O,O),O)

The tree diagram is shown in Fig. 3.96.

Fig. 3.95 The geometric
form of (11) → (12)

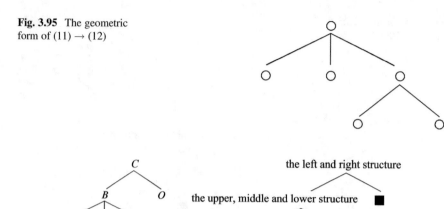

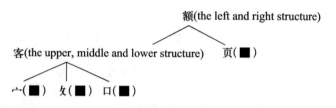

Fig. 3.96 The tree diagram corresponding to the bracket formula C (B(O, O, O), O)

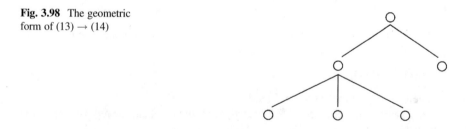

Fig. 3.97 The tree diagram of "额" (/e/; forehead)

Fig. 3.98 The geometric
form of (13) → (14)

For example, the character "额" (/e/; forehead) can be represented as the tree diagram (Fig. 3.97).

Besides, there is another subcategory as shown in the following formula:

14. A(D(O,O,O),O): for example, "辔" (/pei/; bridle).

The structure of (13) → (14) can be summarized in Fig. 3.98.

Another subcategory is shown in the following bracket formula:

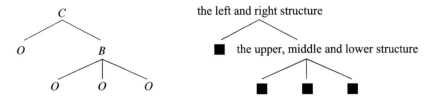

Fig. 3.99   The tree diagram corresponding to the bracket formula C(O,B(O,O,O))

Fig. 3.100   Tree diagram of "樟" (/zhang/; camphor wood)

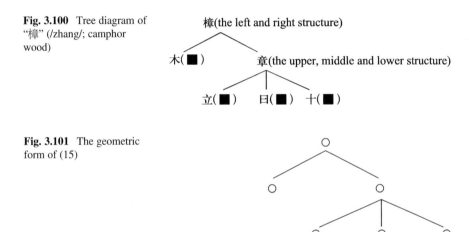

Fig. 3.101   The geometric form of (15)

15. C(O,B(O,O,O))

The tree diagram is shown in Fig. 3.99.

For example, the character "樟" (/zhang/; camphor wood) can be represented as the following tree diagram (Fig. 3.100).

The geometric form is abstracted as follows (Fig. 3.101).

Another subcategory is shown in the following bracket formula, and the tree diagram is shown in Fig. 3.102.

16. A(O,A(C(O,O),O))

For example, the character "荜" (/bi/; Indian long pepper) can be represented in Fig. 3.103.

Besides, there are subcategories, as shown in the following bracket formula:

17. C(O,A(C(O,O),O)): "燃" (/ran/; burn, ignite, light).
18. E(O,A(C(O,O),O)): "腐" (/fu/; rotten, putrid).

The structure of (16) → (18) can be summarized in Fig. 3.104.

There is another subcategory as shown in the following:

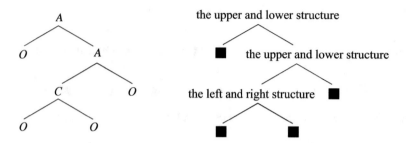

Fig. 3.102 The tree diagram corresponding to the bracket formula A(O,A(C(O,O),O))

Fig. 3.103 The tree
diagram of "荜" (/bi/; Indian
long pepper)

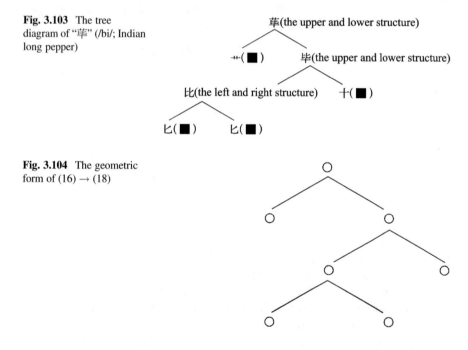

Fig. 3.104 The geometric
form of (16) → (18)

19. G (E (O, A (O, O)), O): for example, "遮" (/zhe/; hide from view, cover up).

To make sure that the readers have understood our approach, we suggest that the readers make a tree diagram of this Chinese character. In the following discussion, we no longer make tree diagrams to save space. We only write the bracket formula of Chinese characters.

3. A formal description of compound characters containing five components

The compound characters containing five components can be divided into 19 subcategories, the form of which is described in the bracket formula as follows:

1. C(O,B(O,C(O,O),O)): for example, "澡" (/zao/; bath).
2. A(O,B(O,A(O,O),O)): for example, "膏" (/gao/; oil, cream).
3. C (O, B (O, O, H (O, O))): for example, "搞" (/gao/; do, be engaged in).
4. A (O, B (O, O, H (O, O))): for example, "蒿" (/hao/; wormwood).
5. C(O,A(C(O,O),C(O,O))): for example, "缀" (/zhui/; sew up, link up).
6. E(O,A(C(O,O),G(O,O))): for example, "魔" (/mo/; devil, demon, magic).
7. D (O, B (O, O, O), O): for example, "渤" (/bo/; Bohai Sea).
8. C(B(O,O,H(O,O)),O): for example, "敲" (/qiao/; knock, strike, beat).
9. A(D(O,A(O,O),O),O): for example, "樊" (/fan/; fence).
10. B(C(O,O),O,C(O,O)): for example, "嚣" (/xiao/; clamor, hubhub).
11. C(A(O,D(O,O,O)),O): for example, "鄑" (/ling/; name of a country in ancient China).
12. C (A (O, O), B (O, O, O)): for example, "蹊" (/xi/; footpath).
13. C (A (C (O, O), C (O, O)), O): for example, "戳" (/chuo/; jab, poke, stamp).
14. A(C(O,O),A(C(O,O),O)): for example, "篮" (/lan/; basket).
15. A(O,C(O,B(O,O,O))): for example, "寝" (/qin/; sleep, bedroom).
16. C (O, E (O, A (O, C (O, O))): for example, "漉" (/lu/; seep through, filter).
17. C(B(O,O,O),A(O,O)): for example, "毂" (/gu/; hub).
18. B (O, O, D (O, O, O)): for example, "赢" (/ying/; win, gain).
19. A(O,G(E(O,A(O,O)),O)): for example, "蘧" (/qu/; pleasantly surprised).

4. A formal description of compound characters containing six components

The compound characters containing six components can be divided into ten subcategories, and the form description is shown in the following bracket formula:

1. C(A(F(O,O), F(O,O)), A(O,O)): for example, "歌" (/ge/; song, sing).
2. A (C (I (O, O), A (O, O)), C (O, O)): for example, "翳" (/yi/; cover, hide).
3. C(B(O,O,O),B(O,O,O)): for example, "豁" (/huo/; slit, break, crack).
4. A(C(O,O),E(O,A(O,C(O,O)))): for example, "麓" (/lu/; foot of a hill or a mountain).
5. C(B(O,O,O), A(O,C(O,O))): for example, "豌" (/wan/; pea).
6. A(C(E(O,A(O,O)),A(O,O)),O): for example, "臀" (/tun/; buttocks).
7. C (O, B (O, O, D (O, O, O))): for example, "瀛" (/ying/; sea, big sea, the world).
8. D (O, A (C (O, O), C (O, O)), O): for example, "衢" (/qu/; road extending in all directions).
9. C (O, B (C (O, O), O, A (O, O))): for example, "骥" (/ji/; fine horse).
10. C (O, B (O, C (O, O), C (O, O)): for example, "灌" (/guan/; irrigate, pour).

5. A formal description of compound characters containing seven components

The compound characters containing seven components can be divided into four subcategories, and the form description is shown in the bracket formula as follows:

1. A(C(B(O,O,O),B(O,O,O)),O):   for   example,   "戆"   (/gang/;   upright   and outspoken).
2. C(E(O,A(O,C(O,O))),A(O,C(O,O))): for example, "麟" (/lin/; unicorn)

3. A(C(A(O,O),E(O,A(O,O)))),A(O,O)): for example, "饕" (/tao/; gourmand, vora-
   cious eater).
4. C (A (O, O), B (O, C (O, O), A (O, O))): for example, "馕" (/nang/; a kind of
   crusty pancake).

6. A formal description of compound characters containing eight and nine
   components

There is only one subcategory for compound characters containing eight components, and there is also only one subcategory for compound characters containing
nine components. The form description is shown in the bracket formula as follows:
   The bracket formula for compound characters containing eight components is

C(B(O,O,O),B(O,C(O,O),A(O,O))): for example, "齉" (/nang/; snuffling).

The bracket formula for compound characters containing nine components is.

C(B(O,O,B(O,O,O)),A(C(O,A(O,O)),O)): for example, "懿" (/yi/; virtuous, moral).

In a word, we can use the formal model of context-free grammar to describe the
structure of Chinese characters. Using a method similar to syntactic analysis, the
Chinese characters are represented either as a tree diagram or as corresponding
bracket formula. In this way, we can automatically analyze or process Chinese
characters, thus promoting the research of Chinese NLP.

Of course, this method is also beneficial to the teaching of Chinese characters to
those whose mother tongue is not Chinese.

3.14   Hausser's Left-Associative Grammar

Roland Hausser (Fig. 3.105), the founder of left-associative grammar (LA), is a
professor of computational linguistics at the University of Erlangen-Nuremberg,
Germany.

He is the author of several books, such as *Surface Compositional Grammar,
Foundations of Computational Linguistics: Human-Computer Communication in
Natural Language*, and *A Computational Model of Natural Language Communication: Interpretation, Inference, and Production in Database Semantics*. He also
published nearly 100 articles. After he created left-associative grammar, he further
proposed database semantics (DBS) and the theory of surface compositional linear
internal matching (SLIM) and established his own unique style in the field of
computational linguistics.

Hausser and I once met in 2002 when the Korean National Commission for
UNESCO held an academic seminar on "Language Issues in the Information Age" in
Seoul, South Korea. Both Hausser and I were both invited to participate in this
seminar and talked during the meeting, during which I had a preliminary understanding of Hausser's unique theory.

Fig. 3.105 R. Hausser

After returning to China, I read his book *Foundations of Computational Linguistics: Human-Computer Communication in Natural Language* and got a further understanding of his theory. In my opinion, Hausser is a computational linguist with an original spirit.

In 2006, Hausser published *A Computational Model of Natural Language Communication: Interpretation, Inference, and Production in Database Semantics.*[15] In this book, he systematically analyzes the main structures of natural languages. Taking English as an example, he analyzes the schematic derivation in the hearer mode and the speaker mode. The analysis in the hearer mode focuses on how to encode the hypotaxis and parataxis as propositional factors in strict linear temporal order and how to analyze the co-reference as a secondary relation based on inference. The analysis in the speaker mode discusses how to perform automatic navigation within the lexicon based on extracted content, how to output the correct word forms and word order according to the grammatical requirements of the corresponding language, how to parse out the appropriate function words, etc. In this book, Hausser builds an English communication system with complete functions but limited coverage, which provides us with a functional framework for theoretical analysis of natural language communication.

Hausser believes that the central task of future-oriented computational linguistics is to study a cognitive machine where humans can communicate freely with computers in their own languages. Therefore, the human-computer communication of natural languages should be the central task of computational linguistics. The research of computational linguistics should model the process of speaker's language generation and hearer's interpretation of language and copy the natural

---

[15] R. Hausser, *A Computational Model of Natural Language Communication: Interpretation, Inference, and Production in Database Semantics*, Springer-Verlag, Berlin, 2006

transmission process of information on the appropriate computer, to construct an autonomous cognitive machine that can communicate freely with humans in natural languages, which is called a robot. To achieve this goal, we must have a deep understanding of the functional model of a natural language communication mechanism.

Hausser's theory of "surface compositionality, time linearity, and internal matching" (SLIM) takes humans as the subject of human-computer communication instead of linguistic symbols, highlighting the dominant role of humans in human-computer communication. The SLIM theory requires the use of fully explicit machinery steps, using logical and electronic means to explain the natural language understanding and natural language generation process. Therefore, the SLIM theory is different from the theories of structuralism, behaviorism, speech act, etc. in modern linguistics and has obvious innovative characteristics.

The SLIM theory emphasizes "surface elements," and its methodological principle is the surface composability. The SLIM theory emphasizes "linear" and uses linear time as its empirical principle. The SLIM theory emphasizes the internal factors of language, taking the internal factors of language as its ontological principle. The SLIM theory emphasizes matching, taking the matching between language and context information as its functional principle. In fact, the acronym SLIM itself comes from the name of these four principles of "surface composition," "linearity," "internal factors," and "matching."

The technical implementation of the SLIM theory is called "database semantics" (DBS). DBS is a rule system that reconstructs natural language understanding and generation into "turn-taking." Turn-taking refers to the conversion from "speaker mode" to "listener mode" or from "listener mode" to "speaker mode."

In the actual communication process of natural languages, the first process is that the natural subject in the listener mode obtains information from another subject or context. The second process is that the natural subject analyzes the information in his own cognition. The third process is that the natural subject thinks about how to respond. The fourth process is that the natural subject makes feedback with language or action.

The input of DBS is similar to the first process, which requires a computer or robot with an external interface. Next, match the contextual and cognitive content, and simulate the second process by using left-associative grammar (LA). This left-associative grammar is in the listener mode, called LA hear. The second variant of left-associative grammar is responsible for searching the appropriate content in the memory lexicon, called LA think. This part of the operation corresponds to the third process. The task of the third variant of left-associative grammar is language generation, called LA speak, which simulates the fourth process as shown below (Fig. 3.106).

In the above figure, the LA hear in the listener mode simulates the second process. The LA think in the speaker mode simulates the third process, and the LA speak simulates the fourth process.

Fig. 3.106 Turn-taking system

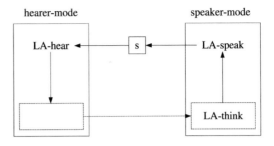

Fig. 3.107 Phrase structure tree

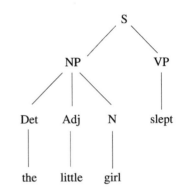

The analysis result of DBS is represented by the DBS graph. The DBS graph is a tree structure, but it is different from the tree structure of phrase structure grammar and dependency grammar.

For example, the English sentence "The little girl slept" is analyzed in phrase structure grammar, and the tree structure is shown in Fig. 3.107.

In the tree structure of this phrase structure grammar, S (sentence) is composed of NP (noun phrase) and VP (verb phrase). NP is composed of DET (determiner), ADJ (adjective), and N (noun), which correspond to the words *the*, *little*, and *girl*. VP corresponds to the word *slept*. The sentence hierarchical and the linear relationship between the words are very clear, but the relationship between the NP and VP that make up S is not clear. It is not stated which one is the head word. The relationship between the DET, ADJ, and N that make up NP is also not clear, which is the head word is not stated. The head of each component in the sentence is not prominent.

The tree structure after analysis with dependency grammar is as follows (Fig. 3.108).

In this tree structure of dependency grammar, all the nodes are specific words, and there are no nodes representing categories such as S, NP, VP, DET, ADJ, N, etc. The dependency relationship between each word is clear. This dependency relationship is binary, and the dominator is the head word and the subordinate word of the dominated. However, the linear order between words is not as clear as the tree structure of phrase structure grammar.

The tree structure after analysis with DBS graph is shown in Fig. 3.109.

Fig. 3.108 Dependency
structure tree

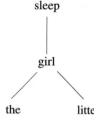

Fig. 3.109 DBS tree
structure

In the tree structure of the DBS graph, the emphasis is on the analysis of the language content. Therefore, there is no node representing the definite article *the*, and the words on the node are all represented by prototype words. The most prominent feature of the DBS diagram is that the connection between nodes in the tree structure of the DBS diagram has its own clear meaning. The connection not only represents the dependency relationship between nodes but also represents different functions according to the different connection directions: vertical line "|" indicates the modifier-modified relationship. For example, in the figure above, *little* and *girl* are connected with a vertical line to indicate that *little* modifies *girl*. The left slash "/" represents the subject-verb relationship. For example, in the figure above, *girl* and *sleep* are connected by a left slash, indicating that *girl* is the subject of *sleep*. Besides, the right slash "\" is also used to indicate the object-verb relationship, and the horizontal line "—"is used to indicate the coordinate relationship. Since different connection directions can represent different functions, such a tree structure represents much more information than the tree structure of phrase structure grammar and that of dependency grammar. This is the most attractive feature of the DBS tree structure.

The above DBS graph shows *little* as the modifier of *girl* and *girl* as the subject of *sleep*, which expresses the semantic relationship between the words in the sentence. Therefore, Hausser calls such a DBS diagram "the semantic relations graph" (SRG).

If the word on each node in the DBS graph is replaced with letters representing their parts of speech, then the semantic relations graph becomes the "part-of-speech signature" (abbreviated as signature). The part-of-speech signature of the previous sentence is shown in Fig. 3.110.

The semantic relations graph and the part-of-speech signature are different representations of the same sentence. They represent the same content in different forms.

Fig. 3.110 The part-of-speech signature

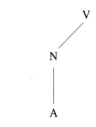

Fig. 3.111 Semantic relationship graph

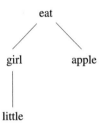

Fig. 3.112 The part-of-speech signature

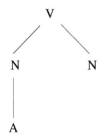

Hausser also proposed two other graphs in his book in 2011: one is the "numbered arc graph" (NAG), and the other is the "surface realization graph." These two graphs respectively show the process and results of how to generate language from the content. The numbered arc graph represents the time linear sequence of activating the semantic relations graph, that is to say, the numbered arc graph can be said to be a semantic relations graph with an added numbered arc to some extent. The surface realization graph shows how to generate the surface form of the language in traversal order.

For example, the semantic relations graph of the English sentence "The little girl ate an apple" is shown in Fig. 3.111.

Since the semantic relations graph (SRG) only represents the content of the sentence, in this SRG, there is no node representing the definite article *the*, nor the node of the indefinite article *an*. The past tense form *ate* is presented as its infinitive verb form *eat*.

In this part-of-speech signature, the words on the node replace the letters that represent their part of speech (Fig. 3.112).

Fig. 3.113 Numbered arc graph

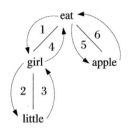

Fig. 3.114 Surface realization graph

1	2	3	4	5	6
The	little	girl	ate	an_apple	•

In this signature, the words on the nodes all replace the letters that represent their parts of speech.

The numbered arc graph (NAG) of this sentence is shown in Fig. 3.113.

Since the numbered arc graph (NAG) is to represent the time linear order of activating semantic relations graph, this time sequence is represented by a numbered arc, which is indicated by a dotted line, and the linear order of time is labeled with a number beside the dotted line: the node *eat* first activates the node *girl* (numbered arc 1); then, the node *girl* activates the node *little* (numbered arc 2). Because the vertical line "|" is used between them, it can be deduced that *little* modifies *girl* (numbered arc 3). Since the node *girl* is connected with the node *girl* with a left slash "/," it can be deduced that *girl* is the subject of *eat* (numbered arc 4); then the node *eat* activates the node *apple* (numbered arc 5). Because a right slash is used between the node *apple* and the node *eat*, it can be deduced that *apple* is the object of *eat* (numbered arc 6). It can be seen that the direction of all numbered arcs representing derivation is bottom-up.

The surface realization graph of the sentence is shown in Fig. 3.114.

These numbers in this surface realization graph indicate the order in which words are generated.

Database semantics (DBS) has two foundations: one is LA grammar, and the other is word bank. LA grammar and word bank are closely integrated with DBS. Hausser compares LA grammar to a locomotive and a word bank to the railway system necessary for train operation.

The word bank stores the contents of words, and its storage form is a non-recursive feature structure called "proplets." The English word "proplet" is taken from the "proposition droplet," which indicates the component of the proposition.

A proplet is a set of "attribute-value pairs." The syntactic and semantic information of each word or sentence element is reflected in the corresponding attribute-value matrix. For example, the attribute-value matrix of the Chinese word "学生" (/xue sheng/; student) is shown in Fig. 3.115.

Such an attribute-value matrix is the "Proplets" of the word bank.

Fig. 3.115 Attribute-value matrix

$$
\begin{bmatrix}
\text{sur} & : & 学生 \\
\text{pyn} & : & \text{xuesheng} \\
\text{noun} & : & \text{student} \\
\text{cat} & : & \text{nr} \\
\text{scm} & : & \text{pl} \\
\text{fnc} & : & \\
\text{mdr} & : & \\
\text{pm} & : & \\
\end{bmatrix}
$$

Fig. 3.116 The calculation process of left-associative grammar

$$
\begin{aligned}
&a \\
&(a) + b \\
&(a + b) + c \\
&(a + b + c) + d \\
&\cdots
\end{aligned}
$$

Left-associative grammar is a method of analysis and calculation from left to right in accordance with the time linear order of natural languages.

Specifically, the first word of each sentence is the first "sentence start" in the entire sentence analysis process, and then input the "next word," and the two are calculated to form a new sentence start, and then it continues to combine with the next input word. This analysis continues until the end of a sentence or a grammatical error occurs. In the case of syntactic or lexical ambiguity, left-associative grammar allows the calculation to continue in parallel on different deduced paths.

Hausser made a comparative analysis of left-associative grammar and phrase structure grammar. He pointed out that left-associative grammar and phrase structure grammar are homogeneous language analysis methods. The difference between them is that phrase structure grammar is based on the "principle of substitution," while left-associative grammar is based on the "the principle of continuation." If "a, b, c, etc." are used to represent language symbols and "+" is used to represent the concatenation, then the calculation process of left-associative grammar can be expressed in Fig. 3.116.

When left-associative grammar is used in a derivation, it always combines words one by one and step-by-step along the left side of the tree structure in the order from left to right and bottom up. The derivation sequence in the tree structure is shown in Fig. 3.117.

Fig. 3.117 Derivation
sequence in the tree
structure

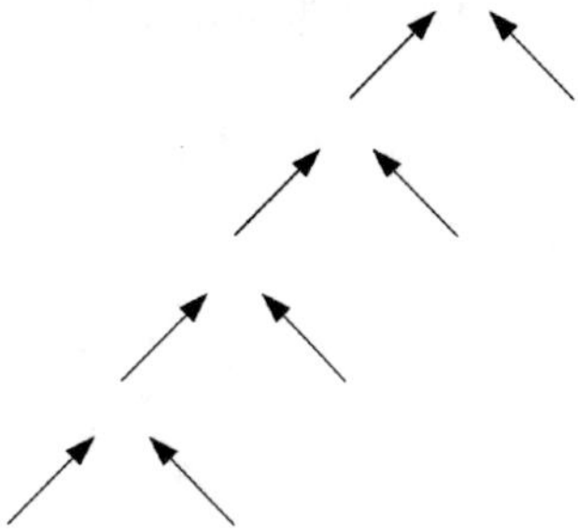

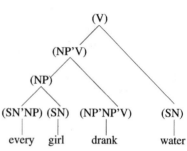

Fig. 3.118 Example of
derivation sequence

(V)

(NP'V)

(NP)

(SN'NP) (SN)   (NP'NP'V)   (SN)

every   girl   drank   water

For example, the derivation sequence of the English sentence "Every girl drunk water" is shown in Fig. 3.118.

It can be seen from this tree structure that the derivation starts from the left. Firstly, *every* and *girl* are combined to form (np), then (np) and *drank* are combined to form (np'v), and finally (np' v) and (sn) are combined to form (v).

The whole derivation process follows the principle of time linearity. The so-called time linearity is linear like time and in the direction of time, that is to say, the derivation should be in the order of time and should be pushed forward along the direction of time.

Obviously, left-associative grammar is a formal model based on phrase structure grammar and at the same time has absorbed some advantages of dependency grammar and database semantics. It has its own obvious innovative features.

Bibliography

1. Chomsky, N. 1956. Three Models for the Description of Language. *IRE Transaction on Information Theory* 2 (3): 113–124.
2. ———. 1957. *Syntactic Structure*. The Hague: Mouton.
3. Chomsky, N., and G.A. Miller. 1958. Finite-State Languages. *Information and Control* 1: 91–112.
4. Chomsky, N. 1959. On Certain Formal Properties of Grammars. *Information and Control* 2: 137–167.

5. ———. 1963. Formal Properties of Grammars. In *Handbook of Mathematical Psychology*, ed. R.D. Luce, R. Bush, and E. Galanter, vol. 2, 323–418. New York: Wiley.

6. ———. 1965. *Aspects of the Theory of Syntax*. Cambridge, MA: MIT Press.

7. ———. 1981. *Lectures on Government and Binding*. Dordrecht: Foris.

8. ———. 1995. *The Minimalist Program*. Cambridge: MIT Press.

9. Earley, J. 1968. *An Efficient Context-Free Parsing Algorithm. Ph.D. Thesis*. Pittsburgh, PA: Carnegie Mellon University.

10. Gang, Wu. 2006. *Generative Grammar Research*. Shanghai: Shanghai Foreign Language Education Press.

11. Humboldt, W. 1997. *On the Difference of Human Language Structure and Its Influence on the Development of Human Spirit* (printed separately in 1836). Chinese translation (translated by Xiaoping Yao). Beijing: Commercial Press.

12. Joshi, A.K., L.S. Levy, and M. Takahashi. 1975. Tree Adjunct Grammars. *Journal of Computer and System Sciences* 10 (1): 55–75.

13. Kay, M. 1980. Algorithm Schemata and Data Structure in Syntactic Processing. In *Proceedings of the Nobel Symposium on Text Processing*. Gothenburg.

14. Woods, W.A. 1970. Transition Network Grammar in Natural Language Analysis. *Communication of the ACM* 13.

15. Wundt, W. 1900. Völkerpsychologie: eine Untersuchung der Entwilcklungsgesetz von Sprache, Mythus, und Sitte. In *Band ii: Die Sprache*. Leipzig: Zweiter Teil.

16. Zhiwei, Feng. 1979. Formal Language Theory. *Computer Science* 1.

17. ———. 1982. From Formal Language Theory to Generative Transformation Grammar. In *Linguistic Research Collection*. Tianjin: Tianjin People's Publishing House.

18. ———. 1994. *Die chinesiscnen Schriftzeichen in Vergangenheit und Gegenwart*. Trier: Wissenschaftlicher Verlag Trier.

19. ———. 2002. Chart Analysis Method. *Contemporary Linguistics* 4.

20. ———. 2003. A Natural Language Analysis Algorithm Without Backtracking. *Language and Character Application* 1.

21. ———. 2006. Using Context-Free Grammar to Describe the Structure of Chinese Characters. *Linguistic Sciences* 5 (3).

22. ———. 2012. *A Concise Course of Natural Language Processing*. Shanghai: Shanghai Foreign Language Education Press.

23. ———. 2013. *Modern Linguistic Schools (Revised Edition)*. Beijing: Commercial Press.

Chapter 4
Formal Models Based on Unification

In the development of NLP, the earliest automatic grammatical analysis theory was phrase structure grammar proposed by American linguist N. Chomsky. Because phrase structure grammar makes the generation of natural language sentences computable, this language theory has been widely used in the computer processing of the natural language.

However, people soon discovered that there are many limitations in phrase structure grammar. The most serious problem is that its generative power is too strong, its ability to distinguish the ambiguous structure is very poor, and it often generates a large number of ambiguous or unqualified sentences. Therefore, scholars have developed new grammatical theories that can avoid these limitations, such as Chinese information MMT model, lexical functional grammar, functional unification grammar, generalized phrase structure grammar, PATR, head-driven phrase structure grammar, definite clause grammar, and so on. In this chapter, we introduce these formal models of natural language processing.

The common feature of these formal models is to use the unification method based on complex features. When unifying, the compatibility of complex features is checked. If they are compatible, unification can be performed. If complex features are incompatible, they cannot be unified. This limits the generation ability of formal grammar and improves the descriptive ability of formal grammar.

4.1 Multiple-Branched and Multiple-Labeled Tree Analysis (MMT)

Chinese scholar Zhiwei Feng introduced the essence of L. Tesnière's dependency grammar and German valence grammar into the research of Chinese-foreign multilingual machine translation research. In view of the weakness of N. Chomsky's phrase structure grammar and the characteristics of Chinese grammar, he proposed

© Springer Nature Singapore Pte Ltd. 2023
Z. Feng, *Formal Analysis for Natural Language Processing: A Handbook*,
https://doi.org/10.1007/978-981-16-5172-4_4

"multiple-branched and multiple-labeled tree analysis" in the early 1980s, which is also known as the "Chinese information MMT model." This model is the earliest attempt of Chinese scholars to study the formal model of NLP.

To improve a binary tree in phrase structure grammar of N. Chomsky, MMT model uses the multiple-branched tree instead of the binary tree.

A multiple-branched tree is a tree diagram with more than two forks on the same node.

Since natural languages usually have the characteristic of dichotomy, binary trees are generally used to describe the hierarchical structure and linear order of natural languages. For example, the subject-predicate structure in Chinese consists of two parts, subject and predicate. The predicate-object structure consists of two parts, the predicate and the object. The modifier-head structure consists of two parts, the modifier and the head. These structures can be described by binary trees.

However, many grammatical forms in Chinese are not easy to describe with binary trees but should be described with the multiple-branched tree. The following are some examples:

1. Pivotal structures

    In the Chinese sentence "我们 | 请 | 他 | 做报告" (/Wo men | qing | ta | zuo bao gao/; We | ask | him | to give a report). 他 (/ta/; he) is the object of 请 (/qing/; ask) and the subject of 做报告 (/zuo bao gao/; give a report). If it is represented by a binary tree, it will overlap, but it is clearly described by a multiple branched tree.
2. Adverbial predicate-object structures

    In the Chinese sentence "努力 | 学习 | 英语" (/Nu li | xue xi | ying yu/; hard | study | English/Study English hard), if it is represented by a binary tree, should it be divided into "努力 | 学习英语" (/Nu li | xue xi ying yu/; hard | study English) first, or should it be divided into "努力学习 | 英语" (/Nu li xue xi | ying yu/; hard study | English) first? Often, people hesitate, and the difficulty of binary tree description can be avoided if it is divided into three parts with a multiple branched tree: "努力 | 学习 | 英语" (/Nu li | xue xi | ying yu/; hard | study | English/Study English hard).
3. Double-object structures

    In the Chinese sentence "给 | 弟弟 | 一本书" (/Gei | di di | yi ben shu/; give | the younger brother | a book), because the verb "给" (/gei/; give) has two objects, it is difficult to describe it by a binary tree but should be described by a multiple branched tree.

Therefore, the characteristics of Chinese determine that it is best to use the multiple-branched tree to describe its sentence structures.

Adopting multiple branched trees can also reduce the amount of programming. Some long sentences, if described by a binary tree, will have as many as ten and eight layers. When the computer processes a multiple-branched tree like this, it needs to be done layer by layer, and the amount of calculation is very large. If described by the multiple-branched tree, the number of the layer is greatly reduced, and the efficiency is improved.

The use of the multiple-branched tree is also conducive to grasping the backbone of the sentence and clearly showing the pattern of the sentence, which is convenient to study and check.

If the multiple-branched tree diagram is regarded as a universal tree format, then the binary tree is a special case of the multiple-branched tree diagram. The so-called multiple branched can be "three-branched," "four-branched," "two-branched," or "one branched." It is a more general form, and "two-branched" is just a special case of "multiple-branched" when the "multiple" of "branch" equals "two."

MMT model also puts forward the concept of the multi-value labeled function of the tree, which uses multiple labels to describe the characteristics of nodes in the tree.

The tree diagram in N. Chomsky's phrase structure grammar is mono-labeled, which makes it difficult for phrase structure grammar to express complicated natural language phenomena, and its analysis ability is too weak and the generation ability is too strong. To overcome this weakness of phrase structure grammar, the MMT model advocates changing the mono-labeled to multiple labels.

In the tree diagram, the function that makes a node correspond to multiple labels is called a multi-value labeled function, denoted as L.

The multi-value labeled function L of the tree diagram can be expressed as follows.

$$L(X) = \begin{pmatrix} y_1 \\ y_2 \\ \cdot \\ \cdot \\ \cdot \\ y_n \end{pmatrix}$$

where X represents a node and $y_1, y_2, \ldots, y_n$ represents the label. For a node X, the function L can map multiple labels $y_1, y_2, \ldots, y_n$ to correspond to it.

Multi-value labeled functions are particularly suitable for describing Chinese, because of the following reasons.

1. There is no simple one-to-one correspondence between phrase types (or parts of speech) and syntactic functions in Chinese sentences. Therefore when describing Chinese sentences, we must give not only the part of speech or phrase type characteristics of its components but also syntactic functional characteristics, so as to avoid ambiguity.

   For example, a noun N plus a verb V can form a subject-predicate structure (such as "小孩/咳嗽" (/xiao hai | ke sou/; child | cough)) and a modifier-head structure (such as "程序/设计" (/cheng xu | she ji/; program | design)). If only N+V is used to describe these structures, it is ambiguous in the syntactic function. We must use a multi-value labeled function, and a subject-predicate structure is N+V, as shown below.

$$\left(\begin{pmatrix} CAT = N \\ \\ SF = SUBJ \end{pmatrix} + \begin{pmatrix} CAT = V \\ \\ SF = PRED \end{pmatrix} \right)$$

where CAT represents the part of speech feature, N and V are the value of CAT, SF represents the syntactic function feature, SUBJ (subject) and PRED (predicate) are the value of SF. So, in the first node, there are two values CAT=N and FS=SUBJ, and there are two values CAT=V and SF=PRED on the second node.

Similarly, the modifier-head structure, which is also N+V, can be described as follows:

$$\left(\begin{pmatrix} CAT = N \\ \\ SF = MODE \end{pmatrix} + \begin{pmatrix} CAT = V \\ \\ SF = HEAD \end{pmatrix} \right)$$

where MODE stands for the modifier, HEAD stands for head, and they are both the value of SF. Thus, there are two values CAT=N and SF=MODF on the first node, and there are two values CAT=V and SF=HEAD on the second node. It can be seen that the use of multi-value labeled function can separate the ambiguity structure N+V into two structures with different syntactic functions, which eliminates ambiguity.

2. Components with the same phrase type (or part of speech) and syntactic function in a Chinese sentence may have different semantic relations with other components in the sentence, and there is no simple one-to-one correspondence between syntactic function and semantic relation. Therefore, when describing Chinese sentences, in addition to the characteristics of the phrase type (or part of speech) and the syntactic function of its constituent components, the semantic relation characteristics should also be given to distinguish them.

For example, if we regard a noun N plus a verb V as a subject-predicate structure with the possibility of being the modifier-head structure in the syntactic function excluded, the N as the subject can be the agent (such as "小王" (/Xiao Wang/) in "小王/工作" (/Xiao Wang | gong zuo/; Xiao Wang | work). It can also be the patient (such as "火车票" (/huo che piao/; train ticket) in "火车票/丢了" (/Huo che piao | diu le/; train ticket | lost). It can also be the result (such as "文章" (/wen zhang/; article) in "文章/写好了" (/Wen zhang | xie hao le/; article | finished). It can also be a tool (such as "左手" (/zuo shou/; left hand) and "右手" (/you shou/; right hand) in "左手/拿纸" (/zuo shou | na zhi/; left hand | holding paper), "右手/拿笔" (/you shou | na bi/; right hand | holding pen). Therefore, in the automatic analysis of Chinese, semantic relation characteristics should also be added so that more labels correspond to the nodes in the tree diagram.

3. The inherent grammatical and semantic features of Chinese words are often of great reference value for judging the nature of the phrase structure. Therefore, in addition to simple features such as the type of phrase (or part of speech) labeled on the nodes of the tree diagram, the inherent grammatical and semantic features of words are labeled, and multiple labels are used to judge the nature of phrases. For example, in the sentence "文章/写好了" (/Wen zhang | xie hao le/; article | finished), if we know that the agent of the verb "写" (/xie/; write) is "a living

person" and the result of "写" (/xie/; write) is "an inanimate cultural product", and we also know that the semantic feature of "写" (/xie/; write) is "inanimate cultural product", then it can be judged that "文章(/wen zhang/; article)" is the result of "写" (/xie/; write).

It can be seen that when the tree diagram analysis method is used to describe Chinese automatically if the multi-value labeled functions are used, the effectiveness of this analysis method can be greatly improved. This multi-value labeled function is a "complex feature set." The MMT model is an important improvement made by Chinese scholars to the N. Chomsky phrase structure grammar. It is a formal model developed by the Chinese-to-foreign language machine translation system and the German-Chinese and French-Chinese machine translation system and other natural language processing systems in the 1980s.

MMT model uses several features and their values to describe Chinese. The complex feature set of Chinese contains several features, and each feature contains several values. This description system consisting of features and their values is called a "feature/value" system. Each language has its own "feature/value" system. Different languages have different "feature/value" systems.

Based on Zhiwei Feng's experience in designing machine translation systems such as FAJRA (Chinese-French\English\Japanese\Russian\German), GCAT (German-Chinese), and FCAT (French-Chinese), he believes that for the automatic analysis and generation of Chinese, the following "feature/value" system can be used.

1. Part of Speech Features and Its Value

Part of speech is one of the complex features that describe Chinese sentences and is labeled as CAT.

CAT can take the following values: nouns, locative words, directive words, time words, distinguishing words, numerals, classifiers, nominative pronouns, predicative pronouns, verbs, adjectives, adverbs, prepositions, conjunctions, auxiliary words, modal particles, onomatopoeias, and exclamations.

For the convenience of computer processing, we also count punctuation marks and formulas as part of speech, so there are 20 parts of speech in Chinese, which are features. CAT can take 20 values.

Each feature value can also take sub-values for further classification. For example, Chinese adjectives can be further divided into two sub-categories, state adjectives and qualitative adjectives. That is to say, the value of adjectives can also take two sub-values: state adjectives and qualitative adjectives. The value of a feature and its sub-values can be regarded as a secondary "feature/value" pair, that is, the value can be regarded as the feature in the secondary "feature/value" pair and the sub-value of the value is regarded as the value in a secondary "feature/value" pair. This means that when there are sub-values, the "value" itself in the "feature/value" pair can also be a secondary "feature/value" pair.

2. Phrase Type Characteristics and its Value

Phrase type is another feature describing Chinese, denoted as K.

The values of K can be verb phrases, noun phrases, adjective phrases, and number phrases, four values in total.

The MMT model incorporates the prepositional phrase in traditional grammar into the noun phrase, because from the perspective of information processing, the preposition in the prepositional phrase is just a sign of the function of the noun phrase behind it, and it is more convenient if it is incorporated into the noun phrase.

3. The Inherent Semantic Features of a Word and Its Value

The inherent semantic feature of words is the semantic category of words, which represents the semantics of isolated words, rather than the semantic relationship between words. The inherent semantic features of words are recorded as SEM.

SEM can take the following values and sub-values:

Objects: its sub-values are the animate, inanimate, organization, and category name.

Materials: its sub-values are equipment, products, and raw materials.

Phenomenon: its sub-values are a natural phenomenon, artificial phenomenon, social phenomenon, and force-energy phenomenon.

Time and space: its sub-values are time and space.

Measure: its sub-values are quantity, unit, and standard.

Abstract: its sub-values are knowledge, concepts, and symbols.

Attribute: its sub-values are property, shape, relationship, and structure.

Action: its sub-values are behaviors, actions, and operations.

These inherent semantic features are labeled on the isolated words in the dictionary and become the inherent semantic attributes of the words themselves. Zhiwei Feng later proposed a better semantic classification system Ontol-MT from the perspective of ontology.

4. The Inherent Grammatical Features of Words and Their Values

Isolated words also have grammatical features. For example, different nouns require different classifiers. Therefore, they have classifier features which are inherent grammatical features. The transitivity of different verbs is different, so transitivity is the inherent grammatical feature of the verb; the "valence" of different verbs is not the same. Therefore, "valence" is another inherent grammatical feature of verbs. "Valence" reflects the requirements of the verb for the words before and after it, but it is the attribute of the verb itself. Therefore, the MMT model regards it as the inherent grammatical features of verbs.

The inherent grammatical features of words are denoted as GRM.

The value of a grammatical feature can also have sub-values. In this case, the value and its sub-values can be treated as "feature/value" pairs. For example, the value of transitivity of the inherent grammatical feature of verbs has two sub-values: "transitive" and "intransitive." We can regard transitivity (denoted as TRANS) as the feature and transitive (denoted as TV) and intransitive (denoted as IV) as the value of this feature. So we get TRANS=TV and TRANS=IV.

"Valence" can also take sub-values: one valence, two valences, and three valences. One-valent verbs can only have one subject, such as "咳嗽" (/ke sou/ ; cough). Two-valent verbs can have one subject and one object, such as "写"

(/xie/; write). Three-valent verbs can have one subject, one direct object, and one indirect object, such as "给" (/gei/; give). The MMT model used "valence theory" to design machine translation systems as early as the 1980s.

5. Syntactic Functional Features

Since there is no clear one-to-one correspondence between phrase types and syntactic functions in modern Chinese, the relationship between them is extremely complicated. In the automatic analysis of Chinese sentences, we must pay attention to the syntactic functional features, which are produced in the automatic analysis of sentences rather than inherent in words or phrases.

The syntactic functional features of the components in a Chinese sentence are denoted as SF.

SF can take the following values: subject, predicate, object, attributive, adverbial, complement, predicative, and head.

The value of SF can have sub-values. For example, the value of an object can have two sub-values: a direct object and an indirect object.

6. Semantic Relation Features

Semantic relation features are not inherent in the words themselves but are obtained through calculations in the process of automatic syntactic and semantic analysis by computer. There is no semantic relationship between isolated words; only two or more words or phrases can produce a semantic relationship. The feature of semantic relation is SM.

SM can take the following values: agent, patient, dative, involved, time, period, time starting point, time ending point, space point, space segment, space starting point, space ending point, initial state, final state, cause, result, tool, method, purpose, condition, function, content, scope, topic, modification, comparison, accompaniment, judgment, statement, addition, etc.

The values of SM can be further subdivided so that each value can also take sub-values.

7. Logical Relationship Features

If a Chinese sentence is taken as a logical proposition, then there is a logical relationship between the predicate of the logical proposition and its arguments. Since each argument of a logical proposition is served by a word or a phrase in a sentence, there is a logical relationship between words or phrases in a sentence. This relationship is what N. Chomsky calls "theta relation" (θ relation), which is represented by LR.

The value of LR is as follows:

Argument 0: it is the deep subject of a sentence
Argument 1: it is the deep direct object of a sentence
Argument 2: it is the deep indirect object of a sentence
The value of a logical relation feature generally has no sub-values.
Each argument plays a thematic role and can only play a thematic role. Each thematic role is played by one argument and can only be played by one argument. Therefore, it is possible to check whether the processed sentence is correct in the

analysis of the logical relationship according to the argument and reveal the logical structure of the whole sentence.

The above-mentioned Chinese "feature/value" system proposed in the MMT model in the early 1980s was not perfect yet and was improved later.

Among the various features listed above, part of speech features, inherent semantic features, and inherent grammatical features of words can all be given independently in the dictionary. They are inherent features of the words and are called "static features" in MMT model. However, the characteristics of phrase type, syntactic function, semantic relationship, and logical relationship do not represent the inherent characteristics of the words. They are the characteristics that are generated when words are connected. The MMT model calls them "dynamic features." This is the most important "Di-State Principle" (DSP) in MMT model. DSP advocates the distinction between static features and dynamic features, which has a guiding role in the design of automatic NLP systems. In actual operation, the computer first queries the static features from the dictionary and then gets the dynamic features based on the static features. In this way, the natural language processing process can be carried out in an orderly manner.

In automatic syntactic and semantic analysis, static features are the basis of computer operations. The computer relies on these static features given in the dictionary in advance and gradually calculates various dynamic features through finite steps, to gradually clarify the relationship between various language components in a Chinese sentence and achieve the purpose of automatic syntactic and semantic analysis.

Among the various dynamic features, the phrase type feature is the easiest to calculate. Generally, based on static features such as the direct descendants of a node in the tree diagram, the inherent grammatical features of the word, and the inherent semantic features of the word, it is not difficult to calculate the phrase type characteristics of the node. Syntactic functional features can only be calculated through broader contextual information, while semantic relation features and logical relation features are the most difficult to calculate, which are often not calculated in one step but through many steps of deduction and reasoning. The quality of a Chinese character automatic analysis and semantic analysis system depends to a large extent on the number and correctness of the syntactic function features, semantic relation features, and logical relation features it calculates. Therefore, how to calculate dynamic features based on various static features is the key to Chinese automatic processing. The study of Chinese grammar and semantics should provide effective rules for this work. In this field, the collaboration of linguists and computer experts is very much needed.

Under the guidance of the "Di-State Principle" (DSP) of the MMT model, Zhiwei Feng proposed that the automatic analysis of Chinese sentences should include the following steps:

1. Segment the input Chinese sentence and determine the boundary between words. This is the so-called automatic segmentation.

2. Find out the static features of each word in the sentence from the dictionary. This is called "automatic tagging for part of speech."
3. According to the grammatical and semantic rules, check the compatibility of these static features, combine the words with compatible static features into phrases, and find the features of phrase types.
4. According to grammatical rules and semantic rules, starting from static features and phrase type features, the syntactic function features are calculated, and the semantic relation features and logical relation features are further calculated.

When checking the compatibility of static features and calculating dynamic features from static features, if the two features are incompatible, the calculation cannot be performed and the calculation fails. If the two features are compatible, the calculation is performed according to the relevant grammatical and semantic rules. Since the features can be calculated when the features do not conflict, the calculated feature information will inevitably increase, and the features contained in each component of the sentence will become more and more abundant. The final features can reflect the nature of the Chinese sentence more comprehensively.

The automatic generation process of Chinese is the opposite. In the machine translation from a foreign language to Chinese, it is generally based on the features of syntactic functions, semantic relations, and logical relations obtained from foreign language analysis, and according to the static features of Chinese words provided by foreign Chinese bilingual machine dictionary, the adjustment of Chinese word order and the necessary part of speech changes (such as the reduplication changes of verbs and adjectives) are carried out, so as to produce qualified Chinese sentences.

Zhiwei Feng used these methods of the MMT model in machine translation experiments such as FAJRA (Chinese-French/English/Japanese/Russian/German, 1981), GCAT (German-Chinese, 1984), and FCAT (French-Chinese, 1984) and obtained good results.

The following are examples of Chinese-foreign machine translation by FAJRA system on IBM-4341 on November 4, 1981. He entered a short text in Chinese and obtained machine translations in five foreign languages, including English, French, German, Japanese, and Russian (Figs. 4.1, 4.2, 4.3, 4.4, 4.5, and 4.6).

The machine translation results of FAJRA system were published at the COLING-82 held in Prague in 1982 and the Southeast Asian Computer Conference

---

汉语输入　　　　4 November 1981
　　语言和通信在人类的生活中起着重要的作用。学者们正在积极地研究语言的生动翻译。他们提出了自动机的理论和形式语言的理论。自动机是能够识别语言的一种抽象机器。语言的规则能够把一个树形图自动地转换成另一个树形图。这个自动翻译系统已经被他们使用了五年。如果我们把这个系统同其他一些系统相比较，就可以看出它的优点。

Fig. 4.1 Chinese input in FAJRA system

English Output

英语输出   4   November 1981

Language and communication play important role in human life. Scholars are actively studying
automatic translation of languages. They have proposed the theory of automaton and the theory of
formal grammar. An automaton is an abstract machine that can recognize language. Grammar rule
can transform a tree graph to another tree graph automatically. This system for automatic
translation had been used by them for five years. If we compare this system with other systems,
then we can see its advantage.

Fig. 4.2 English output of FAJRA system

French Output

法语输出   4   November 1981

Le langage et la communication jouent un rôle important dans la vie humaine. Les
savants sont en train d'étudier activement la traduction automatique des langages. Ils
ont proposé la théorie des automates et la théorie des grammaires formelles. Un
automate es une machine abstraire qui peut reconnaître le langage. La règle de la
grammaire peut transformer automatiquement une arborescence en une autre
arborescence. Ce système de la traduction auotmatique a été utilis par eux pendant
cinq ans. Si nous comparons ce système à d'autres systèmes, alors nous pouvons
voir ses avantages.

Fig. 4.3 French output of FAJRA system

Japanese output

日语输出   4   November 1981

言語と通信は人間の生活に重要な役割を果している。研究者は言語の自動翻訳
を熱心に研究している。彼等はオートマトンの理論と形式文法の理論を提案し
ている。オートマトンは言語を認識することができる一種の抽象機械である。
文法の規則はひとつの木のグラフを別の木のグラフに自動的に変換すること
ができる。自動翻訳のためのこのシステムは彼等によって五年間使われていた。
このシステムを他のシステムと比べると、われわれはその利点をわかることが
できる。

Fig. 4.4 Japanese output of FAJRA system

Russian output	
俄语输出	**4 November 1981**

Язык и коммуникация играют важную роль в жизни человечества. Учёные активно изучают автоматический перевод языков. Они выдвигают теорию автомата и теорию формальной грамматиги. Автомат есть одна абстрактная машина, которая может распознавать язык.Правило грамматиги может автоматически превращать одну древовидную схему на другую древовидную схему. Эта система автоматического перевода использована ими уже пять лет. Если мы сравни ваем эту систему с другимисистем ами, то мы можем видеть еёпреиму шества.

Fig. 4.5 Russian output of FAJRA system

German output	
德语输出	4 November 1981

Die Sprache und die Kommunikation spielen im Leben der Menschen wichtige Rolle. Die Wissenschaftler sind gerade dabei, die automatische Übersetzung der Sprachen aktiv zu studieren. Sie haben die Theorie der Automaten und die Theorie der formalen Grammatiken Vorgeschlagen. Ein Automat ist eine abstrakte Maschine, die die Sprache erkennen kann. Die Grammatikregel kann einen Baumgraphen in einen anderen Baumgraphen automatisch umwandeln. Dieses System zur automatischen Übersetzung war von Ihnen soll fünf Jahren verwendet worden. Wenn wir dieses System mit anderen Systemen vergleichen, dann können wir seinen Vorzug sehen.

Fig. 4.6 German output of FAJRA system

SEARCC-84 held in Hong Kong in 1984. It is the first machine translation system from Chinese to many foreign languages developed by Chinese scholars in the world. Under the technical conditions of the 1980s, it is very valuable to develop such a machine translation system.

4.2   Kaplan's Lexical Functional Grammar

Lexical functional grammar (LFG) was proposed by American linguists R. M. Kaplan (Fig. 4.7) and J. Bresnan in 1982 in "Lexical-functional Grammar: A Formal System for Grammatical Representation." This grammar provides an effective model for the description of the natural language and the expression of grammatical knowledge. It can not only explain the mechanism of children's language acquisition but also explain the behavior of human processing the natural language, so as to meet the needs of natural language computer processing, and has been widely used in natural language processing. Lexical functional grammar also adopts a series of effective methods to overcome the limitations of phrase structure grammar, improve the efficiency of automatic language analysis, and become the most influential formal model of natural language processing.

Lexical functional grammar has two sources: one is the research done by J. Bresnan in the framework of transformational grammar, and the other is the research done by R.M. Kaplan and others in language information processing and psycholinguistics. J. Bresnan felt that transformational generative grammar puts transformation completely in the syntax and could not properly explain many language phenomena. She proposed a model that puts most of the grammar into the lexicon for processing. R.M. Kaplan believes that language processing by the human brain is not completely following transformational generative grammar model and has done a lot of work in computer simulation of human brain processing language. Finally, J. Bresnan and R.M. Kaplan collaborated based on their respective results and proposed lexical functional grammar.

In the early 1970s, N. Chomsky criticized the phenomenon of abusing transformation in language research at that time and advocated that some language phenomena should be dealt with in vocabulary. J. Bresnan is a student of N. Chomsky. She agrees with N. Chomsky and goes further than N. Chomsky. She puts the

Fig. 4.7 R. M. Kaplan

phenomenon that N. Chomsky thinks belongs to the transformation into the vocabulary and does not use transformation at all. Finally, she develops an independent school. The research center of lexical functional grammar was originally at the Massachusetts Institute of Technology. Since 1982, it has been transferred to Stanford University with J. Bresnan.

In terms of language philosophy, J. Bresnan accepts N. Chomsky's view that grammar is psychology. Although N. Chomsky proposed that grammar studies human language knowledge, which exists in the brain and mind, he believes that grammatical rules are not directly reflected in the process of psychological activities. Grammar studies can only use mathematical and logical methods to simulate psychological processes, rather than general psychological experiments. N. Chomsky believes that the study of grammar should focus on the ideal speaker and listener rather than ordinary people; otherwise many factors unrelated to grammar will be involved in the experiment. Therefore, although N. Chomsky regards grammar as a branch of psychology, his research is divorced from psychology. J. Bresnan believes that grammar should be psychology. Every grammatical rule should be embodied in psychological activities and can be regarded as a model of behavior. She advocates "realistic grammar," which is a grammar that embodies psychological activities. This is an extreme psychological view. From this point of view, lexical functional grammar draws on the information processing technology of psycholinguistic experiments and computer science, so lexical functional grammar has become theoretical grammar that should be paid special attention to in language information processing.

Abstractly, the theoretical framework of lexical functional grammar can be expressed in Fig. 4.8.

Conceptual structure is the logical relationship between concepts. Its expression has nothing to do with linguistics. The thematic structure is composed of different thematic roles, and its expression is related to linguistics. The situation to be

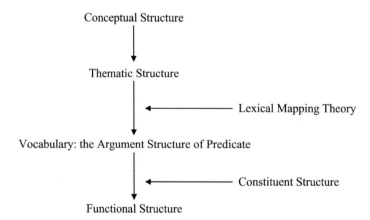

Fig. 4.8 The theoretical framework of lexical functional grammar

expressed by any concept must be represented by one or more roles as arguments, and the argument that is required to appear when each concept is converted into a language expression is called a thematic role. The thematic structure is the skeleton of conceptual structure preserved after language screening, and it is the basis for assigning different semantic roles to each argument relative to the abstract syntactic structure. Vocabulary mapping theory is used to explain the correspondence between topic structure and vocabulary items. After obtaining a complete vocabulary through the lexical mapping theory, it enters the scope of syntax.

A basic idea of lexical functional grammar is that the relationship between the grammatical function and the semantic predicate-argument structure can be changed by lexical rules, but the relationship between the grammatical function and the syntactic structure cannot be changed by any rules. There is no transformational mechanism in the syntactic part. This is "the principle of direct syntactic encoding." This principle stipulates that the grammatical function of the syntactic part cannot be replaced by another grammatical function, so the constituent structure of lexical functional grammar is unitary. In this way, lexical functional grammar has developed a new method of linguistics without transformation.

Lexical functional grammar is mainly composed of three parts: lexicon, syntax, and semantic interpretation. The semantic predicate-argument structure is first assigned to a grammatical function through lexical coding in the lexicon. This connection between semantics and grammatical functions can be transformed in the lexicon through lexical rules. When an entry finally obtains the correct grammatical function coding, it can form a lexical input together with other entries expressing grammatical meaning and enter the syntactic part.

There are two levels of expression in the syntax: the constituent structure (c-structure) and the functional structure (f-structure). When constructing the constituent structure, the nodes of the tree diagram are also attached with "annotated functional equations" and "constraint equations."

The constituent structure is the external structure of language. It represents the sequence of sentence components. It is a tree structure mapped from a set of phrase structure rules. The grammatical function enters the phrase structure rules through syntactic coding and then enters the corresponding position of the tree structure. This level represents the syntactic arrangement and phonetic expression of sentences. The functional structure is the internal structure of language, which expresses the relationship between the various language components and represents the semantics of the sentence. Generally speaking, the expressions of the internal structures of different languages are basically the same, so the functional structures are universal, while the external structures of different languages are very different, so the constituent structures are different. The functional structure and constituent structure are two independent systems with different forms. Lexical functional grammar clearly distinguishes them, describes them part by part, and then combines them to give people an overall view of the structure of language. A constituent structure can be transformed into a functional structure through a functional description. The functional description is composed of a set of equations, which can be easily coded by

Fig. 4.9 The patterns of
lexical functional grammar

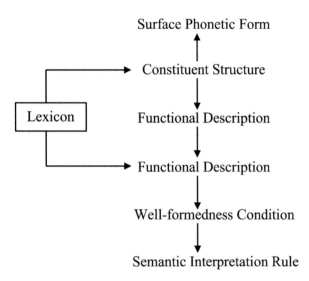

computers. The constituent structure describes the surface structure of language. The
words in the constituent structure carry most of the grammatical information. The
functional equation specifies the method of combining the grammatical information.
After a finite number of steps, the final combination result of the grammatical
information is obtained—the functional structure. To ensure the correctness of the
functional structure, it is necessary to judge the qualification of the functional
structure. Therefore, lexical functional grammar also stipulates "well-formed
conditions."

R. M. Kaplan and J. Bresnan proved that in lexical functional grammar, the
operations from the constituent structure to the functional structure are mathematically decidable, and all operations only need the simple operation of "unification."
The so-called unification means that when the information conflicts, the calculation
fails, and when the information does not conflict, the calculation succeeds. Unification operation is a special form of "union" operation in mathematical logic suitable
for natural language processing. Because of the use of unification operation as the
basic operation method, lexical functional grammar can be easily applied to machine
translation and natural language processing.

In this way, we can express lexical functional grammar more specifically as the
pattern shown in Fig. 4.9.

The constituent structure is a plane of syntactic description in lexical functional
grammar. It is represented by context-free phrase structure grammar, and its form is a
phrase structure tree in the general sense. The nodes on the tree diagram carry the
functional information predicted by the words or phrases in the sentence. This
information is represented by the "functional equation" attached to the symbols on
the right of the grammar rules.

Fig. 4.10 Tree diagram
representation of phrase
structure rules

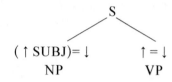

For example, in the following phrase structure rules:

$$S \rightarrow \qquad NP \qquad VP$$
$$(\uparrow SUBJ) = \downarrow \quad \uparrow = \downarrow$$

In the rules, the upward single arrow "↑" and the downward single arrow "↓" are used to indicate the dominance of the category. The upward single arrow "↑" indicates the directly dominating component, and the downward single arrow "↓" indicates the dominated component. These arrows can be used in functional equations. The left side of the equation is the restricted component, and right side of the equation is the restricted value. For example, (↑SUBJ)=↓ is read as "the subject of the directly dominating component is equal to the grammatical function of the directly dominated component," and ↑=↓ is read as "the grammatical function of the directly dominating component is equal to the grammatical function of the directly dominated component." The above phrase structure rule indicates that the sentence S is composed of NP and VP, and the NP before VP is the subject of the sentence. "(↑SUBJ)=↓" below NP is its functional equation, which means that this NP inherits the subject (SUBJ) feature of its parent node S, and "(↑SUBJ)" means that all functional information of NP is the subject function information of S dominating it, and "↓" represents the symbol itself (i.e., the component NP directly dominated by S). The function equation "↑=↓" below VP means that all the function information carried by VP is the function information of its parent node S.

This phrase structure rule can also be represented as a tree diagram in Fig. 4.10. We should pay attention to three problems here:

1. Both the upward arrow and the downward arrow indicate functional information, not nodes.
2. The downward arrow indicates the function information of this node, not the function information of the child nodes under this node.
3. The equal sign not only indicates that the values on both sides are equal but also indicates that the unification operation is performed, that is, the compatibility check is performed before the operation.

Another example, in the following phrase structure rule:

$$NP \quad (DET) \qquad N$$
$$(\uparrow = \downarrow) \quad \uparrow = \downarrow$$

Fig. 4.11 Tree diagram representation of phrase structure rules

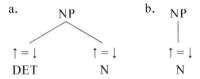

Fig. 4.12 Tree diagram representation of the phrase structure rule

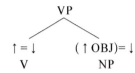

NP has composed of the determiner DET and the noun N. The determiner is an optional component. N inherits the function information of its parent node NP. This grammatical rule represents the following two phrase structure rules:

(a)
$$NP \rightarrow DET \quad N$$
$$\uparrow=\downarrow \quad \uparrow=\downarrow$$

(b)
$$NP \rightarrow N$$
$$\uparrow=\downarrow$$

They can be represented by a tree diagram in Fig. 4.11.

Another example, in the following phrase structure rule:

$$VP \rightarrow V \quad NP$$
$$\uparrow=\downarrow \ (\uparrow OBJ) =\downarrow$$

It means that V has inherited the function information of its parent node VP, and NP has inherited the object (OBJ) feature of its parent node VP. This grammar rule is represented by a tree diagram in Fig. 4.12.

At this time, since V inherits the function information of VP, and VP inherits the function information of S, V also inherits the function information of S, that is, V shares all the information of S. Both the VP of the above rule and the V of this rule have the function equation $\uparrow=\downarrow$. This functional equation makes V, VP, and S share all the information. Therefore, we call the nodes with the function equation $\uparrow=\downarrow$ functional heads. The information carried by the functional headwords is directly incorporated into the functional information represented by their parent nodes. This information is very important. They represent the basic functional pattern of the sentence or phrase being analyzed. ($\uparrow$SUBJ)$=\downarrow$ and ($\uparrow$OBJ)$=\downarrow$ indicate the specific function of the function information represented by the corresponding node in the parent node.

The constituent structure represents the order of words in the surface structure of the sentence, and it is the input part of the phonetic description. The constituent

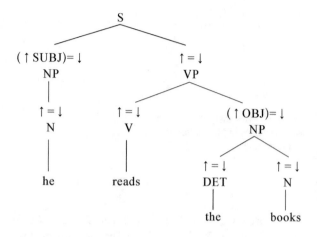

Fig. 4.13 Tree diagram representation of the constituent structure

S'   NP   S
(↑ COMP)= ↓   ⟶   (↑ WH)= ↓   ↑ = ↓
                              ↑ = ⇓

NP   ⟶   e
                              ↑ = ⇑

VP   ⟶   V   S'
                              ↑ = ↓   (↑ COMP)= ↓

Fig. 4.14 Phrase structure rules with double arrows

structure is determined by the phrase structure rules. Every language has its own unique phrase structure rules. In theory, these phrase structure rules can generate any sentence in this language. Map each category represented by the phrase structure rule to the tree diagram, and then the constituent structure of a sentence is obtained.

For example, the constituent structure of the English sentence "He reads the book" can be combined with the above grammatical rules and expressed in Fig. 4.13.

The constituent structure can only be mapped from phrase structure rules. Besides, we have no other means to change the order of words in the constituent structure. Even for the constituent structures of sentences with structural dependency, they must also be generated using phrase structure rules.

For example, the English sentence "I wondered what he read" is a sentence with structural dependency. In this sentence, the object of *read* is *what*, that is, *he read what*. The following are the phrase structure rules used to form the constituent structure of this sentence (Fig. 4.14).

We used double arrows "⇓⇑" in the phrase structure rules. The double arrow is mainly used to indicate the dependency of indirect dominance between categories in

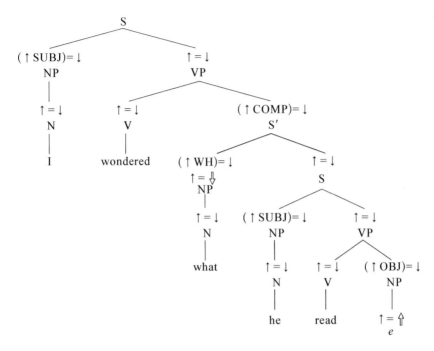

Fig. 4.15 Constituent structure of the sentence

the constituent structure, especially the long-distance dominance relationship. Double arrows must be used in pairs. All components marked with "↓" relationship must be attached to those marked with "↑" relationship, and the existence of "↑" relationship must be based on the existence of "↓" relationship.

In the rules, *e* represents the slot. Through the mapping of the above rules, we can get the constituent structure of the sentence "I wondered what he read" as shown in Fig. 4.15.

Because double arrows must be used in pairs, *e* represents *what*, and the two are connected. It can be seen that the constituent structure can also represent a long-distance dominance relationship.

Phrase structure rules are syntactic rules, and there are also lexical rules. Lexical rules are provided by dictionary information, which has the predictive information of grammatical function and plays an important role in lexical functional grammar. For example, in the following list of vocabulary items:

```
he:   N,  (↑PRED) =' he'
      (↑ABST) = -
      (↑GENDER) =MAS
      (↑NUM) =SING
      (↑PERS) =3
```

```
         (↑CASE) =NOM
read:  V,  (↑PRED) ='read < (SUBJ) (OBJ) >'
         (↑TENSE) =PRESENT
the:  DET,  (↑SPEC) =the
         (↑DEF) =+
book:  N,  (↑PRED) =' book'
         (↑NUM) =SING
```

Lexical functional grammar projects lexical items according to different meanings of words. The information contained in lexical items includes grammatical categories and functional equations. The form of the functional equation is completely consistent with the functional equation in the phrase structure rule, which is convenient for processing language information in a unified way.

In the above lexical items, the "(↑PRED)=' he'" of this lexical item *he* means that its parent node has the function PRED (predicate), and its specific information is *'he'* "(↑ABST)= -" indicates that its parent node has the function ABST (abstract), and its specific information is "-" (not abstract). Therefore, *he* is a concrete object; "(GENDER↑)=MAS" indicates that its parent node has the function GENDER (grammaticality), its specific information is MAS (masculine), "(↑NUM)=SING" means that its parent node has the function NUM (number), and its specific information is SING (singular); "(↑ PERS)=3" indicates that its parent node has the function PERS (person), and its specific information is 3 (third person); and "(↑CASE)=NOM" indicates that its parent node has the function CASE (case), and its specific information is NOM (nominative case). "DET (↑SPEC)=the" of the lexical term *the* indicates that its parent node has the function SPEC (specification), and its specific information is *the* (definite article); "(↑DEF)=+" means its parent node has the function DEF (definite reference), and its specific information is + (definite reference). It is not difficult for readers to understand the meaning of other lexical items from this kind of expression.

What is worth noting here is the PRED of the verb. In lexical functional grammar, the "predicate-argument structure" is used to express the number of arguments in a predicate and the logical semantics represented by each argument. The arguments of the predicate-argument structure are listed in angle brackets "< >." For example, the predicate-argument structure of *read* is "(↑PRED)='READ<(SUBJ)(OBJ)>'," which means that the argument of *read* is the subject (SUBJ) and object (OBJ) of its parent node.

The grammatical information in lexical functional grammar comes from vocabulary after all. The function of the functional structure is only to check whether the structure of the information is reasonable. The function of the constituent structure is only to specify the way of information combination, and the real information with substantial meaning comes from the vocabulary. Therefore, vocabulary plays a decisive role in lexical functional grammar and we must take it seriously.

The lexical items recorded in lexical functional grammar are all morphologically complete. The information in the vocabulary is recorded in the form of "annotated functional equations" and "constraint equations." For example, the English word *persuades* can be recorded as follows:

Fig. 4.16 Attribute-value
matrix

Attribute	Value
A	a
B	b
C	c

```
persuades  V.  (↑PRED)='persuades < (SUBJ) (OBJ) (XCOMP)>'
               (↑OBJ)=(↑XCOMP SUBJ)
            .  (↑SUBJ PER)=c 3
               (↑SUBJ NUM)=c SING
```

where the first two equations are general "functional equations"; they are both annotative, so they are "annotated functional equations." The latter two equations are "constraint functional equations", whose symbol is c, which means "constraint." The first annotated functional equation specifies the predicate-argument relationship of the verb. The verb must carry three arguments: the subject, object, and object complement (XCOMP). The second annotated functional equation stipulates the control relationship between arguments. The object complement of the verb *persuades* XCOMP has no subject, and its logical subject is controlled by the object of its upper predicate (as in the sentence *John persuades Mary to study computational linguistics*, the logical subject of the object complement *to study computational linguistics* is controlled by the object *Mary* of the upper predicate *persuades*). The third equation is a constraint functional equation, which means that the subject of the verb should be a singular third person. The fourth equation is also a constraint functional equation, indicating that the number of the subject of the verb should be singular. The information for the last two equations comes from the ending -s, and the rest comes from the root of the verb *persuade*.

The functional structure is another plane of description in lexical functional grammar. It is an attribute-value matrix, and its basic structure can be shown in Fig. 4.16.

In this attribute matrix, the first column *A*, *B*, *C*, etc. represents the attribute, and the second column *a*, *b*, *c*, etc. represents the value of the corresponding attribute.

Specifically, the functional structure uses square brackets to indicate the hierarchical relationship between the meaningful components in the grammar, to provide necessary information for semantic interpretation at the syntactic level. The first line of the left column in square brackets lists grammatical functions or special grammatical markers, which we call "constraint elements" in general. Corresponding to the constraint components in the horizontal direction are their respective constraint values. There are three forms of constraint values: the simple symbol, semantic form, and sub-functional structure. The sub-functional structure has its constraint components and constraint values, and its constraint value can also have a sub-functional structure, which constitutes the recursive nature of the functional structure. In theory, the functional structure can accommodate sentences of any length.

Fig. 4.17 Functional
structure

$$
\begin{bmatrix}
\text{SUBJ} & \begin{bmatrix} \text{PRED} & \text{'he'} \\ \text{ABST} & - \\ \text{GENDER} & \text{MAS} \\ \text{NUM} & \text{SING} \\ \text{PERS} & 3 \\ \text{CASE} & \text{NOM} \end{bmatrix} \\[2em]
\text{TENSE} & \text{PRESENT} \\[1em]
\text{PRED} & \text{'read } \langle (\text{SUBJ})\ (\text{OBJ}) \rangle\text{'} \\[1em]
\text{OBJ} & \begin{bmatrix} \text{SPES} & \text{the} \\ \text{DEF} & + \\ \text{NUM} & \text{SING} \\ \text{PRED} & \text{'book'} \end{bmatrix}
\end{bmatrix}
$$

Fig. 4.18 Constituent
structure

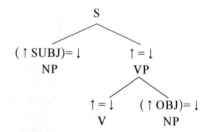

The functional structure of the English sentence "he reads the book" is shown in Fig. 4.17.

In the above functional structure, the SUBJ, TENSE, PRED, and OBJ in the first column on the left are the constraint elements, and their respective constraint values are arranged in the corresponding positions on the right. The constraint value of TENSE "PRESENT" is a simple symbol, the constraint value of PRED is a semantic form, and the constraint values of SUBJ and OBJ are the sub-function structure. In these two sub-functional structures, the first column on the left is still the constraint component, and the column on the right is still the constraint value.

There is a correspondence between the constituent structure and functional structure. This correspondence is the basic basis for the transformation of a sentence's constituent structure into a corresponding functional structure. Next, we will study the corresponding relationship between the constituent structure and functional structure.

For example, see the constituent structure (Fig. 4.18).

The functional structure corresponding to this constituent structure is as follows (Fig. 4.19).

Where pred represents a specific predicate, such as *read*.

$$
\begin{bmatrix}
\text{PRED} & \text{'pred } \langle (\text{SUBJ}) \ (\text{OBJ}) \rangle \text{'} \\
\text{OBJ} & [\quad] \\
\text{SUBJ} & [\quad]
\end{bmatrix}
$$

Fig. 4.19 The functional structure corresponding to the constituent structure in Fig. 4.18

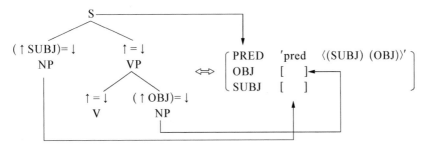

Fig. 4.20 Correspondence between the constituent structure and functional structure in SVO language

There is a correspondence between the constituent structure and the functional structure:

1. Nodes S, VP, and V are the functional heads, since both VP and V have the functional equation ↑=↓ and therefore correspond to the entire functional structure.
2. Node NP with the functional equation (↑SUBJ)=↓ and the node NP with the functional equation (↑OBJ)=↓; because they are not the function heads, they can only correspond to subj [ ] and obj [ ] in the above functional structure, respectively.

This correspondence between the constituent structure and the functional structure can be shown in Fig. 4.20 (the left is the constituent structure, and the right is the functional structure).

This is the constituent structure and functional structure of the SVO language (i.e., the subject-predicate-object structure language).

The functional structure represents the commonality of languages, and the constituent structure represents the differences of languages. Therefore, the functional structure is not affected by the various surface forms of various languages. The constituent structure and functional structure of SOV language (i.e., subject-object-predicate language) can be expressed as follows (Fig. 4.21).

It can be seen that the order of each component in the constituent structure of SOV language is different from that of SVO language. Therefore, the constituent structure reflects the differences of language, while the functional structure of SOV language and SVO language is the same.

Sometimes, to make the constituent structure and functional structure more expressive, the constraint functional equation can be used. This equation does not

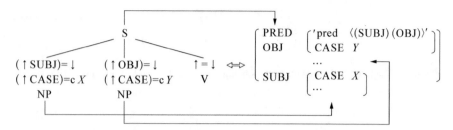

Fig. 4.21 Correspondence between constituent structure and functional structure in SOV language

assign any attribute value but rigidly stipulates that the attribute must have a specified value. For example, to specify whether an NP is singular or plural, countable or uncountable, what kind of case an NP must take, etc., ↑CASE=c X and ↑CASE=c Y in the constituent structure of the above SOV language and [CASE Y] and [CASE X] in the functional structure are all constraint functional equations.

This kind of constraint functional equation can be formulated according to the actual situation of language analysis. In different language analysis systems, their specific interpretations are not the same. In Japanese, ↑CASE=c X means that NP must have a certain case mark X (such as が) to have the function of the subject, and ↑CASE=c Y means that NP must have another case mark (such as を) to have the function of the object.

The transformation of the constituent structure into the functional structure cannot be carried out directly but should be carried out through the intermediary component of functional description. In other words, we should first transform the constituent structure into the functional description and then transform the functional description into the functional structure.

The transformation from the constituent structure to the functional description is divided into three steps.

Step 1: Encode the constituent structure with grammatical function and insert the lexical items. For example, the sentence "he reads the book" becomes the tree diagram in Fig. 4.22 after the first step.

Step 2: Assign the functional variables $(f_1, f_2, \ldots, f_{n-1}, f_n)$ to the S node and other nodes with downward arrows. For example, in the tree diagram above, the function variables $f_1, f_2, f_3, f_4, f_5, f_6, f_7, f_8$ are allocated to the nodes of S, NP, VP, N, V, NP, DET, N, etc. (Fig. 4.23).

Step 3: Replace all the up and down arrows in the constituent structure with functional variables to get the functional description of the sentence. For example, in the above tree diagram, each functional variable is substituted into the up arrow that directly dominates it and the down arrow that is dominated by the up arrow. At this point, the set of all the functional equations in the constituent structure is the functional description of the sentence. For example, in the functional equation (↑SUBJ)=↓, replace ↑ with the functional variable f_1 marked by the upper arrow, and replace ↓ with the functional variable f_2 marked by the lower arrow, to obtain (f1SUBJ)=f2. At node VP in the functional equation ↑=↓,

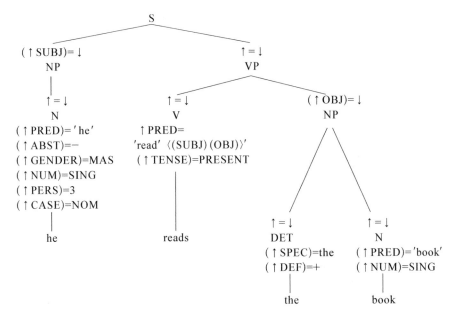

Fig. 4.22 Insert lexical item information

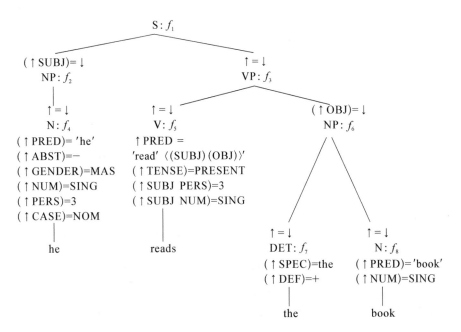

Fig. 4.23 Assign functional variables

replace ↑ with the functional variable f_1 marked by the upper arrow, replace ↓ with the function variable f_3 marked by the lower arrow, obtain $f_1=f_3$, and so on. In this way, we can get the functional description of the above tree diagram as follows:

(a) $(f_1 \text{ SUBJ})=f_2$
(b) $f_1=f_3$
(c) $f_2=f_4$
(d) $(f_4 \text{ PRED})=$' he'
(e) $(f_4 \text{ ABST})=-$
(f) $(f_4 \text{ GENDER})=\text{MAS}$
(g) $(f_4 \text{ NUM})=\text{SING}$
(h) $(f_4 \text{ PERS})=3$
(i) $(f_4 \text{ CASE})=\text{NOM}$
(j) $f_3=f_5$
(k) $(f_5 \text{ PRED}=$'read $<(\text{SUBJ}) (\text{OBJ})>$'
(l) $(f_5 \text{ TENSE})=\text{PRESENT}$
(m) $(f_5 \text{ SUBJ PERS})=3$
(n) $(f_5 \text{ SUBJ NUM}) =\text{SING}$
(o) $(f_3 \text{ OBJ})=f_6$
(p) $f_6=f_7$
(q) $f_6=f_8$
(r) $(f_7 \text{ SPEC})=\text{the}$
(s) $(f_7 \text{ DEF})=+$
(t) $(f_8 \text{ PRED})=$'book'
(u) $(f_8 \text{ NUM})=\text{SING}$

The formal feature of the functional description provides convenience for computer processing. If a sentence is not grammatical, it can be found out quickly by computer operations. For example, if we change *he* in the tree diagram to *they*, the sentence will be ungrammatical. Because if *they* is plural, the corresponding content of its entry should also be plural, that is, $(\uparrow \text{Num}) = \text{PLUR}$. Here, PLUR means plural. Thus, in the functional description, the "$(f_4 \text{ NUM})=\text{SING}$" of the function equation g should be changed to "$(f_4 \text{ NUM})=\text{PLUR}$." However, in this way, there is a contradiction with "$(f_5 \text{ SUBJ NUM}) =\text{SING}$" in the functional equation n. Because from $f_1=f_3$ and $f_3=f_5$, we can get $f_1=f_5$. By replacing f_5 with f_1 in $(f_1 \text{ SUBJ})=f_2$, we can get $(f_5 \text{ SUBJ})=f_2$. By replacing f_5 subj in "$(f_5 \text{ SUBJ NUM}) =\text{SING}$" with f_2, we can get $(f_2 \text{ NUM})=\text{SING}$, and $f_2=f_4$, we get $(f_4 \text{ MUN})=\text{SING}$, but at this time we already have $(f_4 \text{ Num}) = \text{PLUR}$. Therefore, according to the principle of functional consistency, the computer can judge that it is not grammatical to change *he* to *they*, and it is easy to detect grammatical errors. This fact shows that lexical functional grammar as a basic theory of language information processing will be welcomed.

As I mentioned before, in the constituent structure of the sentence "I wonder what he read," e is *what*. This can be reflected by the functional description. The following

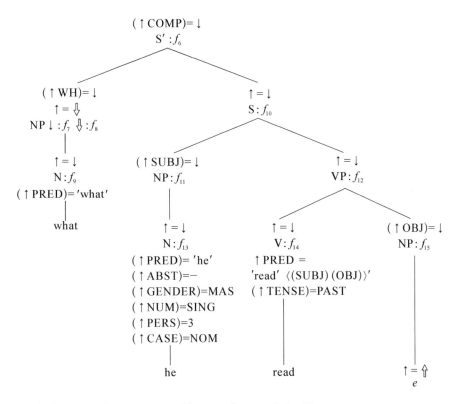

Fig. 4.24 The constituent structure with a long-distance relationship

is the functional description of the fragment "what he read" and the tree diagram obtained through the first two steps (Fig. 4.24).

In the above constituent structure, the double arrows "⇓" and "⇑" have the same functional variable, which confirms that the semantic form "what" should be understood as the second argument of "read." We can get some functional descriptions as follows:

(a) $(f_6\ WH)=f_7$
(b) $f_7=f_8$
(c) $f_7=f_9$
(d) $(f_9\ PRED)=$'what'
(e) $f_6=f_{10}$
(f) $f_{10}=f_{13}$
(g) $(f_{13}\ OBJ)=f_{15}$
(h) $f_{15}=f_8$

The computer can conclude $(f_{10}\ OBJ)=f_8$ from these functional descriptions through simple calculations, which proves that the object of *he read* is *what*.

Fig. 4.25 Functional
structure 1

$$f_2 \atop f_5 \left[\text{SUBJ} \quad {f_2 \atop f_6} \begin{bmatrix} \text{PRED} & \text{'he'} \\ \text{ABST} & - \\ \text{GENDER} & \text{MAS} \\ \text{NUM} & \text{SING} \\ \text{PERS} & 3 \\ \text{CASE} & \text{NOM} \end{bmatrix} \right]$$

Since the functional description is an intermediate component between the constituent structure and functional structure, it can be transformed into a functional structure. The transformation from functional description to function structure is mainly accomplished by two operators: locate and merge. The whole transformation process is a comprehensive analysis process.

Firstly, the location operator determines the position of the names on both sides of the functional equation in the functional structure, and then the merging operator arranges the contents on both sides of the functional equation horizontally according to the format of the functional structure. This process needs to be repeated continuously until all the functional equations in the functional description are calculated and the functional structure is obtained.

The following is a brief description of the transformation process from the constituent structure to the functional structure of the sentence "he reads the book."

Step 1: From the functional equation $(f_1 \text{ SUBJ})=f_2$ and $f1=f3$, we can deduce:

$$f_1 f_3 [\text{SUBJ } f_2 \underline{\quad}]$$

At this time, f_1 and f_3 are merged, and f_2 is determined as the sub-functional description of f_1 and f_3, which is below $f_1 f_3$. The underlined part after f_2 indicates the unknown to be filled in, that is, the constraint value. This value can be determined by the functional equations related to f_2 and f_4.

Step 2: From the functional equation $f_2=f_4$, fill the underlined part in f_2 with the value of f_4, and merge f_2 and f_4. These values of f_4 are:

$(f_4 \text{ PRED})=\text{'he'}$
$(f_4 \text{ ABST})=-$
$(f_4 \text{ GENDER})=\text{MAS}$
$(f_4 \text{ NUM})=\text{SING}$
$(f_4 \text{ PERS})=3$
$(f_4 \text{ CASE})=\text{NOM}$

The results are shown in Fig. 4.25.

where f_1 and f_3 are merged f_2 and f_4 are merged, so f_1 and f_3 are located in the same position, and f_2 and f_4 are also located in the same position.

Step 3: Fill the values of f_5 in f_3 from the function equation $f_3=f_5$, and these values are determined by the functional equation:

Fig. 4.26 Functional
structure 2

$$
f_4 \begin{bmatrix} \text{SUBJ} & f_2 \\ f_6 \end{bmatrix} \begin{bmatrix} \text{PRED} & \text{'he'} \\ \text{ABST} & - \\ \text{GENDER} & \text{MAS} \\ \text{NUM} & \text{SING} \\ \text{PERS} & 3 \\ \text{CASE} & \text{NOM} \end{bmatrix}
$$

$$
f_4 \;\; \text{TENSE} \quad \text{PRESENT}
$$
$$
f_5
$$
$$
f_6 \;\; \text{PRED} \qquad \text{'READ } \langle (\text{SUBJ}) (\text{OBJ}) \rangle\text{'}
$$

Fig. 4.27 Functional
structure 3

$$
f_5 \begin{bmatrix} \text{OBJ} & f_6 \\ f_7 \\ f_8 \end{bmatrix} \begin{bmatrix} \text{SPES} & \text{the} \\ \text{DEF} & + \\ \text{NUM} & \text{SING} \\ \text{PRED} & \text{'book'} \end{bmatrix}
$$

(f_5 PRED='read <(SUBJ) (OBJ)>'
(f_5 TENSE)=PRESENT
They are located in PRED and TENSE of f_3.

From the functional equations (f_5 SUBJ PERS)=3 and (f_5 SUBJ NUM)
=SING, the values of PERS and NUM of SUBJ in f_5 can be filled into the
sub-functional structure of f_3 (i.e., f_1 because they are merged), and there are
PERS and NUM in the sub-functional structure of this SUBJ, and their values
are the same, so the existing values of PERS and NUM can be used instead.
The following functional structure is obtained (Fig. 4.26).

Step 4: From the functional equation (f_3 OBJ)=f_6, fill in the value of f_6 into f_3, and
locate the OBJ of f_3. From the functional equation f_6=f_7 and f_6= f_8, fill in the
values of f_7 and f_8 into f_6 as the values in OBJ of f_3, which are provided by the
following functional equations:

(f_7 SPEC)=the
(f_7 DEF)=+
(f_8 PRED)='book'
(f_8 NUM)=SING,
The results are shown in Fig. 4.27.

Step 5: Fill in the value of OBJ into f_3 to get the functional structure of the whole
sentence as follows (Fig. 4.28).

The functional structure can be used not only to describe complete sentences but
also to describe phrases. In the above functional structures, the values of

Fig. 4.28 Functional
structure 4

$$
f_1 \; f_3 \; f_5 \left\{
\begin{array}{ll}
\text{SUBJ} & f_2 \; f_4 \left[
\begin{array}{ll}
\text{PRED} & \text{'he'} \\
\text{ABST} & - \\
\text{GENDER} & \text{MAS} \\
\text{NUM} & \text{SING} \\
\text{PERS} & 3 \\
\text{CASE} & \text{NOM}
\end{array}
\right] \\[2em]
\text{TENSE} & \text{PRESENT} \\[1em]
\text{PRED} & \text{'read } \langle (\text{SUBJ}) \; (\text{OBJ}) \rangle \text{'} \\[1em]
\text{OBJ} & f_6 \; f_7 \; f_8 \left[
\begin{array}{ll}
\text{SPES} & \text{the} \\
\text{DEF} & + \\
\text{NUM} & \text{SING} \\
\text{PRED} & \text{'book'}
\end{array}
\right]
\end{array}
\right\}
$$

grammatical functions SUBJ and OBJ are also functional structures (we call them sub-functional structures), which are phrases rather than sentences. These grammatical functions are not only the objects described by the functional structure but also the names of the functional structure. In N. Chomsky's phrase structure grammar, all qualified sentences are derived from the initial symbol S, which is a sentence. In this way, phrase structure grammar can describe the sentence. Because the phrase cannot form S, it is unqualified. In lexical functional grammar, a functional structure expressed by NP and a functional structure expressed by S are equally qualified. In this way, lexical functional grammar can successfully describe noun phrases and prepositional phrases such as "a red rose" and "in our classroom." In the automatic parsing of the natural language, partial parsing is often needed. When the input language fragment is not a sentence but a phrase, it can still be processed smoothly. This is a great advantage of lexical functional grammar.

To ensure the mathematical correctness and logical rationality of lexical functional grammar, the functional structure must be restricted by the following qualification conditions:

1. Functional Uniqueness

    In any functional structure, each attribute can have at most one value. For example, the attribute * NUM (number) has two values, singular and plural. However, in a specific functional structure, the value of NUM cannot be both singular and plural. Only one of the two values can be selected.

2. Functional Completeness

    (a) Any functional structure is partially functionally complete, if and only if the functional structure includes all grammatical functions dominated by all its predicates.

(b) Any functional structure is fully functional, if and only if all functional structures in the functional structure are partially functionally complete.

3. Functional Coherence

(a) Any functional structure is locally functionally coherent, if and only if the grammatical functions contained in the functional structure are dominated by a local predicate.

(b) Any functional structure is functionally coherent, if and only if all functional structures in the functional structure are locally functionally coherent.

The uniqueness of function is very similar to the characteristic of mathematical function in mathematics. The correspondence between the domain of the function and the value domain can be many-to-one, but not one-to-many. The attribute in the function definition cannot have more than one value. In fact, the mathematical meaning of the term *function* in English is a function. Lexical functional grammar is essentially a kind of functional grammar. The mathematically functional nature of lexical functional grammar makes it very convenient for computer processing of natural language.

A special one-to-one correspondence is established by the coordination of functional completeness and functional coherence. Every functional structure has the attribute of predicate-argument structure, which represents the predicate-argument relationship of the functional structure and determines the number and type of arguments in the functional structure. In predicate-argument structure, the predicate dominates grammatical functions, and the grammatical functions that can be dominated vary from language to language. These grammatical functions usually include SUBJ, OBJ, COMP, etc. Functional completeness stipulates that every grammatical function defined by predicate-argument structure must appear in the functional structure, while functional coherence stipulates that every grammatical function is dominated by predicate-argument structure. In this way, in lexical functional grammar, the grammatical functions that can be dominated should correspond to the grammatical functions specified by the predicate-argument structure one by one.

The following are some examples that meet well-formedness conditions. They are of functional completeness and coherence:

$$
\begin{bmatrix}
\text{PRED 'pred} <\text{(SUBJ) (OBJ)}>' \\
\text{SUBJ } [\quad] \\
\text{OBJ } [\quad]
\end{bmatrix}
$$

For example, in the Chinese sentence "小王学英语" (/Xiao Wang xue ying yu/; Xiao Wang learns English), "学" (/xue/; learn) is PRED, "小王" (/Xiao Wang/; Xiao Wang) is SUBJ, and "英语" (/ying yu/; English) is OBJ:

$$\begin{bmatrix} \text{PRED 'pred <(SUBJ) (OBJ) (XCOMP)>'} \\ \text{SUBJ [\quad]} \\ \text{OBJ [\quad]} \underline{} \\ \text{XCOMP} \quad \text{PRED 'pred <SUBJ>'} \\ \qquad\qquad \text{SUBJ} \underline{} \end{bmatrix}$$

Where XCOMP stands for object complement.

For example, in the Chinese sentence "小王劝小张休息" (/Xiao Wang quan Xiao Zhang xiu xi/; Xiao Wang persuades Xiao Zhang to rest), "劝" (/quan/; persuade) is PRED, "小王" (/Xiao Wang/; Xiao Wang) is SUBJ, "小张" (/Xiao Zhang/; Xiao Zhang) is OBJ, and "休息" (/xiu xi/; rest) is XCOMP. In this XCOMP, PRED is "休息" (/xiu xi/; rest), and its SUBJ ("小张" (/Xiao Zhang/)) is the OBJ of "劝" (/quan/; persuade), so they are connected by a line.

Below are some examples of the violations of well-formedness conditions.

1. Functionally coherent but not complete

$$\begin{bmatrix} \text{PRED 'pred <(SUBJ) (OBJ)>'} \\ \text{SUBJ [\quad]} \end{bmatrix}$$

SUBJ is the same as SUBJ in PRED but lacks the grammatical function OBJ.

For example, in the Chinese sentence *"小王开" (/Xiao Wang kai/; Xiao Wang open), "开" (/kai/; open) is a transitive verb. It should have SUBJ and OBJ when it is used as PRED, but there is only SUBJ in the sentence but no OBJ, which violates the principle of functional completeness.

2. Functionally complete but not coherent

$$\begin{bmatrix} \text{PRED 'pred <(SUBJ)>'} \\ \text{SUBJ [\quad]} \\ \text{OBJ [\quad]} \end{bmatrix}$$

For example, in the Chinese sentence *"小王咳嗽小张" (/Xiao Wang ke shou Xiao Zhang/; Xiao Wang cough Xiao Zhang), "咳嗽 (/ke shou/; cough)" is an intransitive verb. It can only have SUBJ but not OBJ, but OBJ appears in the functional structure, which violates the principle of functional coherence.

Recently, lexical mapping theory (LMT) has been proposed in lexical functional grammar. According to LMT theory, there is a mapping relationship between the thematic structure and predicate-argument structure in vocabulary. To express this mapping relationship, lexical mapping theory uses two features to classify grammatical functions and thematic roles: one feature is + r (+ restricted), which indicates whether the meaning is restricted or not, with + sign for restricted and − sign for unrestricted, and the other feature is + o (+ objective), which means that the grammatical performance has the property of being the object. If it has the property of being the object, it takes the + sign, and if it does not, it takes the − sign. Using agent$>$beneficiary$>$recipient/experiencer$>$instrument$>$patient/theme$>$locative

Fig. 4.29 Thematic hierarchy

these two features, we can divide the dominated grammatical functions into four categories:

$$\text{SUBJ} : [-r, -o] \quad \text{OBJ} : [-r, +o]$$
$$\text{OBL}_\theta : [+r, -o] \quad \text{OBJ}_\theta : [+r, +o]$$

It can be seen that SUBJ and OBJ have the common feature element $[-r]$, and their semantics are not restricted. The grammatical performance of SUBJ does not have the property of being the object, so it has a feature element $[-o]$. The grammatical performance of OBJ has the property of being the object, so it has the feature element $[+o]$. They naturally form a type of grammatical function. OBJ$_\theta$ is an object with restricted semantics, and θ represents a specific thematic role, so it has a feature element $[+r]$. In a sentence with double objects, OBJ$_\theta$ means indirect object. OBL$_\theta$ means that the semantics is restricted and the grammatical performance is not like a certain grammatical function of the object. The phrase like *of + NP* in English is OBJ$_\theta$, because it can act as a theme, patient, and experiencer but cannot act as an agent.

For example, when the English sentence a is nominalized into a noun phrase b, *of the city* is OBL$_{pt}$, which is the patient, and *by the Romans* is OBL$_{ag}$, which is the agent.

(a) The Romans destroyed the city
　　　SUBJ　　　　　　　OBJ
(b) The destruction of the city by the Romans
　　　　　　　　OBL$_{pt}$　　　OBL$_{ag}$
　　where *of the city* is OBL$_{pt}$, that is, the patient, and *by the Romans* is OBL$_{ag}$, that is, the agent. If we change *from the Romans* to *of the Romans*, we get:
*the destruction of the Romans

It is not well-formed in English. It can be seen from this that *of + NP* is semantically restricted, and is not like an object in grammatical performance. Its grammatical function should be OBL$_\theta$.

Lexical mapping theory also stipulates the thematic hierarchy. For example, this theory proposes the following thematic hierarchy (Fig. 4.29).

Where "/" indicates one of the two (i.e., choose one from the two), and "$>$" indicates the priority relationship of the hierarchy.

The thematic structure of the verb can be constructed according to such hierarchical series.

The theoretical basis of this hierarchical structure is that there is a sequence in the semantic combination of the verb of the predicate and the role, that is, the combination of the role and the predicate verb in the lower position in the hierarchical sequence is before the combination of the role and the predicate verb in the higher position in the hierarchical sequence. Therefore, the role in a lower position is easy to be lexicalized.

This law can be proved from the following phenomena. Idioms are mostly composed of "verb + location," such as *put X to sham, take X to task, go to the dogs*; or "verb + involvement," such as *give X a hand, lend X an ear, ring a bell*; or "verb + involvement + position," such as l*et the cat out of the bag, carry coals to Newcastle*. As the role hierarchy rises, the possibility of forming idioms becomes smaller and smaller.

Another basis of this hierarchical structure theory comes from the grammatical sequence of predicate-verb agreement: the role in the front position of the grammatical sequence is the role in the higher position of the hierarchical sequence. In other words, the higher the hierarchy of the role, the more qualified it is to have an agreement relationship with the verb. Therefore, we can call the role at the highest level in the thematic hierarchy a "logical subject," which is often acted by the agent. Therefore, we can determine which feature elements of [+r] or [+o] can be obtained according to the hierarchy of the thematic role and the situation of each role acting as the agent or patient. The lexical mapping theory not only stipulates the decision-making process of these feature elements but also stipulates that only when the feature elements do not conflict with each other can they be selected to express a thematic role. Besides, this theory also requires that the process of mapping and the assignment of feature elements are monotonic (the latter feature value cannot conflict with the previous feature value) and the function is unique (each function can only correspond to one role at most).

Lexical mapping theory is a new theory of lexical functional grammar. According to the lexical mapping theory, as long as we know the thematic structure of expressing concepts, we can predict the expression of grammatical functions and the predicate-argument structure. And when we get to know the predicate-argument structure of the grammatical function, we can predict the surface structure that may appear in various languages. Therefore, this theory has guiding significance for the computer processing of the natural language.

In summary, lexical functional grammar has the following characteristics:

1. Use attribute value matrix as the basic means of expressing grammatical information.
2. Take unification as the basic method of operation and attribute value as the basic unit of operation.
3. Use the information contained in the vocabulary as the basic source of grammatical information.
4. Use disordered grammatical function as the basic concept of grammatical theory.

With these characteristics, lexical functional grammar overcomes the shortcomings of phrase structure grammar, such as its strong generative ability and weak analytical ability, and it does not adopt the method of transformation as N. Chomsky did. It is unique in contemporary linguistics, which is one of the important achievements of language information processing.

4.3   Martin Kay's Functional Unification Grammar

In 1985, the American computational linguist Martin Kay (Fig. 4.30) proposed the concept of the "complex feature set" in the new grammatical theory "Functional Unification Grammar" (FUG). He believes that the natural language is an information system that is extremely efficient and can accurately express various complex ideas. It is impossible to fully describe natural language sentences using only a single syntactic category in N. Chomsky's phrase structure grammar. It must be described by a complex feature set.

In functional unification grammar, complex feature sets are represented by functional description (FD). FD is composed of a group of descriptors, each of which is a constituent set, a pattern, or an attribute with value, the most important of which is the "attribute/value" pair. In FD, the value of a descriptor can be an atom or another functional description. Therefore, the functional description is defined recursively.

The following is a strict definition of the functional description of the complex feature set: α is a functional description, if and only if α can be expressed as in Fig. 4.31. Where f_i represents the feature name, v_i represents the feature value, and the following two conditions are met:

Fig. 4.30 Martin Kay

Fig. 4.31 Functional description

$$\left\{ \begin{array}{l} f_1 = v_1 \\ f_2 = v_2 \\ \vdots \\ f_n = v_n \end{array} \right\} \quad n \geqslant 1$$

1. The feature name f_i is an atom, and the feature value v_i is either an atom or another functional description.
2. $\alpha < f_i > = v_i$
   $(i = 1, \ldots, n)$
   It is read as: in the set α, the value of feature f_i is equal to v_i.
   Using such a functional description, a complex feature set can be expressed.

A group of descriptors that make up the functional description is written in square brackets, and the order does not matter. In an "attribute/value" pair, the attribute is a symbol, such as NUM (number), SUBJ (subject), OBJ (object), MODF (modifier), HEAD (head), etc. Its value is either a symbol or another functional description. The attribute and its value are connected by an equal sign. Therefore, a = b means that the value of attribute a is b.

For example, the English sentence "We helped her" can be represented by the following functional description (1):

FD（1）:

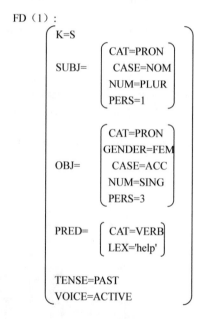

This functional description means: "We helped her" is a sentence (K=S). In this sentence, the subject "we" is a pronoun, nominative, plural, the first person. The object "her" is a pronoun, feminine, accusative, singular, the third person. The predicate "helped" is a verb; the specific word is "help." The tense of the whole sentence is the past tense, and the voice is active. These functional descriptions are the complex feature set of the sentence.

In a functional description, each attribute/value pair is a feature of the object described by FD. If the value is a symbol, then this attribute/value pair is called a basic feature of the functional description. Any functional description can be represented by a table composed of basic features. For example, the functional description (1) above can also be described by the following table FD (2):

```
FD(2) : <K>=S
        <SUBJ CAT>=PRON
        <SUBJ CASE>=NOM
        <SUBJ NUM>=PLUR
        <SUBJ PERS>=1
        <OBJ CAT>=PRON
        <OBJ GENDER>=FEM
        <OBJ CASE>=ACC
        <OBJ NUM>=SING
        <OBJ PERS>=3
        <PRED CAT>=VERB
        <PRED LEX>='help'
        <TENSE>=PAST
        <VOICE>=ACTIVE
```

In FD (2), the symbols in angle brackets <> constitute a path, and each value in the functional description can always be called by a path. It can be seen that the features expressed in FD (2) are the same as those expressed in FD (1), and they are different ways of expressing complex features in the same sentence. However, although FD (1) and FD (2) are two representations of the same functional feature FD, they are different: FD (1) shows the nesting of the functional description, so it emphasizes the structural features of the functional description; FD (2) is a table, which emphasizes the internal component characteristics of the functional description. Both of them intentionally blur the usual differences between features and structures, making functional unification grammar more flexible.

If functional descriptions are treated as nonstructural feature sets, it is possible to deal with them using standard operations of set theory. However, the functional description does not completely obey the operation of set theory. Set theory operations generally do not consider the compatibility of the operation objects, while the functional description must consider such compatibility. If two functional descriptions contain a common attribute, and the value of this common attribute in the two functional descriptions is different, then the two functional descriptions are incompatible. For example, if the functional description F1 contains a basic feature $<A>=x$, and the functional description F2 contains a basic feature $<A>=y$, then F1 and F2 are incompatible unless $x=y$. If the two functional descriptions are incompatible, then when performing the "union" operation in set theory, the result of the operation will not be a qualified functional description. For example, assuming that the sentence described by functional description F1 contains a singular subject, and the sentence described by functional description F2 contains a plural subject, if S1 and S2 are their corresponding basic feature sets, then their union $S1 \cup S2$ is not qualified, because this union of <SUBJ NUM>=SING and <SUBJ NUM>=PLUR is incompatible.

For grammatically ambiguous sentences or phrases, two or more incompatible functional descriptions are needed to represent them. For example, the Chinese sentence "三个学校的实验员来了" (/San ge xue xiao de shi yan yuan lai le/; Three school experimenters have come.) is ambiguous; it has two meanings. One meaning can be expressed by the functional description (3) and the other by the functional description (4).

FD (3)

$$
\begin{bmatrix}
K=S \\
SUBJ= \begin{bmatrix} CAT=NP \\ HEAD='实验员' \\ MODF= \begin{bmatrix} CAT=NP \\ HEAD='学校' \end{bmatrix} \\ QUANT=3 \end{bmatrix} \\
PRED='来' \\
TENSE=PAST \\
VOICE=ACTIVE
\end{bmatrix}
$$

FD (4)

$$
\begin{bmatrix}
CAT=K \\
SUBJ= \begin{bmatrix} CAT=NP \\ HEAD='实验员' \\ MODF= \begin{bmatrix} CAT=NP \\ HEAD='学校' \\ QUANT=3 \end{bmatrix} \end{bmatrix} \\
PRED='来' \\
TENSE=PAST \\
VOICE=ACTIVE
\end{bmatrix}
$$

It can be seen that in FD (3), the sentence means that only three experimenters have come, and these three experimenters are from the same school. In FD (4), the sentence means that some experimenters have come, and these experimenters are from three different schools.

Several incompatible simple functional descriptions, $F_1, \ldots, F_k$, can be combined into a single complex functional description, $\{F_1, \ldots, F_k\}$. The complex functional description represents the union of the object set of components, and the incompatible parts should be enclosed in curly brackets. The following is a complex functional description (5) formed by combining FD (3) and FD (4). It describes the two structural relationships represented by FD (3) and FD (4), respectively:

$$
\text{FD (5)} \begin{bmatrix} \text{CAT=S} \\ \text{SUBJ=} \begin{bmatrix} \text{CAT=NP} \\ \text{HEAD='实验员'} \\ \left\{ \begin{matrix} \begin{bmatrix} \text{MODF=} \begin{bmatrix} \text{CAT=NP} \\ \text{HEAD='学校'} \end{bmatrix} \\ \text{QUANT=3} \end{bmatrix} \\ \begin{bmatrix} \text{MODF=} \begin{bmatrix} \text{CAT=NP} \\ \text{HEAD='学校'} \\ \text{QUANT=3} \end{bmatrix} \end{bmatrix} \end{matrix} \right\} \end{bmatrix} \\ \text{PRED='来'} \\ \text{TENSE=PAST} \\ \text{VOICE-ACTIVE} \end{bmatrix}
$$

The curly braces in FD (5) denote the disjunctive relations between incompatible functional descriptions and sub-functional descriptions. This compact form of complex functional description can describe a large number of incompatible objects. Generally speaking, the grammatical rules in functional unification grammar can be expressed by a unified functional description (6) as follows:

$$
\text{FD (6)} \left\{ \begin{matrix} \begin{bmatrix} \text{CAT=C1} \\ \vdots \end{bmatrix} \\ \begin{bmatrix} \text{CAT=C2} \\ \vdots \end{bmatrix} \\ \vdots \\ \begin{bmatrix} \text{CAT=Cn} \\ \vdots \end{bmatrix} \end{matrix} \right\}
$$

For a system described with this complex feature set, there is no limit to the degree of the detailed description. The more features a description contains, the more specific it is to define the described objects. If some features are removed from a description, it is possible to expand the coverage of the object it describes. Therefore, only by flexibly controlling the number of features and carefully selecting the content of features can we use complex feature sets for a proper description.

In the machine dictionary of machine translation, the definition of each word should not only give its part of speech but also mark its static lexical, syntactic, and semantic features. This is the complex feature set at the word level. With the development of automatic syntactic analysis, not only each word in a sentence is marked with these static features from the dictionary, but also some dynamic features are calculated on each node of the tree diagram representing the hierarchical structure of the sentence, which greatly enrich the content of static features from the dictionary. Of course, these dynamic features should also be marked with complex features. This is the use of complex feature sets at the level of syntactic analysis and semantic analysis. Various complex features in the complex feature set can be inherited from the complex feature labels of the head in the process of phrase merging and can also be dynamically calculated by a computer according to the syntactic and semantic rules. This complex feature set is used in the automatic analysis of the source language, which effectively solves the problem of determining ambiguous structures, and combines the syntactic analysis and semantic analysis through the complex feature set, so as to improve the efficiency of the syntactic and semantic analysis of the source language.

The concept of a complex feature set is similar to the concept of "distinctive feature theory" in phonology. In 1951, R. Jakobson pointed out that all sounds are not monadic, they can be further divided into minimal pairs, and these minimal pairs can be reduced to 12 pairs of distinguishing features. In this way, the undecomposable vowels and consonants in traditional phonology can be transformed into a set of decomposable distinguishing features. This theory makes it possible for us to analyze and identify the structure of phonemes through the method of logical description and raises the theory of phonemes to a new stage. In the early phrase structure grammar, the grammatical categories have no internal structure. They are just like the phonemes before the "distinctive feature theory" was proposed. They are also monadic. After using complex feature sets to describe these syntactic categories, we found that these syntactic categories are not monadic, they also have their structures, so they cannot use a single feature, but must use complex features to describe. Of course, the complex feature sets in language information processing are much richer than the distinguishing features in phonology. They are not only binary opposites but also multivariate opposites. They have not only linear structures but also nested and recursive structures. Therefore, general set theory methods cannot be used to calculate the complex feature sets.

Functional unification grammar uses the unique operation method of "unification" to perform operations on complex feature sets. The term "unification" was originally used in the first-order predicate calculus of mathematical logic. The process of finding the permutation of a certain term for a variable to make the expression consistent is called unification. If there is a permutation S and apply it to each element in the expression set $\{E_i\}$, such that $E_{1s} = E_{2s} = \ldots = E_{ns}$, then the expression set $\{E_i\}$ is said to be unifying; S is called the unifier of $\{E_i\}$ because its function is to simplify the set to a consistent form.

For example, there are two logical terms $A:f(x,y)$ and $B:f(g(y,a),h(a))$; if we use the logical terms $C:x=g(h(a),a)$ and $D:y=h(a)$ to replace the variables x and y in A and B, then after the replacement, both A and B become $f(g(h(a),a),h(a))$, so that A and B become a consistent form. This result is called the unification of A and B. C and D are called the unifier of A and B; A and B are called logical items of unification.

At present, this unification operation has been widely used in high-order logic, computational complexity theory, computability theory, logic programming, and other fields and has been further used in computational linguistics, machine translation, natural language understanding, artificial intelligence, and other fields. One of the reasons why the unification operation is so widely used is the popularity of the logic programming language PROLOG because one of the basic operations that PROLOG is based on in the resolution process of the Horn clause is the unification operation.

In functional unification grammar, the unification operation is used to merge several functional descriptions into a single functional description. Specifically, if two or more simple functional descriptions are compatible, they can be merged into a simple functional description through the unification operation, so that the object described by this functional description is exactly the object described by the previous functional descriptions.

Such unification operation is very similar to the union operation in set theory, but the difference between the unification operation and the union operation is that when incompatible terms are applied to unification operation, the unification fails and an empty set is generated.

The union set obtained by the union operation is a set composed of all the different elements in each set participating in the operation.

For example, $\{A, B\} \cup \{C, B\} = \{A, B, C\}$.

The elements in a set are always regarded as indecomposable atoms in the union operation. Even if the elements are ordered even pairs, such as (f_j, v_j) indicating that the value of feature f_j is v_j, they are still regarded as indecomposable individuals in the union operation, regardless of their internal structure. Suppose

$\alpha = \{(f_1, v_1),(f_2, v_2)\}$
$\beta = \{(f_1, v'_1)\}$

even if $v \neq v'$, the information expressed by α and β conflict with each other; after the union operation, the union set is still

$\gamma = \alpha \cup \beta = \{(f_1, v_1),(f_1, v'_1),(f_2, v_2)\}$.

Although conflicting information is maintained in the union set, from the perspective of information combination and transmission, the union γ obtained is meaningless.

The unification operation must consider the rationality of the operation result. In the unification operation, when the information expressed by α and β conflicts with each other, the unification result is an empty set (denoted as φ), which means the unification fails. If the symbol $\bar{\cup}$ is used to represent unification, then there is $\alpha \bar{\cup} \beta = \varphi$.

Below we give the formal definition of the unification operation in functional unification grammar:

[Definition] Unification operation (operation symbol is represented by $\bar{\cup}$)

1. If both a and b are atoms, then $a\bar{\cup}b = a$, if and only if $a = b$; otherwise $a\bar{\cup}b = \varphi$.
2. If both α and β are complex feature sets, then

   (a) If $\alpha(f) = v$, but the value of $\beta(f)$ is not defined, then $f = v$ belongs to $\alpha\bar{\cup}\beta$.
   (b) If $\beta(f) = v$, but the value of $\alpha(f)$ is not defined, then $f = v$ belongs to $\alpha\bar{\cup}\beta$.
   (c) If $\alpha(f) = v_1$, $\beta(f) = v_2$, and v_1 and v_2 do not conflict, then $f = (v_1\bar{\cup}v_2)$ belongs to $\alpha\bar{\cup}\beta$; otherwise, $\alpha\bar{\cup}\beta = \varphi$. $\alpha\bar{\cup}\beta = \varphi$.

From this definition, we can see that the union operation in set theory is a special case of unification operation. When the elements contained in the object of unification are indecomposable atoms, the result of unification is equal to the union. When the object of unification is a complex feature set with structure, it is necessary to check the compatibility of the features.

Only when the features are compatible the corresponding complex features can be unified. Therefore, the unification operation has two functions: one is to merge the original feature information to construct a new feature structure, which is similar to the union operation in set theory; the other is to check the compatibility of features and the preconditions of rule execution. If the features involved in unification conflict, the unification failure will be declared immediately. It can be seen that the unification operation provides a mechanism to check the restriction conditions while merging the feature information from all aspects. This is exactly what the syntactic and semantic analysis of machine translation needs, so it is welcomed by those who specialize in machine translation.

Let us give an example to illustrate how to perform the unification operation.

Example 1:

$$
\begin{bmatrix} \text{CAT=V} \\ \text{LEX='run'} \\ \text{TENSE=PRES} \end{bmatrix} \bar{\cup} \begin{bmatrix} \text{CAT=V} \\ \text{NUM=SING} \\ \text{PERS=3} \end{bmatrix} \rightarrow \begin{bmatrix} \text{CAT=V} \\ \text{LEX='run'} \\ \text{TENSE=PRES} \\ \text{NUM=SING} \\ \text{PERS=3} \end{bmatrix}
$$

Because the complex features in the two function descriptions involved in the unification operation are compatible, the result of the unification operation is equal to the union of the complex features in the two function descriptions.

Example 2:

$$
\begin{bmatrix} \text{CAT=V} \\ \text{LEX='run'} \\ \text{TENSE=PRES} \end{bmatrix} \bar{\cup} \begin{bmatrix} \text{CAT=V} \\ \text{TENSE=PAST} \\ \text{PRES=3} \end{bmatrix} \rightarrow \text{NIL}
$$

In these two functional descriptions, TENSE=PRES in the first functional description and TENSE=PAST in the second functional description conflict with each other, so the result of the unification operation is NIL, which means unification failure.

Example 3:

$$\left\{ \begin{bmatrix} \text{TENSE=PRES} \\ \text{FORM='is'} \end{bmatrix} \\ \begin{bmatrix} \text{TENSE=PAST} \\ \text{FORM='was'} \end{bmatrix} \right\} \overline{U} \begin{bmatrix} \text{CAT=V} \\ \text{TENSE=PAST} \end{bmatrix} \rightarrow \begin{bmatrix} \text{CAT=V} \\ \text{TENSE=PAST} \\ \text{FORM='was'} \end{bmatrix}$$

The first functional description is a complex one formed by merging two incompatible simple functional descriptions. When it is unified with the second functional description, the compatible feature is taken as the result of the unification operation. Because of the features in the first complex functional description

$$\begin{bmatrix} \text{TENSE=PRES} \\ \text{FORM='is'} \end{bmatrix}$$

It is incompatible with the features in the second functional description, so it is discarded.

Generally speaking, the result of the unification of two complex function descriptions is still a complex function description, in which each item represents a pair of compatible items in the original function description. Therefore,

$$\{a_1, a_2, \ldots, a_n\} \overline{U} \{b_1, b_2, \ldots, b_m\}$$

A functional description in the form of $\{c_1, c_2, \ldots, c_k\}$ is obtained, where each c_h $(1 \le h \le k)$ is the unification result of a pair of compatible terms $a_i = b_j$ $(1 \le i \le n, 1 \le j \le m)$.

It can be seen that the unification operation should have the following properties:

1. In unification operation, information can be added.

   For example,

$$[\text{CAT=NP}] \ \overline{U} \ \begin{bmatrix} \text{AGREEMENT=[NUM=SING]} \end{bmatrix}$$

$$\rightarrow \begin{bmatrix} \text{CAT=NP} \\ \text{AGREEMENT=[NUM=SING]} \end{bmatrix}$$

where the feature AGREEMENT represents an agreement relationship.

2. The unification operation is idempotent.

   For example,

$$[\text{CAT=NP}] \; \bar{\cup} \; \begin{bmatrix} \text{CAT=NP} \\ \\ \text{AGREEMENT=[NUM=SING]} \end{bmatrix}$$

$$\rightarrow \begin{bmatrix} \text{CAT=NP} \\ \\ \text{AGREEMENT=[NUM=SING]} \end{bmatrix}$$

The CAT=NP in the former complex feature set is absorbed into the latter complex feature set.

3. The blank term is the unit element of the unification operation.

For example,

$$[\,] \; \bar{\cup} \; \begin{bmatrix} \text{CAT=NP} \\ \\ \text{AGREEMENT=[NUM=SING]} \end{bmatrix}$$

$$\rightarrow \begin{bmatrix} \text{CAT=NP} \\ \\ \text{AGREEMENT=[NUM=SING]} \end{bmatrix}$$

When the blank item is unified with the complex feature set, it is absorbed by the complex feature.

4. When the feature values are compatible, the same feature can be unified:

For example,

$$\begin{bmatrix} \text{AGREEMENT=[NUM=SING]} \\ \\ \text{SUBJ=[AGREEMENT=[NUM=SING]]} \end{bmatrix} \; \bar{\cup} \; \begin{bmatrix} \text{SUBJ=} & \text{AGREEMENT=[PERS=3]} \end{bmatrix}$$

$$\rightarrow \begin{bmatrix} \text{AGREEMENT=[NUM=SING]} \\ \\ \text{SUBJ =} \begin{bmatrix} \text{AGREEMENT =} \begin{bmatrix} \text{NUM=SING} \\ \text{PERS=3} \end{bmatrix} \end{bmatrix} \end{bmatrix}$$

Since in two complex features before and after the feature values NUM=SING and PERS=3 for the feature SUBJ and feature AGREEMENT are compatible, the following feature is formed after the unification:

$$\left(\begin{array}{l} \text{AGREEMENT=[NUM=SING]} \\ \text{SUBJ} = \left[\text{AGREEMENT} = \left[\begin{array}{l} \text{NUM=SING} \\ \text{PERS=3} \end{array} \right] \right] \end{array} \right)$$

If a natural language is regarded as a system of transmitting and loading information, and it is recognized that the syntactic and semantic components in the natural language can be synthesized of larger components from smaller components, then it is very ideal to use unification as the basic operation of syntactic and semantic analysis. This is because of the following reasons.

First, the information carried by a language unit (such as a sentence or phrase, etc.) can be distributed among various components, and each component can only carry part of the information.

Second, through the unification operation, in the process of combining small components into large ones, the information carried by the small components is also transferred or accumulated to the information carried by the large components. In the process of unification, the information only increases gradually but does not decrease.

Third, because the syntactic and semantic analysis is based on unification as the basic operation, not only the legitimacy of the sentence can be judged by semantic means, but also the syntactic structure and semantic representation of the sentence can be connected more naturally by unification operation.

Fourth, the results of the unification operation of different function descriptions have nothing to do with the order of the operation. No matter which direction the unification starts from, or whether it is the first unification or the last unification, the results of the unification are the same. This disorder of unification is very convenient for parallel processing, and it also makes it possible for us to freely choose the analysis algorithm and the grammar theory for natural language description.

Based on complex feature sets and unification operations, Martin Kay proposed functional unification grammar.

The most important feature of functional unification grammar is the comprehensive and systematic use of complex feature sets in term definition, syntactic rules, semantic rules, and sentence descriptions.

1. The description of the term definition

For example, the English word *saw* has three meanings. In the entry *saw*, three definitions can be given, and the form of each definition is the functional description of the complex feature set FD. See FD (7), FD (8), and FD (9).

FD (7)

$$
\begin{bmatrix}
\text{CAT=V} \\
\text{TENSE=PAST} \\
\text{TRANSITIVITY=MENTAL-PROCESS} \\
\text{ROOT='see'} \\
\text{LEX='saw}
\end{bmatrix}
$$

FD (7) means that saw is the past tense form of the verb *see*, and its meaning is "to see."

FD (8)

$$
\begin{bmatrix}
\text{CAT=N} \\
\text{NUM=SING} \\
\text{LEX='saw'}
\end{bmatrix}
$$

FD (8) means *saw* is a noun, and its meaning is "a cutting tool that has a long blade with a sharp-toothed edge."

FD (9)

$$
\begin{bmatrix}
\text{CAT=V} \\
\text{TENSE=INFINITIVE} \\
\text{TRANSITIVITY=MATERIAL-PROCESS} \\
\text{ROOT='saw'} \\
\text{LEX='saw'}
\end{bmatrix}
$$

FD (9) means *saw* is the infinitive form of the verb *saw*, and its meaning is "to make logs by using a saw."

2. Description of syntactic rules

For example, FD (10) and FD (11) are active and passive rules, respectively.

FD (10):

$$
\begin{bmatrix}
\text{K=S} \\
\text{PATTERNS=(...PREDICATOR} \quad \text{DIRECT-OBJE ...)} \\
\text{SUBJ=ACTOR=[CAT=N]} \\
\text{PREDICATOR=} \begin{bmatrix} \text{CAT=V} \\ \text{TRANSITIVITY=MATERIAL-PROCESS} \\ \text{VOICE=ACTIVE} \end{bmatrix} \\
\text{VOICE=ACTIVE}
\end{bmatrix}
$$

FD (11):

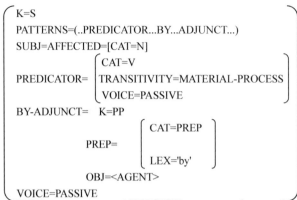

where ACTOR means agent, AFFECTED means patient, and the meaning of other symbols is not difficult to understand from the corresponding English words.

The calling conditions of these two rules are as follows:

(a) K=S for syntactic components;
(b) The predicate verb means a "material process," namely, TRANSITIVETY=MATERIAL-PROCESS.

The value of the feature PATTERNS is ordered, which specifies the basic order of the linguistic elements in the active and passive sentence patterns. The PATTERNS in the active is (...PREDICATOR DIRECT-OBJ...), and the PATTERNS in the passive is (...PREDICATOR...BY-ADJUNCT...). In this way, the position of the language component can be arranged and adjusted according to the value of the feature PATTERNS.

3. Description of sentence structure

For example, the sentence structure of the English sentence "She smashed a brick" can be described by FD (12) (Fig. 4.32).

This functional description not only includes the description of the features and functions of the language components at all levels such as words, phrases, and sentences but also explains the semantic relations of the head verb *smashed* with the actor, the affected, etc.

Martin Kay believes that functional unification grammar is suitable for direct sentence generation. This generation process can start with a synopsis description, then combine the synopsis description with the function description of the grammar rules, and perform the unification operation to generate the complete structure of the sentence.

However, it is difficult to analyze sentences with functional unification grammar, because Martin Kay only regards it as a kind of grammar to describe language competence and does not expect to use this form of grammar directly for sentence analysis. Later, Martin Kay proposed a compiler, which can map the functional description of functional unification grammar into a form suitable for analysis

FD(12):

$$
\begin{bmatrix}
K = S \\
\text{PATTERN} = (\text{SUBJ PREDICATOR DIRECT-OBJ}) \\
\text{TENSE} = \text{PAST} \\
\text{VOICE} = \text{ACTIVE} \\[6pt]
\text{SUBJ} = \text{ACTOR} = \begin{bmatrix}
K = NP \\
\text{PATTERN} = (\text{HEAD}) \\
\text{HEAD} = \begin{bmatrix}
\text{CAT} = \text{PRON} \\
\text{GENDER} = \text{FEM} \\
\text{CASE} = \text{NOM} \\
\text{NUM} = \text{SING} \\
\text{PERS} = 3 \\
\text{LEX} = \text{'she'}
\end{bmatrix} \\
\text{NUM} = \text{SING} \\
\text{DEFINITENESS} = \text{DEFINITE} \\
\text{PERS} = 3
\end{bmatrix} \\[6pt]
\text{PREDICATOR} = \begin{bmatrix}
\text{CAT} = V \\
\text{TRANSITIVITY} = \text{MATERIAL} - \text{PROCESS} \\
\text{VOICE} = \text{ACTIVE} \\
\text{LEX} = \text{'smashed'}
\end{bmatrix} \\[6pt]
\begin{aligned}
\text{DIRECT} - \text{OBJ} = \\
\text{AFFECTED} =
\end{aligned}
\begin{bmatrix}
K = NP \\
\text{PATTERNS} = (\text{DETERMINRE HEAD}) \\
\text{DETERMINER} = \begin{bmatrix}
\text{CAT} = \text{ARTICLE} \\
\text{NUMB} = \text{SING} \\
\text{DEFINITENESS} = \\
\quad \text{INDEFINITE} \\
\text{LEX} = \text{'a'}
\end{bmatrix} \\
\text{HEAD} = \begin{bmatrix}
\text{CAT} = N \\
\text{NUM} = \text{SING} \\
\text{LEX} = \text{'brick'}
\end{bmatrix} \\
\text{NUM} = \text{SING} \\
\text{DEFINITENESS} = \text{INDEFINITE} \\
\text{PERS} = 3
\end{bmatrix}
\end{bmatrix}
$$

Fig. 4.32 Functional description of the sentence

algorithms, and then use R. M. Kaplan's general syntax processor to complete the automatic analysis of sentences. In this way, functional unification grammar can be used for both generation and analysis, becoming bidirectional grammar.

Recently, almost all the grammars used in natural language computer processing have adopted the method of complex feature set and unification operation, so this method has become the mainstream of contemporary language information processing research. In addition to functional unification grammar, generalized phrase structure grammar, lexical functional grammar, head-driven phrase structure grammar, and definite clause grammar all adopt this method.

Generalized phrase structure grammar is based on context-free phrase structure grammar, and its information expression is a restricted "feature/value" system, including simple features and complex features. N. Chomsky once claimed that phrase structure grammar is not suitable for describing the sentence structure of the natural language in a mathematical language. However, G. Gazdar and others pointed out that N. Chomsky made such a conclusion because he made unnecessary restrictions on the formalization of phrase structure grammar, stipulated that only simple markers were used, and excluded the use of complex features. G. Gazdar believes that if we adopt complex features to transform the original phrase structure grammar and develop it into generalized phrase structure grammar instead of generative transformational grammar like N. Chomsky, then this generalized phrase structure grammar will have the universality and generativity of generative transformational grammar while retaining many advantages of phrase structure grammar.

The information structure of lexical functional grammar mentioned above is mainly functional. This functional structure itself is an attribute-value matrix, and this attribute value matrix is a recursive "feature/value" system. Besides, this grammar also has special types of features and information and uses complex feature sets at the lexical level. The functional equation of lexical functional grammar realizes the combination and transmission of complex feature sets among the various nodes of the syntactic structure

Head-driven phrase structure grammar relaxes some restrictions on the context-free feature system in generalized phrase structure grammar by introducing the operation of symbol string around the head and expands the description ability of generalized phrase structure grammar, because the whole sentence takes the head as the core and connects the information of the complex feature set which plays an important role in this grammar.

The symbol in definite clause grammar is a logic item, which can load many kinds of information. Such a structure of loading information is a "feature/value" system. The right part of definite clause grammar rules contains the information of test conditions, which is part of the complex feature set information. The "Horn clause" is widely used in definite clause grammar, and the unification operation is one of the basic operations based on the process of the Horn clause resolution in the PROLOG programming language.

It can be seen that complex feature sets and unification operations are the main trends of language information processing in the twentieth century. At present, in language information processing, there are researches with general methodological significance, such as "complex-feature-based" and "unification-based grammar formalism," which shows that the methods of complex feature sets and unification operations are developing rapidly along different historical clues. In our research on

Fig. 4.33 G. Gazdar

language information processing, we must pay attention to this rather innovative method.

4.4 Gazdar's Generalized Phrase Structure Grammar

Generalized phrase structure grammar (GPSG) is improved phrase structure grammar, which was founded in the late 1970s. The main representatives are the British linguist Gerald Gazdar (Fig. 4.33), Ivan Sag, Ewan Klein, and the American linguist Geoffrey Pullum.

Gazdar's paper on generalized phrase structure grammar first began to circulate in 1979. In 1982, G. Gazdar published the article "Phrase Structure Grammar." In the same year, G. Gazdar and G. Pullum co-authored and published the book *Generalized Phrase Structure Grammar: A Theoretical Synopsis*. In this book, they put forward the basic principles and methods of generalized phrase structure grammar. Since then, G. Gazdar and others have revised and supplemented the original theory and published the book *Generalized Phrase Structure Grammar* (Oxford, Basil Blackwell, 1985), which makes a comprehensive and systematic exposition of generalized phrase structure grammar and which represents the latest achievement of generalized phrase structure grammar.

In the late 1950s, N. Chomsky pointed out the limitations of phrase structure grammar in describing the natural language and proposed transformational generative grammar to overcome these limitations. Since the 1970s, N. Chomsky found that transformational generative grammar has its limitations. Its generation ability is too strong. It can not only generate all human languages but also generate many symbol strings beyond human languages. Therefore, N. Chomsky proposed the government and binding theory to constraint the strong generative ability of transformational generative grammar. However, because transformational generative grammar usually involves the relationship between several sentences, it is very inconvenient to use in machine translation and natural language processing. It is not as good as phrase structure grammar, which analyzes sentence by sentence, and its constituent structure is unitary. A sentence has only one constituent structure, and there is no connection between sentences in the constituent structure, which is very convenient for machine translation grammar analysis and natural language processing. Generalized phrase structure grammar has returned to the standpoint of phrase structure grammar. It advocates that the syntax has only one structural plane. At the same time, it imposes a series of restrictions on phrase structure grammar, which not only gives full play to the advantages of the original phrase structure grammar but also overcomes its limitations.

Generalized phrase structure grammar not only advocates that there is only one plane in syntactic structure but also that every syntactic structure corresponds to a semantic interpretation, which integrates syntactic analysis and semantic explanation. Generalized phrase structure grammar insists on strict formalization and attaches great importance to the study and description of the mathematical nature of grammar, so it is welcomed by natural language processing researchers.

In phrase structure grammar, the tree diagram of the sentence structure is directly formed and interpreted by rewriting rules, and the tree structure can be directly derived from rewriting rules. In generalized phrase structure grammar, the rule system needs to go through a series of well-formedness conditions to connect with the surface structure of the sentence. Each rule only produces a candidate local tree structure. As for whether the tree structure can be accepted or not, it needs to go through a series of well-formedness conditions. Those that pass this test can be accepted, but those that fail this test cannot be accepted. In this way, grammar has changed from a simple derivation process to a step-by-step inspection process, through which unqualified syntactic structures are excluded. This is the fundamental difference between generalized phrase structure grammar and traditional phrase structure grammar.

Generalized phrase structure grammar also refers to Montague grammar for semantic interpretation. They accepted Montague grammar's "rule-to-rule hypothesis" and believed that every syntactic rule in the grammar must have a semantic rule associated with it. The function of the semantic rule is to explain the tree structure derived from the syntactic rule.

When generalized phrase structure grammar performs semantic interpretation, it first translates the syntactic features and syntactic categories on each parent node in the tree structure into connotative logic expressions, and then these expressions are explained by model theory according to Montague grammar.

Syntactic features are the medium through which generalized phrase structure grammar conducts feature restriction, which can be divided into three categories.

The first category is the head feature, including N (noun), V (verb), SUBJ (subject), INV (inversion), AUX (auxiliary verb), AGR (agreement), PRED (predicate), SUBCAT (subcategorization), BAR (bar), SLASH (slash), PLUR (plural),

PERS (person), VFORM (verb form), PFORM (preposition form), PAST (past tense), ADV (adverbial), and LOC (location).

The second category is the foot feature. There are only three: SLASH (slot feature), WH (interrogative and relative pronoun features), and RE (reflexive and reciprocal pronoun features). Among them, SLASH is used to describe the oblique line in the head feature and the slot in the structure in the foot feature. It is used to describe both the head feature and the foot feature. This is the only feature that has the head feature and the foot feature. When SLASH represents the slot in the description structure, its feature value is the category represented by the slot.

The third category is general features, including CASE (case), CONJ (conjunction), GER (gerund), NFORM (noun form), NULL (slot), POSS (possession), COMP (complement component), NEG (negation), REMOR (reflexives), and WHMOR (interrogative words).

The purpose of classifying features into these three different categories is to explain the different attributes of these features in the syntactic description, to explain why these different features are restricted by different rules.

The head feature can diffuse from top to bottom in the tree structure, and the foot feature can percolate from the bottom to the top in the tree structure, but the general feature does not have such diffusivity and permeability.

Generalized phrase structure grammar uses complex features to describe syntax, and all syntactic features are composed of <features, feature values>. A feature has two properties: one is what value it has; the other is what regularity it has with other features in the distribution.

Some features have ultimate values. For example, in English, there are the following features and their ultimate feature values:

```
Feature                    Feature values
BAR (bar)                  {0,1,2}
PERS (person)              {1,2,3}
PLUR(plural)               {+,-}
CASE (Case)                {NOM,ACC}
VFORM (verb form)          {FIN,INF,BAS,PAS,...}
PFORM (preposition form)   {to,by,for,...}
```

In the feature values of CASE and VFORM, NOM means nominative, ACC means accusative, FIN means finite verb, INF means infinitive verb, BAS means prototype verb, and PAS means passive verb.

Other features take a certain syntactic category as their value, so its feature value is the feature of this syntactic category and the feature value of this syntactic category. For example, the feature AGR (agreement feature) takes the syntactic category NP as its value. If the syntactic category NP contains the following features:

{<N,+>, <V,->, <BAR,2>, <PER,3>, <PLU,->},

then the value of the feature AGR representing the agreement relationship is

{<AGR, {<N,+>, <V,->, <BAR,2>, <PER,3>, <PLU,->}>}.

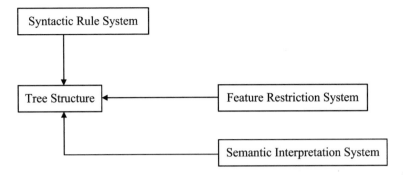

Fig. 4.34 The theoretical framework of generalized phrase structure grammar

Because of this complex feature, it can fully express all kinds of information contained in the sentence and greatly improve the description ability of generalized phrase structure grammar.

One of the characteristics of the syntactic description of generalized phrase structure grammar is to label each node in the tree diagram with feature values. Features can enter the tree diagram in two ways. One is to enter the tree diagram through the direct dominance rules in the syntax, and the features on the tree diagram nodes come from the immediate dominance rules. This feature from the direct dominance rules is called "inherited feature." The other is to enter the tree diagram directly without using syntactic rules. This feature is called the "instantiated feature." Feature acquisition must be restricted by certain principles. On the one hand, the function of these principles is to guide the feature to enter the appropriate node in the tree diagram and, on the other hand, to prevent the occurrence of various erroneous feature assignments. The division of features into inherited features and instantiated features helps to explain language phenomena. This is because some restrictive principles only affect instantiated features but cannot do anything about inherited features.

In a word, generalized phrase structure grammar describes the tree structure of sentences through phrase structure rules and at the same time restricts the tree structure through the feature system, so that it correctly reflects the reality of the language as a whole. This tree structure obtains the model-theoretic semantic interpretation of the sentence through a specific semantic interpretation system.

Therefore, generalized phrase structure grammar can be divided into three parts: a syntactic rule system, a feature restriction system, and a semantic interpretation system. The relationship between them is shown in Fig. 4.34.

Fig. 4.35 Projection of the
main category

X	X'	X''
N	N$'$	NP
V	V$'$	VP
A	A$'$	AP
P	P$'$	PP

4.4.1 Syntactic Rule System

The syntactic rules of generalized phrase structure grammar are the main basis for syntactic description. It is composed of three parts: the numbering part, the direct dominance rule part, and the semantic interpretation part. The general form of syntactic rules is as follows:

$$< n, C_0 \rightarrow C_1, C_2, \ldots C_n; \alpha'(\beta') >$$

where n is the number of subcategorization, the middle part is the direct dominance rule, and $\alpha'(\beta')$ is the semantic interpretation. It can be seen that generalized phrase structure grammar inserts vocabulary into the constituent structure mainly based on the number of vocabulary subcategorization rather than the context. Therefore, this is context-free phrase structure grammar.

The syntactic category of generalized phrase structure grammar is mainly based on "X bar theory." In the theory of X-bar syntax, the traditional phrases such as NP, VP, AP, and PP are regarded as the projection of lexical categories such as N, V, A, and P. "Projection" is the reflection of the category at a more abstract level, and its degree of abstraction is expressed by the bar level of projection. In generalized phrase structure grammar, the lexical category (such as N, V, A, P) is 0-level, and the phrase category (such as NP, VP, AP, PP) is the second-level projection of the lexical category. There is an intermediate level between the lexical category and the phrase category, that is, the first-level projection of the lexical category.

The level of a projection is represented by a superscript or a line over the category of the projection.

For example, the 0-level projection, the first-level projection, and the second-level projection of X can be expressed by superscript as follows:

$$X^0, X^1, X^2$$
$$\text{or} \quad X, X', X''$$

We can also add the horizontal line above X as follows:

$$\mathrm{X}, \overline{\mathrm{X}}, \overline{\overline{\mathrm{X}}}$$

The syntactic categories of X-bar syntax can be divided into two categories: one is the main category and the other is a minor category. The main category is composed of N, V, A, P, and their first- or second-level projection categories. The minor categories are other categories outside the main category, including DET, Comp, CONJ, etc. The main difference between these two categories is that the main category has a projection level value (such as N is 0 level, NP is second level, etc.), while the minor category does not have this value, so the minor category has no projection.

The zero-level, first-level, and second-level projections of the main categories N, V, A, and P are shown in Fig. 4.35.

where the first-level projection of the main category is composed of the main category and its subcategorized components and the second-level projection of the main category is composed of the first-level projection of the main category plus some additional modifier components. They can form NPs, VP, AP, and PP, respectively.

For example, in the verb phrase "sees tables in the room" in the sentence "He sees tables in the room," the zero-level category V of the verb *sees* is itself *sees*. The second-level category V of the verb *sees* is composed of *sees* plus its subcategorized component *tables* (direct object), that is, *sees tables*.

The second-level category V" of the verb *sees* is composed of its first-level category *sees tables* plus the modifier for space *in the room* (adverbial), that is, the verb phrase (VP) "sees tables in the room."

Zero-level category V:	sees
The first-level category V':	sees tables
The second-level category V"(VP):	sees tables in the room

In the generalized phrase structure grammar, in addition to the abovementioned categories, syntactic categories can also be divided into two categories according to whether they have subcategorization features. The subcategorization features are denoted as SUBCAT. All minor category words and the main category words with the first-level have a subcategorization number in the lexicon, that is, the SUBCAT features, which belong to the lexical category. All other main categories with first-level and second-level projections are not included in the lexicon. They have no SUBCAT feature and are non-lexical categories.

The subcategorization feature is a feature that re-differentiates the lexical category. For example, the subcategorization feature of a verb category is the collection of all categories that the category lacks when forming a sentence. In this way, verbs can be divided into intransitive verbs and transitive verbs. If it is an intransitive verb, it lacks the subject to form a sentence, so its subcategorization feature is the subject. If it is a transitive verb, it lacks the subject and the object to form a sentence, so its subcategorization feature is a collection of the subject and object.

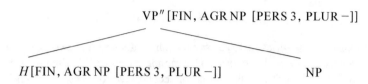

VP″ [FIN, AGR NP [PERS 3, PLUR −]]

H[FIN, AGR NP [PERS 3, PLUR −]]   NP

Fig. 4.36 The circulation of syntactic features in the tree structure

The subcategorization features of a lexical category can be visually represented by a list or a stack. When analyzing the sentence, the items in the subcategorization feature are matched with the components in the sentence being analyzed one by one to get the structure of the sentence. Therefore, subcategorization features play a very important role in automatic syntactic analysis.

Since phrases are projections of vocabulary, there is usually a lexical component in the structure of a phrase as its head. In this way, phrases can be defined as projections of their "internal head." The head largely determines the distribution of the syntactic features within a phrase.

The highest level of a phrase is level 2, which can be written as <BAR, 2>, and the head is level 0, which can be written as <BAR, 0>, or as H (abbreviation for head). Then the syntactic category can be labeled to the corresponding node in the tree structure according to the level of its BAR. The generalized phrase structure grammar further requires the features of the parent node (the node that directly dominates another node) in the hierarchy to agree with the features of the head at its child node (the node directly dominated by the parent node). In this way, the various syntactic features of the vocabulary recorded in the lexicon can be circulated in the tree diagram. For example, in the tree diagram below (Fig. 4.36), the syntactic features of the parent node VP are circulated from the syntactic features of the head (H).

Where FIN represents the finite verb and AGR NP [PERS 3, PLUR −] represents that the third-person and singular features of the head verb must be in agreement with the noun phrase (NP), and these features are all circulated to the parent node verb phrase. The earlier rules of general phrase structure grammar are general phrase structure rules. For example:

VP → V NP PP

This kind of phrase structure rule expresses two structural relationships: one is the direct dominance relationship, and the above rule indicates that VP directly dominates V, NP, and PP; the other is a linear sequence relationship. The above rule also indicates that in VP, V is before NP, and NP is before PP.

Later, researchers of generalized phrase structure grammar canceled such phrase structure rules and replaced them with two rules: one expresses immediate dominance relations, called immediate dominance (ID) rules, and the other expresses before and after position relationship, which is called linear precedence (LP) rules. For example:

ID rule:	VP → V NP PP
LP rule:	V < NP < PP

The former is the ID rule, which only expresses the immediate dominance relationship in the syntactic structure and does not express the word order relationship; the latter is the LP rule, which uses "<" to indicate the before and after position relationship.

Separating immediate dominance rules (ID rules) and linear precedence rules (LP rules) enables the grammar to have greater generalization capabilities. For languages with relatively free word order, it is very cumbersome to express them if they are written using the rules of phrase structure grammar. For example, A is composed of B, C, and D, but the word order of B, C, and D is not restricted. It is written with the rules of phrase structure grammar and has six rules as shown below:

A → B C D
A → B D C
A → C B D
A → C D B
A → D B C
A → D C B

However, writing with the immediate dominance rule of generalized phrase structure grammar requires only the following rule (the symbols A, B, C at the right of the rule are disordered):

A → B C D

At the end of the transfer phase in machine translation, the structure of source language is mainly to express the immediate dominance of the syntactic structure of source language, while the linear precedence of the components of the source language is irrelevant. At this time, it is necessary to separate the immediate dominance rule from the linear precedence rule, so this distinction is very useful in machine translation.

In generalized phrase structure grammar, the immediate dominance rules can be divided into two categories: lexical ID rules and non-lexical ID rules. The rule of the subcategorization feature of the head with SUBCAT is the lexical ID rule. At this time, the value of BAR is 0. The rule of immediate dominance of vocabulary can be expressed as follows:

C → ...H[n],...

where n is the value of SUBCAT, which represents the subcategorization feature of the head, i.e., the component that the head lacks when it forms a sentence which is the syntactic category that the head can dominate, such as the subject, object, etc. C is the non-terminal symbol; H is the head. In this case, the parent node directly dominates the lexical category. For example, the rule

VP″ → H, NP

is a rule that a word immediately dominates. The head $H = V$, that is, the head is the verb, and the verb is a lexical category. NP is the value of SUBCAT of the head, that is, the subcategorization feature of H.

NP is the value of the subcategory of the head H, which is the subcategorization feature of H. The vocabulary category V can be expressed as follows:

$\{<N, ->, <V, +>, <BAR, 0>, <SUBCAT, NP>\}$

The immediate dominance rule of a head which does not have the feature of SUBCAT is called the non-lexical immediate domination rule. The following rule is an example:

$S \rightarrow N'', H[-SUBJ]$

It is a non-lexical immediate domination rule. At this time, N'' is second-level, the head H has non-subject features and does not have subcategorization features, and S represents a sentence.

4.4.2 Meta-Rules

Generalized phrase structure grammar has a mechanism for generating rules from rules, which is called "meta-rule." Meta-rules are mainly used to describe the increase or decrease of the number of child nodes in a parent node or the change of features.

The meta-rule is composed of two parts: the "pattern structure" and "target structure."

The pattern structure can be expressed as follows:

$$P_0 \rightarrow W, P_m$$

where P_0 is the parent node, W is any variable in the category, and P_m is the node immediately dominated by P_0 ($m = 0$ or 1).

The target structure can be expressed as follows:

Fig. 4.37 Meta-rule

$$\text{Pattern structure} \quad P_0 \twoheadrightarrow W, P_m$$
$$\downarrow$$
$$\text{Target structure} \quad a_0 \twoheadrightarrow a_1, a_2, \cdots, a_k$$

Fig. 4.38 The meta-rule for passive in English

$$\text{Pattern structure} \quad VP \twoheadrightarrow W, NP$$
$$\downarrow$$
$$\text{Target structure} \quad VP[PAS] \twoheadrightarrow W, (PP[by])$$

$$a_0 \rightarrow a_1, \ldots, a_k$$

where a_0 and P_0 belong to the same main category, and there can be at most only one a_i which is a variable of W and at most only one a_i which can correspond to P_m. The specific form of the meta-rule is as follows (Fig. 4.37).

The above can be read as if $P_0 \rightarrow W$, P_m is an immediate dominance rule of a word, and then $a_0 \rightarrow a_1, \ldots, a_k$ is also an immediate dominance rule of a word. The purpose of meta-rules is to transform all the immediate dominance rules that conform to the pattern structure into the immediate dominance rules represented by the target structure, thereby increasing the number of immediate dominance rules in the grammar.

For example, the meta-rule for "passive" in English is as follows (Fig. 4.38).

Where W is the category variable, PAS is the feature of VP, and *by* is the feature of PP. It means that in a passive sentence, the verb in the verb phrase is passive, and the preposition in the prepositional phrase is *by*. The parentheses indicate that the part can be omitted, and (PP[by]) indicates that the prepositional phrase PP with *by* in the passive sentence can be omitted.

Apply this meta-rule to the English sentence

He broke the window,

We can get a passive sentence

The window was broken (by him).

In this passive sentence, the original verb *broke* becomes *was broken*, and (by him) can be omitted.

4.4.3   The Feature Restriction System

To restrict the strong generation ability of traditional phrase structure grammar, generalized phrase structure grammar also proposes a "well-formedness definition" to prevent the generation of unqualified structures. This is the feature restriction system.

When projecting from an immediate domination rule to a tree structure, the well-formedness condition should be defined. That is, there is a projection function φ between the rule and the tree structure, which is related to each specific rule to define

Fig. 4.39 Feature restriction

the corresponding local tree structure so that the qualified surface structure can be obtained. This restriction can be illustrated as follows (Fig. 4.39).

Here, C denotes the nodes in a tree structure, which corresponds to the category C in the immediate domination rules. The so-called the projection of rules to tree structures is to reflect the syntactic features contained in the rule in the tree structure. The projection function φ determines which features are allowed and which are not allowed. The correctness of generalized phrase structure grammar is guaranteed by such a feature restriction system.

The projection function φ of the well-formedness definition of the feature restriction system consists of the following principles.

4.4.3.1 Feature Co-occurrence Restriction (FCR)

There are implication relationships between features. When some features appear, they must be accompanied by other features, so that when describing a sentence rule, some accompanying features do not have to be included, and the sentence rule only uses the minimum number of features without reducing the accuracy of generalization. For example, here are two rules for feature co-occurrence restrictions:

1. [INV +] → [AUX +, FIN]
2. [VFORM] → [V +, N −]

Rule (1) states that the inverted feature [INV +] must have both [AUX +] and [VFORM FIN] at the same time. That is to say, the inverted feature and the auxiliary verb feature and the finite verb appear at the same time.

Rule (2) states that the feature of verb form [VFORM] can only be used in the category of verbs ([V +]), not in the category of nouns ([N −]). If the feature of [VFORM] is acquired at the NP node, then it violates the principle of co-occurrence restriction of this feature.

There are 22 restrictions on feature co-occurrence listed in generalized phrase structure grammar. Each node in a tree structure cannot violate these restrictions.

4.4.3.2 Feature Specification Defaults (FSD)

This principle is used to indicate "Default" for certain features. If a feature is defaultable, then the value should be taken according to the general regulations. For example, in generalized phrase structure grammar, there is a default feature which states that the feature [INV] takes a negative value in general, that is:

[INV −]

This means that in general, [INV −] is the default, and the value of the inverted feature [INV +] cannot be arbitrarily introduced into the tree diagram. Only when the subject and predicate are inverted that the inverted feature [INV +] can be introduced into the tree diagram by other means.

Fig. 4.40 Head feature
convention

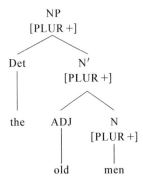

As a whole structure, the grammatical relationship between its various parts of a sentence often shows the consistency of grammatical attributes between the constituent structures. For example, in English, the person and number of the predicate must be consistent with that of the subject, and the person and number of the anaphoric component must be consistent with that of the control component. Therefore, the acquisition of features in a structure is not arbitrary or improvised but is restricted by certain principles that keep the features of the whole structure in harmony. In this respect, the principle of feature restriction includes the principle of head feature convention, the foot feature principle, and the control agreement principle, which are described as follows.

4.4.3.3   Head Feature Convention (HFC)

The feature associated with the head is called the head feature, which is recorded as HEAD. In any local tree structure, the head feature at the child node must be consistent with the feature contained in the head at the parent node. According to the head feature convention, in the immediate dominance rule:

$$C_o \rightarrow \ldots, C_n, \ldots$$

where if C_n is the head of C_o, then the acquired main feature of node C_n should be consistent with that of node C_o. In other words, node C_o must pass all its main features to node C_n. If the head C_n also has its head δ, the obtainable main feature of δ must be the same as that of node C_n according to the principle of the head feature convention. This ensures that the main features can be transferred from top to bottom in the tree diagram. For example, the tree diagram of the noun phrase *the old men* can be represented in Fig. 4.40 after the head feature convention.

In the tree diagram of Fig. 4.40, N′ is the head of NP, and N is the head of N′. The principle of head feature convention ensures that the feature [PLUR +] is transferred from node NP through node N′ to node N. Since neither node Det nor node ADJ is the head, the [PLUR +] cannot be obtained from both nodes.

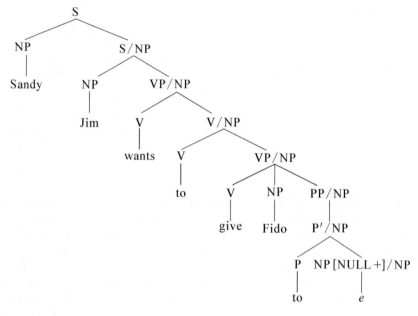

Fig. 4.41 Foot feature principle

4.4.3.4   Foot Feature Principle (FFP)

The foot feature principle applies only to the three foot features SLASH, WH, and RE. The foot feature principle defines that these three features are transferred from the bottom to the top in the tree diagram. According to the foot feature principle, grammar can transfer the acquired foot feature on a node to a parent node, the acquired foot feature on the parent node can continue to transfer up, and so on.

Let us take SLASH as an example. SLASH takes categories as feature values to indicate slots in the structure. C [SLASH C′] denotes a C category that lacks C′, abbreviated as C/C′. According to the foot feature principle, the slot features can be transferred through SLASH. For example, the process of slot transfer can be seen from the tree diagram of "Sandy, Jim wants to give Fido to"; Fido is the name of a dog (Fig. 4.41).

According to the immediate dominance rule

$$P' \rightarrow H, \ NP[NULL+]$$
$$\text{We can get} \quad P' \rightarrow P, \ NP[NULL+]$$

A local sub-tree diagram is created.

According to the feature co-occurrence restriction

$$[NULL+] \rightarrow [SLASH]$$

[NULL +] can get SLASH features. Since SLASH is a foot feature, the slot feature can be transferred upward layer by layer until to the S/NP layer according to the foot feature principle. At this time, according to the immediate dominance rule

S → NP, S/NP

It can be known that S/NP lacks NP that is the slot e transferred from bottom to top. Therefore, slot e refers to the NP *Sandy*.

4.4.3.5   Control Agreement Principle (CAP)

This principle ensures that the features of the two nodes in the structure are consistent. Of these two nodes, one is the control component and the other is the target component. The component that must be consistent with the features of the other nodes is called the target component. The control agreement principle stipulates the following: (1) If the target component C has a control component C' in the same local tree structure, then the value of the control feature of C must be the same as the category of C'; (2) if C does not have a control component C' in the same local tree structure, then the value of the control feature of C must be the same as the value of the control feature of C's parent node. There are two control features: one is AGR, which is an agreement feature, and the other is SLASH, which is an inherited feature, and they all use categories as feature values.

In English, the subject and the predicate are required to be consistent in person, gender, and number. There is an agreement relationship between the subject and the predicate. The control agreement principle is used to control and test this agreement. According to the control agreement principle, in English, to make the functional category VP of the predicate and the argument category NP of the subject functionally consistent, the information of the subject NP must be copied to the predicate VP so that the predicate VP is consistent in person, gender, and number with the subject NP.

4.4.3.6   Linear Precedence Statement (LPS)

There is no order in the immediate precedence rules of generalized phrase structure grammar. Therefore, after the local tree structure is processed by the immediate precedence rules, it is necessary to arrange the pre- and post-order relations among the sibling nodes. This kind of work is controlled by the linear precedence statement. After the rule processing of the linear precedence statement, the sibling nodes in the local tree structure become ordered.

It can be seen that when a rule is projected to a tree structure, it must be restricted by the above well-formedness conditions. This projection must not violate all the feature co-occurrence restrictions (FCR), must compare all the feature specification defaults (FSD), must conform to the head feature convention (HFC), must conform to the foot feature principle (FFP), must conform to the control agreement principle (CAP), and must not violate all the linear precedence statements (LPS). A projection that meets these well-formedness conditions can be regarded as a permissible projection. If every local tree structure in the tree structure passes the test of these well-formedness conditions, then the tree structure is a qualified surface structure, and the sentence generated by grammar can be regarded as a qualified sentence.

When parsing sentences, we should first expand the immediate dominance rules according to the meta-rules and make a partial parsing tree under the condition of satisfying the control agreement principle (CAP), the head feature convention (HFC), and the foot feature principle (FFP). Then we use the feature co-occurrence restriction (FCR) and feature specification defaults (FSD) to check the category features. Finally, we use the linear precedence statements (LPS) to check the surface linear order and complete the automatic parsing of sentences.

As generalized phrase structure grammar sets up these well-formedness conditions, it has effectively restricted the strong generative ability of phrase structure grammar and improved the ability of the grammatical theory to explain language facts. This is an important improvement to N. Chomsky's phrase structure grammar.

The semantic interpretation system of generalized phrase structure grammar adopts the method of intensional logic, which is formed based on Montague grammar. Generalized phrase structure grammar can map the intensional logic expression on the child node to the intensional logic expression on the parent node so that the intensional logic expression on the parent node becomes the result of function application. The referential domain (i.e., the possible referential category) of intensional logic expression depends on the semantic class of the expression. The semantic interpretation of generalized phrase structure grammar is mainly to determine the referential domain of the intensional logical expression. With the referential domain, and given a model, the semantic interpretation of the expression for the model can be obtained.

Generalized phrase structure grammar takes the phrase structure as its only syntactic object and the surface structure as its only syntactic description plane. It expands phrase structure grammar so that the expanded grammar is still phrase structure grammar. Therefore, this kind of grammar is called generalized phrase structure grammar. While establishing grammar, this linguistic theory attempts to reveal the relationship between syntax and semantics and emphasizes both syntax and semantics, which is the goal pursued by generalized phrase structure grammar. Generalized phrase structure grammar is also committed to the exploration of the universality of grammar. The metalanguage based on the grammatical features of a group of known languages can define the grammar of most natural languages, which is of universality. Therefore, this kind of grammar is a grammatical theory with great influence on natural language processing.

Generalized phrase structure grammar uses a series of complex mathematical operations to derive the surface structure of the sentence with semantic interpretation. This kind of grammatical theory is very formal, which facilitates the formal description of the language in the design of natural language processing and machine translation systems. Therefore, generalized phrase structure grammar has been

Fig. 4.42 Stuart M. Shieber

welcomed by natural language processing researchers and is quite influential. This formal model of natural language processing has played a positive role in the development of natural language processing.

4.5 Shieber's PATR

In the 1980s, Stuart M. Shieber of Stanford University (Fig. 4.42) developed PATR. PATR is a computer language used to encode language information, and it is also a formal model of natural language processing.

PATR grammar includes a set of rules and a lexicon.

A PATR rule includes a context-free phrase structure rule and a set of feature constraints. The feature structure related to the components of the phrase structure rule is calculated using the unification method. The terms in the lexicon record the words in the language and their related features. These terms are used to replace the terminal symbols in the phrase structure rules.

The form of the context-free phrase structure rule is as follows:

LHS → RHS_1 RHS_2...

where the LHS (left-hand side) before the arrow is the left part of the rule, which must be a single non-terminal symbol, and the RHS (right-hand side) behind the arrow is the right part of the rule, which is a string of symbols that can include one or more symbols denoted as "RHS_1 RHS_2....". These symbols can be terminal symbols or non-terminal symbols.

Here are some context-free phrase structure rules in English:

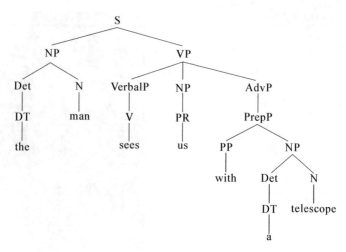

Fig. 4.43 The tree diagram obtained by analysis

```
S        → NP VP (SubCl)
NP       → {(Det) (AdjP) N (PrepP)} / PR
Det      → DT / PR
VP       → VerbalP (NP / AdjP) (AdvP)
VerbalP → V
VerbalP → AuxP V
AuxP     → AUX (AuxP_1)
PrepP    → PP NP
AdjP     → (AV) AJ (AdjP_1)
AdvP     → {AV / PrepP} (AdvP_1)
SubCl    → CJ S
```

where the meanings of symbols such as S, N, V, NP, VP, Det, etc. are already familiar to us and will not be explained. Besides, SubCL represents sub-clause, AdjP represents an adjective phrase, PrepP represents preposition phrase, PR represents pronoun, DT represents determiner, VerbalP represents verb or the combination of a verb and an auxiliary verb, AdvP means adverb phrase, AuxP means auxiliary phrase, AV means adverb, AJ means adjective, PP means preposition, and CJ means conjunction.

On the right part of the rule, the components in parentheses "( )" indicate optional components; the components before and after the slash "/" indicate either-or. If the same component appears repeatedly, it is followed by "_" and a number to show the difference. The components in the curly braces "{ }" appear alternately in groups, and the alternate components are not ambiguous.

Using these rules to analyze the English sentence "the man sees us with a telescope," you can get the tree diagram (Fig. 4.43).

Since the object *us* of *sees* is a pronoun, we can choose PR after the slash in the rule NP→{(Det) (AdjP) N (PrepP)} / PR to get the rule NP → PR. This rule does not

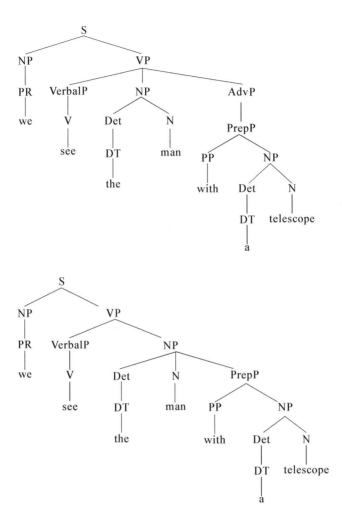

Fig. 4.44 The same sentence gets different analysis results

have a prepositional phrase after PR; we get the analysis result in Fig. 4.43. The sentence means: "This man looks at us with a telescope." However, if we use this context-free phrase structure grammar to analyze the English sentence "we see the man with a telescope," due to the ambiguity of this sentence, the analysis results will get the following two different tree diagrams (Fig. 4.44a, b).

It is because the prepositional phrase (PrepP) "with a telescope" can modify the verb (VerbalP) "sees" and the noun (N) "man," resulting in ambiguity. The analysis results in two tree diagrams with different structures. The first tree diagram means "with a telescope, we look at this man"; the second tree diagram means "Let's look at this man who has a telescope." It can be seen that context-free phrase structure grammar can distinguish sentence ambiguity and is a very effective formal model of natural language processing.

The most serious problem of context-free phrase structure grammar is its overgeneration, which often generates some sentences that do not conform to the grammar. When parsing sentences, because of the overgeneration, some incorrect sentences will be analyzed, which reduces the accuracy of the analysis. For example, using our context-free phrase structure grammar, we can analyze the incorrect English sentence "*he see the man with a telescope" (the verb *see* does not have the ending s) and produce an analysis result similar to that in the tree diagram (Fig. 4.43). This kind of wrong analysis should be avoided in natural language processing.

To overcome this serious shortcoming of context-free phrase structure grammar, PATR-II combines context-free phrase structure grammar with the feature structure and uses the feature structure to control the overgeneration of context-free phrase structure grammar. For example, if we add the plural first-person feature to the verb *see* in the above context-free phrasal structure grammar, the wrong sentence "* he see the man with a telescope" will not be given an analysis result.

The basic data structure of PATR is the feature structure. A feature structure can contain one or more features. A feature consists of an attribute name and an attribute value. The feature structure can be represented by attribute-value matrices. For example, the following is an attribute-value matrix:

```
[ lex: telescope
  cat: N ]
```

where *lex* and *cat* are the attribute names and *telescope* and N are the attribute values of *lex* and *cat*, respectively. The feature structure is enclosed in square brackets. The head of the square bracket indicates the beginning of the feature structure, and the tail of the square bracket indicates the end of the feature structure. In the feature structure represented by the attribute value matrix, each feature occupies a separate line, the attribute name is written in the front, then the colon is written, and the attribute value is written at the end.

The attribute value in the feature structure can be a simple value or a complex value. Simple values are shown in the above example, and the following are examples of complex values:

```
[ lex:     telescope
 cat:     N
 gloss:   `telescope
 head:    [ agr: [ 3sg: + ]
     number: SG
     pos:  N
     proper: -
     verbal: - ]
 root_pos: N ]
```

In this feature structure, the head feature contains another feature structure *agr* (representing agreement), and this feature structure agr contains another embedded feature structure [3sg: +]. In this way, the feature structure is stacked layer by layer.

The components in the feature structure can be described by path. The so-called path is a sequence formed by one or more attribute names in the feature structure. The path is indicated by brackets "< >." For example, in the above feature structure,

```
<head>
<head number>
<head agr 3sg>
```

it's all the path of this feature structure.

Within a feature structure, different paths can share the same value. For example, in the following feature structure,

```
[ cat:  S
  pred: [ cat:  VP
          head: [ agr:  [ 3sg:  + ]
                  finite: +
                  pos:    V
                  tense:  PAST
                  vform:  ED ] ]
  subj: [ cat:  NP
          head: [ agr:  [ 3sg:    + ]
                  case:   NOM
                  number: SG
                  pos:    N
                  proper: -
                  verbal: - ] ] ]
```

the value of the path <head agr> is [3sg: +], and the value of the path <subj head agr> is also [3sg: +]; they have identical value. In this case, they can share the same value [3sg: +]. When two paths share a certain value, label $1 in front of the first path. The path that shares this value with it does not need to write this value again, just quote $1 directly, as shown below:

```
[ cat:  S
  pred: [ cat:  VP
          head: [ agr:    $1[ 3sg:  + ]
                  finite: +
                  pos:    V
                  tense:  PAST
                  vform:  ED ] ]
  subj: [ cat:  NP
          head: [ agr:    $1
                  case:   NOM
                  number: SG
                  pos:    N
```

```
      proper: -
      verbal: - ] ] ]
```

It can be seen that the value of path < head agr > is $1 [3sg: +], and the path <subj head agr> shares this value with it, and it is just recorded as $1. If there are several shared values in a feature structure, we can change the number after $ and record them as $2, $3, etc.

The basic operation of feature structure is "unification." The principle of the unification operation is the same as the principle of unification in functional unification grammar. In the two feature structures, if the attribute values of their shared attributes are compatible, they can be unified. If the attribute values of their shared attributes are incompatible, they cannot be united. Here are some feature structures:

```
(1)
[ agr:  [ number: singular
        person: first ] ]

(2)
[ agr:  [ number: singular ]
 case: nominative ]

(3)
[ agr:  [ number: singular
        person: third ] ]

(4)
[ agr:  [ number: singular
        person: first ]
 case: nominative ]

(5)
[ agr:  [ number: singular
        person: third ]
 case: nominative ]
```

Feature structure (1) can be merged with feature structure (2) to obtain feature structure (4). Feature structure (2) can be merged with feature structure (3) to obtain feature structure (5). However, feature structure (1) and feature structure (3) cannot be merged, because the value of path <agr person> in feature structure (1) is *first* and the value of path <agr person> in feature structure (3) is *third*; hence their values conflict with each other.

To restrict the overgeneration of phrase structure grammar, PATR adds a unification expression to the phrase structure rules to restrict the paragraph and structure rules. The unification expression is composed of the left par and the right part, and the two parts are connected by an equal sign "=".

The left part of the unification expression is a feature path, and the first component of the path is a certain symbol in the phrase structure rule. The left part of the

unification expression is either a simple value or another path. The first component
of this path is also a symbol in phrase structure rules. For example, here are the two
rules of PATR.

```
Rule 1: S → NP VP (SubCl)
        <NP head agr> = <VP head agr>
        <NP head case> = NOM
        <S subj>     = <NP>
        <S head>     = <VP head>

Rule 2: NP → { (Det) (AJ) N (PrepP) } / PR
        <Det head number> = <N head number>
        <NP head>       = <N head>
        <NP head>       = <PR head>
```

In Rule 1, there are four unification expressions to restrict the phrase structure rule
"S → NP VP (SubCl)." The first unification expression requires that the paths <head
agr> of NP and VP are equal, that is, NP and VP must maintain an agreement
relationship (agr). The second unification expression requires NP to be the normative
case (NOM). The three unification expressions require that the subject (subj) of S be
NP. The fourth unification expression requires that the head of S is equal to the head
of VP.

In Rule 2, there are three unification expressions that constrain the phrase
structure rule "NP → {(Det) (AJ) N (PrepP)} / PR." The first unification expression
requires the number of Det and N to be equal, the second unification expression
requires the head of NP and N to be equal, and the third unification expression
requires the head of NP and PR to be equal.

Due to such restrictions of PATR rules, the effect of phrase structure grammar in
natural language processing is improved effectively. Here are some PATR rules.

```
Rule 3: Det -> DT / PR
        <PR head case> = GEN
        <Det head> = <DT head>
        <Det head> = <PR head>

Rule 4: VP -> VerbalP (NP / AdjP) (AdvP)
        <NP head case>   = ACC
        <NP head verbal> = -
        <VP head> = <VerbalP head>

Rule 5: VerbalP -> V
        <V head finite> = +
        <VerbalP head> = <V head>
```

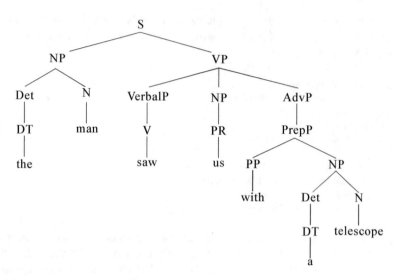

Fig. 4.45 The tree diagram obtained by analysis

```
Rule 6: VerbalP -> AuxP V
    <V head finite> = -
    <VerbalP head> = <AuxP head>

Rule 7: AuxP -> AUX (AuxP_1)
    <AuxP head> = <AUX head>

Rule 8: PrepP -> PP NP
    <NP head case> = ACC
    <PrepP head> = <PP head>
```

From the unification expressions, it is not difficult for readers to understand the restrictions they impose on the rules of the phrase structure.

Using PATR rules to analyze the English sentence "the man saw us with a telescope," we can get the following tree diagram (Fig. 4.45) and the complex feature information on the nodes. The analysis result is much richer than that of phrase structure grammar.

The complex features of node S are as follows:

```
[cat: S
pred:  [cat: VP
     head: [agr: $1[3sg: +]
          finite: +
          pos: V
     tense: PAST
     vform: ED ]]
subj:  [cat: NP
     head: [agr: $1
```

```
case: NOM
number: SG
pos: N
proper: -
verbal: - ]]]
```

It can be seen that the path <subj head agr> and the path <pred head agr> share the attribute value $1, which is [3sg: +]. This is due to the use of PATR Rule 1.

Because in Rule 1 for the phrase structure rule

```
S → NP VP (SubCl),
```

the rule is restricted as follows:

```
<NP head agr>  = <VP head agr>
<NP head case> = NOM
<S subj>       = <NP>
<S head>       = <VP head>
```

Such restrictions cause the path < subj head agr > and the path < pred head agr > to share attribute values.

In the rules of PATR, the variable x can also be used to represent abstractly. For example, we can have the following rules:

X1 → X2 X3
X1(<cat>) = S
X2(<cat>) = NP
X3(<cat>) = VP
X1(<head>) = X3(<head>)
X1(<head subj>) = X2(<head>)

In this rule, X1, X2, and X3 are variables. Such rules can express the following three aspects of information:

1. Linear order of variables: X2 is before X3.
2. The category corresponding to the variable: the category of X1 is S, the category of X2 is NP, and the category of X3 is VP.
3. The relationship between variables: the < head > of X1 is equal to that of X3, and the < head subj > of X1 is equal to that of X2.

The information expressed by this rule is the same as that expressed by Rule 1.

The lexicon of PATR also uses complex features.

For example, the following are the complex features of terms such as *Uther*, *sleeps*, and *sleep*.

```
Uther → [cat: NP
      head: agr: [number: SG
            person: third ]]
```

```
sleeps → [cat: V
      head: [form: finite
           subj: [agr: [number: SG
                  person: third ]]]]
sleep → [cat: V
      head: [form: finite
           subj: [agr: [number: PLUR ]]]]
```

where PLUR means plural.

In automatic syntactic analysis, the computer extracts the complex features of the relevant terms from the lexicon, performs the unification operation, and finally obtains the result of the syntactic analysis.

For example, the sentence *Uther sleep* is ungrammatical, because the number feature value of the verb *sleep* is PLUR, while the number feature value of *Uther* is SG, which is incompatible with each other. The unification fails, and no analysis result is obtained. We have got

Uther sleep → fail

However, for the sentence *Uther sleeps*, since the number feature value of *sleeps* is SG and the person feature value of is *third*, the feature values of *sleeps* and *Uther* are compatible, and their person feature values are also compatible. Therefore, the unification operation can be carried out. In parsing, Rule 2 is used to calculate the feature structure of NP, Rule 5 and Rule 4 are used to calculate the feature structure of VP, and finally, use Rule 1 to calculate the feature structure of the whole sentence. The analysis results are as follows:

```
Uther sleeps → [cat: S
           head: [form: finite
                subj: [agr: [number: SG
                       person: third ]]]]
```

The analysis is successful.

PATR is a better formal model of natural language processing. It has the following advantages.

First, it has simplicity. PATR uses only one operation from beginning to end—the unification operation.

Second, it has flexibility. PATR can also be used in LFG and GPSG for syntactic analysis.

Third, it is declarative. The unification operation in PATR has nothing to do with the order. The result of the operation is the same whether it is first unification or second unification.

Fourth, it has modularity. The rules and lexicon of PATR are modular and easy to debug and use.

Fig. 4.46 I. A. Sag

Fig. 4.47 Phrase structure
of sentence 1

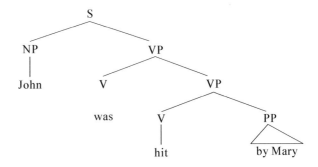

4.6   Pollard's Head-Driven Phrase Structure Grammar

In 1984, C. Pollard and I. A. Sag (Fig. 4.46) proposed head-driven phrase structure grammar (HPSG) in the paper "Parsing Head-driven Phrase Structure Grammar."

Head-driven phrase structure grammar is a formal model of natural language processing proposed based on generalized phrase structure grammar. It inherits the principles of generalized phrase structure grammar and makes important improvements according to the practice of natural language processing. The prominent feature of this new grammatical theory is that it particularly emphasizes the role of the head in grammatical analysis so that the entire grammatical system is driven by

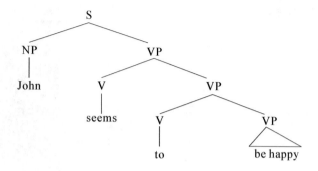

Fig. 4.48 Phrase structure of sentence 2

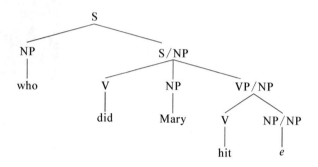

Fig. 4.49 Phrase structure of sentence 3

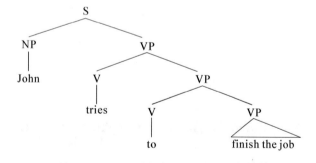

Fig. 4.50 The phrase structure of sentence 4

the head. This kind of grammar shows a strong tendency of lexicalism. Let us look at the following English sentences:

1. John was hit by Mary.
2. John seems to be happy.
3. Who did Mary hit?
4. John tries to finish the job.

The phrase structures of these sentences are shown in Figs. 4.47, 4.48, 4.49, and 4.50.

The *e* on the leaf node of the tree diagram represents the trace of *who*.

According to generalized phrase structure grammar, we can use the following direct dominance rules to generate the above sentence:

1. S → H, NP
2. VP → H, VP
3. VP → H, NP

Obviously, for English, the following rules need to be added to deal with VP:

4. VP → H, NP, NP
5. VP → H, NP, PP
6. VP → H, NP, VP
7. VP → H, NP, S

In these rules, the use of the VP rule is determined by the appearance of the verb as the head. For example, VP must appear after the infinitive *to*, which can be expressed by Rule 2. When the verb *give* has two objects, it can be expressed by Rule 4, etc. It can be seen that the use of rules must consider the basic nature of the head, that is, the value of the subcategorization feature SUBCAT of the head must be considered so that the head can be used to drive the use of rules.

Subcategorization rules are represented by a feature structure list, written as [SUBCAT], which is a subcategorization feature. When we discuss generalized phrase structure grammar, we have said that the subcategorization feature of a verb is the set of all categories that the verb lacks when it forms a sentence. If it is an intransitive verb, it lacks a subject when it forms a sentence. Therefore, its subcategorization feature is subject. If it is a transitive verb, it still lacks the subject and object when forming a sentence. Therefore, its subcategorization features are subject and object. The subcategorization features of words are represented by the feature structure list. The long-distance connection of language units can also be expressed by the principles of universal grammar. All qualified language units should be operated in the way of unification.

Because head-driven phrase structure grammar emphasizes the role of vocabulary (especially the head), according to the subcategorization feature of the head, it is very convenient to connect the grammatical information of the head with the grammatical information of other components in the sentence, so that the information in the whole sentence is connected with the head as the core

Pollard and Sag's head-driven phrase structure grammar systematically summarizes these grammatical phenomena, highlights the status of the head in grammatical analysis, and uses SUBCAT as a list of components to select values and describes in detail the nature of verbs as head one by one. Corresponding to the VP rule of the abovementioned generalized phrase structure grammar, head-driven phrase structure grammar describes the SUBCAT of the head verb as follows:

1. V[SUBCAT <VP, NP>]
   This can describe verbs such as *seem, do, be, try*, etc.
   For example, <u>John</u> **seems** to <u>be happy</u>.
      NP   VP

2. V[SUBCAT <NP, NP>]

This can describe verbs like *love, hit, kill, read*, etc.

For example, <u>John</u> **loves** <u>Mary</u>.
           NP   NP

3. V[SUBCAT <NP, NP, NP>]

This can describe verbs such as *give, send, spare*, etc.

For example, <u>John</u> **gives** <u>Mary</u> <u>a book</u>.
           NP   NP   NP

4. V[SUBCAT <PP, NP, NP>]

This can describe verbs such as *give, send, buy*, etc.

For example, <u>John</u> **gives** <u>a book</u> to <u>Mary</u>.
           NP   NP   PP

5. V[SUBCAT <VP, NP, NP>]

This can describe verbs such as *persuade, expect*, etc.

For example, <u>John</u> **persuades** <u>Mary</u> <u>to leave</u>.
           NP   NP   VP

6. V[SUBCAT <S, NP, NP>]

This can describe verbs such as *expect, believe*, etc.

For example, <u>John</u> **expects** <u>every man</u> <u>to do his duty</u>.
           NP   NP   S

In the SUBCAT value, the last NP is the subject, and the remaining values are the complements in the VP rule above. In generalized phrase structure grammar, the order of the values of SUBCAT is semantically related to the order of verb combination. For English, the order of each value of SUBCAT corresponds to the reverse order of each component in the sentence in most cases.

Using such SUBCAT attributes, the above six NP rules can be expressed as the following two complementary rules and SUBCAT attribute principles.

- Complementary rules

    1. $M \rightarrow H\ C_1$
    2. $M \rightarrow H\ C_2\ C_1$

- SUBCAT attribute principle is as follows.

The SUBCAT value of M should be consistent with the SUBCAT value of H after clearing the part consistent with complement C_1 and C_2 from left to right. That is to say, in the SUBCAT value of H, after removing the parts consistent with the complements C_1 and C_2, the remaining parts should be consistent with the SUBCAT value of M.

For example, in the immediate dominance role

$S \rightarrow H$, NP

where S is equivalent to M and H should be VP; therefore, S can be expressed as V [SUBCAT <>], VP can be expressed as V[SUBCAT <NP>], and C_1 is NP. At this time, NP, which is the SUBCAT value of H, is consistent with another NP, which is

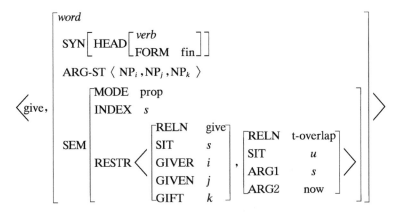

Fig. 4.51 Feature structure of *give*

Fig. 4.52 Specifier SPR and complement COMPS in ARG-ST

the value of C_1, after removing the only consistent part of NP in the SUBCAT value of H. The remaining part is an empty set, so the SUBCAT value of M is also an empty set. It can be seen that this immediate domination rule conforms to the SUBCAT attribute principle. This principle was later developed into the "saturation principle," which we will discuss later.

In head-driven phrase structure grammar, the value of SUBCAT can be changed. For example, to express passive sentences, we can set the following lexical rules to change the value of SUBCAT:

V[SUBCAT <..., NP, NP>] => V[PAS+; SUBCAT <(PP[by],...,NP>]

where the leftmost NP (subject) on the input side corresponds to the PP on the output side and the second NP (object) from the right on the input side corresponds to the rightmost NP (subject) on the output side. PAS+ means the verb is passive.

The feature structure is a means of describing grammatical information. Head-driven phrase structure grammar widely uses complex feature structures to describe the information of words or phrases. The following (Fig. 4.51) is a description of the English word *give*.

Where [...] represents the attribute-value matrix and <...> represents the feature list of the attribute. SYN stands for syntactic structure, and ARG-ST stands for argument structure, which means that the verb *give* can carry three arguments: NP_i, NP_j, and NP_k. SEM stands for semantic structure, including MODE, INDEX, and

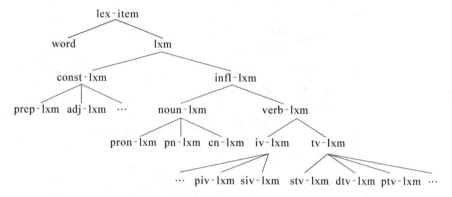

Fig. 4.53 Vocabulary structure of English

RESTR. The MODE has five alternative attribute values: prop (statement), ques (question), dir (imperative), ref (reference), and none. Here, the MODE of *give* is prop. INDEX corresponds to the scenario or event described. Here, *give* conveys an event code s. The RESTR represents a condition that must be met for the event to be established. Here, the conditions that must be met for the *give* event are as follows: i gives k to j in the scenario s; the time of the event is now i, j, and k are respectively related to different arguments of *give* in which NP_i corresponds to GIVER, NP_j corresponds to GIVEN, and NP_k corresponds to GIFT.

Sometimes, ARG-ST can also be described without the argument structure, but with specifier SPR and complement COMPS. For example, *give* can also be described in Fig. 4.52.

Where NP_i is represented by SPR, and NP_j and NP_k are represented by COMPS.

Phrase structure grammar driven by the head adopts the "typed feature structure." The sounds, words, phrases, and sentences in the language belong to different "types," and different attribute features are required to correspond to them. There is objectively a part of speech structure in language.

Head-driven phrase structure grammar holds that there are supertypes and subtypes in the lexical system structure. If there are lexical types T1 and T2, T1 is the upper type of T2 and T2 is the lower type of T1, then:

(a) Every feature suitable for T1 is also suitable for T2.
(b) Every constraint related to T1 affects T2 and lower classes.

Here, the inheritance of constraints specified by a and b is monotonic, that is, no exceptions are allowed in the inheritance process. The monotonousness of constraint inheritance is inconsistent with the actual situation of natural language. For example, nouns in English generally do not have the attribute of case, but pronouns as the lower class of nouns have the attribute of case. Therefore, head-driven phrase structure grammar puts forward the concept of "default inheritance of constraints."

Language has rules, but rules have exceptions. There are two constraint rules: one is inviolable, in that the lower class automatically inherits from the upper class

Fig. 4.54 Basic
information of *dog*

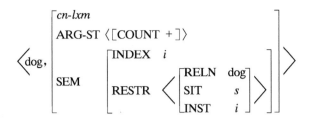

without exception; the other is the default. In the case of default inheritance of constraints, the default constraint rules of the upper class can be overridden and negated by the special and exceptional constraint rules of the lower class. The following is the vocabulary structure of English (Fig. 4.53).

In Fig. 4.53, *lex-item* (lexical item) is the top class. *word* and *lxm* (lexeme) are the direct lower classes of *lex-item*. *word* refers to a combination of sound and meaning with morphological changes. *lxn* is a family of words that does not notice morphological changes. It is an abstract and static prototype word (proto-word). For example, *walk*, *walks*, and *walked* are different words, but they belong to the same *lxm*. lxm is the starting point of language description, and *word* evolved from *lxm*.

According to whether there is a form, *lxm* can be divided into *infl-lxm* (inflecting-lexeme) and *const-lxm* (constant-lexeme).

const-lxm is further divided into prep-lxm and adj-lxm.

infl-lxm is further divided into noun-lxm and verb-lxm.

noun-lxm is further divided into pron-lxm (pronoun), pn-lxm (proper-noun-lexeme), and cn-lxm (common-noun-lexeme).

verb-lxm is further divided into iv-lxm (intransitive-verb-lexeme) and tv-lxm (transitive verb).

iv-lxm is further divided into piv-lxm (prepositional-intransitive-verb-lexeme), siv-lxm (strict-intransitive-verb-lexeme), etc.

tv-lxm is further divided into stv-lxm (strict-transitive-verb-lexeme), dtv-lxm (ditransitive-verb-lexeme), ptv (prepositional-transitive-lexeme), etc.

This lexical system structure simplifies the lexical operation of head-driven phrase structure grammar from two aspects.

First, because a certain class corresponds to a certain attribute feature, nouns will not have transitivity, and adjectives will not have person. Therefore, there is no need to describe the transitivity features of nouns or the person features of adjectives.

Second, the class and its attributes are a regular hierarchical system. As long as we know the position of a symbol in the entire hierarchical structure, we can automatically obtain most of its syntactic and semantic features, and there is no need to describe them one by one.

In the lexical system structure, a complete description of lexemes includes two parts: one is the basic information of lexemes, and the other is the information inherited from the upper class.

Fig 4.55 Attribute feature
structure of *dog*

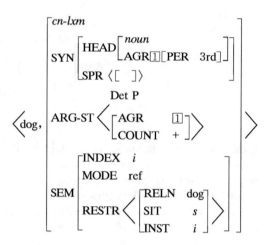

Fig. 4.56 Multiple
inheritance hierarchy

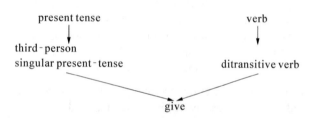

For example, if we want to describe the information of the English word *dog*, we can first describe the basic information of *dog* (Fig. 4.54).

where ARG-ST <[COUNT +]> means that the word *dog* requires a countable specifier to co-occur with it. *Dog* belongs to the cn-lxm category, and it inherits some information of the upper class as its information. The inheritance trajectory is as follows:

lex-item → lxm → infl-lxm → noun-lxm → cn-lxm → dog

In the inheritance process, the default inheritance mechanism of the conventions and constraints of the upper and lower classes must be followed. Add the basic information of the *dog* itself and the inherited information to get the attribute feature structure of *dog* (Fig. 4.55).

What we introduced above is the single inheritance hierarchy. Besides, there is a multiple inheritance hierarchy. In the single inheritance hierarchy, a child node can only obtain information from one parent node, and it cannot effectively describe cross-category language information. In the multiple inheritance hierarchy, a child node can obtain information from several parent nodes and has a more powerful description ability. The following is an example of multiple inheritances of the word *give* (Fig. 4.56).

In Fig. 4.56, *give* obtains third-person, singular, present-tense information from present tense and also obtains ditransitive from the verb. Of course, *give* can also

Fig. 4.57 Plural noun rule

$$\left\langle \boxed{1}, \begin{bmatrix} noun\text{-}lxm \\ \text{ARG-ST } \langle [\text{COUNT} \quad +] \rangle \end{bmatrix} \right\rangle \rightarrow$$

$$\left\langle F_{\text{NPL}}(\boxed{1}), \begin{bmatrix} word \\ \text{SYN} \begin{bmatrix} \text{HEAD} \begin{bmatrix} \\ \text{AGR}[\text{NUM} \quad \text{pl}] \end{bmatrix} \end{bmatrix} \end{bmatrix} \right\rangle$$

Fig. 4.58 The derivational rules of nominalized nouns

$$\left\langle \boxed{1}, \begin{bmatrix} verb\text{-}lxm \\ \text{ARG-ST } \langle \text{NP}_i(,\boxed{2}\,\text{NP}) \rangle \\ \text{SEM} \qquad [\text{INDEX} \quad s] \end{bmatrix} \right\rangle \rightarrow$$

$$\left\langle F\text{-er}(\boxed{1}), \begin{bmatrix} cn\text{-}lxm \\ \text{ARG-ST } \left\langle \text{Det P}(, \begin{bmatrix} \text{PP} \\ \text{P-OBJ} \quad \boxed{2}) \\ \text{FORM} \quad \text{of} \end{bmatrix} \right\rangle \\ \text{SEM} \qquad [\text{INDEX} \quad i] \end{bmatrix} \right\rangle$$

obtain relevant information from other places, and all of the information is added to form the lexical information of *give*.

The lexical rule of head-driven phrase structure grammar is a production device in the form

$$X \rightarrow Y$$

where X is the input, and after the lexical rule operation, the output Y is obtained.

There are two lexical rules: one is inflectional rules, and the other is derivational rules.

The inflectional rules explain how to generate inflectional items from a lexeme. Head-driven phrase structure grammar has many inflectional rules, for example, singular noun rules, plural noun rules, verb past tense rules, verb progressive rules, and so on. Here is the rule for plural nouns (Fig. 4.57).

The input of this rule is noun-lxm, whose specifier feature is [count +], indicating that it is a countable noun. F_{npl} is an inflectional function, it changes a noun from the original form to a plural form, the output class is changed from noun-lxm to *word*, and the attribute obtained is [NUM pl].

The derivational rules explain how to generate another related lexeme from one lexeme. The following are the derivational rules for nominalized nouns (Fig. 4.58).

The parentheses ( ) in the rule ARG-ST means optional, indicating that the input is a transitive verb. In the output, verb-lxm becomes cn-lxm, which means that a common noun is derived from a verb. F-er is a morphological function, which means that when outputting nouns, add -er at the end of the verb. The input verb and output noun have the same scenario INDEX; they are both i. For example, in the scenario of "driving," the scenarios of *drive* and *driver* are the same. This can be understood from the following example sentence:

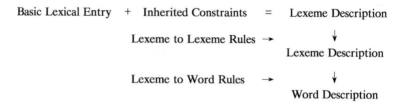

Fig. 4.59 The operation of the lexical system

He discovered the oxygen → the discoverer of oxygen

where *oxygen* is changed from the complement of the verb *discover* to the object of the preposition *of* after the noun *discoverer*, which is represented by a label [2].

Such lexical rules make lexical operations easier and the description of vocabulary clearer. We can explain some syntactic phenomena with the help of such lexical rules, which embodies the spirit of lexicalism.

The operation of the lexical system of head-driven phrase structure grammar can be described as follows (Fig. 4.59).

It can be seen that head-driven phrase structure grammar has a distinct lexicalist tendency. This formal model pays special attention to the role of the head. According to the subcategorization features of the head, it is possible to connect the grammatical information of the head with the grammatical information of other components in the sentence, making the information in the whole sentence connect with the head. Complex features are used to represent all kinds of information of sentences, which provides convenience for computer processing of natural language. This grammar theory has been applied in some machine translation systems and has strong vitality.

In this kind of grammar, all language units are represented by feature structures. Feature structures are used to describe phonetic, syntactic, and semantic information, which are represented as [PHON], [SYNSEM]. By combining these feature values, we can determine the grammatical relationship between sound and the meaning of language units. Grammar is also expressed in the form of feature structures, which are well-formedness conditions of language units.

The main difference between head-driven phrase structure grammar and generalized phrase structure grammar is that in head-driven phrase structure grammar, special attention is paid to the role of vocabulary. Vocabulary forms a hierarchical structure through a unified formal method. The information in the hierarchical structure can circulate and inherit from each other. In all the syntactic information, lexical information accounts for a large proportion, while the real syntactic information only accounts for a small proportion.

In the early model of head-driven phrase structure grammar, the structure of a sentence can be formally described by a sign. The simplest expression includes two parts: [PHON] and [SYNSEM]:

Fig. 4.60 The basic
structure of SYNSEM

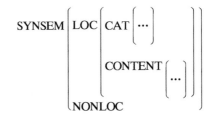

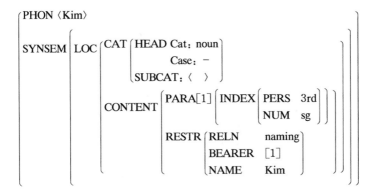

Fig. 4.61 Description of the proper noun

$$
\begin{bmatrix}
\text{PHON} < \quad > \\
\text{SYNSEM}
\end{bmatrix}
$$

where [PHON] is the phonetic part of the sentence. For example, the phonetic part of the sentence "Kim saw the girl" can be expressed as:

PHON <Kim, saw, the, girl>

[SYNSEM] is the syntax (SYNtax) and semantics (SEMantics) part of the sentence, and its basic structure can be described in a similar expression as follows (Fig. 4.60).

In the syntactic and semantic part, LOC means local, which is used to record the information of the actual position in the sentence, and NON-LOC means no local, which is used to record the slot information with a long-distance relationship. LOC is further divided into CAT and CONTENT. CAT means category, which explains the morphological and syntactic features of sentence components, and CONTENT means content, which explains the semantic features of sentence components. For example, the expression of the proper noun *Kim* in English can be described in Fig. 4.61.

In the above expression, the phonetic part of PHON is Kim, and the syntax and semantics of the SYNSEM have only overt components and no covert components. The CAT of the overt component records the category feature (Cat) of HEAD as

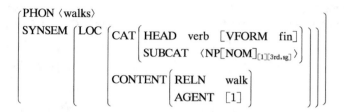

Fig. 4.62 Description of the verb

noun. The case feature is "-" (no case), the SUBCAT (subcategorization) feature is
<>, the CONTENT of the overt component records the meaning of Kim (i.e.,
semantic feature), PARA represents the parameter, and its INDEX (indexing) has
PERS (person) and NUM (number). PERS is the third person (3rd); NUM is the
singular (sg). The RESTR stands for parameter restriction, which includes the
following three items: RELN (relation), BEARER (represents the bearer), and
NAME (represents the name). RELN is naming (to name, i.e., give a name to the
person), label [1] after BEARER, which means that its parameters are the same as
PARA(1), and Kim after NAME is the name given to the bearer. These features
express the phonetic, syntactic, and semantic features of the word Kim.

For another example, the expression of the English verb *walks* can be described as
follows (Fig. 4.62).

In the above expression, the PHON part of phonics is *walks*, and the syntax and
semantics of the SYNSEM part have only overt components and no covert components. The CAT of the overt component records that the HEAD feature is the verb,
and its verb form is the finite verb [VFORM fin], and the SUBCAT records the
subcategory of *walk* as <NP[NOM] [1] [3rd, sg]>, which is a nominative case (NOM),
third person (3rd), singular (sg) noun phrase; the parameter takes the label [1]. The
meaning of the overt component CONTENT records its relationship (RELN) as
walk, and its agent (AGENT) parameter takes label [1]. We know that the parameter
in the proper noun *Kim* also takes [1], so the subcategory of *walk* takes Kim's
parameter [1].

The expression of the structure of the phrase *Kim walks* can be described as
follows (Fig. 4.63).

In the above sentence expression, the PHON part is *Kim walks*, and the SYNSEM
part records the syntax and semantics of the phrase. It is worth noting that the DRTS
(daughters) part is added to the phrase expression to describe the information of the
child nodes of the phrase. Child nodes are divided into two types: HEAD-DRT and
COMP-DRTS. HEAD-DRT is the child node of the head, which describes the
features of *walks* in this phrase, and COMP-DRTS is the child node of the complement, which describes the features of *Kim* in the phrase. It can be seen that, except
for the difference in SUBCAT, the feature value of the HEAD in the phrase is the
same as the feature value of the HEAD of the child node. They are shared structurally because the phrase and child node of the head are located at different levels; their
subcategories should be different. At the phrase level, SUBCAT is <>. At the level

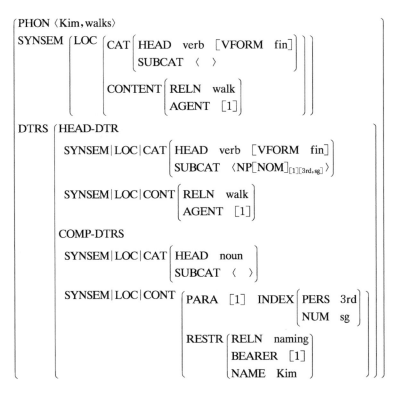

Fig. 4.63 Description of the phrase structure

of the child node of the head, SUBCAT is <NP[NOM] [1] [3rd, sg]>, which requires a nominative, singular, and third-person NP as the complement. This complement is described in COMP-DRTS.

To save space, DRTS adopts a concise representation method. Instead of using brackets in SYNSEM and LOC, it uses "|".

$$\text{SYNSEM|LOC|CAT} \begin{bmatrix} \text{HEAD} & \text{verb [VFORM fin]} \\ \text{SUBCAT <NP[NOM]}_{[1][3rd, sg]}> \end{bmatrix}$$

It represents the bracket expression.

$$\text{SYNSEM} \begin{bmatrix} \text{LOC} \begin{bmatrix} \text{CAT} \begin{bmatrix} \text{HEAD} & \text{verb [VFORM fin]} \\ \text{SUBCAT <NP[NOM]}_{[1][3rd, sg]}> \end{bmatrix} \end{bmatrix} \end{bmatrix}$$

From the structural expression of *Kim walks*, we can see that in the phrase with head, the feature value of the HEAD of the phrase is structurally shared with the head

Fig. 4.64 Contribution principle

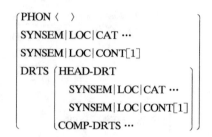

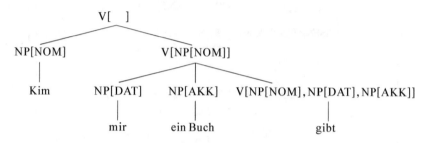

Fig. 4.65 Tree diagram of a German phrase

feature value of the child node of the head. This is the most important principle of lexical information circulation in head-driven phrase structure grammar, which is called the "head feature principle."

Because the level of the phrase is also the level of the parent node, we can express this "head feature principle" in another way.

In a phrase with a head, the feature value of the HEAD of the parent node is structurally shared with the feature value of the head of the child node.

The principles of head-driven phrase structure grammar for lexical information circulation are as follows.

- The Contribution Principle: In a phrase with a head, the CONTENT feature value of the parent node is equivalent to that of the CONTENT of the child node of the head.

  This means that the CONTENT feature value of the parent node comes from the child node of the head, that is to say, the child node of the head must contribute the feature value to its parent node.

  For example, in the expression *Kim walks*, the feature value of the CONTENT of the parent node is as follows:

$$\text{CONTENT} \begin{bmatrix} \text{RELN walk} \\ \text{AGENT [1]} \end{bmatrix}$$

  It is contributed by the feature value of CONTENT in the child node of the head.

  The contribution principle can be described in Fig. 4.64.

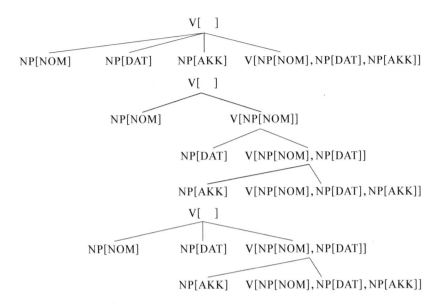

Fig. 4.66   Another combination of the tree diagram

The CONT[1] of the parent node comes from the CONT[1] of the child node of the head.

• The Saturation Principle: In a phrase with a head, the value of the SUBCAT of the parent node is equal to the value of the SUBCAT of the child node of the head minus the relevant feature value on the complement node. For example, the tree structure diagram of the German phrase "Kim mir ein Buch gibt" (Kim gives me a book) is shown in Fig. 4.65.

In the tree diagram of Fig. 4.65, the value of SUBCAT of each node is labeled in square brackets behind it. NOM means nominative case, DAT means dative case, and AKK means accusative case. If V[ ] is the parent node, the SUBCAT value of the child node of the head V[NP[NOM]] minus its complement NP [NOM] value [NOM] which is [ ], the result of which is exactly the value of the parent node SUBCAT. If V[NP[NOM]] is the parent node, the value of SUBCAT of the child node of the head V[NP[NOM],NP[DAT],NP[AKK]] which is [NP [NOM],NP[DAT],NP[AKK]] minus the value [DAT] and [AKK] of its compliments NP[DAT] and NP[AKK], the result of which is exactly equal to the SUBCAT value [NP[NOM]] of the parent node V[NP[NOM]].

Regardless of the leaf nodes of the tree diagram, the tree diagram above can also be changed to the form shown in Fig. 4.66.

No matter how we change the combination of the tree diagram, the value of SUBCAT of the child node of the head minus the relevant value of the child node of the complement, the result must be equal to the value of SUBCAT of the parent node. This shows that the value of SUBCAT of the child node of the head is saturated. It cannot be increased anymore, and it is already in a saturated state.

$$
\begin{bmatrix}
\text{SYNSEM}\,|\,\text{LOC}\,|\,\text{CAT}\begin{bmatrix}\text{HEAD}[\,n\,]\\ \text{SUBCAT }\langle[1]\cdots[m]\rangle\end{bmatrix}\\[4pt]
\text{DTRS}\begin{bmatrix}\text{HEAD-DRT }\begin{bmatrix}|\,\text{SYNSEM}\,|\,\text{LOC}\,|\,\text{CAT}\,|\,\text{HEAD}[\,n\,]\\ |\,\text{SYNSEM}\,|\,\text{LOC}\,|\,\text{CAT}\,|\,\text{SUBCAT}\langle[1]\cdots[m],[n]\rangle\end{bmatrix}\\[6pt] \text{COMP-DRTS }\langle n\rangle\end{bmatrix}
\end{bmatrix}
$$

Fig. 4.67 Saturation principle

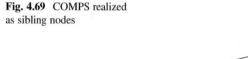

Fig. 4.68 Head-complement rules

Fig. 4.69 COMPS realized
as sibling nodes

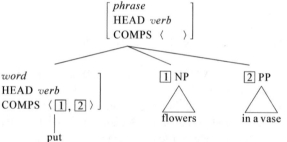

The saturation principle can be described as follows (Fig. 4.67).

It can be seen that after subtracting the <n> in the SUBCAT of COMP-DRTS from the <[1]...[m],[n]> in the SUBCAT of the HEAD-DRT, it is exactly equal to the value of the SUBCAT of the parent node <[1]...[M]>.

Besides, there are "QSTORE-inheritance Principle," "SPEC Principle," and "NONLOCAL Principle."

The "QSTORE-inheritance Principle" indicates that the information of the head complement is temporarily stored in logical quantifiers, which can penetrate to the top of the tree diagram during analysis. "SPEC Principle" describes the relationship between the value of the modifier SPEC of the child node of the non-head and the semantic features of the child node of the head. "NONLOCAL Principle" indicates the transfer relationship between the feature value of the distant nonlocal component and the feature value of its parent node, etc. These principles are the principles of universal grammar. We will not go into details here.

In 1999, I. Sag and T. Wasow adopted different rules and principles to describe head-driven phrase structure grammar in "Syntactic Theory: A Formal Introduction." Their description is more intuitive and concise. Next, we introduce the rules and principles of head-driven phrase structure grammar that they describe.

Fig. 4.70 Head-specifier rules

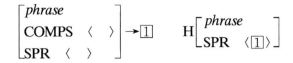

Fig. 4.71 The determiner of the specifier SPR is bound with the specifier John

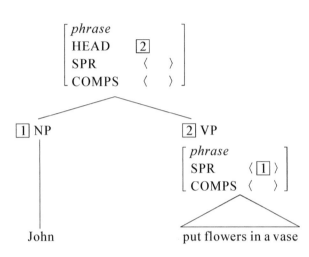

The rules proposed by I. Sag and T. Wasow are as follows.

- Head-Complement Rules

   Complements are syntactically required co-occurrence component of the head, which is represented by COMPS. COMPS is an attribute feature list, and the order of its components matches the order in the actual sentence. For example, the value of COMPS of the word *put* is <NP, PP>, and the value of COMPS of the word *give* is <NP, NP>. In COMPS, we use "(...)" to indicate optionality, such as eat [COMPS (NP)]; we use "|" to indicate "or," such as deny [COMPS NP|P]. The rules are shown in Fig. 4.68.

   The head-complement rule requires all complements to be realized as sibling nodes of the head. For example, "put flowers in a vase" can be analyzed in Fig. 4.69.

   In Fig. 4.69, COMPS is implemented as a brother node:

- Head-Specifier Rules

   The specifier is the subject of the verb head. In head-driven phrase structure grammar, the determiner of the noun head is represented by the attribute of SPR. Like COMPS, SPR is also a list of attribute features. The rules are shown in Fig. 4.70.

   It can be seen from the figure that in the head-specifier rule, the child class of the head is the phrase; and in the head-complement rule, the child class of the head is the word. This means that the head-complement rule always occurs before the head-specifier rule, and the head is always bound to the complement first and

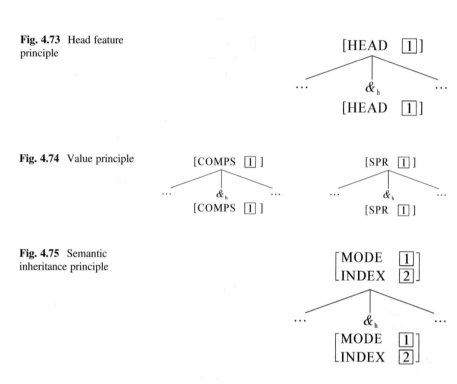

Fig. 4.72 Head-modifier rules

Fig. 4.73 Head feature principle

Fig. 4.74 Value principle

Fig. 4.75 Semantic inheritance principle

then with the specifier as a phrase. For example, "John put flowers in a vase" can be analyzed the form shown in Fig. 4.71.

- Head-Modifier Rules

  Modifiers are the components that modify the head. In head-driven phrase structure grammar, the attributes of MOD are used to express the function of the modifier, and MOD is also a list of attribute features. For example, the MOD attribute of an adjective is [MOD NP], and the MOD attribute of an adverb is [MOD VP]. The rules are as follows (Fig. 4.72).

  Besides, there are coordination rules. We will not go into details here.

  I. Sag and T. Wasow further developed the principles of the "head feature principle," "contribution principle," and "saturation principle" mentioned earlier and summarized these principles into the following principles:

- Head Feature Principle

  In any headed phrase, the head feature value of the father node and the head feature value of the child node are unified. Its form is described in Fig. 4.73.

- The Value Principle

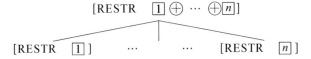

Fig. 4.76 Semantic combination principle

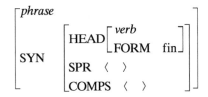

Fig. 4.77 The initial symbols of head-driven phrase structure grammar

In a headed phrase, unless otherwise specified, the feature values of the specifier SPR of the father node and the compliment COMPS are the same as those of the child node, so as to ensure that the properties of SPR and COMPS of the father node are consistent with those of the child node, as shown in Fig. 4.74.

The head feature principle and the value principle are about syntax. The following two principles are about semantics.

- The Semantic Inheritance Principle

  In a headed phrase, the MODE and INDEX feature values of the father node are the same as those of the child node of the head, as shown in Fig. 4.75.

- The Semantic Combination Principle

  In a complete phrase structure, the value of the RESTR of the parent node is equal to the sum of the RESTR values of all its child nodes ("sum" is represented by the symbol ⊕), as shown in Fig. 4.76.

Besides, there are argument realization principle, anaphoric agreement principle, binding principle, etc. We will not go into details here.

In context-free phrase structure grammar, the initial symbol of all phrase structure rules is S (sentence), and sentence generation starts from S. However, in head-driven phrase structure grammar, there is no concept of S, and its initial symbol is phrase that satisfies the constraint conditions, as shown in Fig. 4.77.

The head of this phrase is a verb, its form is finite, it is fully saturated, and the values of SPR and COMPS are empty. Head-driven phrase structure grammar uses this method to define the initial symbols, making the whole theory perfect and unified.

The expression of head-driven phrase structure grammar (HPSG) includes three parts: SYNSEM, DTRS, and PHON. Compared with the rules of context-free phrase structure grammar (CFG), SYNSEM of head-driven phrase structure grammar describes the restriction features of the syntax and semantics of phrases or words, which is roughly equivalent to the information in the left part of context-free grammar rule but contains more information. DRTS of head-driven phrase structure grammar constitutes the features of each component of phrases, and each such component can be complete head-driven phrase structure grammar. DRTS is equivalent to the information on the right part of context-free grammar rules, but it does not contain information about the order of these components. PHON of head-driven phrase structure grammar describes the order of the components in DRTS and the pronunciation of these components. This part is equivalent to the order information of the right part in context-free grammar rules. From the comparison, it can be seen that head-driven phrase structure grammar is still context-free phrase structure grammar in essence, but this grammar contains richer information and is a new development of phrase structure grammar.

Next, we illustrate how to use head-driven phrase structure grammar to analyze natural language automatically.

The general process of the bottom-up analysis algorithm of head-driven phrase structure grammar is as follows:

1. Unify the lexical expressions of the words in the input sentence with those in the dictionary.
2. Until there is no word to unify, unify the expression that has been unified with the expression of the child node of the phrase or with the expression of the phrase in the grammar until the sentence S is saturated.
3. If all expressions are unified, and all PHON values in all expressions are explained, the entire structure of sentence S is constructed.
4. Otherwise, the analysis fails.

Let us illustrate the analysis process of the sentence "Kim walks."

- The words in the input sentence "Kim walks" only describe their pronunciation and position in the sentence.

   ① [PHON < (0 1 kim) >]
   ② [PHON < (1 2 walks) >]

   (0 1 kim) means that *Kim* is in the position from 0 to 1 in the sentence; (1 2 walks) means that *walks* is in the position from 1 to 2 in the sentence.
- Unify ① with the expression of Kim in the dictionary to get

   ③ [PHON < (0 1 kim) >
        SYNSEM [CAT [HEAD noun SUBCAT < >]
        CONTENT [INDEX *1* [PERS 3rd NUM sg]]
        CONTENT [RESTR { [RELN naming BEARER *1* NAME Kim] }]]]

   From this, we learn some information about the meaning of Kim (this is a person named Kim) and some information about the syntactic properties (singular, third person).
- Unify ② with the expression of *walks* in the dictionary. We get

   ④ [PHON < (1 2 walks) >
        SYNSEM [CAT [HEAD [VFORM fin]
             SUBCAT < [CAT [HEAD noun SUBCAT < >]

```
                        CONTENT [INDEX *1* [PERS 3rd NUM sg]]]>]
              CONTENT [RELN walk WALKER *1*]]]
```

From this, we learn that *walks* is an act of walking. It is a finite verb that requires a subject to be an actor of walking but does not require an object.

• We have the following grammatical rule, which is only applicable when VP is an intransitive verb. The rule can be written in our expression as follows:

```
    [SYNSEM [CAT [HEAD *1* SUBCAT <*2*>]
                CONTENT *4*]
        DRTS [HEAD-DRT [SYNSEM [CAT [HEAD *1* SUBCAT <*2*>]
                               CONTENT *4*]
                    PHON *3*]
            COMP-DRTS < >]
        PHON *3*]
```

1, *2*, *3*, *4* in this rule are some temporary parameters, which are used to simplify the writing of the rule; the meaning is as follows:

```
    *1* = [VFORM fin]
    *2* = [CAT [HEAD noun SUBCAT < >] CONTENT [INDEX *1* [PERS 3rd NUM
sg]]]
    *3* = (1 2 walks)
    *4* = [RELN walk WALKER *1*]
```

Unify ④ and HEAD-DRT in this rule; we get the following results:

```
⑤ [SYNSEM [CAT [HEAD [VFORM fin
        SUBCAT < [CAT [HEAD noun SUBCAT < >]
                CONTENT [INDEX *1* [PERS 3rd NUM sg]]]>]
            CONTENT [RELN walk WALKER *1*]]
        DRTS [HEAD-DRT [SYNSEM [CAT [HEAD [VFORM fin] SUBCAT <...>]]
                       CONTENT [...]
                    PHON < (1 2 walks) >]
            COMP-DRTS < >]
        PHON < (1 2 walks) >]
```

Now we have a VP with the intransitive verb *walks* as the head.

• We also have the following grammatical rule, which indicates that a saturated phrase can contain a head phrase and a complement before the head phrase. Because the VP here only requires one subject, this rule is used. The rule can be written in our expression as follows:

```
⑥ [SYNSEM [CAT [HEAD *1* SUBCAT < >]
        CONTENT *4*]
    DRTS [HEAD-DRT [SYNSEM [CAT [HEAD *1* SUBCAT <*2*>]
                       CONTENT *4*]
            PHON *3*]
        COMP-DRTS < [PHON *5*
```

```
                SYNSEM *2*] >]
        PHON (*5* < *3*)]
   In this rule *5* = (0 1 Kim).
```

Unify the previous result (5) with the HEAD-DTR in this rule; we get the following result:

```
⑦[SYNSEM [CAT [HEAD [VFORM fin SUBCAT < >]]
         CONTENT [RELN walk WALKER *1*]]
   DRTS [HEAD-DRT [SYNSEM [CAT [HEAD [VFORM fin]
                    SUBCAT < [CAT [HEAD noun SUBCAT < >]
                              CONTENT [INDEX *1*
                                       [PERS 3ʳᵈ NUM sg]]]>]
                    CONTENT [RELN walk WALKER *1*]]
              PHON < (1 2 walks) >]
         COMP-DRTS < [PHON *5*
                    SYNSEM [CAT [HEAD noun SUBCAT < >]
                           CONTENT [INDEX *1*]]]>]
   PHON <*5* < (1 2 walks) >]
Here, *1* = [PERS 3ʳᵈ NUM sg]
```

Now we have a sentence (the subcategory is zero), but the subject of this sentence (the complement in the expression) has no pronunciation information.
• Unify ③ and COMP-DRTS in ⑦ to get

```
⑧[SYNSEM [CAT [HEAD [VFORM fin SUBCAT < >]]
         CONTENT [RELN walk WALKER [PERS 3ʳᵈ NUM sg]]]
   DRTS [HEAD-DRT [SYNSEM [CAT [HEAD [VFORM fin]
                    SUBCAT < [CAT [HEAD noun SUBCAT < >]
                              CONTENT [INDEX *1*
                                       [PERS 3ʳᵈ NUM sg]]]>]
                    CONTENT [RELN walk WALKER
                 [PERS 3ʳᵈ NUM sg]]]
              PHON < (1 2 walks) >]
         COMP-DRTS < [PHON < (0 1 Kim) >
                    SYNSEM [CAT [HEAD noun SUBCAT < >]
                           CONTENT [INDEX [PERS 3ʳᵈ NUM sg]]]]>]
   PHON < (0 1 Kim) < (1 2 walks) >]
```

At this point, the subject of the sentence has pronunciation information, and the entire sentence is analyzed.

The above analysis process is more difficult to read. To help readers understand the effect of head-driven phrase structure grammar on language information processing, we use a more concise way to describe the process of analyzing natural language sentences with head-driven phrase structure grammar.

We will no longer write complete feature expressions, and the categories of words and phrases are all expressed in such a way as "NP."

Let us analyze the English sentence "Sue the guy with the mustache," where Sue is ambiguous. When used as a noun, it is a person's name, but when used as a verb, it means "accusation."

The bottom-up analysis process is as follows:

1. *Sue* can be a noun or a verb. First of all, treat it as a noun and get

```
N: Sue
```

2. noun can be used as the head of NP to get

```
NP:[HEAD [N: Sue]]
```

3. NP can be used as the subject complement COMP of sentence S to get

```
S: [HEAD?
COMP1 [NP: [HEAD [N: Sue]]]
MOOD declarative]
Declarative means declarative sentence.
```

4. For *Sue*, we cannot continue the analysis. So, go back to the input sentence and take the word *the*, which is a determiner. The determiner must be the HEAD of a DetP, and a DetP must be the complement COMP of NP. "MOD" means that NP has an optional modifier.

```
Det: the
DetP: [HEAD [Det: the]]
NP: [HEAD ?
COMP [DetP: [HEAD [Det: the]]]
(MOD)]
```

5. Moving on, we have to go back to the input sentence and find the next word *guy*. *Guy* must be a noun, which is the HEAD of NP and requires a complement (COMP) DetP.

```
N: Guy
NP: [HEAD [N:guy]
COMP [DetP: [HEAD [Det:the]]]
   (MOD)]
```

6. This NP cannot form a sentence. Let us go back to the input sentence and continue to analyze the words *with*, *the*, *mustache*, and so on. They are preposition, determiner, and noun, respectively, forming a prepositional phrase (PP).

```
Prep: with
PP: [HEAD [Prep: with
   COMP ?]
```

```
Det: the
DetP: [HEAD [Det: the]]

NP: [HEAD ?
   COMP [DetP: [HEAD [Det: the]]]]

N: mustache

NP: [HEAD [N: mustache]
   COMP [DetP: [HEAD [Det: the]]]]

PP: [HEAD [Prep: with]
   COMP [NP: [HEAD [N: mustache]
         COMP [DetP: [HEAD [Det: the]]]]]]
```

7. PP can be used as the modifier of NP, so we get

```
NP: [HEAD [N:guy]
   COMP [DetP: [HEAD [Det:the]]]
   MOD [PP: [HEAD [Prep: with
         COMP [NP: [HEAD [N: mustach]
               COMP [DetP: [HEAD [Det: the]]]]]]]]]
```

At this time, this complex NP has been processed. The analysis continues.

8. The words have all gone through, but S has not found the HEAD, so we have to go back to the first word *Sue*. This time we use *Sue* as a verb, so this sentence becomes an imperative sentence, and the sentence has an implied subject *you*.

```
V: sue

VP: [HEAD [V:sue]
   COMP ?
   (MOD)]

S: [HEAD [VP: [HEAD [V: sue]
      COMP ?
      (MOD)]]
   COMP [HEAD [N: you]
      PHON < >]
   MOOD imperative]
```

9. Now, we go back to the input sentence and get an analysis result:

```
S: [HEAD [VP: [HEAD [V: sue]
      COMP [NP [HEAD [N: guy]
         COMP [DetP: [Det: the]]]
         MOD [PP: [HEAD [Prep: with]
               COMP [NP: [HEAD [N: mustache]
                     COMP [DetP: [HEAD [Det: the]]]]]]]]]]
```

```
       (MOD)]]
 COMP [NP: [HEAD [N: you]
     PHON < >]]
 COMP2
 MOOD imperative]
```

10. If we want to get all possible analysis results, the above results also have ignored one result, which is the case of PP modifying the verb phrase. At this time, NP only contains *the guy*, which is a simple noun phrase. Obviously, this result is syntactically valid but semantically unreasonable.

```
S: [HEAD [VP: [HEAD [V: sue]
        COMP [NP [HEAD [N: guy]
            COMP [DetP: [Det: the]]]]]]
        MOD [PP: [HEAD [Prep: with]
             COMP [NP: [HEAD [N: mustache]
                    COMP [DetP: [HEAD [Det: the]]]]]]]]]]
   COMP [NP: [HEAD [N: you]
       PHON < >]]
   MOOD imperative]
```

The top-down analysis process is as follows:

1. We have only two rules about S, one describing the declarative sentence, the other describing the imperative sentence.

```
 S: [HEAD ?
   COMP ?
   MOOD declarative]
```

```
S: [HEAD ?
 COMP [NP: [HEAD [N: you]
       PHON< >]]
 MOOD imperative]
```

2. Go further down from the top S of the tree, there are only two nonempty NP and two nonempty VP.
   The two NP are as follows:

```
 S: [HEAD ?
   COMP [NP: HEAD [N]]
   MOOD [declarative]
```

```
S: [HEAD ?
 COMP [NP: [HEAD [N]
       COMP [DetP]]]
 MOOD declarative]
```

The two VPs are as follows:

```
S: [HEAD [VP: [HEAD [V]]
    COMP [NP: [HEAD [N: you]
           PHON < >]]
    MOOD imperative]
```

```
 S: [HEAD [VP: [HEAD [V]
          COMP [NP]]]
    COMP [NP: [HEAD [N: you]
          PHON < >]]
    MOOD imperative]
```

3. Follow the branch of the tree to get the following results:

```
    S: [HEAD ?
     COMP [NP: [HEAD [N: sue]]
     MOOD declarative]
```

```
 S: [HEAD ?
  COMP [NP: [HEAD [N]
          COMP [DetP [HEAD [Det]]]]]]
  MOOD declarative]
```

```
 S: [HEAD [VP: [HEAD [sue]
          COMP [NP]]]
    COMP [NP: [HEAD [N: you]
          PHON < >]]
    MOOD imperative]
```

Continue with the top-down analysis, so we can get the results; I will not repeat here, so readers can try their analysis.

In recent years, the research on head-driven phrase structure grammar (HPSG) is very hot in the field of natural language processing at home and abroad. The first conference was held in Copenhagen, Denmark, in 1994; the second in Tübingen, Germany, in 1995; the third in Pittsburgh, USA, in 1996; the fourth in Cornell University, USA, in 1997, the fifth in Saarbrücken, Germany, in 1998; the sixth in Edinburgh, UK, in 1999; the seventh in Berkeley, USA, in 2000; the eighth in Trondheim in 2001; the ninth in Seoul, South Korea, in 2002; and the tenth in Michigan, USA, in 2003. Besides, international seminars on head-driven phrase structure grammar have been held in Marseilles, France, and Poznan, Poland. It can be said that head-driven phrase structure grammar is a hot topic in current international natural language processing research based on the rationalist approach.

Why does this grammar attract the attention of so many scholars at home and abroad? We believe that this is because head-driven phrase structure grammar reflects some important ideas of current language information processing based on

Fig. 4.78 A. Colmerauer

the rationalist approach, which is in line with the trend of world academic development. At present, the study of head-driven phrase structure grammar is continuing to be discussed on the following issues.

First, it emphasizes the restriction of grammar and tries to describe the human language model as a system of feature structure restriction. It implements strict lexicalism so that the structure of words and phrases is dominated by some independent rules and principles.

Second, it focuses on the description of concrete and surface-oriented structures, tries to avoid those abstract structures (such as empty categories, functional mapping, etc.), and puts the description of constituent structures in an important position.

Third, the organization of grammar should also reflect the geometric structure of sentences. The linguistic information organized according to the hierarchical relationship helps to predict some linguistic phenomena that are absolutely impossible in structure.

Fourth, it tries to localize the choice of the head. The choice of the lexical head is limited to the subject, complement, and modifier of SYNSEM. The choice of category and the agreement of the head are controlled by the localized feature selection.

Fifth, the lexical features in the grammar are rich. These features are not simply listed but are obtained through the inheritance and transfer of features in the tree diagram. All lexical features are organized into a hierarchy with an inheritance relationship.

Sixth, the types of phrases are also dealt with by the hierarchical method of inheritance, which unifies the processing methods of different types of structures. On this basis, the general concept of "construction grammar" is established.

4.7   Pereira and Warren's Definite Clause Grammar

In 1975, A. Colmerauer (Fig. 4.78) and R. Kowalski proved that context-free phrase structure grammar can be translated into "definite clause." The definite clause is a restricted subset of first-order predicate logic.

In this way, the problem of syntactic analysis of a word string of a language can be transformed into a problem of using a set of definite clause axioms which is used to describe a certain language to prove theorems. In 1980, F. Pereira and D. Warren of the University of Edinburgh in the United Kingdom published a paper "Definite clause grammars for language analysis—a survey of the formalism and a comparison with augmented transition networks," formally proposed definite clause grammar (DCG), and proved that definite clause grammar is extended context-free grammar. The grammar maintains a series of important characteristics of context-free grammar, and its description ability is at least not lower than procedural augmented transition network grammar. This paper also clarified a very important fact, that is, the grammar rules expressed in definite clauses can be directly transformed into Prolog after a simple transformation. Because the grammar rules expressed in definite clauses are the executable programs of Prolog, they can be directly interpreted by the Prolog system. Since the compilation system or interpretation system of the Prolog language itself has constituted an efficient top-down parser, the grammar rules and dictionaries written with definite clause grammar can directly become Prolog programs without designing a separate parser. Since Prolog is a declarative programming language, it has been used to implement many large-scale applications. After the birth of Prolog, it has become the mainstream programming language in the field of artificial intelligence in Europe. The fifth-generation computer in Japan also uses Prolog as the core programming language of machine reasoning. The natural combination of definite clause grammar and Prolog language makes definite clause grammar attractive and becomes a popular formal language in language information processing.

The basic idea of definite clause grammar is that grammatical symbols are not only atomic symbols but also generalized logical items. For example, the following rule in context-free grammar

sentence → noun_phrase, verb_phrase

indicates that a sentence consists of two parts: noun phrase and verb phrase. In definite clause grammar, this rule can be expressed as follows: if there is a noun phrase and a verb phrase, then there is a reasoning process of a sentence, which is expressed with a first-order predicate logic formula

$$(\forall U)(\forall V)(\forall W)[np(U) \wedge vp(V) \wedge concatenate(U,V,W) \rightarrow S(W)]$$

where $\forall$ means universal quantifier, $\wedge$ is logical conjunction, and $\rightarrow$ means implication. The three-argument predicate *concatenate* (U, V, W) takes the true value if and only if the word string W is the result of the adjacency operation of the word string U and V. Therefore, the meaning of the above logic formula is as follows: for any string U, V, and W, if U is a noun phrase, V is a verb phrase, and W is formed by the sequence of U and V, then W is a qualified declarative sentence defined by this grammatical rule. The essence of this logical deduction is equivalent to proving the following theorem:

There is a syntactic structure S, which makes the word string W an analysis that satisfies the grammatical rule set P.

Although there are many similarities in form between the rules of context-free phrase structure grammar and the rules of definite clause grammar, there are great differences in essence. Context-free phrase structure grammar is just language description grammar, while definite clause grammar is a kind of inference grammar of a language. In this way, definite clause grammar has realized the transformation from descriptive formal grammar to inferential logical grammar, thus making a qualitative leap in context-free phrase structure grammar.

The logical meaning of definite clauses is clear and the form is concise, which brings great convenience to the program design. From the perspective of logic programming, definite clauses can be regarded as rules with at most one predicate on the left. For example, the above definite clause grammar rule can be written as

sentence(s0,s):- noun_phrase(s0,s1), verb_phrase(s1,s)

where s0, s1, and s are pointers to strings. This definite clause rule can be interpreted as follows: if between s0 and s1 is a noun phrase, between s1 and s is a verb phrase, then between s0 and s is a sentence. It can be seen that the definite clause rules specifically express the reasoning process of the sentence.

As there is a natural connection between definite clause grammar and Prolog language, we will directly use the labels and terms of the Prolog language to define definite clauses.

The data object of the Prolog language is called "term." An item can be a constant, a variable, or a compound item.

Constants include integers and atoms. Integers include 0, 1, 2, 12, 99, etc. Atoms are generally represented by English lowercase letters or other strings, such as john, mary, isa, plural, np, =,:-,[], etc. Like other programming languages, constants are used to represent certain basic objects.

Variables are represented by a string of symbols whose initials are English capital letters, such as X, A06, Result, C-, etc. A variable usually refers to a specific, undetermined object.

Compound items are data objects with a certain structure. The most common compound items in Prolog are predicates and tables.

A predicate consists of a predicate name and one or more arguments. For example, np(X) is a one-place predicate. If X is a noun phrase, the value of np (X) is true; otherwise, it is false. For another example, isa(X, Y) is a two-place predicate. If X is a subordinate concept of Y (e.g., "golden monkey" is a subordinate concept of "animal"), the predicate takes the truth value.

Each argument in a compound term can itself be a compound term.

Fig. 4.79 Hierarchical
structure

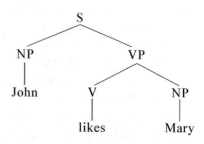

For example, the syntactic structure of the sentence "John likes Mary" can be expressed as a compound term as follows:

s(np(john),vp(v(likes),np(mary)))

where each argument of s is a compound term, which describes the following hierarchical structure of the syntactic tree (Fig. 4.79).

The boundary of a table is indicated by square brackets, and the elements in the table are separated by commas. Therefore, an empty table is represented by the atom "[ ]". A table composed of integers 1, 2, 3 can be expressed as [1–3]. Each element in a table can also be a table. For example, in [a,[b,c]], the first element is a, and the second element is the table [b,c]. If the head and tail of the table are represented by the variables H and L, respectively, the table can be denoted as [X|L], where L is the remaining table in subtraction to the head $H = X$ in this table, in which L is called the "remaining table." Therefore, in the table [1–3], if the header $X = 1$, the remaining table is $L = [2, 3]$.

Another concept in Prolog is the clause.

A logic program consists only of a series of clauses. In logic programming, the so-called horn clause was proposed. The horn clause is also called a definite clause. The definite clause consists of a head and a body. The "head" of the definite clause can only contain zero or one predicate, and the "body" of the definite clause can contain zero or more predicates. The clause defined in this way has the following three forms:

1. For a clause with a nonempty head and body, its general form is as follows:

   P:- Q, R, S.

   where the atom ":-" that separates the head and body is read as "if," the predicate Q, R, S on the right is the condition of this clause, and the comma "," between the predicates indicates conjunction. The single predicate P on the left is the result of the clause, and each clause ends with a period ".". Such a clause is a rule, which can be interpreted declaratively as

"If Q, R, and S are all true, then P is true."

Since the result of a clause is completely definite, it is called a "definite clause." The head of this definite clause can only contain one predicate at most. The above clauses can also be explained in a procedural way like explaining a program as follows:

"In order to meet the target P, the targets Q, R and S must be met at the same time."

2. A clause with an empty body is recorded as

P.

Obviously, such a clause is a special case of the rule, indicating that P is unconditional. Therefore, it is a fact that can be interpreted declaratively as

"P is true."

It can also be explained procedurally as

"Object P must be met."

3. The clause with an empty head is recorded as

?:- P, Q.

It can be explained declaratively as

"Are P and Q true?"

Or procedurally explained as

"Try to meet goals P and Q."

Generally speaking, all clauses contain variables. Even if the variables in different clauses have the same name, they are also independent of each other. Therefore, the domain governed by a variable is limited to the clause in which it is located.

The Prolog program is composed of the above facts and rules. Prolog questions are equivalent to query statements in man-machine dialogue. Here is a simple program:

```
male (john)
male (bill)
female (mary)
parent-of (mary, john)
mother-of (X,Y):-parent-of (X,Y), female(X).
```

The first four lines are all facts, indicating that john is male, bill is male, mary is female, and mary is john's parent (parent-of). Line 5 is the inference rule, meaning: If X is Y's parents and X is female, then X is Y's mother.

The above facts and rules constitute the Prolog database. The following is the query entered by the user and the answer of the machine in the Prolog environment.

```
User asks: ?:- parent-of (mary, john)
    (Is mary john's parents?)
Machine answers: Yes
    (Yes. Note: There is this fact in the program)
User asks: ?:- parent-of (bill, john)
    (Is bill john's parents?)
Machine answers: No
    (No. Note: There is no such fact in the program.)
The user asked: ?:- mother-of (mary, john)
    (Is mary john's mother?)
Machine answers: Yes
    (Yes. Note: Although there is no such fact in the program, this
conclusion can be derived according to the rule.)
The user asked: ?:- mother-of (X, john)
    (Who is john's mother?)
Machine answers: mary (It is mary. Note: this conclusion can be derived
according to the rule.)
```

The rule form of definite clause grammar is as follows:

<non-terminal symbol> → <rule body>

where the non-terminal symbol is a word or phrase label, which is represented by Prolog atoms. The rule body consists of one or more entries, separated by commas. Each entry is either a non-terminal symbol or a sequence of terminal symbols. If it is a sequence of terminal symbols, use the Prolog table to label, and each of the terminal symbols can be any Prolog item.

The following is a set of rules for definite clause grammar:

s → np, vp.
np → n.
vp → v, np.
n → [john].
n → [wine].
v → [likes].

The right part of the last three rules is the terminal symbol, which is represented by Prolog's "table."

To transform the rules of definite clause grammar into the clause form of Prolog language, we only need to replace each non-terminal symbol with a two-place predicate with the same name, where each variable is a table and the second argument represents the remaining table of the first argument.

The following is the Prolog program obtained after transformation:

```
s (X, Y) :-np (X, Z) , vp (Z, Y) .
np (X, Y) :-n (X, Y) .
vp (X, Y) :-v (X, Z) , np (Z, Y) .
```

```
n([john|X],X).
n([wine|X],X).
v([likes|X],X).
```

Run this program, and we can get the following man-machine dialogue results:

```
User asks: ?:- s([john, likes, wine],[])
    (Is "john likes wine" a sentence?)
Machine answers: Yes
User asks: ?:- np([john, likes, wine], X)
    (In a string, after subtracting what, it is a noun phrase np?)
Machine answers: X=[likes, wine]
    (After deducting the remaining table [likes, wine], the remaining
[john] is the noun phrase np)
```

It can be seen that definite clause grammar is very useful in natural language human-machine dialogues, especially when using Prolog language to write man-machine dialogue programs. Because of the direct relationship between definite clause grammar and Prolog language, the rules are particularly convenient to write.

To improve the descriptive ability of definite clause grammar and overcome the shortcomings of context-free phrase structure grammar, definite clause grammar has made the following improvements to context-free phrase structure grammar.

First, in the rules of definite clause grammar, non-terminal symbols can be compound items with multiple variables, which can carry information about the context, transformation, structures, etc., so that the syntactic and semantic information can be transferred as variables inside the rules like complex features, thus realizing the context-dependent constraint mechanism and greatly increasing the ability of definite clause grammar to describe the complex features of the natural language.

Second, the right part of the definite clause grammatical rules can introduce test conditions and actions that do not belong to the grammar itself and further increase the constraint power of the rules.

In this way, although definite clause grammar uses context-free phrase structure grammar, its description ability is equivalent to type 0 grammar defined by N. Chomsky. Definite clause grammar is an important improvement of N. Chomsky's phrase structure grammar from the perspective of logical programming. It is an outstanding achievement of contemporary language information processing research.

Bibliography

1. Pollard, C., and I. Sag. 1987. *Information-Based Syntax and Semantics*. Chicago: The University of Chicago Press.

2. ———. 1994. *Head-Driven Phrase Structure Grammar*. Chicago: The University of Chicago Press.

3. Sag, I., and T. Wasow. 1999. *Syntactic Theory: A Formal Introduction*. Stanford: Center for the Study of Language and Information.

4. Shieber, S.M. 1984. The Design of a Computer Language for Linguistic Information. In *Proceedings of 10th International Conference on Computational Linguistics*, 362–366. Stanford: Stanford University.

5. ———. 1985. Using Restriction to Extend Parsing Algorithms for Complex-feature-based Formalisms. In *Proceedings of the 22nd Annual Meeting of the Association for Computational Linguistics*, 145–152. Chicago: University of Chicago.

6. ———. 1986. An Introduction to Unification Based Approaches to Grammar. In *CSLI Lecture Notes Series*, vol. 4. Stanford: Center for the Study of Language and Information, Stanford University.

7. Yunfang, Wu. 2003. Introduction to HPSG Theory. *Contemporary Linguistics* 3.

8. Zhiwei, Feng. 1982. Chinese-French/English/Japanese/Russian/German Multilingual Automatic Translation Experiment. *Language Studies* 2.

9. ———. 1983. Analysis of Chinese Sentences with Multi-Branch and Multi-Label Tree Diagram. *Journal of Artificial Intelligence* 2.

10. ———. 1990. Complex Features in Chinese Sentence Descriptions. *Journal of Chinese Information Processing* 3: 20–29.

11. ———. 1990. Lexical Functional Grammar and Its Role in Computational Linguistics. *China Computer Users* 11.

12. ———. 1990. Description of Complex Features for Chinese Language. In *Proceedings of COLING'90, Helsinki*.

13. ———. 1991. Martin Kay's Functional Unification Grammar. *Linguistics Abroad* 2: 34–42.

14. ———. 1991. On Potential Ambiguity in Chinese Terminology. In *Proceedings of TSTT'91, Beijing*.

15. ———. 1992. Chinese Information MMT Model. *Language Application* 4: 21–30.

16. ———. 1992. The Challenge of Computational Linguistics to Theoretical Linguistics. *Language Application* 1: 81–97.

17. ———. 1994. The Calculation Method of the Multi-Value Label Set in the Chinese Information MMT Model. *Information Science* 15 (3): 14–25.

18. ———. 2001. Head-Driven Phrase Structure Grammar. In *Linguistic Issues Collection*, vol. 1. Changchun: Jilin People's Publishing House.

19. ———. 2004. Conversion from Constituent Structure to Functional Structure in LFG. *Language Application* 4: 105–112.

Chapter 5
Formal Models Based on Dependency and Valence

Valence is the potential combining ability of words. Nouns, verbs, and adjectives all have the potential combining ability, and they all have valence. When a word with this potential combining ability enters a sentence, it forms a dependence relation between words in the sentence, which is called "dependency" for short.

Therefore, "dependency" is a one-way binary relation between words in a language. The direction of dependency is from the governor to the dependent, which can be represented by an arrow.

In NLP, "dependency" and "valence" are two important concepts. In this chapter, we first introduce the origin of the concept of "valence", then introduce dependency grammar, and finally introduce valence grammar. Dependency grammar and valence grammar are the theoretical basis of many formal models of NLP. In this section, some of the practical applications in NLP and related formal models are also discussed.

5.1 Origin of Valence

As early as the twelfth century, the linguist Petrus Helias put forward the "verb center theory" in his work. He believed that different verbs require a different number of sentence components. The necessary components of verbs are usually nominal. These components are necessary to construct a *perfectio constructionis* (Latin: complete structure). This "verb center theory" points out the requirements of verbs for sentence components and implies the concept of "valence."

Johann Werner Meiner, known as the greatest general linguist in Germany in the eighteenth century, clearly divided predicates (verbs) into univalent verbs, bivalent verbs, and trivalent verbs in his work in 1781. However, he did not use the word

© Springer Nature Singapore Pte Ltd. 2023
Z. Feng, *Formal Analysis for Natural Language Processing: A Handbook*,
https://doi.org/10.1007/978-981-16-5172-4_5

"valence" directly; he used the German word *seitig-unselbständig*,[1] but its definition is almost the same as the modern definition of "valence" for the verb.

In 1934, the Austrian linguist Karl Bühler said in his published work *Sprachtheorie* (Language Theory) that "There is selective affinity in every language; adverbs look for their own verbs, and other words do the same. In other words, words in a certain part of speech open up one or more slots around themselves, and these slots must be filled by other types of words." Karl Bühler's[2] insights on "slots" reveal the essence of "valence." Although he has never used the term "valence," scholars who study valence theory generally regard him as a pioneer in the study of valence theory.

In 1948, Soviet linguist Solomon D. Kacnel'son first proposed the term "valence." He said, "In every language, fully and effectively concretized words are not simple words, but words with specific syntactic potential, which make words only be used in a strictly limited way." The development stage of grammatical relations predetermined such a way. Words appear in a sentence in a certain way and combine with other words, which can be called "syntactic valence."[3]

Forty years later, Kacnel'son's understanding of valence changed. He said "valence can be defined as a kind of syntactic potential contained in the lexical meaning of a word, which means that the ability to relate to other words is determined by the content word. We use valence (combining ability) to reveal those hidden in the meaning of the word and need to use certain types of words in the sentence to perfect the meaning of the word. According to this view, not all content words have a valence. Only those words that make people feel incomplete and need to be complete have valence."[4]

Kacnel'son especially emphasizes the "potential" of "valence." He believes that the obvious grammatical categories, functions, and relations "are expressed through syntactic morphology," while the potential grammatical categories, functions, and relations are implied in the syntactic combination and semantics of words. He said, "Grammar is like an iceberg, most of which are underwater." Therefore, to study these potential grammatical phenomena, "valence" as a means of expressing potential syntactic relations is of special significance.

In 1949, A.W. de Groot, a Dutch linguist, also used the concept of "valence" in his book *Structural Syntax* and systematically described the syntactic system based on the concept of valence. However, limited by being written in the Dutch language, this book is rarely known. Groot wrote in his book, "compared with other parts of speech, the possibility of using certain parts of speech is limited, that is, parts of speech have different syntactic valence. Valence is the possibility of being limited by

---

[1] Ágel, Vilmos. *Valenztheorie*. Tübingen: Narr, 2000: 21–25.

[2] Bühler, Karl. *Sprachtheorie. Die Darstellungsfunktion der Sprache*. 3. Auflage. Stuttgart: Lucius & Lucius, 1934/1999:173.

[3] Kacnel'son, Solomon. D. O grammatičeskio kategorii. In: Vestnik Lenningradskogo Universiteta, serija istorii, jazyka i literatury 2. Leningrad. p. 114–134. 1948.

[4] Kacnel'son, Solomon. D. Zum Verständnis von Typen der Valenz. in: Sprachwissenschaft 13, 1–30. 1988.

Fig. 5.1 Tesnière

other words or limiting other words."[5] He used the terms *valentie* (valence) and *syntactische valentie* (syntactic valence) in his syntactic research. Groot believes that not only words have "valence," other structures in the language also have "valence"; not only verbs have "valence" but also all other parts of speech, such as nouns, articles, numerals, exclamations, prepositional phrases, and so on. This is a kind of "pan valence" point of view.

In NLP, "valence" is a very important concept, and we will trace the origin of this concept in this section, which helps to deepen our understanding of "valence" in NLP.

5.2 Tesnière's Dependency Grammar

Dependency grammar (*grammaire de dependance*), also known as "subordination grammar," was proposed by the French linguist L. Tesnière (Ténière, 1893–1954, Fig. 5.1). The concept of "valence" in dependency grammar became the origin of valence grammar. Tesnière is neither the only scholar nor the first to use the concept of "valence" in the world, but there is no doubt that because of his work on dependency grammar, the term "valence" has become so widely known. Therefore, we believe that Tesnière can be regarded as "the father of valence theory."

Tesnière is a famous French linguist in the first half of the twentieth century. Born on May 13, 1893, he taught at the University of Strasbourg and the University of Montpellier, studying Slavic languages and general linguistics.

The main job of Tesnière is to establish a general theory of dependency grammar. He conducted many comparative studies on languages, including ancient Greek,

---

[5] de Groot. A.W. Structurele syntaxis. Den Haag: Servire. 1949, p114.

ancient Roman, Romanian, Slavic, Hungarian, Turkish, and Basque. He once deeply regretted not being able to quote Eastern languages in his works. In 1934, he published "How to Build a Syntax" (*Comment construire une Syntaxe*) in "Bulletin de la Faculté des Lettres de Strasbourg," which expounds his basic arguments of dependency grammar. Beginning in 1939, he began to write *Élément de Syntaxe Structurale (Basics of Structural Syntax)*,[6] a masterpiece of dependency grammar, which took him more than 10 years to complete while writing and modifying. And the book was completed in 1950. Unfortunately, this masterpiece was not published before his death. Tesnière passed away on December 6, 1954. Later, his friends compiled his posthumous manuscripts. The first edition of the book *Basics of Structural Syntax* was published in 1959, and the second edition was published in 1965.

In addition to the book *Basics of Structural Syntax*, Tesnière has written some papers on Slovenian, such as "Slovenian Dual Number Forms" (*Les formes du duel en Slovene*), "Language Atlas for the Study of Slovenian Dual Number Forms Language Map" (*Atlas linguistique pour servir à l'étude du duel en slovènel*), and so on.

The basic concepts of dependency grammar are "connexion" and "translation." In this section, we will focus on these two basic concepts.

5.2.1 Connexion

The French sentence *Alfred parle* (Alfred is talking) is composed of two forms: *Alfred* and *parle*. However, when French speakers say this, it doesn't mean that there is one person named *Alfred* on the one hand and another person is speaking on the other but refers to the action of *Alfred* making a speech, and the speaker is *Alfred*. The relationship between *Alfred* and *parle* is not expressed through two separate forms of *Alfred* and *parle*. Instead, it is expressed through syntactic connection, which is "connexion." It is the "connexion" that connects *Alfred* and *Parle*, making them a whole. Tesnière said: "This situation is the same as that in chemistry. Chlorine and sodium combine to form a sodium chloride compound (table salt), which is completely different from the nature of chlorine or sodium. 'Connexion' endows sentences with 'rigorous organization and breath of life,' which is the 'lifeline' of a sentence. 'The so-called sentence making is to establish a variety of connexions between a group of words and give them life.' On the other hand, to understand a sentence, it means to grasp the various connexions that connect different words."[7]

Connexion should be subject to the hierarchy (*hiérarchie*) principle, that is, connexion should establish the dependency relationship between words in a

---

[6]L. Tesnière. Éléments de Syntaxe Structurale, Paris : Klincksieck, 1959.

[7]L. Tesnière. Éléments de Syntaxe Structurale, Paris : Klincksieck, 1959.

Fig. 5.2 Schema of "Alfred
mange une pomme"

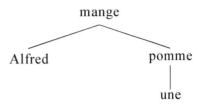

Fig. 5.3 The verb is the
center of the sentence

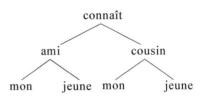

sentence. This dependency can be represented by a "schema" (*stemma*). For example, the French sentence *Alfred mange une pomme* (Alfred ate an apple) can be represented by Fig. 5.2.

Here, the verb *mange* (eat) is the *noeud* (node) of the sentence. *Alfred* and *pomme* depend on the verb *mange*, and they are placed below *mange*; *une* depends on *pomme*, which is placed below *pomme*.

Tesnière believes that the verb is the center of the sentence. It governs other components, but it is not governed by any other components. Therefore, he treats the subject and the object equally and puts them under the dominance of the verb. For example

Mon jeune ami connaît mon jeune cousin.
(My young friend knows my young cousin.)

The diagram is in Fig. 5.3.

Both the subject phrase and the object phrase are listed under the node of the verb *connaît*. These two phrases can be adjusted to each other. Therefore, the following passive sentences can be formed:

Mon jeune cousin est connu de mon jeune ami.
(My young cousin is known by my young friend.)

An inevitable corollary of the hierarchy principle is that all dependent components depend on their governor. For example, let us compare:

In Fig. 5.4, the subject noun phrase *mon vieil ami* (my old friend) in P1 becomes the object noun phrase in P2. The object noun phrase *cette fort jolie chanson* (this very beautiful song) in P1 becomes the subject noun phrase in P2, and they are all dependent components of the verbs.

Tesnière believes that structural order (*ordre structural*) and linear order (*ordre linéaire*) should be distinguished. For example, the phrase *un petit garçon* (a little boy) is related to the phrase *un garçon poli* (a polite boy) in the same structural order (Fig. 5.5).

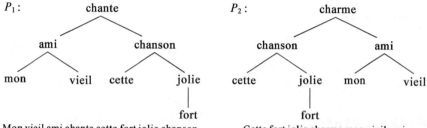

Mon vieil ami chante cette fort jolie chanson.   Cette fort jolie charme mon vieil ami.
(My old friend is singing this very beautiful   (This very beautiful son charmed my old
song.)   friend.)

Fig. 5.4 Governors and dependent components

Fig. 5.5 Structural order

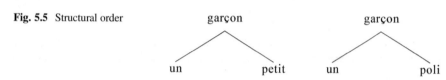

The noun *garçon* is the governor in Fig. 5.5, and the adjectives *petit* and *poli* both
depend on this noun. However, the linear order of the two phrases is different: in *un
petit garçon*, the adjective is on the left side of the noun *garçon*; in *un garçon poli*,
the adjective is on the right side of the noun *garçon*. Obviously, the structural order
is two dimensional, while the linear order is one dimensional.

One of the important problems in syntactic theory is to determine the rules that
change the two-dimensional structural order into one-dimensional linear order and
those rules that lead one-dimensional linear order to two-dimensional structural
order. The order of *garçon poli* is centrifugal or descending, and the adjective *poli*
drops away from the central noun *garçon*. The order of *petit garçon* is centripetal or
ascending, and the adjective petit rises toward the central noun garçon. Some
languages have a centripetal tendency, while others have a centrifugal tendency.
For example, in English, the modifier of a noun tends to rise toward the modified
central noun, and in French, many of the modifiers of a noun drop away from the
modified central noun with a centrifugal tendency.

In the schema showing the order of sentence structure, the noun phrase and
adverb phrase are directly under the verb node. The noun phrase forms "actant,"
and the adverb phrase forms "circonstants."

The meaning of "circonstants" is self-explanatory, while the meaning of "actant"
must be defined.

Tesnière defines the actant as follows:

> The actant is a thing or thing with a certain name or a certain way, which can participate in
> the process through a very simple name or a negative way.[8]

---

[8]L. Tesnière. Éléments de Syntaxe Structurale, Paris : Klincksieck, 1959.

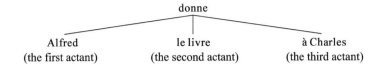

Fig. 5.6 Actants

Fig. 5.7 Comparison of
verbs to dramas

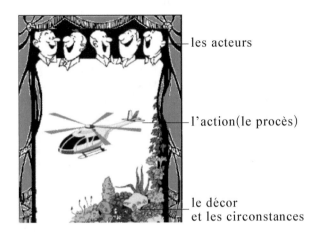

The number of actants cannot exceed three: subject, object 1, object 2.
For example:

Alfred donne le livre à Charles.
(Alfred gave the book to Charles.)

In this sentence, there are three actants that depend on the verb *donne*: the first actant is *Alfred*, acting as the subject; the second actant is *livre*, acting as object 1; and the third actant is *à Charles*, acting as object 2. The diagram is as follows (Fig. 5.6).

Theoretically, the number of circonstants can be infinite. For example:

Ce Soir, je passerai vite, chez lui, en sortant du bureau, pour. . . .
(Tonight, I come out of the office and will go to his house soon for. . . .)

where *Ce Soir*, *vite*, *chez lui*, *en sortant du bureau*, *pour*, etc. are all circonstants.

Tesnière pointed out, "The verb node, which occupies the central position in most European languages, represents a complete drama. Like most real dramas, they must have a plot, mostly characters and scenes."

"If we move the situation in dramas to the structural syntax, the plot, characters and scenes become verbs, actants elements and circonstants."

Regarding Tesnière's metaphor of a verb as a drama, someone made the following picture to vividly illustrate Tesnière's metaphor (Fig. 5.7).

In this picture, *les acturs* are characters, *l'action (le procès)* is the plot, and *le décor et les circonstances* is the scene. The plot is equivalent to the verb, the character is equivalent to the actant, and the scene is equivalent to the circonstant.

Tesnière's metaphor about verbs and dramas is very vivid. Japanese scholar Sugayama Kensei translated the valence into "the combined valence" in two Japanese articles on verb valence, the actant into "co-performance element," and the circonstant into "the condition element"; the necessary actant is translated as the "obligatory co-acting element," the optional actant is translated as "the arbitrary co-acting element," and the free circonstant is translated as "the free adding element."[9]

Tesnière also said, "You can compare a verb to an atom with hooks, which are used to attract the same number of actants as its dependent components. The number of hooks that a verb has, that is, the number of actants that the verb can control, constitutes what we call the valence of the verb."

The number of actants determines the number of valences of the verb. If there is no actant, it is a zero-valent verb; if there is one actant, it is a univalent verb; if there are two actants, it is a bivalent verb; and if there are three actants, it is a trivalent verb. For example:

```
zero-valent verb (Verbes avalents):
    Il pleut                        zero actant
    (it's raining)

univalent verb (Verbes monovalents):
    Il dort                         one actant
    (He fell asleep)

bivalent verb (Verbes bivalents):
    Il mange une pomme              two actants
    (He ate an apple)

trivalent verb (Verbes trivalents):
    Il donne son livre à Charles    three actants
    (He gave the book to Charles)
```

Tesnière explained that: "It should be pointed out that it is not always necessary to require the verb to carry all the actants following the valence or to make the verb reach a saturated state. Some valences can be left unused or vacant."

In addition to the abovementioned connexions, there is also a potential connexion, which is a semantic connexion rather than a structural connexion. Potential connexions are indicated by dotted lines in the diagram. For example:

---

[9]Sugayama Kensei. Some notes on verb valency in Englsih I, II. Collection of essays from Kobe Foreign Language University, 1984.4/1988.1.

Fig. 5.8 Potential
connexion

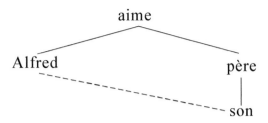

Fig. 5.9 The dependency
relation of the part of speech

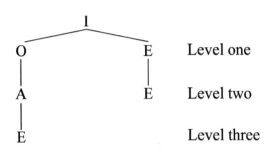

Alfred aime son père.
(Alfred loved his father.)

   In this sentence, the word *son* (his) is not only structurally related to its dependent word *père* (father) but also semantically related to *Alfred*, as shown in Fig. 5.8.

5.2.2 Translation

Tesnière proposed four basic parts of speech: verbs, nouns, adjectives, and adverbs. The verb is represented by I, the noun is represented by O, the adjective is represented by A, and the adverb is represented by E. The dependency relation between them is shown in Fig. 5.9.

   This scheme can be complicated by "translation." In the phrase *le livre de Pièrre* (The book of Pierre), *de Pièrre* is structurally related to *levre*, which acts as an adjective. In this way, we can think that the preposition *de* translates the noun *Pièrre* into an adjective in the discourse.

   This can be illustrated as follows (Fig. 5.10).

   At this time, *de* is the translator, Pièrre is the translate, and they together form a translation. According to the parts of speech involved in translation, Tesnière divides translation into first-degree translation and second-degree translation. If the ones to be translated are the noun (O), adjective (A), and adverb (E), then this kind of translation is a first-degree translation. As in the above example, it is a first-degree translation. If the one that is to be translated is a verb (1) and the verb itself is the governor rather than the governed, then the translation is a second-degree translation. For example, in the sentence:

Fig. 5.10 The preposition
turns a noun into an
adjective

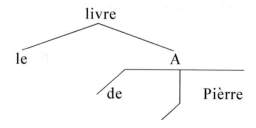

Fig. 5.11 Translation of the
verb into the noun by *que*

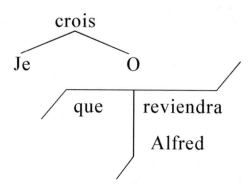

Je crois qu'Alfred reviendra.
(I'm sure Alfred will come back.)

Alfred reviendra replaced the position of the noun, and the verb *reviendra* was
translated into a noun by *que*. Therefore, this kind of translation is a second
translation.

This can be seen in Fig. 5.11.

Within the first- and second-degree translations, Tesnière also distinguished
simple translations and complex translations. If the translation merely translates
one component to another, it is a simple translation. For example, the above cases
are simple translations. If the translation can continuously translate from one component to another and then from this component to other components, that is, it is
first translated to component C1, then from component C1 to component C2, and
then from component C2 to component C3, and so on, until it reaches component
Cn, then this kind of translation is a complex translation. For example, in *trancher
dans le vif* (cut into thin slices), the translation of the word *vif* is a complex
translation: the adjective *vif* is translated by the translate *le* into a noun, the function
of *le vif* is equivalent to an adverb in terms of its relationship with the verb *trancher*,
and its translator is *dans* (see Fig. 5.12).

In theory, there are six types of translation:

```
O>A;  O>E;  A>O;
A>E;  E>O;  E>A。
```

Fig. 5.12 Complex
translation

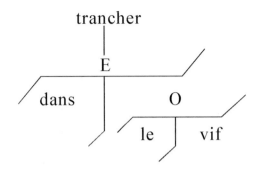

In these six types of translation, the translator is either a preposition, a suffix, or a label. And the translator can also be empty. In the following example, the prepositional translate is annotated with PREP, suffix translate with suffix SUFF, labeled translate with INDICE, and empty translate with ø. For example:

```
        PREP
O>A:  un poéte /de/ génie (genius poet)

        SUFF
    un poéte gen /ial (genius poet)

        ø
    là question/ /type (typical question)

        PREP
O>E:  I1 se bat/avec/courage
      (he fought bravely)

        ø
    cette année/ /il se bat
    (He's fighting this year)

        INDICE
A>O:  /le /vif (meat)

        SUFF
    La beau/té/ (beautiful)

        SUFF
A>E:  Courageus/ement/ (bravely)

        ø
    Sentir bon/ / (scented)

        INDICE
E>O:     /le /bien (benefits)
```

```
      PREP
E>A: le mode /d'/aujourd'hui
     (today's fashion)


        ∅
un homme bien / / (a decent person)
```

Tesnière's dependency grammar has attracted increasing attention from linguists. Computational linguists who are engaged in NLP especially advocate this grammar and regard it as an important formal model. Dependency grammar is playing an increasingly important role in automatic translation and human-computer dialogue research. Professor B. Vauquois at Grenoble University of Science and Medicine in France used dependency grammar to design a multilanguage automatic translation system in his GETA automatic translation laboratory.

5.3   Application of Dependency Grammar in NLP

Tesnière's dependency grammar has been welcomed by NLP researchers. In 1980, when Chinese scholar Zhiwei Feng studied machine translation at the Institute of Applied Mathematics (IMAG) of Grenoble University of Science and Medicine in France, he used dependency grammar to design a Chinese-French/English/Japanese/German/Russian multilingual automatic translation system. He introduced Tesnière's concept of "valence" into the study of machine translation and proposed a preliminary Chinese valence system. In this system, he divided the actants of verbs and adjectives into three types, agent, patient, and benefactive, and divided circonstants into time points, time period, the start of time, end of time, space point, time distance, the start of space, terminal of time space, initial state, final state, reason, result, goal, instrument, manner, scope, condition, content, comparison, comitative, degree, adjunct, modifier, etc. Together, 27 were used to establish a multilanguage automatic syntactic analysis system. For some nouns expressing concepts and feelings, their valences are also given.

He also combined dependency grammar with phrase structure grammar. In the tree diagram representing the structural relationship, the position of the head word is indicated. Head (GOV), pivot (PIVOT), and other nodes are used to represent the head word. GOV represents the head word of the phrase, and PIVOT represents the head word of the entire sentence. This may be the earliest successful attempt by Chinese scholars to use dependency grammar for natural language computer processing.

After Zhiwei Feng returned to China, he wrote an article to introduce dependency grammar.[10] This is the first time in China to introduce dependency grammar directly according to the original French text of Tesnière. Unfortunately, it was difficult to

---

[10]Feng Zhiwei. The dependency grammar of Tesnière. Foreign linguistics, 1983,(1): 63–65.

Fig. 5.13 Phrase
structure tree

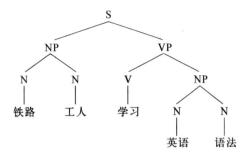

speak alone at the time, and there were very few responders. In the 1980s, for 10 years, the concepts of dependency and valence were almost ignored in China's NLP field. Since the 1990s, Chinese NLP researchers have begun to use dependency grammar to process Chinese automatically and have achieved very good results. Consequently, this important grammar has become popular in the Chinese language information processing field and has received extensive attention. Facts have proven that dependency grammar is indeed a better theoretical grammar for NLP.

Compared with phrase structure grammar, dependency grammar has no phrase level. Each node corresponds to the word in the sentence. It can deal with the relationship between words in the sentence, and the number of nodes is greatly reduced. It is easy to label the part of speech directly and has the advantages of simplicity and clarity. Especially in the automatic labeling of corpus text, it is more convenient to use than phrase structure grammar.

For example, if the Chinese sentence "铁路工人学习英语语法" (/Tie lu gong ren xue xi ying yu yu fa/; Railroad workers learn English grammar.) is represented in phrase structure grammar, its structure is a phrase structure tree (Fig. 5.13).

If it is represented in dependency grammar, its structure is a dependency tree (Fig. 5.14).

Obviously, the structure of the dependency tree is much more concise than the phrase structure tree, and the level and the number of nodes are reduced. Therefore, dependency grammar is welcomed by NLP researchers.

If the dependency relationship between the nodes is determined in the phrase structure tree, the dominant word is called the main word, and the dependent word is called the subordinate word. The phrase structure tree can be transformed into a dependency tree through the following steps:

1. Starting from the leaf nodes, first attribute the nodes representing specific words to the nodes representing parts of speech.
2. Then, from the bottom up, attribute the main word to the parent node.
3. Finally, the central main word of the whole sentence is attributed to the root node.

In this way, a dependency tree equivalent to the phrase structure tree can be obtained.

Fig. 5.14 Dependency tree

For example, in the above phrase structure tree, "铁路(/tie lu/; railroad)" is first attributed to node N that governs it, "工人(/gong ren/; worker)" is attributed to node N that governs it, and "学习(/xue xi/; learn)" is attributed to node V that governs it. "英语(/ying yu/; English)" is attributed to node N that governs it, and "语法(/yu fa/; grammar)" is attributed to node N that governs it. Then, the main word "工人(/gong ren/; worker)" in NP "铁路工人(/tie lu gong ren/; railroad worker)" is attributed to its parent node NP, "学习(/xue xi/; learn)" is attributed to its parent node VP, and the main word "语法(/yu fa/; grammar)" in NP "英语语法(/ying yu yu fa/; English grammar)" is attributed to the parent node NP. Finally, the central main word "学习(/xue xi/; learn)" of the whole sentence is attributed from node VP to root node S, and the above dependency tree that is completely equivalent to the phrase structure tree is obtained.

This shows that dependency grammar and phrase structure grammar are equivalent. Through finite steps, it is not difficult for us to realize the mutual transformation between phrase structure grammar and dependent grammar.

American linguist D. G Hays published the paper "Grouping and Dependency Theory" in 1960. Hays proposed dependency analysis according to the characteristics of machine translation. Although Hays's dependency analysis was proposed independently, this analysis has much in common with Tesnière's dependency grammar in terms of basic principles. This kind of analysis attempts to formally establish the dependency between words in a sentence, which is more formal than Tesnière's theory.

For example, in English, the relationship between the article (Art) and the noun (N) is like this: the noun is the head word, the article is the dependent word, and the article is located on the left side of the noun. This dependency relationship is illustrated in Fig. 5.15.

Fig. 5.15 Hays's dependency relationship representation method

The dependent word is written under the head word. If the dependent word is located on the right side of the head word, it is written under the right side.

This dependency can also be represented by symbols. Assuming that X_i is the head word, $X_{j1}, X_{j2} \ldots, X_{jk}$ are the left-hand dependent words of X_i (X_{j1} is on the left), and $X_{jk+1}, X_{jk+2}, \ldots X_{jn}$ are the right-hand dependent words of X_i (X_{jn} is on the right), then the grammatical rules between X_i and its dependent words can be written as follows:

$$X_i \left(X_{j1}, X_{j2} \ldots X_{jk}, *, X_{jk+1}, X_{jk+2}, \ldots, X_{jn} \right)$$

where * represents the position of the head word relative to the dependent word. This rule is denoted as rule (1).

In addition to this form of rules, there are two forms of rules, denoted as (2) and (3):

(2) X_i (*): indicates that X_i has no dependency in the sentence, which is the terminal rule
(3) *(X_i): indicates that X_i is not a dependent word of any word, that is, X_i is the head word of the whole sentence, which is an initial rule

Using these three rules, we can formally express the relationship between the head word of the sentence and its dependent words and create a tree diagram of the dependency relationship of the sentence to show the syntactic structure of the sentence and achieve the purpose of automatic syntactic analysis.

In 1970, the American computational linguist J. Robinson proposed four axioms of dependency grammar:

1. Only one component of a sentence is independent.
2. Other components in the sentence are directly dependent on a certain component.
3. No one component can depend on two or more components.
4. If component A directly depends on component B and component C is located between A and B in the sentence, then component C depends on either A, B, or a component between A and B.

In 1987, K. Schubert developed a multilingual machine translation system DLT from the perspective of language information processing and proposed 12 principles of dependency grammar for language information processing:

1. Syntax is only related to the form of language symbols.
2. Syntactic study of the formal features at all levels from morpheme to discourse.
3. Words in the sentence are related to each other through dependency.
4. Dependency is a directed co-occurrence relationship.
5. The syntactic form of a word is reflected through morphology, word formation, and word order.
6. The syntactic function of a word with respect to other words is described by dependency.
7. A phrase is a linguistic unit that has an aggregation relationship with other words and phrases as a whole, and there is a syntactic relationship between each word in the phrase, forming a language combination.

8. There is only one dominant word in a language combination, and this dominant word represents the connection between the language combination and other components in the sentence.
9. The main dominant word of the sentence governs other words in the sentence without being governed by any word. In addition to the main dominant word, other words in the sentence can only have one word that directly governs it.
10. Each word in the sentence only appears once in the dependency relationship structure.
11. The dependency relationship structure is a real tree structure.
12. Empty nodes should be avoided in the dependency structure.

Schubert's 12 principles contain Robinson's 4 axioms and expand the dependency relationship to the field of morpheme and discourse. It is more computable and operable and more suitable for the requirements of NLP.

The dependency relationship can be represented by a tree diagram. The tree diagram that represents the dependency relationship is called a "dependency tree." This kind of dependency tree is a formal description of the sentence structure in machine translation. Therefore, it is necessary for us to further study the various relationships between nodes in the dependency tree.

The relationship between the nodes in the dependency tree mainly includes dominance and precedence.

If there is a series of branches connecting them from node x to node y and all branches in the series have the same direction from x to y from top to bottom, then we say that node x governs node y. For example, in the dependency tree for the sentence "铁路工人学习英语语法" (/Tie lu gong ren xue xi ying yu yu fa/; railroad workers learn English grammar), the node labeled 学习 (/xue xi/; learn) governs the nodes labeled 工人 (/gong ren/; worker) and 铁路 (/tie lu/; railroad). The node labeled 工人(/gong ren/; worker) governs the node labeled with 铁路 (/tie lu/; railroad); the node labeled with 学习 (/xue xi/; learn) also governs the nodes labeled with 语法(/yu fa/; grammar) and 英语(/ying yu/; English), and the node labeled with 语法(/yu fa/; grammar) governs the node labeled with 英语(/ying yu/; English).

The two nodes in the dependency tree can be sorted from left to right only when there is no dominance between them. In this case, there is precedence between the two nodes. For example, in the previous dependency tree, the node labeled 工人 (/gong ren/; worker) precedes the nodes labeled 语法(/yu fa/; grammar) and 英语 (/ying yu/; English). There is no dominance between the two nodes labelled 工人 (/gong ren/; worker) and 语法 (/yu fa/; grammar). There is also no dominance between the two nodes of 工人(/gong ren/; worker) and 英语(/ying yu/; English). Similarly, the node labeled 铁路(/tie lu/; railroad) precedes the nodes labelled 语法(/ yu fa/; grammar) and 英语(/ying yu/; English) there is no dominance between the two nodes labeled 铁路(/tie lu/; railroad) and 语法(/yu fa/; grammar), and there is also no dominance between the two nodes labeled 铁路(/tie lu/; railroad) and 英语(/ ying yu/; English).

Based on the practice of machine translation research, Zhiwei Feng proposed that the dependency tree should satisfy the following five conditions:

1. **Simple node condition**: In the dependency tree, there are only terminal nodes and no non-terminal nodes. That is, all the nodes in the dependency tree represent specific words that appear in the sentence.
2. **Single parent condition**: In the dependency tree, all nodes have only one parent except the root node.
3. **Single root condition**: A dependency tree can only have one root node, which is the only node without a parent node in the dependency tree. This root node governs all other nodes.
4. **Non-intersection condition**: The branches in the dependency tree cannot intersect each other.
5. **Mutually exclusive conditions**: Between the nodes in the dependency tree, the dominance from top to bottom and the precedence from left to right are mutually exclusive. That is, if there is dominance between two nodes, there can be no precedence between them.

The five conditions of the dependency tree more vividly describe the relationship between the nodes in the dependency tree, which are more intuitive than the 4 axioms of J. Robinson and the 12 principles of K. Schubert and are more convenient to use in machine translation.

It is very good to use dependency grammar for automatic analysis because in the dependency tree obtained by the analysis, there are few levels and the number of nodes is small, which clearly shows the dependency relationship between each word in the sentence. However, when the dependency tree is used for automatic generation, the dependency tree that represents the sentence hierarchy must be transformed into a linear natural language sentence. According to the fifth condition (mutual exclusion condition) of the dependency tree, between the nodes in the dependency tree, the dominance and precedence are mutually exclusive. From the dominance between nodes, the precedence between them cannot be directly deduced. Therefore, we should also put forward appropriate generative rules according to the characteristics of the word order in the specific natural language to turn the dependency tree that represents structural relationships into sentences that represent linear relationships. In this regard, the generative rules of various natural languages are different. For example, Chinese modifiers should generally be placed before the head component, while certain modifiers in French should be placed after the head component. The object in active Chinese sentences should generally be placed after the predicate, and the object in Japanese should be placed before the predicate.

Therefore, compared with phrase structure grammar, dependency trees also have shortcomings. In the component structure tree of phrase structure grammar, since the precedence between the terminal nodes directly reflects the order of words, as long as the words on the terminal node are taken in sequence, the sentence can be directly generated. Therefore, in terms of automatic generation, the dependency tree is not as convenient as the component structure tree of phrase structure grammar. To compensate for this shortcoming of dependency trees, Chinese scholars combined phrase structure grammar with dependency grammar in machine translation research, which solves the problem of automatic sentence generation.

Based on the equivalence of dependency grammar and phrase structure grammar, Zhiwei Feng and others developed an English-Japanese machine translation system E-to-J in the 1980s. According to the characteristics of English and Japanese, phrase structure grammar is used for English analysis. In English analysis, phrase structure grammar-based shift-reduce algorithm and Tomita algorithm are used to prune, share, and compress the local ambiguity of the phrase structure tree to give play to the advantages of phrase structure grammar in the analysis of English. After the English analysis was completed, the English phrase structure tree was converted into an English dependency tree, and English words were converted into corresponding Japanese words. Finally, dependency grammar is used to adjust the Japanese word order, and Japanese words are generated according to Japanese morphological rules. In the dependency tree representing the Japanese sentence structure, all the main words of each phrase are on the parent node, the central main word of the sentence is on the root node, and the central main word of the sentence in Japanese happens to be at the end of the entire sentence. In this way, when generating Japanese, we only need to take words from left to right, from bottom to top, so that we can get Japanese sentences that conform to the rules of Japanese word order, greatly simplify the rules of Japanese generation, which is very convenient and gives full play to the advantages of dependency grammar in generating Japanese. This English-Japanese machine translation system was commercialized and launched in the Japanese market in November 1998.

In 1984, British linguist Richard Hudson proposed "word grammar" (WG[11]). WG is formal grammar based on dependency grammar. In WG, grammar is a network composed of all the words in a language. Hudson believes that grammar has no natural boundaries, that is, there are no grammar or even language modules. The grammar network is only part of the entire network of vocabulary knowledge, and it is closely related to the subnets of encyclopedia knowledge, social structure, and pronunciation in this network. Hudson points out that there is no essential difference between "grammar" and "vocabulary" in terms of description, but "grammar" deals with general patterns, while "vocabulary" describes facts about a single morpheme. From the formal point of view, although the general pattern involves parts of speech, the method of expression is not different from the method of describing morphemes (Hudson 2003).

In the WG network, the relationships among words include *is-a* relations, part relations (part-whole relations), and various dependency relations. Dependency is the most important relationship in the WG network.

---

[11] The latest information of WG can be obtained from the following address: "An Encyclopedia of English Grammar and Word Grammar":http://www.phon.ucl.ac.uk/home/dick/enc-gen.htm

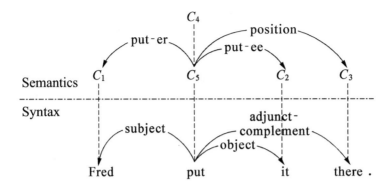

Fig. 5.16 WG analysis diagram

Here is an example of the WG processing the verb *put*:

```
PUT
PUT is a verb.
stem of PUT =<put>.
whole of ed-form of PUT = stem of it.
NOT: whole of ed-form of PUT = <put> + mEd.

sense of PUT = put.
PUT has [1] object.
PUT has [1] adjunct-complement.
NOT: PUT has [0-0] complement.
type of sense of adjunct-complement of PUT = place.
referent of adjunct-complement of PUT = position of sense of it.
referent of object of PUT = put-ee of sense of it.
```

According to the English description, readers can easily understand the syntactic and semantic features of *put*. We won't explain it here.

The following is a WG analysis diagram of the example sentence "Fred put it there" that includes *put* (Fig. 5.16).

From the WG analysis diagram of this example sentence, we can see that the lower layer represents the result of syntactic analysis, the upper layer represents the result of semantic analysis, and the result of semantic analysis is expressed through dependency. *Fred* is the subject of *put*, and the dependency is put-er (*Fred* is the agent of *put*). *It* is the object of *put*, and the dependency is put-ee (*it* is the patient of *put*). *There* is the adjunct complement of *put*, and the dependency is position (*there* is the position of *put*). For each syntactic component, there is a corresponding dependency analysis result. In the whole WG, syntactic analysis and dependency analysis are closely linked, and the analysis and description of dependency are important issues of WG.

In NLP, the results of dependency analysis are expressed using dependency tags. The Stanford parser automatic syntactic analysis system developed by Stanford University in the United States can perform phrase structure analysis and dependency analysis. When performing dependency analysis, they use predicate logic expressions to express the dependency between the governor word and the dependent words. In the parentheses of the predicate logic expression, the governor word is written before the dependent word:

Predicate (governor word, dependent word)

The main tags for the Stanford parser to represent dependency are as follows, which can act as predicates in predicate logical expressions:

root—ROOT
It represents the root of the sentence dependency tree. The fake node ROOT is used to represent the governor. In the dependency tree, the root node number is 0, which is a virtual number. The number of real words in the sentence starts from 1.
For example, in "I love French fries," there is root (ROOT, love).

In "an honest man," there is root (ROOT, man).

dep—dependent
If the system cannot accurately determine which of the two words is dependent, it can be tagged as dep. If the system encounters weird grammatical structures, has analysis errors, or encounters a long-distance dependency that is difficult to analyze, we can use the tag dep.
For example, in "Then, as if to show that he could. . .," if the relationship between *show* and *if* is not clear, we can tag it with dep(show, if).

aux—auxiliary
Auxiliaries do not serve as main verbs in a sentence. For example, modal verbs, or verbs such as *be, do, have*, etc. that express grammatical relations such as tense and aspect, are all tagged with aux.
For example, in "Reagent has died," there is aux(died, has).

In "He should leave," there is aux(leave, should).

auxpass—passive auxiliary
Passive auxiliary verbs are not the main verbs in the sentence. It contains passive information.
For example, in "Kennedy has been killed," there is auxpass(killed, been).

In "Kennedy was/got killed," there is auxpass(killed, was/got).

cop—copula
cop represents the relationship between the complement of the linking verb (copula) and the linking verb in the sentence.
For example, in "Bill is big," there is cop(big, is).

In "Bill is an honest man," there is cop(man, is).

The dependency tags of arguments are agent, complement, object, and subject. The complement, object, and subject can be further subdivided.

agent—agent

Agent represents the complement of the passive verb introduced by the preposition *by*, which is the actor of the action. This tag is only used in the collapsed dependency tree to replace prep_by. The agent tag is not used in the basic dependency tree.

For example, in "The man has been killed by the police," there is an agent (killed, police).

In "Effects caused by the protein are important," there is an agent(caused, protein).

The dependency tags for complement can be further subdivided into acomp, ccomp, and xcomp.

acomp—adjectival complement

The adjective complement of a verb is an adjective phrase that functions as a complement.

For example, in "She looks very beautiful," there is an acomp(looks, beautiful).

ccomp—clause complement with internal subject

The clause complement of a verb or adjective has an internal subject, and this internal subject functions like the object of the verb or adjective. The clause complements with internal subjects of nouns are limited to nouns such as *fact* or *report*. Such clause complements with internal subjects are generally definite.

For example, in "He says that you like to swim," there is a ccomp(says, like).

In "I am certain that he did it," there is a ccomp(certain, did).

In "I admire the fact that you are honest," there is a ccomp (fact, honest).

xcomp—clause complement with external subject

The clause complement of a verb or adjective is a clause or a predicate without a subject complement. The reference of the subject must be determined by the argument outside xcomp. This complement is always indefinite.

For example, in "He says that you like to swim," there is an xcomp(like, swim).

In "I am ready to leave," there is an xcomp(ready, leave).

In "Sue asked George to respond to her offer," there is an xcomp(asked, respond).

In "I consider him a fool," there is an xcomp(consider, fool).

In "I consider him honest," there is an xcomp(consider, honest).

The dependency tags representing the object can be further subdivided into dobj, iobj, and pobj.

dobj—direct object

The direct object of a verb or verb phrase is a noun phrase that acts as the accusative of a verb.

For example, in "she game me a raise," there is a dobj(give, raise).

In "they win the lottery," there is a dobj(win, lottery).

iobj—indirect object
> The indirect object of VP is a noun phrase that acts as the dative of a verb.
> For example, in "she gave me a raise," there is an iobj(give, me).

pobj—object of preposition
> A prepositional object is the head word of the noun phrase after the preposition or adverbs such as *here* and *there*. Unlike Penn Treebank, Stanford parser uses words such as *including* and *concerning* as quasi-prepositions.
> For example, in "I sat on the chair," there is a pobj(on, chair).

The dependency tags representing the subject (subj—subject) can be further subdivided into nsubj, nsubjpass, csubj, and csubjpass.

nsubj—nominal subject
> The noun subject is a noun phrase that acts as a syntactic subject in a sentence. The governor of nsubj is not always a verb. When the verb is a copula, the root of the sentence (the governor) is not the copula but the complement of the copula, which can be an adjective or a noun.
> For example, in "Clinton defeated Dole," there is a nsubj(defeated, Clinton).

In "The baby is cute," there is a nsubj(cute, baby).

nsubjpass—passive nominal subject
> The subject of a passive noun is a noun phrase that serves as the syntactic subject of a passive sentence.
> For example, in "Dole was defeated by Clinton," there is a nsubjpass (defeated, Dole).

csubj—clause subject (clausal subject)
> The clause subject is the clause that serves as the syntactic subject in the sentence, that is, the clause itself serves as the subject. The governor of csubj is not always a verb. When the verb is a copula, the root of the sentence (governor) is not the copula but should be the complement of the copula. In the following sentence, *what she said* is the clause subject.
> For example, in "What she said makes sense," there is a csubj(makes, said).

In "What she said is not true," there is a csubj(true, said).

csubjpass—passive clausal subject
> The subject of a passive clause is a clause that serves as the syntactic subject of a passive sentence. In the following example sentences, "that she lied" is the clause subject.
> For example, in "That she lied was suspected by everyone," there is a csubjpass(suspected, lied).

The dependency of modifiers (mod—modifier) can be further subdivided into amod, advmod, appos, advcl, det, predet, preconj, vmod, mwe, poss, etc.

amod—adjectival modifier

The adjective modifier of the noun phrase NP is any adjective phrase used to modify the meaning of NP.

For example, in "Sam eats red meat," there is an amod(meat, red).

In "Sam took out a 3 million dollar loan," there is an amod(loan, dollar).
In "Sam took out a $3 million loan," there is an amod(loan, $).

advmod—adverbial modifier

The adverbial modifier of a word is an adverb or adverb phrase (ADVP), which is used to modify or limit the meaning of a word.

For example, in "genetically modified food," there is an advmod(modified, genetically).

In "less often," there is an advmod(often, less).

appos—appositional modifier

The appositive modifier of NP is the noun phrase to the right of the first NP, which is used to identify or modify NP. Appos also includes instances in parentheses and abbreviations in these structures.

For example, in "Sam, my brother, arrived," there is an appos(Sam, brother).

In "Bill (John's cousin)," there is an appos(Bill, cousin).
In "The Australian Broadcasting Corporation (ABC)," there is an appos (Corporation, ABC).

advcl—adverbial clause modifier

The adverbial clause modifier of the VP or sentence S is a clause that modifies the verb (including the time clause, result clause, condition clause, purpose clause, etc.).

For example, in "The accident happened as the night was falling," there is an advcl(happened, falling).

In "If you know who did it, you should tell the teacher," there is an advcl (tell, know).
In "He talked to him in order to secure the account," there was an advcl(talked, secure).

det—determiner

The determiner relationship is the relationship between the head word in an NP and its determiner.

For example, in "The man is here," there is a det(man, the).

In "Which book do you prefer?," there is a det(book, which).

predet—predeterminer

The predeterminer relationship is the relationship between the head word in an NP and the word before the determiner in NP and is used to modify the meaning of the determiner.

For example, in "All the boys are here," there is a predet(boys, all).

preconj—preconjunct

The preconj represents the relationship between the head word in an NP and the words appearing at the beginning of the conjunct (such as *either*, *both*, *neither*, etc.).

For example, in "Both the boys and the girls are here," there is a preconj (boys, both).

vmod—reduced nonfinite verbal modifier

The reduced nonfinite verbal modifier is the participle or infinitive form of the verb. vmod is at the beginning of the phrase (the phrase often has some argument components, such as the verb phrase (VP)), which is used to modify the meaning of a noun phrase or another verb.

For example, in "Points to establish are...," there is a vmod(points, establish).

In "I don't have anything to say to you," there is a vmod(anything, say).

In "Truffles picked during the spring are tasty," there is a vmod(truffles, picked).

In "Bill tried to shoot, demonstrating his incompetence," there is a vmod(shoot, demonstrating).

mwe—multiword expression modifier

The multiword modification relationship mwe is used in multiword idioms, and the function of these idioms is equivalent to a word. In the ordinary multiword structure, it is difficult to add any other relations to it, or after adding other relations, the meaning of the multiword structure is not clear. At present, mwe is mainly used in the following structures: *rather than*, *as well as*, *instead of*, *such as*, *because of*, *in addition to*, *all but*, *such as*, *because of*, and *due to*.

For example, in "I like dogs as well as cats," there is an mwe(well, as).

In "He cries because of you," there is an mwe(of, because).

poss—poss modifier

poss is used to denote the possessive relation in a noun phrase.

For example, in "their offices," there is a poss(offices, their).

In "Bill's clothes," there is a poss(clothes, bill).

cc—coordination

The coordinate relation (cc) is the relationship between the connective component and its coordinate conjunctions. Note: in different dependency grammars, the way to deal with the coordinate relationship is different. Stanford parser uses one of the conjunctions (usually the first conjunction) as the head word of a connective. The conjunction can also appear at the beginning of a sentence. This conjunction can also be tagged as cc, which is a subordinate of the root predicate of a sentence.

For example, in "Bill is big and honest," there is a cc(big, and).

In "They either ski or snowboard," there is a cc(ski, or).

In "And then we left," there is a cc(left, And).

conj—conjunct

conj represents the relationship between two components connected by coordinate conjunctions (such as *and*). Stanford parser's treatment of connectives is asymmetric: the head word of the conj relationship is the first connective component, while the other connective component is subordinate to the first connective component through the conj relationship.

For example, in "Bill is big and honest," there is a conj(big, honest).

In "They either ski or snowboard," there is a conj(ski, snowboard).

expl—expletive [there]

The existential relationship is used to represent the existential word *there*. In the existential relationship, the main verb of the sentence acts as the governor.

For example, in "There is a ghost in the room," there is an exp(is, There).

When analyzing the dependency of a sentence, Stanford parser first tags the words in the sentence according to the natural number order to indicate the position of the word in the sentence. When outputting the analysis result, each word should carry the number of its positions in the sentence. For example, the sentence "My dog also likes eating sausage" is numbered as follows:

```
My dog also likes eating sausage
1  2    3    4     5      6
```

ROOT represents the root of the dependency tree. It is a virtual node, numbered 0. The results of the dependency analysis of this sentence are as follows:

```
poss(dog-2, My-1)
nsubj(likes-4, dog-2)
advmod(likes-4, also-3)
root(ROOT-0, likes-4)
xcomp(likes-4, eating-5)
dobj(eating-5, sausage-6)
```

It can be seen from the analysis that *dog-2* governs *My-1*, and the dependency between them is governed by modifier poss; *likes-4* governs *dog-2*, and the dependency between them is noun subject nsubj, *like-4* also governs *also-3*, and the dependency between them is advmod; *ROOT-0* governs like-4, and the dependency between them is root; *likes-4* governs *eating-5*, and their dependency is xcomp with external subject; and *eating-5* governs *sausage-6*, and the dependency relationship between them is the direct object dobj. Through these predicate logic expressions, the results of dependency analysis can be clearly expressed.

5.4   Valence Grammar

In the early 1960s, German scholars introduced Tesnière's dependency grammar into German studies. Dependency grammar is generally called "valence grammar" (*Valenzgrammatik*) in Germany. At that time, the German valence grammar study was mainly concentrated in Leipzig in East Germany and Mannheim in West Germany, which were called Leipzig School and Mannheim School, respectively.

The leader of the Leipzig School is Gerhard Helbig. He and W. Schenkel edited and published the first valence dictionary in human history entitled the *German Verb Valence and Distribution Dictionary* in 1969. Starting from this verb dictionary, they edited and published an adjective valence dictionary (1974) and a noun valence dictionary (1977). In addition to a large number of articles, the Leipzig School also published a collection of essays on valence. Helbig, G. published *Probleme der Valenz- und Kasustheorie* (Tübingen: Niemeyer, 1992), and Welke, K. published *Einführung in die Valenz-und Kasustheorie* (Leipzig: Bibliographisches Institut, 1988). The two publications are considered to be essential readings for the study of valence theory. The contribution of the Leipzig School is mainly in valence theory.

Helbig believes that "valence refers to the abstract relationship between the verb and its governed components. Syntactic valence refers to the ability of a verb to create a certain number of slots around it and to fill them with necessary or optional mitspielers" [1, pp. 49–50].

Helbig proposed the concepts of "the complementary element" (Ergänzungen) and "the explanatory element" (Angaben). The complementary element is roughly equivalent to Tesnière's actant, and the explanatory element is roughly equivalent to Tesnière's circonstant.

Helbig believes that not only complementary elements and explanatory elements should be distinguished but also obligatory complementary elements and optional complementary elements should be distinguished. The valence of a verb is formed by adding up the number of obligatory and optional complementary elements. Complementary elements can be determined by the deletion method. The specific method is to delete each component in a sentence in turn. If after deleting a component the sentence structure is still correct, it means that the deleted component is not obligatory; otherwise, the component is obligatory. In the sentence processed by the deletion method, the last remaining component is the number of complementary elements that this verb can govern. The components deleted by the deletion method can be collectively referred to as optional components, which are composed of two components with different properties: obligatory complementary elements and explanatory elements. Because the complementary element is used when calculating the valence of verbs, it is necessary to separate it from the explanatory element. Helbig uses a reduction method to identify explanatory elements, but the effect is not ideal.

The judgment of complementary elements and explanatory elements and the distinction between obligatory complementary elements and optional complementary elements are important for anyone who constructs a valence dictionary.

Zifonun and others introduced a method of judging obligatory complementary elements, explanatory elements, and optional complementary elements. Following the following flow chart, the problem of defining the most "complementary elements/explanatory elements" (Ergänzungen/Angaben, E/A) in Germany can be solved (Fig. 5.17).

Put the E/A candidate components to be determined into the flow chart as the starting point. The first test is R-Test (deletion test). If it cannot be deleted, it can be

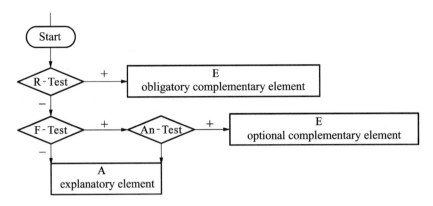

Fig. 5.17 Judgment flow chart of E/A

determined that it must be an obligatory complementary element. Then, an F-test (substitution test) was performed on the remaining components. The specific method is to substitute the test object with a variable, i.e., an indefinite personal pronoun such as someone, something, and a place. An inferential relationship is formed between the deleted component and the sentence with an indefinite word. If it cannot be substituted, it is judged as an explanatory element. If it can be substituted, an An-Test (rewriting test) is performed. An-Test rewrites the tested component as "und das X" (where X should indicate the component to be tested) and then determines whether the sentence is correct. If the sentence is not correct, X is judged as an optional supplementary element; otherwise, it is judged as an explanatory element.

The core figure in Mannheim school is Ulrich Engel of the Institut für Deutsche Sprache (IDS). Although they edited the valence dictionary of German verbs, the main contribution of this school lies in the research and practice of whether the principle of dependency can be used to describe the main phenomena in a language completely. The achievements in this area are Engel's two German grammar books [2, 3]). U. Engel established a perfect German valence grammar system in these works. He defined complementary elements as the set of dominant elements in the subcategorization of verbs to form a sentence and made a detailed classification and discussion on complementary elements and explanatory elements. His grammar may be the first one that only uses the principle of dependency to describe the grammar of a certain language. Engel regards valence as a dominant power of verbs in subcategorization. He believes that the difference between complementary elements and explanatory elements is that the former is only possessed by certain parts of speech in subcategorization, while all parts of speech can have explanatory elements. The obligatory complementary element is an indispensable component in grammar, and even if there is no optional element, it will not produce an ungrammatical sentence. The obligatory element must be complementary, while the optional element can be either explanatory or complementary. Whether an element is explanatory or complementary is determined by its governor. In 1980, Engel translated

Tesnière classic works of dependency grammar into German, which is helpful for German scholars to study the classical works of dependency grammar.

H. Schumacher, a scholar of the German Research Institute, edited the *Verb Valency Classification Dictionary*, which adjusted the types of complementary elements. The dictionary was published in 1986 and is a monograph on the study of German verb valence. W. Teubert of the institute extended the concept of "valence" to nouns and studied the valence of German nouns in depth. In 1979, he published a monograph *The Valence of Nouns*, which is the earliest work on the valence of nouns.

Valence can be understood from three different levels: logic, syntax, and semantics.

1. **Logical valence**: German scholar W. Bondzio believes that in the process of building syntactic structures, the meaning of vocabulary provides a decisive premise. The vocabulary itself has the possibility of connection, and its ability to connect comes from the semantic characteristics of words. The core of the concept of word meaning reflects the relationship between various phenomena in reality outside the language.

   For example, the meaning of the German word *verbinden* (connect) indicates the relationship between the linker, the object to be connected, and the components to be connected with the object. The meaning of the word *besuchen* (visit) in German indicates the relationship between the visitor and the interviewee.

   Bondzio believes that valence is a characteristic of word meaning, which opens up a certain number of slots in the meaning of a word, and this slot is valence. Valence embodies a kind of logical semantic relationship. He advocated using the term "vacancy" in predicate logic to express the relationship of word meaning. The meaning of the German word *verbinden* (connect) contains three slots, and the meaning of the German word *besuchen* (visit) contains two slots. The number of slots is determined by the meaning of the word. The slot generated based on the meaning of the word is "valence," and the number of slots contained in the meaning of a word is the number of valences of the word. This kind of valence determined by the logical relationship of word meaning is called logical valence.

   In different languages, the number of logical valences represented by the same concept is the same. In Chinese, the verb 联接(/lian jie/; connect) is also trivalent, and the verb 访问(/fang wen/; visit) is also bivalent. However, in a specific language, how to realize the logical relationship depends on the specific method of expression of the language.

2. **Syntactic valence**: The manifestation of logical valence in a specific language is not the same. The different forms of expression are determined by the specific form of the specific language. The manifestation of logical valence in a specific language is syntactic valence. For example, the logical valence of the verb *helfen* (help) in German is trivalent: the helper, the person being helped, and the content of the help provided. The logical valence in German is that the predicate verb needs conjugation, the helper is represented by the nominative case, the person

being helped is represented by the dative case, and the help provided is represented by the preposition structure formed by *bei*. The German for "He helps me with my work" is "Er hilft mir bei der Arbeit."

The logical valences of synonyms in the same language are the same, but they often have different syntactic valences. For example, the German words *warten* and *erwarten* both mean "wait." The logical valence is the same. They are both bivalent verbs, and there are two slots: the waiter and the waited. However, the waited for *warten* should be represented by *auf*, which constitutes a preposition structure, while the waited for *erwarten* is represented by the accusative case. Compare:

Er wartet auf seine Freundin
Er erwartet seine Freundin
    The meaning of these two sentences is "he is waiting for his girlfriend."

3. **Semantic valence**: Semantic valence refers to whether the words used as complementary elements are semantically compatible with verbs. Semantic valence often has different characteristics in different languages. For example, 喝汤(/he tang/; drink soup) can be said in Chinese. The complement 汤(/tang/; soup) is semantically compatible with the verb 喝(/he/; drink). However, in German, *suppe* (soup) and *trinken* (drink) are incompatible. German does not say *eine Suppe trinken* (to drink soup) but to say *eine Suppe essen* (to eat soup), but in Mandarin Chinese, you cannot say 吃汤(/chi tang/; eat soup). This semantic valence also reflects the characteristics of different languages.

Based on decades of experience, Helbig summed up six steps for constructing valence dictionary entries:

1. Analyze the logical semantic structure of the predicate corresponding to the verb and determine the number of lexicalizable arguments that form a complete predicate structure.
2. Label the semantic features of the verb.
3. Label the semantic case for verbs, that is, assign clear semantic roles to those arguments obtained in the first step, such as agent, recipient, location, tool, etc.
4. Perform semantic referential analysis on lexicalizable arguments and perform semantic labeling such as [±animate], [± human], [± abstract].
5. This step addresses the problem of mapping from the semantic level to the syntactic level. There are two things to consider: one is based on the functional components of the sentence, such as subject and object, and the other is based on the morphology of the sentence components, such as the case of the noun and the type of prepositional phrase, which is the qualitative description of the actant (complement).
6. Give the quantitative description of the actant (complement) of a given word, that is, to give the valence of the verb. We should distinguish between obligatory complementary elements and optional complementary elements (1992:153–155).

The six steps proposed by Helbig to determine valence are of great value not only for the construction of valence dictionaries but also for the construction of the valency lexicon.

For example, let us construct a valence entry for the German verb *wohnen* (live). wohnen: Er wohnt in Köln (he lives in Cologne)

Er wohnt am Bahnhof (he lives at the station)

Follow the steps below to construct the valence entry for *wohnen*:

1. The logical semantic structure of *wohnen* is **R** a b, and its number of semantic slots is 2, which are a and b, respectively.
2. The semantic features of *wohnen* are as follows:

   - Predicate features related to valence: [+static] [+relation][-symmetric] [+appearance] [+location]
   - Predicate features unrelated to valence: [+location] [+house] [+fixed] . . .

3. The semantic case of *wohnen*:
   a → state owner
   b → locative case
4. Semantic referential analysis of the argument of *wohnen*:
   a → [human]
   b → [+specific], [-inanimate], [+fixed]; [location], [building]. . .
5. The mapping from argument to syntax level:
   Argument mapping to sentence components:
   a → Subj
   b → Adv
   Argument mapping to the case or phrase type:
   a → Sn (nominative case)
   b → pS (prepositional phrase)
6. The number of actants for *wohnen* is 2, which is a bivalent verb expressed as *wohnen₂*.

Schumacher (1986) of the Mannheim School dealt with the German verb *herstellen* (manufacture, produce) in the following steps:

1. Give the sentence structure of the verb. For example, the sentence structure of *herstellen* is "herstellen NomE AkkE (PrapE aus/mit)."[12] This sentence structure means that *herstellen* needs a first-case complement and a fourth-case complement in the sentence. These two complements are obligatory. An optional prepositional complement can also appear in a sentence, usually introduced by the preposition aus or mit. This kind of optional complement is indicated in the dictionary with brackets.

---

[12] In German examples, NOM "denotes the nominative case, the first case," Akk "the accusative case, the fourth case," dat "the dative case, the third case," and Gen "the genitive case, the second case."

> *Der* a$_{NomE}$ stellt den x$_{AkkE}$ (*aus/min dem* y$_{PrapE}$) her.

Fig. 5.18 Structure format of a sentence

> a bewirkt absichtlich, daß es auf der Voraussetzung von y dazu kommt, daß *es x gibt*.

Fig. 5.19 Paraphrase with the rewriting method

2. Give the sentence format of the structure. Each complement is represented by the letters a, x, y, etc. In the lower right corner of the letter, the abovementioned abbreviation form is used to indicate the syntactic type of the complement, and the complement is treated as a masculine noun. Each case is expressed as far as possible with the definite article. For example, the structural format of *herstellen* is shown in Fig. 5.18.

   The meaning of this sentence format is "a makes x (with y)."
3. Use the "rewriting method" to paraphrase the sentence format. For example, the so-called a (with y) to make x can be interpreted by the "rewriting method" (Fig. 5.19).

   This rewriting paraphrase means: "With the prerequisites of *y*, *a* purposefully makes *x* appear."
4. Semantic description of various complements in the sentence format, such as the first complement *a* can be a "capable individual," "collective," or "institution," the fourth complement *x* is "artifact (as a commodity)," and the prepositional complement *y* can be "object" or "material."
5. Discuss the ability of verbs to form passive.
6. In the process of interpreting verbs, the example is one of the central parts.
7. Explore the possibility of verb derivation from the perspective of "word formation."
8. Each dictionary entry corresponds to only one meaning of a verb, but it is necessary to point out other meanings of this verb.

From the format of Helbig and Schumacher's valence dictionary, we can see some similarities between the two. For example, both contain syntactic and semantic elements, and the valence structure does not reflect the surface linear order.

The difference between the two is that Helbig's description method is from semantics to syntax, semantics is the main means to determine the valence, and the syntactic valence is ultimately obtained. Although Schumacher did not mention in detail how he obtained the valence of a word, it can be seen that his description method is influenced by Engel. It starts from the surface (syntax) of the sentence to obtain the sentence structure. The function of semantics here is more choice restriction than the basis of determining valence.

5.5 Application of Valence Grammar in NLP

The study of valence theory by German scholars is welcomed by language information processing researchers. The German-Chinese machine translation system
GCAT developed by Zhiwei Feng in 1983 applied the achievements made by
German scholars at that time.[13] In this German-Chinese machine translation system,
the relationship between language components is not only syntactic but also logical
and semantic. It has consciously accepted German valence scholars' theory on the
distinction between logical valence, syntactic valence, and semantic valence. This
GCAT German-Chinese machine translation system also established the principle of
establishing the dominant relationship of sentence components based on the lexical
meaning of words. It was also obviously influenced by the idea of German valence
scholars that the meaning of a word determines the slots of a verb.[14]

Next, we introduce several formal models based on valence grammar, which are
very helpful for NLP.

Computational linguistics scholars Petr Sgall, Jarmila Panevová, Eva Hajicová,
and others from Prague University in the Czech Republic put forward functional
generative descriptions (FGDs). This is a multilevel formal model of NLP in which
valence plays a key role.

Hajicová and Sgall pointed out, "If dependency is regarded as a basic relationship, then the syntactic characteristics of lexical units can be described in terms of its
optional or obligatory dependent components. This description can include restrictions on the combination of words, their relationship between the surface structure of
the sentence, etc. The broad valence framework includes all complementary elements and explanatory elements, while the narrow valence framework only considers the complementary elements and the necessary explanatory elements."[15] Over
the years, these researchers at the University of Prague have not only theoretically
proven the feasibility and accuracy of FDG but also constructed many workable NLP
systems.

The Valency Lexicon of Czech Verbs (VALLEX 1.0), which was published in
2003, contains 1400 Czech verbs and may be the largest practical valency lexicon
available. In addition to the general purpose of language research, Vallex is also used
in the following NLP fields:

1. It helps to ensure the consistency of the valence structure of the Prague Dependency Tree (PDT) bank.

---

[13]Zhiwei Feng. Design principle and method of German-Chinese machine translation GCAT
system. *Journal of Chinese Information Processing*, 1988, (3).

[14]Zhiwei Feng. German-Chinese machine translation GCAT system. Language Modernization,
Volume 10, 1990.

[15]Sgall Petr, Eva Hajicová, and Jarmila Panevová. *The Meaning of the Sentence in Its Semantic and
Pragmatic Aspects*. Dordrecht: D. Reidel. 1986.

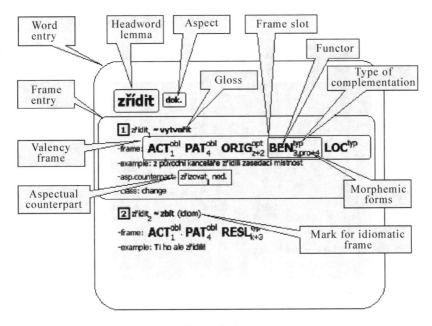

Fig. 5.20 An entry zřídit and its composition in Vallex

2. It is helpful for automatic syntactic analysis. Without the help of valence information, it would be difficult for a parser to distinguish the syntactic structure of
the following two sentences: "He began to love her" and "He forced her to walk."
3. The valency lexicon helps to generate the semantic structure representation of the
input sentence.
4. It is helpful to construct a verb valence dictionary in an automatic way.

The following is an entry zřídit (establish, set) and its composition in Vallex[16]
(Fig. 5.20).

As seen from Fig. 5.20, an entry in Vallex has very rich content, including head
word lemma, aspect, gloss, frame slot, functor, type of complementation, morphemic
form, mark for idiomatic frame, frame entry, valency frame, aspectual
counterpart, etc.

It is worth mentioning that Vallex not only provides the traditional print version
but also builds the xml format and html version, which is very meaningful for the
sharing, communication, and use of the valency lexicon. In particular, the interactive
interface built on top of html files, although it is not highly technical, is very
convenient for people to use (Fig. 5.21).

Through this interactive interface, we can easily browse the content of the
valency lexicon according to different indicators and conduct quantitative and

---

[16] Refer to http://ckl.mff.cuni.cz/zabokrtsky/vallex/1.0/doc/vallex-doc.html

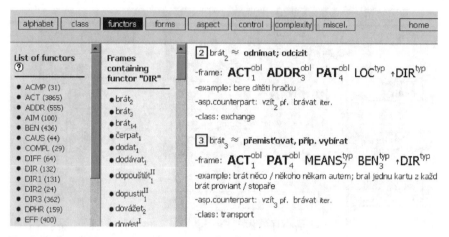

Fig. 5.21 Interactive interface of Vallex

qualitative analysis on the valence structure of various verbs. For example, if the user wants to query the valence function of *brát*, he can click functors, and the interactive interface will display its various valence functions, such as ACT, ADDR, PAT, LOC, DIR, etc.

Valence grammar generally does not consider the linear order of words in a sentence. However, in NLP, the linear order of words is also very important. Therefore, it is necessary to study the automatic processing of word order.

In the early 1970s, Stanley Starosta established a syntactic theory called Lexicase (1988), which can effectively deal with the linear order of words in valence analysis.

Starosta believes that "grammar is a lexicon. The properties of a word related to grammar are explained in its vocabulary matrix. These properties define the 'environment' in which the word can appear. The 'environment' here does not only refer to the linear environment. It also includes a hierarchical dependency environment." He also said that "context attributes as part of lexical representation make phrase structure rules no longer necessary. The context attribute is similar to an atomic valence, which states which words can be attached to a given word as dependents to form molecules called 'sentences.' Context attributes can belong to syntax, semantics and morphology."[17]

Starosta gave the definition of "valence" in Lexicase: "Most parts of speech in Lexicase are identified by one or more context attributes, which limit their valence. The valence attribute indicates the combination potential of words and other words, which includes required and optional dependency connections, linear prepositions and other requirements. Every word contains the qualification of a word sequence. Only when each word in the string can become the governor or dependency of other

---

[17] Starosta, Stanley. *The Case for Lexicase: An Outline of Lexicase Grammatical Theory*. London and New York: Pinter Publishers. 1988.

Fig. 5.22 The linear order in Lexicase

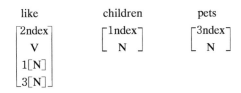

words and the valence of each word is satisfied is the phrase qualified."[18] This shows that valence is a lexical attribute, which reflects the potential ability of a word to combine with other words. The purpose of our research on valence is to realize this potential ability. Anything can reflect its value only in use, and valence is no exception. Through the realization of the "valence," we can generate a larger language unit, which can be used to test whether the string is qualified and why it is qualified from syntax, semantics, and even pragmatics.

The following is a representation of Lexicase's analysis of the English sentence "Children like pets." We can see that in Lexicase, the linear order of words is reflected in the final analysis result. For example, as seen from the following example, *like* is a verb with a linear order of 2, dominating two nouns at 1 and 3 (Fig. 5.22).

Obviously, these representations are the results of the instantiation of specific sentences. If in the lexicon, the attribute representation is not instantiated; at this time, lexical items can also be used to represent and distinguish linear relationships. The following is an example of the Japanese postposition から (kara) and the English preposition *from*:

1. から (*kara*)[@ndex,P,+sorc,?[N],?[N]<@]
2. *from* [@ndex,P,+sorc,?[N],@<?[N]]
   where the position of the word that has not been instantiated is indicated by @ and the required component N is represented by ?. The order of the positions of the required components is limited by "<". If you want to analyze and identify a Japanese string "学校から" (gakkoo kara, from school) and an English string *from school*, then the instantiated [1, 2] become
3. 学校(*gakkoo*)[1ndex,N]
   から (*kara*)[2ndex,P,+sorc,1[N],1[N]<2]
4. *from* [1ndex,P,+sorc,2[N],1<2[N]]
   school [2ndex,N]

The combination condition is fully satisfied, so the input string is qualified.

Lexicase also uses vocabulary rules to determine whether the order between Det, Adj, and N in English is grammatical. For example, if there is a string *old this house*, we use lexical rules to determine whether it is grammatical. In the lexicon of Lexicase, a *house* as the head word or governor has the following format:

---

[18] Starosta Stanley. Lexicase Grammar. In Àgel,Vilmos; Eichinger,Ludwig; Eroms,Hans-Werner; Hellwig,Peter; Heringer,Hans-Jürgen; Lobin,Henning (eds.). *Dependenz Und Valenz: Ein Internationales Handbuch Der Zeitgenösischen Forschung,* Berlin:De Gruyter. 2003. p. 526–545.

<u>house</u> [@ndex,N,?[Det],?[Adj],?[Det]<@,?[Adj]<@,$\underline{\underline{?}}$[Det]$\underline{\underline{<?}}$[Adj]]

The input string is analyzed according to the lexicon, and the following results are obtained:

<u>house</u> [3ndex,N,2[Det],1[Adj],2[Det]<3,1[Adj]<3,$\underline{\underline{2}}$[Det]$\underline{\underline{<1}}$[Adj]]
<u>old</u> [1ndex,Adj]
<u>this</u> [2ndex,Det]

Because 2 is not less than 1, the input string is not qualified.

Hellwig, a German computational linguist, combined valence and unification and proposed "dependency unification grammar" (DUG). Valence is one of the core concepts of DUG.

Hellwig believes that "syntax is almost the combination ability of words. Words are not only fillers of an existing structural pattern but also the real source of the pattern. From a formal point of view, the core concept of dependency grammar is complementation. A head element and some components that can improve the head element form a standard syntactic structure. In the real world, the natural language is used to assign attributes for certain things and describe the relationship between them. Therefore, words can be divided into two categories: one that expresses relations and the other that refers to things. If there is no complement, the words expressing relations will be incomplete. However, the number and types of syntactic structures suitable for filling the specific vacancy are predictable. If the ability to predict complements plays the leading role in the formal system of syntax, then our approach and systems belong to dependency grammar."[19]

Since the goal of DUG is machine-oriented, a list is used to represent language knowledge and analysis results. The following is the list for the English sentence "The robot picks up a big red block" (Table 5.1).

The "<" and ">" in DUG indicate the linear order between the head word and its complements: "<" means "before," and ">" means "behind."

If we turn the above table 90° clockwise and connect each head item and its complements with a line, it is not difficult to obtain a tree diagram (Fig. 5.23).

In 2007, Chinese scholars Haitao Liu and Zhiwei Feng proposed the formal model of "probabilistic valency pattern" (PVP) theory.[20]

According to PVP theory, valence is a fundamental attribute of a word.[21] In a broad sense, valence refers to the ability of a word to combine with other words. This ability is a potential ability. Its realization in a sentence is restricted by syntactic,

---

[19] Hellwig Peter. Dependency Unification Grammar. In Àgel,Vilmos; Eichinger, Ludwig; Eroms, Hans-Werner; Hellwig,Peter; Heringer,Hans-Jürgen; Lobin,Henning (eds.), *Dependenz Und Valenz: Ein Internationales Handbuch Der Zeitgenösischen Forschung,* Berlin:De Gruyter, 2003.

[20] Haitao Liu, Zhiwei Feng. Probabilistic valency pattern theory of natural language processing [J], *Linguistic Science*, 2007, (3): 32–41.

[21] In fact, valence should be regarded as a universal attribute of linguistic units. Only words or parts of speech are mentioned here for the convenience of discussion.

Table 5.1 A list that shows the results of sentence analysis

(string[•] role[illocution] lexeme[statement'] category[sign] utterance[+]

   (<string[picks] role[predication] lexeme[pick] category[verb] form[finite] tense [present]
   voice[active] person[it, U] s_type[statement] adjacent[+] margin[left]

      (< string [robot] role [subject] lexeme [robot] category [noun] number [singular] person[it, C]

         (< string [The] role [determination] lexeme [definite'] category [determiner]
         number[singular, C])

      (>string[up] role[phrasal_part] lexeme[up] category[particle])

      (>string[block] role[dir _ object] lexeme[block] category[noun] number [singular] person[it]

         (< string [a] role [determination] lexeme [indefinite'] category [determiner]
         number[singular, C])

         (<string[big] role[attribute] lexeme[big] category[adjective] use [attributive])

         (<string[red] role[attribute] lexeme[red] category[adjective])))

semantic, and pragmatic factors. In a broad sense, valence refers to the ability of verbs and other parts of speech that require complements. Figure 5.24 is a schematic diagram of a valency pattern where W represents a word and C1–C3 are complements needed to complete or clarify the meaning of W. A1–A3 are adjuncts that can further explain or limit W, and G is the potential governor of W. The diagram also shows that the cohesive force of a word can be divided into centripetal force (input) and centrifugal force (output). Centripetal force indicates the ability of a word to be governed by other words, and centrifugal force is its ability to govern other words.[22] Once W appears in the real text, it opens up some slots that need to be filled. In other words, while it has the potential to open up specific slots, it also predicts the number and types of complements needed. At the same time, when W enters the specific text, it also shows whether it can meet the needs of other word dependents. Whether the real combination can take place depends on whether the combination requirements

---

[22] The metaphor of centrifugal force and centripetal force is used here to better explain the problem of words forming sentences.

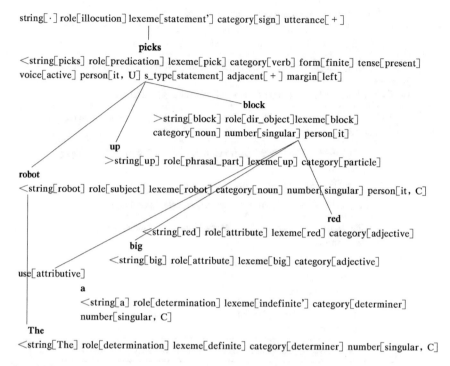

string[·] role[illocution] lexeme[statement'] category[sign] utterance[+]

picks
<string[picks] role[predication] lexeme[pick] category[verb] form[finite] tense[present]
voice[active] person[it, U] s_type[statement] adjacent[+] margin[left]

block
>string[block] role[dir_object]lexeme[block]
category[noun] number[singular] person[it]

up
>string[up] role[phrasal_part] lexeme[up] category[particle]

robot
<string[robot] role[subject] lexeme[robot] category[noun] number[singular] person[it, C]

red
<string[red] role[attribute] lexeme[red] category[adjective]

big
<string[big] role[attribute] lexeme[big] category[adjective]

use[attributive]

a
<string[a] role[determination] lexeme[indefinite'] category[determiner]
number[singular, C]

The
<string[The] role[determination] lexeme[definite] category[determiner] number[singular, C]

Fig. 5.23 Tree diagram showing the results of sentence analysis

Fig. 5.24 Schematic
diagram of valency pattern

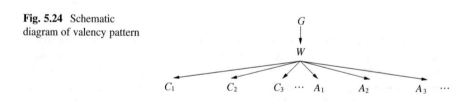

of syntax and semantics can be met so that the restriction of syntactic and semantic features will become a part of the valence.

In the word of the valency lexicon, not only should the valence of the word be described quantitatively, but qualitative research should also be carried out. Specifically, it is necessary to study the quantity, type, nature, and realization conditions of the valence. In terms of quantity, it should include not only the nominal complements necessary for traditional valence but also other components that can improve the word. In terms of types and properties, semantic relations and semantic features need to be considered. In terms of realization, syntactic, semantic, and even pragmatic models are under consideration. The word in the valency lexicon, which is constructed on this basis, has hierarchical characteristics. Based on different application fields, valence attributes such as syntax, semantics, and pragmatics can be used to restrict the realization of valence. Of course, the number of constraints used

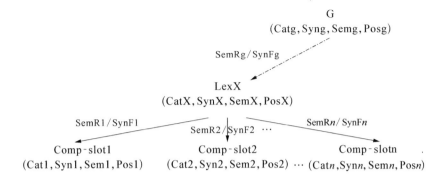

Fig. 5.25   Valence representation framework

has a direct impact on the efficiency and accuracy of analysis and understanding. The following is a valence representation framework similar to a tree structure (Fig. 5.25).

In Fig. 5.25, LexX represents the current word, Cat represents the category, Syn represents the syntactic feature, Sem represents the semantic feature, Pos represents the part of speech feature, and Comp-slot represents the slot of the complement. In this framework of valence representation, all the factors related to semantics can also be eliminated, thus forming a pure form of dependency parsing model based on valence. After such a pure syntactic model generates a dependency structure tree, it needs a semantic mechanism to select the most suitable result from the ambiguous structure. Valence belongs to the semantic-syntactic category. Semantics not only play a role in determining the valence but also play a restricting role in the realization of valence. The early combination of semantics and syntax makes the results of analysis and understanding clearer and can be processed and disambiguated in the process of understanding, which is in line with the human language understanding mechanism. The valency lexicon model can contain only simple syntactic information, semantic information, and even pragmatic and scene information. This information determines the level of constraint when combining words with words. According to the needs of different application fields and understanding accuracy, these levels of information can be used alone or in combination. Therefore, this valency model can be seen as a multilevel descriptive format of part of speech information.

Valence is the potential ability of a word to combine with other words, and it is a static description of a word. When a word enters a specific context, this potential ability is realized, and a dependency relation is formed. Obviously, the dominable dependency relation of a part of speech is not balanced. Although a certain part of speech can theoretically govern other types of words through several dependency relations, the possibility of these dependencies is not the same. For example, the possibility of a noun as a "subject" and "object" is obviously much greater than when it is used as a "predicate." This means that the concept of quantity can be introduced into the syntactic valency pattern of parts of speech, and the strength of

Fig. 5.26 Schematic
diagram of the probabilistic
valency pattern (PVP)

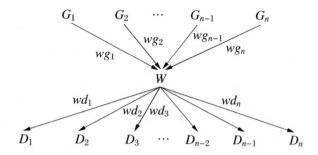

the dependency relation can be labeled by the corpus. If there are more dependency relations, the higher values we will obtain and vice versa. The cohesive force (valence) of a word can be divided into two types: centripetal force (input) and centrifugal force (output). Centripetal force means that a word is governed by other words, and centrifugal force is its ability to govern other words. This ability can be qualitatively described by the number and quantity of the dependent relations that a part of speech can govern or can be governed, or a more accurate quantitative description can be obtained through the corpus. In this way, from a practical point of view, some statistical-based language information processing systems can be better constructed. The introduction of the concept of probability to the valency pattern is also necessary for the establishment of a more universally meaningful language processing or understanding model because "a large number of language facts have proved that language is a probabilistic thing. In the process of language understanding and generation, probability plays a role in the process of access, ambiguity resolution and generation in the field of syntax and semantics, probability is of great significance to the gradient of categories, the judgment of syntactic qualification and the interpretation of sentences."[23] After introducing probability, the above valency pattern becomes a kind of "probabilistic valency pattern" (PVP). In PVP, when describing a word or part of speech, we should not only use a qualitative method to describe what kind of dependency relations it can control but also give the weight or probability distribution of these dependencies in a quantitative way, such as what is the probability of a noun as the subject and what is the probability of a noun as the object.

PVP is used to describe the schematic diagram of the valency pattern in Fig. 5.25, and the following figure can be obtained.

In Fig. 5.26, W is still a part of speech or a specific word, and $G_1, G_2, \ldots G_n$ is n kinds of dependency relations that can govern W. $D_1, D_2, \ldots D_n$ is n kinds of dependency relations that W can govern. $wg_1, wg_2, \ldots wg_n$ is the probability of the corresponding dependency relations governed by W, which is the weight. Obviously, $wg_1 + wg_2 + \cdots + wg_n = 1$; $wd_1, wd_2 \ldots wd_n$ are the probabilities of the corresponding dependency relations in the total dominance of W. $wd_1 + wd_2 + \cdots + wd_n = 1$. In the

---

[23] Rens Bod, Jennyfer Hay and Stefanie Jannedy. Probabilistic Linguistics. Cambridge/Mass: The MIT Press. 2003.

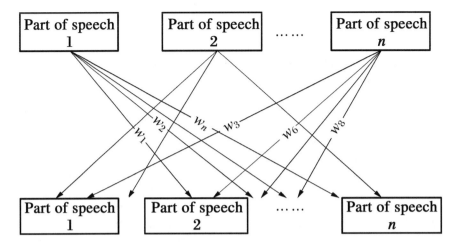

Fig. 5.27 Probability distribution of dependency relations

syntactic analysis driven by the valency pattern, there can be more than one dominating component, while the governed can only accept the government of one word above it. In other words, although the dominance and dominance of a word or a part of speech are not evenly distributed, the governed relationship is exclusive, that is, a word cannot have two or more governors at the same time.

The probability distribution of dependency relations can also be described as in Fig. 5.27.

Assuming that a grammar contains n parts of speech, theoretically, there can be $n \times (n - 1)$ possibilities for the realization of any kind of dependency D in this grammar, but in reality, there is almost no such D. For example, subject relations are mostly formed between verbs and nouns, but not between numerals and quantifiers. In this way, if the impossible combinations are removed, the remaining combinations will vary in quantity. Figure 5.27 is a reflection of this idea. The part of speech at the top of the figure represents the governor, and the bottom part of the figure represents the dependent. The connection line between the parts of speech indicates that a dependency relationship D can be formed between them. The label w_i on each line represents the probability of this connection in the total composition of the relationship $w_1 + \cdots + w_i = 1$. Of course, the parts of speech in this figure can also be specific words, and this is just for ease of expression.

The introduction of the above quantitative method into the description of valence can better reflect the role of probability statistics in language analysis and provide a better explanation for the metaphor of centrifugal force and centripetal force in valency patterns because force has not only direction but also size. The probabilistic valence pattern (PVP) also helps to explain why the frequency of each dependency is different when we calculate dependency statistics on a text. In this way, we can better combine the idea of "dependency is realized valence" with probability and statistics methods in language research. It is also possible to better describe idioms and fixed collocation language units by using PVP because in such a structure, the structural strength between the various parts is very strong, and it is difficult to separate them by general methods. It is obviously beneficial to study the collocation strength of the fixed collocation structure and the theoretical explanation of the garden path sentence based on PVP.

If the dependency relation and the parts of speech of modern Chinese are combined, a preliminary model of the modern Chinese part of speech combination ability can be formed, that is, the "PVP of Chinese parts of speech." In the structure diagram below, the strength of the dependency relation is represented by lines with different thicknesses,[24] that is, the probability in PVP.

For parts of speech with strong combination power, such as verbs, adjectives, and nouns, the input and output are expressed separately. The relation shown by the arrow pointing outward in Fig. 5.26 indicates the relationship that can be governed by the part of speech, and the relation shown by the arrow pointing inward indicates that the part of speech can satisfy this relation. The former can be regarded as the active combination of parts of speech, which is the ability to open up slots; the latter can be regarded as the passive combination of parts of speech, which is the ability to fill slots. For the sake of simplification, we only give the combination ability of major categories of words and classify some subclass attributes into the major categories. In the specific implementation, this point needs to be noted.

In the following figures and tables, various labels representing the dependency relationships are basically abbreviated based on the corresponding English words. For example, subj is the abbreviation of the subject, indicating the subject; obj is the abbreviation of the object, indicating the object; etc. Different from Stanford parser's dependency labels, these dependency labels are designed according to the characteristics of Chinese, as shown in Table 5.2.

The thickness of the arrow in Fig. 5.28 represents the probability of PVP.

The PVP of verbs is as follows (Fig. 5.28).

It can be seen that the verb governs the subject (subj) with the greatest probability, followed by the object (obj) and then the complement (comp). The verb is most likely to be governed by the sentence (S), followed by the complement (comp), that is, the verb is often used to fill the slot of the sentence and the slot of the complement.

The PVP of nouns is as follows (Fig. 5.29).

Nouns are basically governed by other components and are often used to fill in the slots of the subject (subj) and slots of the object (obj).

The PVP of prepositions is as follows (Fig. 5.30).

It can be seen that prepositions often govern the prepositional object (pobj) and are often used to fill the slots of adverbials (adva) and complements (comp).

The PVP of numerals is as follows (Fig. 5.31).

---

[24] Because of the lack of accurate statistical data, we can only use the thickness of lines to describe the framework model. The thickness of lines is basically drawn by our language intuition. After having enough statistical data, we can also give an accurate description.

Table 5.2 Dependency relation labels

Type	Label	Type	Label
Main governor	S	Sentential object	SentObj
Subject	SUBJ	Auxiliary verb	ObjA
Object	OBJ	Coordinating mark	C-
Indirect object	OTU2	Adverbial	AVDA
Subobject	SUBOBJ	Verb adjunct	VA
Subject complement	SOC	Attributer	ATR
Prepositional object	POBJ	Topic	TOP
Postpositional complement	FC	Coordinating adjunct	COOR
Complement	COMP	Epithet	ERA
Complement of usde "的"	DEC	Numeral adjunct	MA
Complement of usdi "地"	DIC	Aspect adjunct	TA
Complement of usdf "得"	DIC	Adjunct of sentence end	ESA
Object of Pba "把"	BaOBJ	Parenthesis	InA
Plural complement	PLC	Clause adjunct	CR
Ordinal complement	OC	Correlative adjunct	CsR
Complement of classifier	OC	Particle adjunct	AuxR
Construction of Pbei "被"	BeiS	Punctuation	Punct

It can be seen that numerals often govern the explanatory element of cardinal number (ma) and ordinal number complements (oc), and they are used to fill the slot of the quantifier complements (qc) with the greatest probability.

The PVP of quantifiers is as follows (Fig. 5.32).

The quantifier often governs the quantifier complement (qc), and it has the greatest probability of filling the slot of the predicative (atr).

This kind of research has deepened our understanding of valence from a quantitative perspective.

In the NLP system based on the valency pattern, the words in the lexicon exist in a free state, and these free words have the ability to combine with other words. This ability is potential but objective when words are in an isolated state. Once triggered, that is, when receiving instructions to understand or generate, the intelligent agent as a brain or computer copies a copy of the involved words that were originally in a free state from the lexicon into a temporary workspace. After the words enter the workspace area, they try to combine with other words. This is a process of revealing the potential.

The realization process of valence is slightly different due to the difference between generation and recognition.

In the process of generation, the intelligent agent selects words (usually verbs) that can represent the core content of the generation according to the plan in advance. The appearance of verbs constitutes the basic framework of the whole sentence. Then, the intelligent agent can select other words from the lexicon according to this framework. At this time, the index selected is still the combination ability of words.

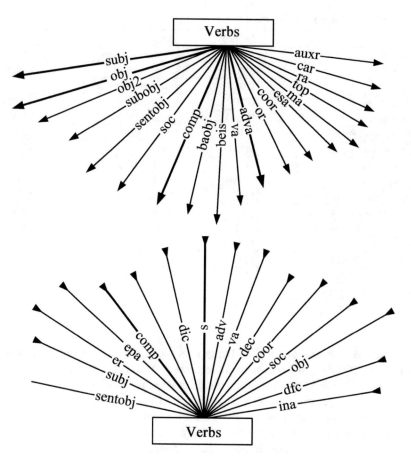

Fig. 5.28 The PVP of verbs

In the process of recognition, two methods are available. One is that after all the words to be input have entered the workspace area, they will be given all kinds of information according to the corresponding items in the lexicon and then start the activity of looking for relatives (verb guided strategy can be used). If these words can form an organic whole, the recognition is successful. Another method is that when the first input word is received, the relevant information is extracted from the lexicon immediately. In the subsequent reading process, the strategy of reading in and analyzing is adopted so that when the input ends, the result will be produced. If the valency pattern is given the probability, the system can produce the understanding results of different scores. Of course, probability can be used as a real-time disambiguation method in the analysis.

Knowledge of the lexical combination ability in the lexicon can be extracted from the text and language use manually or automatically. The valence of words is something that can be learned from the past or existing experience, so that the

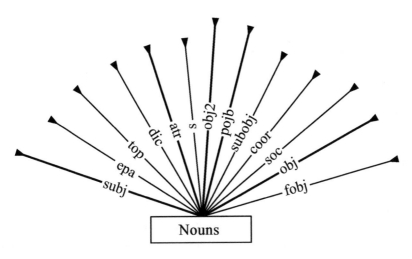

Fig. 5.29 The PVP of nouns

Fig. 5.30 The PVP of prepositions

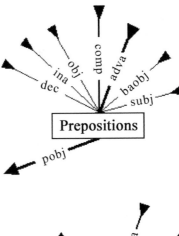

Fig. 5.31 The PVP numerals

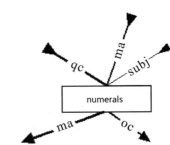

process of understanding or generating language based on valence is an experience-based method.

When generating sentences, words in the free state are combined into an organic whole according to their valence in the temporary workspace. It is a two-dimensional or three-dimensional structure. Due to the limitation of human organs, it needs to

Fig. 5.32 The PVP of
quantifiers

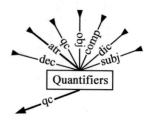

transform the two-dimensional or three-dimensional structure into a linear one-dimensional sequence, which needs to be completed by using some constraints. These constraints vary from language to language. These constraints can be lexical, syntactic, semantic, and pragmatic.

In the analysis, although the linear constraints are useful in checking the eligibility of the syntax, the result of analysis and understanding is a two-dimensional representation, and the valence of the word plays a greater role. As a result, it is possible to make the computer correctly understand some input that is not in line with syntax, which will be beneficial to improve the robustness of the system. Therefore, the valence-based dependency analysis strategy is a semantically oriented analysis and understanding. For example, "I read the book," "Book I read," "Read the book I," "Book reads me," and other combinations according to the valence (semantic combination ability) of the word can be judged or understood as "I read the book." After considering the linear order constraints, those inputs that do not conform to the syntax are eliminated. In this way, a system can be constructed to measure the degree of understanding based on the number of constraints.

It should be noted that if the valence (slot) of a word in a sentence is combined with other words in a continuous discourse, it is easy to derive the filling component through the context. These elements can be omitted in general according to the validity of communication. This situation often occurs in scenes such as daily conversations. At this time, it cannot be said that these sentences with omitted components are not qualified. Borrowing from Tesnière's drama analogy, this omission of components can be called the "serial drama" effect in the realization of valence. Therefore, in the study and determination of valence, simple sentences out of context should be the main target.

To make the system more controllable and make the theoretical model more effective and general, a valency pattern describing a certain part of speech can be introduced to simplify and refine the construction and use of the lexicon. In this case, the calling of a word is a two-stage process. First, the valency pattern of the corresponding part of the speech subcategory is instantiated, and then the valency pattern of the specific part of speech is brought into the workspace.

The above process is shown in Fig. 5.33. In Fig. 5.33, a valence relationship is composed of two elements: the component or structure to be perfected and some other components that can be perfected. The former is the head word, and the latter is the complement. The dependency relationship is a realized valence relationship, but it should be noted that if the definition and scope of valence are explained in a narrow

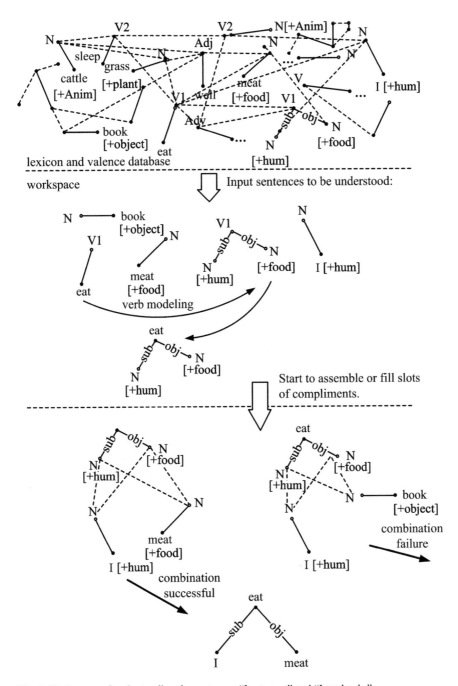

Fig. 5.33 Process of understanding the sentences "I eat meat" and "I eat books"

sense, then valence is only a subset of the dependency relationship. Whether it is defined as the ability to require complements or as the dominance ability of a part of speech subcategory, valence and other realizations only cover part of the dependency relationship. In other words, to construct a complete valence-based language understanding model, it is not enough to consider complements only.

Figure 5.33 roughly illustrates the process of understanding the sentences "I eat meat" and "I eat books." Only a very limited structure is dealt with here.

As seen from Fig. 5.33, in the lexicon and valence database, the part of speech information, semantic information, and valence information of words are stored. For example, the part of speech for "book" is N, the semantics is [+object]; the part of speech for "meat" is N, the semantics is [+food]; and the part of speech for "eat" is V1, and V1 requires its subject to be [+hum], its object is [+food]. After inputting the sentences "I eat meat" and "I eat books" to be understood, verb-guided relative seeking combinations start in the workspace area to carry out combinations and fill in the slot of complements. The "I eat meat" combination was successful, but the "I eat book" combination failed.

Obviously, using this narrow valency pattern, it is still impossible to express and analyze the sentence of "eat meat" with whom, when, and where. This point will be seen more clearly, especially in the generation of sentences. This limitation of valence stems from the semantic characteristics of valence. What it cares about is how to improve the minimum semantic requirements of the activity of "eating." Other explanatory things are powerless and uninterested.

The above is a brief introduction to the PVP formal model, and the feasibility of the model is discussed below.

To verify the feasibility of this model, a formal method and system are needed to describe the PVP model. Although there exist many theories and methods for the formalization of dependency grammar at present, many of them are mostly developed from the formal method of phrase structure. If only focusing on the acquisition of binary dependency, these methods are not only feasible but also effective (Nivre 2006).[25] Because the PVP syntactic analysis model essentially requires a declarative formal system to describe it, using these methods to describe the PVP model always feels like cutting the feet to fit the shoes. If you want to use not only the information at the syntactic level in syntactic analysis but also other attributes in the PVP valency pattern, then the formal system suitable for the PVP model should also be a progressive one based on complex features and constraints (unification). At the same time, the system should also be able to give a complete description of the PVP valency pattern, including distinguishing some new concepts, such as the dominating force and the governed force in the valency pattern.

Taking these needs into consideration, Haitao Liu and Fengguo Hu[26] chose XDG (Extended Dependency Grammar) and XDK (Extensible Dependency Grammar

---

[25] Nivre, J. Inductive Dependency Parsing. Dordrecht: Springer. 2006.

[26] Haitao Liu, Fengguo Hu. Chinese Dependency Parsing Based on valence pattern, ICCC07 proceedings, Wuhan, 2007.

Development Kit) developed by Debusmann and others at Saarland University in Germany as the formal system and implementation platform to simulate PVP's dependency analysis architecture based on valency patterns (Debusmann/Duchier/Kruijff 2004).[27]

XDG is a grammatical formal theory based on multidimensional graph description. In XDG, grammar is regarded as a graph description. In this way, analysis and generation can be regarded as a kind of graph configuration problem, which can be solved by constraint programming. The graph used by XDG is the well-known dependency structure graph in dependency grammar. Different from the concept of parallel grammatical analysis that XDG itself intends to realize, they did not adopt the multidimensional structure of XDG but introduced different constraints in the syntactic dimension because this is also a basic principle of PVP theory, namely, all other features at different levels serve for syntactic analysis. The process of using XDK for Chinese syntax analysis is as follows. First, write the processing formal rules in the form allowed by XDG, and follow the general principles (see the previous part) to write the rule, then transfer it into the XDK system, and the machine will automatically analyze the sentences The following dependency tree graphs capture the output of the automatic parsing system. Because Mozart, the programming language of XDK, cannot deal with Chinese characters, they use Chinese Pinyin to represent Chinese characters as a temporary substitute.

Haitao Liu and Fengguo Hu (2007) divided the Chinese syntax analysis experiment into two parts. The first part deals with simple sentences, and the second part deals with slightly more complicated structures. In the first part of the study, their test was divided into three stages:

- There are no restrictions in the first stage.
- The second stage has only semantic restrictions.
- The third stage has both semantic restrictions and word order restrictions.

Through this division, we can discover the influence of different constraints or factors on Chinese dependency syntactic analysis. This further improves the research of the PVP model from a rule-based perspective.

In the first stage, they conducted an analysis experiment without any restriction. The so-called without any restriction means that only the valence (dominance and dominance ability) of the word, the part of speech used in the analysis, and the dependency relationship are given. The analysis results of the sentences "我睡觉" (/wo shui jiao/; I sleep) and "睡觉我" (/shui jiao wo/; Sleep I) are as follows (Fig. 5.34).

Of course, in the first stage of the experiment, since no restrictions were imposed, not only "人"(/ren/; humans) can sleep but also "肉"(/rou/; meat) and "苹果"(/ping guo/; apple) can sleep.

Let us look at the machine's analysis of "我吃肉" (/wo chi rou/; I eat meat) (Fig. 5.35).

---

[27]Debusmann, R.; Denys Duchier and Joachim Niehren. The XDG Grammar Development Kit. Second International Mozart/Oz Conference, MOZ 2004, Charleroi. 2004.

Fig. 5.34 Analysis results of "I sleep" and "Sleep I" without any constraint

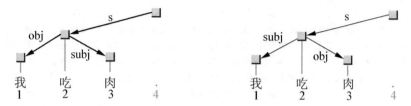

Fig. 5.35 Analysis result of "I eat meat" without semantic features

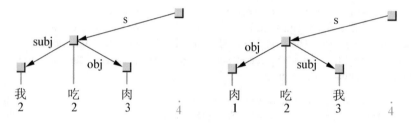

Fig. 5.36 Analysis result of "I eat meat" after adding semantic features

In the first stage of the experiment, "肉吃我" (/rou chi wo/; meat eat I) is also possible. Why is this so? Because both "I" and "meat" have a nominal valency pattern, nouns can be used as both subjects and objects. When "meat" is used as the subject, the result is "meat eat me." As far as the current Chinese knowledge of the system is concerned, "I eat meat" and "meat eats I" are the same, and there are two analysis results, namely, "I" and "meat" can be used as both object and the subject of "eat."

In the second phase of the experiment, they gave the nouns some simple semantic features, the purpose of which is to observe the semantic limitation of the ability to solve such problems. After adding semantic features, neither "apple" nor "meat" can sleep. So what changes do "I eat meat" and "meat eat me"? The analysis results they got are shown in Fig. 5.36.

After adding semantic features, no matter how the word order changes, there is only one analysis result: "I" is always the subject and "meat" is always the object. This shows that the introduction of semantic features plays a positive role in resolving ambiguity in syntactic analysis. At the same time, it can also be seen

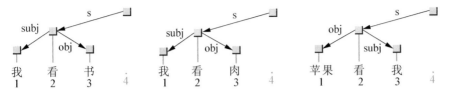

Fig. 5.37 After adding semantic features, the analysis results of "书" (/shu/; book), "肉" (/rou/; meat) and "苹果"(/ping guo/; apple) are all the objects

that no matter where the "meat" goes, it cannot escape the fate of being eaten. It is always the object. Now, not only "书" (/shu/; book) cannot eat "我" (/wo/; I), "我" (/wo/; I) cannot eat "书" (/shu/; book) either. Because "书" (/shu/; book) are used to "看" (/kan/; read/see), of course not only "书" (/shu/; book) can be "看" (/kan/; read/ seen), "肉" (/rou/; meat) and "苹果"(/ping guo/; apple) can also be "看" (/kan/; read/ seen). The analysis results are shown in Fig. 5.37.

In the second stage of the experiment, whether it is "书" (/shu/; book) and "肉" (/rou/; meat) in "书看我" (/shu kan wo/; books read I) or "肉吃我" (/rou chi wo/; meat eats I), the system considers them to be objects. However, there are still problems with the word order in the analysis results, for example, In "苹果看我" (/ping guo kan wo/; apples see me), although "苹果"(/ping guo/; apple) is analyzed as an object, it is before the verb "see", and the linear order is wrong.

In the third stage of the experiment, they further introduced word order constraints. Now, strings such as "睡觉我" (/shui jiao wo/; sleep I), "肉吃我" (/rou chi wo/; meat eat I), "我苹果吃" (/wo ping guo chi/; I apple eat) and other strings will no longer have analysis results. The only correct ones are "我吃肉" (/wo chi rou/; I eat meat) and "我看书" (/wo kan shu/; I read books) (Fig. 5.38).

When the machines reach this level of understanding, the key parts of the grammar files they use are as follows (Table 5.3).

In the second part of the experiment, to limit the syntactic analysis to the syntactic level as much as possible, they conducted a syntactic analysis experiment using only valence patterns and word order constraints for some long sentences with more complex structures. It is rather complicated, so we will not talk about it.

Through the above experiments, Haitao Liu and Fengguo Hu (2007) not only verified the feasibility of the PVP probabilistic valency pattern theory proposed by Haitao Liu and Zhiwei Feng but also gained a further understanding of the role of semantic features and word order in the analysis of Chinese syntax. At the same time, they also proved that in the multidimensional XDG, it is feasible to use only one dimension (syntactic dimension), plus the valency pattern and word order constraints of words (classes), to solve the Chinese analysis problem. The studies reviewed above are very enlightening for the application of valence grammar in NLP.

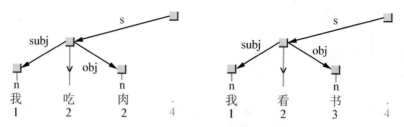

Fig. 5.38 Analysis result after adding word order constraints

Table 5.3 The key parts of the grammar files

defclass "v_id"{ dim yn {in: {s?} out: {subj!} on: {V} govern: {subj: {hum}}}}	Define the valency pattern of the verb, where *in* is the ability to the governed, *out* is the dependency relation to be governed, and *govern* introduces the semantic requirements of the word class for subj
defclass "V2" Word{ "v_id" dim lex {word: Word} dim syn {out: {obj!}} govern: {obj: {food}}}}	Define the valency pattern of the subclass of bivalent verbs. V2 is a divalent verb, which requires obj to the *food*
defentry{"V2"{Word: "chi"}}	Give part of speech attribute to the input verb *"chi"* (eat). The word class attribute of *"chi"* is V2

Bibliography

1. Vilmos, Ágel. 2000. *Valenztheorie*, 21–25. Tübingen: Narr.
2. Engel, Ulrich. 1982. *Syntax Der Deutschen Gegenwartssprache. Zweite Auflage*. Berlin: Schmidt.
3. ———. 1992. *Deutsche Grammatik*. Beijing: Beijing Language Institute Press.
4. Haitao, Liu and Zhiwei, Feng. 2007. The Probability Valency Pattern in Natural Language Processing. *Linguistic Sciences* 3: 32–41.
5. Haitao, Liu and Fengguo, Hu. 2007. Chinese Dependency Parsing Based on Valency Pattern. In *ICCC07 Proceedings*, Wuhan.
6. Haitao, Liu, R.A. Hudson, and Zhiwei, Feng. 2009. Using a Chinese Treebank to Measure the Dependency Distance. *Corpus Linguistics and Linguistic Theory* 5 (2): 161–175.
7. Helbig, G., and W. Schenkel. 1978. *Wörterbuch zur Valenz und Distribution deutscher Verben*. Leipzig: Bibliographishes Institut.
8. Helbig, G. 2002. *Linguistische Theorien der Moderne*. Berlin: Weidler Buchverlag.
9. Hudson, R.A. 2004. *An Encyclopedia of English Grammar and Word Grammar* [EB/OL]. http://www.phon.ucl.ac.uk/home/dick/enc-gen.htm.
10. Song, Gao and Zhiwei, Feng. 2011. Research on Text Clustering Based on Dependency Tree Bank. *Journal of Chinese Information Processing* 3: 59–63.
11. Tesnière, L. 1959. *Eléments de la syntaxe structural*. Paris: Klincksieck.

12. Zhiwei, Feng. 1983. Tesnière's Dependency Grammar. *Linguistics Abroad* 1: 63–65.
13. ————. 1998. Some Formal Characteristics of Dependency Grammar. In *Proceedings of 1998 International Conference on Chinese Information*, Beijing, 237–243.
14. ————. 1998. The Effect of Dependency Grammar on Machine Translation Research. *Journal of Foreign Languages* 1: 18–21.
15. ————. 1999. Deambiguity Strategy of Trans-Classed Word in E-to-J Machine Translation System. *Journal of Chinese Information Processing* 5: 14–27.
16. ————. 2014. Tesnière and Dependency Grammar. *Modern Chinese* 11:1–9.
17. ————. 2019. Functional Generative Description Theory of the Prague School. *Modern Chinese* 7: 124–127.

Chapter 6
Formal Models Based on Lexicalism

Differences between languages are mostly found in lexis. Due to the importance of lexis in linguistic research, lexicalism began to emerge, and building lexical resources has gained wide attention in NLP.

This chapter explores several lexicalism-based formal models. Specifically, lexicon-grammar and link grammar will be introduced first, followed by lexical semantics and knowledge ontology. After that, some details will be presented regarding the most important formalized lexical resource, i.e., WordNet.

6.1 Gross's Lexicon-Grammar

Based on lexical studies, Maurice Gross (1934–2001), a French linguist as shown in Fig. 6.1, published *Grammaire transformationnelle du français, syntaxe du verbe* in 1968, *Methodes en syntaxe* in 1975,[1] *Grammaire transformationnelle du français* in 1977, and *Evidence in Linguistics* in 1979 and put forward lexicon-grammar, which is a lexicalism-based formalized linguistic theory.

Born in Sedan, France, in 1934, Maurice Gross graduated from Institut supérieur d'industrielle de Paris as a major in military engineering. From 1961 to 1962, he studied linguistics at the Massachusetts Institute of Technology (MIT) under the supervision of Noam Chomsky. From 1964 to 1965, he went to University of Pennsylvania to study under Zellig Harris. After graduation, he taught at MIT. He engaged himself in NLP research after he returned to France. In 1968, he founded Laboratoire Automatique de Documentation Linguistique (abbreviated as LADL) at Université Paris Diderot-Paris 7 and acted as director of the lab. In 1975, Maurice Gross proposed lexicon-grammar and later modified the theory in 1979. Therefore, he was perceived as the founder of lexicon-grammar.

---

[1] Maurice Gross, Methodes en syntaxe, Paris, Hernamm, 1975.

© Springer Nature Singapore Pte Ltd. 2023
Z. Feng, *Formal Analysis for Natural Language Processing: A Handbook*,
https://doi.org/10.1007/978-981-16-5172-4_6

Fig. 6.1 Maurice Gross

The following is the theoretical basis and the operating principles of lexicon-grammar. The former will be presented first.

Maurice Gross studied under both Noam Chomsky and Zellig Harris, but he was influenced more by Harris' structural linguistics. Therefore, structural linguistics is the theoretical basis of lexicon-grammar.

1. Lexicon-grammar adheres to Saussure's pure-linguistic viewpoint that language is the only and the real object of linguistics, holds that language should be studied for and in terms of language itself, defines language as a special social phenomenon featuring many characteristics of natural phenomena, and argues that language should be studied from the perspective of its internal structure. In other words, lexicon-grammar perceives language as a symbol system of sound-meaning combination and strictly limits non-language factors (such as social factors, cultural factors, and psychological factors) to a manageable scope. Lexicon-grammar aims to create room unique to linguistics and discuss facts related to internal and external interpretations of language structure within the scope of experience. Its purpose is to provide application researchers with a system easy to operate. According to lexicon-grammar, the internal interpretation of language structure is a lexicon-oriented investigation of linguistics, while the external interpretation belongs to a subjective study of linguistics. Therefore, the dialectical relationship between the two should be treated in a proper way.

2. Lexicon-grammar uses the methodologies of structuralism. The characteristics shared by the methodologies of structuralism in the twentieth century include that language is a system of structure, that the inter-relationships between various elements of language structures should be explored, that synchronic research should be attached importance to, and that formal analysis and description should be stressed. Linguists' task is to describe language by paying attention to the integrity of description, the limitations of descriptive methods, and the importance of syntactic studies. Syntactic studies should include viewpoints such as classification, transformation, and function.

3. Lexicon-grammar adopts the transformational method of empiricism. It holds that language research should aim to deal with all the empirical data, the core of which is categories of syntactic pattern pairs because categories show the hierarchical

relationship between sentences, while syntactic pattern pairs imply the transformational relationship between sentences.

4. The central argument of lexicon-grammar is that lexicon and grammar, the two components of language, are equally important and necessary. Interaction between the two should be explored systematically. Syntactic features of lexical units are the primary reason for variations in co-occurrence and coexistence in sentences. The conditions of co-occurrence and co-existence of different language forms should be made clear in the interaction between lexicon and grammar.

5. In terms of the relationship between theory and practice, lexicon-grammar holds that research methods should be guided by application value. It rejects those methods where research is premised on hypotheses and application is neglected.

6. Lexicon-grammar advocates the autonomy of syntax and adheres to the belief that semantic apriorism should be discarded in syntactic descriptions to minimize semantic descriptions and achieve semantic minimalism. Only in this way can linguists manage the interaction between syntactic and semantic factors in sentences and describe syntax in a more systematic and accurate manner. Maurice Gross firmly believed that syntax could be formalized for operating value to a large extent, whereas semantics could never be formalized independently of syntax. He did not reject considering semantics but advocated semantic minimalism.

7. Lexicon-grammar upholds the seeking-truth-from-facts spirits advocated in natural science research, including innovation, empirical attitudes, and doubt. Lexicon-grammar also holds that all linguistic theories and methods should be tested by language facts. Linguists should start from the situation in which linguistics has not developed into an exact science, winnow out some research methods, design new methods, and combine induction and deduction in an organic way.

The seven points above are the theoretical bases of lexicon-grammar.

In the following are its operating principles.

These principles are detailed and clear. By adhering to empiricism, lexicon-grammar clarifies some basic facts concerning descriptions of grammar and inductively sets out the operating principles and order for classification and reclassification. The operating basis, background, intention, and methods of lexicon-grammar are listed below.

1. The operating basis is the verification principle grounded on experience and empiricism of objectivism. The verification principle grounded on experience emphasizes that any concept and theory should be based on observable facts and verified by experience. Objectivism stresses a reasonable separation of the subject and the object during the process of knowing. The subject's knowledge should faithfully reflect the characteristics of the object, excluding subjective factors such as attitudes, emotions, beliefs, and values as much as possible.

2. The operating background is Post-Harrisism. Like other structuralism linguists, Harris has invariably attached importance to formal features of language, the core

concept of which is distribution. Distribution refers to the set of all possible positions, or in other words, the environment, where a certain unit or feature may occur in a discourse. Harris makes efforts to improve the status of syntax, reorganize linguistics, and try to render it as exact as a natural science. He limits grammatical research to the sentence level. Specifically, he advocates the use of formal methods and avoids neither oral materials nor exceptions to perform intuition-based starting-with-structure linguistic research, leaving the content of sentences (semantics) in a less important position. His central argument is that syntactic facts cannot be observed effectively without the framework of kernel sentences because only within this kind of framework can the interaction be fathomed among constituents of a sentence, its internal semantic structure, and the external distribution of different language forms. Maurice Gross inherits Harris's academic tradition and believes in post-Harrisism. He holds that oral materials and counterexamples cannot be processed without intuition. No effort without considering oral materials and counterexamples is helpful for a formal description of language.

3. The operating intention of lexicon-grammar is to build four interrelated mechanisms: description, verification, classification, and corpus.

   The description mechanism includes:

   (a) A diachronic mechanism to describe a language systematically
   (b) Concentration on the empirical conditions of the formation and occurrence of sentences
   (c) A lexicon-driven as-exhaustive-as-possible description, which can completely describe all the language phenomena in a large-scale corpus composed of authentic texts
   (d) The establishment of a sentence-based grammatical description mechanism, where the lexicon can be examined in sentences to verify syntactic combinational rules
   (e) A description of the syntactic patterns of kernel sentences that can satisfy sentence-completing conditions

   The verification mechanism puts the grammatical rules proposed by linguists in a formalized system in which the lexicon and grammar interact with each other and then verifie the operability of these rules.

   The classification mechanism endeavors to establish a set of theories regarding corpus processing to collect facts more systematically, investigate the complementary relationship between concepts and retrospection, and probe into the hierarchical relationship hidden in corpora and its various forms.

   The corpus mechanism believes that corpora are the only research object of linguistics. Corpora should be characterized by reoccurrence of samples, openness, and formalized output. A vocabulary base and a grammar base should also be constructed.

4. The operating methods of lexicon-grammar consist of lexical processing, grammatical processing, matrix design, and expert intervention.

Lexical processing includes identifying kernel words, determining the senses of relevant words, and assessing the legality of syntactic performance. In addition, lexical processing emphasizes that idiomatic words should be identified, that entries should be made for those non-idiomatic kernel words, and that the entries should be grounded on syntactic formal criteria. To conduct thorough research, words should be observed one by one, and each feature should be determined separately.

For instance, *book* in the following sentences should be established as different entries:

Bob booked a seat for the show.
The police booked the thieves.
Bob booked a room for Tom.

The meanings and uses of *booked* in the above three sentences are different, so *booked* should be listed as three entries. Maurice Gross studied 6000 French verbs and made 12,000 entries for them.

In grammatical processing, lexicon-grammar advocates that syntactic research should have a clearly defined framework.

Different verbs have different obligatory complements. Even for the same verb, its different uses may require different obligatory complements. Only by describing verbs individually in the lexicon system can obligatory and optional complements be marked effectively. By complements, we mean occurring conditions or sentence-completing conditions. Similarly, only by directing and controlling syntactic analysis for each lexical entry can the interaction between lexicon and grammar be understood in its essence. This is the essential feature of the methodology of lexicon-grammar.

Another important concept of lexicon-grammar, transformation, is closely related to distribution. Syntactic transformation involves not only the set of sentences composed of the same word classes but also the features of the constituent words.

For example, the following transformational rule exists between English active and passive sentences:

$$NP_0 \ V \ NP_1 = NP_1 \ be \ V_{pp} \ by \ NP_0$$

If V is the word *eat*, then we have

$$NP_0 \ eat \ NP_1 = NP_1 \ be \ eaten \ by \ NP_0$$

For *eat*, the transformation above is correct.
If V is the word *require*, the transformation also holds.
The passive form of "This report requires a lot of attention"
is
"A lot of attention is required by this report."

However, if V is the word *deserve, got,* or *receive,* the transformation above no longer holds.

We can have the following active sentences.

"This report deserved a lot of attention."
"This report got a lot of attention."
"This report received a lot of attention."

But we cannot transform them into

*A lot of attention is deserved by this report.
*A lot of attention is got by this report.
*A lot of attention is received by this report.

It can be observed from the above examples that if we replace the abstract symbols in transformational rules with specific words, the rules sometimes may hold (for instance, *eat* and *require*) and sometimes may not (such as *deserve, got, receive*). Different lexical features can play a decisive role in determining whether a transformational rule holds. Therefore, the importance of words should be recognized, and lexicon-grammar should be built on the basis of words. This is the essence of lexicon-grammar.

Matrix design, which includes the layout of rows and columns, is the key to the formalization of lexicon-grammar. Columns are about properties of syntactic patterns, distributive properties, semantic properties, and relevant transformational attributes, which may be marked by "+" or "−". Rows stand for predefined lexical entries. Each row of a single matrix represents the syntactic paradigmatic relations of the corresponding lexical entry.

When lexicon-grammar analysis is performed, the matrix receives an input of one lexical entry, processes it, and outputs the results of the syntactic analysis, as shown in Fig. 6.2.

With an experiential model such as the matrix, linguistic researchers can immediately identify the syntactic distributive properties of a specific word and obtain the results of the syntactic analysis.

For instance, we establish the following matrix for subjects and objects of the predicate verbs A, A', and A".

In Fig. 6.3, the distributive properties of the subjects are a_1 and a_2, while those of the objects are a_3, a_4, and a_5. When different predicates are inputted, they may select

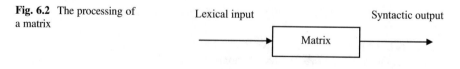

Fig. 6.2 The processing of a matrix

Lexical input   Syntactic output

Matrix

Subject		Predicate	Object		
a_1	a_2		a_3	a_4	a_5

Fig. 6.3 An instance of a matrix

Subject		Predicate	Object		
a_1	a_2		a_3	a_4	a_5
+	−	A	+	+	−
+	−	A'	−	+	−
+	+	A"	+	−	+

Fig. 6.4 Syntactic descriptions

different properties of subjects and objects. Researchers can then use the matrix to obtain their syntactic information and the results of syntactic analyses at the output end (shown in Fig. 6.4).

If A is the input predicate, the distributive properties of the output sentence are $a_1 + a_3 + a_4$. If A' serves as the input, the properties are $a_1 + a_4$. When the input becomes A", the properties turn out to be $a_1 + a_2 + a_3 + a_5$.

Maurice Gross assumes that syntactic acceptability is intuitively higher than semantic acceptability. Therefore, syntactic acceptability is more reliable. Once an error is made, it can be corrected according to objective linguistic facts. In lexicon-grammar, syntactic acceptability is determined through expert intervention.

Expert intervention stresses expert-guided processing of corpora, which are collected systematically from different sources. Lexicon-grammar requires an organic combination of expert intervention, corpus construction, and computer technology. The key point of expert intervention is to judge the acceptability of a given sentence according to understandability and reoccurrence. This operating principle can let researchers know where to start, where to finish, what steps to go through, at what stage the current study is, and how to move on. It organically combines both macro-considerations and micro-treatments.

Maurice Gross has conducted fine-grained research on French verbs. With a solid mathematical foundation, he was able to engage himself in computational linguistics research. From the perspective of computational linguistics, he has made 19 valency pattern matrices for 3000 French verbs, every sense of which is listed as a lexical entry. Each of the 19 matrices represents one or two basic patterns of "verb + complement." As the compatibility of the valency patterns is well designed, each matrix can in fact reflect multiple valency patterns. Maurice Gross used approximately 100 valency features to analyze the 3000 verbs and classify them into 2000 categories. Maurice Gross's work has laid a firm foundation for compiling an NLP-oriented dictionary of grammatical information. Until 1990, Maurice and his LADL lab had already analyzed 6000 words and designed 81 matrices to describe 31,000 lexical entries.

In 1994, Maurice Gross made a summative account of lexicon-grammar in *Constructing Lexicon-grammar*, pointing out that "(. . ., only because) we have operated in the framework of lexicon-grammar, that is, in a framework where a methodological enumeration of facts is required. Actually, lexicon-grammar representation can be viewed as a verification of the fact that the various uses of the dictionary entries of a language are satisfactorily described in terms of a given grammar, namely, that no relation between sentences which are obviously related to each other is left unaccounted for by the rules of the grammar."[2]

Generally, lexicon-grammar has the following prominent features:

1. On the basis of surface forms and with matrices as the media to convey language information, the grammatical rules of a language are described by delineating the properties of individual words. Quantitative and constant descriptions are made for matrix formats and valency, respectively.
2. Considering oral materials and counterexamples and using intuition, lexicon-grammar emphasizes syntactic acceptability and pays appropriate attention to semantic factors.
3. Lexicon-grammar endeavors to conduct an exhaustive lexicon-driven study, which attaches great importance to the unique properties of words and emphasizes increasing the lexical coverage as much as possible.
4. With kernel sentences that meet sentence-completing conditions being the basic concepts, lexicon-grammar verifies syntactic combinational rules in sentences, places in the dominant position the various formal relations between constituents of sentences at the structure level, and excludes pragmatic factors such as conversational situations and rhetorical factors such as discourse analysis.

In conclusion, lexicon-grammar adheres to "quantitative formats, constant valency, few semantic factors, and broad lexical coverage," showing the lexicalism tendency in modern linguistics.

6.2   Link Grammar

Link grammar was proposed by D. Sleator and D. Temperley (see Fig. 6.5) in 1991 in *Parsing English with a Link Grammar, Technical Report of Carnegie Mellon University, CMU-SC-91-196.*

The construction of link grammar is very similar to categorial grammar in that it underlines the importance of lexical properties and thus reflects a strong tendency of lexicalism. As categorial grammar has been detailed in Chap. 2, it is not difficult for readers who are familiar with categorial grammar to understand the principles of link grammar. Link grammar can facilitate language engineering and serve as an attractive new formal model of language information processing.

Link grammar is composed of a group of words, each of which has a linking requirement. A linking requirement is contained in the corresponding entry of a link grammar dictionary. To analyze the syntactic structure of a sentence, linking computation should be performed on the linking features of words according to the linking requirements. Therefore, link grammar can be regarded as a grammar based on the linking features of words.

---

[2]Maurice Gross, Constructing Lexicon-Grammar, 1995.

Fig. 6.5 D. Sleator and
D. Temperley

The linking between words should be described with a link, which consists of a link head and a link base. Analogously, a link is similar to a circuit, which means that the link head is the plug and the link base functions as the socket. In link grammar, if two words can be legally linked, they should carry the same type of link, with one carrying the link head and the other carrying the link base, so that the link head can be properly plugged into the link base.

For example, in "the delegation yesterday visited the museum," the words *delegation, yesterday, visited,* and *museum* can be described through connectors as follows.

Delegation: Its connector is ((), (s)). To the left of the connector is the link base, (), which is now empty. Its right side is the link head, which is an s(subject) link, implying that the word needs to be linked to the right to a word with an s link base.

Yesterday: Its connector is ((), (t)). To the left is the link base, (), which is now empty. Its right side is the link head, a t(temporal) link, implying that the word needs to be linked to the right to a word with a t link base.

Visited: Its connector is ((t, s), (o)). To the left of the connector is a (t, s) link base. From the back to the front are t and s, suggesting that the word needs to be linked to the left to a word with a t link head and then again to the left to a word with an s link head. To the right of the connector is the link head, which is an o(object) link, indicating that the word needs to be linked to the right to a word with an o link base.

Museum: Its connector is ((o), ()). To the left of the connector is an o link base, implying that the word needs to be linked to the left to a word with an o link head. Its right side is an empty link base ().

If the link head of a connector can be plugged into a link base of the same type, the linking requirement of the connector is satisfied. If the linking requirements of the connectors of all the words in a sentence are satisfied, a set of links that link these words is called a linkage of the sentence. The linkage of the sentence *the delegation yesterday visited the museum* is presented in Fig. 6.6.

Fig. 6.6 An example of a
linkage

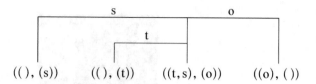

$$(( ), (s))   (( ), (t))   ((t, s), (o))   ((o), ( ))$$

The connector of *the delegation* requires a rightward link to a word with an s link base. The connector of *yesterday* requires a rightward link to a word with a t link base, while the connector of *visited* first requires a leftward link to a word with a t link head. The linking requirement of *yesterday* is thus satisfied. The second linking requirement of the connector of *visited* is a leftward link to a word with an s link head, which exactly corresponds to the connector of *the delegation*. Therefore, *visited* can be linked to *yesterday* first and then to *the delegation*. Additionally, the connector of *visited* also requires a rightward link to a word with an o link base, while the connector of *the museum* can fully satisfy the condition. Hence, *visited* is linked to *the museum*. In this manner, all the links of the sentence have been created. It can be seen from Fig. 6.6 that the linkage includes three links, represented by s, t, and o, with each link head being plugged into its mating link base and all the linking requirements being satisfied.

Another example "The cat chased a snake" can be described with connectors as follows.

The: Its connector is $((), (d))$, which has an empty link base $()$ to its left and a link head (d) to its right, indicating that the word requires a rightward link to a word with a d link base.

Cat: Its connector is $(((d), (s)) \vee ((d, o), (s)))$. In this connector, $((d), (s))$ and $((d, o), (s))$ are called disjuncts, the relationship between which is disjunctive (represented by $\vee$). The left part of $((d), (s))$ is the link base (d), which means that the word requires a leftward link to a word with a d link head, while the right part of the disjunct is the link head (s), which looks for a rightward link to a word with an s link base. Regarding the disjunct $((d, o), (s))$, its left is a (d, o) link base, implying that the word first requires a leftward link to a word with a d link head and then looks for another leftward link to a word with an o link head. Its right is an s link head, requiring a rightward link to a word with an s link base.

Chased: Its connector is $((s), (o))$. Its left part is an s link base, requiring a leftward link to a word with an s link head, while its right part is an o link head, looking for a rightward link to a word with an o link base.

A: Its connector is $((), (d))$. Its left part is an empty link base $()$, while its right part is a d link head, which means that the word requires a rightward link to a word with a d link base.

Snake: Its connector is composed of two disjuncts $((d), (s) \vee (d, o), ())$. For the disjunct $((d), (s))$, its left is a d link base, which means that the word looks for a leftward link to a word with a d link head, while its right is an s link head, requiring a rightward link to a word with an s link base. For the other disjunct, $((d, o), ())$, its left part is the (d, o) link base, which looks for a leftward link first to a

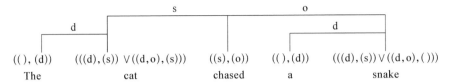

Fig. 6.7 Another example of a linkage

word with a d link head and then a leftward link again to a word with an o link head. Its right part is an empty link head ().

In light of the properties of these connectors, we can link them and obtain the linkage of the sentence *The cat chased a snake* (Fig. 6.7).

During the process of constructing a sentence, for connectors that include two or more disjuncts, only one of them can satisfy the linking requirements because the relationship between any two disjuncts is disjunctive. Take the connector of *cat*, for instance. Only the disjunct ((d), (s)) can satisfy the linking requirement so that it can be linked leftward to *the* first and then rightward to *chased*. Another example is the connector of *snake*. Only the disjunct ((d, o), ()) can satisfy the linking requirement. It is connected to *a* on its left and then linked leftward further to *chased*.

In a strict sense, link grammar consists of a group of words and their connectors, which in turn are composed of a series of disjuncts (the logical OR operation). Formally, link grammar can be represented as

$$w = (d_1 \lor d_2 \lor \ldots \lor d_k)$$

$$d = ((l_1, l_2, \ldots, l_m), \ (r_n, r_{n-1}, \ldots, r_1))$$

$$\text{here } d \in \{d_1, d_2, \ldots, d_k\}$$

$(l_1, l_2, \ldots, l_m)$ is called the left list, while $(r_n, r_{n-1}, \ldots, r_1)$ is called the right list. The word w that carries the disjunct d can be linked to the words on both sides. Specifically, words connected to the left of w must match $(l_1, l_2, \ldots, l_m)$, allowing neither repetition nor omission. The same principle applies to words that are connected to the right of w. For the selected disjunct $d = ((l_1, l_2, \ldots, l_m), (r_n, r_{n-1}, \ldots, r_1))$, the distance between w and the words that are connected to l_i monotonically increases, while the distance between w and the words that are linked to r_j monotonically decreases.

In other words, if l_i and r_j of a given word w are arranged as follows:

$$l_m, \ldots, l_2, l_1, w, r_n, r_{n-1}, \ldots, r_1$$

then the disjuncts of w can be described as

$$(l_1, l_2, \ldots, l_m), \ (r_n, r_{n-1}, \ldots, r_1)$$

The linkage of a sentence should satisfy the following four conditions:

1. Planarity: The links drawn above the words in the sentence do not cross.
2. Connectivity: The links can connect all the words of the sentence.
3. Ordering: When the left-side connectors of a disjunct are traversed from left to right, their leftward words to be connected must proceed from near to far. Similarly, for the right-side connectors of the disjunct, they must also be arranged from left to right as their rightward words to be connected proceed from near to far.
4. Exclusion: Only one link is used to connect a pair of words, or in other words, no two or more links can connect the same pair of words.

Compared with context-free grammars, word-based grammatical systems, such as link grammar, can help to obtain statistics regarding the relationship between words more easily. If the occurrence frequencies of the pairs of words that are linked together can be acquired from a corpus composed of large-scale authentic texts, the statistics can facilitate researchers' decision-making process when they encounter some linking ambiguities in syntactic analysis so that an optimal analysis with the highest probability can be selected.

6.3 Lexical Semantics

A lexicon has a highly systematic structure, which determines what words can mean and how they can be used. The structure consists of relations between words and their meanings, as well as the internal structure of individual words. This kind of lexical research on the systematic and meaning-related structure is called lexical semantics.

From the perspective of lexical semantics, a lexicon is not a finite list of words but a highly systematic structure.

Before moving on, some new terms will be introduced because these terms that have been used so far in this book are too vague. For example, the term *word* has been used in so many different ways that it is difficult to clarify its meaning. Therefore, *word* is replaced with *lexeme*, which is a single entry in a lexicon. A lexeme is a combination of an orthographic form, a phonological form, and a form of symbolic meaning representation. From the perspective of lexical semantics the lexicon is thus not only a finite list of lexemes but also a mechanism to generate infinite meanings. The meaning component of a lexeme is called a sense.

Between a lexeme and its sense exist very complicated relations, which can be described with homonymy, synonymy, polysemy, and hyponymy.

Homonymy

A relation between lexemes that have the same form but unrelated meanings is called homonymy. Lexemes between which such a relation holds are called homonyms.

For example, *bank* has two meanings as follows:

1. A financial institution in *A bank can hold the investments in an account in the client's name*. It is denoted as bank$_1$.
2. A sloping mound in *the agriculture development on the east bank, the river will shrink even more*. It is denoted as bank$_2$.

bank$_1$ and bank$_2$ are unrelated in meaning. In terms of their etymologies, bank$_1$ comes from Italian, while bank$_2$ derives from Scandinavian languages.

Homonyms are of two types.

Homophones: Lexemes with the same pronunciation but different spellings. Examples are wood, would; be, bee; and weather, whether.

Homographs: Lexemes with the same orthographic form but different pronunciations. An instance is bass [bæs]—bass [beis]. The former is a kind of eatable fish with stings, while the latter refers to a low tone.

In NLP, homonymy should be attached importance to.

- In spelling correction, homophones can lead to incorrect spelling. For example, *weather* can be mistakenly spelled as *whether*.
- In speech recognition, homophones can increase the difficulty of recognition. For instance, *to*, *two*, and *too* have similar pronunciations, which are hard to differentiate.
- In a text-to-speech system, homographs, such as bass [bæs] and bass [beis], may cause an incorrect transformation because of their different pronunciations.

Polysemy

Polysemy refers to the phenomenon that a single lexeme has multiple related meanings. Lexemes with multiple meanings are called polysemes. The meanings of polysemes are interrelated, while the senses of homonyms are irrelevant to each other.

For example, *head* is polysemic in English. It has the following senses:

1. Part of the body containing the brain, eyes, ears, nose, and mouth
2. The front part of an object, as in *the head of the bed*
3. Brain, as in *Can't you get these facts into your head?*

Sense 2 derives from sense 1, while sense 3 is a narrowing of sense 1. The senses are obviously inter-related. Usually, two methods can be used to judge whether the senses of a lexeme are related.

- Etymology criteria: Two lexemes are polysemic when the etymologies of their senses are related. They are homographs if no connection is found. As the etymologies of bank$_1$ and bank$_2$ are different, their senses are irrelevant to each other and should be regarded as homographs.

- Zeugma criteria: Combine two senses that need to be judged with a conjunction and put them into a sentence. If the sentences make sense, then they are polysemes. Otherwise, they are homographs.

For example, in sentence *Which of those flights serve breakfast?*, the sense of *serve* is to offer food to someone, whereas in sentence *Does ASIANA serve Philadelphia?*, its sense is to work for. With the Zeugma criteria, when the two senses are combined with the conjunction *and* the resulting sentence is **Does ASIANA serve breakfast and Philadelphia?*, this sentence seems a little weird and thus illegal. Therefore, *serve* cannot be used before *breakfast* and *Philadelphia* at the same time. Although the two senses are not quite related to each other, it cannot be decided yet whether they are polysemes or homographs.

Compared with etymology criteria, Zeugma criteria are only a reference instead of a reliable means to identify polysemes or homographs. Nevertheless, this method can help to measure the semantic distance between the senses of polysemes.

Look at the following sentences:

1. *They play soccer.* Here, *play* means to do sport that helps a person pass time pleasantly.
2. *They play basketball.* In this sentence, *play* carries the same sense as *play* in sentence 1.
3. *They play the piano.* The sense of *play* in this sentence is to perform a musical instrument.
4. *They play doctors and nurses.* The sense of *play* here is that children amuse themselves by pretending to play some role in the games.

With Zeugma criteria, we can make up the following sentences to estimate the semantic distance between different senses.

They play soccer and basketball. This sentence makes sense, so the senses of *play* in sentences 1 and 2 are quite close.
*They play soccer and the piano. This sentence is somewhat weird, so the semantic distance between *play* in sentences 1 and 3 is longer.
** They play soccer and doctors. This sentence is very strange. It shows that the semantic distance between *play* in sentences 1 and 4 is the longest.

For a sentence created by using Zeugma criteria, the weirder it appears, the less acceptable it is. Therefore, Zeugma criteria are an effective means to measure the semantic distance between lexemes.

In linguistics, it is very important to distinguish between homographs and polysemes. However, in NLP, as homographs and polysemes are about the phenomenon that one lexeme carries more than one sense, both can lead to semantic ambiguity and be treated as a word sense disambiguation (WSD) task. It is hence not necessary to differentiate the two.

Synonymy
In traditional linguistics, if two lexemes have the same sense, then synonymy is established between the two. Obviously, this kind of definition is too vague and useless for identifying synonyms in NLP.

In NLP research, synonymy can be defined according to substitutability. In one sentence, if two lexemes can substitute each other without changing the meaning or the acceptability of the sentence, the two lexemes can then be perceived as synonyms. Compared with the preceding definition, this definition is more helpful.

For example, as *big* and *large* in *How big is that plane?* and *Would I be flying on a large or small plane?* are substitutable without changing the meaning or the acceptability of the two sentences, synonymy holds between *big* and *large*.

Nevertheless, if substitutability is regarded as a must in all environments, there will be few true synonyms in English. As a result, the requirement for substitutability cannot be too high. It is more realistic if a weaker notion of synonymy is used, which allows two lexemes to substitute each other in some environment.

Substitutability is related to the following four factors.

- Polysemy

    For instance, the sentence *Miss Kim became a kind of big sister to Mrs. Park's son* is acceptable, while the sentence **Miss Kim became a kind of large sister to Mrs. Park's son* is weird. The reason is that *big* in the first sentence carries the sense of being older as one of its multiple senses, while *large* does not. As a result, *big* and *large* cannot substitute each other in this environment.

- Shades of Meaning

    For example, the sentence *What is the cheapest first class fare?* is acceptable, whereas the sentence *What is the cheapest first class price?* seems odd to some extent. The source of the oddity is that *fare* is better suited to the costs of services, while *price* is usually more appropriate for the cost of tickets.

- Collocational Constraints

    An example is that the sentence *They make a big mistake* is acceptable, while the sentence *They make a large mistake* is a little weird. The reason is that when describing a serious mistake, *big* is usually preferred instead of *large*. In other words, *mistake* tends to collocate with *big* rather than *large*.

- Register

    Register refers to the influence of social factors such as politeness and social status on the use of words. Differences in register can affect the selection of synonyms.

In NLP research, shades of meaning, collocational constraints, and register of synonyms can have obvious effects on the quality of machine translation. These factors should be considered so that appropriate synonyms can be selected.

Hyponymy

If one lexeme is a subclass of another lexeme, then hyponymy holds between them. An example is the relationship between *car* and *vehicle*. Hyponymy is asymmetrical. The more specific lexeme is called a hyponym of the more general lexeme, while the more general lexeme is a hypernym of the more specific lexeme. Therefore, *car* is a hyponym of *vehicle* and conversely *vehicle* is a hypernym of *car*.

The notion of hyponymy can be explored using restricted substitution.

Consider the following schema:

This is a X => That is a Y

If X is a hyponym of Y, then in any situation where the left sentence is true, the right sentence must also be true, as in the following:

This is a car => That is a vehicle.

The purpose of generating a new sentence is not to replace the original sentence but to serve as a diagnostic test for hyponymy. Therefore, this is merely a restricted substitution.

For terms such as ontology, taxonomy, and object hierarchy, hyponymy is very useful. An ontology usually refers to a normalized description of the conceptual system derived from the analysis of a domain or microworld. Taxonomy is a special arrangement of the elements of an ontology into a tree-like classification structure. In computer science, the notion of an object hierarchy is based on such a concept: objects from an ontology, when arranged in a taxonomy, can receive or inherit the features of their ancestors in the taxonomy. Of course, the notion makes sense only when the elements of a taxonomy are complex structured objects with inheritable features. Therefore, hyponymy relations themselves do not constitute an ontology, category structure, taxonomy, or object hierarchy. However, hyponymy is an approximate representation of these structures. It will be useful for the following discussions of ontology and WordNet.

6.4   Ontology

If we analyze objects in a domain, determine the relations among them, and obtain a set that can describe in a clear, formal, and shareable manner the system of concepts represented by objects in the domain, then the set is in fact the norm of a conceptual system, which can be perceived as the ontology of the domain.

As human beings began to study ontology more than 2000 years ago, the term has acquired various definitions. Some are made from speculative philosophy, while some are given from the perspective of knowledge classification. Recently, some other pragmatic definitions have been proposed for computer reasoning purposes.

Oxford English Dictionary defines ontology as the science or study of being. Obviously, this definition is too broad because it endeavors to study and establish sciences for everything that exists. Nevertheless, it is a classical philosophical definition of ontology.

What are things? What is essence? When things change, does their essence remain? Does any concept exist outside our minds? How should entities in the world be classified? These are the questions that ontology attempts to answer. As a result, ontology is about the science or study of being.

As early as the ancient Greek period, philosophers sought to uncover the essence of things when they changed. For example, when a plant seed grew into a tree, it was no longer a seed but a tree. Then, the question arose whether the essence of the tree included the essence of the seed. Parmenides argued that the essence of things was independent of our senses. It appeared that the seed had become a tree, but its essence remained unchanged. Accordingly, the seed in its essence did not grow into a tree, but our senses made us feel that it was a seed at first and then a tree. Aristotle (Fig. 6.8) believed instead that the seed was nothing but a tree that had not yet fully grown up. During the process, the tree did not change its essence but its form, from a not-fully-grown-up tree (a potential tree) to a completely-grown-up tree (a tangible tree). On that account, the seed and the tree had the same essence. This example illustrates that the essence of things is what ontology aims to reveal. Additionally, Aristotle differentiated various modes of being and established a system of categories, including substance, quality, quantity, relation, action, passion, place, time, active, and passive. This system of categories is the earliest conceptual system.

In medieval times, scholars fell into two schools, i.e., realism and nominalism, when discussing the relations between things and their names. Realism asserted that the two were the same, while nominalism argued that names were only words that were used to refer to things. In the late period of medieval times, most scholars tended to hold that names were merely symbols of things. For instance, the name *book* was a symbol to refer to any entity that was a book. This belief was the starting point of modern physics, in which different symbols were used to represent different features of the physical world (e.g., V for velocity, L for length, E for energy, and so on). These features were concepts or categories in physics.

In 1613, the German philosopher R. Goclenius, in *The Dictionary of Philosophy* that he compiled in Latin, coined the term *ontologia* by combining *onta* (meaning *beings*), which is the plural form of the Greek word *on* (meaning *being*), and *logos* (meaning *a study of*). As ontologia is the equivalent of the English word *ontology*, the dictionary is seen as the earliest Western literature that mentioned ontology. In 1636, the German philosopher A. Calovius, in *Metaphysics of God*, perceived

Fig. 6.8 Aristotle

ontologia as the synonym of metaphysica (the equivalent of metaphysics in English), thereby connecting ontologia closely with Aristotle's metaphysics. Additionally, the French philosopher R. Descartes clearly named the first philosophy that studied ontology the ontologia of metaphysics. Hence, ontologia became a part of metaphysics. From the perspective of discipline classification, the German philosopher G. von Leibniz and his inheritor C. Wolff regarded ontologia as a branch of metaphysics so that ontologia became a relatively independent philosophical discipline. In Chinese works of philosophy, the term *ontologia* is usually translated into 本体论(/ben ti lun/; ontology; literally the ontology theory). However, in Chinese NLP practice, 知识本体(/zhi shi ben ti/; ontology; literally knowledge ontology) is probably a more suitable term. Therefore, the term ontology will be adopted in the following discussion.

The German philosopher Emmanuel Kant (Fig. 6.9) asserted that the essence of things was not only determined by themselves but also influenced by how human beings perceived or understood the things.

Kant raised a question about what kind of structure our minds might rely on to capture the outside world. To answer this question, Kant put forward categorical classification and established his own framework of categories, which included quantity, quality, relation, and modality. Each of the four categories consisted of three subcategories. Quantity fell into unity, plurality, and totality; quality into reality, negation, and limitation; relation into inherence, causation, and community; and modality into possibility, existence, and necessity. Kant believed that our minds could classify things in accordance with the framework of categories to perceive the outside world. For example, the author of the book Zhiwei Feng belongs to subcategories such as unity, reality, and existence, so he can be perceived as a single, real, and existing man. In addition, database designers can employ Kant's approach to establish categories for things and manage data according to the categories. For instance, designers can build categories such as name, gender, occupation, residence

Fig. 6.9 Emmanuel Kant

of one's paternal grandfather, and so on for an employee database, which can then use these categories to provide personnel management service. This instance shows that Kant's research on the framework of categories lays a solid foundation for ontology research. However, noteworthily, his framework of categories is different from Aristotle's system of categories. In *Critique of Pure Reason*, Kant clearly expressed his disagreement with Aristotle's ten categories.

In 1991, the American computer expert R. Niches and his colleagues proposed a new idea to establish an intelligent system when they were engaged in a knowledge sharing project supported by DARPA (Defense Advanced Research Projects Agency). They believed that an intelligent system was composed of two parts: ontology and problem-solving methods (PSMs). Ontology was concerned with static knowledge, involving shared knowledge and knowledge structure in a specific domain, while PSMs dealt with dynamic knowledge, i.e., information about how to reason in one domain. An intelligent system could be constructed when PSMs used static knowledge in ontology to reason dynamically. Such an intelligent system was a de facto knowledge base, the core of which was the ontology. For this reason, scholars in computer science have shown great concern for ontology.

In 1990, the Chinese scholar Zhiwei Feng proposed the bi-state theory, which held that static and dynamic labels should be combined in machine translation systems. Static labels represented context-free features of words such as word class features and inherent semantic features, which could be stored in a machine-readable dictionary, whereas dynamic labels included syntactic-functional labels, semantic relation labels, and logical relation labels that were solved by computers through utilizing static labels and the context of words. Static information should be formulated according to the norms of word classes and semantic systems, whereas dynamic labels should be created in accordance with generative rules, the basic format of which was a condition-action pair. Therefore, machine-translation-oriented linguistic research should focus on setting out the conditions of the rules. Here, the norms of word classes are in fact the norms of grammatical information, while the norms of semantic systems are the norms of conceptual systems, i.e., ontology.

Briefly, Feng's bi-state theory could be described as:

A machine-readable dictionary based on grammatical information and static labels for ontology + dynamic label solving based on generative rules = a machine translation system

For comparison, Niches' conception could be expressed as:

Static ontology + dynamic PSMs = a knowledge base

Obviously, Feng's bi-state theory about the combination of static and dynamic labels is very similar to Niches' idea of combining static ontology and dynamic PSMs.

In the late twentieth and early twenty-first centuries, ontology research has become an important field in computer science. Its primary task is to study things in the world (such as physical objects and events) and the formal attributes and classification of the categories representing the things (such as concepts and features). Obviously, ontology research in computer science is based on the above classical research on ontology, yet with great development. Therefore, it is necessary to redefine ontology in the field of computer science. Some of the definitions are given below.

In artificial intelligence studies, Gruber in 1993 defined ontology as "an explicit specification of conceptualization." As the definition is relatively specific and easy to operate with, it is widely used in ontology research.

In 1997, Borst made some small modifications to Gruber's definition and defined ontology as "a formal specification of a shared conceptualization."

On the basis of the above two definitions, Studer in 1998 defined ontology more clearly as "a formal explicit specification of a shared conceptualization."

In this definition, the so-called conceptualization refers to an abstract model of concepts related to describing some phenomena in the objective world; "explicit" means that types of the concepts in use and constraints on how to use the concepts are clearly defined; "formal" requires that the ontology in question should be machine readable; the meaning of "shared" is that the knowledge described in the ontology is owned not by any individual exclusively but by all the members of a community.

Specifically, if a knowledge field is abstracted into a system of concepts, which in turn is represented as a shared word list, where word senses and relations among the words can be explicitly described and agreed upon by experts in the field, then the word list is an ontology in that field. As a tool to extract, understand, and process domain knowledge, ontology can be used in any specific discipline or domain. After a strict formalization and with the help of powerful computers, ontology can organize all the knowledge of human beings into an ordered knowledge network.

Human beings may have different perceptions of the term ontology, and hence, different types of ontologies are engendered.

A common ontology usually starts from epistemology. The roots of concepts are usually very abstract, such as time, space, event, state, object, and so on.

A domain ontology is an abstraction of domain knowledge, whose concepts are more specific and convenient for formalization and sharing. For instance, a domain-specific ontology of botany and a domain-specific ontology of archaeology recently developed by Chinese scholars belong to domain ontologies.

A language ontology often takes the form of a word list, where conceptual relations among words or terms are described. An instance is WordNet. If the conceptual nodes of a language ontology are all technical terms, the ontology is called a terminology ontology. Terms are the mark left by scientific and technological development in natural languages. Where there's science and technology, there're terms. Therefore, a terminology ontology is very important for processing domain knowledge.

A formal ontology has a strict classification system of concepts and terms. By following some principles and criteria, it endeavors to clearly define explicit and implicit relations between concepts and clarify the constraints on and the logical relations between concepts. After some abstraction and extraction, a domain ontology or a terminology ontology can develop into a formal ontology.

Ontologies can help to analyze and formalize domain knowledge systematically so that it can be processed by computers. In addition, ontologies can also help to realize interpersonal and human-computer knowledge sharing. For semantic analyses in NLP, ontologies can provide all kinds of information about words, reveal various semantic relations among words, and serve as the source of knowledge.

Currently, dozens of ontology development tools are available with various functions. They differ in their ability to support and express ontologies. Differences can also be found in their scalability, flexibility, and usability. Some of the well-known tools include Protégé-2000, OntoEdit, OilEd, and Ontolingua. As a widely used ontology tool, Protégé-2000 is a piece of free and open-source Java-coded software that can support many ontology formats with the help of different plug-ins.

Zhiwei Feng designed the ontology system ONTOL-MT when conducting Japanese-Chinese machine translation research. The initial concepts of the ontology included entity, time, space, quantity, action-state, and attribute. Under the six initial concepts were subordinate concepts placed at different levels.

The basic structure of ONTOL-MT is presented as follows (Fig. 6.10).

The primary concepts in ONTOL-MT can be defined as follows.

Entity: an ontology that can be extended in space (including thinking space) and time

Thing: an ontology that can be extended mainly in space (including thinking space)
Concrete: things with shape, color, and mass
Abstract: things without shape, color, and mass
Affair: an ontology that can be extended mainly in time, referring to all the activities in human beings' daily life, all the social phenomena (including political, military, legal, economic, cultural, or educational phenomena) and the natural phenomena related to human beings

Time: a continuous system that consists of past, present, and future events, serves as an objective form of being, and indicates the continuity of movements and changes of matter

Time point: a point of time
Period: a span of time with both a starting point and an ending point
Time attribute: attributes of time (such as year, month, day, hour, minute, second, millisecond, and so on)

Space: another objective form of being, which can be extended in different dimensions

Place: an objective form of being described by length, width, and height, or in other words, the location where activities take place
Distance: separation in terms of space or time
Way: the route from one place to another
Direction: including east, south, west, north, up, down, and so on

Quantity: the amount of something and its measurement

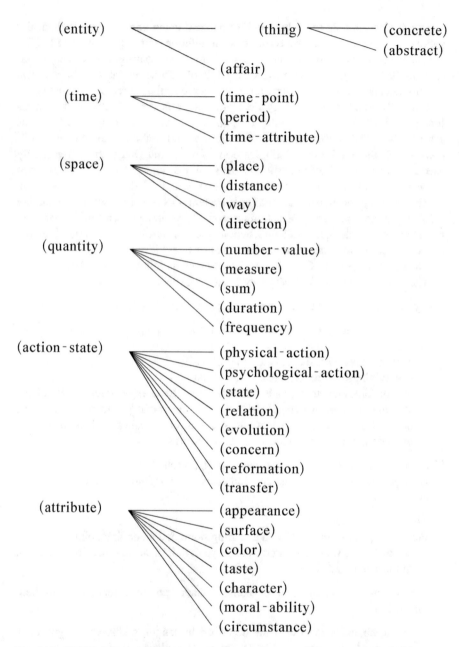

Fig. 6.10 ONTOL-MT

Number-value: an amount that is expressed by number
Measure: temperature, length, weight, usage amount, and so on
Sum: the amount of money
Duration: the amount of time
Frequency: the frequency of events

Action-state: the activities or conditions of human beings or things

Physical action: the physical activities performed by human beings or things
Psychological action: psychological activities performed by human beings or animals
State: the condition shown by human beings or things
Relation: the state of the interaction among things
Evolution: the action that things change from being simple to being complicated or from being primitive to being advanced
Concern: the state that one thing concerns or involves another
Reformation: the action that makes things change or differ
Transfer: the action that moves things from one place to another

Attribute: the qualities and relations that things are characterized by

Appearance: the outward physical attributes of human beings or things
Surface: the attributes of phenomena that can be observed from appearance
Color: the visual impression generated by production, reflection, or transmission of light waves
Taste: the qualities that tongues can recognize
Character: the qualities that differentiate one thing from another
Moral ability: the qualities of human beings' morality and ability
Circumstance: the qualities of the external environment

Above are the primary high-level concepts in ONTOL-MT. Due to space constraints, many other subordinate concepts cannot be listed here. Obviously, the initial concepts in ONTOL-MT are deeply influenced by Aristotle's system of categories and thus seem very close to the categories in his system. The ontology also reflects the world view that everything moves and exists in time and space with some attributes and quantity. In other words, although ONTOL-MT was designed for developing machine translation technologies, it inherited Aristotle's system of categories, reflected our world view, and strongly exhibited humanity.

As the concepts in the ontology of ONTOL-MT are in fact the inherent semantic features of words, which are independent of context, these concepts can be used to represent the inherent semantic features of words in machine-readable dictionaries that are compiled for machine translation. For example, in Japanese-Chinese machine translation systems, the inherent semantic features of words can help distinguish Japanese homonyms.

The word きしゃ is a homonym in Japanese. From the perspective of machine translation, it is also a polyseme, which can mean a reporter, a train, or to return to

one's company. In a Japanese sentence きしゃ は きしゃ で きしゃ した, each き
しゃ has a distinct meaning. For convenience of description, the first きしゃ is
marked as きしゃ$_1$, the second as きしゃ$_2$, and the third as きしゃ$_3$. は is the
subject particle; で is the contextual particle; and した is an auxiliary verb that
indicates the past tense after a verb. Therefore, the above sentence can be rewritten as
follows:

きしゃ$_1$ は きしゃ$_2$ で きしゃ$_3$ した

Aside from the rewriting step, the following information can be stored in a
machine-readable dictionary.

If the semantic feature of きしゃ is [HUMAN], then it is translated into 记者 (/ji
zhe/; reporter) in Chinese.
If the semantic feature of きしゃ is [VEHICLE], then it is translated into 火车(/huo
che/; train) in Chinese.
If the semantic feature of きしゃ is [MOVEMENT], then it is translated into 回公司
(/hui gong si/; to return to one's company) in Chinese, and its semantic framework is [HUMAN] は [VEHICLE] で [MOVEMENT].

Semantic features such as [HUMAN], [VEHICLE], and [MOVEMENT] are all
concepts in the ontology of ONTOL-MT.

In the sample sentence, as した comes after きしゃ$_3$, きしゃ$_3$ must be a
predicate verb, whose semantic category is [MOVEMENT]. Accordingly, its Chinese translation should be 回公司 (/hui gong si/; to return to one's company).

By comparing the sample sentence きしゃ$_1$ は きしゃ$_2$ で きしゃ$_3$ した with
the semantic framework of きしゃ$_3$ [HUMAN] は [VEHICLE] で [MOVEMENT],
the following information can be obtained.

Situated before は, the semantic category of きしゃ$_1$ is [HUMAN]. Therefore, its
Chinese translation should be 记者 (/ji zhe/; reporter), and きしゃ$_1$ should be the
subject of the predicate verb きしゃ$_3$.

Standing before で, the semantic category of きしゃ$_2$ is [VEHICLE]. Therefore,
its Chinese translation should be 火车 (/huo che/; train), and きしゃ$_2$ should be the
manner adverbial of the predicate verb きしゃ$_3$.

Through the above analysis, the correct Chinese translation of each きしゃ can
be acquired. After transformational and generative operations, the Chinese translation of the sample sentence can be 记者乘火车回公司 (/Ji zhe cheng huo che hui
gong si/; the reporter returned to the company by train).

The example shows that the semantic features in the ontology of ONTOL-MT can
be very helpful for differentiating homonyms and identifying ambiguities. Such
semantic features can also be applied to speech recognition and speech translation.
For these reasons, ontology research and design is regarded as one of the foundations
of machine translation and should be paid enough attention to.

Based on ONTOL-MT, Zhiwei Feng compiled a dictionary of synonyms and
developed ONTOL-MT2, a synonym marking system.

Enlightened by P. M. Roget's *Thesaurus of English Words and Phrases* (London,
1851), L. V. Berrey's *Roget's International Thesaurus, Third Edition* (New York,

1962), and R. Hallig and W. von Wartburg's *Begriffssystem als Grundlage für die Lexikographie* (Versuch eines Ordnungsschemas, Berlin, 1963), Zhiwei Feng integrated all the lexical entries in *Thesaurus of Chinese Synonyms* into ONTOL-MT and constructed ONTOL-MT2, where concepts were divided into 14 categories represented by ABCDEFGHIJKLMN.

A (human): advanced animals that can manufacture and use tools
B (natural things): natural things with shape, color, or mass
C (artificial things tool): man-made things without shape, color, or mass
D (abstract things): things without shape, color, or mass
E (affair): things that can be extended in the dimension of time
F (time): a continuous system that consists of past, present, and future events, serves as an objective form of being, and indicates the continuity of movements and changes in matter
G (space): another objective form of being, which can be extended in different dimensions
H (quantity): the amount of something and its measurement
I (physical action): the physical activities performed by human beings or things
J (psychological action): the psychological activities performed by human beings or things
K (social activity): collective activities attended by human beings and related to social phenomena (such as political, military, legal, economic, cultural, and educational phenomena)
L (phenomena-state): the conditions shown by human beings or things
M (attribute): the qualities and relations that things are characterized by
N (others): conjunctions, interjections, adverbial particles, greetings, onomatopoeia, and so on.

Each of the categories above could fall into multiple subcategories. On the basis of ONTOL-MT2, a synonym thesaurus can be made. At present, researchers at Ludong University are now compiling *Thesaurus of Synonyms (A New Edition)* according to ONTOL-MT2.

The following section is about a well-known language ontology, WordNet.

6.5 WordNet

As a database about lexical relations in English, WordNet can also be perceived as a language ontology. Developed by G. A. Miller, R. C. Beckwick, C. Fellbaum, and their colleagues at Princeton University in 1985, it can be accessed by visiting its website http:// www.cogsci.princeton.edu/~wn/.

To build WordNet, Miller et al. proposed the following three hypotheses.

First, the separability hypothesis states that lexical elements can be separated from language and studied independently.

Second, the patterning hypothesis states that human beings have the tendency to pay special attention to the systematic patterns and relations exhibited by the senses of words.

Third, the comprehensiveness hypothesis states that it is necessary for the system to store human beings' lexical knowledge in WordNet as much as possible.

These hypotheses indicate that Miller et al. endeavored to separate words from language, adopt a formulaic approach, and collect lexical knowledge as much as possible to build WordNet.

Although WordNet includes descriptions of compound words, phrases, idioms, and collocations, its basic units are still words. WordNet consists of three databases, one each for nouns and verbs and a third for adjectives and adverbs. A complete sense entry in WordNet is composed of the corresponding word, its synonyms, their definitions, and some examples of its usage.

WordNet makes no distinction between homonymy and polysemy. As a polysemic word can have several senses, obviously there are more senses than words in WordNet.

A considerable number of words and senses are stored in WordNet. The size of WordNet 1.6 is given in Table 6.1.

In the following, nouns, adjectives, adverbs, and verbs in WordNet will be described.

Nouns in WordNet

Due to polysemy, 94,474 nouns in WordNet can indicate 116,317 senses (lexicalized concepts).

As the basic semantic relation in WordNet, synonymy is identified according to the fundamental principle discussed in Sect. 6.3. Two entries are regarded as synonyms in WordNet if they can replace each other in some context. A set of synonyms is called a SYNSET. An example of a SYNSET is listed below:

```
{chump, fish, fool, gull, mark, patsy, fall guy, sucker, schlemiel, soft
touch, mug}
```

This SYNSET is defined as a person who is gullible and easy to take advantage of. Each lexical entry in this SYNSET can, therefore, express the notion in some situations. Senses of many entries in WordNet are composed of this kind of SYNSET. Specifically, the sense of each entry in a SYNSET includes the SYNSET itself, its definition, and example sentences.

Table 6.1 The size of WordNet

Category	Number of words	Number of senses
Noun	94,474	116,317
Verb	10,319	22,066
Adjective	20,170	29,881
Adverb	4546	5677

From a more theoretical point of view, each SYNSET can express a lexicalized notion in a language. WordNet achieves this by organizing the lexical entries that can express the notion into a list rather than by using logical terms. This perspective reveals that it is SYNSETs instead of lexical entries or individual senses that participate in most of the semantic relations among nouns in WordNet. For ease of description, usually only some representative words in a SYNSET are used to represent the SYNSET.

In the following, three other semantic relations, including hyponymy, meronymy, and antonymy, will be discussed.

Hyponymy

Hyponymy in WordNet corresponds directly to the notion of hyponymy discussed in Sect. 6.3. More specific words are hyponyms of more generic words, while the latter are reversely hypernyms of the former.

For example, birds are hypernymous robins, whereas robins are hyponymous birds.

According to hyponymy, nouns can be organized into a lexical hierarchy.

For example, as WordNet defines robin as a migratory bird that has a clear melodious song and a reddish breast with gray or black upper plumage, one hypernym of robin is thus bird. Birds in WordNet are defined as warm-blooded egg-laying animals with feathers and forelimbs modified as wings. Therefore, one hypernym of bird is animal. To trace the hyponymy in WordNet further, the definition of animal is found to be an organism capable of voluntary movement and possessing sense organs and cells with non-cellulose walls. Accordingly, a hypernym of animal is organism, which in turn is defined as a living entity.

In the above relations, each word represents a SYNSET, which is connected through superordinate or subordinate relations to a more generic or specific SYNSET. To find a series of more generic or specific SYNSETs, users can simply follow a hyponymy chain to search upward or downward.

Of note, hyponymy represents relations between word senses instead of word forms. For example, when trees are regarded as a kind of plant, both trees and plants denote a type of living organism rather than other senses as in tree graphs and manufacturing plants.

In one word, hyponymy is a relation between particular senses of words, representing a relation between lexicalized concepts. In WordNet, the pointer "@->" is used to connect SYNSETs in hyponymy relations. An instance is {robin, redbreast} @-> {bird} @-> {animal, animate_being} @-> organism, life_form, living_thing}.

In mathematics, @ is transitive and asymmetric. Its semantic relation can be interpreted as IS-A or IS-A-KIND-OF. The sign -> means pointing upward.

When a less generic sense points to a more generic sense, the process is called generalization, which means pointing from a specific sense to a generic one. Generalization, denoted by @->, can be written as Ss @-> Sg.

When a more generic sense points to a less generic sense, the process is called specification, which means pointing from a generic sense to a specific one. Specification, denoted by ~->, can be written as Sg ~-> Ss.

As features of concepts can be inherited in hyponymy relations, hyponymy can be used for reasoning purposes. For instance, if Rex is a collie, then Rex is a dog; if Rex is a dog, then Rex is an animal; and if Rex is an animal, then Rex is capable of voluntary movement. In this manner, hyponymy relations can form an upward chain, where concepts become increasingly generic. When the chain comes to the most generic concept, the concept is a primitive semantic component, called a unique beginner in WordNet.

The noun database in WordNet used 25 unique beginners. They were

```
{act, activity}
{animal, fauna}
{artifact}
{attribute}
{body}
{cognition, knowledge}
{communication}
{event, happening}
{feeling, emotion}
{food}
{group, grouping}
{location}
{motivation, motive}
{natural object}
{natural phenomenon}
{person, human being}
{plant flora}
{possession}
{process}
{quantity, amount}
{relation}
{shape}
{substance}
{time}
```

In its later versions, WordNet rearranged the 25 unique beginners into the following 11 beginners (represented by bold type).

As shown in Fig. 6.11, the 11 unique beginners are entity, abstraction, psychological feature, natural phenomenon, activity, event, group, location, possession, shape, and state.

The word *bass* has two distinct senses: sense 3 and sense 7. The hyponymy chains of the two senses are given below. Notably, the two chains are completely separated, but they join at entity, which is a unique beginner.

```
Sense 3
bass, basso
(an adult male singer with the lowest voice)
=> singer, vocalist
  => musician, instrumentalist, player
    => performer, performing artist
      => entertainer
```

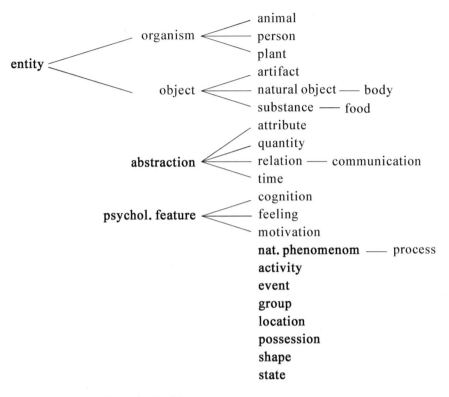

Fig. 6.11 Unique beginners in WordNet

```
=> person, individual, someone
  => life form, organism, being
    => entity, something
  => causal agent, cause, causal agency
    => entity, something
```

```
Sense 7
bass -
(the member with the lowest range of a family of musical instruments)
=> musical instrument
  => instrument
    => device
      => instrumentality, instrumentation
        => artifact, artefact
          => object, physical object
            => entity, something
```

The first chain starts from an adult male singer with the lowest voice, whose immediate hypernym is singer, a more generic concept. Following the chain upward leads to more generic concepts such as musicians, performers, entertainers, persons, life forms, and entities.

The second chain, which starts from the member with the lowest range of a family of musical instruments, has a completely different path leading to concepts such as musical instruments, instruments, devices, instrumentality, artifacts, and objects but also eventually ends up with the same unique beginner, i.e., entity.

It can thus be noted that at the top of the two hierarchical systems of concepts is entity, which is one of the 11 unique beginners in WordNet.

Meronymy

The part-to-whole relation in WordNet is called meronymy. Meros, which means part, derives from Greek.

In meronymy relations, the word that is the part is called a meronym, denoted S_m, while the word that serves as the whole is a holonym, denoted S_h. Obviously, if S_m is the meronym of S_h, then S_h is the holonym of S_m.

WordNet also makes use of W_m and W_h to represent a meronym and a holonym and employs "is a part of" and "has a" to describe the meaning of the part-to-whole relation. If the proposition is acceptable that W_m is a part of W_h, then W_m is a meronym of W_h. If it is acceptable that W_h has W_m as a part, then W_h is a holonym of W_m.

Meronymy relations have mathematical properties similar to those of hyponymy relations, as both are transitive and asymmetric. For example, a finger is a part of a hand, while a hand is a part of an arm, which in turn is a part of a body.

According to Winston and Chaffin's research in 1987, meronymy relations can fall into the following six types.

Component-object: e.g., branch-tree
Member-collection: e.g., tree-forest
Portion-mass: e.g., slice-cake
Stuff-object: e.g., aluminum-airplane
Feature-activity: e.g., paying-shopping
Place-area: e.g., Princeton-New Jersey

WordNet uses only three of the six types, which are component-object, member-collection, and stuff-object, denoted #p->, #m->, and #s->. To be more specific

W_m #p-> W_h: W_m is a component of W_h.
W_m #m-> W_h: W_m is a member of W_h.
W_m #s-> W_h: W_m is the stuff that W_h is made of.

Antonymy

Antonymy refers to the relations between words that are opposite to each other. Though antonymy is not a fundamental approach to organizing meanings of nouns in a language, WordNet still takes it into account. Therefore, a description of its representations is necessary.

Antonymy relations are indicated with "!->". For example, [{man} !-> {woman}] means *man* is an antonym of *woman*, while [{woman} !-> {man}] suggests that *woman* is an antonym of *man*.

Antonyms usually share the same immediate hypernym. An instance is that human is the immediate hypernym of *men* and *women*.

Adjectives in WordNet

In WordNet, 20,170 adjectives are subsumed under 29,881 senses (lexicalized concepts).

As any word that modifies a noun is perceived as an adjective in WordNet, adjectives in WordNet include not only adjectives in traditional grammar but also nouns, present participles, past participles, prepositional phrases, and even clauses. For noun phrases such as *a large chair* and *a comfortable chair*, large and *comfortable* are adjectives in traditional grammar and are naturally counted as adjectives in WordNet. In addition, the italicized words, phrases, and clauses in the following examples are also seen as adjectives in WordNet:

kitchen chair, *barber* chair (nouns in traditional grammar)
the *creaking* chair (a present participle in traditional grammar)
the *overstuffed* chair (a past participle in traditional grammar)
chair *by the window* (a prepositional phrase in traditional grammar)
the chair *that you bought at the auction* (a clause in traditional grammar)

In WordNet, 16,428 adjectives have SYNSETs that include adjectives, participles, and prepositional phrases in traditional grammar.

Adjectives can fall into descriptive adjectives and relational adjectives.

- Descriptive adjectives: such as *big, beautiful, interesting, possible*, and *married*
  A descriptive adjective can assign the value of some attribute to the noun it modifies. The construction *X is Adj* means that there exists an attribute A such that $A(X) = Adj$. For example, the sentence *the package is heavy* denotes that there exists an attribute *WEIGHT* such that *WEIGHT* (*package*) = *heavy*, as *heavy* and *light* are values of WEIGHT. WordNet uses a pointer to connect an adjective with the noun it modifies.
- Relational adjectives: such as *electrical*
  As relational adjectives derive from nouns, the two groups are related to each other. For instance, the relational adjective *electrical* is related to the noun *electricity*.

Antonymy is the basic semantic relation to describe adjectives. An example is good—bad.

Descriptive adjectives have two salient features, i.e., bipolarity and gradeness of their attributes. The two are explained as follows.

Bipolarity: an attribute of a descriptive adjective tends to be polarized.
  The attributes of antonymous adjectives are opposite to each other. For instance, the antonym of *heavy* is *light*, as they indicate the two opposite values of the attribute WEIGHT.

In WordNet, bipolarity is described with the symbol !->, which means IS-ANTONYMOUS-TO. Take *heavy (vs. light)* and *light (vs. heavy)* as examples. The two can be rewritten as

heavy !-> light
light !-> heavy

In WordNet, if a word has two senses, then it is treated as two word forms labeled with two numbers. For example, *hard* can mean *solid* and *difficult*, thus marked as *hard₁* and *hard₂* respectively. The antonym of *hard₁* is *soft*, while *easy* is opposite to *hard₂*.

In English, words that directly indicate opposite meanings are called antonyms, such as *heavy/light* and *weighty/weightless*. There also exist indirect antonyms. An instance is *ponderous*. It is hard to tell what word is its antonym. However, *ponderous* and *heavy* indicate similar senses because any noun that can be modified by *heavy* can also be modified by *ponderous*. As *heavy* is opposite to *light*, *light* can then be perceived as an approximate antonym of *ponderous* through the mediation of *heavy*. In other words, the opposition conveyed by the word pair *ponderous/light* is established not directly but through the mediation of *heavy*. Accordingly, *ponderous* and *light* are an instance of indirect antonyms. From the lexical perspective, although *ponderous/light* is not an antonym pair, an antonymy relation can be established through the mediation of *heavy* between the concepts indicated by the two words. In WordNet, similar senses mean *is similar to*, described with the pointer &->. The reasoning process of finding indirect antonyms can therefore be exemplified as follows:

As *heavy* !-> *light* and *ponderous* &-> *heavy* hold, *ponderous* !-> *light* holds.

Antonyms of all the descriptive adjectives in English are likely to be found because even for those adjectives whose antonyms are hard to determine, their indirect antonyms can be determined in this manner.

Antonyms and indirect antonyms can be arranged in a bipolar cluster, as instanced below (Fig. 6.12).

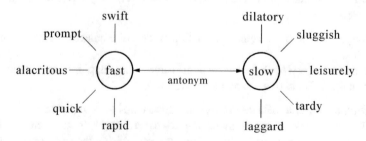

Fig. 6.12 A bipolar cluster

In the bipolar cluster above, its head SYNSET is *fast/slow*. One half of the cluster takes *fast* as the head word, whereas *slow* is the head word of the other half. Around the head words are words with similar meanings, called satellite SYNSETs. The satellite SYNSETs of *fast* are *swift*, *prompt*, *alacritous*, *quick*, and *rapid*, meaning a high speed. In contrast, the satellite SYNSETs of *slow* include *dilatory*, *sluggish*, *leisurely*, *tardy*, and *laggard*, implying a low speed. The whole bipolar cluster is concerned with the attribute of SPEED.

In a bipolar cluster, as different antonym pairs indicate opposite senses or closely related senses, they can represent different values of a single attribute. For example, antonym pairs such as *large/small* and *big/little* determine the attribute SIZE. Its values in WordNet are represented by one half of a bipolar cluster as *large (vs. small)* and *big (vs. little)* and by the other half of the bipolar cluster as *small (vs. large)* and *little (vs. big)*.

The adjective database in WordNet includes 1732 bipolar clusters. On either side of each bipolar cluster are words that have antonymy relations with words on the other side. In other words, as each word has its corresponding antonyms in a bipolar cluster, the 1732 bipolar clusters denote 1732 similar senses when only one side of each cluster is taken into account and 3464 similar senses if both sides are considered. The number of senses in bipolar clusters is thus approximately the number of senses of adjectives in WordNet.

Gradeness: Adjectives in WordNet can be graded according to different attributes, as exemplified by the following adjectives that are graded in line with SIZE, LIGHTNESS, QUALITY, BODY-WEIGHT, and TEMPERATURE (Fig. 6.13).

This kind of grading shows the similarity between the senses of adjectives, and the attributes described by these adjectives can indicate directionality or, put it another way, dimensions. Therefore, adjectives in WordNet can be imagined as hyperspace with a myriad of dimensions, each of which has one end that is closely attached to the origin of the hyperspace.

Relational adjectives are related to nouns in terms of semantics or morphology, though not very directly in the latter case.

For example, *musical* is related to *music*, whereas *dental* has some connections with *tooth*.

SIZE	LIGHTNESS	QUALITY	BODY-WEIGHT	TEMPERATURE
Astronomical	snowy	superb	obese	torrid
huge	white	great	fat	hot
large	ash-gray	good	plump	warm
...	gray	mediocre	...	tepid
small	charcoal	bad	slim	cool
tiny	black	awful	thin	cold
infinitesimal	pitch-black	atrocious	gaunt	frigid

Fig. 6.13 Gradeness of adjectives

Therefore, nouns can often be modified by relational adjectives or nouns that the adjectives derive from. For instance

A relational adjective + a noun: a noun + a noun

Atomic bomb: *atom bomb*
Dental hygiene: *tooth hygiene*

The differences between relational adjectives and descriptive adjectives are as follows.

Relational adjectives do not involve the attributes of the nouns they modify, so they are irrelevant to attributes.

Relational adjectives cannot be graded, so *the very atomic bomb* is an illegal expression.

Most relational adjectives have no immediate antonyms.

Due to these differences, relational adjectives cannot be included in clusters and characterized by polarity. In WordNet, the documents of relational adjectives consist of 2823 SYNSETs. Each relational adjective has one pointer pointing toward the corresponding nouns. For example, relational adjectives *stellar* and *astral* point toward *star*, *celestial body*, or *heavenly body*.

Adverbs in WordNet

WordNet includes 4546 adverbial forms, which are subsumed under 5677 senses (lexicalized concepts).

Most adverbs are derivatives created by adding the suffix *-ly* to adjectives. For example, adverbs such as *beautifully*, *oddly*, *quickly*, *interestingly*, and *hurriedly* derive from *beautiful*, *odd*, *quick*, *interesting*, and *hurried*. Other adverbs are derivatives generated by adding suffixes such as *-ward*, *-wise*, and *-ways*, such as *northward*, *crosswise*, and *sideways*.

In WordNet, these derivative adverbs point to their corresponding adjectives through a pointer that denotes DERIVED-FROM.

Verbs in WordNet

In WordNet, there are 10,319 verbs, which are subsumed under 22,066 senses (lexicalized concepts).

The verb database of WordNet involves 14 semantic fields: motion, perception, contact, communication, competition, change, cognition, consumption, creation, emotion, possession, body care and function, social behavior, and interaction.

Pulman (1983) suggested that *be* and *do* should be the root nodes of all verbs in a conceptual system, where *be* represents static verbs and *do* stands for action verbs. However, the two verbs convey multiple meanings and are thus inconvenient for serving as the root nodes of all the verbs. WordNet does not follow Pulman's suggestion because both *be* and *do* in WordNet have 12 senses. For instance, *be* indicates different senses in *To be or not to be, that is the question* and *Let him be, I tell you*. So does *do* in *do my hair* and *do my room in blue*. Therefore, the two words cannot be taken as the root nodes of all the verbs.

WordNet version 1.5 includes 11,500 verb SYNSETs.

Verbs in a single semantic field can hardly be subsumed under one initial concept. Some semantic fields should be described with several independent tree structures.

For example, motion verbs can be classified into $move_1$ and $move_2$. The former refers to motion with displacement, while the latter refers to motion without displacement.

Verbs that mean possession can be subsumed under three concepts, represented by three SYNSETS, i.e., {give, transfer}, {take, receive}, and {have, hold}.

Verbs that denote communication can fall into verbal communication and non-verbal communication (such as hand gestures).

The relationship between verbs in WordNet can be described with entailment. Given two verbs V_1 and V_2, V_1 entails V_2 if the behavior indicated by the sentence *someone V_1* logically entails the behavior expressed by *someone V_2*.

An instance is that, as the behavior indicated by *He is snoring* entails the behavior indicated by *He is sleeping*, the verb *snore* entails the verb *sleep*. Logically, if the first sentence holds, then the second sentence also holds.

Entailment between verbs has the following characteristics:

- Entailment is unidirectional. If a verb V_1 entails another verb V_2 and they are not synonyms, then V_2 cannot entail V_1.
- If two verbs entail each other, then they must be synonyms. That means they have the same sense.
- Negation can change the direction of entailment. *Not sleeping* entails *not snoring*, but *not snoring* does not entail *not sleeping*.
- Contradictions arise if the entailed verb is negated. If the sentence *he is snoring* entails the sentence *he is sleeping*, then *he is snoring* is contradictory to *he is not sleeping*.
- Verbs with entailment are connected with each other in terms of time. For instance, *drive* and *ride* are related to each other in terms of time. If you *drive*, then you must *ride* at the same time.
- Inclusion in terms of time can be found in the entailment. The time for *snoring* is part of the time for *sleeping*. The former is included in the latter, though the two are not always the same. If you stop sleeping, then you must also stop snoring (but you can continue sleeping without snoring). In other words, for two verbs connected through entailment, one includes the other in terms of time. During the time span when verbs V_1 and V_2 occur, if V_1 occurs but V_2 does not, then the time for V_2 to occur is properly included in the time for V_1 to occur.

The distribution of verb senses in WordNet can be described with coordinates. In a rectangular coordinate system, if the y axis indicates the number of senses of a lexeme and the x axis represents the number of polysemous words, the distribution of verb senses can be described in Fig. 6.14.

The figure shows that the number of polysemous verbs is relatively small in WordNet and that most verbs have only one sense.

As a language ontology, WordNet provides abundant lexical semantic information, which is very useful for semantic analysis in NLP.

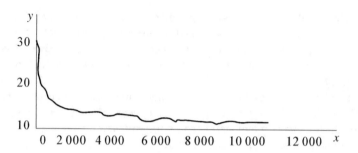

Fig. 6.14 The distribution of verb senses in WordNet

6.6   HowNet

HowNet was developed by Chinese scholars Zhendong Dong and Qiang Dong. As a system to describe knowledge in dictionaries, HowNet describes Chinese and English words in a relatively independent manner. The correspondence between the two groups of words is established on the basis of the attributes they share. With its size being expanded, HowNet now includes 33,069 Chinese words (41,791 concepts) and 38,774 English words (48,834 concepts).

The development of HowNet falls into five phases, i.e., the conceptual design phase from 1988 to 1993, the experimental phase from 1993 to 1997, the engineering realization phase from 1997 to 1999, the modification phase from 1999 to 2003, and the application phase from 2003 until now. After having studied issues such as how to compute conceptual correlations and conceptual similarities, researchers are now planning to design a new version of HowNet.

In HowNet, each record is composed of the concept of a word and its description. A record includes seven items, each of which consists of two parts connected with one equal sign =. On the left side of the equal sign is the domain name of data, while on the right side is the value of data. Their arrangement is as follows:

```
W_C = a Chinese word
G_C = the POS of the Chinese word
E_C = an example of how to use the Chinese word
W_E = an English word
G_E = the POS of the English word
E_E = an example of how to use the English word
Def = the conceptual category and attributes of the word
```

The conceptual category and attributes are the most important information in a knowledge dictionary. Located in the first position on the right side of the equal sign, the conceptual category information is separated from the following attributes by using a comma. Besides, attributes are also separated from each other by a comma.

Some examples are given in the following:

```
W_C = 医生 (/yi sheng/; an equivalent of doctor in Chinese)
G_C=NOUN
E_C=
W_E=doctor
G_E=NOUN
E_E=
Def = humans|人类(/ren lei/), medical|医(/yi/), *cure|医治(/yi zhi/),
#disease|疾病(/ji bing/), addressable|称(/cheng/)
```

The first six items are self-evident, but the last item Def should be explained. The first position on the right side of the equal sign is humans, indicating that doctors belong to the category of humans. The attributes of doctors include belonging to the medical field (medical), performing medical treatment behavior (*cure where * means the agent-event relationship), treating diseases (#disease, where # denotes the subject-relevant relationship), and serving as an addressing term (addressable).

```
W_C = 医院 (/yi yuan/; an equivalent of hospital in Chinese)
G_C=NOUN
E_C=
W_E=hospital
G_E=NOUN
E_E=
Def = institute - place|场所(/chang suo/), +cure|医治(/yi zhi/),
#disease|疾病(/ji bing/), medical|医(/yi/)
```

Regarding the Def above, the first position on the right side of the equal sign is institute-place, which shows that a hospital is an institute-place. Its attributes include being an institute-place for medical treatment (+cure, where + means the place-event relationship), treating diseases (#disease), and belonging to the medical field (medical).

```
W_C = 看病 (/kan bing/; an equivalent of seeing a patient in Chinese)
G_C=VERB
E_C=
W_E=see a patient
G_E=VERB
E_E=
Def = cure|医治(/yi zhi/), content=disease|疾病(/ji bing/), medical|医
(/yi/)
```

For the Def above, the first position on the right side of the equal sign is cure, which suggests that seeing a doctor belongs to the category of cure. Its attributes consist of diagnosing diseases (content = disease) and belonging to the medical field (medical).

The word 看病(/kan bing/) can also mean seeing a doctor in Chinese, which can be described as follows:

```
W_C = 看病 (/kan bing/; an equivalent of seeing a doctor in Chinese)
G_C=VERB
E_C=
W_E=see a doctor
G_E=VERB
```

```
E_E=
Def = request|要求(/yao qiu/), result-event=cure|医治(/yi zhi/),
#medical|医(/yi/)
```

For the Def above, the first position on the right side of the equal sign is request, which implies a necessary attribute, i.e., the resultative event cure (result event = cure). Another attribute is belonging to the medical field (# medical where # denotes relevant).

```
W_C=健壮(/jian zhuang/; an equivalent of tough in Chinese)
G_C=ADJ
E_C=
W_E=tough
G_E=ADJ
E_E=
Def=situation-value|状况值(/zhuang kuang zhi/), physique|体格(/ti ge/),
strong|强(/qiang/), desired|良(/liang/)
```

Regarding Def above, the initial position of the right side of the equal sign is a situation value. This conceptual category has attributes such as a strong physique (physique, strong) and a desired condition (desired).

Interconnected in HowNet, these concepts form a network (Fig. 6.15):

The network shows that the agent of the verb *cure* is *doctor*, whose attributes such as patient, content, fee, institute-place, and instrument are *a person suffering from illness*, *disease*, *medical expense*, *hospital*, and *medicine*, respectively. Regarding the verb phrase *pay to*, its agent, possession, and object are *a person suffering from illness*, *medical expense*, and *hospital*, respectively.

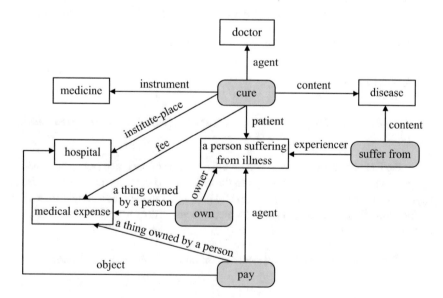

Fig. 6.15 A network composed of concepts

These examples indicate that the descriptions of words in HowNet are clearer than the definitions in dictionaries. In fact, the former is a formalization of the latter. This formalization can facilitate describing the concepts of words by reorganizing their attributes and attribute values. In this manner, the descriptive ability of HowNet is strengthened.

Designers of HowNet believe that everything (material, spiritual, or eventive) in the world is constantly moving and changing in the dimensions of time and space, usually changing from one state to another and taking the form of changes in its attribute values. Therefore, HowNet divides conceptual categories into three subcategories: N, V, and A. Category N includes entity, attribute, and unit. Specifically, entity comprises time, space, part, and things that usually move or change and fall into material, mental, and eventive types. As a very important class, attribute is ubiquitous. A person can have attributes such as gender, age, nationality, health condition, level of education, intelligence, and personality. A thing can have attributes such as size, weight, color, mass, and function. Nothing in the world can exist without an attribute, nor can any attribute be described independently of a thing. Category V consists of events, which can be classified into static events and behavior. Category A includes values of different attributes. The attribute values in category A correspond strictly with the attributes in category N. An attribute value cannot make sense without considering its attribute. Neither can an attribute be found without a value. For example, category A includes being smart as an attribute value, which points to the attribute of intelligence in category N.

HowNet does not treat nouns, verbs, and adjectives directly as category N, category V, and category A. Generally, in English, entity, attribute, time, space, everything, part, and unit in category N correspond to nouns; events in category V correspond to verbs and some adjectives; and attribute values in category A correspond to adjectives and adverbs. However, the corresponding relation in English does not completely hold in Chinese. That is why HowNet is perceived as a knowledge dictionary describing meanings of words.

In HowNet, the conceptual category in the Def item of a word represents the main attribute of the concept involved. Organized into a hierarchical structure indicating hyponymy relations, such a main attribute reveals the essence of the concept. For example, the main attribute of the concept "doctor" is human, while that of the concept "hospital" is institute-place. The two concepts are differentiated from each other by their main attributes. Besides, the main attribute of the concept "doctor," human, takes "animal" as its superordinate concept. In this manner, the main attribute is put into a hierarchical structure describing hyponymy relations.

However, hyponymy relations do not hold among non-main attributes, which include attribute values (such as male, female, old, young, kind, evil, and so on) in category A and the field where the target word is used (such as industry, commerce, medicine, and so on).

The distinction between main and non-main attributes is not absolute. The main attribute of a concept can sometimes become a non-main attribute of another concept. For example, for the concept "doctor" in category N, cure is a non-main attribute, but it is the main attribute of the concept "seeing a patient" in category V and thus a conceptual category.

HowNet processes main and non-main attributes according to the following principles:

1. The attributes of a superordinate concept can be inherited by its subordinate concept; the subordinate concept has at least one attribute that the superordinate concept does not have.
2. Each concept in the dictionary must have a main attribute that serves as the conceptual category. The main attribute is placed in the initial position on the right side of the equal sign. A concept can have several or no non-main attributes. Non-main attributes are placed after the main attribute and separated from it with a comma.
3. When the category of a concept and its hyponymy relations need to be identified, the criteria for classification should be consistent. For example, utensils can fall into furniture, stationery, cosmetics, tea sets, and so on according to their purposes of use; they can also be classified into ceramics, pottery, glass, and so on in line with their materials. However, the two criteria cannot be used at the same time.
4. When a main attribute is used as a non-main attribute, all or part of its original non-main attributes can be preserved, but it will lose its position as an indicator of hyponymy relations in the hierarchical system. As a result, its superordinate or subordinate concepts can no longer be inferred.

In summary, HowNet describes concepts in a formalized manner and organizes concepts and their attributes into a coherent knowledge system. These treatments are valuable for computers to process natural languages.

6.7 Pustejovsky's Generative Lexicon Theory

Generative lexicon theory (GLT) was proposed by Professor Pustejovsky (Fig. 6.16) at Brandeis University in the United States in 1991. When his monograph *The Generative Lexicon* was published in 1995, the framework of GLT had basically been established.[3]

By applying the generalized generative method to research on word senses and other related fields for the first time, GLT solved some difficult problems in lexical semantics. After more than 20 years of development, GLT has been widely used in studies on various languages, becoming increasingly mature and influential. Based on the creative uses of words, GLT devises an approach to representing word senses, focuses on how to formalize and compute word senses, and endeavors to explain from the generative perspective the different or creative uses of words in a specific

---

[3] Pustejovsky, James, *Generative Lexicon*. Cambridge: MIT Press, 1995.

Fig. 6.16 Pustejovsky

context. It has now become an important lexical semantics-based formal model for NLP. In recent years, Chinese linguists have begun to pay attention to GLT and have made attempts to apply this model to construct large-scale language knowledge databases and corpora for Chinese.[4]

The fundamental idea of GLT is that the senses of a lexical item in the lexicon are relatively stable but may be extended through some generative mechanisms at the sentence level in a specific context. The primary objective of GLT is to study linguistic phenomena such as polysemy, semantic ambiguity, and meaning shifts.

GLT is mainly composed of two parts. One is the representation of the senses of lexical items in the lexicon. The other is the generative mechanism of meaning at the sentence level. Therefore, the theory is named generative lexicon theory.

In lexicon, representing the senses of a lexical item includes four aspects, i.e., argument structure, event structure, qualia structure, and lexical typing structure.

1. Argument structure: The structure includes the number and types of arguments and explains how arguments are mapped onto syntactic expressions.
2. Event structure: Types of events include state, process, and transition. For example, *like* belongs to state, *run* to process, and *build* to transition. Event structure should also state clearly which event is the core event and how events are combined, such as the sequence of the events.
3. Qualia structure: The structure describes the object of a lexical item by specifying what the lexical item is made of, what it points to, how it is generated, and what purpose or function it is used for. Qualia structure is concerned with four features of lexical items: constitutive quale, formal quale, telic quale, and agentive quale.

---

[4]Song Zuoyan. The latest development of Generative Lexicon Theory. *Essays on Linguistics*, volume 44: 202-221. Beijing: The Commercial Press, 2011.

The four features are usually called the constitutive role, the formal role, the telic role, and the agentive role.

(a) The constitutive role describes the relation between an object and its constituents, such as material, weight, and part. The constitutive role also describes what other things the object in question can constitute. For instance, the constitutive role of *house* should specify that a house is made of materials like bricks, cement, and rebar; the constitutive role of *hand* should specify that a hand is a combination of fingers, a palm, and an arm and make clear that a hand is part of human body.

(b) The formal role describes how an object distinguishes itself from other objects within a larger cognitive domain. The formal role includes orientation, magnitude, shape, color, and dimensionality. An object can be differentiated from other objects according to its formal role.

(c) The telic role describes purposes and functions of objects. These purposes and functions are of two types, i.e., direct telic and purpose telic. The former concerns those purposes and functions through which human beings can be directly related to an object. For example, the direct telic of *beer* is drinking, as it can directly form a verb-object construction *drink beer*. The latter type concerns the purposes and functions that can be achieved with the assistance of a thing. For instance, the purpose telic of *knife* is cutting. The role is indicated in English by using the preposition *with*, like *cut with a knife*. The telic role can also describe the social functions of human beings. The telic role of a word denoting human beings specifies what social functions its referent has. An instance is that the telic role of the role-defining noun *printer* is a person who provides printing service.

(d) The agentive role includes factors involved in the origin or creation of an object, describing how the object is formed or produced, such as creation or cause-effect relations. For example, a book is written by its author, so the agentive role of *book* is writing. For the situation-defining noun *passenger*, its agentive role is taking a bus or an airplane because the agentive role makes him or her a passenger. Similarly, regarding *plaintiff*, which is another situation-defining noun, its agentive role is filing a complaint because the agentive role makes him or her a plaintiff.

The qualia structure of some lexical items can include all the four roles. For instance, the lexical item *roman* takes *story* as its constitutive role, *book* as the formal role, *read* as the telic role, and *write* as the agentive role. However, not every lexical item can have all the roles.

Qualia structure describes the things, events, or relations related to a lexical item and manifests its relations with its typical predicates. As a representation of overlapping categories, qualia structure provides lexical items with function labels, connects lexical items with conceptual networks, and serves as the organizing principle of concepts.

The lexical semantic expression of a lexical item α can be represented as follows.

ARGSTR in Fig. 6.17 means argument structure, so ARG1=x implies that argument1 is x; EVENTSTR is event structure, so E1:e1 refers to event1; QUALIA denotes qualia structure, with its constitutive role, formal role, telic role, and agentive role respectively represented by CONST = what x is made of, FORMAL = what x is, TELIC = function of x, and AGENTIVE = how x came into being.

For example, the lexical semantic expression of the lexical item *book* can be described as follows.

Figure 6.18 shows that *book* has two arguments, namely, physical object (physobj) and information (info). The lexical item *book* is a lexical conceptual paradigm (abbreviated as lcp) that combines the two arguments. Its formal role is *hold* (y, x), which means the physical object y holds the information x. Its telic role is *read* (e, w, x.y), implying that for e and w, the function of *book* is reading a book with the formal role of x.y (the physical object y holds information x). Its agentive role is *write* (e', v, x.y), suggesting that a book is written (v) by e' through putting information x into the physical object y.

Another instance is the lexical semantic expression of the lexical item *kill*, which is given as follows.

Figure 6.19 indicates that *kill* has two arguments, namely, an individual (ind) and an animal physical object (animate_in d). The lexical item *kill* includes two sub-events. One is the process of killing (e1: process), and the other describes the state of being dead (e2: state). The former is the core of the whole event. As a causative lcp, *kill* takes the action of killing as its agentive role (kill_act) and the state of being dead as its formal role (dead).

Fig. 6.17 The lexical semantic expression of a lexical item α

$$
\alpha \\
\text{ARGSTR} = \begin{bmatrix} \text{ARG1} = x \\ \cdots \end{bmatrix} \\
\text{EVENTSTR} = \begin{bmatrix} E_1 : e_1 \\ \cdots \end{bmatrix} \\
\text{QUALIA} = \begin{bmatrix} \text{CONST} = \text{what } x \text{ is made of} \\ \text{FORMAL} = \text{what } x \text{ is} \\ \text{TELIC} = \text{function of } x \\ \text{AGENTIVE} = \text{how } x \text{ came into being} \end{bmatrix}
$$

Fig. 6.18 The lexical semantic expression of the lexical item *book*

$$
\text{book} \\
\text{ARGSTR} = \begin{bmatrix} \text{ARG1} = x : \text{info} \\ \text{ARG2} = y : \text{physobj} \end{bmatrix} \\
\text{QUALIA} = \begin{bmatrix} \text{fino} \cdot \text{physobj\_1 cp} \\ \text{FORMAL} = \text{hold}(y, x) \\ \text{TELIC} = \text{read}(e, w, x. y) \\ \text{AGENTIVE} = \text{write}(ee', v, x. y) \end{bmatrix}
$$

Fig. 6.19 The lexical
semantic expression of the
lexical item *kill*

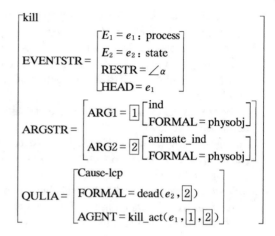

$$
\text{kill}
\begin{bmatrix}
\text{EVENTSTR} =
\begin{bmatrix}
E_1 = e_1 : \text{process} \\
E_2 = e_2 : \text{state} \\
\text{RESTR} = \angle_\alpha \\
\text{HEAD} = e_1
\end{bmatrix} \\[2em]
\text{ARGSTR} =
\begin{bmatrix}
\text{ARG1} = \boxed{1}
\begin{bmatrix}
\text{ind} \\
\text{FORMAL} = \text{physobj}
\end{bmatrix} \\[1em]
\text{ARG2} = \boxed{2}
\begin{bmatrix}
\text{animate\_ind} \\
\text{FORMAL} = \text{physobj}
\end{bmatrix}
\end{bmatrix} \\[2em]
\text{QULIA} =
\begin{bmatrix}
\text{Cause-lcp} \\
\text{FORMAL} = \text{dead}(e_2, \boxed{2}) \\
\text{AGENT} = \text{kill\_act}(e_1, \boxed{1}, \boxed{2})
\end{bmatrix}
\end{bmatrix}
$$

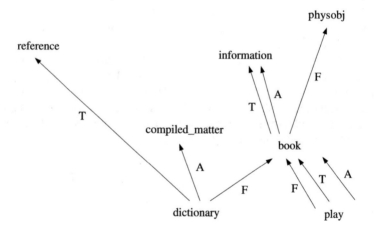

Fig. 6.20 The inheritance relationship in an instance of lexical typing structure

4. Lexical typing structure describes the position of a lexical item in a type system, i.e., the type that the lexical item belongs to. It determines how this lexical item is related to other lexical items, or in other words, the inheritance relationship among lexical items. Word senses in this system are directly connected with common sense. In the earlier frameworks of GLT, lexical typing structure was called lexical inheritance structure. An instance of lexical typing structure is shown in Fig. 6.20, with T, A, and F representing the telic role, the agentive role, and the formal role, respectively.

A word can inherit its features from multiple upper-level words. Figure 6.20 shows that the word *dictionary* inherits its telic role *consulting* from *reference*, its agentive role *compiling* from *compiled_matter*, and its formal role *holding* from *book*. It does not inherit the telic role of *book*, which is *reading*, because *reading a dictionary* does not sound as natural as *consulting a dictionary*. The figure above also demonstrates that the word *play* inherits from *book* its formal, telic, and agentive roles, while the word *book* inherits its telic and agentive roles from *information* and its formal role from *Phys_obj*.

Of all the four types of structure (argument structure, event structure, lexical typing structure, and qualia structure) in GLT, qualia structure receives the most attention. As such structure is unique to GLT, a more detailed explanation is needed.

The idea of qualia structure derives from Aristotle's four causes of knowledge. Aristotle believed that "ALL men by nature desire to know"[5] and that "Wisdom is knowledge about certain principles and causes"[6]. As a discipline about knowledge, philosophy aims to uncover the causes why things come into being and change. Aristotle put forward a theory on the types of explanatory factors. The theory assumed the existence of explanatory conditions and factors and classifed the reasons why things came into being and changed into the following four causes.

1. The material cause is the material that makes up and always exists in a thing. In other words, the material cause is the raw material that a thing is made of, such as bricks for a house, wood for a bed, bronze for a bronze statue, and so on.
2. The formal cause is the form of a thing's inherent or fundamental structure. The formal cause is the pattern or principle, on the basis of which a thing is constructed. Examples are the blueprint or prototype of a house in an architect's mind, the structure of a bed, and the configuration or outline of a bronze sculpture.
3. The efficient cause or the moving cause refers to the thing that enables other things to move or change. It is the driving force that shapes materials into a certain form. The efficient cause can be an architect who builds a house out of bricks, a craftsman who makes a bed or sculpture, or even the behavior of making the bed or sculpture.
4. The final cause is the purpose for which a thing is created or changed. Aristotle pointed out that the final cause was the best end of a thing, just like building a house for residence, creating a bed for sleeping, making a sculpture for appreciation, and so on.

The four types of causes above are called Aristotle's four causes.

Of all four causes, the material cause is the foundation on which a thing is formed. However, as the material cause is passive, only when the driving force needed by the formal cause takes effect and complies with the purpose determined by the formal cause can the material be changed into a certain form. Aristotle asserted that "For at least the substratum itself does not make itself change; e.g. neither the wood nor the bronze causes the change of either of them, nor does the wood manufacture a bed and the bronze a statue, but something else is the cause of the change. And to seek this is to seek the second cause, as we should say,-that from which comes the

---

[5] Aristotle. *Metaphysics*, translated by Ross W. D. NuVision Publications, LLC, 2005.
[6] Aristotle. *Metaphysics*, translated by Ross W. D. NuVision Publications, LLC, 2005.

beginning of the movement."[7] In this sense, the formal cause includes the moving cause and the final cause. Therefore, Aristotle later reduced his four causes to the material cause and the formal cause. In Part 7, Book 2 of *Physics*, Aristotle stated that "The causes, therefore, are these and so many in number. Now, the causes being four, it is the business of the physicist to know about them all, and if he refers his problems back to all of them, he will assign the 'why' in the way proper to his science the matter, the form, the mover, 'that for the sake of which'. The last three often coincide; for the 'what' and 'that for the sake of which' are one, while the primary source of motion is the same in species as these … The question 'why', then, is answered by reference to the matter, to the form, and to the primary moving cause. For in respect of coming to be it is mostly in this last way that causes are investigated – 'what comes to be after what? what was the primary agent or patient?' and so at each step of the series."[8]

Aristotle believed that the four causes he put forward could explain the cause of everything. As early as more than 2300 years ago, it was amazing that Aristotle could make such an in-depth analysis of causes of things. Aristotle's four causes display what reasoning can achieve in exploring the most common phenomena and their root causes.

Pustejovsky gained insight from Aristotle's four causes and applied them to GLT. He developed the four causes into the four features of lexical items, i.e., the constitutive quale, the formal quale, the telic quale, and the agentive quale, named them after the constitutive role, the formal role, the telic role, and the agentive role respectively, and put forward the qualia structure. All these demonstrated Pustejovsky's great wisdom.

Over the past 10 odd years, Pustejovsky and other scholars, based on the telic role of the qualia structure, have endeavored to divide lexical items into natural types, artifactual types, and complex types and have constructed a system of semantic types.

GLT holds that human beings' cognitive ability is reflected in language, especially in the mental lexicon, which is a complex, dynamic, and coherent knowledge system and an interface between structural linguistic operations and generative combinative rules. Lexical items in the mental lexicon fall into natural types, artifactual types, and complex types according to the senses they denote.

1. Natural types: Natural types are a basic concept that is concerned with the formal role and the constitutive role of the qualia structure. A natural type inherits its formal role from its superordinate type. As the basis of other types, natural types take words from the material domain as their predicates. For example, *rabbit* in the following sentence is a noun belonging to the natural type.

   The rabbit died.

---

[7] Aristotle. *Metaphysics*, translated by Ross W. D. NuVision Publications, LLC, 2005.

[8] Aristotle. *Physics*, translated by Hardie R. P. and Gaye R. K., LLC, 2005.

2. Artifactual types: The concept of function is added to artifactual types, so each
   artifactual type inherits its telic role from its superordinate type. As a basic type,
   artifactual types combine the agentive role and the telic role and take as predicates
   words related to the two roles. The biggest difference between natural types and
   artifactual types is that artifactual types are characterized by intentionality, while
   natural types are not. For instance, sentence a is acceptable, whereas sentence b is
   weird because *good* is an evaluation connected with intentionality and *chair* and
   rock belong to artifactual types and natural types, respectively.

   (a) This is a good chair.
   (b) *This is a good rock.

   Artifactual types also need to inherit their formal roles, which in turn are
related to natural types. Accordingly, for a specific noun, it necessarily has
connections with both natural types and artifactual types. An instance is *beer*,
which is a combination of the natural type *liquid*, the agentive role *brew*, and the
telic role *drink*. Another instance is *knife*, where the natural type *phys* is combined
with the agentive role *make* and the telic role *cut*. The two concepts can be
represented as follows:

beer: (liquid $\otimes_A$ brew) $\otimes_T$ drink
knife: (phys $\otimes_A$ make) $\otimes_T$ cut

   In the above expressions, $\otimes$ is the tensor type constructor, which introduces a
role of the qualia structure into a type so that the role becomes part of the type.
   A third example is *beverage*, whose ground type, or natural basis in other
words, is *liquid*. It is also an artifactual type with a telic role *drink*. Therefore, the
meaning of beverage can also be regarded as a tensor type, denoted by liquid $\otimes$
drink$_T$. Beverages can fall into several subcategories according to their functions
(Fig. 6.21).
   These examples reveal that, through inheritance, artifactual types can obtain
various telic roles. Some of the roles are quite close, while others are far from
each other. Take *coffee* for example. It has two telic roles. One is "drink" inherited
from beverage and denoted by b (the abbreviation of *beverage*). The other is
"wake-up" denoted by $b \otimes e_T^3$. As coffee plays the wake-up role only when a
person drinks it, its inherited telic role, drink, can be seen as an agentive role
embedded in the telic role of its qualia structure, denoted as

Fig. 6.21 Subcategories of
beverage

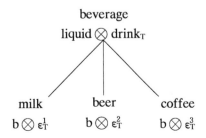

coffee:liquid $\otimes_T$ drink $\otimes_T$ wake-up.

Therefore, the lexical semantic expression of coffee can be represented as follows (Fig. 6.22).

Nouns denoting human beings can also be classified into natural types and artifactual types. The two types are shown on the left and right sides of the figure below. Both *doctor* and *surgeon* are found to be nouns of artifactual types (Fig. 6.23).

3. Complex types: In GLT, complex types are also called dot objects because each dot object is represented by a dot connecting natural types and artifactual types. A dot object inherits its roles from two or three natural types or artifactual types.

Complex types are labeled with lexical conceptual paradigms (abbreviated as lcp). An lcp is a meta-entry into which the different senses of a word can be combined so that the size of the lexicon can be reduced to a large extent.

Fig. 6.22 The lexical semantic expression of coffee

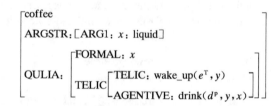

Fig. 6.23 Type inheritance of natural types and artifactual types

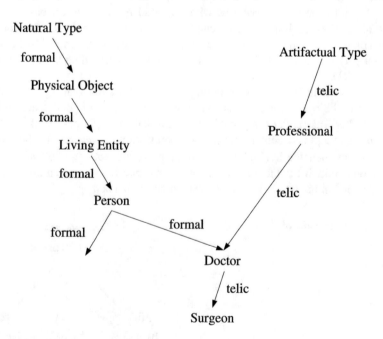

In Fig. 6.20, *book* is a complex type, *phys·info*, represented by a combination of *phys_obj* and *information*, the relationship between which is shown by the formal role of *book* as *hold*.

Other examples are

EVENT·INFO:lecture, play, seminar, exam, quiz, test
EVENT·PHYSOBJ:lunch, breakfast, dinner, tea
EVENT·(INFO·SOUND):concert, sonata, symphony, song

The lexical item *lecture* is a complex type combined by EVENT and INFO, denoting both an event and a thing carrying information. As a complex type combined by EVENT and PHYSOBJ, the lexical item *lunch* can mean both an event following a chronological order and specific food items. Similarly, the lexical item *concert* can be interpreted in the same manner.

Classification of lexical items into the three semantic types is basically made for nouns. Verbs and adjectives can also fall into the three types according to their relationships with the semantic type of nouns. For example, in *the rabbit died*, as *rabbit* belongs to the natural type, *died* is a verb of the same type. In this manner, the Tripartite Concept Lattice is formed. Figure 6.24 shows the upper-level concepts of the three semantic types. The concept at the top level is structured into three domains, i.e., entity, event, and quality, each of which is in turn structured into natural, artifact, and complex types. The lattice evolves from a simple to a more complex form.

Examples of the three categories are given below:

1. Nouns

   Natural types (N): rock, water, woman, tiger, tree
   Artifactual types (A): knife, beer, husband, dancer
   Complex types (C): book, lunch, university, temperature

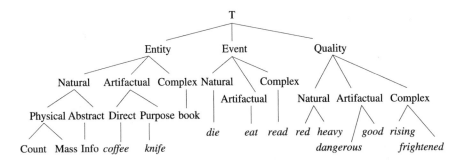

Fig. 6.24 The Tripartite Concept Lattice

2. Verbs

   Natural types (N): fall, walk, rain, put, have
   Artifactual types (A): donate, spoil, quench
   Complex types (C): read, perform

3. Adjectives

   Natural types (N): red, large, flat
   Artifactual types (A): useful, good, effective
   Complex types (C): rising, frightened

As the most salient feature of GLT's semantic descriptions of lexical items, the qualia structure combines the senses of nouns with experiential knowledge, connects nouns with verbs, and, in particular, introduces the telic role into the classification of semantic types. The specific features and contributions of GLT can be summarized as follows:

1. Daily experiential knowledge is connected with meanings of lexical items through the qualia structure. Linguistic and non-linguistic knowledge has been a thorny issue in semantic research. Conventional semantics makes a clear distinction between linguistic and non-linguistic knowledge and excludes the latter from linguistic research. In contrast, cognitive linguistics believes that there is no clear borderline between linguistic and non-linguistic knowledge; frame semantics also holds that the background of non-linguistic knowledge should be incorporated into language understanding. However, not all daily experiential knowledge has linguistic value. Through the constitutive role, formal role, telic role, and agentive role of the qualia structure, GLT includes the experiential knowledge related to word senses into its semantic descriptions of lexical items and provides an interface between experiential knowledge and linguistic knowledge. Research has shown that these roles can interpret many linguistic phenomena and thus are of great systemic value in linguistics.

2. Natural types are differentiated from artifactual types. For verbs related to nouns, GLT pays more attention to those that have telic roles. In addition, based on telic roles, GLT classifies nouns into natural types and artifactual types. The fundamental distinction between the two types can cause differences in linguistic forms, which are detailed in the following.

   (a) Artifactual types rather than natural types can achieve co-predication. For example:

       *That is a dog and a cat.
       That is a pen and a knife.
       She is a teacher and a mother.

(b) When modified by an adjective, natural types allow only one interpretation of the adjective, but artifactual types can enable it to be interpreted in more than one way. For instance:

beautiful flower (*beautiful* only means having beauty)
long record/disk (*long* can describe the length of the object or the time for playing the record)

(c) Natural types need to obtain coerced meanings from the context, while artifactual types can provide the context with coerced meanings. For example, in sentence *a* below, as *tree* is a natural type, *began* has no default interpretation and needs to be explained according to the context. Therefore, the meaning it obtains is coerced. In sentence *b*, *book* is an artifactual type, so *began* can be interpreted in a default manner as writing or reading. It is the artifactual type *book* that provides the context for the semantic interpretation of *began*.

a. I began the tree.
b. I began the book.

Natural types can be identified with the help of opposition structures such as *male/female* or *alive/dead* and predicates belonging to natural types such as *swimming, flying, walking*, and so on. Artifactual types are more about functional behavior and are thus somewhat arbitrary, varying from one language to another.

Before Pustejovsky, many scholars had already observed the distinction between natural types and artifactual types. In the semantic categories of WordNet and HowNet, natural and man-made things were also put in two distinct categories.

GLT's contribution is that the distinction between natural types and artifactual types is connected with verbs and formalized. GLT uses the semantic expressions of nouns to describe verbs and extends this approach to nouns denoting human beings and even to adjectives. With the distinction between natural types and artifactual types made at each level of language, GLT reconstructs the system of semantic types.

3. Multiple inheritance is used. A word is not simply placed in the tree structure of GLT but designed to inherit different qualia roles from different branches of the tree structure in a bottom-up manner so that repeated placement can be avoided.

GLT believes that word senses, which are relatively stable, can only change when words are combined. This kind of change is realized by the generative mechanisms in semantics.

In 1995, Pustejovsky classified the generative mechanisms in semantics into three types, namely, type coercion, selective binding, and co-composition. In recent years, the generative mechanisms in semantics have undergone some changes and have included type coercion into the mechanisms of argument selection in grammar. Therefore, arguments can be selected using three generative mechanisms of argument selection. The three mechanisms can help to interpret the syntactic and pragmatic features of a lexical item in word combinations. In this sense, the generative mechanisms in semantics are in fact the generative mechanisms of argument selection.

In the following, the three generative mechanisms of argument selection will be explained:

1. Pure selection refers to the phenomenon that the type required by a function is exactly the type to which the argument belongs.
2. Type accommodation means that the type a function requires is inherited from the superordinate argument.
3. Type coercion means that the type a function requires is imposed on the argument. Type coercion is realized through two approaches, i.e., exploitation and introduction:

   • Exploitation: The requirement of a function can be satisfied by exploiting part of the argument-type structure.
   • Introduction: The type that a function requires is introduced into the argument.

Figure 6.25 describes the environment where different generative mechanisms in semantics apply. For the purpose of meaning generation, pure selection applies only when the argument type matches the required type. Similarly, type accommodation works only in the case that the argument type and the required type belong to the same type domain. Type coercion works if their type domains are different. When the argument type is more complicated than the required type, exploitation is selected. Otherwise, type introduction is adopted.

In Fig. 6.25, Sel denotes pure selection; Acc stands for type accommodation; Exploit represents exploitation of type coercion; and Intro indicates introduction of type coercion.

The above generative mechanisms of argument selection can be exemplified as follows.

1. Pure selection. To select and generate the argument in the following sentence, *fall* requires an argument type denoting a physical object, which can be directly satisfied by *rock*. Therefore, this is an instance of pure selection.

The rock fell.

The required type of lexical items Argument type	Natual	artifactual	Complex
Natual	Sel/Acc	Intro	Intro
artifactual	Exploit	Sel/Acc	Intro
Complex	Exploit	Exploit	Sel/Acc

Fig. 6.25 The environment for the three generative mechanisms of argument selection

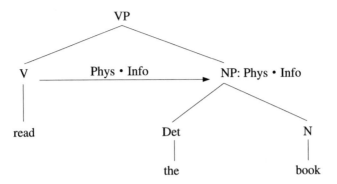

Fig. 6.26 An instance of pure selection

To select and generate arguments for the sentence below, *read* requires the noun it combines with belong to the complex type, Phys•Info. As *book* can directly satisfy the requirement, the sentence is another instance of pure selection (Fig. 6.26).

John read the book.

2. Type accommodation. To select and generate arguments for the following sentence, *wipe* requires its object argument to have a surface. Although *hands* cannot directly satisfy the requirement, it can inherit a surface from its superordinate type, which is Phys (physical object). Therefore, the sentence is an example of type accommodation (Fig. 6.27).

Mary wiped her hands.

3. Type coercion. To select and generate arguments in sentence *a* below, *burn* requires the noun it combines with should be of the natural type, Phys (physical object). Although *book* belongs to the complex type, Phys•Info, part of its type

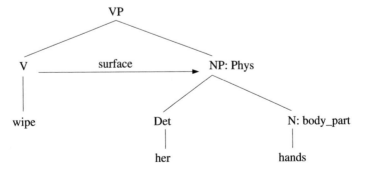

Fig. 6.27 An example of type accommodation

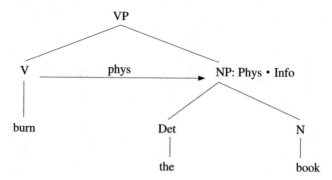

Fig. 6.28 An example (a) of type coercion: exploitation

structure can meet the requirement. Accordingly, sentence *a* exemplifies exploitation of type coercion (as illustrated in Fig. 6.28).

(a) The police burned the book.

To select and generate arguments in sentence *b*, *believe* requires the noun it combines with should be information. The requirement can be met by part of the type structure of *book* (Phys•Info). Therefore, sentence *b* is another instance of exploitation (as illustrated in Fig. 6.29).

(b) Mary believed the book. (type coercion: exploitation)

When selecting and generating arguments for the following sentence, *read* requires its object argument to be of the complex type, Phys•Info, but *rumor* belongs to the Info type, and cannot satisfy the requirement. The mechanism of type coercion can introduce a new type, Phys•Info, into *rumor*, which therefore implies a physical object carrying the information, such as a newspaper. This sentence exemplifies introduction of type coercion (as illustrated in Fig. 6.30).

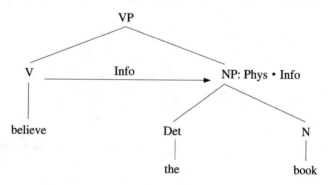

Fig. 6.29 An example (b) of type coercion: exploitation

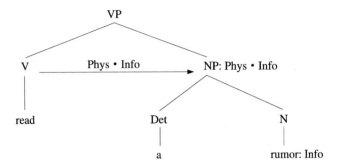

Fig. 6.30 Type coercion: introduction

Mary read a rumor about John. (type coercion: introduction)

   To select and generate arguments for the following sentences, *begin*, as an eventive verb, requires its complement to be an eventive argument, which is syntactically represented as a VP (read the book/write the book). Sentences *a* and *b* can meet this semantic-selection criterion and thus belong to pure selection. However, a type mismatch arises in sentence *c*, as the complement of *begin* syntactically takes the form of an NP referring to an object (the book). Therefore, *begin* will coerce the NP to shift into an eventive type. The coercion is realized through the agentive role *write* or the telic role *read* of the noun *book*. This sentence is also an instance of introduction, which introduces an eventive type into the physical object *book* (as illustrated in Fig. 6.31).

(a) John began writing/reading the book.
(b) John began to write/read the book.
(c) John began the book. (John began to write the book or John began to read the book.)

The improvement made by GLT in the generative mechanisms in semantics mainly includes that it makes a distinction between pure selection and type coercion

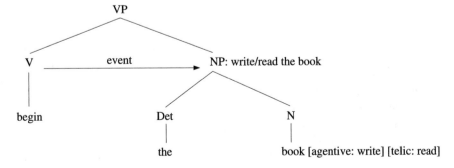

Fig. 6.31 Type coercion: introduction

and makes use of the two mechanisms to deal with type matches and mismatches, respectively. In particular, it stresses the use of type coercion to solve some problems about semantic ambiguity or vagueness.

When an argument is selected and generated, type coercion is an important semantic operation that can change the argument into the type meeting the requirement of the function involved. Without the operation, a type mismatch will arise. In the case of type coercion, the sense of a lexical item may change in two ways as follows.

1. Domain-preserving. For example, in the following sentence, the lexical item *chicken* changes from a countable noun into an uncountable noun, but its domain (entity) is preserved.

   There's chicken in the soup.

2. Domain-shifting, which can be subcategorized into

   (a) An entity shifts to an event:
       I enjoyed the beer. (I enjoyed drinking the beer)
   (b) An event shifts to an interval:
       before the party started. (before the interval of the party started)
   (c) An entity shifts to a proposition:
       I doubt John. (I doubt John's words)

Recent years have witnessed the rapid development of GLT, as an increasing number of scholars have engaged themselves in GLT research. In 2009, The Fifth International Conference on Generative Approaches to the Lexicon was convened. For Pustejovsky, he led his research group to build a corpus-based semantic system—Brandeis Semantic Ontology (BSO)—by making use of GLT. Now, the Type Lattice of BSO includes 3500 semantic type nodes and more than 40,000 polysemic words, which consist of 29,000 nouns, 5000 verbs, and 6000 adjectives. In addition, Pustejovsky and his colleagues, based on GLT, created a Generative Lexicon Markup Language (GLML) and made efforts to perform a semantic annotation for corpora. They used GLML to tag the corpora not with semantic cases such as agent and patient but with semantic types of nouns (like the artifactual or eventive type), the combination between nouns and predicates (type selection or type coercion), and the corresponding qualia roles (the formal role, the constitutive role, the telic role, and the agentive role).

As a lexicalist formal model, GLT underscores both generation and lexicon by combining the two in a tactful way. It plays a very important role in NLP, especially in online retrieval.

An online retrieval process basically includes submitting a retrieval request, sending the request, screening and classifying texts, searching the index, selecting webpages, ranking the webpages, and presenting the result.

A retrieval research group at Google pointed out that "A retrieval request is sent to thousands of data centers and then matched according to its keywords. After that, the results obtained are ranked according to hundreds of indicators. The complicated process is usually finished within one second, although each keyword of a Google retrieval request has to travel 2400 kilometers (1500 miles) on average between the user's computer and a data center."[9]

The description above shows that multiple analyses lie behind online retrieval, which seems to be a simple behavior accomplished within a second. The background operations of retrieval fall into high-level and low-level analyses. The former attempt to analyze the user's search intent in a top-down manner, while the latter involve structural and semantic analyses of keywords in a bottom-up approach. The two types of analyses make up most of the semantic analyses in retrieval.

Currently, users tend to use noun phrases when they submit their retrieval requests. When a user submits a noun phrase for retrieval, GLT can be used to automatically analyze the meaning of the noun phrase and help a retrieval system to better understand the ontological meaning of the noun phrase and identify the user's search intent.

For example, when a user inputs the Chinese noun phrase "蔬菜大王" (/shu cai da wang/; literally vegetable king) as a search term, his or her search intent is likely to obtain news reports about a person crowned as "蔬菜大王" (/shu cai da wang/; literally vegetable king). Therefore, the ontological meaning of "蔬菜大王" (/shu cai da wang/; literally vegetable king) should be determined first. Based on GLT, a retrieval system can analyze its formal role, constitutive role, telic role, and agentive role. Through GLT's generative mechanisms of argument selection, the system can find that the noun phrase is ambiguous because the qualia roles of "蔬菜" (/shu cai/; vegetables) and "大王" (/da wang/; king) indicate that the phrase can denote a person famous for purchasing/selling, planting, or even eating vegetables. With the help of GLT, the system can obtain multiple semantic interpretations of the noun phrase "蔬菜大王" (/shu cai da wang/; literally vegetable king), provide different search results for the user to select, and finally determine his or her search intent.

Despite these remarkable advantages, controversies still exist concerning GLT. To name just a few: Is GLT's approach to semantic description acceptable? Do the telic role and the agentive role belong to language knowledge? Should more features be added to the qualia structure? Do type shifts really occur in the case of type coercion? These questions warrant further investigation.

However, it can never be denied that GLT, which proposes a new idea of and a new approach to formalization, can better explain some language phenomena and thus serve as a formal model with unique characteristics for NLP.

Bibliography

1. Gomez-Perez, Asuncion. 2004. *Ontological Engineering with Examples from the Areas of Knowledge Management, e-Commerce and Semantic Web*. London: Springer.

---

[9]Translated from a science news report of Sina (http://www.sina.com.cn) on March 12, 2012.

2. Borst, W. N. 1997. *Construction of Engineering Ontologies. The Netherlands: Centre for Telemetica and Information Technology*. Enschede: University of Tweenty.
3. Bloch, B., and G.L. Trager. 1942. *Outline of Linguistic Analysis*, 60. Baltimore: Linguistic Society of America.
4. Chunxia, Zhang. 2004. Domain-Specific Formal Ontology of Archaeology and Its Application in Knowledge Acquisition and Analysis. *Journal of Computer Science & Technology* 19 (3): 290–301.
5. Church, K.W., and F. Hanks. 1989. Word Association Norms, Mutual Information, and Lexicography. In *ACL-89*, Vancouver, BC, 76–83.
6. Dagan, I., L. Lee, and F.C.N. Peraira. 1999. Similarity-Based Models of Cooccurrence Probabilities. *Machine Learning* 34 (1–3): 43–69.
7. Firth, J.R. 1957. *A Synopsis of Linguistic Theory 1930-1955*.
8. Gross, M. 1968. *Grammaire transformationnelle du français, syntaxe du verbe*. Paris: Larousse.
9. ———. 1975. *Methodes en syntaxe*. Paris: Hernamm.
10. ———. 1977. *Grammaire transformationnelle du français, syntaxe du nom*. Paris: Larousse.
11. Gruber, T.R. 1993. A Translation Approach to Portable Ontologies. *Knowledge Acquisition* 5 (2): 199–220.
12. Gu, Fang, et al. 2004. Domain-Specific Ontology of Botany. *Journal of Computer Science & Technology* 19 (2): 238–248.
13. Harris, Z. 1951 *Methods in Structural Linguistics*.
14. ———. 1954. Distributional Structure. *Word* 10: 146–162.
15. ———. 1963. *Structural Linguistics*.
16. Hocket, C.F. 1954. Two Models of Grammatical Description. *Word* 10: 210–233.
17. Joos, M. 1950. Description of Language Design. *JASA* 22: 701–708.
18. Jurafsky, D., and J.H. Martin. 2018. *Speech and Language Processing, An Introduction to Natural Language Processing, Computational Linguistics, and Speech Recognition*. 2nd ed. Trans Zhiwei Feng and Le Sun, Chinese Version. Beijing: Publishing House of Electronics Industry.
19. ———. 2017. *Speech and Language Processing, An Introduction to Natural Language Processing, Computational Linguistics, and Speech Recognition*. 3rd ed.
20. Mikolov, T., K. Chen, G. Corrado, et al. 2013. Efficient Estimation of Word Representation in Vector Space. *Computer Science*.
21. Miller, G., R. Beckwith, C. Fellbaum, D. Gross, and K. Miller. 1990. Introduction to WordNet: a On-Line Lexical Database. *International Journal of Lexicography* 3 (4): 235–244.
22. Miller, G. 1995. WordNet: a Lexical Database for English. *Communication of the ACM* 38911: 39–41.
23. Nida, E.A. 1975. *Componential Analysis of Meaning: An Introduction to Semantic Structures*. The Hague: Mouton.
24. Osgood, C.E., G.J. Suci, and P.H. Tannenbaum. 1957. *The Measurement of Meaning*. Champaign: University of Illinois Press.
25. Rohde, D.L.T., L.M. Gonnerman, and D.C. Plaut. 2006. An Improved Model of Semantic Similarity Based on Lexico-Occurrence. *Communications of ACM* 8: 627–633.
26. Salton, G. 1971. *The SMART Retrieval System: Experiments in Automatic Document Processing*. Englewood Cliffs: Prentice Hall.
27. De Ferdinand, Saussure. 1916. *Cours de Linguistique Générale*. Paris: Laussane.
28. Studer, R., V.R. Benjiamins, and D. Fensel. 1998. Knowledge Engineering: Principle and Methods. *IEEE Transaction on Data and Knowledge Engineering* 25 (1–2): 161–197.
29. Swadesh, M. 1934. The Phonemic Principle. *Language* 10: 117.
30. Xiusong, Zhang, and Ailing Zhang. 2009. An Introduction of Generative Lexicon theory. *Contemporary Linguistics* 11 (3): 267–271.
31. Zhendong, Dong, and Qiang Dong. 2006. *HowNet and the Computation of Meaning*. Singapore: World Scientific Publishing.

32. Zhiwei, Feng. 1999. *An Introduction to Applied Linguistics*. Guangzhou: Guangdong Education Publishing House.
33. ———. 2001. *Basics of Computational Linguistics*. Beijing: The Commercial Press.
34. ———. 2001. *Explorations into Computational Linguistics*. Harbin: Heilongjiang Education Publishing House.
35. ———. 2003. *A New Theory of Applied Linguistics*. Beijing: Modern World Press.
36. ———. 2004. *Research on Machine Translation*. Beijing: China Translation Corporation.
37. ———. 1999. Review on Link Grammar. *Applied Linguistics* 8 (4): 3–5.
38. ———. 2018. Parallel Development of Machine Translation and Artificial Intelligence. *Journal of Foreign Languages* 41 (6): 35–48.
39. Zuoyan, Song. 2011. The Latest Development of Generative Lexicon Theory. In *Essays on Linguistics*, vol. 44, 202–221. Beijing: The Commercial Press.

Chapter 7
Formal Models of Automatic Semantic Processing

The computer processing of the natural language also includes semantic analysis in addition to lexical and syntactic analyses.

There are different ways to deal with the relationship between semantic analysis and syntactic analysis in the existing NLP systems. Some systems adopt the syntax-before-semantics approach, while others adopt the syntactic-semantic integration approach.

The so-called syntax-before-semantics approach means that in the natural language analysis system, independent syntactic analysis is carried out first to obtain the syntactic representation of the input sentence, and then the semantic representation of the input sentence is obtained through independent semantic analysis. Syntactic analysis basically makes use of lexical and syntactic information, although some necessary semantic information attached to words and phrases should also be of some use. The program design of this kind of system does not depend on a specific domain, which has good transferability and extensibility.

The so-called syntactic-semantic integration approach means that in the natural language analysis system, instead of setting up a single syntactic module, syntactic analysis and semantic analysis are parallel. Alternatively, the semantic representation of input sentences can be directly obtained according to some semantic patterns. This kind of system can effectively deal with sentences with some grammatical errors or with some incomplete information and can directly obtain the semantic interpretation of sentences according to their semantic clues. However, due to insufficient syntactic information, semantic analysis does not always work well.

Regardless of which approach is adopted, semantic analysis is essential. Therefore, semantic analysis, like syntactic analysis, is the most basic functional module of NLP.

The core subject of AI is the study of knowledge expression, and knowledge is actually a meaningful collection of symbols that reflect the state of the world. Knowledge expression is inseparable from semantic analysis. The issue of expressing the meaning of sentences in the natural language is integrated into the

© Springer Nature Singapore Pte Ltd. 2023
Z. Feng, *Formal Analysis for Natural Language Processing: A Handbook*,
https://doi.org/10.1007/978-981-16-5172-4_7

issue of knowledge expression. The study of semantics in the natural language will inevitably have an important impact on the theory of knowledge expression in AI.

In this chapter, we mainly introduce formal models of automatic semantic processing, such as sememe analysis, semantic fields, semantic networks, Montague semantics, preference semantics, concept-dependency theory, meaning-text theory, deep cases, and frame semantics. Finally, it introduces methods of word sense disambiguation (WSD).

7.1   Sememe Analysis

As early as the early 1940s, L. Hjelmslev, representative of the Danish school of structuralism, put forward the idea of sememe analysis. In the 1950s, American anthropologists, F. G. Lounsbury and W. H. Goodenough, also advocated sememe analysis when they studied senses of kinship words. In the early 1960s, American linguists J. J. Katz and J. A. Fodor proposed interpretive semantics, which introduced sememe analysis into linguistics to provide semantic features for generative transformation grammar.

Sememes are the basic elements of senses, the distinguishing features of rational senses of words. The rational senses of a word are the sum of its semantic features. For example, the rational senses of "elder brother" (哥哥/ge ge/) in Chinese are the sum of sememes such as [+person] [+relative] [+kinship] [+elder brother] [+male]; the rational senses of "younger brother" (弟弟/di di/) in Chinese are the sum of such sememes as [+person] [+relative] [+kinship] [−elder brother] [+male]; the rational senses of "elder sister" (姐姐/jie jie/) in Chinese are the sum of such sememes as [+person] [+relative] [+kinship] [+elder brother] [−male]; and the rational senses of "younger sister" (妹妹/mei mei/) are the sum of the sememes of [+person] [+relative] [+kinship] [−elder] [−male]. The sign "+" means positive, and the sign "−" means negative. The sememe [−older] means [+young], and the sememe [−male] means [+female].

The sememe "elder brother" [+elder brother] is in comparison with the sememe [−elder brother], while the sememe "elder brother" [+male] is in comparison to sememe [−male]. The English kinship word "brother" has no comparison of age. The word "brother" can be used to express both "elder brother" and "younger brother" in Chinese. Therefore, English does not have the sememes [+elder] and [−elder]. As there is no contrast between men and women in Zhuang language, there are no such sememes as [+male] and [−male] in the language.

The sememes of a group of words can be represented by a sememe matrix. The ordinate represents the word, and the abscissa represents the sememe. The intersection of the vertical and horizontal coordinates is marked either with "+" or "−." For example, the sememe matrix of kinship words in Chinese is as follows (Fig. 7.1).

In modern Chinese dictionaries, the definitions of the abovementioned kinship words are as follows:

	[person]	[relative]	[kinship]	[elder]	[male]
elder brother	+	+	+	+	+
younger brother	+	+	+	−	+
elder sister	+	+	+	+	−
younger sister	+	+	+	−	−

Fig. 7.1 Sememe matrix of kinship words

Elder brother: a man older than himself with the same parents (or only the same father or mother)
Younger brother: a man younger than himself with the same parents (or only the same father or mother)
Elder sister: a woman older than herself with the same parents (or only the same father or mother)
Younger sister: a woman younger than herself with the same parents (or only the same father or mother)

If we compare the sememe matrix of the above kinship words with their definitions in the modern Chinese dictionary, we can see that the sememe matrix reflects the basic semantic features of the corresponding kinship words and that they are equivalent to the definitions in the dictionary.

Therefore, sememe analysis is a good method for formal semantic description.

In a sememe matrix, signs "+" and "−" are generally marked with binary opposition, but sometimes, other marking methods may also be used when binary opposition fails. For example, E. A. Nida, an American linguist, listed the following sememe matrix when he analyzed the semantics of the seven verbs representing human body movements in English, such as "run" and "walk" (Fig. 7.2).

In this sememe matrix, the sememe [one limb always touching the ground] has binary opposites, which are represented by "+" and "−"; as the sememe [order of limbs touching the ground] has no binary opposition, the numbers "1-2-1-2" are used, indicating the rotation of lower limbs (to move one's left foot first and then the right one or to move one's right foot first and then the left one). The numbers "1-1-1/2-2-2" mean that the lower limbs do not rotate, the numbers "1-1-2-2" mean that the left foot and right foot rotate every two times, and the numbers "1-3-2-4" represent the rotation of the upper and lower limbs. As the sememe [number of limbs touching the ground] does not have binary opposition, either number is used to represent the number of limbs in contact with the ground.

Sememe analysis has made considerable achievements in the analysis of kinship words and military rank words, whose application is still expanding. However, to date, there has been no application of sememe analysis to analyze the whole vocabulary system of a language.

	One limb always touching the ground	Order of limbs touching the ground	Number of limbs touching the ground
run	–	1—2—1—2	2
walk	+	1—2—1—2	2
hop	–	1—1—1/2—2—2	1
skip	–	1—1—2—2	2
jump	–		2
dance	+	various and rhythmic	2
crawl	+	1—3—2—4	4

Fig. 7.2 Sememe matrix of limb activity

In computer processing of the natural language, the construction of a machine dictionary is a very important task. A machine dictionary, also known as an electronic dictionary, is a dictionary that can be accessed by computer at will on disk, on CD, or on EPROM (erasable programmable read-only memory), which stores a variety of information needed for NLP, including phonetic, grammatical, and semantic information. Semantic information in machine dictionaries is usually specified by directly storing the rational senses of each word, enumerating and explaining the corresponding concepts of each word as ordinary dictionaries do. However, such a method not only takes up a large amount of storage space but also makes it difficult either to distinguish rational senses among synonyms or near-synonyms or to determine the collocation relations between words.

If sememe analysis is used to build a machine dictionary, these problems can be solved.

First, a smaller number of sememes can be used to formalize a large number of senses that are inexhaustibly enumerated in a machine dictionary, since lexical entries are no longer stored in terms of their senses but in terms of sememes. Of course, sememes are also quite numerous, as they represent the vast, diverse world. So far, we don't know how many sememes there are in modern Chinese (it might take some time to solve this problem). For practical purposes, in NLP systems, we can build sememe systems in different fields and, for different purposes, decompose sememes from concepts according to relevant requirements or adopt a goal-driven approach to tentatively build the sememe system. When establishing a sememe system, we should follow the principles of clarity, connectedness, completeness, interpretability, comprehensibility, and economy.

Second, by analyzing and comparing the sememes in different sememe sets in machine dictionaries, the computer can easily determine the subtle differences in senses of different words.

For example, by means of sememe analysis, the sememe expressions of the three Chinese words "army (陆军/lu jun/)," "navy (海军/hai jun/)," and "air force (空军/kong jun/)" are as follows:

Army: [army]{[on land] [combat]} f{[usually composed of] [infantry] [artillery] [armored force] [engineering force] [railroad force] each [professional force]}
Navy: [army] {[at sea] [combat]} f{[usually composed of] [surface ships] [submarines] [naval aviation] [Marine Corps] each [professional units]}
Air force: [army]{[in the air] [combat]} f{[usually composed of] each [aviation force] [ground force of the air force]}

In the above sememe expressions, sememes are written in square brackets, and sememes of the same type or sememes matching one another are written in the same curly braces. The letter "f" is the structure symbol, meaning "scope of application." The word "each" is not a sememe but a sign, which means that the marked sememe can be decomposed into several similar sememes.

From the above sememe expressions, we can clearly see that the three words *army*, *navy*, and *air force* share sememes such as [army] [combat]. The differences are as follows:

- Their combat areas are different. The sememe of the army is [on land], the sememe of the navy is [at sea], and the sememe of the air force is [in the air].
- Their compositions are different. The sememes of the army are {[usually composed of] [infantry] [artillery] [armored force] [engineering force] [railroad force] each [professional force]}, the sememes of the navy are {[usually composed of] [surface ships] [submarines] [naval aviation] [Marine Corps] each [professional force]}, and the sememes of the air force are {[usually composed of] each [aviation force] [ground force of the air force]}.

For another example, the sememe expressions of the two Chinese words *hand* (手/shou/) and *foot* (脚/jiao/) are as follows:

Hand: [organ] [human body] {[located in...]} [+upper limb] of [end]} [able to use tools]
Foot: [organ] [human body] {[located in...] [−upper limb] of [end]} [able to move]

Among them, "of" between the sememes is a sign of possession.

From their sememe expressions, we can see that the two words *hand* and *foot* share sememes such as [organ] and [human body]. The differences are as follows:

- Their positions are different. The sememes of "hand" are {[located in...] [+upper limb] of [end]}, whereas the sememes of "foot" are {[located in...] [−upper limb] of [end]}.
- Their functions are different. The function of the "hand" is [able to use tools], and the function of the "foot" is [able to move].

For another example, the sememe expressions of the four Chinese words "炒," "熘," "炸," and "煎" (/chao, liu, zha, jian/) are as follows:

炒 (/chao/; stir-fry): [−water][−large amount of oil][+keep stirring][−add starch syrup]

熘 (/liu/; quick-fry): [−water][−large amount of oil][+ keep stirring][+add starch syrup]

炸 (/zha/; deep-fry): [− water] [+large amount of oil] [−keep stirring]

煎 (/jian/; fry): [− water] [−large amount of oil] [−keep stirring]

From their sememe expressions, we can see that the four Chinese words "炒"(/chao/; stir-fry), "熘"(/liu/; quick-fry), "炸"(/zha/; deep-fry), and "煎"(/jian/; fry) share the same sememe [−water], that is, no water is used in cooking. The difference is that the amount of oil used is small [−large amount of oil] for the three words "炒"(/chao/; stir-fry), "熘"(/liu/; quick-fry), and "煎"(/jian/; fry), while for the word "炸"(/zha/; deep-fry), the amount of oil used is large [+large amount of oil]. These two words "炒"(/chao/; stir-fry) and "熘"(/liu/; quick-fry) share the same sememe [+keep stirring], whereas the sememe of these two words "炸"(/zha/; deep-fry) and "煎"(/jian/; fry) is [−keep stirring]. The sememe of the word "炒"(/chao/; stir-fry) is [−add starch syrup], and the sememe of the word "熘"(/liu/; quick-fry) is [+add starch syrup].

Since the sememe expression is a formalized representation of the senses of a word, it is easy for the computer to determine the similarities and differences in the senses of words and find their subtle differences.

Third, through sememe analysis, the computer can learn what kind of semantic restrictions should be imposed on the collocation of words.

For example, in the sememe expressions of the words *speak* and *think*, the actor of the action is required to bear the sememe of [+person], while the sememe expressions of the words *chair* and *fish* do not contain the sememe of [+person]. Therefore, in general, sentences such as "The chair is thinking" or "The fish is talking" are not semantically valid, although they are grammatically correct. This will help the computer judge whether the sentence is semantically reasonable.

Of course, under certain conditions, such as in fairy tales, the words *chair* and *fish*, which do not contain the sememe of [+person], can also be used with the words *talk* and *think*. At this time, sentences such as "The chair is thinking" and "The fish is talking" can be semantically valid. However, it is only in fairy tales that words such as *chair* and *fish* temporarily acquire the sememe of [+human] for specific purposes. However, this is not allowed under normal circumstances. Sometimes, to achieve the rhetorical effect, we can compare animals to humans. When we say "The Yellow River is roaring," the nonanimal "Yellow River" temporarily obtains the sememe of [+animal]. When we say that "The weasel pays a new year's visit to the chicken," the animal "weasel" temporarily obtains the sememe of [+human]. This is called a metaphor. But under normal circumstances, we can't speak in that way. The fact that metaphors exist is not enough to deny the fact that words must have certain semantic restrictions in combination. Therefore, effective semantic restrictions of words in combination are still necessary.

However, we should not take metaphors lightly. Metaphors are a common phenomenon in the natural language and have always been an important part of rhetorical research. For example, the sentence "The wheel of history rolls on" means that the trajectory of history rolls on like a wheel. It's a metaphor. In this metaphor, the concept of a "wheel" is used to compare the concept of a "historical development trajectory." We are familiar with the concept of the word *wheel*, which is a concrete and intuitive concept that is easy to understand, while the concept of the phrase "historical development trajectory" is an abstract concept that is not easy to understand. Through the metaphor of "wheel," we gain a clearer and more vivid understanding of the abstract and less easily understood concept of the "trajectory of historical development."

In rhetoric, metaphor is a kind of "figure of speech." A complete metaphor is generally composed of "vehicle" and "ontology." Vehicles are usually conceptual categories that we are familiar with, the ones that are concrete, intuitive, and easy to understand. On the other hand, ontology is the conceptual category that we only know later, the one that is abstract and not easy to understand. In our example above, "wheel" is the vehicle, and "trajectory of historical development" is "ontology."

In cognitive linguistics, vehicles are called the source domain, and ontologies are called the target domain. In the example above, the word *wheel* is the source domain, and the phrase "trajectory of historical development" is the target domain. The cognitive power of metaphor lies in mapping the schema structure of the source domain onto the target domain so that people can obtain a clearer understanding of the target domain through the schema structure of the source domain. Therefore, cognitive linguistics holds that metaphor is not only a rhetorical device but also a way of thinking of human beings.

Metaphor exists even in terminology known for its rigor.

Terminology is the crystallization of human scientific knowledge in the natural language, and it is an important product of human cognitive activities. Therefore, there should be metaphors in terminology, an important way of naming that helps people understand the target domain more clearly through the source domain.

To illustrate the role of metaphors in naming, we use terminology in computer science as examples.

The term "fire wall" in computer science is metaphorically named. Its source domain refers to the wall used to prevent fire in the building; its target domain refers to a kind of security facility between the Internet and the user's equipment. Through identification and screening, the fire wall can prevent unauthorized or potentially destructive external access, although there is no such real or concrete "fire wall" in computer science. Through the source domain of a "fire wall," people can understand the abstract concept of "a kind of security facility between the Internet and the user's equipment" more clearly.

In computer science, there is another terminology called "virus," whose source domain refers to pathogens smaller than bacteria with genetic and mutation characteristics that have no cellular structure. Generally, they can pass through filters that block bacteria and can only be seen by an electron microscope. Its target domain is a harmful and destructive program. Through the source domain of "virus," people can realize that once a "virus" program is run on the computer that will be infected with a virus, like a living being, bringing disaster to the user.

The terminology "tree" in computer science is also metaphorically named. Its source domain refers to the generic term for woody plants. Its target domain is a nonlinear structure that represents the branching relationship between nodes in computer algorithms. Through the source domain of the "tree," people can imagine this abstract nonlinear structure as a tree in nature to obtain a clearer understanding of this concept.

In computer science, there are many other metaphorically named terms, such as "slot, network, desktop, recycle bin."

In the *Introduction to Modern Terminology*,[1] Zhiwei Feng pointed out that the naming of terms should follow principles such as accuracy, monosemy, systematicness, correctness, conciseness, motivation, stability, and productivity. Does the use of metaphors to name terms contradict these principles? Personally, I don't think it is contradictory. Because metaphor is an important way of thinking for human beings, this way of thinking should, of course, be used in the naming of terms. Using metaphors to name terms is consistent with these principles and it can also better implement them.

A few years ago, when we were discussing the term "menu" in computer science, some scholars suggested that the term "menu" in computer science does not include "dish," which is inconsistent with the fact. Therefore, they strongly opposed the use of the term "menu" and advocated the use of "selection list." Later, academia vigorously promoted the term "selection list" and opposed the use of "menu." However, among most computer users, the term "menu" is still widely used, while the term "selection list" is difficult to popularize. The source domain of the term "menu" is a list of vegetables, fish, etc., cooked for rice or wine. Its target domain is a table with several optional items. The menu displayed on the computer screen can be selected by the user with a cursor, just as easily as someone ordering a meal. The term "menu," named metaphorically, is accurate, clear, and vivid, which conforms to the term-naming principles. Therefore, it is popular among the majority of users and has not been replaced by the term "selection list," promoted vigorously by academia.

This shows that we can name terms metaphorically in the term naming. As metaphor is an important way of thinking for human beings, it cannot be avoided in naming terms.[2]

Since metaphors cannot be ignored in term naming, of course, metaphors cannot be ignored in NLP. Currently, we have made some achievements in NLP of metaphors.

---

[1] Zhiwei Feng. *Introduction to Modern Terminology*. The Commercial Press, 2011.

[2] Zhiwei Feng. Metaphors in Term Naming. *Research on Scientific and Technological Terminology*, 2006, (3):19-20.

7.2 Semantic Field

To analyze sememes of a given language, it is first required to establish a semantic field for the lexical system of the language.

The term "semantic field" was proposed by a German scholar called G. Ipsen in 1924. In the early 1930s, J. Trier, another German scholar, proposed the theory of the systematic semantic field. He cooperated with L. Weisgerber, a student of his, in his research in the 1930s. After World War II, J. Trier continued to study the theory of the semantic field. However, the influence of semantic field theory was very limited in the 1930s and 1940s. It was not until the 1950s when Chomsky put forward transformational generative grammar and when American anthropologists put forward sememe analysis methods that the theory of the semantic field started to attract widespread attention.

Ipsen graduated from the University of Leipzig in 1922 with a doctorate in psychology. His teacher, F. Krügers, is the heir to the professorship of the famous psychologist Wundt at the University of Leipzig, the founder of Leipzig School of Gestalt psychology. Krügers pointed out that there is Gestalt in consciousness, which can be further distinguished on the basis of Gestalt perception. In 1924, under the influence of Gestalt theory, Ipsen pointed out that "words cannot appear alone in a language but should be arranged according to their senses, forming a word group.... According to the characteristics of the entire word group, it is organized into semantic field, like a mosaic with an interconnected structure in *Der alte Orient und die Indogermanen*."[3] The term "Bedeutungsfeld" (semantic field in English) was first proposed.

In 1927, Weisgerber argued that a word does not exist in people's consciousness in isolation in *Die Bedeutungslehre – ein Irrweg der Sprachwissenschaft?*. Instead, it is usually composed of one or some interrelated sets with some structure(s) together with other words with similar concepts.[4] To express this set of words, Weisgerber uses the term "Wortfeld" (word field in English).

In 1931, Trier integrated Ipsen's "semantic field" and Weisgerber's "word field" into a complete theoretical system in *German Vocabulary in the Intelligent Semantic Domain: The History of the Language Field (Der Deutsche Wortschatz im Sinnbezirk des Verstandes: Die Geschichte eines sprachlichen Feldes)*. He pointed out that "every word is between its related concepts. These words form a self-contained structure together with the word that summarizes them".[5] Trier classifies

---

[3] G. Ipsen. *Der alte Orient und die Indogermanen*, J. Friedrich & J. Hofmann et al. (eds.) Stand und Aufgabe der Sprachwissenschaft – Festschrift für Wilhelm Streitberg, Heidelberg: Winter, p225, 1924.

[4] L. Weisgerber. Die Bedeutungslehre – ein Irrweg der Sprachwissenschaft? *Germanisch-Romanische Monatsschaft*, 1927 (15), p161-168.

[5] J. Trier. Der Deutsche Wortschatz im Sinnbezirk des Verstandes: Die Geschichte eines sprachlichen Feldes, Bd I, Von den Anfangen bis zum Beginn des 13 Jahrhunderts. Heidelberg: Winter, 1931, p31.

semantic fields and word fields as the language field (Das Sprachliche Feld). In 1934, he defined the word "field" in *Das Sprachliche Feld: Eine Auseinandersetzung* as follows: "Field is the language reality that exists between individual words and the overall vocabulary. As a localized overall field, some fields combine with other words to form a common feature with a larger structure, while others are divided into smaller common features with other words".[6] These common features enable individual words to interact with the entire field. In this way, individual words can be combined into larger structures or divided into smaller language units.

In recent years, Chinese scholars have also begun to study the semantic field of Chinese. Professor Yande Jia from Peking University systematically proposed the semantic field theory of Chinese in the book *Chinese Semantics* published in 1992. On the basis of previous studies, Professor Pu Zhang at the Institute of Language Information Processing of Beijing Language and Culture University proposed the concept of the field type in light of the practice of natural language computer processing, which further deepened the study of the Chinese semantic field.

The word *field was* originally a physical term, such as electric field, magnetic field, gravitational field, etc. The physical field, an interaction field, is one of the basic forms of matter that takes up a certain amount of space and has spatiality. Later, it was further extended to mean that a space area distributed with a certain physical quantity or a mathematical function that does not necessarily have the form of material existence. The concept of the field is further blurred but still has spatial property.

Semantic field, the system of sense formation, is based on the relation field of concepts, which is a completely fictitious and immaterial space field formed by senses. The spatial nature of the semantic field is reflected in the distribution of sememes constituting the senses. A sense always interacts with other senses in the semantic field. Generally, a number of closely related senses, usually under a generic name, constitute the semantic field.

The semantic field can be further divided into lexical fields and associative fields. The lexical field is static, which shows a paradigmatic relationship between senses; the associative field is dynamic, which shows a syntagmatic relationship between senses. The semantic field we deal with in this section is mainly lexical. For the sake of convenience, we refer to the lexical field as a semantic field when it does not hinder readers' understanding. We will further explain the associative field in the semantic networks.

Lexical field is a static semantic field in which the relationship between senses is a kind of clustering relationship. The following is a list of the various semantic fields based on senses:

Bird field: eagle, starling, peacock, seagull...
Animal field: elephant, deer, horse, cow, sheep, tiger, ant...
Human field: senior, man, worker, youngster, soldier...

---

[6]J. Trier. Das sprachliche Feld: Eine Auseinandersetzung, Neue Jahrbücher für Wissenschaft und Jugendbildung, 1934 (10), p132.

Cooking field: boil, braise, stew, stir-fry, fry, quick-fry, deep-fry...
Kinship field: father, elder brother, uncle, grandpa, sister-in-law...
Color field: red, orange, yellow, green, blue...
Physical state field: solid, liquid, gas, colloid...
Abstract field: thought, plan, will, character...

These semantic fields can be further subdivided. For example, kinship field can be further subdivided according to the relationship, direct line, collateral line, paternal line, etc., to form smaller semantic fields. Semantic fields formed after subdivision are called subfields, and those that cannot be further subdivided are called small subfields. These semantic fields can also be further generalized and merged. For example, animal field and plant field can be further generalized as biological field, and semantic field formed after generalization is called mother field.

Different types of semantic fields are called field types. Major field types in Chinese are as follows:

7.2.1   Taxonomic Field Type

In the taxonomic field, each sense in the same semantic field refers to things in the same category, to the same kind of movement, or to something with the same traits. Taxonomic field type is generally of multilevel. For example, the semantic field of printing is of taxonomic field type (Fig. 7.3).

In the semantic field, the sense of the upper level is called superordinate, and the sense of the lower level is called subordinate. The superordinates next to each other are called direct superordinates, and the subordinates next to each other are called direct subordinates. The sense of the lowest level no longer contains other senses and is called the base level, while the superordinate at the uppermost level has no upper level and becomes the top level. The sense of the same level is called co-level. Several variants of the same sense are called coordinate senses. For example, [wife],

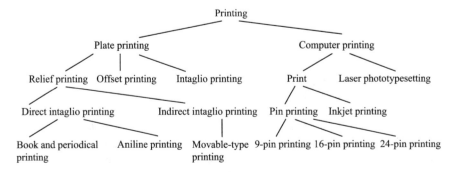

Fig. 7.3 Taxonomic field type

[madam] and [better half] are coordinate senses, where [wife] is the main sense, and [madam] and [better half] are variant senses.

Semantic relationship of the taxonomic field type has the following characteristics:

First, there is a possessive relationship between the superordinate and the subordinate. The superordinate represents the domain of the semantic field, whereas the subordinate represents the classification in the field. The sense at the middle level is both the classification of its superordinate and the domain of its subordinate. For example, in Fig. 7.3, "printing" at the top level is the superordinate, meaning that the domain of this semantic field is "printing." A small classification of printing, "24-pin printing," is the subordinate, the base level of the superordinate "printing." "Plate printing" at the middle level is both the classification of its superordinate and the domain of its subordinate. Therefore, "relief printing," "offset printing," and "intaglio printing" all belong to "plate printing."

Second, the subordinate can inherit the basic sememes of its superordinate. For example, "9-pin printing," "16-pin printing," and "24-pin printing" all inherit the basic sememes of the superordinate "printing." "Print" and "laser phototypesetting" are both subordinates of "computer printing," which inherits the basic sememes of their common superordinate "computer printing," while "computer printing" and "plate printing" are different forms of printing, which also inherit the basic sememes of their common superordinate "printing." In the taxonomic field type, the higher the superordinate, the fewer its common sememes; the lower the subordinate, the more common sememes inherited. The higher the superordinate, the larger the field it contains; the lower the subordinate, the smaller the field it contains. The base level no longer constitutes a new semantic field, which is the smallest subfield. The superordinate at the top level is called the largest mother field.

7.2.2 Component Field Type

The component field type is also a basic field type. In the component field, senses of each word in the same semantic field do not refer to things in the same category or to the same kind of movements or something with the same traits. Any subordinate is a component of its superordinate. The component field is also hierarchical. For example, the following semantic field representing the structure of "car" is of the component field type (Fig. 7.4).

The semantic relationship of the component field type has the following characteristics:

First, the relationship between the superordinate and the subordinate is that of whole and part. The superordinate represents the whole, and the subordinate represents the components of the whole. For example, the superordinate "car" means the whole, whereas the subordinate "gearbox" means a component of the whole. The

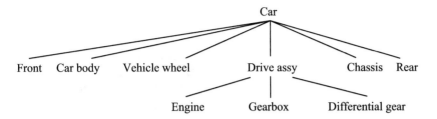

Fig. 7.4 Component field type

sense at the middle level is both the component of its superordinate and the whole of the subordinates. For example, "drive assy" at the middle level is both a component of the superordinate "car" and the superordinate of the subordinates, "engine," "gearbox," and "differential gear."

Second, in the component field type, it is not the subordinate that carries the sememes of its superordinate. Instead, it is the superordinate that extracts some sememes from its subordinate to be integrated. For example, the superordinate "building" is composed of "door" and "window." The component "door" has functional sememes such as [access] and [locking], and the component "window" has sememes such as [lighting] and [ventilation]. Therefore, "building" can extract the sememes [access] [locking] [lighting] [ventilation] from its subordinates "doors" and "windows" to be integrated into its own sememes. Of course, not all sememes representing functions can be transferred from the subordinate to the superordinate. For example, in "building," there is a component of "light bulb," whose function sememe [luminescence] cannot be transferred to the superordinate "building." It is only a function sememe of the superordinate "building." It can be seen that the overall functions can be extracted from the functions of components, but it is not equal to the sum of the functions of its components.

7.2.3   Ordered Field Type

The taxonomic field type and the component field type are basic field types, whereas the ordered field type is not. The ordered field is a special field type based on the taxonomic field type and the component field type. All levels in an ordered field are in order. In addition to the transferring relationship between the superordinate and its subordinates in taxonomic field or component field types, there is also an orderly relationship among senses at the co-level. This order can be expressed in terms of time, space, quantity, degree, scope, or rank. For example, the subordinates of "military ranks," such as "Second Lieutenant, Lieutenant, Captain, Senior Captain, Lieutenant Commander, Lieutenant Colonel, Colonel, Major General, Lieutenant

General, General, Senior General, Marshal, and Grand Marshal," have a strict hierarchical order.

The characteristics of semantic relations in the ordered field type are as follows:

First, senses at the same level are arranged in an orderly sequence, reflecting the orderliness of the objective world. For example, seasonal names "spring, summer, autumn, winter" that reflect the chronological order are ordered, with "spring" being before "summer" and "autumn" being after "summer."

Second, some senses in an orderly sequence are closed, and such closed ones can be recycled. For example, "spring, summer, autumn, and winter" in the four seasons of the year are cyclical and endless. There is neither a beginning nor an end.

Some senses in an orderly sequence are nonclosed, and nonclosed senses cannot be recycled. For example, senses that express academic degrees, such as "bachelor's degree, master's degree, and doctor's degree," are nonclosed. Such senses cannot be recycled as there is no end to learning.

7.2.4   Opposition Field Type

The opposition field type is not a basic field type but a special field type in which there is an antagonistic relationship between the senses at the co-level, such as "hard" or "soft," "on" or "off," "attack" or "retreat," "birth" or "death," and "male" or "female." The opposition can be manifested in terms of nature, state, movement direction, movement result, location, time, and so on. For example, the senses "hard" and "soft" are opposites in matter state, the senses "attack" and "retreat" are opposites in the movement direction, and the senses "life" and "death" are the beginning or end of life, the opposition of the time in which life and death are located.

The characteristics of the opposition field type are as follows:

First, for some senses at the co-level in the opposition field type, there is an either-or relationship without an intermediate state. This opposition is called opposite opposition. For example, the senses "on" or "off" are either "on" or "off" without the intermediate state. The senses "birth" or "death" are either "birth" or "death" with no intermediate state, respectively.

Second, there are cases where more than two senses at the co-level occur in the opposition field type. The two opposites are at the poles of the co-level string, between which there is an intermediate state. This kind of opposition is called polar opposition. For example, the senses "attach" or "retreat," there is a state of "stop" that neither attacks nor retreats.

7.2.5 Synonymous Field Type

The synonymous field type is a special field type in which the rational senses of the coordinative sense and variant sense are exactly the same. Only the semantic sememes attached to their rational senses are different in terms of style, color, etc., such as "calculating machine" and "electronic computer," "hesitate" and "hold hack," "wife," "madam," and "better half," and so on.

Strictly speaking, the synonymous field type only involves the relationship between coordinative senses and variant senses. It cannot yet become an independent field type.

The abovementioned different field types constitute the total semantic field, in which the relationship among these field types mainly has the following types.

Nested Relations
The sub-taxonomic field is nested under the generic taxonomic field type, and the subcomponent field is nested under the generic component field type. For example, in the taxonomic field, "biological field," there are sub-taxonomic fields, such as "animal field" or "plant field." Similarly, in animal fields, there are subfields, such as "bird," "beast," "insect," or "fish." For another example, in the component field "human being," there are subcomponent fields, such as "head," "neck," "torso," and "limbs." Similarly, in the subcomponent field "limbs," there are subfields, such as "upper limbs" and "lower limbs." Again, nested in the subcomponent field, "upper limb," are subfields such as "hand" and "arm."

A nested relationship reflects the relation between the same field types.

Cross Relationship
In some taxonomic field types or component field types, senses at the co-level are either ordered or opposite. For example, in the taxonomic field, the subordinates of "military rank," such as "Second Lieutenant," "Lieutenant," and "Captain," are of the ordered field type. The subordinates of "hand," such as "finger," "palm," and "the back of the hand," are of the ordered field type.

Cross relation reflects the relationship between different field types.

Transitive Relationship
A transitive relationship means that senses in one field are transferred to senses in another. For example, in a component field, the senses of "person," as a whole, is composed of such components as head, neck, torso, limbs, internal organs, etc. In a taxonomic field, the subordinates of "people" are "men, women, whites, blacks, old people, middle-aged people, young people, juveniles"; "Chinese, Americans, Germans, etc."; "soldiers, workers, businessmen, etc."; etc. If transitive relationship

between the words "person" in the component field and "people" in the taxonomic field is established, all kinds of "people" in the taxonomic field can have the component senses of "person" in the component field, if all component senses of "person" are transferred to the various senses of "people" in the taxonomic type.

Obviously, the transitive relationship is the relationship between different field types.

Associative Relationship

Associative relations occur between different field types or between different subfields of the same field type. For example, the senses "navy, sea, warship, and naval port" can produce associative relationships among "soldiers, natural environment, weapons, and military facilities." Associative relations can be used in the semantic analysis of sentences, revealing the relationship between senses of words in a sentence to help computers understand the meaning of the sentence.

The semantic field formed by associative relationships is called the associative field type, which reflects dynamic combination relationships among word senses. Combination relationships can be described by a semantic network. Since the content of semantics is the content of concepts, concepts are directly used to express the senses of words in the semantic network.

7.3 Semantic Network

The semantic network was proposed by American psychologist M. R. Quillian in 1968 when he was studying human associative memory. In 1972, American artificial intelligence experts R. F. Simmons and J. Slocum first used semantic networks in the NLU system. In 1977, American artificial intelligence scholar G. Hendrix proposed the idea of block semantic networks, combining logical representations of semantics with case grammar and decomposing complex problems into several simple subproblems. Each subproblem is represented by a semantic network, which can make various complex inferences in NLU. This has greatly advanced the research on NLU.

A semantic network can be represented by a directed graph. And it is formed by connecting some triplets (node 1, arc, node 2) represented by a directed graph.

Nodes represent concepts, and marked arcs are directional. In the triplet, the arc points from node 1 to node 2, where node 1 is primary and node 2 is secondary. The direction of the arc reflects the priority, and the mark on the arc represents the attribute of node 1 or the relationship between node 1 and node 2 (Fig. 7.5).

A triplet in a semantic network can be shown as follows:

In this way, a semantic network composed of several triplets can be expressed in Fig. 7.6.

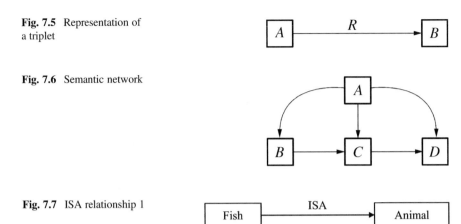

Fig. 7.5 Representation of a triplet

Fig. 7.6 Semantic network

Fig. 7.7 ISA relationship 1

From the perspective of logical representation, a triplet in a semantic network is equivalent to a binary predicate. Therefore, the triplet

(node 1, arc, node 2)

can be written as a binary predicate

P (Individual 1, Individual 2)

where Individual 1 corresponds to node 1, Individual 2 corresponds to node 2, and the arc and its mark indicating the relationship between node 1 and node 2 are embodied by the predicate P.

Therefore, a semantic network composed of several triplets is equivalent to a set of binary predicates.

We can regard semantic networks as units of knowledge. The memory of the human brain is realized by storing a large number of semantic networks.

In AI, relationships among concepts in semantic networks are mainly represented by predicates such as ISA, PART-OF, and IS.

The predicate ISA represents a "concrete-abstract" relationship, where the concrete concept belongs to a given abstract concept. Therefore, ISA is a kind of subordination relationship that is embodied in a certain level of classification. The nodes of the concrete level can inherit the attributes of the nodes at the abstract level.

For example, the proposition that "Fish is an animal" can be expressed in Fig. 7.7.

As animals have the attributes of "moving," "eating," and "breathing," fish also have such attributes. In addition, "fish" have special attributes such as "breathing with gills," "living in water," and "having fins," but some animals do not have those attributes. The fact that "fish" is a node at the concrete level whereas "animal" is a node at the abstract level shows that the nodes of the concrete level can inherit the

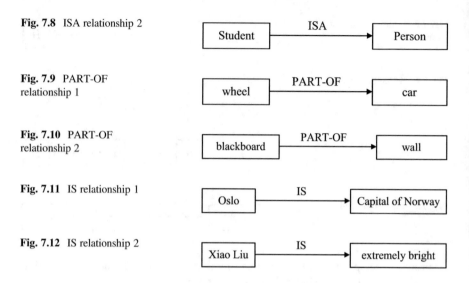

Fig. 7.8 ISA relationship 2

Fig. 7.9 PART-OF relationship 1

Fig. 7.10 PART-OF relationship 2

Fig. 7.11 IS relationship 1

Fig. 7.12 IS relationship 2

attributes of the nodes at the abstract level, but not the otherwise. This is the "attribute inheritance rule" in the ISA relationship.

For another example, the proposition "The student is a person." can be expressed as follows (Fig. 7.8).

A person has attributes such as "ability to make tools," "ability to use tools," "ability to work," and "higher animals." Therefore, students also bear such attributes. In addition, students have the attribute "studying at school," while other persons may not have such an attribute. Obviously, this proposition also follows the "attribute inheritance rule" in the ISA relationship.

The predicate PART-OF represents the "whole-part" relationship, in which the part is contained in the whole. Therefore, PART-OF is also an inclusive relationship. In the PART-OF relationship, the attributes of the lower nodes cannot be inherited from one another. The "attribute inheritance rules" in the ISA relationship cannot be established in the PART-OF relationship.

For example, the proposition "The wheel is part of a car" can be expressed as Fig. 7.9 where "wheel" does not necessarily carry certain attributes of "car."

For another example, the proposition "There is a blackboard on the wall" can be expressed as Fig. 7.10.

Here, the attributes of the blackboard and the wall have almost nothing in common.

The predicate IS is used to indicate that a node is an attribute of another node.

For example, the proposition "Oslo is the capital of Norway" can be expressed in Fig. 7.11.

For another example, the proposition "Xiao Liu is extremely bright" can be expressed in Fig. 7.12.

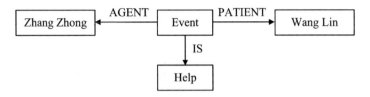

Fig. 7.13 Semantic network of events 1

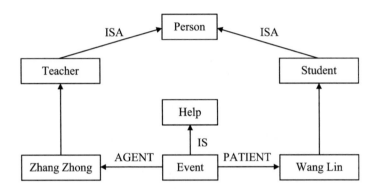

Fig. 7.14 Semantic network of events 2

The relationship between nodes is diverse. The three most common relationships are ISA, PART-OF, and IS. For computer processing of the natural language, these three relationships are far from sufficient.

As mentioned above, a semantic network is composed of a set of binary predicates, which may represent an event. An event is an objective reality reflected by a combination of several concepts. Events can be divided into three types: narrative, descriptive, and expressive events. When a semantic network is used to express events, the relationship between nodes in the semantic network can also include AGENT, PATIENT, LOCATION, TIME, and so on.

For example, the event "Zhang Zhong helped Wang Lin" can be expressed in Fig. 7.13.

If Zhang Zhong is a teacher and Wang Lin is a student, then the semantic network can be expressed in Fig. 7.14.

The reasoning mechanism for the semantic network system is generally based on network matching. According to the questions raised, a partial network can be formed, where the variables represent the objects to be sought. The process of query answering is to query the matching operation from the local network to the network knowledge base. If the match is successful, the replacement value of the output variable is "Yes," and if the match is not successful, "No" is the output.

For example, if the event "Zhang Zhong helped Wang Lin" is stored in the semantic network knowledge base, the purpose of the query is to determine "whom did Zhang Zhong help." According to the network in Fig. 7.14, the matching is successful, and the result of the match is obtained. The replacement value is "Wang Lin," that is, "Whom = Wang Lin."

When the theories and methods of semantic networks are applied to the automatic processing of Chinese, it is necessary to conduct an in-depth research on the predicate in binary predicates in light of the characteristics of the Chinese language, fully revealing the semantic relations in Chinese.

With the development of the Web and the overall implementation of projects such as linking open data,[7] the idea of semantic Web has been adopted on the Web, and the semantic Web has been established. As the semantic Web uses ontology to express the relationship between concepts, semantic information annotation of documents is actually based on ontology. At present, the number of semantic Web data sources has surged, and a large amount of resource description framework (RDF) data has been released. The Web is changing from the document Web, which contains only Web pages and hyperlinks between Web pages to the data Web containing a large number of entities and rich relationships between entities. In this context, search engine companies such as Google, Baidu, and Sogou have built a "knowledge graph" based on it to improve search quality, thus kicking off the prelude to semantic search.

According to incomplete statistics, Google Knowledge Graph contains 500 million entities and 3.5 billion facts so far (represented in the form of "entity-attribute-value" and "entity-relation-entity"). As Google Knowledge Graph is globally oriented, it contains multilingual descriptions of entities and related facts, mainly in English. Baidu and Sogou also launched knowledge graphs for Chinese search. Knowledge in their knowledge bases is mainly described in Chinese, but the scale is slightly smaller than that of Google Knowledge Graph.

To improve the quality of the Web search, knowledge graphs must not only contain high-quality commonsense knowledge but also be able to discover and add new knowledge in a timely manner. At present, the knowledge graph covers the most commonsense knowledge by collecting structured data from encyclopedia websites and various vertical websites. The quality of these data is high, but the update is slow. On the other hand, the knowledge graph also enriches the description of entities by extracting AVP (attribute-value pairs) of related entities from various semistructured data (such as HTML tables). In addition, discovering new entities or new entity attributes through the Web query log can also continuously expand the coverage of the knowledge graph. Moreover, the knowledge graph can also obtain knowledge data through data mining methods. Compared with high-quality commonsense knowledge, more knowledge data can be extracted through data mining, which can better reflect current users' query demands and discover the latest entities or facts in a timely manner. However, the quality of these knowledge data is relatively poor, in addition to containing some errors. To settle such issues, we can use the redundancy of the Internet to evaluate the credibility of these knowledge data

---

[7] http://linkeddata.org/

through voting or other aggregation algorithms in the subsequent mining and add them to the knowledge graph through manual verification.

The knowledge data obtained by using the above method are only the candidate entities (concepts) and their attribute associations obtained from various types of data sources to construct knowledge graphs, which form isolated extraction graphs. To build a true knowledge graph, we also need to integrate those isolated information.

Therefore, we cannot build a knowledge graph just on the data level. We need to further build a knowledge graph on the schema level. Schema, the refinement of knowledge, follows a predetermined pattern to build a knowledge graph, which is helpful to the standardization of knowledge and which is more conducive to subsequent processing such as queries.

Building a knowledge graph schema is equivalent to building an ontology for it. The most basic knowledge ontology includes concepts, concept levels, attributes, attribute value types, relations, relation domain concept sets, and relation range concept sets. In addition, additional rules or axioms can be added to represent more complex constraints at the schema levels.

The construction of a most basic ontology is very challenging when faced with such a large-scale and domain-independent knowledge base. The method commonly used by companies, such as Google, is a combination of both top-down and bottom-up approaches.

Here, the top-down approach refers to the preconstruction of ontology through an ontology editor. The construction of ontology should use schema information extracted from high-quality knowledge obtained from encyclopedias and structured data. The Google Knowledge Graph schema is modified on the basis of the Freebase schema it acquired. The Freebase schema defines domain, type, and topic. Each domain has several types, each of which contains multiple topics and is associated with multiple properties. These properties specify the attributes and relationships that the topics in the current type need to include. Such a defined schema can be used to extract new entities (or entity pairs) belonging to a certain type or satisfying a certain property.

The bottom-up approach uses various techniques, especially through search logs and Web tables to extract the identified categories, attributes and relationships, and then merges these high-confidence schemas into the knowledge graph. Schemas that do not match the categories, attributes, and relationships in the original knowledge graph can be added as new schemas to the knowledge graph and then manually filtered.

In the construction of the knowledge graph, the top-down method is conducive to extracting new examples, ensuring the quality of the extraction, while the bottom-up method is conducive to discovering new schemas. The two methods are complementary. For more details about the knowledge graph, you can refer to Chap. 12 of this handbook.

7.4   Montague's Semantics

Montague's semantics is a new language theory that uses intensional logic to describe the semantic content of sentences. Around 1970, American mathematical logician R. Montague (1932–1971), together with others, applied intensional logic to the study of the natural language and concentrated the studies in the two fields of generative grammar and intensional logic into Montague's semantics, creating a new way of studying the natural language with formal methods of modern logic.

Montague points out that, theoretically, there is no difference between a natural language and a highly formalized artificial language (logical language). The syntax and semantics of these two languages can be described within the same theoretical system. Of course, if a theory is to formally describe the natural language with rich and colorful meanings, it must first have a high degree of mathematical accuracy. Therefore, Montague believes research on the natural language is a branch of mathematics rather than a branch of psychology as Chomsky does.

The theory of Montague's semantics embodies the basic idea of Frege's principle, which proposes that the overall meaning of a sentence is a function of the meaning of its parts and the way in which they are combined. Montague extends the "meaning" of Frege's principle to "structure," further proposing that the overall structure of a sentence is a function of the structure of its constituents and the way in which they are combined. Therefore, in Montague's semantics, the syntactic form, intensional logical expression, and semantic referent of a sentence all start from the basic unit and are determined through syntactic rules, translation rules, and semantic rules in an ascending manner. Syntax, translation, and semantics, the three major parts, are homomorphism. In Montague's semantics, if there is a syntactic rule, there must be a translation rule to translate the phrase it deals with into an intensional logical expression, and then a semantic rule determines the semantics of this intensional logical expression. The ambiguity is resolved through different combinations and the use of different syntax and semantic rules. This is the "rule-to-rule hypothesis," a hypothesis of Montague's semantics.

Montague's semantics first separates the meaning of words or phrases from their carriers. Meanings are called meaningful expressions (abbreviated as ME), and their carriers are called basic expressions (abbreviated as B). MEs are given, and their specific referents depend on specific models. Bs are also given, and their forms vary from one language to another.

Montague's semantics is mainly composed of three parts: syntax, translation, and semantics.

Syntax includes a set of categories and a set of syntactic rules. Its function is to form sentences from words in the lexicon. The categories define a syntactic category for Bs. The function of syntactic rules is to turn Bs into phrases and then to synthesize smaller phrases into larger ones. In relation to the categories of Bs or phrases at the input end, it specifies the category of the phrase at the output end and the syntactic order of the phrases at the output end. This set of rules can be used again, gradually combining phrases until a sentence is generated, the whole process of which is represented by a tree structure. From syntactic point of view, every member of the lexicon has a B, which does not include meaning but which is just a form of expression. Each B has a category determined by its syntactic characteristics. According to syntactic rules, each B is a phrase that, with other phrases, can form a larger phrase, the largest of which is a sentence. The linear arrangement of Bs in a phrase and their collocation are determined by syntactic rules.

The category in Montague's semantics is not a collection of nouns, verbs, and adjectives but a set of basic e and t categories and the relationship between them. Basic categories are e and t, while the others are derived categories. Category e represents individual expressions or entity expressions in certain types of things in the natural world, which is different from nouns or noun phrases in traditional grammar. No corresponding units can be found in Chinese or English. For example, "chair" does not belong to category e because "chair" is just a concept that can refer to the set of all the chairs in the world. Only the word that represents a specific chair in the set belongs to the e category. The t category represents a language unit with a truth value called a truth value expression or a declarative sentence. The other categories are derived from the basic categories e and t. Montague's semantics stipulates that if A and B are category markers, then A/B and A//B are all category markers. Here, A and B are variables. If we set A = t and B = e, then t/e and t//e are all category markers; if we set A = t/e and B = e, then t/e/e and t/e//e are all category markers. As such a definition is recursive and repeated, Montague's semantics can determine infinite category markers. Since syntax and semantics in Montague's semantics are homomorphic, the syntactic category corresponds to the semantic category in the semantics. Semantic categories can be identified in the model through semantic rules, so categories can be connected with objective things. Using this recursive method to define categories actually lays the foundation for determining the connection between categories and objective things.

In Montague's semantics, translation includes a set of translation rules to translate phrases into intensional logical expressions. The translation process strictly follows the process of sentence generation. Every syntactic rule has a corresponding translation rule.

Semantics is based on intensional logic, the essence of Montague's semantics. The intensional logic of Montague's semantics includes two aspects, syntax and semantics. The syntactic aspect of semantics consists of a set of semantic systems and syntactic rules. The semantic category is obtained from the category of the expression by the corresponding function. Syntactic rules stipulate the semantic category after the various phrases are combined. The semantic category of a complete intensional logical expression can be calculated using this set of rules. The syntactic aspect of semantics mainly deals with the combination of intensional logical structure constituents. If the referent set of one constituent is not in the referent set of another, then they cannot be combined. The semantic aspect mainly handles the issue of semantic referent with a set of semantic rules. Using this set of semantic rules, the semantic referent of the intensional logical expression in a specific model can be obtained.

The semantic theory of Montague's semantics based on intensional logic has the following three characteristics:

1. It describes the truth condition of a sentence and determines under what conditions the meaning of a sentence is true or false. Therefore, Montague's semantics is a kind of truth-conditional semantics.
2. Semantic referents derived from semantic rules are relative to specific models, and semantic values of sentences or phrases are variable in different models. Therefore, Montague's semantics is model-theoretic semantics.
3. What it refers to can include things that do not exist in the real world. Truth value is closely related to time and space. To judge whether a sentence is true or not, it must refer to the specific time and place where the speech act occurs. With time and space parameters, Montague's semantics can express things that do not exist in the real world (such as "dragon, kylin, unicorn") in the model (they only have connotations without extensions). Therefore, Montague's semantics is a possible-world semantics.

The ambiguity of the readings between de re (about things) and de dicto (about what is said) has been discussed in philosophy. Montague's grammar provides a unique explanation for this. The reading of de re refers to the existence of a certain individual and that individual has certain characteristics, which is a kind of matter-based reading, whereas de dicto reading refers to a conceptual individual and that individual has certain characteristics, which is a kind of "speech-based" reading. For example, the English sentence "John seeks a unicorn" can be read in two different ways, depending on the syntactic rules. The de re reading presupposes that there is a unicorn, and John is trying to find it, while the de dicto reading is an inaccurate reading. John is not looking for a specific unicorn; he is just looking for an imaginary animal like a unicorn. This latter reading of the word "seeks" can refer to looking for things that do not exist in the real world.

The mathematical description of Montague's semantics is more formal. Here, we only introduce its basic ideas by way of examples without ideas that are too formalized.

Montague's semantics has two sources. One is N. Chomsky's generative transformation grammar, and the other is intensional logic proposed by Louis. Combining these two research results, Montague uses intensional logic to describe the deep structure of a sentence. At each level of the sentence, a corresponding intensional logical expression can be obtained, which can be used to express the logical expression of the deep structure of the sentence.

For example,

$$\text{the man walks} \tag{7.1a}$$

According to generative transformation grammar, the deep structure of this sentence can be represented by the following tree diagram (7.1b) (Fig. 7.15).

$$\text{the} \to \lambda P \lambda Q \{\exists x(P(x) \wedge Q(x)) \wedge \quad \forall x \quad \forall y \, ((P(x) \wedge P(y)) \to x = y)\} \tag{7.1b}$$

Fig. 7.15 Tree diagram
(7.1b)

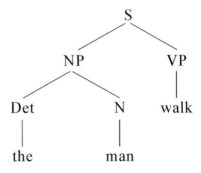

Fig. 7.16 Tree diagram
(7.2b)

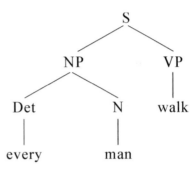

It can be seen from the tree diagram that the sentence S can be rewritten as the noun phrase NP and the verb phrase VP, and the noun phrase NP can be rewritten as the determiner Det and the noun N. According to word insertion rules, the lexical string "the man walk" is obtained. To obtain the surface structure of the sentence, it is necessary to make a morphological change, converting "walk" into "walks." Finally, the sentence "The man walks" is obtained.

For another example,

$$\text{every man walks} \qquad\qquad (7.2\text{a})$$

The deep structure of this sentence can be represented by the tree diagram (7.2b) (Fig. 7.16).

$$\text{every} \rightarrow \lambda P \lambda Q \quad \forall x\, (P(x) \rightarrow Q(x)) \qquad\qquad (7.2\text{b})$$

It can be seen from the tree diagrams that the deep structures of the sentence (Eq. 7.2a) and the sentence (Eq. 7.1a) are exactly the same. The difference between them lies in the descendants of Det with one being "the" and the other being "every." This difference cannot be explained only from Chomsky's generative transformation grammar.

To explain this difference, Montague uses the intensional logical method to translate the deep structure of the sentence. This kind of translation is carried out in the tree diagram in a top-down manner, translating the items on the relevant nodes in the tree diagram into corresponding intensional logical expressions.

First, translation starts from the lexical item at the end of the tree diagram (7.1b):

the $\rightarrow$ $\lambda P \lambda Q\{\exists x(P(x) \wedge Q(x)) \wedge \forall x \; \forall y((P(x) \wedge P(y)) \rightarrow x = y)\}$
man $\rightarrow$ man
walk $\rightarrow$ walk

Now, we will explain the above translation expressions.

First, we explain the symbols $\lambda P \lambda Q$.

The expression $\lambda x \; x + 1$ represents a function of adding 1. For example,

$$(\lambda x \; x + 1) \, 2 = 2 + 1 = 3$$

The expression $\lambda x \; x > 0$ represents a function of >0. For example,

$(\lambda x \; x > 0) \, 3 = 3 > 0$ is a true proposition;
$(\lambda x \; x > 0) - 2 = -2 > 0$ is a false proposition.

Generally speaking,

The expression $(\lambda x...x...) \, a = ...a...$ is a set satisfying the property of ...x...

In addition, $\lambda x \; x + 1 = \lambda y \; y + 1$ means that the function $\lambda x \; x + 1$ plus 1 can also be written as $\lambda y \; y + 1$.

The symbol after λ is a variable, which can be written as x, y, or other symbols.

$\lambda P \lambda Q$ in the translation expression of the definite article "the" represents the two properties of P and Q. $\exists \, x(P(x) \wedge Q(x))$ indicates that there is a certain x, which satisfies both property P and property Q. $\forall x \; \forall y(P(x) \wedge P(y))$ means that for any x and any y, both x and y have the property of P at the same time. "$\rightarrow$" is the sign of implication, which means "if..., then...." The expression $(x = y)$ means x and y are equal. The translation expression of the definite article "the" shows that property P is unique. If x has properties P and Q, and if y and x have properties P at the same time, then x and y are equal. This translation expression properly explains the meaning of the definite article "the."

The item "man" is translated into "man." The one on the left is the "man" in English, and the one on the right is the constant "man" in intensional logic.

The translation of the item "walk" is the same as that of "man."

Starting from $(\lambda x...x...) \, a$, we obtain the property of ...a..., which is called "λ-conversion." The above expression $(\lambda x \; x + 1) \, 2 = 2 + 1 = 3$ is the λ-conversion.

λ-conversion is the key to the translation calculation of Montague's semantics.

Next, starting from the intensional logical expression of "the," we continue to translate other items in the tree diagram (7.1b) by using λ-conversion. From "the" and "man" in an upward direction, we obtain the qualifier DET and noun N, respectively. Then, if we continue to proceed in an upward direction, we can obtain the noun phrase NP composed of "the" and "man." To obtain the intensional logical expression of NP, we substitute "man" into the logical expression of "the." We get

$$[\lambda P \lambda Q\{\exists x(P(X) \wedge Q(x)) \wedge \quad \forall x \quad \forall y((P(x) \wedge P(y)) \rightarrow x = y)\}] \qquad (7.3)$$

By means of λ-conversion, the property P is replaced by "man." We get the following expression:

$$\lambda Q\{\exists x(man(x) \wedge Q(x)) \wedge \quad \forall x \quad \forall y((man(x) \wedge man(y)) \rightarrow x = y)\}_{man} \quad (7.4)$$

The item "walk" goes up to NP. NP is combined with VP to form the sentence S. We get

$$[\lambda Q\{\exists x(man(x) \wedge Q(x) \wedge \quad \forall x \quad \forall y((man(x) \wedge man(y)) \rightarrow x = y)\}]_{walk} \quad (7.5)$$

By means of λ conversion, property Q is replaced by a "walk". We get

$$\exists x((man(x) \wedge walk(x)) \wedge \quad \forall x \quad \forall y((man(x) \wedge man(y)) \rightarrow x = y \quad (7.6)$$

Equation (7.6) is the intensional logical expression of sentence S, which explains the intensional logic of the sentence "the man walks."
The explanation is as follows:

There is a certain x. If x has the properties of both "man" and "walk," and if x has the property of "man" for any x and any y, then x = y.

For the tree diagram (1.2b), we have

every → λPλQ ∀x(P(x) → Q(x))
man → man
walk → walk

If "man" is put into the intensional logical expression of "every," there is

$$[\lambda P \lambda Q \quad \forall x(P(x) \rightarrow Q(x))]man \quad (7.7)$$

By means of λ-conversion, the property P is replaced by "man." We get

$$\lambda Q \quad \forall x(man(x) \rightarrow Q(x)) \quad (7.8)$$

If "walk" is put into Eq. (7.8), there is

$$[\lambda Q \quad \forall x(man(x) \rightarrow Q(x))]_{walk} \quad (7.9)$$

By means of λ-conversion, property Q is replaced by "walk." We get

$$\forall x(man(x) \rightarrow walk(x)) \quad (7.10)$$

(7.10) is the intensional logical expression of sentence S, which explains the intensional logic of the sentence "every man walks."
The explanation is as follows:

For any x, if it has the property of "man," then it has the property of "walk."

It can be seen that two different sentences with the same tree diagram obtained by Chomsky's generative transformation grammar can be transformed into different intensional logical expressions by means of λ-conversion of Montague semantics. Therefore, the interpretation of natural language phenomena with Montague's semantics is more profound than that with Chomsky's generative transformation grammar, as the intensional logical expression of Montague's semantics is a deeper structure, a kind of logical deep structure, than that of generative transformation grammar.

Montague also incorporates the meaning of the natural language into intensional logic by means of truth-conditional semantics, model-theoretic semantics, and possible-world semantics, establishing the semantic theory of Montague's semantics.

As Montague's semantics combines syntax and semantics, any tree diagram that expresses the syntactic structure of a sentence obtained through syntactic analysis can be interpreted as a corresponding intensional logical expression with Montague's semantics to represent its semantic content. Therefore, in some current MT systems, Montague's semantics is used to semantically associate the source language with the target language for MT between two languages.

The advantages of MT using Montague's semantics are as follows:

First, in Montague's semantics, the conversion of sentences to intensional logical expressions and interpretations of these expressions are all the results of mechanical processes, which are carried out under various tough constraints. Therefore, it is easy to be implemented by computer. For example, the English sentence,

$$\text{no student has a textbook} \tag{7.11}$$

Its corresponding intensional logical expression is

$$\forall x[\text{student}(x) \rightarrow \sim \exists y[\text{have}(x, y) \land \text{textbook}(y)] \tag{7.12}$$

The meaning of this intensional logical expression is as follows:

For any x, if x is a college student, then there is no such y, so x has y, and y is a textbook.

The following steps must be taken to obtain such an intensional logical expression.

Step 1: Syntactic analysis

According to dictionary items and syntax generation rules, the input sentence is analyzed to obtain a tree diagram representing its structure. The following tree diagram (Fig. 7.17) shows the analysis result of the sentence (Eq. 7.11).

When constructing the tree diagram, the following dictionary items and syntactic rules are used.

Fig. 7.17 Tree diagram

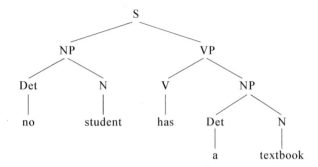

```
Dictionary items:
  Det (determiner):
  {a, no, the, ...}
  N (noun):
  {student, textbook, ...}
  V (verb):
  {has, ...}

Syntactic rules:
  R1: S → NP + VP
  R2: VP → V + NP
  R3: NP → Det + N
```

The tree diagram notation is equivalent to the following parenthesis notation.

$$R1(R3(no, student), R2(has, R3(a, textbook))) \qquad (7.13)$$

Formula (7.13) expresses the syntactic analysis result of sentence (Eq. 7.11).

Step 2: The results of the sentence analysis are interpreted as intensional logical expressions.

The transformation rules used to transform each dictionary item and syntactic rules into intensional logical expressions in the first step are called interpretation rules. Interpretation rules are used to explain each part in parentheses of formula (7.13) equivalent to the tree diagram.

The interpretation rules for dictionary items are as follows:

```
Det:
no => λPλQ[∀x[P(x) → ~Q(x)]]
a => λPλQ[∃y[P(y)∧Q(y)]]
N:
textbook => textbook
student => student
V:
has => have
```

The interpretation rules regarding syntactic rules are as follows:

$$R1(NP, VP) \Rightarrow NP'(VP')$$

$$R2(V, NP) \Rightarrow \lambda u[NP'(\lambda v[V'(u, v)])]$$

$$R3(Det, N) \Rightarrow Det'(N')$$

Among them, α' represents the interpretation result of α. For example, NP' represents the interpretation result of NP.

According to this interpretation rule, the part "no, student" in formula (7.13) can be explained as follows:

$$R3(no, student \Rightarrow no\ (student)$$

$$\Rightarrow (\lambda P \lambda Q[\forall x[P(x) \rightarrow \sim Q(x)]](student)$$

This is because at this time, there are

$$Det = no, N = student.$$

In this way, each part in formula (7.13) can be explained by using interpretation rules. It can be seen that it is entirely possible to analyze sentences in a strict mechanical way by using Montague's semantics.

Second, λ-conversion is proposed in Montague's semantics. By means of λ-conversion, the intensional logical expression of the entire sentence can be finally obtained.

Although the theory of λ-conversion is very esoteric, its operation rules are very simple. The operation method is extremely intuitive, providing great convenience for semantic interpretation of sentences.

Next, we substitute interpretation rules into formula (7.13) and try to obtain the intensional logical expression of sentence (Eq. 7.11) by means of λ-conversion.

```
R1(R3(no, student), R2(has, R3(a, textbook)))
≡ (λPλQ[∀x[P(x) → ~Q(x)]](student))
(λu[λPλQ[∃y[P(y)∧Q(y)]](textbook)
(λv[have(u, v)])])

≡λQ[∀x[student(x) → ~Q(x)]]
(λu[λQ[∃y[textbook(y)∧Q(y)]]
(λv[have(u, v)])])

≡λQ[∀x[student(x) → ~Q(x)]]
(λu[∃y[textbook(y)∧λx[have(u, v)(y)]]])

≡λQ[∀x[student(x) → ~Q(x)]]
λu[∃y[textbook(y)∧have(u, y)]]
```

$\equiv \forall x[student(x) \rightarrow \sim\lambda u[\exists y[textbook(y) \land have(u, y)]](x)]$

$\equiv \forall x[student(x) \rightarrow \sim\exists y[textbook(y) \land have(x, y)]]$

In the above explanation, the sign "$\equiv$" indicates semantic equivalence. The intensional logical expression of the sentence is very clearly derived by means of λ-conversion.

For the Chinese language, we can also start from formula (7.13) to obtain the Chinese translation expression (7.13) by using interpretation rules and λ-conversion. Here, the only difference lies in the need to formulate a set of separate word interpretation rules for Chinese.

For example, for the above English sentence (Eq. 7.11), the corresponding Chinese interpretation rules are as follows.

```
no => λPλQ[+negative(Q(任何一个(/ren he yi ge/)P也(/ye/))))]
a => λPλQ[Q(一本(/yi ben/)P)]
textbook => 教科书(/jiao ke shu/)
student => 大学生(/da xue sheng/)
have => λuv(u有(/you/)v)
```

If we copy exactly the interpretation rules of syntactic rules and substitute the above rules into formula (7.13), we can obtain

```
R1(R3(no, student),R2(has,R3(a, textbook)))
≡((λPλQ[+negative(Q(任何一个(/ren he yi ge/)P也(/ye/))))])(大学生(/da
xue sheng/)))
(λx[((λPλQ[Q(一本(/yi ben/)P)])(教科书(/jiao ke shu/)))
(λy[λuv[u有(/you/v)v](x, y)]])])
≡λQ[+negative(Q(任何一个大学生也(/ren he yi ge da xue sheng ye/))))]
(λx[λQ[Q(一本教科书(/yi ben jiao ke shu/))]
(λy[x有(/you/)y])])
≡λQ[+negative(Q(任何一个大学生也(/ren he yi ge da xue sheng ye/))))]
(λx[x有一本教科书(/you yi ben jiao ke shu/)])
≡+negative(任何一个大学生也有一本教科书(/Ren he yi ge da xue sheng ye you yi
ben jiao ke shu/))
≡任何一个大学生也没有一本教科书(/Ren he yi ge da xue sheng ye mei you yi ben
jiao ke shu/)
```

In this case, we obtain the Chinese sentence "任何一个大学生也没有一本教科书" (/Ren he yi ge da xue sheng ye mei you yi ben jiao ke shu/; No college student has a textbook).

Starting from formula (7.13), we can obtain the intensional logical expression of English by using English dictionary items, interpretation rules, and λ-conversion. Similarly, also starting from formula (7.13), we can obtain the Chinese translation of formula (7.13) by using the corresponding Chinese word interpretation rules, together with other original interpretation rules, and λ-conversion. The only difference is that the corresponding interpretation rules are formulated separately for the Chinese words. That is, for both English and Chinese, except for the rules about word items, the interpretation rules of other items are common, which leaves sufficient room for simplifying and optimizing the rules of English-Chinese MT.

By means of λ-conversion, the English input sentence (Eq. 7.11) can also be expressed as the following expression through formula (7.13).

$$no(student)[\lambda x[a(textbook)(\lambda y[have(x, y)])]] \qquad (7.14)$$

Compared with formula (7.13), formula (7.14) is more concise, through which we can obtain the intensional logical expressions of English sentences such as (7.12) by using the interpretation rules for dictionary items, and we can also obtain the corresponding Chinese translation. Therefore, we take formula (7.14) as the processing matrix and call it "English-oriented formal representation" (EFR), an intermediate language in English-Chinese MT. When translating, the input English sentence is changed into EFR, first, and then the Chinese sentence is generated by EFR.

Montague's semantics transforms the deep structure of sentences represented by tree diagrams into intensional logical expressions, thereby revealing certain semantic content of sentences. This grammatical theory is of great value to natural language information processing, logic, and even cognitive science.

Montague proposes, in his paper entitled "The Proper Treatment of Quantification in Ordinary English" (1974), the famous PTQ (the Proper Treatment of Quantification in Ordinary English) system to calculate the semantic value of sentences.

Specific steps are as follows:

Step 1 A limited fragment English is selected, from which a dictionary containing 9 derived categories (including basic categories e and t, 11 in all) and 17 syntactic rules is extracted. According to the combination principle, it starts with the vocabulary, the simplest items, and proceeds to combine them into complex ones one level after another.

The 11 categories are as follows:

Category	Definition	Basic expression
t	Basic category	None
e	Basic category	None
IV	t/e	Run, walk, talk, rise, change
T	t/IV	John, Mary, he
TV	IV/T	Find, lose, eat, love, be, seek
IAV	IV/IV	Rapidly, slowly, voluntarily
CN	t//e	Man, woman, fish, unicorn, friend
t/t		Necessarily
IAV/T		In, about
IV/t		Believe that, assert that
IV//IV		Try to, wish to

The above derived categories can be recursively defined by the basic categories e and t. For example,

$IV=t/e$

$TV=IV/T=t/e/T=t/e/(t/IV)=t/e/(t/(t/e))$

The 17 syntactic rules are represented through S1 to S17.

S1 is a rule for processing simple noun phrases, S2 is a rule for processing quantified noun phrases ("every," "the," or "a" + noun), and S3 is a rule for processing noun phrases modified by clauses. S4 is a rule for dealing with the subject-predicate collocation of the sentence; S5 is a rule for dealing with the predicate-object collocation of the sentence. S6 is a rule for processing prepositional phrases, S7 is a rule for processing verb phrases with clauses, S8 is a rule for processing verb phrases with infinitives, S9 is a rule for processing sentences modified by adverbs, and S10 is a rule for processing verb phrases modified by adverbs. S11 to S13 are rules for processing conjunctive or disjunctive phrases connected by "and" or "or", S14 to S16 are quantification rules, and S17 includes rules for processing time and notation systems.

Step 2 Each of the 17 syntactic rules of fragment English corresponds to a translation rule. A total of 17 intensional logic translation rules translate each language item in fragment English into an intensional logical expression within the intensional logic language so that each language item corresponds to an intensional logical expression. Finally, the complicated language expressions in fragment English are translated into complex intensional logical expressions.

Step 3 According to the semantic interpretation rules of intension logic, the semantic value of the intensional logical expression in the given model is calculated. This semantic value is a semantic interpretation of fragment English expression.

The intensional logic theory of Montague semantics is based on truth-conditional semantics, which requires that the meaning of sentences be described from the perspective of truth conditions and that the truth conditions of sentences be investigated in relation to the abstract mathematical model of the external world.

Seen from the standards of linguistic methodology, the formalized features of Montague's semantics are mainly manifested both as limited fragments in research and highly mathematical processing.

The description of the natural language in Montague's semantics is strictly limited to restricted fragments. In PTQ, only declarative sentences are studied, only active voice is considered, and only nine syntactic categories are listed, each of which only involves a few words. It is under such strict conditions that Montague's semantics can describe the natural language. Montague points out, "I limit my description to a very restricted scope, partly because I don't know how to deal with phenomena outside it. However, this also helps keep the system simple and helps clarify some of its characteristics. Now everyone already knows how to broadly expand and deal with this limited description from various perspectives." Montague's semantics not only accurately describes fragment English but also gradually expands this limited fragment to achieve the goal of gradually approaching the entire natural language.

The highly mathematical processing features of Montague's semantics are manifested in the extensive use of mathematical logic and set theory. In Montague's semantics, the syntactic structure generation of sentences is regarded as an algebraic operation, and the simple-to-complex process of the natural language's semantic combination is regarded as another algebraic system operation. The corresponding relationship between syntactic algebra and semantic algebra is a kind of mathematical isomorphism. In the PTQ system, from the syntactic structure of English to the translation of intensional logical formulas, recursion is used to describe it step-by-step. The syntactic category of the natural language is interpreted as the individual, truth value, and function in the intensional logic. The semantic combination of the natural language is expressed as the function operation in mathematics, and the meaning of the natural language is described as the truth conditions from the perspective of the model. In addition, Montague's semantics emphasizes the overall simplicity and coordination and pays attention to perfection and refinement of the system, which also shows the highly mathematical processing features of this grammar.

Nishita and others of Kyoto University in Japan used Montague's semantics to develop an English-Japanese MT system, which achieved some success. This system is divided into three stages: English analysis, English-Japanese transfer, and Japanese generation. In the stage of English analysis, the input English text is analyzed to obtain the English intensional logical expression. In the transfer stage, English and Japanese vocabulary conversion and some simple structural transformations are carried out to change the English intensional logical expression into a Japanese expression. In the Japanese generation stage, the Japanese phrase structure is generated from the intensional logical expression, and then after its morphological processing, the Japanese output text is obtained. The use of the intensional logical expression of Montague's semantics as an intermediate expression method reduces the difficulty of automatic language analysis and generation to a certain extent, as English and Japanese belong to two different language families with different grammatical structures.

In 1986, Zhiwei Feng implemented an English-Chinese MT model on computer based on Montague's semantics. The model could only process fragment English and limited Chinese generation. This is the first practical test of Montague's semantics by Chinese NLP scholars on computer.[8] Montague's semantics is also used in generalized phrase structure grammar to describe the semantic interpretation of sentences. This kind of grammar has broad application prospects in NLP.

7.5 Wilks' Preference Semantics

In 1874, Y. A. Wilks (Fig. 7.18) proposed the theory of preference semantics when developing the English-French MT system.

---

[8]Zhiwei Feng. The Application of Montague's Grammar in Machine Translation. *Modern Library and Information Technology*, 1987, (4): 39-42.

Fig. 7.18 Y. A. Wilks

There are five semantic units in preference semantics. In addition, there are rules for constructing sentences from smaller units to larger units.

The five semantic units are as follows:

- Semantic elements
- Semantic formulas
- Bare templates
- Templates
- Paraplates

Semantic elements composed of semantic formulas are used to describe the semantics of words. Bare templates and templates are composed of semantic formulas to describe the semantics of simple sentences. Paraplates are used to describe the semantics of larger units and sentences.

These units are further described below:

1. Semantic elements: Semantic elements defined by Wilks are 80 semantic units, which are used to represent semantic entities, states, properties, and actions. These elements can be divided into the following five groups (capital English letters denote semantic elements):

    (a) Semantic entities: MAN, STUFF, SIGN, THING, PART, FOLK, STATE, BEAST, and so on
    (b) Actions: FORCE, CAUSE, FLOW, PICK, BE (existence), and so on
    (c) Properties (type identifier): KIND(feature), HOW, and so on
    (d) Types: CONT (container), GOOD, THRU(hole), and so on
    (e) Cases: TO(direction), SOUR(source), GOAL, LOCA(location), SUBJ(subject), OBJE(object), IN(inclusion), POSS(possession), and so on.

In addition, the semantic element with an asterisk in front of it indicates category. For example, *ANI means living semantic elements, such as MAN, BEAST, and FOLK; *HUM means the semantic elements of human beings, such as MAN and FOLK; *PHYSOB means categories that include semantic elements such as MAN and THING, but it does not include the category STUFF; *DO means the category of semantic actions. The use of asterisks can simplify the writing of semantic elements.

When selecting semantic elements, the following principles should be followed:

(a) Comprehensiveness: Semantic elements should comprehensively express and distinguish the meanings of different words.
(b) Independence: No semantic element can be defined by other semantic elements.
(c) Noncircularity: No semantic elements can be defined by one another.
(d) Primitiveness: Semantic elements cannot be further decomposed in meaning; that is, any semantic element cannot be defined by a smaller semantic element.

Wilks notes that semantic elements based on these principles are almost exactly the same as the high-frequency content words in Webster's dictionary.

2. Semantic formulas: Semantic formulas are composed of semantic elements and parentheses at both ends of the formulas. Semantic elements must be arranged in a certain order in the semantic formulas, the most important semantic element of which is always arranged at the right end, which is called the semantic formula head. The head dominates other semantic elements in the semantic formula either directly or indirectly. The semantic element that can be used as the semantic formula head can also appear in the middle of the formula. For example, CAUSE can be located at the beginning of the formula "drink" because "drink" can be regarded as an action leading to certain consequences. However, in the formula "box," the element "CAUSE" can also appear in the middle of the formula because the meaning of the formula "box" is "to hit someone, the purpose of which is to cause him to feel painful."

To avoid adding new semantic elements to the semantic formula, two semantic elements can form a subformula. For example, the subformula FLOW STUFF means "liquid," and the subformula THRU PART means "hole."

Here is an example of semantic formulas.

The semantic formula "drink" is as follows:

$$\text{Drink (action)} \rightarrow ((*\text{ANI SUBJ})(((\text{FLOW STUFF})\text{OBJE})((\text{SELF IN})$$
$$((((*\text{ANI}(\text{THRU PART}))\text{TO})(\text{BE CAUSE})))))$$

The semantic element "CAUSE" on the far right end of the formula is the head. The whole semantic formula is made up of several nested subformulas, each of which is not only an explanation of the case relationship but also an explanation of the formula head. In each subformula, there is a certain dependency between the two items in parentheses, which is a further explanation of the type. For example, *ANI in the above example is a description of the agent type. There is no dependency relationship between subformulas, but the order of subformulas in the semantic formula is very important. For example, in a semantic formula, a description of the patient is considered to be the object of all the actions to the right of the formula.

Next, we decompose the semantic formula "drink" into subformulas to explain their meanings, respectively.

Subformulas	Case/ action	Value	Interpretation
(*ANI SUBJ)	SUBJ	*ANI	The preference subject is a living object.
((FLOW STUFF) OBJE)	OBJE	(FLOW STUFF)	The preference object is liquid.
(SELF IN)	IN	SELF	The container is the subject itself.
((*ANI(THRU PART))TO)	TO	*ANI(THRU (PART))	The direction of action is the hole in the human body (mouth).
(BE CAUSE)	CAUSE	BE	Actions are of the type that causes existence.

According to the semantic formula, the meaning of "drink" can be understood as follows. "Drink" is a verb, the preference subject of action is a living object (*ANI SUBJ), the preference object of action is liquid or flowing substance ((FLOW STUFF)OBJE), the action causes the liquid to exist in the living object itself (SELF IN), and the liquid enters the body through a special hole in the living object (TO indicates the directional case relationship).

Here, preference is very important. SUBJ represents the preference subject of the action, and OBJE represents the preference object of the action. However, preference cannot be regarded as a rigid rule. Normal conditions should be selected first. If normal conditions cannot be selected, abnormal conditions should be selected. In this way, we can deal with issues, such as metaphors. For example, the following sentences are all "abnormal" metaphors, but they are acceptable.

To drink gall and wormwood.
(To drink gall and wormwood → extremely hate something)
The car drinks gasoline.
(The car drinks gasoline → to fuel the car)

The semantic formula "fire at" is as follows:

Fire at (action) → ((MAN SUBJ)((*ANI OBJE)(STRIKE GOAL)

((THING INSTR)((THING MOVE)CAUSE)))))

The subformulas of the semantic formula "fire at" are explained as follows:

Subformulas	Case/action	Value	Interpretation
(MAN SUBJ)	SUBJ	MAN	The preference subject of the action is human.
(*ANI OBJE)	OBJE	*ANI	The preference object of the action is a living thing.
(STRIKE GOAL)	GOAL	STRIKE	The goal of the action is to strike at the living thing.

The semantic formula "grasp" is as follows:

$$grasp(action) \rightarrow ((*ANI\,SUBJ)((*PHYSOB\,OBJE)(((THIS\,(MAN\,PART))\,INSTR)$$
$$(TOUCH\,SENSE))))$$

The subformulas of the semantic formula "grasp" are explained as follows:

Subformulas	Case/action	Value	Interpretation
(*ANI SUBJ)	SUBJ	*ANI	The preference subject of the action has life.
(*PHYSOB OBJE)	OBJE	*PHYSOB	The preference object is the object.
((THIS (MAN PART)) INSTR)	INSTR	(THIS(MAN PART))	The tool of the action is part of the human body (hand).
(TOUCH SENSE)	SENSE	TOUCH	The action has actual contact.

Therefore, "grasp" means that the action of touching the object and the preference subject of the action is living objects, and the tool of the action is part of the human body, the hand.

Here are a few other examples of semantic formulas:

$$policemen \rightarrow ((FOLK\,SOUR)(((((NOTGOOD\,MAN)OBJE)PICK)(SUBJ\,MAN)))$$

This semantic formula can be represented by a tree diagram in Fig. 7.19.

This means that "policeman" is a person who finds out the bad guys from the folk.

$$big \rightarrow ((*PHYSOB\,POSS)(MUCH\,KIND))$$

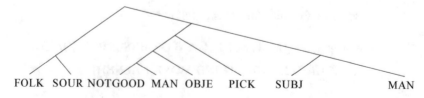

FOLK   SOUR NOTGOOD MAN OBJE   PICK   SUBJ   MAN

Fig. 7.19 Tree diagram of the semantic formula 1

Fig. 7.20 Tree diagram of
the semantic formula 2

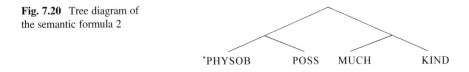

*PHYSOB   POSS   MUCH   KIND

MAN   SUBJ   MAN   OBJE   TELL   FORCE

Fig. 7.21 Tree diagram of the semantic formula 7.13

This semantic formula can be represented by a tree diagram in Fig. 7.20.

From this, we can see that the property (KIND) represented by "big" is the preference one of the objects (*PHYSOB), while the general substance (STUFF) cannot be modified by "big" (we cannot say "big substances") because the property (KIND) of "big" is (MUCH).

Interrogate $\rightarrow$ ((MAN SUBJ)((MAN OBJE)(TELL FORCE)))

This semantic formula can be represented by a tree diagram in Fig. 7.21.

From this, it can be seen that "interrogate" means forcing someone to explain something, giving priority to person-to-person action.

3. Bare templates: A sequence that can be intuitively explained is called a bare template composed of the semantic formula heads of the subject, the action, and the object, which takes the following form:

$$N_1\text{--}V\text{--}N_2$$

where N_1 is the semantic formula head of the subject. V is the semantic formula head of the action, and N_2 is either the semantic formula head of the object or the semantic element (KIND).

In essence, bare templates suggest the semantic categories of the main sentence components, such as subject, predicate, and direct object (or predicative).

For example, the bare template of the sentence "He has a compass" is as follows:

MAN—HAVE—THING

For another example, the sentence "The old salt is damp" is ambiguous, whose two templates are as follows:

One of the templates is MAN—BE—KIND, which means "The old sailor is depressed."

The other template is STUFF—BE—KIND, which means "the time-worn salt is slightly wet."

Bare templates composed of these three semantic elements can record all sentences, even those whose predicates are expressed by intransitive verbs. If the predicate is an intransitive verb, a fictitious node DTHIS can be used to replace N_2 in the bare template. DTHIS, a dummy element, does not correspond to anything in the sentence. For example, the sentence "He travels" can be expressed as the following bare template:

$$MAN—DO—DTHIS$$

4. Templates: If formula heads can form a bare template, then the sequence composed of other formulas on which these formulas may be attached is called a template of the original fragment.

   For example, the sentence "Small men sometimes father big sons" (sometimes small men are the fathers of big sons) can be expressed in the following two different formula sequences. Now, the formula heads and the words in the sentence are shown one by one.

Small	men	sometimes	father	big	sons
KIND	MAN	HOW	MAN	KIND	MAN
KIND	MAN	HOW	CAUSE	KIND	MAN

Of the two sequences, CAUSE is the formula head when the word "father" is used as a verb (meaning "to cause life").

The first sequence cannot form a bare template because its triple element sequence is not intuitively explained, while the MAN CAUSE MAN in the second sequence can be intuitively interpreted as "human causes human existence," so it is a bare template, the core part of the sentence template. It also becomes the sentence template.

It should be pointed out that the template does not only include formula heads. It is actually a network composed of the formulas, whose heads are the core parts. Some ambiguity can only be resolved after the initial establishment of the template and the extended analysis. For example, in the sentence

"The old salt drinks wine,"

the word "salt" has two meanings, "sailor" and "salt."

The first meaning of the word "salt" results in the template that follows:

MAN-INGEST-THING

The second meaning of the word "salt" can be expressed in the template that follows:

STUFF-INGEST-THING

Due to the existence of two templates, the meaning of this sentence cannot be obtained immediately, so further analysis is necessary. It can be seen from the formula "drink" that the action of the verb "drink" should take living beings as the subject. Therefore, in the first template MAN-INGEST-THING, "sailor" is the preference meaning, as the closeness of the connection between the first and second items increases, excluding the template STUFF-INGEST-THING. Accordingly, the sentence means "The old sailor drinks wine."

For another example, in

"policeman interrogated the crook,"

the word "crook" has two meanings, "rascal man" and "shepherd stick."

If the first meaning of the word is taken, the sentence template is as follows:

MAN-FORCE-MAN

If the second meaning of the word is taken, the sentence template is as follows:

MAN-FORCE-THING

From the formula "interrogate," we can learn that this action prioritizes people as the object, so the first template is selected and the second template is excluded. Accordingly, the meaning of this sentence is "the police interrogated the rascal man."

5. Paraplates: Paraplates are templates combined usually in the following two ways.

   (a) Use fictitious nodes. For example, when the verb is an intransitive object, an indirect object can be introduced according to the dummy direct object (it is obviously a fictitious node), or the adverbial can be introduced by using the deep case information in the template.

   (b) Determine the relationship between deixis and anaphora. This often requires the template to have sufficient semantic information. For example, in the following sentences,

   > "Give the bananas to the monkeys, although they are not ripe. They are hungry,"

The first "they" refers to bananas, and the second "they" refers to monkeys. This is because the semantic formula "ripe" satisfies the condition of the dominant component in the formula "bananas," while the semantic formula "hungry" satisfies the condition of the semantic formula "monkey."

For another example, in the sentence

"John took a bottle of whisky, came to the rock, and drank it," "it" refers to whisky rather than bottle or rock. This is because the action "drink" prioritizes liquid as its object. Here, whisky is liquid, and neither bottle nor rock is liquid.

Anaphora is a very difficult problem in language information processing, which can be solved relatively smoothly by using the method of preference semantics.

In addition to the various semantic units mentioned above, the rule of common-sense reasoning is also used in preference semantics. This kind of commonsense reasoning rule is generally used when more information than what is contained in semantic formulas, templates, and paraplates is needed. For example, in the sentence

"The soldiers fired at the women, and I saw several of them fall,"

it is impossible to judge by the above five semantic units whether "them" refers to soldiers or women because both soldiers and women could fall down. In this case, preference semantics can adopt the following commonsense reasoning rules:

$$(1(\text{THIS STRIKE})(*\text{ANI2})) \leftrightarrow ((*\text{ANI2})(\text{NOTUP BE})\text{DTHIS})$$

in which the subformula (NOTUP BE) means "fall down," and DTHIS is a dummy element that fills in the blank here to make it consistent with the normal form.

The meaning of this commonsense reasoning is that "If 1 hits animate 2, it is likely to fall." The "women" in the sentence are alive and are the objects of the soldiers' firing. Therefore, according to the rules of commonsense reasoning, "women" rather than "soldiers" should fall.

Wilks applies preference semantics to MT of natural languages and he uses stereotypes, as well. In his English-French MT system, the stereotypes include English entries, their semantic forms, and French entries (French nouns are also marked with their grammaticality) when English entries correspond to French entries one by one. For example,

private	(MASC simple soldat)
odd	(impair)
build	(construire)
brandy	(FEMI eau de vie)

However, in more complex dictionaries, selection rules must be added in addition to the above information. For example, the English word "advise" has two French equivalents, "concealer à" and "conseiller." To make a choice between the two, the formula head of the object in the given verb should be taken into consideration. If the formula head is MAN or FOLK, then "conseiller à" is chosen; if the formula head is STATE or STUFF, "conseiller" is chosen. Then, the stereotype is written as follows:

(ADVISE(CONSEILLER A(FN1 FOLK MAN))(CONSEILLER(FN2 ACT STATE STUFF)))

in which the two functions FN1 and FN2 are used when making selections. Their functions are to distinguish between two different translations of French. For example, in the sentence "I advise John to have patience," as the object of "advise" is (MAN), "consulter à" is chosen when it is translated to French. In the sentence "I advise patience," "conseiller" is chosen when it is translated to French because the object of "advise" is STATE. These can all be done automatically at a higher level by constructing a function of French sentences.

Such stereotypes can be used not only for words but also for phrases. For example, there are three translations of English phrase "out of" in French, "de," "par," and "en dehors de." When making selections, semantic information of the verb that dominates the phrase "out of" and characteristics of the deep case relationship between the dominating fragment and the dominated fragment should be taken into account.

The automatic language analysis process with preference semantics can be divided into the following steps:

1. Segmentation: The paragraph is used as the processing unit. The entire paragraph is divided into several fragments according to keywords, such as indicator symbols, connectives, and prepositions. For example,

I advise him/to go
I want him/to go
John likes/eating fish
The old man/in the corner/left
The key is/in the lock
He put the list/in the table
I bought the wine,/sat on a rock,/and drank it

   in which "/" represents the split point between fragments.
2. Pickup: Extracted fragments are matched with bare templates to see which bare template the corresponding fragment conforms to. When there is more than one bare template it conforms, all bare templates that match the fragment should be determined.
3. Extend: The bare template is extended into a network of templates. The template is then used as the framework to establish the relationship between words within the segmentation. If more than one bare template is obtained in PICKUP, preference should be developed according to the degree of semantic connection of each bare template when establishing the relationship.
4. Tie: The connection is established among the templates, and the templates are tied into a paraplate. At this time, the connection is established outside the segmentation, that is, between segmentations. The main tasks of Tie are as follows:

   (a) Establish deep case connections between templates.
   (b) Establish the connection between the dummy element and the word it replaces.
   (c) Resolve remaining ambiguities.
   (d) Settle the issue of pronoun anaphora.

The preference semantic analysis of the text can be realized after the abovementioned four stages: segmentation, pickup, extension, and tie.

Obviously, the most striking features of Wilks's preference semantics are as follows:

First, language analysis does not go through intermediate stages such as morphological analysis and syntactic analysis. Instead, both morphological and syntactic information are expressed through semantic information, leaving behind traditional syntactic analysis. The entire analysis is firmly rooted in semantics, making the automatic analysis of the natural language a complete semantic analysis system.

Second, the semantic description of each fragment of the text, from words to entire paragraphs, can be performed uniformly with semantic elements and parentheses.

Of course, preference semantics is not without its shortcomings. Undoubtedly, it is a well-considered means of describing semantics of the natural language. More importantly, Wilks not only put forward the idea of preference semantics but also implemented this theory in the MT system. Therefore, the value of preference semantics for language information processing cannot be ignored.

7.6   Schank's Conceptual Dependency Theory

In 1973, American computational linguist R. Schank (Fig. 7.22) proposed conceptual dependency (CD) theory, which is used to describe the meaning of phrases and sentences in the natural language.

In 1975, R. Schank developed the MARGIE system (Meaning Analysis, Response Generation and Inference of English) based on CD theory in the Artificial Intelligence Laboratory of Stanford University, providing an intuitive model of

Fig. 7.22 R. Schank

NLU. In the same year, with cooperation of Professor R. Abelson of the Department of Psychology at Yale University, he established the SAM system (Script Applier Mechanism) at Yale University in the United States. In 1978, R. Wilensky developed the PAM system (Plan Applier Mechanism). They used these systems to understand simple stories written in natural languages, showing the practical value of CD theory. They successively proposed a series of static and dynamic memory models, such as scripts, plans, goals, and MOPs (Memory Organization Packets), and further designed some well-known story understanding systems, such as FRUMP (Fast Reading Understanding and Memory Program) and IPP (Integrated Partial Parser), making the theory of CD a theory that has a significant impact on language information processing.

This section first introduces the basic principles of this theory and then describes MARGIE, SAM, PAM, FRUMP, IPP, and other systems developed on the basis of this theory.

The proposal and application of CD theory is a challenge to the traditional NLU model. This theory advocates an integrated processing model that integrates syntax, semantics, and inference, which is closer to people's understanding of the natural language. The processing efficiency is relatively high due to the comprehensive use of knowledge, including that of linguistics and that of the external world, in the initial stage of processing.

CD theory has three important principles:

First, for any two sentences with the same meaning, no matter what language the two sentences belong to, there is only one semantic expression for them.

As far back as 1949, W. Weaver, the natural science division director of the Rockefeller Foundation of the United States, proposed that when a machine translates language A into language B, it can start from language A and then convert it to language B through an interlingua, which is common to all mankind. Schank extremely admired Weaver's ideas.

Second, any information contained in a sentence necessary for understanding should be explicitly expressed in CD theory.

Such explicit expressions generally use CD expressions composed of a limited number of semantic primitives. These semantic primitives can be divided into basic actions and basic states.

Basic actions include:

PTRANS: This refers to the transfer of the physical position of an object. For example, the action "go" means that the actor himself wants to perform PTRANS, that is, PTRANS itself goes somewhere, and the action "put" means that the actor himself puts an object somewhere, that is, to PTRANS an object somewhere.

ATRANS: It refers to the transfer of abstract relationships such as possession, ownership, or control. For example, the action "give" refers to the ATRANS of possession relationship or ownership, that is, to ATRANS something to someone; the action "take" is to ATRANS something to oneself. The action "buy" is composed of two concepts that are mutually causal. One is the ATRANS of money, and the other is the ATRANS of commodities.

$$\text{John} \Leftrightarrow \text{ATRANS} \xleftarrow{\quad O \quad} \text{book} \xleftarrow{\quad R \quad} \begin{array}{l} \rightarrow \text{Mary} \\ - \text{John} \end{array}$$

Fig. 7.23 CD expression

INGEST: It refers to the fact that something is brought into the body of an animal.
The object of the INGEST is usually food, fluid, or gas. For example, actions such
as "eat, drink, smoke, breathe," etc. are all INGEST.

PROPEL: It refers to the use of physical strength on something. For example, actions
such as "push, pull, and kick" are all PROPEL.

MTRANS: It refers to the transfer of spiritual information between people or within
one person. For example, the action "tell" is the MTRANS between people; the
action "see" is the MTRANS from the eyes to the brain within the individual.
Similarly, actions such as "remember, forget, and learn" are all MTRANS.

MBUILD: It refers to the process in which new information is derived from given
information. For example, actions such as "decide, conclude, imagine, and
consider" are all MBUILD.

In 1977, Schank and Abelson listed 11 basic actions. In addition to the six actions
mentioned above, the other five are MOVE, GRASP, EXPEL, SPEAK, and
ATTEND. In addition, DO is used to represent a dummy action (an action in
general).

The conceptual relationship among these basic actions is called dependency. The
number of dependencies is also limited, and each dependency is represented with a
special arrow on the graph. For example, the CD expression of the sentence "John
gives Mary a book" is shown in Fig. 7.23.

In the expression, John, book, and Mary are called conceptual nodes. A basic
action represented by this node is ATRANS, which refers to the transfer of this
abstract relationship of the action "give." The three-way arrow marked with R
indicates the dependency of acceptance or giving among John, Mary, and book
because Mary got a book from John. The arrow marked with O indicates the
dependency of the "object," that is, the book is the target of ATRANS.

The number of basic states in CD theory is relatively large. Some of them are
listed below:

HEALTH: It represents the health status, the value of which ranges from -10 to $+10$.			
Dead (-10)	Seriously ill (-9)	Ill (-9 to -1)	Uncomfortable (-2)
Normal (0)	Good ($+7$)	Completely healthy ($+10$)	
FEAR: It represents the state of fear, the value of which ranges from -10 to 0.			
Creepy (-9)	Fear (-5)	Worry (-2)	Calm (0)
MENTAL–STATE: It represents the mental state, the value of which ranges from -10 to $+10$.			
Crazy (-9)	Frustrated (-5)	Upset (-3)	Sad (-2)
Normal (0)	Delightful ($+2$)	Happy ($+5$)	Ecstatic ($+10$)
PHYSICAL–STATE: It represents the physical state, the value of which ranges from -10 to $+10$.			
Dead (-10)	Severely injured (-9)	Slightly injured (-5)	Broken (-5)
Injured (-1 to -7)	Normal ($+10$)		

For example,

Mary HEALTH(−10)	Mary is dead.
John MENTAL−STATE(+10)	John is ecstatic.
Vase PHYSICAL−STATE(−5)	The vase is broken.

In addition, basic states also include CONSCIOUSNESS, ANGER, HUNGER, DISGUST, SURPRISE, etc.

Basic states are also used to represent the relationship between objects that cannot be measured with a numerical scale. For example, CONTROL, PART-OF, POS-SESSION, OWNERSHIP, CONTAIN, PROXIMITY, LOCATION, PHYSICAL-CONTACT, etc.

Basic actions and basic states can be combined. For example, the sentence "John told Mary that Bill was happy" can be expressed in terms of the basic action and the basic state instead of the expression with arrows above, as shown below:

John MTRANS (Bill BE MANTAL-STATE(+5)) to Mary

In the expression, MTRANS means that John transfers certain spiritual information to Mary, that is, "John tells Mary," and MENTAL-STATE (+5) means that the mental state is good, that is, "Bill is happy," which is the content of spiritual information transfer.

This sentence can also be expressed in terms of the basic action and the basic state as follows:

```
(MTRANS (ACTOR John)
  (OBJECT (MENTAL-STATE (OBJECT BILL)
  (VALUE 5)))
  (TO Mary)
  (FROM John)
  (TIME PAST))
```

Readers can easily understand the meaning of these expressions if they follow our previous explanation.

The following are examples of two sentences expressed in this way.

1. John gave Mary a book.

   (ATRANS (ACTOR John)
   (OBJECT book)
   (TO Mary)
   (FROM John)
   (TIME PAST))

2. John killed Mary.

   (HEALTH (OBJECT Mary)
   (VALUE −10)
   (CAUSE (DO (ACTOR John))))

Making inference is very important in the process of NLU. This is not only because the ambiguity of individual words or syntactic structure in a sentence needs to be resolved by making inferences but also because the information contained in the sentence is expected to be found through reasoning. Schank et al. established the following five rules for deriving causality in his CD theory:

1. An action can cause a change in the state.
2. A state can make an action possible.
3. A state can make an action impossible.
4. A state can activate a mental event, and an action can also stimulate a mental event.
5. Mental events can be the cause of an action.

The following details the application of the explicit expressions:

1. From any

   (ATRANS (ACTOR x) (OBJECT y) (TO z) (FROM w)),
   it can be deduced that
   Premise: w owns y [equivalent to POSSESSES (ACTOR w
               (OBJECT y))]
   Results: z possesses y.

   Allow z to take advantage of some functions of y.
   w no longer possesses y.

2. And from any

   (PTRANS (ACTOR x) (OBJECT y) (TO z) (FROM w)),
   it can be deduced that
   Premise: y was originally at w [equivalent to (LOCATION (OBJECT y)
               (LOC w))]
   Results: y is now at z.

   Permission: If z is the place where an object is stored, then y can now take advantage of the function of the object.
   y is no longer at w.

3. Again, according to the given state (POSSESSES (ACTOR x) (OBJECT y)), we can deduce the reasons for an action:

(ATRANS (ACTOR ?) (OBJECT y) (TO x) (FROM ?))

The reason that x POSSESSEs y is because an ACTOR gives x the ATRANS of y from itself.

Third, in the expression of the meaning of the sentence, it is necessary to show as much information as possible what is implicit in the sentence.

For example, the sentence "John eats the ice cream with a spoon" can be expressed with a more complex CD expression in Fig. 7.24.

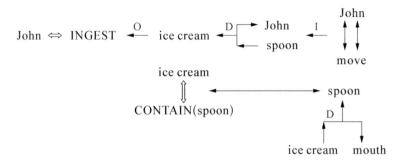

Fig. 7.24 Complex CD expression

In Fig. 7.24, the arrow marked with D represents the direction dependency, and the arrow marked with I represents the tool dependency. It is worth noting that the word "mouth" does not exist in the original sentence, but it enters the CD expression as a concept node, which is a fundamental difference between the CD network and the derivation tree generated during analysis. According to the third principle of CD theory, John's mouth exists implicitly in the meaning of the sentence as the acceptor of ice cream. Whether it is expressed in words or not, John must use his mouth when he eats ice cream, so it should be expressed in the CD expression.

Of course, such an expression can also express the meaning in a more detailed way, as the meaning hidden in the sentence is inexhaustible. For example, this sentence can also be interpreted as follows.

> John INGESTs the ice cream by TRANSing the ice cream on a spoon to his mouth, by TRANSing the spoon to the ice cream, by GRASPing the spoon, by MOVing his hand to the spoon, by MOVing his hand muscles.

Of course, there is no need to carry out such extensions endlessly under normal circumstances. In general, the expression is extended to meet our requirements.

Compared with structure-oriented systems, CD expressions have many advantages for tasks such as paraphrasing and question answering.

For example,

"Shakespeare wrote *Hamlet*."
"The author of *Hamlet* was Shakespeare."

These two sentences can be expressed in the same CD expression as they have the same meaning. Generally, CD expressions do not depend on syntax, which is quite different from the early phrase structure grammar and transformation grammar. According to Schank, CD theory has some psychological effects, reflecting the perceptual concept of people's cognitive activities.

Schank et al. have also proposed higher-level knowledge structures such as scripts, plans, goals, and themes based on these basic principles of CD theory.

Script is a standardized sequence of events used to describe people's activities (such as going to restaurants or seeing a doctor). It is a unique knowledge package that people have in a fixed sequence of events that may be activated under specific occasions. Schank and Abelson assumed that these scripts can be used to establish the context of the event when understanding the story and therefore can be used to predict the situation of the event it represents. For example, for the event of "going to a restaurant," we can create a RESTAURANT script, which includes basic activities such as entering a restaurant, finding a seat, ordering food, etc. People can make inferences based on these basic activities. For example, for the sentence "John went out to dinner," people can expect John to order food first, then eat, and finally pay the bill and walk out of the restaurant, according to the RESTAURAT script.

```
What follows is the RESTAURANT script.

Characters: customer, server, cashier
Props: restaurant, table, menu, food, check, tip, payment

Events: 1. Customer goes to restaurant
        2. Customer goes to table
        3. Server brings menu
        4. Customer orders food
        5. Server brings food
        6. Customer eats food
        7. Server brings check
        8. Customer leaves tip to server
        9. Customer gives payment to cashier
       10. Customer leaves restaurant

Key event: 1
Main concept: 6
```

Two events in the script are particularly important. One is the key event, which must be matched first before sentence analysis starts; the other is the main concept, which is the goal of the story narrated by the script. In the RESTAURANT script, the key event is "customer goes to restaurant," which is the event to be matched first; the main concept is "customer eats food," which is the goal of this script.

When analyzing a story, we should match the events in the story with the events in the script in a certain order. Because the sequence of events in the script is in line with common sense, we can intuitively understand how people understand a story when matching.

The sequence of actions that must (or may) be taken to achieve a certain goal in a given situation is another kind of more general knowledge package, which Schank and Abelson call "plan," "goal," and "theme." For example, when a person wants to use a tool, he must first know where the tool is stored, then approach it, and hold it in his hand. Having completed these steps, he can use the tool. In the knowledge structure of the "plan," goal USE is divided into three subgoals, namely, D-KNOW, D-PROXIMITY, and D-CONTROL, and the possible actions taken to realize these subgoals are also included.

"Plan" is the means that the characters in the story take to achieve their goals. If the story is understood through a "plan," it is necessary to determine the goals of the characters and the actions taken to reach their goals. For example,

John wanted to go to a movie. He walked to bus stop.

John's direct goal is "go to a movie," D-goal (read as "delta goal"), which is the embodiment of a more general goal. For example, the D-goal of "go to a movie" can be the concretization of a more general goal "going to somewhere." The more general goal "going to somewhere" does not necessarily mean "going to a movie," but it may also be "going to a restaurant," "going to school," or "going to work." This general goal is "plan."

"Plan" may also include means to achieve a general goal. For example, to realize the plan of "going to somewhere," such means as "riding a horse," "riding a bicycle," "riding a motorcycle," "driving a car by oneself," or "walking" can be taken to reach this goal.

These plans are put together to form a "plan box," in which information about various goals and various means is stored.

When understanding a story, as long as you calculate the interaction between the plot and the information stored in the plan box, you can understand the goal of a story. In this way, when there is difficulty in matching one story to another with the script, the "plan box" can provide information about the general goal, which will be unlikely to cause failure in understanding the story.

The process of using "plan" to understand the story is first to determine the goal of the character, then to determine the D-goal that leads to the main goal, and then to match the action of the character with the plan box that stores the D-goal to obtain some understanding of the story.

"Theme" is the background information on which our foresight is built. In this background information, there must be a certain goal of the character. For example, if there is a LOVE theme, which is about John and Mary falling in love, such a theme must include the goal of protecting each other from harm.

A theme should enumerate a series of characters and explain the situation of these characters and the actions taken to address the situation contained in the theme. The goal of the theme is to complete these actions.

Schank and Abelson proposed seven types of goals, the important ones of which are the following:

1. A-goals (Achievement goals): For example, good health means having an A-goal in terms of health.
2. P-goals (Preservation goals): For example, to protect someone is to have a P-goal in terms of health or mental state.
3. C-goals (Crisis goals): This is a special P-goal for which some action must be taken immediately.

The LOVE theme can be expressed with several such goals. Here, we use the symbols suggested by Schank and Abelson to write out this theme.

Let X be the lover, Y be the loved one, and Z be the other person.

Situations	Actions
Z cause Y harm or C-Health(Y)	A-Health (Y) and possible cause Z harm
not-LOVE (X, Y)	A-Love (Y,X)
X and Y did not love each other yet	X has an A-goal to Y in terms of love
General goals	A-Respect (Y)
	X has an A-goal to Y in term of respect
	A-Marry (Y)
	X has an A-goal to Y in term of marriage
	A-Approval (Y)
	X has an A-goal to Y in term of approval

The process of understanding a story with the knowledge structures of "plan," "goal," and "theme" is roughly as follows:

1. Use knowledge structure such as "plan" and "theme" to identify the goal of the story.
2. Use "plan" to find the subgoals to reach the goal and take corresponding actions.
3. Look for the above subgoals and actions in the successive input of the story and explain the story accordingly.

The Sam and PAM systems use this kind of knowledge structure to understand the story. Such systems interpret the story through the above process and answer questions about the goal and action of the characters.

The relationships among "script," "plan," "goal," and "theme" are as follows:

1. Theme leads to goal.
2. When the goal is recognized, a plan can be initiated if the actions are consistent with the realization of the goal.
3. Script is a standardized mode of events.
4. Script is special, and plan is general.
5. Script is the source of plan.
6. Plan is one of the ways to express people's goals, which are implied in scripts and which only represent actions.
7. If there is a key event in script, the key event needs to match the input sentence pattern. However, if there is no key event in plan, each plan falls under one purpose.

Using higher-level knowledge structure such as "script," "plan," "goal," and "theme," Schank and others have successively developed the MARGIE, SAM, PAM, MOPs, FRUMP, and IPP systems.

Now, we will introduce these systems one by one.

The MARGIE system written with LISP1.6 is divided into three parts.

The first part is the concept analysis program designed by Ch. Riesbeck. Its task is to convert English sentences into CD expressions. First, some surface structures of the sentence should be obtained. If they are found, the corresponding actions will be implemented, which mainly include three aspects of information: (1) what to look for in the input, (2) what to do with the input just found, and (3) how to convert the input surface structures into CD expressions. This concept analysis program is very flexible. It does not rely much on syntax when working and has high execution efficiency.

The second part is the inference program designed by Ch. Rieger. It receives a sentence that has been converted into a CD expression, makes inferences in terms of the relevant information stored in the memory of the system, and deduces a large number of facts from the sentence. CD theory believes that understanding a sentence involves much more information than what is expressed in the superficial string of the sentence. There are 16 types of references in the program, including cause, effect, explanation, function, etc. The knowledge needed for making inferences is represented in the form of semantic networks in the memory.

The following is an example of the inference process:

From the sentence "John hit Mary," the following sentences can be deduced by inference rules.

John was angry with Mary.
Mary might hit John back.
Mary might get hurt.

For any given input sentence, a large number of sentences may be deduced using inference procedures. To avoid excessive and endless deduction, restrictions have been imposed on the inference program.

The third part is the text generation program designed by N. Goldman. This program can convert internal CD expressions into output English sentences.

The text generation uses the following two methods.

1. Discriminative network: It is used to distinguish different word meanings. This method can select the appropriate word according to the English context to make it suitable for the requirements of the output text. It is particularly good for the selection of verbs, so the meaning of the output verb is very appropriate, which improves the quality of the output.
2. Augmented Transition Network (ATN): This network can transform CD expressions into linear word symbol sequences, thereby outputting the surface linear structure of sentences.

The MARGIE system operates in two modes, the inference mode and the paraphrase mode. The inference mode is to receive a sentence and reason it out, explaining a sentence in as many ways as possible. For example, for a given input sentence,

John killed Mary by choking her.

The following sentences can be obtained by way of the paraphrase mode:

John strangled Mary.
John choked Mary, and she died because she was unable to breathe.

Because the MARGIE system uses CD expressions to express the meaning of sentences, the surface structure of the sentence disappears immediately after the sentence is processed, and further work is done by completely using CD symbols. Moreover, all sentences with the same meaning can be represented by a standard CD expression, making sentence paraphrasing and question answering easier.

The SAM and PAM systems use scripts and plans to understand simple stories written in the natural language. Both systems use CD theory to analyze the story written in English as the internal expression of the story, that is, the CD expression of each English sentence in the story. Both systems can paraphrase the stories and use these paraphrases for intelligent reasoning.

The difference between the SAM system and the PAM system lies in different processing procedures after they establish CD expressions.

The SAM system uses the method of matching the story with the script to understand the story. After the matching is completed, the SAM system can summarize the story.

The matching within the SAM system is completed by three different modules, PARSER (the analysis module), MEMTOK (the storage module), and APPLY (the script module).

PARSER generates corresponding CD expressions for each sentence. However, it cannot make much inference. For example, when the input sentence is

The hot dog was burned. It tasted awful,

PARSER cannot recognize that "it" refers to hot dog.

Such tasks are completed by MEMTOK, which can make inferences about the characters, places, and events in the story. During the inference process, relevant information is added. In this way, MEMTOK can recognize that "it" in the latter part of the sentence refers to the hot dog in the previous part of the sentence.

APPLY has three functions.

The first function is to remove the sentence from the analysis module PARSER and to check whether it matches the current script, whether it matches other scripts that affect it, or whether it matches any other scripts in the database. If the matching is successful, it executes the second function.

The second function is to predict the events that may occur after the sentence is successfully matched and estimate what other events will happen.

The third function is to further specify certain steps in the current script involved in the story.

When the entire story is rewritten into CD expressions using the above method, the SAM system generates a summary of the story and answers questions related to it. The system can summarize the stories in English, Russian, German, Spanish, and Chinese.

The following is an example of understanding the story with the SAM system. Enter the original text:

John went to a restaurant. He sat down. He got mad. He left.

The paraphrase results are:

John was hungry. He decided to go to a restaurant. He went to one. He sat down in a chair. A waiter did not go to the table. John became upset. He decided he was going to leave the restaurant. He left it.

If we compare the paraphrase made by the SAM system with the original input text, we can see that the paraphrase interprets some of the obscure connections beyond the sentences in the original text. It is worth noting that the SAM system is able to infer that John left the restaurant because he wasn't being served properly, which is inferred from the RESTAURANT script, because in this script, event 3 is "server brings menu." In other words, according to the script, when John, the main character, sits down, the waiter should come to the table to serve. It cannot be seen in the input text that the waiter has come to the table to serve. Therefore, the SAM system infers from the script that reflects people's common sense that when the waiter does not come to serve, John will be angry; that is, because there is no event 3, John is angry. The SAM system uses its inference function to determine the reason why John is angry.

The PAM system based on the concept of a "plan" is another story understanding system designed by Wilensky in 1978. Its method is to determine the goal of the tasks in the story and to interpret the subsequent actions to achieve the goal and D-goal of these actions.

Specifically, the process of understanding a story with the PAM system is as follows:

1. Determine the goal.
2. Determine the D-goal that helps to reach the goal.
3. Analyze the input that has been expressed as CD expressions stored in the "plan box." Match the D-goal with the CD expression in the "plan box," and use relevant themes for reference to understand the content of the story.

For example, the input is the following sentences:

John wanted to rescue Mary from the dragoon.
John loves Mary.
Mary was stolen away by a dragoon.

Assuming that the dragoon stole Mary to hurt her, then character X will have an A-goal in terms of health and may harm character Z, if character Z wants to harm character Y, and if character Y is the lover of the main character X, according to the LOVE theme. In this way, the PAM system can infer that John rescues Mary to protect Mary's safety. In the input sentence, this goal is not explicitly stated.

The determination of the character's goal in the PAM system is as follows:

1. Point out what has been explicitly stated in the sentences of the story.
2. Define these as D-goals.
3. Make reference to determine the goal of the character according to the theme mentioned in the story.

From the designer's perspective of the PAM system, to understand a story is to determine the goals of each character in the story and to interpret the actions of these characters as a means to achieve these goals. The PAM system first accepts written English sentences and then converts them into CD expressions. It explains each sentence with the goals, predicts the D-goals and the actions taken to achieve these goals, or uses the action itself to explain the sentence so that the D-goal becomes the task to be realized. At the end of the process, the PAM system summarizes the story and answers questions about the characters' goals and actions.

Schank and Abelson pointed out that people use both of the means, "script" and "plan," when understanding stories. In addition to such packages, another type of knowledge is needed. That is abstract knowledge.

Taking the knowledge structure of scripts as an example, there may be very similar scenarios in different scripts, but the knowledge for a specific environment cannot be applied to another similar environment because each belongs to its own scripts. For example, in the two scripts of "going to the internal medicine outpatient department" and "going to the dental outpatient department," there will be similar scenarios, such as registration, waiting for a doctor, paying fees, and filling the prescription. However, such common knowledge stored in two different scripts cannot be shared by the two scripts. Obviously, this kind of knowledge storage method is a huge waste of computer memory space.

If one type of knowledge that can be shared by a variety of different environments is called abstract knowledge, then psychological experiments and people's intuition both show that there is another type of knowledge structure in the process of understanding stories, which can simultaneously accommodate the abovementioned packages and abstract knowledge. Schank calls such knowledge structures memory organization packages (MOPs), in which abstract knowledge that can be shared by various environments will be stored in a unique place so that it can be retrieved by different MOPs.

If we call the script "going to the outpatient department of internal medicine" $-DOCTOR and the corresponding MOPs M-DOCTOR, we can further understand the structural characteristics of MOPs by comparing the two expressions.

```
$-DOCTOR:
Have-Medical-Problem
Make-Appointment
Go
Enter
Waiting-Room
Treatment
Pay


M-DOCTOR:
M-Professional-Office-Visit
  Have-Problem
Make-Appointment
GO
    Enter
Waiting-Room
    [Get-Service]
M-Contract
    Negotiate
[Get-Service]
Pay
```

Two generalized MOPs are included in M-DOCTOR, namely, M-Professional-Office-Visit and M-Contract. The former summarizes the general event sequences that may occur in the case of going to the internal medicine outpatient department or dental outpatient department or going to the law firm to find a lawyer, while the latter summarizes the general knowledge about the contract and payment of fees between the relevant business parties in society.

The CD expression, script, and plan belong to a static memory, while MOPs are a kind of dynamic memory with self-modifying ability. It can transform the experience gained from specific events into abstract general experience, which reflects the process of human learning. MOPs, a knowledge representation model, simulate the human learning function.

Any language understanding system needs to convert the input text into a machine internal meaning representation. In the past, the method of language information processing was to first perform syntactic analysis to find a certain formal description of the syntactic structure of the input sentence (e.g., a tree diagram representing the syntactic structure) and then to pass the analysis results to another semantic extraction program to obtain the semantic representation of the input sentence.

Schank and his colleagues argue that this separation of parsing is unnecessary and does not conform to the psychological process of people understanding the language. They advocate combining syntactic and semantic knowledge to transform input statements into internal representations of a machine all at once. They call this analysis method an integrated conceptual analysis model.

In fact, this idea of integration has been reflected in the conceptual analysis program written by Riesbeck for the MARGIE system. After appropriate extension, this conceptual analysis program becomes ELI (English Language Interpreter), which serves as the public front end for many story understanding systems (such as SAM and PAM) constructed under the guidance of Schank. The task of ELI is to directly map input sentences into CD expressions, and then knowledge structures such as scripts or plans are used to perform deductive inferences on the input CD expressions.

The basic approach used by Schank and Riesbeck in the ELI program is called expectation. They believe that when a person utters a word or hears a word, he or she will foresee that other words have already appeared or will appear one after another. This expectation is based on what he has understood so far and on his knowledge about the language and the world. In the process of reading, people constantly predict what they might read next based on such expectations and use them to eliminate ambiguity and understand the text being read.

Schank further includes inference needed in the process of understanding into the analysis program, realizing the integration of syntax, semantics, and inference. Intuitively, people's understanding of the natural language is such a highly unified process. People often make certain necessary inferences based on the fragments that have been read and understood before they finish reading the sentence.

The first integrated program, FRUMP, was designed by DeJong in 1977. FRUMP does not process the input news story word by word but browses the input text to find what it is interested in. These things are often important information that the FRUMP system intends to state in the summary of the story. The FRUMP system uses the sketchy script as its knowledge representation model, with each type of news having a corresponding sketchy script. The entire comprehension process is expectation-driven. Once a sketchy script corresponding to the input news story is found, the analysis is completely guided by this sketchy script. The expectation attached to the specified sketchy script indicates what information the script wants to look for, with the rest being completely ignored. For example, in a sketch script about a natural disaster, the information it looks for is date, location, nature of the disaster, number of casualties, rescue situation, etc. If you find this information in the input news story, you understand the story.

In essence, the analysis program of the FRUMP system can hardly be separated from its inference program. The system has 2300 words and 60 sketchy scripts, whose processing speed is very fast. The CPU time of analyzing a story on a DEC's PDP20/50 computer is only 8.5 s, while it takes one minute for such a story to be transmitted from the associated press (AP). Therefore, the FRUMP system is fully capable of processing part of AP news stories in real time.

Since the story understanding of the FRUMP system is based on the content of predesigned sketchy scripts, errors might occur in understanding if some important plots are ignored during the design of the sketchy script. Therefore, it needs to be improved. The IPP system designed by M. Lebowitz in 1980 overcomes this defect in the FRUMP system.

The IPP system uses MOPs as the knowledge structure, which has a high degree of abstraction and which can automatically summarize general conclusions from the stories read. Some of MOPs in the IPP system are predesigned, and there are also some new MOPs refined by the system through induction. Therefore, the memory model of the IPP system is dynamic and has a preliminary learning function.

The expectation-driven IPP system also embodies an integrated design concept. The lexical entries in its dictionary are divided into three types: words that are analyzed immediately, words that are temporarily skipped, and words that are completely ignored. Therefore, only the words, not the whole sentence, can be ignored so that some unforeseen important plots can be found and dealt with when dealing with the story, effectively overcoming the defects of the FRUMP system.

The subject matter of stories understood by the IPP system is limited to news about terrorism. Its dictionary has 200 words and can successfully analyze news stories extracted from various newspapers.

In 1976, Lames Meehan designed the TALE-SPIN system, which can automatically compose simple stories.

The process of writing a story with TALE-SPIN is divided into three steps:

Step 1: Determine the content of the story.
Step 2: Build a model by using CD theory, write a program, and add it to the existing system.
Step 3: Run the system and find the errors or shortcomings of the system to provide a reference for program improvement.

For example, if a user tries to use TALE-SPIN to write a story about "thirsty," the system needs to have a preliminary dialogue with the user to determine the characters and related facilities in the story. When the program is running, the story begins when the character feels thirsty.

The story written with TALE-SPIN is as follows:

> Once upon a time George ant lived near a patch of ground. There was a nest in an ash tree. Wilma bird lived in the nest. There was some water in a river. Wilma knew that the water was in the river. George knew that the water was in the river. One day Wilma was very thirsty. Wilma wanted to get near some water. Wilma flew from her nest across a meadow through a valley to the river. Wilma drank the water. Wilma was not thirsty anymore.
>
> George was very thirsty. George wanted to get near some water. George walked from his patch of ground across the meadow through the valley to a river bank. George fell into the river. George wanted to get near the valley. George couldn't get near the valley. George wanted to get near the meadow. Wilma wanted George to get near the meadow. Wilma wanted to get near George. Wilma grabbed George with her claw. Wilma took George from the river through the valley to the meadow. George was devoted to Wilma. George owed everything to Wilma. Wilma let go of George. George fell to the meadow. The end.

This simple story written automatically with TALE-SPIN is still very vivid.

In 1979, Carbonell wrote a POLITICS system. This system is composed of several computer programs that are closely related to one another. The system tries to simulate people's ideological interpretations of international political events and simulates the dialogue of the US Senate on some politically sensitive issues. For this reason, POLITICS simulates the different opinions of conservatives and liberals in the Senate in the dialogue and evaluates news events based on such opinions. It has constructed its own belief system and a series of goal trees and has built a hierarchical system according to the relative importance of political events or beliefs.

The formal representation of political ideology must include various ideological interpretations of political events required by the computer inference mechanism, and the simulation system must model different ideological behaviors, which suggests the capability of CD theory for NLU.

The following is a dialogue with the POLITICS system on the incident of "The US Congress expects to pass the Panama Canal Treaty":

Conservative Views:

Q1: Should the United States approve the treaty?

A1: NO, THE TREATY IS BAD FOR THE UNITED STATES.

Q2: Why is the treaty bad for the United States?

A2: THE UNITED STATES WOULD LOSE THE CANAL TO PANAMA AND THE UNITED STATES WILL BE WEAKER.

Q3: What might happen if the United States loses the Canal?

A3: RUSSIA WILL TRY TO CONTROL THE CANAL.

Q4: Why would Russia try to take over the canal?

A4: RUSSIA WANTS TO EXPEND ITS MILITARY CONTROL. THE PANAMA CANAL HAS HIGH MILITARY VALUE.

Q5: How might this happen?

A5: THE UNITED STATES MAY NOT BE ABLE TO STOP ANYONE TAKING OVER THE PANAMA CANAL. TORRIJOS IS A COMMUNIST. TORRIJOS WILL LET RUSSIA CONTROL PANAMA.

Q6: Why should the United States worry about Russia taking over the canal?

A6: BECAUSE RUSSIA WANTS TO CONTROL THE WORLD.

Q7: What should the United States do to stop Russia from taking over the Canal?

A7: CONGRESS SHOULD VOTE AGAINST THE PANAMA CANAL TREATY.

Liberal Views:

Q1: Should the United States approve the treaty?

A1: YES. THE PANAMA CANAL TREATY IS GOOD FOR THE UNITED STATES.

Q2: Why is the treaty good?

A2: THE PANAMA CANAL TREATY IMPROVES RELATIONS WITH LATIN AMERICAN COUNTRIES.

Q3: What happens if the United States keeps the canal?

A3: THIS WILL CAUSE DISCONTENT AND CONFLICT IN PANAMA AND LATIN AMERICA.

Q4: Why would this lead to conflict?

A4: THE CANAL ZONE IS A UNITED STATES COLONY. LATIN AMERICA DOES NOT LIKE COLONIALISM. THE UNITED STATES WOULD MAINTAIN COLONIALISM.

Q5: What if Russia tries to take over the canal?

A5: RUSSIA DOES NOT WANT CONFLICT WITH THE UNITED STATES. RUSSIA WILL STAY OUT OF THE CANAL, IF THE UNITED STATES DEFENDS IT. THE UNITED STATES DEFENDING THE CANAL IS PART OF THE TREATY.

The Panama Canal issue was a very complex international political issue during the Cold War in the 1970s. Of course, computers have a very limited understanding of such a complex issue. However, the understanding mechanism for such political events of the POLITICS system is general, which can be used to deal with other planning issues that are as complicated as political events.

7.7 Mel'chuk's Meaning ↔ Text Theory

The process of language generation starts with meaning, goes through syntactic processing, and finally outputs linear texts, which is a meaning (смысл in Russian) ↔ text (текст in Russian) process. Meaning ↔ text theory (MTT) has conducted an in-depth study of this process. Therefore, we are here to introduce this theory.

MTT was proposed by A. K. Zolkovski and I. A. Mel'chuk in Moscow. Their earliest article entitled "On semantic synthesis (of text)" was included in the 19th volume of *"The Problem of Cybernetics"* published in Russia in the 1960s. In 1977, Mel'chuk left Moscow and went to Montreal University in Canada, where he established Observatoire de Linguistique Sens-Texte, a special group for in-depth research on MTT, ultimately forming a school.

MTT claims that the natural language is a logical tool to establish the correspondence between meaning and text. Although this view seems to be acceptable to everyone, most theories in modern linguistics have not yet adopted such a theory to establish natural language models.

What is language? To answer this question, three basic hypotheses are proposed in MTT.

Hypothesis 1: The correspondence between meaning and text in the natural language is a many-to-many one.

Hypothesis 2: The correspondence between meaning and text in the natural language can be described by formal logical tools, which should reflect the natural speech activities of speakers.

Hypothesis 3: Since the correspondence between meaning and text is very complicated, some intermediate levels, such as syntactic level and morphological level, must be distinguished in the process of speech.

Hypothesis 1 shows that the so-called description of the natural language (L) is the description of the corresponding relationship between the meaning set of L and the text set of L. F. Saussure once proposed that linguistic signs include two aspects, signifie and significance. Hypothesis 1 of MTT is very close to Saussure's view. The signifie is equivalent to meaning, and the significance is equivalent to text.

Hypothesis 2 shows that the natural language must describe the correspondence between meaning and text; construct a meaning-text model (MTM), which must simulate the speaker's language activities; and describe how the speaker converts what he wants to say (i.e., meaning) into what he says (i.e., text) in a specific way when the speaker speaks. Mel'chuk claims that "Linguists should try their best to

Semantic Representation (SemR) or Meaning

⇕

Deep-syntactic representation (DSyntR)

⇕

Surface-syntactic representation (SSyntR)

⇕

Deep-morphological representation (DMorphR)

⇕

Surface-morphological representation (SMorphR)

⇕

Deep-phonological representation (DPhonR)

⇕

Surface-phonological representation (SphonR) or Text

Fig. 7.25 Seven levels from meaning to text

propose a set of formal rules for expressing meaning or some formal interpretation rules to establish the correspondence between meaning and text." The text referred to by Mel'chuk here includes all sentences in communication, not just written sentences.

Hypothesis 3 shows that the correspondence between meaning and text includes some intermediate levels. There are seven levels as is shown in Fig. 7.25.

The level of semantic representation (SemR) is the meaning level, and the level of surface-phonological representation (SPhonR) is the text level. In this way, the correspondence between meaning and text can be divided into six modules: The correspondence of SemR to DSyntR is the semantic module, the correspondence of DSyntR to SSyntR is the deep syntax module, the correspondence of SSyntR to DMorphR is the surface syntax module, the correspondence of DMorphR to SMorphR is the deep-morphological module, the correspondence of SMorphR to DPhonR is the surface-morphological module, and the correspondence of DPhonR to SPhonR is the phonology module. The transformation from meaning to text is not realized directly but through various intermediate levels. The MTM with the above six modules is a hierarchical and systematic model.

Different levels of representation have different properties. Semantic representation is a multidimensional graph because semantic representation is multidimensional, whereas syntactic representation is a two-dimensional tree because syntactic representation is two-dimensional. Morphological representation is one-dimensional, so it is a one-dimensional string.

The transformation process from meaning to text is the process from a multidimensional graph, through a two-dimensional tree, and finally to a one-dimensional string. For example, the semantic representation (meaning) of the sentence "Peter wants to sell his blue car" is shown in Fig. 7.26.

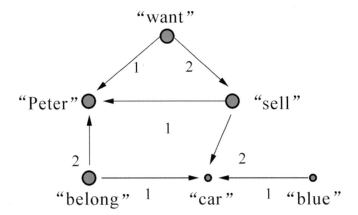

Fig. 7.26 Semantic representation

This semantic representation is a multidimensional directed graph. The mark on the node in the figure is called the semanteme, a semantic unit, which corresponds to the meaning of a word in the language. From a mathematical point of view, the semanteme is equivalent to a functor, whose argument is called the semantic actant. The functor without argument is called the semantic name, which is generally a specific noun. The semanteme and its semantic actant are connected by arrows. This kind of connection is called semantic dependency. The arrow pointing to the ith semantic actant of the semanteme is marked with i. The order of the number of semantic actants is not arbitrary; instead, the semantic actants are numbered roughly based on the syntactic requirements when speaking. The semantic representation in Fig. 7.26 shows that the semanteme "want" has two semantic actants, "Peter" and "sell." In the semantic representation, "sell" itself is also a semanteme with two semantic actants, "Peter" and "car"; "belong" is a semanteme that represents the relationship of belonging. It has two semantic actants, "car" and "Peter"; "blue" is a semanteme with only one semantic actant, "car"; and "Peter" and "car" are both semantic names, neither of which has a semantic actant. The relationships in this directed graph are intricate, forming a very complex network. It should be noted that this semantic representation only represents the meaning of the utterance and its surface form. Although the semanteme "belong" does not appear in the surface form, it expresses the belonging relationship, indicating that "car" belongs to "Peter." This relationship is very important to the meaning of an utterance, even though "belong" does not appear in the surface form.

The directed graph (Fig. 7.26) is a simplified version. In fact, the semantic features of each semanteme constitute a directed graph connected from all sides to form a very complex and three-dimensional network.

This semantic representation is processed by the semantic module and the deep syntax module. The surface-syntactic representation (Fig. 7.27) is the result of the transformation of the semantic representation SemR to the deep syntactic representation DSyntR and then the transformation of the deep syntactic representation

Fig. 7.27 Surface-syntactic
representation

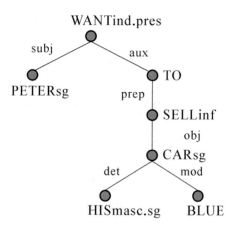

DSyntR to the surface-syntactic representation SSyntR by the semantic module and the deep syntax module, respectively.

This surface-syntactic representation is a two-dimensional dependency tree. Here, MTT does not use the phrase structure tree but uses the dependency tree because the phrase structure tree, in addition to the two-dimensional dominance relationship (i.e., the dependency relationship) between nodes, also represents the one-dimensional linear relationship between nodes. This means that the phrase structure tree does not distinguish between the syntactic structure and the morphological structure. MTT, however, strictly distinguishes syntactic structures from morphological structures. Syntactic structures express only a two-dimensional dependence relationship, but they do not express a one-dimensional linear relationship. In this respect, MTT different from phrase structure grammar is consistent with dependency grammar.

The surface-syntactic representation (Fig. 7.27) shows that the root of the dependency tree is WANTind.pres in the present tense and that its subject (Subj) is PETERsg, which is a singular noun that also governs TO and SELL. In the surface-syntactic representation, TO is a preposition prep, SELLinf is an infinitive verb, and the object (Obj) dominated by SELL is CARsg, which is a singular noun. Again, in this representation, the qualifier (det) dominated by CAR is HISmasc.sg, which is a masculine singular pronoun that replaces the semanteme "belong" in the semantic representation, indicating the belonging relationship between CAR and PETER. Therefore, the semanteme "belong" has disappeared from the surface-syntactic representation; the modifier (mod) dominated by CAR is BLUE. This dependency tree representing the dependency relationship between nodes does not represent the order between nodes, so it is two-dimensional rather than one-dimensional.

This surface-syntactic representation SSyntR is transformed to the deep-morphological representation DMorphR and is then transformed from the deep-morphological representation DMorphR to the surface-morphological representation SMorphR by the surface syntax module and the deep morphology module, respectively. The resulting surface-morphological representation is as follows:

PETERsg	WANTind.pres.sg	TO	SELLinf	HISmasc.sg	BLUE	CARsg

This surface-morphological representation is a one-dimensional string of symbols, in which each of the words in order carries its corresponding grammatical information.

Having obtained the surface-morphological representation, the written MT system can directly take the words in the surface-morphological representation and then output them as translation results after some morphological changes according to the morphological information obtained in the words. If it is the speech MT system, the surface-morphological representation also needs to be processed by the surface-morphological module and the phonology module to convert it first into the deep-phonological representation and then into the surface-phonological representation to obtain the speech output of the sentence.

MTT can describe the generation process in MT and can be used as the theoretical basis for research on automatic generation of MT.

Of course, MTT can also be used to describe the analysis process in NLP. As we can see in Fig. 7.25, the connection between the various levels is bidirectional, from meaning to text, or vice versa. The process from text to meaning is the analysis process of the natural language. Therefore, MTT can be applied both to the generation of the natural language and to the analysis of the natural language. From the perspectives of the processes of generation and analysis, MTT is also an MTM (meaning-text model), an important formal model of NLP.

Mel'chuk emphasizes that MTM is a transformation device rather than a generation device. This is the fundamental difference between MTT and Chomsky's generative grammar. The basic working principle of MTM is to perform synonym conversion. Using the principle of conversion between synonymous phenomena, MTM generates a large number of synonymous structures at various levels. These synonymous structures are then passed through various filtering devices to eliminate structures that do not conform to the rules of the natural language, filtering out the qualified texts. The most prominent feature of MTM is its transformation.

All the conversion between meaning and text is a one-to-many relationship. Therefore, Mel'chuk has set up eight types of filters to filter the analysis and generated results at various levels. The eight filters are as follows:

1. General-type filter: It removes all deep syntactic structures containing artificial fictional words in semantic synthesis results.
2. Congeneric filter: It removes all deep syntactic structures containing dummy keywords in synonymous structures.
3. Filter that guarantees semantic valence saturation and syntactic valence saturation: It removes the deep syntactic structure that does not satisfy the valence.
4. Filter that limits the combining performance of words or phrases: It eliminates irregular vocabulary combinations.
5. Word order rule filter: It proposes unqualified word orders in certain language environments.

6. Filter that restricts surface-syntactic components: It removes unqualified syntactic components in the surface-syntactic structure.
7. Filter that restricts morphology or word formation: It removes syntactic components that are unqualified in morphology or word formation.
8. Filter that optimizes the text: It removes the text that is rhetorically unqualified.

In MTM, most of these filters are implemented, and only the filter that optimizes the text is still in its preliminary design stage. Due to the use of these filters, it is easy to deal with ambiguity, the core issue of NLP, at all levels.

Mel'chuk once said, "MTM should do the same thing, that is, to transform a given meaning into a text that expresses this meaning (so this model is transductive)." The original text of this passage is in French and is recorded as follows. "Un MST (Modele Sens-Texte) doit faire la même chose : traduire un sens donne en un texte qui l'exprime (voila pourquoi ce modele est 'traductif')." Here, Mel'chuk emphasizes the importance of transduction (French : traductif).

S. Kahane from the University of Paris 7 proposed transductive grammar based on Mel'chuk's thought and the idea of MTT. Kahane compares his transductive grammar to a transducer. He believes that the main function of transductive grammar is to correspond to the set of structures at different levels in MTM. Suppose S and S′ are two sets of structures at different levels (such as the set of graphs, the set of trees, or the set of symbol strings); then, transductive grammar G between S and S′ is formal grammar that links the elements in the set S with the elements in the set S′. As a formal grammar, transductive grammar G includes a finite set of rules called corresponding rules, which connect the structural fragments composed of elements in S with those of elements in S′ to correspond to each other. For structure S and structure S′ connected by G, G can also define a certain part of structure S and structure S′ and perform a one-on-one mapping between the fragments of the two parts. Obviously, this kind of transductive grammar is very different from general grammar in that it not only studies issues at a certain level in the language but is also dedicated to exploring the problem of transduction at different levels in MTM. Therefore, transductive grammar is a kind of meta-grammar formalism, which is of course valuable for further in-depth research on the theory of automatic generation in MT.

7.8   Fillmore's Deep Case and Frame Semantics

A semantic theory proposed by American linguist C. Fillmore (1929–2014, Fig. 7.28) is a deep case, which is also called case grammar. Although it is named grammar, it is actually a semantic theory, which has been widely used in NLP.

The development of case grammar can be divided into two stages. The first stage was from the late 1960s to the early 1970s. In this stage, only the case analysis plane is used as a tool to connect the underlying semantic expression of the sentence with the characteristics of the situation described by the sentence, with no consideration

Fig. 7.28 C. Fillmore

given to the deep grammatical relationship plane. The main works published by Fillmore in the first stage are *Toward a Modern Theory of Case* in 1966, *The Case for Case* in 1968, and *Some Problems for Case Grammar* in 1971. After the mid-1970s, case grammar entered the second stage. In this stage, a deep grammatical relationship plane was added to explain semantic and syntactic phenomena in addition to the case analysis plane. The main works in the second stage include *The Case for Case Reopened* and *Topics in Lexical Semantics* published in 1977. Studies in these two stages constitute the system of case grammar theory and have a great impact on language information processing.

Fillmore believes that a sentence in the natural language has a deep structure that reflects its theme. This deep structure is composed of a verb as the central component and several noun phrases. Each noun phrase is associated with the central verb in a specific relationship, which is called a case relation. Here, the case referred to by Fillmore is not a case in traditional grammar but a case in a deep structure.

In traditional grammar, the case is associated with morphological changes of nouns. Nouns with different cases have different morphological changes. For example, Russian nouns have six cases, and German nouns have four cases. Each case is associated with a specific morphological change. From the point of view of traditional grammar, English and French nouns have no morphological change systems, so they have no cases. However, this does not mean that there are no grammatical meanings such as "agent," "receiver," "tool," "giving," and "location" in English and French. Although these grammatical meanings do not have to be expressed through morphological changes of noun endings, they can be expressed through other grammatical forms. Different languages have different expressions. For example, such grammatical meanings in English and in French can be expressed through prepositions, and in Japanese, they can be expressed through auxiliary words. In addition, some languages do not express them through morphological changes of nouns but through verbal changes. To study the case relation from the perspective of deep structure, it is necessary to abandon morphological changes attached to nouns. Instead, the term "case" is used to refer to the syntactic and semantic relations in the deep structure.

Fillmore believes that grammatical relationships that exist in the deep structure in the standard theory, such as subject, direct object, indirect object, prepositional object, etc., are actually concepts of the surface structure. What is needed in the deep structure is not the surface grammatical relations but the deep syntactic and semantic relations, such as agent, patient, tool, location, and so on. In other words, every noun phrase (including individual nouns and pronouns) has a certain case in the deep structure. After proper transformation, these cases become subject, object, prepositional phrase, etc. in the surface structure. In languages where nouns have morphological changes, they become the surface cases of different forms of nouns. Therefore, Fillmore called his theory case grammar.

Fillmore pointed out that "the substantial amendment I want to propose to the theory of transformational grammar can be attributed to the reintroduction of the case system as a conceptual frame. This time, however, the difference between the deep structure and the surface structure has been clearly understood. The basic structure of a sentence consists of a verb and one or more noun phrases. Each noun phrase is associated with the verb in a certain case."[9]

In case grammar, a sentence includes two parts, modality and proposition. If we use S to denote a sentence, M to denote modality, and P to denote proposition, we can write

$$S \to M + P$$

The component P can be extended to a category of a verb and one or more cases. If the verb is represented by V and if the category of the case is represented by C_1, C_2..., C_n, we can write

$$P \to V + C_l + C_2 + \ldots + C_n$$

[9]C. Fillmore. *The Case for Case*, 1968, Chinese translation: 《Ge Bian》 (translated by Mingyang Hu), The Commercial Press, 2018.

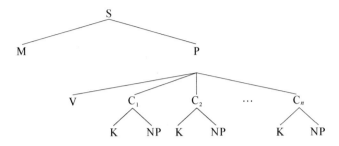

Fig. 7.29 Representation of a sentence by case grammar

Each case category can be represented by a case mark (denoted as K, which is the abbreviation of German Kasus (case)) plus a noun phrase (denoted as NP), namely,

$$C \rightarrow K + NP$$

In this way, a sentence expressed by case grammar can be drawn as the tree graph (Fig. 7.29).

What needs to be explained here is modality M in case grammar, which is different from modality in the traditional sense. Modality in the traditional sense mainly means possibility, necessity, etc., while modality in case grammar mainly refers to the tense, aspect, and voice of verbs, as well as affirmation, negation, imperative, question, exclamation, statement, etc.

Fillmore said that "the concept of case includes a set of universal and presumptive internal concepts equivalent to some types of judgment that human beings can make about what happens around them, such as who did this thing, whom this thing happened to, and what has been changed."

The case types proposed by Fillmore are agentive, instrumental, objective, locative, dative, and factitive. In case grammar, the case is a basic tool to explain the relationship between semantics and syntax, but it is very difficult to determine a list of cases, a complete and clear list of which Fillmore himself has never made. In different articles, the number of cases varies, and even their names often vary, too. We found that Fillmore proposed a total of 13 cases from 1966 to 1977. In addition to the original types, agentive, instrumental, objective, locative, dative, and factitive, eight other cases were added, such as experiencer, source, goal, time, path, benefactive, comitative, and permanence/transition case (essive/translative). The original case, factitive, is merged into Goal.

Here are some common cases and their simple definitions given by Fillmore.

- Agentive (A): This refers to the typical doer of the action that can be detected by the action determined by the verb. The doer of the action is generally a living person or thing. For example, the word "He" in the sentence "He laughed" is A.
- Instrumental (I): This refers to an inanimate force or object involved as a factor for the action or state determined by the verb. For example, the phrase "a knife" in the sentence "He cut the rope with a knife" is I.

- Dative (D): This refers to a living being affected by an action or state determined by the verb. For example, the word "He" in the sentence "He is tall" is D.
- Factitive (F): This refers to the object or living being formed by the action or state determined by the verb or to the object or living being understood as part of the meaning of the verb. For example, the phrase "a dream" in the sentence "John dreamed a dream about Mary" is D.
- Locative (L): This refers to the location or spatial direction of an action or state determined by the verb. For example, the word "house" in the sentence "He is in the house" is L.
- Objective (O): This refers to the things affected by the state or the thing determined by the verb. It is the thing represented by the noun, whose function is determined by the meaning of the verb itself. For example, the word "book" in the sentence "He bought a book" is O. The objective was later renamed patientive.
- Benefactive (B): This refers to the living object for which the action determined by the verb serves. For example, the word "Mary" in the sentence "He sang a song for Mary" is B.
- Source (S): This refers to the source of things affected by the action determined by the verb or to the starting position in the process of position change. For example, the word "Mary" in the sentence "I bought a book from Mary" is S.
- Goal (G): This refers to the end point of the object or the terminal position in the process of position change determined by the verb. For example, the word "Mary" in the sentence "I sold a car to Mary" is G.
- Comitative (C): This refers to the companion determined by the verb, who completes the action together with A. For example, the word "Mary" in the sentence "He sang a song with Mary" is C.

The Fillmore's definitions of cases are abstract. We can better understand their meanings through the following sentences:

For example,

1. John opened the door.
    John in the sentence is A.
2. The door was opened by John.
    John in the sentence is also A.
3. The key opened the door.
    The key in the sentence is I.
4. John opened the door with the key.
    The key in the sentence is also I.
5. John used the key to open the door.
    The key in the sentence is still I.
6. John believed that he would win.
    John in the sentence is D.
7. We persuaded John that he would win.
    John in the sentence is also D.
8. It was apparent to John that he would win.
    John in the sentence is still D.

9. Chicago is windy.
   Chicago in this sentence is L.
10. It is windy in Chicago.
    Chicago in this sentence is also L.

It can be seen that none of these cases corresponds to the surface relationship (such as subject, object, etc.) in a given language. They are all deep cases.

Each word in the vocabulary can have a series of features in addition to its own semantics. Case grammar focuses on features of nouns and verbs.

Features of nouns required by a particular case can be specified by mandatory rules. For example, any noun N in the phrase A or D must have the feature [+Animate], which can be written as

$$N \rightarrow [+\text{Animate}]^{A.D}[X—Y]$$

Features of verbs depend on the case arrangement provided by the whole sentence, which can be expressed by case frames. For example, the verb "run" can be inserted into the case frame [—A], the verb "sadden" can be inserted into the case frame [—D], the verbs "remove" or "open" can be inserted into the case frame [—O +A], the verbs "murder" or "terrorize" can be inserted into the case frame [—D+A], and the verb "give" can be inserted into the case frame [—O+D+A].

The same verb can appear in different case frames. For example, the verb "open" can appear in the case frame [—O].

The door opened.

The verb "open" can also appear in the case frame [—O+I].

The wind opened the door.

It also can appear in the case frame [—O+I+A].

John opened the door with a chisel.

To express these different situations, all the candidate components that can be selected on demand are enclosed in parentheses in case frames so that the case frame of the verb "open" can be abbreviated as

$$+[—O \ (I) \ (A)]$$

This case frame means that O (objective) must be used for the verb "open," while I (instrumental) and A (agentive) are optional.

Fillmore also proposes a method of transforming the deep structure of the sentence into the surface structure in case grammar (Fig. 7.30).

The subject in the surface structure comes from different deep cases, and the process of transforming the deep case in the deep structure into the subject in the surface structure is called subjectivization. Case grammar stipulates if there is A,

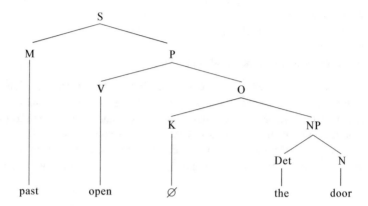

Fig. 7.30 B of a sentence

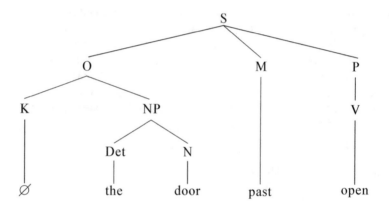

Fig. 7.31 O movement to the beginning of the sentence

then A be the subject; if there is no A but I, then I be the subject; and if there is neither A nor I, then O be the subject during subjectivization.

For example, B of a sentence is shown in Fig. 7.30 above.

It can be seen from Fig. 7.30 that the modality (M) of this sentence (S) is past and that the proposition (P) is composed of the verb V and the category O (objective) of the case. In this expression, the case mark K of this case category is empty (Ø), and the noun phrase NP is composed of "the" (definite article) and "door." In B of this sentence, there is neither A nor I, so O is the subject.

First, O is moved to the beginning of the sentence, as shown in Fig. 7.31 above.

Then, the subject preposition and the case mark are deleted. After the subject preposition Ø and the case mark K in Fig. 7.31 are deleted, Fig. 7.32 is obtained.

Finally, the tense "past" is added to the verb "open" to obtain the surface form (Fig. 7.33).

At the surface level, the verb "open" is changed to its past tense form "opened" so that the sentence "The door opened" is obtained.

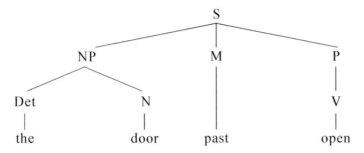

Fig. 7.32 Deletion of subject preposition and case mark

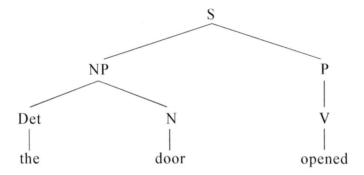

Fig. 7.33 Surface form

Let's look at a slightly more complicated example. B of the sentence is as follows (Fig. 7.34).

It can be seen from Fig. 7.34 that there are A, D, and O in the deep case of this sentence. According to the subjectivization rule, A is chosen as the subject and is moved to the beginning of the sentence because there is A in the deep case of the sentence (Fig. 7.35).

Then, the subject preposition and the case mark of the subject are deleted. After deletion of the subject preposition "by" and the case mark K in Fig. 7.35, Fig. 7.36 is obtained.

In Fig. 7.36, as O is used as the direct object of the verb "give," the preposition of the direct object and the case mark should be deleted. After the deletion of the preposition of the direct object Ø and the case mark K, Fig. 7.37 is obtained.

Finally, to obtain the surface form (Fig. 7.38), the tense "past" is added to the verb "give."

In this way, the sentence "John gave the books to my brother" is obtained.

In the above sentence, the verb "give" takes A as its subject, which is a regular choice. However, there are other alternative choices, which means that the verb "give" can also take either O or D as its subject. Then, the feature [+passive] is added to the verb. After adding [+passive], V loses the feature of deleting object

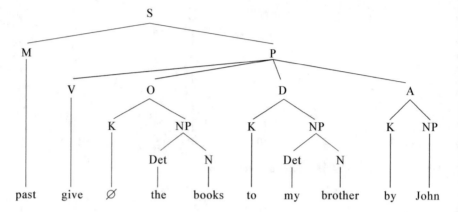

Fig. 7.34 A slightly more complicated example

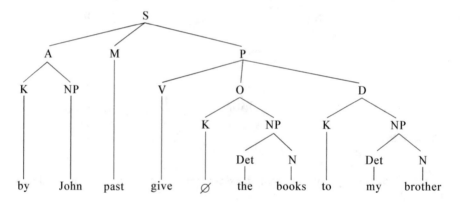

Fig. 7.35 A movement to the beginning of the sentence

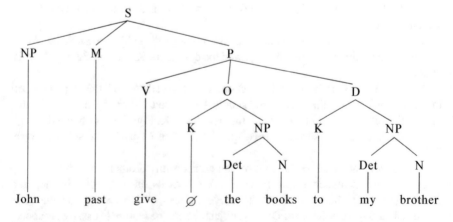

Fig. 7.36 Deletion of the preposition "by"

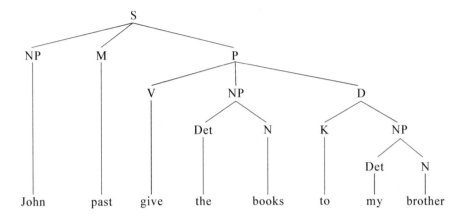

Fig. 7.37 Deletion of the preposition of the direct object and its case mark

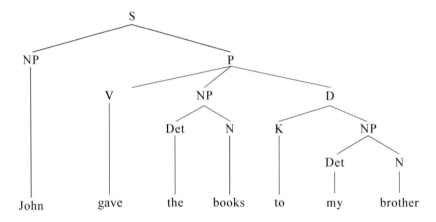

Fig. 7.38 Addition of tense "past" to the verb

prepositions. It is required automatically to insert a "be" in component M and to fill in a special passive form "given."

When O is used as the subject, the conversion process is as follows:

First, O in Fig. 7.34 is moved to the beginning of the sentence, as shown in Fig. 7.39.

Then, the subject preposition and the case mark are deleted. In Fig. 7.39, the subject preposition Ø and the case mark K are deleted to obtain Fig. 7.40.

Then, "be" is inserted in M to get Fig. 7.41.

Finally, the tense "past" is merged into "be," "be" is changed to "were," and then "give" to "given" to obtain the surface form (Fig. 7.42).

In this way, the sentence "The books were given to my brother by John" is obtained.

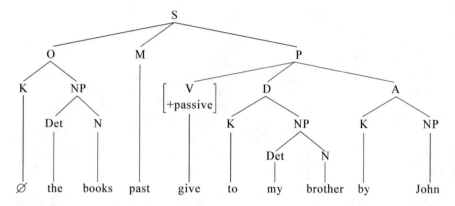

Fig. 7.39 O movement to the beginning of the sentence

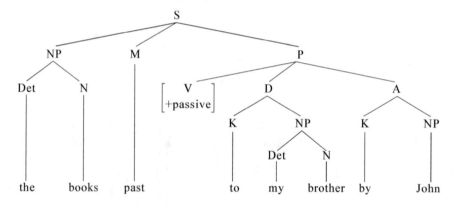

Fig. 7.40 Deletion of the subject preposition and the case mark

Another alternative choice (an irregular one) is to use D as the subject. The conversion process is as follows.

First, D in Fig. 7.34 is moved to the beginning of the sentence. Figure 7.43 is obtained.

Then, the subject preposition and the case mark are deleted. After deletion of the subject preposition "to" and the case mark K in Fig. 7.43, Fig. 7.44 is obtained.

Then, "be" is inserted in M to get Fig. 7.45.

In Fig. 7.45, O is used as a direct object. The preposition Ø and case mark K of the direct object are deleted. The verb "give" is changed to "given." Figure 7.46 is obtained.

Finally, the tense "past" is merged into "be,", changing "be" to "was." The surface form is obtained.

In this way, the sentence "My brother was given the books by John" can be obtained.

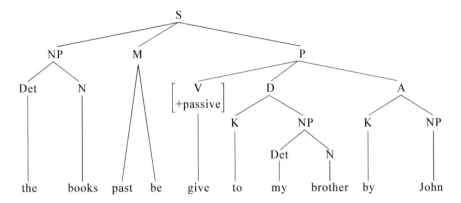

Fig. 7.41   Insertion of "be" in M

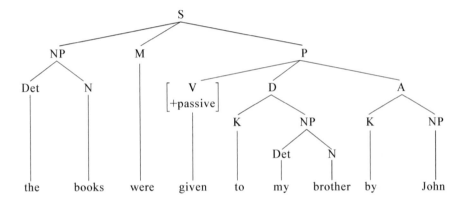

Fig. 7.42   Surface form

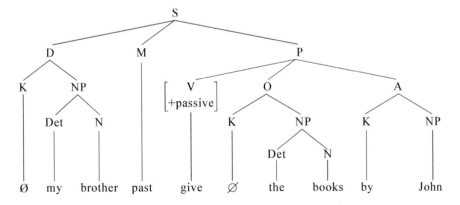

Fig. 7.43   D used as the subject

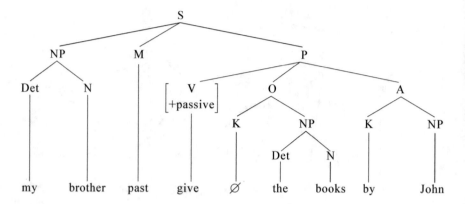

Fig. 7.44 Deletion of the subject preposition and the case mark

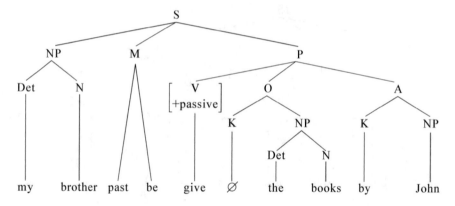

Fig. 7.45 Insertion of "be" in M in Fig. 7.44

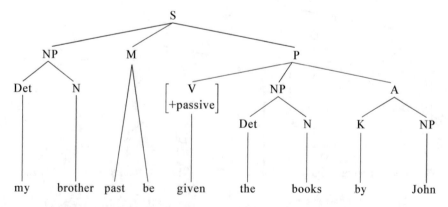

Fig. 7.46 Deletion of the preposition Ø and case mark K of the direct object and the change of "give" to "given"

Fillmore's case grammar has improved the traditional concept of "case," which has been quite innovating and refreshing. The function of deep case is universal and applicable to all natural languages. Case grammar can reveal deep semantic relations and can be used to infer the surface structure. As Fillmore said, "Knowing the case relationship, you can relate it to the syntactic structure of the actual sentence. For example, What is the predicted subject? Can it form a subject predicate structure? Can we determine what the direct object is? What are the surface markers of these elements? In a given language, which elements should be separated? Which elements refer to the same thing? What is the word order in the sentence? ... In a word, once the case of the sentence structure is described, various inferences can be made about the relationship and nature of the surface sentence."[10] Because of this, case grammar has attracted the attention of linguistic circles all over the world ever since it was proposed, especially in the research of language information processing and AI, and it has achieved certain application effects.

Thus far, we have mainly presented the research on case grammar in its first stage. After the mid-1970s, the development of case grammar entered the second stage, in which the following modifications were made. The structure of the case role in the first stage is referred to as the underlying structure composed of case roles. The underlying structure is transformed to obtain the surface structure in the first stage. In the second stage, the underlying structure composed of case roles must pass through the distribution of grammatical relations such as deep subjects and deep objects before it is transformed to obtain the deep structure, which is then converted to the surface structure through conversion. In this way, each sentence has two analysis planes, case roles and grammatical relations. These two planes connect the sentence with the events described by the sentence and explain the semantic and syntactic phenomena of the sentence.

Fillmore proposes that sentences describe scenes in which participants assume case roles and constitute the underlying structure of sentences. After the choice of perspective, some participants enter the perspective and become the nucleus of the sentence. Each nuclear element determines its grammatical relationship according to the salience hierarchy. Other participants may not be able to enter the sentence, even if they appear in the sentence. They can only become peripheries.

Scenes are the real world outside of the language, such as objects, events, states, behaviors, changes, and people's memory, feeling, and perception of the real world. Every word, phrase, and sentence in a language is a description of the scene. When people utter a word, a phrase, or a sentence, they identify a scene and highlight or emphasize a part of that scene. For example, the verb "write" describes a scene in which a person holds a pen to make it move on the surface of an object, leaving traces on the surface of the object. In this scene, there are four entities (i.e., four participants), the person who makes the behavior, the tool by which the behavior is carried out, the surface of the object that bears the behavior, and the trace left by the

---

[10] Feisheng Ye. "Talk of Professor Lakoff and Professor Fillmore about American linguistics" (Part II, Fillmore's talk). *Linguistics abroad*, 1982, (3):1.

behavior on the surface of the object. This is the entire scene described by a single verb "write" when there is no context, that is, all the imagination generated by a single verb "write" or all the imagination that the word "write" prompts us to have without context. The function of a sentence is to highlight the principal entity being described. If I say to you, "Xiao Wang is writing," then the scene elicited by this sentence will be different. According to this sentence, you know that this is the scene of an event in the real world. When you hear this sentence, you will create a scene in which Xiao Wang is holding a pen, moving it on the surface of an object, leaving traces on it. There are still four entities in this scene: the writer (Xiao Wang), the writing instrument (pen), the surface of the writing object (paper), and the traces left on the surface (characters). However, in this scene, the entity of the writer, Xiao Wang, is highlighted. If I say "Xiao Wang is writing a letter," the scene that this sentence generates still has only four entities, but it highlights two entities, the writer (Xiao Wang) and the traces (letter) left on the surface. If I say "Xiao Wang writes on the blackboard with chalk," this sentence again triggers four entities, but it highlights three entities, the writer (Xiao Wang), the writing tool (chalk), and the surface of the object (blackboard). If I say "Xiao Wang wrote a mathematical formula on the blackboard with chalk," again, this sentence triggers four entities. Unlike the previous three sentences, these four entities are all prominent: the writer (Xiao Wang), traces left on the surface (mathematics formula), the writing tool (chalk), and the surface of the object (blackboard).

Semantics is connected with the scene, but the scene is not equal to semantics. The scene can enter the language only through the perspective of the language user and can be connected with semantics. Every sentence or speech we utter has a specific perspective. At any point of a speech, we consider a scene from a special perspective. When the whole scene is under consideration, we generally only pay attention to a certain part of the scene. For example, there were four participants in a business event: buyer, seller, money, and goods. Sometimes, the participant "money" can be further analyzed into cash and credit. A prototype business event should include the above, but when we talk about this event, a single sentence we use requires us to choose a special perspective for the event. For example, if you want to put the seller and goods in the perspective, you use the verb "sell"; if you want to put the buyer and money in the perspective, you use the verb "buy," and so on. In this way, when someone hears and understands a certain sentence, he has in his mind a scene that covers all the necessary aspects of a business event. Only certain aspects of the event are identified and placed in the perspective.

The elements that enter the perspective become the nucleus elements of a sentence. Each nucleus element often has a grammatical relationship in the deep structure, acting either as the subject or direct object of a sentence. The elements that do not enter the perspective do not necessarily appear in the sentence. Even if they appear in the sentence, they are only the peripheries of the sentence usually introduced by prepositions, adverbials, or clauses.

The saliency hierarchy of the nuclear elements in a sentence is different. Fillmore proposes the following principles to determine the saliency hierarchy of the nucleus elements:

1. The saliency hierarchy of active elements is higher than that of non-active elements.
2. The saliency hierarchy of causal elements is higher than that of non-causal elements.
3. The saliency hierarchy of human (or living) perceivers is higher than that of others.
4. The saliency hierarchy of the elements that have been changed is higher than that of the elements that have not been changed.
5. The saliency hierarchy of complete or personalized elements is higher than that of part of an element or that of non-personalized elements.
6. The saliency hierarchy of the actual physical shape is higher than that of the background.
7. The saliency hierarchy of definite elements is higher than that of indefinite elements.

The saliency hierarchy here is arranged in a descending order. Therefore, the saliency hierarchy of the active element is higher than that of any other element, and the saliency hierarchy of the causal element is higher than that of any other element except for the active element. The saliency hierarchy of human (or living) perceivers is higher than that of any other element except for the active and causal elements and so on.

Therefore, the saliency hierarchy should be considered when the grammatical relationship of the nucleus elements is determined.

When the nucleus element is determined to be one, the highest element in the scene is the subject. When there are two nuclear elements, the subject and the direct object should be assigned according to their relative positions in the saliency hierarchy, with the subject being higher and the direct object being lower. When the subject of a verb has been determined, the thing with a higher saliency hierarchy has priority, if the direct object can be selected from the other two elements. If the two elements are of the same saliency hierarchy, either of them can enter the perspective. However, the classification of the saliency hierarchy is still in its hypothetical stage. As Fillmore puts it, "at this stage, it's all speculation."

The deep case in case grammar is universal and is suitable for describing sentences in various natural languages. Once case grammar is used to describe the sentence structure, various inferences can be made about the surface relationship and nature of the sentence, such as inferring what the subject is, whether it can form a subject-predicate structure, or how the word order in the sentence should be arranged.

Case grammar widely used in NLP has become an important NLP formal model, and it has played an important role in MT, AI, and other fields.

In 1977, Fillmore pointed out that different verbs that can describe the same business event can choose different ways to express the participants of the event. For example, a transaction involving $3 and a sandwich between John and Tom can be described in any of the following ways.

(a) John **bought** the sandwich from Tom for three dollars.
(b) Tom **sold** John the sandwich for three dollars.
(c) John **paid** Tom three dollars for the sandwich.

In these sentences, the verbs "buy, sell, and pay" express business events from different perspectives, and to achieve the perspective, different mappings between potential participants and thematic roles are chosen. We can see that these three verbs have completely different mappings, which suggests that the semantic role of the verb must be listed in the dictionary entry of the verb and that it cannot be predicted from the underlying conceptual structure.

Based on these facts, many researchers believe that it is necessary to list all the possibilities of syntactic and semantic combinations of each verb in the dictionary of the NLP system instead of relying solely on the correspondence between syntactic functions and semantic relations to carry out simple logical reasoning to solve the problem of semantic analysis. Moreover, the possibilities of syntactic and semantic combination of verbs should be described by frames.

Since the correspondence between syntactic function and semantic structure in a language differs from word to word, Fillmore came to realize that it is necessary to describe the corresponding relationship between syntactic function and semantic structure for specific words and to establish a frame for describing syntactic function and semantic structure. Based on this understanding, Fillmore proposed frame semantics at the end of the twentieth century, shifting from case grammar to FrameNet. Thus, FrameNet has become another NLP formal model based on case grammar.

FrameNet is a project hosted by Fillmore. The main members of the project team are Srini Narayanan, Dan Jurafsky, Mark Gawron, Collin Baker, the project manager, and Sue Atkins, the lexicographer consultant. The purpose of this project is to study the relationship between grammatical function and conceptual structure (i.e., semantic structure) in English and to establish a vocabulary knowledge base for NLP. This project was continuously funded by the US National Scientific Foundation (NSF) for many years. The title of the project is NSF ITR/HCI # 0086132: "FrameNet++: An online lexical and semantic resource and its application in speech and language technology" (September 2000-August 2003). Due to the great impact of this project, it continued after August 2003 and continued to achieve new results.

Thanks to the corpus, FrameNet is now building an online English vocabulary resource based on the theory of frame semantics. As of October 2005, FrameNet contains at least 7600 lexical units, including verbs, nouns, and adjectives, covering a wide range of semantic domains. For every sense of every lexeme, the possibilities of its semantic and syntactic combination, its valences, have been described in detail. These valences are obtained by manually annotating example sentences or automatically organizing and collating the annotated results.

The central idea of frame semantics is that the description of the meaning of a word must be related to the semantic frame. The frame is a graphical representation of the conceptual structures and patterns of belief, practice, system, and imagination. It provides a basis for the interaction of meaning in a certain speech community.

The tasks that FrameNet has established for itself are as follows:

1. Describe the conceptual structure or frame to which a given lexical unit belongs.
2. Extract sentences containing a certain word from the corpus and select examples from which we can illustrate the lexical unit with a given meaning.
3. Label the selected sentences by assigning frame-related tags (i.e., frame elements (FEs)) to phrases in sentences that contain the lexical unit.
4. Prepare the final annotation summary report, concisely showing the possibility of each lexical unit in combination, which is called the valence description.

As the format of the FrameNet database is independent of the development platform, it can be displayed through the network and other interactive means.

Next, we will illustrate semantic frameworks with a simple example to give you a better idea. Here is a set of words related to the frame called "revenge." The lexical units that evoke the meaning of "revenge" include avenge, avenger, get back (at), get even (with), retaliate, retribution, revenge (noun), revenge (verb), and vengeance. "Revenge" must be related to a certain punishment imposed in response to undeserved suffering. An "AVENGER" imposes a certain "PUNISHMENT" on an "OFFENDER" in response to the bad things that the offender did in the early days, that is, some kind of "INJURY." "AVENGER" may be the "INJURED PARTY," that is, the person who has been hurt, or maybe not. The judgment of "INJURY" caused by "OFFENDER" has nothing to do with the law, which requires a distinction between the concept of revenge and legally permissible "punishment." The events and participants in the revenge scene, such as "AVENGER" and "PUN-ISHMENT," are called FEs.

Take a look at the following annotated sentences that contain the lexical units of the frame "revenge."

1. [Ethel AVENGER] eventually **got even** [with Mildred OFFENDER] [for the insult to Ethel's family INJURY].
2. Why hadn't [he AVENGER] sought to **avenge** [his child INJURED PARTY]?
3. Yesterday [the Cowboys AVENGER] **avenged** [their only defeat of the season INJURY] [by beating Philadelphia Eagles 20–10 PUNISHMENT].
4. The Old Bailey was told [he AVENGER] was desperately in love and wanted to **get back** [at the woman OFFENDER] ["for ending their relationship" INJURY].
5. [The USA AVENGER] **retaliated** [against the harassment of its diplomats INJURY] [by expelling 36 staff from the Iraqi embassy in Washington on Aug. 27 PUNISHMENT].

It is obvious from the examples above that we have various FEs needed to annotate the main participants. Now, we can consider how different FEs are implemented in the language, that is, how FEs are related to syntactic elements. Sometimes, different lexical units have different possibilities.

Take the verb in the above frame as an example. In the active sentence, "AVENGER" is the subject, and "OFFENDER" typically appears in a prepositional phrase. The lexical form of the preposition depends on the lexical unit. The preposition "with" goes with "get even," as shown in Example (1), and the preposition "at" goes with "get back," as shown in Example (4). "INJURY" mostly appears in prepositional phrases with "for," but it can also be the direct object of the verbs, such as "revenge" and "avenge." The expression "INJURY" can be understood from the perspective of the original event (such as my brother's murder), or it can also be understood from the impact on the injured party (such as my brother's death). "PUNISHMENT" is typically expressed as a "by phrase" containing the gerund complement. Finally, "INJURED PARTY" is sometimes expressed as an independent element, especially as the direct object of "avenge," as in Example (2).

In contrast, some elements have a more specific semantic connection with the verb frame in a syntactic structure with the core of the verb. Therefore, FrameNet distinguishes between core FEs and noncore FEs. Although there is a considerable overlap with the distinction between argument and adjunct traditionally made by syntacticians, the two are not the same. The traditional distinction is mainly based on assumptions about syntactic configuration and syntactic phenomena, such as extraction. The concept of FrameNet is mainly semantic, focusing on whether a concept is necessary to understand the meaning of the frame. In FrameNet, the valence mode closely related to the description of verbs is only based on the core FEs. Non-core FEs include various types of peripheral modifiers, which are more or less coordinated with various types of events or states. An example of the noncore FE is the adverbial of time "yesterday" in Example (3). Although any "revenge" behavior obviously has the attributes of space and time, the modifier "yesterday" has no specific meaning to the verb "avenge." In FrameNet, the basic valence description of the related verb includes only those core FEs. Although FrameNet's secondary goal is to provide at least part of the semantic analysis of the sentence examined, annotators often annotate these elements with appropriate FE tags (time, place, etc.).

The semantic frame is a structure similar to a "script," in which the various elements of the structure are connected by the meaning of lexical units.

Each frame is a collection of FEs, which include frame participants and frame props and thematic roles. Frame semantics of the lexical unit should describe the FE combination and the FE distribution in the frame within a given sense.

Each sense should describe its valence, which should not only express the set information of the FE combination but also the information of its grammatical function and its phrase type testified in the relevant corpus.

Annotated sentences are an integral part of a database. They are annotated in the XML language and are the basis for lexical entries. Such a format supports searching by using frames, FEs, and their combinations.

The FrameNet database can be used either as a dictionary or as a thesaurus.

When the FrameNet database is used as a dictionary, the information for word entries includes the following:

- The definition of the word: Definition mostly comes from *the Concise Oxford Dictionary* (10th Edition, COD).
- Annotated sentences: These sentences are from the corpus and must have been carefully selected by linguists to be explained in the dictionary's annotation by LexUnit Report.

- FE table: This table describes the occurrence of FEs in the annotation by the LexUnit Report and the syntactic relationship they represent.
- Valence mode: This mode explains the valence modes that the word can have and explains the corresponding phrase types and syntactic functions of FEs in each valence mode.
- Index: It is arranged in an alphabetical order.

When the FrameNet database is used as a thesaurus, each word is linked to the semantic frame to which it belongs, and the frame in turn is linked to the vocabulary and other related frames.

The corpus used by FrameNet is the British National Corpus (BNC) containing 100 million words, which has been licensed by Oxford University Press (OUP). Semantic annotation is carried out using MITRE's Alembic Workbench. Syntactic annotation is performed by using the annotation program developed on their own, which annotates each phrase with information on its grammatical function and its phrase type. Each entry in FrameNet can be linked with other vocabulary resources, including the SYNSET of WordNet and the subcategorization frame of COMLEX.

All the arguments of each entry including the thematic roles, its phrase types, and its grammatical functions should be listed in FrameNet.

FrameNet includes several domains, each of which includes several frames defined by several thematic roles.

For example, in the early form of FrameNet, the domain of COGNITION includes the following three frames:

- STATIC COGNITION FRAME: such as believe, think, understand, etc.
- COGITATION FRAME: such as brood and ruminate
- JUDGMENT FRAME: such as respect, accuse, admire, and rebuke

In each frame of the COGNITION domain, there is a thematic role, COGNIZER, which can be referred to by different names in different frames. For example, in the JUDGMENT frame, the name of the reference to COGNIZER is called JUDGE. In addition, the thematic roles in the JUDGMENT frame include EVALUEE, REASON, and ROLE. The meanings of these thematic roles can be seen from the following example sentences about the verb "respect" (words representing thematic roles are marked in square brackets).

JUDGE: [John] **respects** Kim for being so brave.
EVALUEE: John **respects** [Kim] for being so brave.
REASON: John **respects** Kim [for being so brave].
ROLE: John **respects** Kim [as a scholar].

These thematic roles are the FEs of the corresponding frames.

In FrameNet, each entry is also annotated with its phrase types (such as NP and PP) and with its syntactic functions (such as Subj and Obj).

For example, the verb "appreciate," which expresses judgment, has both senses of dynamic cognition and static cognition. Its frames are as follows:

--Sense of dynamic cognition, which means "to be thankful or grateful for"

a. JUDGE	REASON	EVALUEE
NP/Subj	NP/Obj	PP(in)/Comp
I still appreciate	good manners	in men.
b. JUDGE	EVALUEE	REASON
NP/Subj	NP/Obj	PP(for)/Comp
I could appreciate	it	for the music alone.
c. JUDGE	REASON	
NP/Subj	NP/Obj	
I appreciate	your kindness.	
d. JUDGE	EVALUEE	ROLE
NP/Subj	NP/Obj	PP(as)/Comp
I did not appreciate	the artist	as a dissenting voice.

-- Sense of static cognition, which means "understand"

a. COGNIZER	CONTENT	
NP/Subj	Sfin/Comp	
They appreciate that communication is a two-way process.		
b. COGNIZER	CONTENT	
NP/Subj	Swh/Comp	
She appreciated	how far she had fallen from grace.	

From these example sentences, we can also see that there is a correspondence between the thematic role and the syntactic function (or phrase type). Thematic roles, such as JUDGE or COGNIZER, are generally the subjects (Subj) in the active sentences. The thematic role, ROLE, is generally a prepositional phrase PP with "as" as the preposition, and the thematic role, CONTENT, is generally the clause (S). Such information is very useful for syntax-driven automatic semantic analysis.

In FrameNet, the kernel dependency graph (KDG) can be used to represent the basic features of the entry dependency relationship while ignoring the elements that have nothing to do with the dependency relationship. For example, the KDG of the sentence "The professor demonstrated the proof to the class" (with the definite article being omitted) is as follows (Fig. 7.47).

In the annotation, it is worth noting that the syntactic core of a phrase is not always the most important frame activator and that the syntactic core of dependent phrases is not always the most important indicator of the meaning of these phrases. These phenomena include the following.

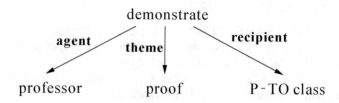

Fig. 7.47 Kernel dependency graph 1

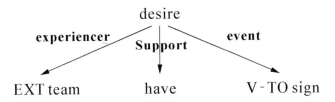

Fig. 7.48 Kernel dependency graph 2

1. Support verbs: The syntactic core of a verb plays a limited role in semantics. The main frame introducer is the noun related to the support verb.

    Light verbs, such as "have, do, make, take, and give," are the most obvious examples of support verbs. These verbs are used most frequently and can be used with a large number of event nouns, but they have little semantic contribution to the scene evoked by the noun, for example, "have desire, have an argument, make an argument, make a complaint, give a speech," etc.

    Except for light verbs, other support verbs and event nouns have a narrow range of collocation. For example, the verb "pay" goes with "attention," and the verb "say" goes with "prayers."

    In these cases, the support verb is not the core of the predicate of KDG, but the event noun should be taken as the core of the predicate.

    For example, the KDG of the sentence "The team has the desire to sign the player" is shown in Fig. 7.48.

    In this sentence, the phrase "the team" is introduced as an external argument (annotated as EXT) and serves as the subject of the verb "have." Therefore, we add EXT before the core of the FE, experiencer, which is shown by changing the arrow direction to indicate that syntactically, the noun "desire" is still the dependency element supporting the verb "have."

2. Null instantiated FE: Sometimes, the core FE is neither the dependency element of the predicate nor can it be found by slot filling. Therefore, the conceptual element perceived obviously has no corresponding form in the sentence. This is called a null instantiated FE. They are of three types:

    (a) Construct null instantiated FE (CNI): For example, the subject omitted in the imperative sentence and the agent in the "by phrase" omitted in the passive sentence are all CNIs.
    (b) Definite null instantiated FE (DNI): The missing elements could have been understood in the text or the context.

        For example, "the place where John left" in the sentence "John left" must be available from the context. Its core frame graph is as follows (Fig. 7.49).
    (c) Indefinite null instantiated FE (INI): The natural type or semantic type of the default element can be understood. There is no need to retrieve or establish a specific textual reference.

Fig. 7.49 Definite null
instantiated FE (DNI)

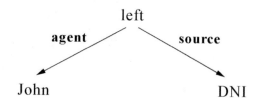

Fig. 7.50 Indefinite null
instantiated FE (INI)

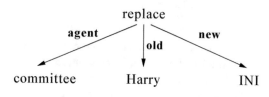

Fig. 7.51 Transparent noun
"kind"

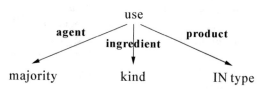

Fig. 7.52 Replacing kind
with asbestos

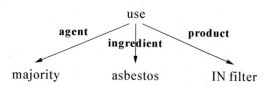

For example, the sentence "The committee replaced Harry with Susan"
becomes "The Committee replaced Harry" after omitting the prepositional
phrase "with Susan." The core frame graph is shown in Fig. 7.50.

3. Transparent nouns: When the syntactic core element of a noun phrase represents
   the quantitative one, type or container, its complement contains the semantic core
   of the noun phrase.

   For example, the noun "pins" in "several pins of water," the noun "kind" in "a
   kind of asbestos," and the noun "type" in "this type of filter" are all transparent
   nouns. In the core frame graph, we should select nouns that are semantically
   related to transparent nouns as the core.

   If the core frame of the sentence "The majority of tobacco producers use a kind
   of asbestos in this type of filter" can be drawn as follows, its semantics will be
   very vague (Fig. 7.51).

   However, if the noun "kind" is replaced with the noun "asbestos," as shown in
   the following graph, much more information is provided (Fig. 7.52).

4. FE fusion: Information related to two FEs is expressed by one element. In some
   frames, pair FEs are so closely linked that it is grammatically permissible to omit

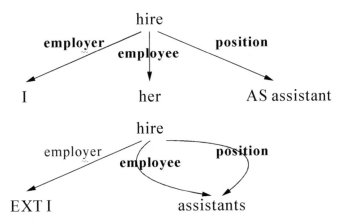

Fig. 7.53 FE fusion

one of them because the omitted FE can be inferred from the other implemented FE.

For example, of the two sentences, "I hired [her EMPLOYEE] [as my assistant POSITION]" and "I expect to hire two new assistants EMPLOYEE + POSITION," FEs, EMPLOYEE and POSITION, merge in the second sentence. Their core frame is as follows (Fig. 7.53).

In FrameNet, it is necessary to conduct in-depth research on annotated sentences and valence modes of these sentences. Thus, its research group has developed software tools needed, which can automatically generate two reports from the annotated corpus, "annotation by LexUnit Report" and "Lexical Entry Report." These two automatically generated reports can help researchers conduct further research.

In automatically generated annotation by LexUnit Report, the FE table of the lexical unit is first listed, and then example sentences containing the lexical units annotated with these FEs are displayed. The example sentences are automatically extracted from the corpus.

For example, annotation by LexUnit Report of the lexical unit "avenge" in the revenge frame is as follows:

The FE Table includes the following.

AVENGER
INJURED PARTY
INJURY
OFFENDER
PUNISHMENT

Example sentences with the lexical unit "avenge" are as follows:

1. [Swegen AVENGER] is also to have invaded England later to AVENGE [his brother INJURED PARTY]. [DNI PUNISHMENT] [DNI OFFENDER]
2. With this, [ElCid AVENGER] at once AVENGED [the death of his son INJURY] and once again showed that any attempt to reconquer Valencia was fruitless while he still lived. [DNI PUNISHMENT] [DNI OFFENDER]
3. His secret ambition was for the Argentine ban to be lifted so [he AVENGER] could get to England and AVENGE [Pedro's death INJURY] [by taking out the England and especially one poker-faced Guards Officer PUNISHMENT]. [DNI OFFENDER]
4. In article 3 of the agreement, [each AVENGER] had promised to AVENGE [the violent death of the other INJURY] [with the blood of the murderer PUNISHMENT]. [DNI OFFENDER]
5. Suddenly he walked back to me and said [I AVENGER] ought to AVENGE [my father's death INJURY] and that he could help me. [DNI PUNISHMENT] [DNI OFFENDER]
6. [The Trojans AVENGER] wish to AVENGE [the death of Hector INJURY]; their misplaced values mean that patience in adversity is impossible. [DNI PUNISHMENT] [DNI OFFENDER]
7. "We know the conditions here and [we AVENGER] want to AVENGE [that World Cup defeat INJURY]," he said, referring to South Africa's 64-run with in New Zealand. [DNI PUNISHMENT] [DNI OFFENDER]

We can see that FEs are annotated in these example sentences extracted automatically. Among them, DNI is a definite null instantiated FE. Although it does not appear in the example sentence, it should still be annotated.

Through the seven example sentences annotated above, we can summarize two valence modes of the lexical unit, "avenge."

1. [AVENGER]-[INJURED PARTY]-[PUNISHMENT]-[OFFENDER]
2. [AVENGER]-[INJURY]-[PUNISHMENT]-[OFFENDER]

If we automatically extract more annotated example sentences from the corpus, we can also come up with the third valence mode.

3. [AVENGER]-[INJURED PARTY]-[INJURY]-[PUNISHMENT]-[OFFENDER]

These three valence modes reflect the syntactic and semantic characteristics of the lexical unit, "avenge." Obviously, such valence modes are very valuable for NLP.

FrameNet's software tools can also automatically generate Lexical Entry Reports, which include an FE syntactic realization table and valence mode table of the lexical unit. These two tables summarize the FE syntactic implementation and the valence modes of lexical units.

The FE syntactic realization table lists all the core FEs of a lexical unit, the number of annotated examples, and their syntactic implementation.

For example, the FE syntactic realization table of the lexical unit "avenge" is shown in Table 7.1.

Table 7.1   The FE syntactic realization table of the lexical unit "avenge"

Frame element	Number of annotated examples	Syntactic realization
AVENGER	33 exx	NP. Ext 25 exx ... 7 exx Poss, Ext 1 exx
INJURED PARTY	14 exx	NP. Ext 4 exx NP. Obj 11 exx
INJURY	21 exx	NP. Ext 4 exx PP. Comp 2 exx NP. Obj 13 exx ... 2 exx
OFFENDER	33 exx	PP Comp 5 exx ... 30 exx
PUNISHMENT	33 exx	PPing. Comp exx PP. Comp 3 exx ... 25 exx

Among them, exx represents instances that appear in the corpus. For example, 33 exx in the first line indicates that 33 instances of FE, AVENGER, appear in the corpus.

The valence mode table of the lexical unit describes phrase types (such as NP, VP, etc.) and syntactic functions (such as Ext, Obj, Comp, etc.) of FEs in the mode, respectively.

Table 7.2 is the valence mode table of the lexical unit "avenge", which shows the distribution of its phrase types and syntactic functions in the three valence modes.

These annotations by LexUnit Reports and Lexical Entry Reports automatically generated by the software provide us with sufficient language information in an intuitive way, which helps us to conduct an in-depth analysis of and research on the syntactic and semantic functions of relevant lexical units.

In addition to these software tools that can automatically generate annotated corpus-based reports, the FrameNet research group has also developed a powerful network-based database query tool called FrameSQL. The tool was developed with the help of Professor Hiroaki Sato of Senshu University, Japan, and it is available through a Web page linked to FrameNet. FrameSQL can help users realize database queries of multiple search parameters, such as frame name, FE name, syntax function, etc. For example, you can query all sentences of any frame in the form of prepositional phrases with an FE called "PUNISHMENT."

Readers interested in FrameNet can visit the following website: http//www.icsi. berkeley.edu/~framenet.

We have described the developmental process from case grammar to FrameNet. From this, we can see that Fillmore has advanced a lot the research on the thematic role relationship. We believe these advances are mainly reflected in the following three aspects:

Table 7.2 Valence mode of the lexical unit "avenge"

Number of annotated examples	Valence mode				
2 exx TOTAL	[Avenger] –	[injured party] –	[Injury] –	[Punishment] –	[Offender]
2 exx	NP	NP	PP	PPing	—
	Ext	Obj	Comp	Comp	—
12 exx TOTAL	[Avenger] –	[Injured Party] –	[Punishment] –		[Offender]
2 exx	—	NP	—		—
	—	Ext	—		—
1 exx	—	NP	—		PP
	—	Ext	—		Comp
6 exx	NP	NP	—		
	Ext	Obj	—		—
1 exx	NP	NP	PP		—
	Ext	Obj	Comp		—
1 exx	NP	NP	PP		—
	Ext	Obj	Comp		—
1 exx	NP	NP	PPing		PP
	Ext	Obj	Comp		—
19 exx TOTAL	[Avenger] –	[Injury] –	[Punishment] –		[Offender]
3 exx	—	NP	—		—
	—	Ext	—		—
1 exx	—	NP	PP		—
	—	Ext	Comp		—
1 exx	NP	—	—		—
	Ext	—	—		—
11 exx	NP	NP	—		—
	Ext	Obj	—		—
1 exx	NP	NP	PP		—
	Ext	Obj	Comp		—
1 exx	NP	NP	PPing		—
	Ext	Obj	Comp		—

First, FEs used in FrameNet are richer and more specific than the 13 cases proposed in case grammar, so it is more convenient to describe the syntactic and semantic functions of words, which helps us gain a better understanding of the relationship between thematic roles.

Second, linguistic facts that the research on case grammar relies on are mainly based on the linguists' own language knowledge and their intuitive feelings about the language, which are inevitably subjective and one-sided, while the research on FrameNet is carried out on the basis of a large-scale annotated corpus, which objectively reflects the true features of language phenomena and helps to avoid subjectivity and one-sidedness.

Third, the research method of case grammar mainly relies on the introspection of linguists and their insight into language phenomena, while the research on

FRAMENET ANNOTATION:

[Buyer Chuck] *bought* [Goods a car][Seller from Jerry][Payment for $1 000].

[Seller Jerry] *sold* [Goods a car][Buyer to Chuck][Payment for $1 000].

PROPBANK ANNOTATION:

[Arg0 Chuck] *bought* [Arg1 a car][Arg2 from Jerry][Arg3 for $1 000].

[Arg0 Jerry] *sold* [Arg1 a car][Arg2 to Chuck][Arg3 for $1 000].

Fig. 7.54 Annotation examples of FrameNet and PropBank 1

FrameNet uses various software tools run on computer, such as annotation by LexUnit Report and Lexical Entry Report, automatic generation tools, and Web-based database query tools. These software tools have become powerful assistants for researchers and improved the efficiency of research work.

Based on the Penn Treebank, Martha Palmer of the Department of Computer and Information Science, University of Pennsylvania in the United States, and others annotated the valence relationship of the verbs in the Penn Treebank and established Proposition Bank (PropBank). PropBank's work is similar to that of FrameNet, but what it annotates is not FE in the valence mode but the argument in the proposition (Arg). For example,

Chuck bought a car from Jerry.
Jerry sold a car to Chuck.

These two sentences are annotated in FrameNet and PropBank as follows (Fig. 7.54).

As seen from the annotation examples in Fig. 7.54, FrameNet classifies "bought" and "sold" into the event, COMMERCE (business activity), the FEs of which are buyer, goods, seller, and payment. FrameNet uses these FEs to annotate these two sentences. It can be seen from the annotation results of FrameNet that although the expressions of the two sentences are different, their FEs are the same, so the semantic contents they express are also the same. PropBank does not classify "bought" and "sold"; instead, it treats the two sentences as two propositions and uses logical arguments, Arg0, Arg1, Arg2, and Arg3, to annotate them. The arguments of "bought" and "sold" are different. For example, Arg0 in the first sentence is Chuck, but Arg0 in the second sentence is Jerry, etc.

The annotation results of the sentences in active voice are presented. Now, let us look at the following sentences in passive voice:

A car was bought by Chuck.
A car was sold to Chuck by Jerry.
Chuck was sold a car by Jerry.

FRAMENET ANNOTATION:

[Goods A car] was *bought* [Buyer by Chuck].

[Goods A car] was *sold* [Buyer to Chuck][Seller by Jerry].

[Buyer Chuck] was *sold* [Goods a car][Seller by Jerry].

PROPBANK ANNOTATION:

[Arg1 A car] was *bought* [Arg0 by Chuck].

[Arg1 A car] was *sold* [Arg2 to Chuck][Arg0 by Jerry].

[Arg2 Chuck] was *sold* [Arg1 a car][Arg0 by Jerry].

Fig. 7.55 Annotation examples of passive sentences 2

Fig. 7.56 Comparison between PropBank and FrameNet

PropBank		FrameNet
buy	*sell*	COMMERCE
Arg0: buyer	Arg0: seller	Buyer
Arg1: thing bought	Arg1: thing sold	Seller
Arg2: seller	Arg2: buyer	Payment
Arg3: price paid	Arg3: price paid	Goods
Arg4: benefactive	Arg4: benefactive	Rate/Unit

Their annotation results are shown in Fig. 7.55.

In passive sentences, FEs of FrameNet are still "buyer", "goods", and "seller", as shown in Fig. 7.55. Although the expressions of the three sentences are different, FEs of each word annotated in the three sentences are consistent. In PropBank, the subject can no longer be annotated as Arg0 but as Arg1 or Arg2, as they are sentences in passive voice. Moreover, the arguments Arg0, Arg1, and Arg2 of "bought" and "sold" are also different.

In PropBank, Arg0 of "bought" is the buyer, Arg1 is the thing bought, Arg2 is the seller, Arg3 is the price paid, and Arg4 is benefactive. Arg0 of "sold" is the seller, Arg1 is the thing sold, Arg2 is the buyer, Arg3 is the price paid, and Arg4 is the benefactive. In PropBank, the arguments for "bought" and "sold" are different. In FrameNet, "bought" and "sold" both belong to the COMMERCE event, and their FEs are always the same. The comparison is shown in Fig. 7.56.

From this comparison, it can be seen that FrameNet has better description and interpretation capabilities for language phenomena than PropBank does.

7.9 Word Sense Disambiguation Methods

In NLP, word sense disambiguation (WSD) is a very tough issue, as polysemy is a common phenomenon in any language. Additionally, it is difficult to find the general rules for the distribution of senses in polysemous words. Generally speaking, disambiguation of polysemous words involves many factors, such as context factors, semantic factors, situational factors, and even common sense in daily life, the handling of which is precisely the most difficult problem for computers.

As early as when MT was first introduced, the famous American mathematical logician Bar-Hillel pointed out in 1959 that fully automatic, high-quality MT (FAHQMT) is impossible (Detailed information can be found in Chap. 1). He believes that the problem of WSD will always perplex research on MT in its embryo. Therefore, FAHQMT was not only impossible at the technical level at that time but also impossible to realize in a long time.

In MT, senses of polysemy words in two languages often have an intricate and complicated situation. For example, the English word "leg" can refer to the legs of human beings, those of animals, those of chairs, or a boat's journey of sailing against the wind. The word "foot" in English can refer to the feet of people and those of chairs. The word "paw" means the claws of animals and clumsy or dirty hands of people. These three polysemous words have a very intricate intersection with the senses of the French words "jambe" (leg), "pied" (foot), "pate" (claw), and "etape" (a journey), as shown in Fig. 7.57.

This intricate and complicated situation of word senses brings great difficulties when selecting the sense of polysemous words in English-French MT.

Since 1959, scholars have done much work in polysemous word disambiguation research. Although the problem of WSD is far from being solved completely, the achievements over the past 40 years have allowed us to see the dawn of hope.

The methods of WSD can be summarized as follows:

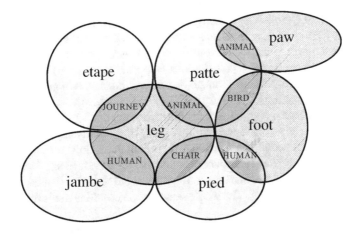

Fig. 7.57 Intricate intersection of word senses in English and French

7.9.1 WSD by Selecting the Most Common Sense

The early MT system does not have the WSD function. Although various senses of polysemous words in the machine dictionary are listed, the most common sense prioritizes the others. This method can handle some polysemous words and achieves certain disambiguation purposes, but WSD efficiency is not high, which is one of the important reasons behind the poor translation quality of early MT systems. For example, in the test sentence proposed by Bar-Hillel in 1959 (Sect. 1.2, Chap. 1), the most common sense is selected when the word "pen" is translated, as the most common sense of the word "pen" is a long thin object that one uses to write in ink. Jokingly, the translation turns out to be "The box was in the instrument used for writing."

7.9.2 WSD by Using Parts of Speech

Senses of some polysemous words are related to the parts of speech to which they belong, as different word senses often belong to different parts of speech. Therefore, if the parts of speech of these polysemous words can be determined, the WSD problem will be easily solved.

For example,

Face: When the word "face" is a verb, its sense is "to be positioned opposite someone or something"; when it is a noun, its sense is "the front part of your head from your chin to the top of your forehead where your mouth, eyes, nose, and other features are." In the sentence "The house faces the park," there is a noun phrase both in front of the word "faces" and after it, which suggests the word "faces" in the sentence is a verb, so its sense is "to be positioned opposite something." The whole sentence means "The house is positioned opposite the park." In the sentence "She pulled a long face," there is an adjective modification of the word "face," suggesting that the word "face" in the sentence is a noun, which refers to the front part of your head from your chin to the top of your forehead where your mouth, eyes and nose are. The sentence means "She pulled a long face (She looked sad)."

May: When the word "may" is an auxiliary verb, its sense is to give permission to someone to do something or to ask for permission (if it is used at the beginning of the sentence, the first letter is capitalized; in other cases, the first letter is not capitalized). When the word "May" is a noun, the first letter of which is capitalized, its sense refers to the month following April and preceding June. In the sentence "May I help you?," the word "May" is an auxiliary verb, so its sense is to ask for permission. In the sentence "May Day is first day of May," the word "May" is a noun, so its sense is the fifth month of the year. The whole sentence means "May 1st is the first day of the fifth month of the year."

Can: When the word "can" is used as an auxiliary verb, it means that someone has the ability to do something; when it is used as a noun, it refers to a metal container in which something, such as food, drink, or paint is put. In the sentence "She can speak German," the word "can" is used before the verb "speak" and after the personal pronoun "she," suggesting that it is used as an auxiliary verb, which means that someone has the ability to do something. The whole sentence means "she has the ability to speak German." In the sentence "He opened a can of beans," the word "can" is preceded by an indefinite article, followed by a preposition, indicating that it is used as a noun, which means a metal container. The whole sentence means "He opened a metal container in which beans are put."

Will: When the word "will" is used as an auxiliary verb, it is used to indicate that you hope, think, or have evidence that something is going to happen or be the case in the future; when it is used as a noun, it means the ability to control your thoughts or actions in order to achieve what you want to do. In the sentence "It will rain tomorrow," there is a pronoun in front of the word "will" and a verb after it, indicating that it is an auxiliary verb, so it means that you have evidence that something is going to happen." The whole sentence means "You have evidence that it is going to rain tomorrow." In the sentence "Free will makes us able to choose our way of life," the word "will" is preceded by an adjective, followed by a third-person present tense verb, suggesting that it is used a noun, so it refers to the ability to control your thoughts or actions to achieve what you want to do. The whole sentence means "We have the ability to choose our way of life."

Kind: When the word "kind" is used as a noun, it means "a particular variety or type of something or someone"; when it is used as an adjective, it means "being gentle, friendly, or generous." In the sentence "I like that kind of book," the word "kind" is used after the demonstrative "that" and before the preposition "of," indicating that it is used as a noun. Its sense is a particular variety or type of something or someone. The whole sentence means "I like that type of books." In the sentence "It was very kind of you to do it," the word "kind" is used after the adverb "very" and before the preposition "of," suggesting that it is used as an adjective. Its sense is "being gentle, friendly, or generous," and the whole sentence means "It was very friendly of you to do it."

If we have an efficient part-of-speech tagging system that can correctly determine the parts of speech of polysemous words, we can use it to determine the sense of polysemous words to achieve the purpose of WSD. However, when there are many different senses of polysemous words in the same parts of speech, this method, WSD by using parts of speech, is powerless because we still need to choose the appropriate senses among different senses after its part of speech of the word has been determined.

For example, the polysemous word "works" can be used both as a verb and as a noun. When it is used as a verb, its sense is "to do something that involves physical or mental effort"; when it is used as a noun, its sense can either be "factory" or "a thing produced as a result of work." In the sentence "My daughter works in an office," the word "works" is used after the noun phrase "my daughter" and before the preposition "in," indicating it is used a verb, so its sense is "to do something that involves physical or mental effort." The whole sentence means "My daughter does something that involves physical or mental effort in an office." However, when the word "works" is found to be used as a noun whose sense has not been finally determined, an embarrassing dilemma might occur. For example, in the two sentences "It is a gas works" and "I read the works of Shakespeare," the word "works" can be regarded as a noun. However, we still cannot decide whether the sense of the word "works" in the first sentence is "factory," or it is "a thing produced as a result of work" in the second sentence. Then, we also need to disambiguate word sense according to selectional restrictions of the context. For example, we can prescribe that when the word "works" is used with a noun that expresses fuel, its sense can be determined to be "factory," and when the word "works" is used with the name of a writer, its sense can be determined to be "a thing produced as a result of work." Then, WSD can be resolved in light of such selectional restrictions.

7.9.3 WSD Based on Selectional Restrictions

The main knowledge sources for WSD are selectional restrictions and semantic type hierarchies, which are used to remove inappropriate senses to reduce the number of ambiguities in semantic analysis.

Katz and Fodor (1963) were the first to study selectional restrictions. Hirst (1987) applied selectional restrictions to computer processing.

Take the disambiguation of the word "dish" for example. Let's have a close look at the following passage:

In our house, everybody has a career, and none of them includes washing *dishes*," he says. In her tiny kitchen at home, Mr. Chen works efficiently, stir-frying several simple *dishes*, including braised pig ears and chicken livers with green peppers.

The word "dishes" in the former sentence refers to physical objects for eating, while the word "dishes" in the latter sentence refers to food that is prepared in a particular style. Their selectional restrictions are different. The former is PATIENT of "wash," which should be washable, and the latter is PATIENT of "stir-fry," which should be edible. The predicate chooses the correct sense of its ambiguous argument and removes the sense that cannot be matched. Therefore, the idea of selectional restrictions is actually that "you shall know a word by the company it keeps.

When the predicate is ambiguous, the ambiguity can be eliminated according to the senses of its argument. For example,

Well, there was the time *served* green-lipped mussels from New Zealand.
Which airlines *serve* Denver?
Which ones *serve* breakfast?

The verb "serve" in the former sentence requires a certain food as its PATIENT, the verb "serve" in the second sentence requires a place name or group as its PATIENT, and the verb "serve" in the third sentence requires a certain meal as its PATIENT. If we are sure that the words "mussel, Denver, and breakfast" are unambiguous, we can eliminate the ambiguity of the verb "serve" by their senses.

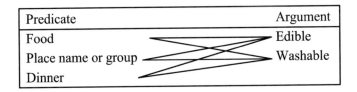

Fig. 7.58 Selectional restrictions

If the predicate and its arguments are both ambiguous, the possibility of selection is greatly increased. For example,

I'm looking for a restaurant that *serves* vegetarian *dishes*.

If the word "serve" has 3 senses and the word "dish" has 2 senses, this sentence should have 3 × 2 senses. In this case, the correct choice must be made jointly based on the selectional restrictions of its predicate and argument (Fig. 7.58).

Therefore, this sentence means "I am looking for a restaurant that sells vegetarian food."

WSD based on selectional restrictions requires the use of two aspects of knowledge in semantic analysis:

- Semantic-type hierarchies
- Selectional restrictions

These two aspects of knowledge can be obtained from WordNet. The information on the semantic-type hierarchies can be obtained from the hypernymy of the relevant word, and the information on selectional restriction is obtained by linking the Synset of the relevant word with the argument of the predicate. If we obtain these two aspects of knowledge from WordNet, we can use the selectional restriction to resolve WSD.

However, the selectional restriction is limited in the following aspects:

- It is difficult to determine the scope of the selectional restriction of the relevant word when the selectional restriction is too general.

  For example,

What kind of *dishes* do you recommend?
     It is difficult for us to decide whether the selectional restriction of the word "dishes" is "washable" or "edible" in this sentence.

- In a negative sentence, the negative relationship clearly violates the selectional restriction, while the sense of the sentence is legal.

  For example,

People realized you can't *eat* gold for lunch if you're hungry.
     In the sentence, the phrase "eat gold" obviously violates the selectional restriction of the word "eat" because gold is not edible. However, this sentence is completely legal because of the presence of the negative word "can't."

- When the event described in the sentence is an unusual event, the sentence is still completely legal despite violating the selectional restriction.

  For example,

  In his two championship trials, Mr. Kulkirni *ate* glass on an empty stomach, accompanied only by water and tea.

  　　The word "glass" in the sentence is not edible, which violates the selectional restriction of the word "eat," but this sentence is still legal.

- A metaphor or a metonymy in a sentence is a great challenge to the selectional restriction.

  For example,

  If you want to *kill* the Soviet Union, get it to try to *eat* Afghanistan.

At this time, the typical selectional restrictions of the PATIENT of the predicate "kill" and "eat" are completely invalid. However, the semantic legitimacy of this sentence is beyond doubt.

　　In 1987, Hirst pointed out that all legal example sentences that violate selectional restrictions would lead to the failure of WSD. Therefore, he suggested that the concept of preference should be introduced into the study of selectional restriction rather than a rigid stipulation.

　　In 1997, Resnik proposed the concept of selectional association, a probability measure of the strength of association between a predicate and the category of argument dominated by the predicate. Resnik combines the hypernymy relationship in WordNet with the verb-argument relationship in the annotated corpus to calculate the strength of selectional association. Resnik uses selectional association for WSD. The algorithm chooses the argument with the highest selectional association between the predicate and the superordinate of the argument as the correct sense of the argument. Its drawback is that it can only be used when only the argument is ambiguous while the predicate is not.

7.9.4　Robust WSD Methods

The methods introduced previously all belong to the so-called "rule-to-rule approach." In addition to the so-called "rule-to-rule approach," there is a "stand-alone approach," a kind of robust WSD method. The robust stand-alone approach to WSD relies on part-of-speech tagging to minimize the requirements for information to achieve "stand-alone" and allow the machine to learn and obtain information by itself.

　　This machine learning method requires active training of the system so that the system itself can perform WSD.

　　The word to be disambiguated is called the target word, and the text in which the target word is embedded is called the context. The input is initialized as follows:

- The input text should be annotated with parts of speech.
- The context can be regarded as a language fragment of varying lengths surrounding the target word.
- The words in the context should be lexically analyzed, and the words with derivational endings should be reduced to their original forms.
- Preferably, the text should have undergone local syntactic analysis or dependency relationship analysis to reflect the topic role relationship or other grammatical relationships.

After such initialization, the input text is further refined into a set of features containing relevant information. The main steps are as follows:

- Carefully select relevant linguistic features.
- Formally describe (or encode) these features according to the requirements of the learning algorithm.

Most learning systems use simple feature vectors encoded by using numbers or part-of-speech tags.

Linguistic features used to train the WSD system can be roughly divided into two categories:

- Collocation features
- Co-occurrence features

The collocation feature encodes the context around the target word and requires specific location features that reflect the grammatical nature of these words. Typical features, such as words, root forms, and parts of speech, can often isolate the specific sense of the target word for processing.

For example,

An electric guitar and *bass* player stand off to one side, not really part of the scene, just as a sort of nod to gringo expectations perhaps.

We take the words both before and after the feature word "bass" and their part-of-speech tags as feature vectors, which are expressed as follows.

[guitar, NN1, and, CJC, player, NN1, stand, VVB]

The co-occurrence feature does not consider the precise location information of adjacent words. Instead, it takes the words themselves as features. The value of the feature is the number of times the word appears in the environment surrounding the target word. The environment of the target word is generally defined as a fixed window centered on the target word, in which the occurrence frequency of the notional word should be calculated.

For example, for the target word "bass," we select its 12 co-occurring words from the corpus and mark their frequency of appearance in a specific window.

The 12 co-occurring words are fishing, big, sound, player, fly, rod, pound, double, runs, playing, guitar, and band.

In the above sentence, the fragment "guitar and bass player stand" is chosen as the window, whose feature vector is as follows:

[0, 0, 0, 1, 0, 0, 0, 0, 0, 0, 1, 0]

According to this feature vector, it can be determined that the sense of the word "bass" is a bass instrument since the values of the fourth co-occurrence word "player" and the eleventh co-occurrence word "guitar" in the feature vector are all 1.

In robust WSD systems, collocation features and co-occurrence features are usually used together.

7.9.5   Supervised Learning Approaches

Supervised learning approaches can be further divided into the naïve Bayes classifier and the decision list classifier.

7.9.5.1   Naïve Bayes Classifier

The naïve Bayes classifier is based on comprehensive consideration of multiple features for WSD instead of a specific feature. This method calculates the most likely sense of a polysemous word in a given context. The calculation formula is as follows:

$$s = \arg\max_{s \in S} P(s|V)$$

where S is the set of word senses, s represents every possible sense in S, and V represents the vector in the input context.

The calculation formula directly based on the vector is as follows:

$$s = \arg\max_{s \in S} P(s) \prod_{j=1}^{n} P(v_j|s)$$

In 1992, Gale et al. used this method to test six English polysemous words, "duty," "drug," "land," "language," "position," and "sentence," for WSD, and the accuracy rate reached approximately 90%.

7.9.5.2   Decision List Classifier

The decision list classifier makes a decision table according to different equivalence classes of co-occurrence words and then uses the decision table to determine the best word sense in the input vector.

For example, the following decision table can be made to determine the sense of the target word "bass."

Rule		Sense of the target word
The word "fish" appears in the window	→	bass1
striped bass	→	bass1
The word "guitar" appears in the window.	→	bass2
bass player	→	bass2
The word "piano" appears in the window.	→	bass2
The word "tenor" appears in the window.	→	bass2
sea bass	→	bass1
play/V bass	→	bass2
The word "river" appears in the window.	→	bass1
The word "violin" appears in the window.	→	bass2
The word "salmon" appears in the window.	→	bass1
on bass	→	bass2
bass are		bass1

Among them, bass1 means fish and bass2 means music. If detection is successful, the corresponding word sense is selected. If detection fails, the next detection is carried out. In this way, detection proceeds to the end of the decision table, whose default value is the maximum possible sense.

This decision table can be used to eliminate the sense of "fish" from the sense of "music" in the target word "bass." The first detection indicates that if the word "fish" appears in the input, bass1 is chosen as the correct answer. Otherwise, the next item is detected until the return value is true. If the default value at the end of the decision table is detected, the return value is true.

The items in the decision table are arranged according to the features of the training corpus. In 1994, Yarowsky proposed a method to calculate the log-likelihood ratio of each pair of eigenvalues in the decision table. According to the calculated ratio, the order of sense1 and sense2 in the decision table was adjusted to determine the sequence of eigenvalues in the whole decision table. The calculation formula is as follows:

$$\text{Abs}\left(\text{Log}\left(\frac{P(\text{sense}_1|f_i = v_j)}{P(\text{sense}_2|f_i = v_j)}\right)\right)$$

where v is the eigenvector of sense and f is the absolute frequency of sense.

According to this formula, the decision table with the best arrangement can be obtained by comparing pairs of eigenvalues. Yarowsky (1996) obtained a 95% correct rate of WSD by using this method.

7.9.6   Bootstrapping Approaches to WSD

To overcome the problem of supervised learning approaches, the need to train a large number of annotated corpora, Hearst in 1991 and Yarowsky in 1995 proposed bootstrapping approaches. This approach does not need to train a large number of corpora, only relying on a relatively small number of examples with each determined sense of a word depending on a small number of annotated examples. With these examples as seeds, a supervised learning method is used to train the corpus to obtain the initial classification. Then, these initial classifications are used to extract a large number of training data from the untrained corpora, and the process is repeated until satisfactory accuracy and coverage are obtained.

The key to this method is to create a large number of training data from a small seed set, which is then used to create a new and more accurate classification. Every time this process is repeated, an increasing number of training corpora is obtained; a decreasing number of non-annotated corpora remains.

The initial seed of the bootstrapping approach can be generated by using different methods.

In 1991, Hearst used a simple manual annotating method to obtain a small set of examples from the initial corpus. His method has the following three advantages.

- The seed instances are reliable, which ensures that machine learning has a correct foothold.
- The examples selected by the analysis program are not only correct but can also be used as the prototype of each sense.
- Training is simple and feasible.

In 1995, Yarowsky proposed the principle called "One Sense per Collocation," which works quite well. His method is to choose a reasonable indicator as the seed for each sense. For example, "fish" is chosen as the seed for identifying the sense of "bass1" and "play" as the seed for identifying the sense of "bass2."

Here is an example:

play -- bass2

We need more good teachers—right now, there are only a half a dozen who can *play* the free *bass* with ease.

An electric guitar and *bass play*er stand off to one side, not really part of the scene, just as a sort of nod to gringo expectation perhaps.

fish -- bass1

The researchers said the worms spend part of their life cycle in fish such as Pacific salmon and striped *bass* and Pacific rockfish or snapper.

Saturday morning I arise at 8:30 and click on "America's best known *fisherman*," giving advice on catching *bass* in cold weather from the seat of a *bass* boat in Louisiana.

There are two ways for Yarowsky to choose seeds. One is through a machine-readable dictionary, and the other is to use statistical methods to select seeds based on collocation relationships. His correct rate of ambiguity resolution for 12 polysemous words is 96.5%.

7.9.7   Unsupervised WSD Methods

Unsupervised methods avoid using corpora with sense tagging through training. Instead, they only use unlabeled corpora as input, and these corpora are clustered according to their similarity, which can be used as a representative of the feature vector of the component. Clustering based on similarity can be used to classify instances without feature coding after manual semantic tagging.

For example, the senses of the English polysemous word "bank" are bank1 and bank2. In the untrained corpus, the word "money" appears in one context, the word "loan" appears in the second context, and the word "water" appears in the third context. The number of co-occurrences with other words in different contexts is their correlation vector, as shown in Table 7.3.

From the distribution of the number of co-occurrences (correlation vector), we can see the closeness of the similarity of these three words. The similarity between "water and loan or money" is far less than that between "money and loan." In other words, the correlation vector between "money and loan" is greater than that between "money and water" and that between "loan and water." In this way, we can cluster the words "money and loan" together, which is labeled as "bank1." Obviously, the sense of bank1 should be the bank, an institution where people or businesses can keep their money. If the word "water" is counted as an independent cluster labeled as "bank2," the sense should obviously be the raised area of ground along the edge of a river, canal, or lake.

The method used frequently is agglomerative clustering, in which each of the N training instances is assigned to a cluster. Then, the two most similar clusters are successively combined into a new cluster in a bottom-up manner until the expected index is reached.

The unsupervised approach has the following shortcomings, as it does not use manually labeled data:

- It is impossible to know what the correct sense is in the training corpus.
- The obtained clusters are often very different in nature from the senses of the training examples. They do not agree with one another.
- The number of clusters is almost always inconsistent with the number of sense items of the target word that needs to be disambiguated.

In 1992 and 1998, Schütze successively used unsupervised methods to disambiguate polysemous words. The obtained results were very close to those obtained by using supervised methods and bootstrapping methods, reaching a 90% accuracy rate. However, the number of polysemous words tested is very small.

Table 7.3 Number of co-occurrences

	bank	building	loan	money	mortgage	river	water
loan	150	20	70	100	50	10	40
money	600	500	100	400	50	30	70
water	15	400	40	70	1	400	500

Table 7.4 Comparison of ambiguity resolution results

Words	Number of sense items	WSD correct rate by vector clustering	WSD correct rate by selecting the most common sense item
tank/s	8	95	80
plant/s	13	92	66
interest/s	3	93	68
capital/s	2	95	66
suit/s	2	95	54
motion/s	2	92	54
ruling	2	90	60
vessel/s	7	92	58
space	10	90	59
train/s	10	89	76

In 1992, Schütze also used the method of vector clustering for WSD, comparing the WSD results of vector clustering with those obtained by selecting the most common sense (Table 7.4).

The results obtained by vector clustering are much better than those obtained by selecting the most commonsense item used in early MT systems.

7.9.8   Dictionary-Based WSD Approach

The biggest problem with the above methods is the size of the data. Now we shall discuss the dictionary-based WSD.

Many WSD tests involve 2–12 words, and the largest test involves 121 nouns and 70 verbs (Ng and Lee 1996). Therefore, scholars have come up with the idea of using a machine-readable dictionary by a dictionary-based approach because the machine-readable dictionary can provide sense items and the definition context of the corresponding sense items for WSD.

In 1986, M. Lesk first used dictionary definitions for WSD. The definition of dictionary entries in the machine-readable dictionary is actually an existing source of knowledge. When the degree of affinity between two words is estimated, the two words that appear in the definition of the machine-readable dictionary at the same time can be compared. If there are common words in the definitions of the two words, it can be inferred that the affinity between them is greater so that the optimization can be made accordingly. He compares the definitions of the senses of polysemous words and selects the sense with the largest coverage context as the correct one. For example,

In the phrase "pine cone," the word "cone" is a polysemous word. We compare the definitions of the word "pine" in the dictionary with the definition of the word "cone" as follows:

Pine	1	Kinds of *evergreen trees* with needle-shaped leaves
	2	Waste away through sorrow or illness
Cone	1	Solid body which narrows to a point
	2	Something of this shape whether solid or hollow
	3	Fruit of certain *evergreen trees*

We choose cone 3 as the correct sense of the polysemous word "cone" in the phrase "pine cone" because in the definition of cone 3, the words "evergreen and tree" coincide with the words "evergreen and tree" in the definition of pine 1. Lesk selected some primary linguistic data from the book *Pride and Prejudice* and from articles in *AP Newswire* for his hypothesis testing, and WSD accuracy rate was found to be 50–70%.

For another example, in English, the word "pen" is a polysemous word, which can be understood as "an instrument used for writing with ink" or "a small area with a fence around it in which farm animals are kept for a short time." In the machine-readable dictionary, the definition of the word "pen" is "an enclosure in which domestic animals are kept," and the definition of word "sheep" is "there are many breeds of domestic sheep." If there are both "pen" and "sheep" in a sentence, the sense of the word "pen" should be "an enclosure in which *domestic* animals are kept" instead of "an instrument used for writing with ink," as there is a common word "domestic" in definitions of these two words, thus resolving the ambiguity.

K. Jensen and J. L. Binot use definitions of words in online dictionaries to resolve the case ambiguity of English prepositions.

For example, the English preposition "with" can be used to mean the INSTRU-MENT or PART-OF relationship, which gives rise to case ambiguity. In the English sentence "I ate a fish with a fork," the word "fork" is defined as "an instrument for eating food," in which the function of instrument is the same as that of the preposition "with," so it can be judged that the function of the preposition "with" in this sentence should be INSTRUMENT. Therefore, the sense of this sentence should be "I use a fork as an instrument to eat fish."

In another English sentence, "I ate a fish with bones," the word "bone" is defined as "a part of animal" in the machine-readable dictionary. In the machine-readable dictionary, the definition of the word "fish" is "a kind of animal," which is the same as the preposition "with," denoting the PART-OF relationship, so it can be judged that the function of preposition "with" in this sentence is the PART-OF relationship, so the sense of this sentence should be "I ate a fish with its bones."

The main difficulty of this method is that the definitions in the dictionary are often too short to provide sufficient contextual information for WSD. For example, in *the American Heritage Dictionary*, there is no deposit in the definition of the word "bank," and there is no bank in the definition of the word "deposit." However, these two words are closely related. Now, some dictionaries have subject codes, which seem to be able to make up for this defect because the words "bank" and "deposit" can be classified as the subject of EC (economics). Guthrie reported that he used the subject codes of LDOCE (*Longman's Dictionary of Contemporary English*, 1978) to resolve ambiguities and increased the accuracy rate from 47% to 72%.

Over the past 40 years, although NLP has made great achievements in WSD, it seems that it is still difficult for scholars with their proposed methods to determine the sense of the word "pen," a small area with a fence around it, in the sentence "The box was in the pen," a test sentence proposed by Bar-Hillel in 1959. WSD is indeed a very difficult problem. Unremitting efforts should be made before the WSD problem can be truly resolved. Undoubtedly, past achievements have given us a glimmer of hope; however frail, it is an early dawn, which is encouraging because it heralds the bright future of NLP.

Bibliography

1. Brown, P. F. et al. 1991. Word-Sense Disambiguation Using Statistical Methods. In *Proceedings of ACL 29*.
2. Fillmore, C. 1968. The Case for Case. In *Universals in Linguistic Theory*, ed. Emmon Bach and Harms, 1–88. New York: Holt-Rinehart-Winston.
3. ———. 1985. Frames and the Semantics of Understanding. *Quaderni di Semantica* 6 (2): 222–253.
4. Gale, W., K. Church, and D. Yarowsky. 1992. A Method for Disambiguating Word Senses in a Large Corpus. *Computer and Humanities* 26.
5. Lesk, M.E. 1986. Automatic Sense Disambiguation: How to Tell a Pine Cone from an Ice Cream Cone. In *Proceedings of the 1986 SIGDOC Conference*. New York: Association for Computing Machinery.
6. Mel'chuk, I.A. 1979. *Studies in Dependency Syntax*. Ann Arbor: Karoma Publishers.
7. Мельчук, И.А. 1995. *Русский язык в модели <смысл текст>*. Москва.
8. Montague, R. 1973. The Proper Treatment of Qualification in Ordinary English. In *Formal Philosophy: Selectional Papers of Richard Montague*, ed. R. Thomasson, 247–270. New Haven: Yale University Press.
9. Quillian, M.R. 1968. Semantic Memory. In *Semantic Information Processing*, ed. Minsky, 227–270. Cambridge: MIT Press.
10. Schank, R.C. 1972. Conceptual Dependency: A Theory of Natural Language Processing. *Cognitive Psychology* 3: 52–631.
11. Schank, R.C., and C.K. Reisbeck. 1977. *Scripts, Plans, Goals and Understanding*. New York: Lawrence Relbaum.
12. Wilks, Y. 1975. A Preferential, Pattern-Seeking, Semantics for Natural Language Reference. *Artificial Intelligence* 6 (1): 53–74.
13. Yarowsky, D. 1995. Unsupervised Word Sense Disambiguation Rivaling Supervised Methods. In *Proceedings ACL 33*.
14. Zhiwei, Feng. 1985. Montague Grammar. *Journal of Foreign Languages (Journal of Heilongjiang University)* 2: 1–6.
15. ———. 1986. Application of Mathematical Logic Methods in Machine Translation. In *Collection of Logic and Language*. Beijing: Language Publishing House.
16. ———. 1987. The Application of Montage Grammar in Machine Translation. *Modern Library and Information Technology* 4: 39–42.

17. ———. 1987. New Methods of Language Research in Machine Translation and Human-machine Dialogue. *Information Science* 1: 9–26.
18. ———. 1996. *Computer Processing of Natural Languages*. Shanghai: Shanghai Foreign Language Education Press.
19. ———. 1998. Characteristics and Difficulties of Semantic Analysis of Chinese Syntax from the Perspective of Chinese-English Machine Translation. In *Proceedings of the Symposium on Chinese Computing and Metrology*. Hong Kong: City University of Hong Kong.
20. ———. 2004. Research on Word Sense Disambiguation Methods. *Terminology Standardization and Information Technology* 1: 31–37.
21. ———. 2006. From Case Grammar to FrameNet. *Journal of PLA University of Foreign Languages* 3: 1–9.
22. ———. 2008. The Orderliness of Concepts—The Conceptual System. *Chinese Terminology for Science and Technology* 4: 12–15.
23. ———. 2013. *Schools of Modern Linguistics (Revised Edition)*, 486–524. Beijing: The Commercial Press.
24. Zhiwei, Feng, and Li Li. 2007. Understanding and Construction of FrameNet. In *Frontiers of Content Computing Research and Application*, 314–319. Beijing: Tsinghua University Press.
25. Zhiwei, Feng, and Yunhua Qu. 2006. Classification and Semantic Interpretation of Chinese Tense and Aspects. *Journal of Zhejiang University (Edition of Humanities and Social Sciences)* 3: 169–175.

Chapter 8
Formal Models of Automatic Situation and Pragmatic Processing

Systemic functional grammar holds that a language has both situational and internal contexts and that situation plays an important role in language understanding. Since different sentences are often used to express the same message due to different situations, systemic functional grammar is a kind of linguistic theory that studies different sentence expressions according to functional differences of situations. It has been widely used in NLP. Pragmatics is the study of the relationship between the language and the context in which it is used. As the context of language use includes ontologies such as people and things, pragmatics involves studying how to use the language to indicate or refer back to people and things. Pragmatics also involves the formation of the structure of an utterance and the study of how the listener understands the conversation because the context of language use also includes the context of the utterance. Research on formal models of automatic pragmatic processing has achieved preliminary results.

This chapter is devoted to an introduction to formal models of automatic processing of situation and pragmatics, describing systemic functional grammar, speech act theory, and conversation intelligent agents.

8.1 Basic Concepts of Systemic Functional Grammar

Systemic functional grammar was proposed by British linguist M. A. K. Halliday (1925–2018, Fig. 8.1).

Halliday was born in Leeds, Yorkshire, England, in 1925. In his youth, he majored in Chinese Language and Literature at the University of London. He studied at Peking University in China from 1947 to 1949 under the guidance of Changpei Luo. From 1949 to 1950, he studied at Lingnan University under Li Wang's supervision. After returning to Britain, he studied for a doctorate under the guidance of J. R. Firth (1890–1960). In 1955, having completed his doctoral dissertation entitled "The Language of the Chinese Secret History of the Mongols," he was

© Springer Nature Singapore Pte Ltd. 2023
Z. Feng, *Formal Analysis for Natural Language Processing: A Handbook*,
https://doi.org/10.1007/978-981-16-5172-4_8

Fig. 8.1 Halliday

awarded doctorate of Philosophy from Cambridge University. After that, Halliday taught at the University of Cambridge, University of Edinburgh, University of London, Yale University, Brown University, and University of Nairobi, Kenya. From 1972 to 1973, he was a researcher at the Advanced Research Center of the Stanford Academy of Behavioral Sciences in California, United States, and from 1973 to 1975, he was a professor of linguistics at Illinois State University. Then, Halliday moved to Australia and helped establish the Department of Linguistics at the University of Sydney and served as the head of the department. Halliday has been successively awarded the corresponding academician of the British Academy of Sciences, the academician of the Australian Academy of Humanities, the honorary academician of the European Academy of Sciences, and the lifetime honorary professor of the University of Sydney. He has also been awarded the honorary doctorate by universities such as the University of Nancy in France, the University of Birmingham in the United Kingdom, the University of Athens in Greece, Macquarie University in Australia, Lingnan University in Hong Kong, Cardiff University in the United Kingdom, and the Central Institute of English and Foreign Languages in India.

Halliday inherited and developed the functionalist theory advocated by the London School of Linguistics represented by his teacher Firth. Influenced by B. Malinowski, L. Hjelmslev, and Whorf, he established and developed a unique systemic functional grammar.

The key points of Firth's functionalist language theory are as follows:

1. In addition to the context within the language, the language also has its situational context.

   Firth's language theory was greatly influenced by B. Manlinowski. While conducting anthropological fieldwork in the Trobriand Islands of Papua New Guinea in the South Pacific, B. Manlinowski found that it was very difficult to translate the native speakers' utterances into English. For example, a man rowing a canoe called his oars *wood*. One can hardly understand the word *wood* without taking into consideration the context in which the word *wood* was uttered. Therefore, he believes that it is impossible to translate the terms and utterances in the language used by one culture into the language used by another culture. The language is by no means a self-contained system. Languages have evolved in relation to the specific requirements of society. Therefore, the nature and use of a language reflect the specific characteristics of a society. He said, "Utterances and their contexts are closely intertwined with each other. The context in which an utterance is uttered is essential for understanding that utterance." He went on to say, "The meaning of a word cannot be derived passively from the contemplation of this word itself. Instead, it is always necessary to refer to a specific culture and to analyze the functions of words before they can be inferred."[1] Therefore, in general, the meaning of an utterance can only be derived in the context of a given culture, especially in the context of the situation in which it occurs. By "cultural context," B. Manlinowski refers to the social culture in which the speaker lives. By "situational context," B. Manlinowski means something that is actually happening at the time when an utterance is issued, that is, the context in which the speech occurs.

Firth also used the term "situational context" suggested by B. Manlinowski, but he defined it more precisely.

Firth believed that verbal behavior includes the following three feature categories:

(a) Characteristic features of the participants: who they are, what kind of personality they have, and what kind of relevant characteristics they possess

- Verbal behavior of the participants
- Behaviors other than the verbal behavior of the participants

(b) Related things and nonverbal and nonpersonality events
(c) Effects of verbal behavior[2]

Behaviors other than verbal behaviors, nonverbal and nonpersonality events, effects of verbal behavior, and so on, mentioned here are situational contexts.

Therefore, he argued that languages should be viewed as "social processes." A language, he said, is "a form of human life, and that it is not just a set of conventional signs and symbols." "As we continue to live," he added, "we must continue to learn, step-by-step, the various forms of the language which serve as the conditions of our society, and that we are supposed to know what roles we play and what we have to say in relation to the roles we are playing. To act effectively and courteously is to speak appropriately in the context of a

---

[1] B. Malinowski, *The Problem of Meaning in Primitive Language*, p307, 1923.
[2] J. R. Firth, *A Synopsis of Linguistic Theory*, 1957.

situation. Therefore, the concept of the restricted language must be put forward."
He also said, "Social people can play various and interconnected roles and that
they don't appear to conflict or to be incompatible with one another... In order
to study linguistics, a social person should be regarded as one who can use
various restricted languages."[3] Here, the so-called restricted language refers to
the appropriate words spoken by people according to their respective industries,
identities, statuses, or circumstances. Firth argued that the heterogeneity and
unconnectedness of the language go beyond what most people would like to
admit. There are as many languages as there are specialized systems of human
behavior and as many specialized social behaviors associated with a given
language. People may have a variety of identities, sometimes being yokels and
sometimes being people of the educated class. They all have different languages.

Logicians tend to believe that words and propositions have meaning in
themselves regardless of the "speaker" or the "situational context." Firth pointed
out that this is not true. "I believe that speech cannot be separated from the social
context in which it occurs," he said. "Every utterance of the modern spoken
language should be considered to have a context in which it is spoken and that it
should be studied in relation to the typical participant in some generalized
situational context."[4]

2. Speech has both contextual and formal meanings.

Firth emphasized that the purpose of linguistics is to interpret meaning. He
said, "The primary task of descriptive linguistics is to state meaning."[5] There are
two meanings, contextual and formal. The reason why he makes such a distinction is that he believes that speech has its situational context and internal context
as well. The situational meaning comes from the context of the situation, and the
formal meaning comes from the internal context of the language. The situational
meaning is the function of the language in the context of the situation, which was
proposed by Firth, who followed B. Manlinowski's viewpoint, as is previously
mentioned. The formal meaning was proposed by Firth, who had been inspired by
the idea that linguistic signs have value advocated by Ferdinand de Sausurre
(1857–1913). What is the formal meaning then? Firth said that "I advocate
decomposing meaning or function into a series of components. To determine
each function, we should start with the relation between a certain language form
or component and a certain context. That is to say, the meaning of a certain
language form should be seen as a complex of contextual relations, while
phonetics, grammar, or semantics deals with its relevant components placed in
the proper context."[6]

---

[3] J. R. Firth, *The treatment of language in general linguistics*, p146, 1959.

[4] J. R. Firth, *Papers in Linguistics*, 1934–1951, p226.

[5] J. R. Firth, *Papers in Linguistics*, 1957, p190.

[6] J. R. Firth, *Papers in Linguistics*, 1934–1951, p19.

In Firth's view, the formal meaning can be expressed in three levels, collocation level, grammatical level, and phonetic level.

Here, collocation means that certain words are often used together with certain other words. Firth said, "The fact that 'Meaning depends on collocation' is an abstraction in relation to the composition, which has no direct connection with the ways used to analyze the meaning conceptually or mentally. For example, one of the meanings of the word *night* denotes the collocation relation with the word *dark*, and one of the meanings of the word *dark* is naturally the collocation relation with the word *night*."[7] The noun *cow* is often used with the verb *milk*. These two words are often used in ways that follow. They are milking the cows, or cows give milk. However, the words *tigress* or *lioness* hardly go with the word *milk*. Native speakers of English will never say *They are milking the tigresses, or *Tigresses give milk. It can be seen that at the collocation level, the formal meaning of the word *cow* is different from those of tigress and lioness.

There are also formal meanings at the grammatical level. For example, in the grammatical category of quantity that nouns denote, there are only singular or plural forms in some languages (such as English), and in some other languages, there are singular, double, or plural forms (such as Old Cyrillic). And, in still some other languages there are four forms, singular, double, large, or small plural (such as Fijian). In this way, the formal meaning of the singular number in English is different from that of Old Cyrillic and that of Fijian. In English, the singular is only opposed to the plural. In Old Cyrillic, the singular is opposed to the double and the plural; in Fijian, the singular is opposed to the double, large, and small plural numbers.

At the phonetic level, there are also formal meanings. Suppose there are three vowels [i], [a], and [u] in one language and five vowels [i], [e], [a], [o], and [u] in another language, the formal meaning of the vowel [i] in the first language is opposite to [a] and [u], and the formal meaning of the same vowel in the second language is opposite to [e], [a], [o], and [u]. The formal meanings of the two are different.

Firth's idea of the situational meaning comes from B. Manlinowski, and his idea of the formal meaning originates from Sausurre. He combined the views of these two masters into one, creating a unique one, which made it shine in a different way with great brilliance.

3. Language has two aspects, structure and system.

In Firth's theory, the words "structure" and "system" have specific meanings. Structure refers to the syntagmatic ordering of elements of language components, while system is a set of paradigmatic units that can be replaced at one position in the structure. The structure is horizontal, whereas the system is vertical, as shown in Fig. 8.2.

There are structures and systems at the grammatical, phonetic, and collocation levels.

---

[7] J. R. Firth, *Papers in Linguistics*, 1957, p196.

Fig. 8.2 Structure and system

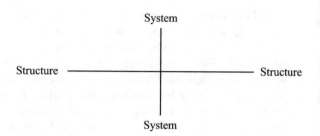

At the grammatical level, for example,

John greeted him.
John invited him.
John met him.

The structure of these three sentences is SVO (subject + verb + object), and their structure is the same. In this same structure, the verbs can be *greet, invite*, or *meet*, and the three together form a system.

At the phonetic level, for example, there are four English words, *pit, bit, pin*, and *pen*, whose structure is C_1VC_2 (consonant$_1$ + vowel + consonant$_2$). In this structure, [p] and [b] can appear at position C_1, [i] and [e] can appear at position V, and [t] and [n] can appear at position C_2, which, therefore, constitutes three different systems.

At the collocation level, for example,

Column A	Column B
Strong argument	Powerful argument
Strong tea	Powerful whiskey
Strong table	Powerful car

The structure here is A + N (adjective + noun). However, in Column A, three nouns *argument, tea*, and *table* appear after the adjective *strong*, and the three nouns belong to one system; in Column B, three nouns *argument, whiskey*, and *car* appear after the adjective *powerful*, and all three nouns belong to another system. For native speakers of English, neither *strong whiskey nor *powerful tea is allowed; otherwise, the system will be messed up.

4. Polysystemic theory and prosodic theory of phonemes

Firth's phoneme theory has two characteristics, polysystemic and prosodic.

We will first introduce the polysystemic theory. According to Firth's concept of systems, a system in phonology is a general term for several interchangeable sounds that can appear in a position in a certain structure. For example, the three words *skate* [skeit], *slate* [sleit], and *spate* [speit] all share the same structure, $C_1C_2VC_3$ (consonant$_1$ + consonant$_2$ + vowel + consonant$_3$); and [k], [l], and [p] can appear at position C_2, forming a system. The description of phonemes in American descriptive linguistics uses the monosystemic analysis method. For example, [t^h] in the word *team* is exhaled, which appears at the beginning of the word; [t] in the word *steam* is not exhaled, which appears after [s]. Therefore, [tʰ] and [t] are classified as a phoneme |t|, and [tʰ] and [t] are allophones of the phoneme |t|. However, the use of the monosystemic analysis method is sometimes quite limited. For example, there are 11 consonants, [p], [b], [t], [d], [t], [d], [tj], [dj], [k], [g], and [?], which may appear at the beginning of a Javanese word, whereas at the end of a word, only four consonants can appear, [p], [t], [k], and [?]. If the monosystemic analysis method is followed, the four consonants at the end of the word and four out of the 11 consonants at the beginning of the word should be combined into four phonemes. However, does the [t] at the end of the word and the [t] at the beginning of the word fall into the same phoneme? Or is it a phoneme with [t] or [tj] at the beginning of a word? It's hard to figure it out. If a polysystemic analysis method is adopted to establish two consonant systems with one being the initial consonant system and the other the final consonant system, it will be much easier to describe. Now we will introduce the prosodic theory of phonemes. Firth believes that in a language, distinctive phonetic features cannot all be summarized in one segment position. For example, intonation is not in the position of a segment, which, instead, governs entire phrases and sentences. If the sentence "Has he come?" is uttered with a rising tone, this rising tone is not limited to the positions of the segments |h|, |æ|, and |z| of the word *has*, nor is it limited to the positions of the segments |h|, |i|, |k|, |ʌ|, and |m| of the words *he* and *come*. The tone governs the entire interrogative sentence. This kind of component straddling the segment is called "prosody." Prosodic components can span a part of a syllable, the entire syllable, or a word, a phrase, or a sentence. Intonation is one of the prosodic components. For example, the compound word *roman meal* made from semolina or rye flour mixed with flaxseed has eight phonemes |romən mil|. If the method of American descriptive linguistics is followed, each phoneme must be described in ways that follow. The phoneme|r| is voiced, apical, and curled; the phoneme |o| is voiced, round labial, and central vowel; the phoneme |m| is voiced, bilabial, and nasal, and so on. When all eight phonemes are described, the voicing feature is repeated eight times, which seems to be repeating and pointless. In fact, voicing is shared by all eight phonemes, and it spans the entire segment of the compound word *roman meal*. Therefore, Firth also regards voicing as a prosodic component, a description method that is both concise and clear. We can learn from Firth's article that prosodic components specified by Firth include pitch, intensity, length, vowels, and soft palate, in addition to intonation. Firth calls what remains after removing the prosody from the phonemic units phonematic units. For example, if voicing of |romən mil| is removed, the eight phonematic units remain. What we have introduced so far is Firth's functionalist linguistic theory.

Halliday, a student of Firth, inherited the idea of functionalism of the London School of Linguistics and further proposed systemic functional grammar.

Halliday's systemic functional grammar inherits and develops Firth's functionalism theory in the following three aspects.

1. Halliday developed Firth's theory of situational contexts and proposed the concept of "register."

Halliday implements Firth's theory of situational contexts into specific language structures. He believes that the contexts of the situation are composed of three parts: held, mode, and tenor. "The held refers to the whole event in which an utterance functions, and the purpose of the speaker or the writer. Therefore, it includes the theme of the utterance. Mode is the function of an utterance in an event. Therefore, it includes the channels of the language use (temporary or prepared speech or writing), as well as the style or rhetoric of the language (narration, preaching, persuasion, socializing, etc.). The tenor refers to the role type in communication, that is, a set of permanent or temporary corresponding social relations among participants in language use. The held, mode, and tenor together constitute the linguistic context of an utterance."[8]

Semantics in a language can be divided into three functions: ideational, textual, and interpersonal.

The ideational function, which refers to the content of speech, can be further divided into experiential and logical functions. The experiential function acts in relation to the content of the speech. It is the speaker's reflection of the external environment and his experience of the various phenomena in the external world and the internal world of his self-consciousness. Logical functions are merely the expression of abstract logical relations obtained indirectly from one's experience. The ideational function analysis of the sentence "This picture was written by John" is as follows: The phrase *this picture* is Goal, the phrase *was written* is Action, and the phrase *by John* is Actor. They represent the content of speech and transitivity relations, which are determined by the held in the context of language use.

The interpersonal function denotes a kind of role relationship, which involves both the role played by the speaker in the context and the role assigned by the speaker to other participants. For example, when asking questions, the speaker himself plays the role of the questioner, the one who requests information; at the same time, he assigns the listener to the role of the answerer, the one who provides information. For another example, when issuing a command, the speaker himself acts as the sender of the command, the one who assumes the role of a higher-level identity to give orders, and at the same time, he assigns the listener to act as the command-receiver, the one who assumes the role of a lower-level identity to take orders. Different speakers, due to their different relationships with the listener, adopt different tones when speaking to the same listener, while the same speaker also adopts different tones when speaking to different listeners. Therefore, the ideational function analysis of the sentence "This picture was written by John" is as follows. The phrase *this picture* represents the past behavior, which is the modal part of the sentence; the phrase *written by John* represents the content, the propositional part of the sentence. From the

---

[8]M. A. K. Halliday & R. Hosan, *Cohesion in English*, Longman, p22, 1976.

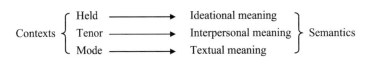

Fig. 8.3 The context determines the choice of semantics

perspective of the syntactic function analysis, the phrases *this picture, were written* and by *John* were the subject, predictor, and adjunct of the sentence, respectively. They represent the role relationship of each constituent in the sentence. Such role relationships are determined by the tenor in the context of language use.

The textual function makes what the speaker says work in the context of language use and reflects the need for coherence in the use of the language. It includes how to make a sentence that relates to the previous sentence, how to choose a topic to speak on, how to distinguish new information from information already known by the listener, and so on. It is an effect-giving function, without which neither ideational nor interpersonal functions of the sentence can be realized. The textual function of the sentence "This picture was written by John" is analyzed as follows. In the sentence, *this picture* is the theme, and *written by John* is the rheme. From the perspective of the given or new information, the meaning unit *this picture was written* is the given information, and the meaning unit *by John* is the new information. They indicate the effectiveness of sentence components. Such effectiveness is determined by the mode of communication in the context of language use.

When the features of the situational contexts of language use are reflected in the language structure, the held tends to determine the choice of the ideational meaning, the tenor tends to determine the choice of the interpersonal meaning, and the mode tends to determine the choice of the textual meaning, as shown in Fig. 8.3.

In this way, Halliday put the context of language use into the semantics of the language itself and specified the relationship between contexts and the language.

On this basis, Halliday presented the concept of registers. Register is a language variation caused by the change of contexts in the language use. The held, tenor, and mode, the three components of the contexts, can generate new registers. Different helds can generate different registers, such as scientific English, nonscientific English, and other registers. Scientific English can be further subdivided into metallurgical, geological, mathematical, physical, chemical, agricultural, medical English, and so on. The differences among these registers are mainly manifested in the differences in terms of lexical, transitive, and logical relations among different levels of the language structure. Differences in tenors can produce registers such as formal English, informal English, and formal or informal English with different degrees in between, and so on. Registers such as advertising, humorous, and social English can also be generated. The differences among these registers are mainly manifested in the tone, modality, and attitude of the speaker expressed in his choice of words. Differences in modes can generate registers such as spoken English or written English. Differences among these registers are mainly manifested in the differences of the topic structure of the sentence (theme or rheme), information structure (new or given information), and coherence (reference, substitution, omission, connection, etc).

In language use, a variation of the register is usually the result of several changes in the context. In the actual use of the language, the three components, held, tenor, or mode, are changing all the time. The changes in them work together to produce a wide variety of registers. The language is nothing more than a highly abstract concept.

2. Halliday developed Firth's theory of "structure" and "system" and redefined them, proposing systemic grammar.

Halliday insists on studying language from two perspectives, system and function. Halliday revises Firth's view that "the system or selection is carried out within the structure of the language and therefore the structure is primary." Halliday argues "The concept of systems applies to all levels[9] from top to bottom and that there are systems, not structures, at all levels." In this way, he shifts from scale and category grammar to systemic grammar.

Systemic grammar proposed by Halliday includes four basic categories: unit, structure, classification, and system. We will explain them one by one.

(a) Unit

The unit of the language forms a hierarchy, which is also a classification system. The relationship between units presents a hierarchical distribution from the highest (largest) to the lowest (smallest). Each unit contains one or more units (one size smaller) immediately below it. For example, units in English are sentences, clauses, phrases, words, and morphemes. The rank of a unit is its position in the hierarchy.

(b) Structure

In grammar, the category set up to illustrate the similarity between consecutive facts is called the structure, which is a linear arrangement of symbols where each symbol occupies a bit and where each different symbol represents a component. Each unit in a structure is made up of one or more units that are one level lower than it/them, and each of these components has its own special function. For example, an English clause consists of four words that act as subject, predicate, complement, and adjunct, respectively, represented by S, P, C, and A. All clauses can be composed of them, such as SAPA (subject-adjunct-predicate-adjunct), ASP (adjunct-subject-predicate), SPC (subject-predicate-complement), ASPCC (adjunct-subject-predicate-complement-complement), and so on. At the phrase level, there are a group of phrases that Halliday call the modifier, head, and qualifier, represented by M, H, and Q, respectively. If possible structures are in the forms of H (head), MH (modifier-head), HQ (head-qualifier), and MHQ (modifier-head-

---

[9]By the word *level*, Halliday refers to different levels of language, such as discourse, sentences, clauses, phrases, words, and morphemes.

qualifier), these structures can be expressed by the formula (M)H(Q), where the elements in brackets are optional.

(c) Classification

A group of members of a certain unit can be classified according to their roles in the structure of a higher unit. For example, English phrases can be classified into verb phrases, noun phrases, and adverbial phrases. The verb phrase is used as the predicate in the clause, the noun phrase is used as the subject or complement in the clause, and the adverbial phrase has the function of an adjunct in the clause. Their classifications are based on the role that the members of the phrase play in the clause. Generally, if a unit has such basic structures as XY, XYZ, YZ, or XYZY, the basic classification of the next level of the unit is "classification acting on X," "classification acting on Y," and "classification acting on Z."

The structure and classification can be viewed as one parameter and the unit as the other, whose relation can be theoretically determined. Classifications, such as structures, are related to units, and classifications are always classifications of members of a unit. The relation between classification and structure usually remains unchanged. Classification is always determined in relation to the structure of an upper-level unit, whereas the structure is always determined in light of the classification of a lower-level unit.

(d) System

Halliday pointed out that the "system" is a network composed of a set of characteristics. If the conditions for entering the system are met, one feature is selected, and only one feature is selected. Any choice made from the features formed in a particular system network constitutes a description of the system of a certain unit. It can be seen that the system, from its external form, is a list that can be effectively selected by the speaker. The various relationships among systems can be represented by a network of the system. The system exists in all layers of the language, such as the semantic layer, the grammatical layer, and the phonemic layer, which all have its own system to express its semantic potential.

From the point of view of systemic grammar, a speech act is a process of simultaneous selection from a huge number of interrelated, alternative components.

Suppose there is a system including features a and b, and feature a or b must be selected, which can be represented as Fig. 8.4.

If system (1) contains features a and b and if system (2) contains features x and y, feature a in system (1) is a condition for its entry into system (2). That is, if feature a is selected, feature x or y must be selected, which can be expressed in Fig. 8.5.

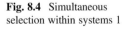

Fig. 8.4 Simultaneous selection within systems 1

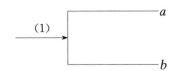

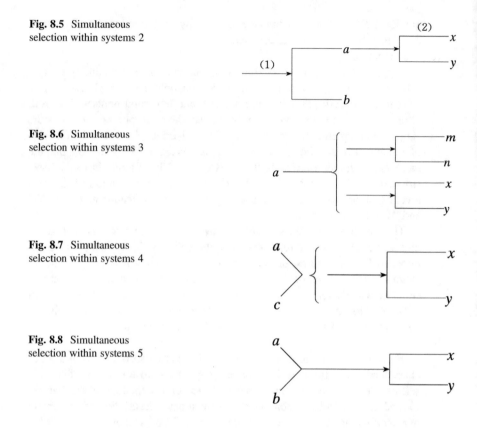

Fig. 8.5 Simultaneous selection within systems 2

Fig. 8.6 Simultaneous selection within systems 3

Fig. 8.7 Simultaneous selection within systems 4

Fig. 8.8 Simultaneous selection within systems 5

If under the same condition a, features m/n and the features x/y occur simultaneously, the relation among them can be expressed in Fig. 8.6.

One must choose x or y under the condition that both a and c are selected, which can be expressed in Fig. 8.7.

One must choose x or y under the condition that a or b is selected, which can be expressed in Fig. 8.8.

As a result, a system network can be formed, which can clearly describe the structure of sentences. For example, a system network of time expressions in English is shown in Fig. 8.9.

This system network can accurately explain whether the following sentences are grammatical.

   I. Is it six yet?
  II. I think it's about half past.
 III. It was five after ten.
 IV. He got there at eight minutes to twelve.
  V. *He got there at eight before twelve.
 VI. *It was half past ten o'clock.

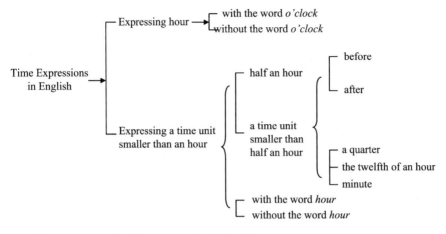

Fig. 8.9 System network of time expressions in English

Sentence I is correct because in the system network, the classification "hour" can be used without the word "o'clock." Sentence II is correct because in the system network, a unit smaller than an hour is also used instead of the unit word "hour." Sentence III is correct because in the system network, the classification unit "representing units smaller than hours" can first enter "units smaller than half an hour." Then, it proceeds to enter units of "the twelfth of an hour" (i.e., 5 min) without using the word "minute." However, under the same condition of "a unit smaller than half an hour," either the words "after" or "before" should be used. Sentence III uses the word "after," so it is correct. Sentence IV is also correct because in the system network, the classification unit "representing a unit smaller than the hour" can first enter the unit less than half an hour and then simultaneously enter "before" and "minute." Sentence V is incorrect because in the system network, when one enters the "unit less than half a point," one should select either "one-quarter hour" or "one-twelfth hour" or "minute." It is incorrect, as no choice was made among any of them. Sentence VI is also incorrect because in the system network, if one enters "a unit smaller than an hour" and then proceeds to enter the subclassification unit representing the "half point," the use of "o'clock" is allowed. Only in the classification representing "hour" can the word "o'clock" be included. Therefore, Sentence VI is incorrect.

The system network of systemic grammar must be carefully constructed to represent the structure of the language accurately and correctly.

Systemic grammar regards speech acts as a process of simultaneous selection among a large number of mutually related alternatives. If the system network representing this selection process is elaborated and accurate, formalized methods can be used to describe the language in detail. In turn, systemic grammar can be practically applied in NLP. American artificial intelligence expert T. Winograd used systemic grammar in the NLU program. SHRDLU was developed in 1974 and achieved great success. The SHRDLU program understands the words typed into a computer terminal in plain English and conducts human-computer conversations by answering questions. It instructs robots to play with blocks and to move simple geometric objects in English. Halliday's systemic grammar greatly develops the theory of functional grammar about systems and develops functional grammar into systemic functional grammar.

3. Halliday proposed three scales of grammatical analysis: rank, exponence, and delicacy.

Halliday calls the measure of syntactic analysis the scale. To link the classifications to one another, three abstract scales, rank, exponence, and delicacy, are used. On the scale of the rank, there are various layers of units ranging from sentences to morphemes arranged in a logical order from the highest unit to the lowest one. The description of the sentence is complete only when the description of the morpheme is completed and vice versa. The scale of the exponence is the extent of the laddered-shaped abstraction to which it connects concepts in grammar to authentic linguistic data. The scale of the exponence descends when moving from a more abstract concept to concrete authentic linguistic data. The scale of the delicacy reflects the degree of subdivision of structure and classification. Delicacy is a cline, which is a continuum with potentially infinite graduations. At one end of the continuum, there are the fundamentals of structure and classification, and at the other end, there is the theoretical point beyond which no new grammatical relations can be derived.

Halliday believed that the classification of a language item should be based on the scale of delicacy, from general to special, giving an approximate scale to the options at each choice point. For example, sentences can be classified into declarative and imperative sentences. If the sentence is declarative, it can be further classified into either an affirmative sentence or an interrogative sentence. If the sentence is a question, it can be further classified into a general question or a special question. The concept of delicacy can also be applied to the semantic layer. For example, in the transitive system, processes can be subdivided into physical, mental, relational, and verbal processes, in which mental processes can be further subdivided into sensory, reactive, and cognitive processes. At each choice point, the choice of alternatives takes probability into account. If there are multiple standards and if the relevant standards intersect with one another when further subdivision is required, it is necessary to give different parameter values and make appropriate adjustments according to different situations. If the distinction of classifications is so subtle that the description is concerned only with the critical criterion to the exclusion of others, the description comes to an end. For example, clauses are distinguished step-by-step by the scale of delicacy. When their grammatical distinctions come to an end at a certain point, lexical distinctions follow. At this stage, whether their formal items are arranged in the system or not, the further relations between them can only be lexical relations, and a lexical theory must be used to explain that part of the language forms that grammar fails to deal with.

Systemic functional grammar includes two parts: systemic grammar and functional grammar. It is not a simple synthesis of the two grammars but two inseparable aspects within the framework of a complete language theory. Systemic grammar emphasizes that a language, as the internal underlying relationship of a system, is a system network composed of several subsystems that are connected with meaning and that can be continuously selected by its users. It is also called the meaning potential. As a kind of symbol, the language must make corresponding choices in each layer of its semantic functions when expressing the meaning that the speaker intends to express. Functional grammar emphasizes that a language is a tool for social communication and that language systems are gradually formed as a result of long-term communication to achieve various semantic functions. When people need to make choices in the language system in communication, they also carry out function-motivated activities.

Therefore, systemic functional grammar not only studies the structure of the language symbol system with its internal subsystems but also studies functions of the language in use and how these functions can be performed. Halliday said that his systemic functional grammar was most concerned with such questions as "how people decipher highly condensed everyday speech, and how they use social systems to decipher it."

In summary, the core ideas of Halliday's systemic functional grammar are as follows:

1. The Idea of Meta-functions

   Halliday divides the semantics of the language into three functions: ideational, interpersonal, and textual.

   Such classification connects the language with its external environment and explains the internal relations of the language. Halliday believes that the nature of the language determines people's requirements for the language, that is, the functions that the language must perform. Although this variety of functions has infinite possibilities, there are a number of finite abstract functions inherent in the language itself, which are called meta-functions. Halliday believes that ideational, interpersonal, and textual functions all have the nature of meta-functions, the meanings of which are as follows:

   (a) Ideational meta-functions

      Ideational meta-functions include the experiential function or the function of what is called the "content" and the logical function. These functions are related to the propositional content of expression.

   (b) Interpersonal meta-functions

      Interpersonal meta-functions are composed of functions that help establish and maintain the interaction between the speaker and the listener. As speech is a meaningful activity of social people, a means of doing things, as well as behaviors and acts, it reflects the different status and relationships among people.

   (c) Textual meta-function

      Textual meta-function is related to the appropriate presentation of an ongoing utterance. This includes issues such as thematization and the refer-ent. The basic unit of a language in use is not a grammatical unit such as a word or a sentence but a "discourse," which expresses ideas in a more complete manner than words or sentences do.

In systemic functional grammar, the three aspects of ideational, interpersonal, and textual meta-functions are integrated into one, and there is no priority among them.

2. The Idea of Being Systemic

Sausurre et al. treat a language merely as a collection of symbols. However, Halliday disagrees about the way in which the language has been treated by them. He holds:

(a) The language should be explained by a regular source of meaning potentials because the language is not a collection of all grammatical sentences.
(b) The structure is the underlying relationship of a process derived from the potential, which can be better expressed by the aggregation relationship. The language system is a network for semantic selection. A structure can be generated when each step of the relevant system is realized.
(c) Systems exist at all layers of the language, each of which has its meaning potential.

3. The Idea of Hierarchy

Halliday believes that a language is a structure with multilayer interrelated systems, including content, expression, and entity layers. He holds:

(a) The language has layers, including at least the semantic layer, lexical grammar layer, and phonological layer.
(b) Among different layers, there exists a "realization" relation, which means that the choice of meaning (at the semantic layer) is realized by the choice of the form (at the lexical grammar layer), and the choice of the form is reflected in the choice of the entity (at the phonological layer).
(c) The entire language system is a multiple code system in which one system can lead to another; then, the other system leads to another one, the process of which repeats.
(d) By adopting the concept of hierarchy, people can extend their understanding of the nature of the language to what goes beyond the language itself. The semantic layer of the language system is actually the embodiment of the context, that is, the behavior or the social symbol sublayer.

4. The Idea of Functions

The functional idea of Halliday belongs to the concept of semantics, where the function is the discrete part of the formalized meaning potential and the semantic component that plays a specific role in constituting a semantic system, while the component or structure of lexical grammar is only its format of the expression. For example, the sentence "The little girl broke her glasses at school" can be analyzed in Table 8.1.

In this way, expressions and semantics they express can be clearly divided into different layers, which can be analyzed as "actor-process-goal-context" at the

Table 8.1 Ideational functions and lexical grammar

Ideational function: Transitivity	The little girl broke her glasses at school			
	Actor	Process	Goal	Context
Lexical grammar	Noun phrase	Verb	Noun phrase	Pre. phrase

ideational functional layer and "noun phrase-verb-noun phrase-prepositional phrase" at the lexical grammar level. We will go into the details of each of these parts later.

Halliday believes that the transitivity of the language is only a component of semantics, which can be described at the surface level where consistency is not required. At the ideational meta-function layer, there is the normality of expressing positive or negative, and each semantic system, such as interpersonal meta-functions and textual meta-functions, can express semantics.

5. The Idea of Contexts

Halliday believes that if people treat the language as a whole, they must determine the criteria for distinguishing the semantic systems beyond the language itself; that is, they must rely on the context to determine whether the linguistic data belonging to the same semantic type share the same meaning. The social context or situation is also part of semantics such as the language itself. The concepts of the social context, situational context, and interaction theoretically are the same as those of knowledge and thinking; that is, interaction can explain linguistic knowledge.

6. The Idea of Approximation or Probability

Halliday has derived approximative or probabilistic ideas from information theory. He holds:

(a) One of the inherent characteristics of the language is probabilistic. This probabilistic feature is most obvious when people choose vocabulary. For example, when choosing a word that expresses a flat part at the side of a road for people to walk on in English, some people tend to use the word *sidewalk,* while others prefer to use the word *pavement.*

(b) People can master the use of the language only from the relative probability. When this principle is extended to the description of the grammatical system, there is also a probability problem with the use of various sentence patterns. To master the use of different forms of language items, it is necessary to accurately distinguish the relationship between semantics and specific contexts.

(c) The probabilistic nature of the language shows that differences among different registers may be formed due to their different probabilities at the lexical grammar level. This probability is related to the exact degree of the different semantics to be expressed. This probability depends on the extent of accuracy to which different expressions intend to mean.

8.2   Application of Systemic Functional Grammar in Natural Language Processing

Systemic functional grammar, an important linguistic theory, has been widely used in NLP. Therefore, it is also an important NLP formal model. Here, we illustrate its application in NLP.

In NLP, we can use acyclic directed graphs containing an and/or logical relationship to represent the grammar. Such a grammar is called system networks, as shown in Fig. 8.10.

A simple system network is shown in Fig. 8.10 by way of an example. Here, the largest curly bracket represents the "and" (i.e., parallel) system, and the straight vertical line represents the "or" (i.e., disjoint) system. Therefore, each clause can

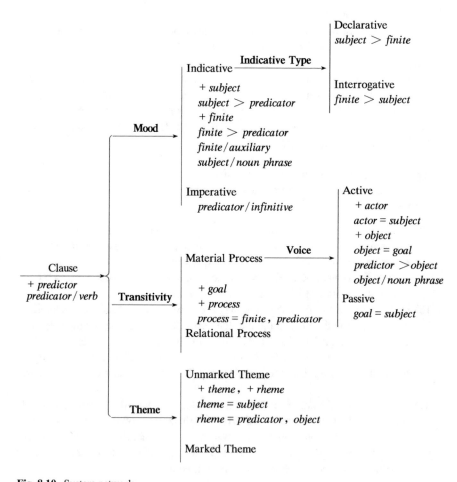

Fig. 8.10 System network

have the characteristics of mood, transitivity, and theme at the same time. However, it is unlikely to be both indicative and imperative and can only be one of them.

Systemic functional grammar uses realization statements to establish the mapping between features specified grammatically (e.g., indicative, imperative) and syntactic forms. Each feature in the network has a set of realization statements, which are used to specify constraints on the final expression. The realization statements of each feature are represented by a set of italicized sentences below the feature in the system network. The realization statement set allows the syntax to be used to constrain the structure of the expression as it traverses the system network. The simple operation symbols used are as follows:

+X: Insert function X.

For example, in Fig. 8.10, the realization statement for the feature "Clause" is "+predicator", which indicates that a predicator needs to be inserted in the clause.

X = Y: Combine functions X and Y.

This means that grammar is allowed to establish a hierarchical functional structure by assigning different functions to the same part of the expression. For example, the realization statement for the feature "Active" is "actor = subject," which means that the sentence in the active voice merges the actor and the subject, whereas the realization statement for the feature "Passive" is "goal = subject," indicating that the passive clause merges the goal and the subject.

X > Y: Place function X in a position before function Y.

For example, the realization statement "subject > predicator" means that the subject of the sentence is placed before the predicator.

X/A: Classify function X and lexical or grammatical feature A into one category.

For example, the realization statement "predicator/verb" means classifying the function of "predicator" and "verb" into the same category; that is, this predicator function must be a verb in terms of its lexical features.

For a given system network, the generation procedure is as follows:

- Traverse the network from left to right; select the correct feature and execute the relevant realization statement.
- Establish an intermediate representation, which must satisfy the constraints imposed by the realization statements executed during the traversal.
- Specify any function that is not fully specified by recursively calling the grammar at a lower level.

In Chinese-English MT, for example, after the analysis of the Chinese sentence "系统将把文件存储起来" (/Xi tong jiang ba wen jian cun chu qi lai/; The system will save the document), the predicator-argument structure of this sentence is obtained. The computer judges that the predicator of this sentence is "存储" (/cun chu/; to save), which means process, the argument of the actor is "系统" (/xi tong/; system), and the argument of the goal is "文件" (/wen jian/; document). This speech act represents an assertion in which the future tense is used. Such information can be expressed as follows:

"存储" (/cun chu/; to save): process
"系统" (/xi tong/; system): actor
"文件" (/wen jian/; document): goal
Speech act: assertion
Tense: future (future tense)

After the lexical conversion from Chinese to English, the Chinese words "存储"(/cun chu/) are converted to "save," "系统"(/xi tong/) to "system," and "文件"(/wen jian/) to "document." In this way, we can obtain the following as the initial information for English sentence generation:

process:	save-1
actor:	system-1
goal:	document-1
speech act:	assertion
tense:	future

Options such as save-1, system-1, and document-1 indicate that they are dictionary options and that the words marked with "-1" suggest that the system might also choose other synonyms to replace them. The information given above shows that the English sentence we want to generate should be an assertive sentence with the future tense.

Now, we can use the system network in Fig. 8.10 to generate the English sentence based on the information obtained.

The generation starts from the sentence feature "Clause" in the system network. The realization statements for this feature are +predicator and predicator/verb, which means that a predicator needs to be inserted and classified as a verb. Therefore, the verb *save* is inserted.

Then, it proceeds to the mood system. The correct option for a system is selected through simple queries or decision-making networks related to the system. Because the input description specifies that this is an assertive sentence, the mood system chooses indicative and declarative features, the realization statements of which are +subject, subject > predicator, +finite, and finite > predicator, which means inserting subject and finite functions and arranging them in the order of subject, finite, and predicator. In this way, we obtained the functional structure (Table 8.2).

Then, it enters the transitivity system. If we assume that the feature of "save-1" is the material processing process, the transitivity system selects the feature of "material process," the realization statements of which are +goal, +process, process = finite, and predicator, which means inserting goal and process functions and merging finite and predicator. As the passive voice is not specified in the input, the system selects the feature of the active voice, the realization statements of which are +actor, actor = subject, +object, object = goal, predicator > object, and object/noun phrase, which means inserting the actor and merging it with the subject;

Table 8.2 The mood system

Mood	Subject	Finite	Predicator

Table 8.3 The transitivity system

Mood	Subject	Finite	Predicator	Object
Transitivity	Actor	Process		Goal

Table 8.4 The theme system

Mood	Subject	Finite	Predicator	Object
Transitivity	Actor	Process		Goal
Theme	Theme	Rheme		

Table 8.5 The multilayered structure

	The system	Will	Save	The document
Mood	Subject	Finite	Predicator	Object
Transitivity	Actor	Process		Goal
Theme	Theme	Rheme		

inserting the object, merging it with the goal, and placing it after the predicator, respectively; and that the object is a noun phrase. The results are shown in Table 8.3.

Finally, as there is no description about the theme in the input information, the theme system selects the feature of an unmarked theme, the realization statements of which is +theme, +rheme, theme = subject, rheme = predicator, and object, which means inserting the theme and rheme, merging the theme with the subject, and merging the rheme with the predicator and the object, respectively. The results obtained are a complete functional structure shown in Table 8.4.

At this time, the generation process also needs to recursively enter the lower levels of the grammar multiple times to completely specify phrases, dictionary items, and word forms. The noun phrase network will use a method similar to the one given here to generate the noun phrases, *the system* and *the document*. The auxiliary verb network will insert the term *will* into the system. The selection of lexical items, *systems, documents, and saves,* can be handled in a variety of ways. The generated English sentence is "The system will save the document."

Systemic functional grammar expresses this sentence as a multilayered structure shown in Table 8.5.

Here, the mood layer indicates that the sentence is a simple declarative sentence with subject, finite verb, predicator verb, and object, in which "the system" is the subject, "will" is the finite verb, "save" is the predicator verb, and "the document" is the object.

The transitivity layer means that the subject "system" is the actor of the saving process, the object "document" is the goal, and "will save" is the process.

The theme layer means that "the system" is the theme or focus of the sentence, and "will save the document" is the rheme of the sentence.

These three layers deal with different sets of functions that are related to different meta-functions.

In the previous section, we introduced that Halliday divides semantics of the language into three different meta-functions, namely, interpersonal, ideational, and textual. The mood layer, the transitivity layer, and the theme layer are closely related to the three basic meta-functions in systemic functional grammar.

Because the mood layer determines whether the speaker is asserting, commanding, or asking, it is related to the interpersonal meta-function of establishing or maintaining an interactive relationship between the speaker and the listener.

As the transitivity layer represents the predicator-argument structure in the sentence, where "system" is the actor, that is, the agent, and "document" is the goal, that is, the patient, it is, therefore, related to the ideational meta-function of expressing the propositional content.

The theme layer represents such issues as thematization or referents. In our example, the theme layer clearly shows that "the system" is the theme of the sentence. Therefore, it is related to textual meta-functions suitable for the current expression.

As seen from the above example, systemic functional grammar treats a language as a resource that represents meaning in the context and expresses sentences as a collection of functions and rules for the mapping between these functions and their grammatical forms. The automatic generation of the natural language is closely related to the three basic meta-functions in systemic functional grammar. Such a theory has important methodological value and has extensive influence on the study of NLP.

8.3 Speech Act Theory and Conversation Intelligent Agent

Speech act theory in pragmatics was put forward by a group of philosophers.

L. Wittgenstein (1889–1951, Fig. 8.11) is a major representative in analytical philosophy, whose philosophy is primarily concerned with the language. He wants

Fig. 8.11 L. Wittgenstein (1889–1951)

to reveal what happens when people communicate and express themselves, and he maintains that the essence of philosophy is the language, the expression of human thought, and the foundation of the entire civilization. Therefore, the essence of philosophy can only be found in the language. He has deconstructed the sole essence of traditional metaphysics and has found a new direction for philosophy. However, he also believes that it is impossible to create a strict language that can express philosophy because the speech of daily life, the foundation and source of philosophy, is endless. Therefore, the essence of philosophy should be derived from daily life. Daily life is like a game (Spiel in German), a free activity without purposes and rules. We must understand the language while playing the game. Therefore, he proposed "language game theory" (Sprachspiel in German).

He advocates in his representative work *Tractatus Logico-Philosophicus* published in 1922 that philosophy should be a linguistic problem and that philosophy must face the language directly. He argues that everything that can be said should be explained and that everything that cannot be said should keep silent because philosophy is simply to make things clear. What is silence? Silence is to keep your mouth shut to what is in front of you or what is in your mind or to keep your words in your mind instead of expressing them. So, in what circumstances should you remain silent? Wittgenstein believes that silence should be maintained when the subject is something unspeakable. For example, it is difficult to explain a philosophical theory that contains only a few words thoroughly and clearly even if thousands of words are used. Although you have an understanding of it in your mind, you can't find the right words to explain this theory to the extent as you take it, resulting in your no way to put the theory clearly in words. For another example, when you talk about such empty things as "life" or "ideal," it is difficult to speak clearly, even if you speak eloquently. As everyone has different ideas, which, more often than not, leads to different interpretations of things, open talks about "life" or "ideal" will also vary and be multifarious without an accurate, unified, and clear answer. Such things that differ from reality are called "mysteries" by Wittgenstein. In Wittgenstein's mind, the best choice for you is to remain silent when confronted with the mysteries, as it is impossible for you to express them clearly. Therefore, a language can only play its role when it is in its actual use. Wittgenstein proposed in *Philosophical Studies* that "the meaning of a word is its usage in the language." "What does the word *five* mean?" he said. "I wasn't talking about anything at all; it's only about how the word *five* is used." "Think of the sentence as a tool and its meaning as its use," he added. "You should not ask for the meaning of a word," he argues, but for its use. This is Wittgenstein's idea that meaning is use.

Influenced by Wittgenstein's ideas, J. L. Austin (1911–1960, Fig. 8.12) proposed speech act theory in the 1950s.

In 1962, J. L. Austin published *How to Do Things with Words*, in which he put forward an important idea of "doing something in saying something."

He divides speech acts into performatives and constatives. Performatives can be divided into happy and unhappy performatives. A happy performative speech act is uttered under the condition of felicity, whereas an unhappy act is uttered under the

Fig. 8.12 J. L. Austin

condition of infelicity. There are six proper conditions for a happy performative speech act:

1. There must be an agreed process that has agreed effects, including certain words spoken by certain people in a certain situation. Violations of this rule are called nonplays.
2. In a given context, the specific people and circumstances must be appropriate for the execution of the specific procedure invoked. Violations of this rule are called misapplications.
3. All involved in the speech acts must implement such procedures correctly. Violations of this rule are called flaws.
4. All involved in the speech acts must fully implement such procedures. Violations of this rule are called hitches.
5. Those who follow these procedures are often those who have some ideas or feelings or those who conduct ceremonies for the speakers. Therefore, both those involved and those implementing the procedure must, in fact, share such ideas or feelings, and all those involved must carry them out intentionally. Violations of this rule are called insincerities.
6. All those involved did so later. Violations of this rule are called infraction.

Austin believes that violating any of these six rules is deemed to be an unhappy performative speech act.

According to Austin, an important feature of a dialogue is that the utterance in the dialogue is an act performed by the speaker. This is especially obvious in the following performative sentences.

1. I name this ship the Titanic.
2. I second that motion.
3. I bet you five dollars it will snow tomorrow.

When someone in authority utters sentence (1), like any other behavior that can change the world, it has the effect of changing the state of the world, resulting in the ship bearing the name Titanic. Verbs, such as *name* or *second* that can perform these actions, are called performative verbs, and Austin calls these actions speech acts. Austin's research has a great impact because speech acts are not limited to a small type of action words. He has further made a detailed and an in-depth demonstration of performatives with both grammatical and lexical standards.

However, as Austin failed to find a unified standard for performatives, he analyzed speech acts only from the perspectives of "say something" and "do something."

Austin pointed out that in an authentic speech, any sentence uttered is nothing more than the following three types of speech acts.

- Locutionary acts: The act of conveying an intended meaning when a sentence is uttered
- Illocutionary acts: The act of asking, answering, or promising, etc., when a sentence is uttered
- Perlocutionary acts: The act of having a specific effect (often intentional) on the listener's feelings, beliefs, or behavior when a sentence is uttered.

The purpose of distinguishing these three types of speech acts is to emphasize illocutionary acts.

Austin explained, for example, that when the speaker utters the following sentence (4), it has the illocutionary force of protest and has the effect of making the listener stop doing something or annoying the listener.

4. You can't do that.

He holds that if you want to test which verbs are the obvious performative ones, it is better to distinguish those verbs that have the obvious illocutionary force when a performative sentence is uttered.

Therefore, Austin divides speech acts into the following five categories according to their illocutionary force.

1. Verdictives: They refer to any verdicts, estimates, inferences, or evaluations implied by the speaker when a sentence is uttered. The verdictive is used to deliver judgment.
2. Exercitives: They refer to the execution, order, guidance, or urge implied by the speaker when a sentence is uttered. The executive is to exert influence or use of power.
3. Commissives: They refer to the promise, guarantee, intention, or support for a certain action plan implied by the speaker when a sentence is uttered. The commissive is to assume obligations or to express intention.
4. Behabitives: They refer to the speaker's response to other people's behavior, such as apologies, congratulations, thanks, or resentment, including attitudes toward other people's past or present behavior when a sentence is uttered. The behabitive is to express the speaker's attitude.

Fig. 8.13 J. R. Searle

5. Expositives: They refer to the speaker's opinions, arguments, clarification, etc., when a sentence is uttered. The expositive is to clarify the reason, argument, or opinion.

The term "speech act" is often used to describe the fact that an utterance implies an intended action.

Philosopher J. R. Searle (Fig. 8.13) was a student of Austin. He learned from Austin and inherited the speech act theory that was being established and then further developed it, making a significant contribution to the philosophy of the language. Searle became a member of the American Academy of Arts and Sciences for his outstanding research and won the National Presidential Award for Humanities in 2004.

Searle revised Austin's classification of speech acts in 1975 and proposed classifying all speech acts into the following five categories.

1. Assertives: The speaker's statements about something (suggestion, proposal, oath, boasting, inference, etc.)
2. Directives: The speaker's statements that make the listener do something (inquiry, order, request, invitation, suggestion, begging, etc.)
3. Commissives: The speaker's statements that make promises for future behavior (promises, plans, swears, bets, objection, etc.)
4. Expressives: The speaker's statements that express the speaker's mental state of something (thanks, apologies, welcome, grief, etc.)
5. Declarations: The speaker's statements that result in a change in the outside world (including many examples, such as "I resign," "You are fired," etc.).

Searle also analyzed the grammatical structure of these five speech acts in English. He believes that English sentences with these five speech acts generally contain a main clause with a performative verb and a clause.

For example, the statement "I order you to leave" is a directive, the statement "I promise to pay you the money" is a commissive, the statement "I apologize for stepping on your toe" is an expressive, and the statement "I find you guilty as charged" is a declaration.

Austin and Searle's research laid the foundation of speech act theory, which completely changed people's views on the nature and function of the language and has had a profound impact. This theory has become the theoretical basis for the study of conversation intelligent agents in NLP.

The language itself has always been a sign of humanity and perception, whereas conversation or dialogue is the most basic and privileged platform on which a language can be fully employed. Of course, conversation or dialogue is also the first thing we learn about speech acts when we were little kids. Whether we order meal for lunch, buy stamps, participate in business meetings, chat with relatives and friends, book air tickets, or complain about the weather, it is the conversation or dialogue that keeps us afloat.

In NLP, the conversations or dialogues between humans and computers are called conversation intelligent agents. The term "conversation" also includes "dialogue" because most of the conversations take the form of a dialogue. Conversation intelligent agents involve automatic speech processing, an advanced issue of automatic speech processing.

A conversation intelligent agent is a program that can communicate with users in the natural language, through which you can book tickets, answer questions, or reply to emails. Many of these issues are also related to business meeting summarization systems or to other oral comprehension systems.

As the conversation intelligent agent has to understand the meaning of a conversation, it is a kind of speech act denoting meaning. As the conversation intelligent agent has to communicate with its users, it is also a kind of speech act denoting an intended action. Conversation intelligent agents are meant to automatically book tickets, answer questions, or reply to emails, and they are, therefore, speech acts. In this way, speech act theory has become one of the theoretical bases for the study of conversation intelligent agents.

Figure 8.14 shows the basic architecture of a conversation intelligent agent system with speech recognition, NLU, natural language generation, text-to-speech synthesis, dialogue manager, and task manager, six components in all.

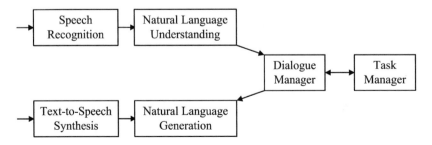

Fig. 8.14 Basic architecture of a conversation intelligent agent system taken from the book *Speech and Language Processing* by D. Jurafsky et al. (First Edition, 2000)

Speech recognition and NLU extract meaning from the user's conversational input. Natural language generation and text-to-speech synthesis map the results obtained by the conversational intelligent agent system to speech and output the result of the dialogue. Dialogue manager and task manager together control the entire working process of the conversation intelligent agent system.

Specifically, speech recognition accepts voice signals. Such voice signals are generally received through the microphone of a telephone, PDA (personal data assistant), or a laptop computer of the user. These voice signals are then converted into word strings, which are input into the conversation intelligent agent system. NLU generates a semantic representation suitable for the dialogue according to the word string entered. Natural language generation generates corresponding words and sentences according to the obtained semantic representation and gives these words and sentences the necessary prosody. Then, text-to-speech synthesis synthesizes a waveform graph with the words and sentences and their prosodic annotations received, and it outputs the result of the conversation in the form of speech.

Dialogue manager and task manager control the entire architecture and structure of the conversation intelligent agent system. Dialogue manager receives input from speech recognition and NLU maintains a given state, interacts with task manager, and passes the output to the natural language generation and text-speech synthesis. Therefore, in the conversation intelligent agent system, the role of dialogue manager is crucial.

The study of speech acts is based on the speech act theory proposed by Austin and Searle. However, recent research, especially on the establishment of computer automatic dialogue systems, has extended the concept of speech acts to the extent that the study of speech acts is based on more types of conversational forces that speech can have. This kind of enriched speech act with more conversational forces is called dialogue acts or conversational moves. A dialogic act tagging program that has been implementing recently is called the Dialogue Act Markup in Several Layers (DAMSL) system, which catalogs various layers of dialogue information. Two of the layers, the forward-looking function and backward-looking function, are extensions of speech acts. Although the DAMSL tag set is hierarchical and only focuses on the processing of those types of dialogue acts that are likely to occur in task-oriented dialogues, the forward function is still closely related to the speech act theory proposed by Austin and Searle. The explanation of the forward-looking function tagging is shown in Table 8.6.

In the forward-looking function, the tag INFLUENCE-ON-ADDRESSEE is equivalent to Searle's directives, and the tag INFLUENCE-ON-SPEAKER is equivalent to Austin's commissives, which suggests that DAMSL still has a close relationship with speech act theory.

The backward-looking function of DAMSL focuses on the relationship in relation to previous dialogue by other speakers, including proposals to be accepted or rejected (since DAMSL focuses on task-oriented dialogue), as well as the common ground for dialogue or dialogue repair (Table 8.7).

What follows is an example dialogue tagged by the forward- and backward-looking functions of DAMSL.

Table 8.6 Forward-looking function tagging in DAMSL

Forward-looking function tagging	Explanation of forward-looking function tagging
STATEMENT	A claim made by the speaker
INFO-REQUEST	A question by the speaker
CHECK	A question for confirmation information
INFLUENCE-ON-ADDRESSEE	(=Searle's directives)
OPEN-OPTION	A weak suggestion or listing of options
ACTION-DIRECTIVE	An actual command
INFLUENCE-ON-SPEAKER	(=Austin's commissives)
OFFER	Speaker offers to do sth (subject to confirmation)
COMMIT	Speaker is committed to doing sth
CONVENTIONAL	Other
OPENING	Greetings
CLOSING	Farewells
THANKING	Thanking or responding to thanks

Table 8.7 Backward-looking function tagging in DAMSL

Backward-looking function tagging	Explanation of backward-looking function tagging
AGREEMENT	Speaker's response to previous proposal
ACCEPT	Accepting the proposal
ACCEPT-PART	Accepting some part of the proposal
MAYBE	Neither accepting nor rejecting the proposal
REJECT-PART	Rejecting some part of the proposal
REJECT	Rejecting the proposal
HOLD	Putting off response, usually via subdialogue
ANSWER	Answering a question
UNDERSTANDING	Whether speaker understood previous
SIGNAL-NON-UNDER	Speaker did not understand
SIGNAL-UNDER	Speaker did understand
ACK	Demonstrated via continuer or assessment
REPEAT-REPHRASE	Demonstrated via repetition or reformulation
COMPLITION	Demonstrated via collaborative completion

What is shown in Fig. 8.15 is part of a dialogue about air travel, in which C represents customer, A represents intelligent agent, [assert] represents confirmation, [info-req, ack] represents question and continuer, [assert, open-option] represents confirmation and option suggestions, [check, hold] means verifying the question, [check, ack] means verifying and continuer, and [accept, ack] means accepting and proceeding, respectively. We chose this dialogue because it belongs to the area of travel planning, which has been the focus of many recent studies on conversation intelligent agents.

Speech act theory provides a pragmatic theoretical basis for conversation intelligent agents.

[ASSERT]	C_1: ... I need to travel in May.
[INFO-REQ, ACK]	A_1: And, what day in May do you want to travel?
[ASSERT, ANSWER]	C_2: OK uh I need to be there for a meeting that's from the 12th to the 15th.
[INFO-REQ, ACK]	A_2: And you're flying into what city?
[ASSERT, ANSWER]	C_3: Seattle.
[INFO-REQ, ACK]	A_3: And what time would you like to leave Pittsburgh?
[CHECK, HOLD]	C_4: Uh-hmm I don't think there's many options for non-stop.
[ACCEQP, ACK] [ASSERT]	A_4: Right. There's three non-stops today.
[INFO-REQ]	C_5: What are they?
[ASSERT, OPEN-OPTION]	A_5: The first one departs PGH at 10:00 a.m. arrives Seattle at 12:05 their time. The second flight departs PGH at 5:55 p.m., arrives Seattle at 8:00 p.m.. And the last flight departs PGH at 8:15 p.m. arrives Seattle at 10:28 p.m..
[ACCEQP, ACK]	C_6: OK, I'll take the 115 flight on the night before on the 11th.
[CHECK, ACK]	A_6: On the 11th?
[ASSERT, ACK]	OK. Departing at 5:55 p.m. arrives Seattle at 8:00 p.m., U.S. Air flight 115.
[ACK]	C_7: OK.

Fig. 8.15 The DAMSL tagging taken from the book *Speech and Language Processing* by D. Jurafsky et al. (First Edition, 2000)

The idea of conversation intelligent agents is fascinating. Such conversation intelligent agent systems as ELIZA, PARRY, or SHRDLU have become the most well-known examples of the NLP technology. The current applications of conversational intelligent agents also include air travel information systems, voice-based restaurant guide systems, and phone interfaces for emails or calendars. One of the important components of this type of conversation intelligent agent is dialogue manager, whose functions include controlling the conversation flow, determining at a high level how the conversation should be conducted on the side of the intelligent agent, asking questions or making statements, and determining when the questions should be presented.

"If we want to analyze the language, we have to think about forms of expression," said R. Carnap, a mathematical logician, in his book *Introduction to Semantics* published in 1942.[10] He holds that "we do not have to deal with both the speaker and the meaning of the words, although these factors will be involved whenever we use the language. With respect to the language we are talking about, we can always extract one or two of these factors to address. Therefore, we need to distinguish among three fields of language study. If, in a language, a reference explicitly refers to the speaker, or, in more general terms, to the user of the language, then such a study

---

[10]R. Carnap, *Introduction of Semantics*, Cambridge, MA: Harvard University Press, 1942.

is relegated to the field of pragmatics (in this case, whether the relation between the reference and the referent is involved has no effect on this classification). If we only analyze the forms of the expression without taking into consideration the users of the language and the referents, we are in the realm of semantics. Finally, if we only analyze the relation between the linguistic expressions without taking into consideration the referent, we are in the field of logical syntax." It can be seen that the field of pragmatics is broader than that of semantics or that of syntax, so the study of pragmatics is more difficult.

In NLP, the study of formal models of pragmatics is still quite limited. Now an emerging research field is computational pragmatics, whose application prospects are very attractive. Further exploration is expected.

Bibliography

1. Halliday, M.A.K. 1973. *Explorations in the Functions of Language*. New York: Elsevier.
2. Halliday, M.A.K., and C.M.I.M. Matthiessen. 1999. *Construing Experience Through Meaning: A Language-Based Approach to Cognition*. London: Continuum.
3. Halliday, M.A.K. 2000. *An Introduction to Functional Grammar*. Beijing: Foreign Language Teaching and Research Press.
4. ———. 2002. *Linguistic Studies of Text and Discourse*. Continuum: London.
5. Jurafsky, D., and J. Martin. 2000. *Speech and Language Processing*. Hoboken: Prentice Hall. *An Overview of Natural Language Processing* (Chinese trans: Feng, Zhiwei, and Sun, Le). Beijing: Publishing House of Electronics Industry, 2005.
6. Martin, J.R. 1992. *English Text: System and Structure*. Philadelphia: John Benjamins.
7. Shushan, Cai, and Chongli Zou. 2010. *Research on the Formal Theory of Natural Language*. Beijing: People's Publishing House.
8. Zhiwei, Feng. 1996. *Computer Processing of Natural Languages*. Shanghai: Shanghai Foreign Language Education Press.
9. ———. 1985. *Mathematical Linguistics*. Shanghai: Shanghai Knowledge Publishing House.
10. ———. 2002. *Exploration of Computational Linguistics*. Harbin: Heilongjiang Education Press.
11. ———. 2003. *New Theory of Applied Linguistics: Three Pillars of Applied Language Research*. Beijing: Contemporary World Press.
12. ———. 2005. *Research on Machine Translation*. Beijing: China International Translation and Publishing Corporation.
13. ———. 2014. Speech Act Theory and Conversation Intelligent Agents. *Studies on Foreign Languages* 1: 21–36.
14. ———. 1992. The Challenge of Computational Linguistics to Theoretical Linguistics. *Application of Language and Script* 1: 81–97.
15. ———. 2007. On the Eight Characteristics of Language Signs. *Journal of College of Chinese Language and Culture of Jinan University* 1: 37–50.
16. ———. 2013. *Schools of Modern Linguistics (Updated Edition)*. Beijing: The Commercial Press.
17. Zhuanglin, Hu, Yongsheng Zhu, Delu Zhang, and Zhanzi Li. 2005. *Introduction to Systemic Functional Linguistics*. Beijing: Peking University Press.

Chapter 9
Formal Models of Discourse Analysis

Most NLP studies focus on language phenomena at the word or sentence level, paying less attention to the relationships between sentences. However, the natural language usually appears not as a collection of independent sentences but of interrelated sentence groups, which are called a discourse. Currently, the wide use of computers is witnessed in discourse processing. Against this backdrop, discourses encompass not only monologues and dialogues but also human-computer interactions (abbreviated as HCI).

Participants in a monologue are one speaker (such as the author of this book) and one or multiple listener(s) (correspondingly, readers of this book). The communication in a monologue is unidirectional, from the speaker to the listener(s).

After reading a passage, you may discuss it with your friend. The discussion takes the form of a free bidirectional discourse called a dialogue. When engaged in a dialogue, each participant takes turns assuming the role of a speaker and a listener. Different from a monologue, a dialogue is usually composed of various communicative acts, such as asking questions, giving answers, making corrections, and so on.

The third type of discourse, HCI, is quite different from a dialogue, partly because computer systems have limitations in dealing with free dialogues. Systems for HCI usually constrain a dialogue by adopting strategies that can generate a restrictive interpretation of a user's utterance and thus help computers to make sense of it. While processing the three types of discourses shares a multitude of problems, the discourses require different processing techniques due to their unique characteristics. Processing the three types of discourses automatically is very complicated because automated discourse analysis involves not only intra-sentential but also inter-sentential and sentence-speaker relations.

In this chapter, we will explain some problems common to automated discourse analysis. In addition, some techniques for formal discourse analysis will be detailed to address reference resolution, textual coherence, and rhetorical structure in different types of discourses.

© Springer Nature Singapore Pte Ltd. 2023
Z. Feng, *Formal Analysis for Natural Language Processing: A Handbook*,
https://doi.org/10.1007/978-981-16-5172-4_9

9.1 Reference Resolution

What follows are some examples in English-Chinese machine translation that need to be processed with discourse analysis techniques:

(a) I saw the soldiers aim at the women, and I saw several of them fall.
(b) The council refused the women a permit because they advocated violence.
(c) Sue wants to put the key under the doormat. When she lifted it up, a cockroach quickly scampered across the path.

In *a*, does *them* refer to *soldiers* or *women*? When translated into Chinese, it should be rendered as "他们" (/ta men/; the equivalent of masculine *them* in Chinese) if it denotes soldiers and "她们" (/ta men/; the equivalent of feminine *them* in Chinese) if meaning women. Similarly, in *b*, they can refer to *council* or *women*. In the former case, *they* should be translated into "他们" (/ta men/), while in the latter, "她们" (/ta men/) is the appropriate translation. If its referent is not clarified in the source text, an unambiguous translation will be impossible. In *c*, *it* can stand for either *key* or *doormat*. If the word is directly translated into "它" (/ta/; the equivalent of *it* in Chinese) without indicating its referent, the whole sentence will be quite confusing. The above examples show that how to resolve reference expressions should be investigated in machine translation research.

Let's look at another example.

(d) John went to Bill's car dealership to check out a Benz. He looked at it for about an hour.

What do *He* and *it* refer to respectively? Anyone who speaks English can easily infer that *He* represents John instead of Bill and *it* is a Benz automobile rather than Bill's car dealership. However, it is difficult for computers to make such inferences. Without reference resolution, machine translation would be out of the question.

In this section, we will discuss some issues concerning reference. But before that, we need to define some terms.

Reference: The process in which a speaker uses a language expression such as *John* or *he* to refer to an entity such as a person named John.

Referring expression and referent: A referring expression is a natural language expression that is used to refer, while a referent is the entity to which a referring expression refers. Accordingly, in the above example, *he* is a referring expression and *John* serves as its referent. For simplification, a referring expression is usually said to point to an object. For instance, we can say *he* points to *John*. But we should bear in our minds that the speaker in fact makes an act which uses *he* to refer to *John*.

Corefer: The act that two referring expressions refer to the same entity. In the example above, *John* and *he* corefer.

Antecedent: After an entity is referred to by a referring expression, if another expression is used to refer to the same entity, the preceding expression is the antecedent of the following one. For instance, in *d*, after the referring expression *John* refers to the person John, *he* also represents John. Therefore, *John* is the antecedent of *he*.

Anaphoric: Anaphora is the phenomenon that a referring expression is used to refer to an entity that has already been introduced into the discourse. The referring expression is called an anaphoric. Accordingly, *He* and *it* are anaphorics in *d*.

The natural language has provided speakers with various means to refer to an entity. If your friend owns a Benz car, you have many options available to denote it. When the discourse context varies, you may use *it, this, that, this car, that car, the car, the Benz,* or *my friend's car* to refer to the Benz car. However, you can never choose freely in any context. Take the Benz car for example. You cannot use *it* or *the Benz* if the listener knows nothing about your friend's car. Neither of the two expressions is acceptable if the car has not been mentioned previously or the car is not near the discourse participants. The reason is that each referring expression implies a different message about a place, which the speaker assumes the referent occupies within the hearer's set of beliefs. A summation of such beliefs forms the hearer's mental model of the ongoing discourse, which is called a discourse model. The discourse model includes representations of the entities mentioned in the discourse and the relationships they hold.

Next, let us elaborate on syntactic and semantic restrictions.

Any algorithm that can successfully resolve a referring expression should sort out all the potential referents on the basis of some relatively strict restrictions. Some of the restrictions are described as follows.

Number Agreement: A referring expression and its referent should agree in number. For the English language, it means that a distinction should be made between singular and plural references. Figure 9.1 is a classification of English pronouns according to the number they imply.

The following examples are used to illustrate the restriction of number agreement:

John has a new Benz. It is red. (*It* and *Benz* both indicate a singular.)
John has three Benzs. They are red. (*They* and *Benzs* are both plural.)
*John has three Benz. They are red. (The first sentence is ungrammatical because *Benz* is not plural.)
*John has three new Benzs. It is red. (The sentence is ungrammatical because *It* does not agree in number with *Benzs*.)

Singular	Plural	Unspecified
She, her, he, him, his, it	We, us, they, them	You

Fig. 9.1 Number agreement of English pronouns

	First person	Second person	Third person
Nominative	I, we	You	He, she, they
Accusative	Me, us	You	Him, her, them
Genitive	My, our	Your	His, her, their

Fig. 9.2 Person and case agreements of English pronouns

Masculine	Feminine	Nonpersonal
He, him, his	She, her	It

Fig. 9.3 Gender agreement of English pronouns

Person and Case Agreement: English has three types of personal pronouns: first person, second person, and third person. The details are given in Fig. 9.2.

Additionally, the selection of English pronouns is also restrained by case agreement. Different forms of pronouns are required at different positions in a sentence. For example, he, she, and they appear in the subject position; him, her, and them occur in the object position; genitives should be used in his Benz, her Benz, and their Benz. This classification is also presented in Fig. 9.2.

The following sample sentences account for the restrictions imposed by person agreement:

You and I have Benzs. We love them.
John and Mary have Benzs. They love them.
*John and Mary have Benzs. We love them.

(Person disagreement occurs as *We* is used to represent *John and Mary*.)

*You and I have Benzs. They love them.
(Person disagreement occurs as *They* is used to represent *you and I*.)

Gender Agreement: A pronoun should also agree in gender with its referent. English third-person pronouns are grouped into masculine, feminine, and nonpersonal pronouns. Different from other languages, the first two groups in English can only apply to animate entities. Some of them are listed in Fig. 9.3.

The two sentences below illustrate how gender agreement works:

John has a Benz. He is attractive. (he = John, not the Benz)
John has a Benz. It is attractive. (it = the Benz, not John)

Syntactic Constraint: When a referring expression and its potential antecedent occur in the same clause, reference is likely to be constrained by their syntactic relation. For example, pronouns in the following sentences are subject to the constraints within the square brackets:

John bought himself a new Benz. [himself = John]
John bought him a new Benz. [him ≠ John]
John said that Bill bought him a new Benz. [him ≠ Bill]
John said that Bill bought himself a new Benz. [himself = Bill]
He said that he bought John a new Benz. [He ≠ John; he ≠ John]

English pronouns like himself, herself, and themselves are called reflexives. To put it simply, a reflexive corefers with the subject of the immediately embedding clause (as in *John bought himself a new Benz*, himself and *John* corefer), while a nonreflexive pronoun cannot corefer with the subject (as in *John bought him a new Benz*, him and *John* do not corefer). Additionally, a full noun phrase like John cannot corefer with the subject of the most immediate clause nor with the subject of a higher-level clause (as in *He said that he bought John a new Benz*, *John* corefers with neither *He* nor *he*).

Selectional Restriction: The restriction imposed by a verb on its argument can be used to resolve the pronoun involved. An instance is the following utterance.

John parked his Benz in the garage. He had driven it around for hours.

It in the above utterance has two potential referents, that is, *Benz* and *garage*. However, for the verb *drive*, it requires its direct object to be an entity that can be driven, such as a car, a truck, or a bus, rather than a garage. Therefore, the fact that *it* serves as the object of *drive* imposes a selectional restriction on the potential referents of *it*.

A selectional restriction may be lifted in a metaphorical sentence, as in the following example:

John bought a new Benz. It drinks gasoline like you would not believe.

Although the subject of the verb *drink* is usually animate, *it* can refer to *a new Benz* here because of a metaphorical use.

Of course, a more general selectional restriction is also possible. In that case, reference resolution tends to be much more difficult. Please look at the following utterance:

John parked his Benz in the garage. It is incredibly messy, with old bikes and car parts lying around everywhere.

Almost for sure, *it* here refers to *garage* because a car is not spacious enough so that it cannot be scattered with old bikes and car parts. To resolve *it* here, a listener needs to know about the typical size of a car and a garage and what is typically placed in the two.

Here is another example: Beverly Hills is a clean city located in southern California, United States, and surrounded by Los Angeles. Adjacent to Hollywood, it is usually known as a residential area of movie stars. Therefore, *it* in the following utterance is believed to refer to the Benz car:

John parked his Benz in downtown Beverly Hills. It is incredibly messy, with old bike and car parts lying around everywhere.

The above instance shows that in discourse analysis, almost all the knowledge shared by discourse participants can be used to resolve a pronoun. Such a huge amount of encyclopedic knowledge can hardly be made full use of in NLP.

Next, we will discuss some preferences that should be considered in resolving pronouns.

Recency: Most of the theories concerning reference have elaborated on this concept. It refers to the phenomenon that entities introduced by a recent utterance are more salient than those in an utterance further back. Therefore, in the following example, the referent of *it* is more likely to be *Benz* rather than *Mazda*:

John has a Mazda. Bill has a Benz. Mary likes to drive it.

Grammatical Role: Many theories specify a salience hierarchy of different entities in a sentence. Specifically, the entities in the subject position are more salient than those in the object position, which in turn are more salient than those in subsequent positions. In the utterances below, pronouns can be explained with this hierarchy. Although the first sentence in each example conveys a roughly similar propositional meaning, the preferred referent of the pronoun *He* varies with the subject in each case. *He* refers to John in the first utterance and Bill in the second. For the third one, both John and Bill occur in the subject position and enjoy the same salience, so the referent of *He* is unclear.

John went to the Benz dealership with Bill. He bought a Mazda. [he = John]
Bill went to the Benz dealership with John. He bought a Mazda. [he = Bill]
John and Bill went to the Benz dealership. He bought a Mazda. [he = ??]

Repeated Mention: An entity that is the focus of the prior utterance is more likely to be the focus of the subsequent utterance. Therefore, a reference to the entity is more likely to be pronominalized. For example, in the following utterance, the first two sentences focus on John. Although the subject of the third sentence is Bill, *He* in the final sentence should refer to John, as it is a repeated mention.

John needed a car to get to his new job. He decided that he wanted something sporty. Bill went to the Benz dealership with him. He bought a Mazda. [he = John]

Parallelism: Parallelism can result in a strong preference, as is shown in the following example:

Mary went with Sue to the Benz dealership. Sally went with her to the Mazda dealership. [her = Sue]

According to the hierarchy of grammatical roles previously mentioned, *Mary* is more salient than *Sue* and thus more likely to be the referent of *her*. However, *her* should refer to *Sue* because of the parallelism brought by *went with Sue* in the first sentence and *went with her* in the second sentence.

In the following utterance, no parallelism occurs, so *her* in the second sentence should refer to *Mary* in the first sentence:

Mary went with Sue to the Benz dealership. Sally told her not to buy anything. [her = Mary]

Verb Semantics: Some verbs may place a semantic emphasis on one of their argument positions. This emphasis can lead to a biased interpretation of their subsequent pronouns. Try to compare the following utterances:

John telephoned Bill. He lost the pamphlet on Benz. [He = John]
John criticized Bill. He lost the pamphlet on Benz. [He = Bill]

The two utterances appear to differ only in the verbs in their first sentence, yet *He* is resolved to John in the first utterance but Bill in the second. This results from the implicit causal relationships indicated by the two verbs. To be more specific, the implicit cause of the "criticizing" event is thought to be its object, Bill, which is the patient of the verb, while the implicit cause of the "telephoning" event is probably its subject, John, which is the agent of the verb. Such causal relationships bring more salience to the entity in the argument position indicating the implicit cause.

Noun Semantics: Sometimes, the referent of a pronoun should be resolved according to the attributes of the nouns that the pronoun potentially refers to. Try to analyze the following example:

The computer outputs the data; it is fast. [it = computer]
The computer outputs the data; it is stored in ASCII. [it = data]

We can identify the referents of *it* in the above two utterances according to the attributes associated with computer (speed [fast or slow]) and data (storable [yes or no]). In the first utterance, as *fast* is a value of computers' attribute *speed*, *it* should refer to *computer*. However, in the second utterance, *store* is an attribute of data, so *it* should refer to *data*.

In the following, some algorithms will be briefed for pronoun resolution.

To date, no algorithm for pronoun resolution can successfully explain all the preferences mentioned above and resolve the contradictions between them. However, Lappin and Leass devised a straightforward algorithm that considered many of the preferences. The algorithm adopts a simple weighting method and integrates recency and syntax-based preferences. Here, we will describe a simplified version of the Lappin-Leass algorithm, which can help resolve third-person nonreflexive pronouns. Generally, the Lappin-Leass algorithm performs two operations, that is, discourse model updating and pronoun resolution. First, when a noun phrase referring to a new entity is found, a representation for it should be added to the discourse model, and the salience value of the noun phrase should be calculated. The salience

Salience factors	Weight
Sentence recency	100
Subject emphasis	80
Existential emphasis	70
Direct object emphasis	50
Indirect object and oblique complement emphasis	40
Non-adverbial emphasis	50
Head noun emphasis	80

Fig. 9.4   Salience factors of Lappin-Leass algorithm

value is the sum of all the weights assigned by a group of salience factors. Figure 9.4 is a list of some salience factors and their corresponding weights.

Whenever the Lappin-Leass algorithm processes a new sentence, the weight assigned by each factor to the entity in the discourse model will be reduced to half its original value. This operation works together with the effect brought by the sentence recency weight (the initial weight is 100 and will be reduced to half its value each time a new sentence is processed) to capture the recency preference.

The hierarchical relationship among the following five factors illustrates a preference scheme for different grammatical roles.

Subject > existential predicate nominal > object > indirect object or oblique > demarcated adverbial PP

The five factors can be exemplified by the positions of the italicized phrases in the following sentences:

A *Benz* is parked in the lot. (subject)
There is *a Benz* is parked in the lot. (existential predicate nominal)
John parked *a Benz* in the lot. (object)
John gave *his Benz* a bath. (indirect object)
Inside *his Benz*, John showed Susan his new CD player. (demarcated adverbial PP)

The demarcated adverbial PP, which is represented as the non-adverbial emphasis in Fig. 9.4, is assigned a weight of 50. The head noun emphasis factor can penalize referents embedded in larger noun phrases and increase the weights of un-embedded referents. Therefore, "a Benz" or "his Benz" in the above examples will receive a weight of 80 points for being a head noun, while "a Benz" in the example below will not get the same weight as it is embedded in a subject noun phrase:

The owner's manual for a *Benz* is on John's desk.

The contributions of all these factors to the salience of a referent are based on the attributes of the noun phrases that denote the referent. Of course, it is very likely that some noun phrases in the preceding discourse refer to the same entity, but each is assigned a different level of salience. Therefore, we need an approach that can integrate the contribution of each noun phrase. To solve the problem, the Lappin-Leass algorithm provides each referent with an equivalence class, which contains all

Role parallelism	35
Cataphora	-175

Fig. 9.5 Salience weights of pronouns in the Lappin-Leass algorithm

the noun phrases that have been resolved to the referent. The weight assigned by a salience factor to a referent is the weights assigned by the factor to all the members of the corresponding equivalence class. The salience weight of a referent is thus calculated by adding up the weight of each factor. One salience factor scopes over a sentence, so if a possible referent is referred to in the current sentence and the preceding one, its weight will be computed separately according to sentence recency. If a referent is mentioned repeatedly in the same sentence, its weight will be calculated only once. As a result, if a referent is mentioned more than once in the preceding discourse, its salience will increase. This is an example of repeated mentions that have been discussed in the preferences considered in pronoun resolution. If we update the discourse model with new potential referents and recalculate their salience values, we should resolve all the pronouns in this new sentence. To achieve this, we employ another two salience weights. One can reward the grammatical role parallelism between a pronoun and its potential referent. The other can penalize cataphoric reference. Their weights are given in Fig. 9.5. Different from the other preferences, the two weights cannot be calculated independently of the pronoun. Therefore, they cannot be calculated during the updating of the discourse model. We will use the *initial salience value* and the *final salience value* to represent the weight of a referent before and after the factors are applied.

Now, we will explain in detail how the Lappin-Leass algorithm resolves a pronoun.

If the discourse model has been updated and the initial salience values of the above referents have been calculated, the steps to resolve a pronoun can be described as follows:

1. Collect all the potential referents.
2. Remove the referents that disagree with the pronoun in gender and number.
3. Remove the referents that cannot pass the intra-sentential syntactic coreference constraint.
4. Calculate the total salience value of the referents by adding the existing salience values that have been calculated during the updating of the discourse model (the sum of the applicable values in Fig. 9.4) to the applicable values in Fig. 9.5.
5. Select the referent that has the highest salience value. If the highest value is shared by more than two referents (two included), select the closest referent according to their string positions.

The above steps can be illustrated with the help of the following utterance:

John saw a beautiful Benz at the dealership. He showed it to Bob. He bought it.

To begin with, we process the first sentence *John saw a beautiful Benz at the dealership* by collecting all the potential referents in it and calculating their initial salience values. Figure 9.6 details the contribution of each salience factor to salience.

No pronoun needs to be resolved in the first sentence, so we move on to process the second sentence by dividing the total values by 2 to reduce the salience values. The *phrase* column gives the equivalence class of referring expressions for each referent, as is shown in Fig. 9.7.

In the second sentence *He showed it to Bob,* its first noun phrase is *He.* As *He* refers to a male person, step two of the resolution algorithm limits the potential referent to *John.*

Now we need to update the discourse model. First, add the pronoun *He* to the equivalence class of *John* (denoted as He_1 to differentiate it from other possible occurrences of he). As *He* occurs in the second sentence while *John* occurs in the first sentence, their salience factors do not overlap. The pronoun in the current sentence has the following salience factors: recency = 100, subject = 80, non-adverbial = 50, and nonembedded head noun = 80. The total value of 310 is then added to 155, which is the current weight for *John.* Therefore, *John*'s total value is updated to 465 (Fig. 9.8).

	Recency	Subject	Existential Noun	Object	Indirect Object	Non-adverbial	Head Noun	Total
John	100	80				50	80	310
Benz	100			50		50	80	280
Dealership	100					50	80	230

Fig. 9.6 Referents in the first sentence and their initial salience values

Referent	Phrase	Value
John	{John}	155
Benz	{a beautiful Benz}	140
Dealership	{the dealership}	115

Fig. 9.7 Equivalence classes of the three referents and their salience values

Referent	Phrase	Value
John	{John, He_1}	465
Benz	{a beautiful Benz}	140
Dealership	{the dealership}	115

Fig. 9.8 The updated salience value of John when processing the second sentence

The second noun phrase in the second sentence is the pronoun *it*, whose potential referent is *Benz* or *dealership*. To calculate the final salience values, we add the applicable weights in Fig. 9.5 to the above initial salience values first. Since neither potential referent would lead to cataphora, this factor does not work. For the parallelism preference, as both *a beautiful Benz* and *it* occupy the object position in the first and second sentences respectively (whereas *the dealership* is not an object in the third sentence), role parallelism occurs. We then add 35 to the weight of *Benz*, which becomes 175, while the weight of *dealership* is still 115. Therefore, we choose *Benz* to be the referent of *it*.

Now the discourse model should be updated again. Because *it* occupies a nonembedded object position, its weight should be $100 + 50 + 50 + 80 = 280$. The value is added to 140, the current weight of *Benz*, and thus updated to 420 (Fig. 9.9).

The last noun phrase in the second sentence is *Bob*, which introduces another discourse referent. Since it is in an oblique argument position, whose weight is 40, *Bob* is assigned a weight of $100 + 40 + 50 + 80 = 270$ (Fig. 9.10).

Now, we come to the last sentence "He bought it." For one more time, we cut the current weights in half (Fig. 9.11).

Readers can verify that the referent of *He* is John and *it* refers to Benz.

The weights adopted by the Lappin-Leass algorithm were acquired by an experiment on a corpus of computer training manuals. The algorithm, when collaborating with other filtering algorithms, could achieve an accuracy of 86% if applied to an untrained corpus within the same genre.

Referent	Phrase	Value
John	{John, He$_1$}	465
Benz	{a beautiful Benz, it$_1$}	420
Dealership	{the dealership}	115

Fig. 9.9   The updated discourse model after processing *it* in the second sentence

Referent	Phrase	Value
John	{John, He$_1$}	465
Benz	{a beautiful Benz, it$_1$}	420
Bob	{Bob}	270
Dealership	{the dealership}	115

Fig. 9.10   The updated discourse model after processing *Bob* in the second sentence

Referent	Phrase	Value
John	{John, He_1}	232.5
Benz	{a beautiful Benz, it_1}	210
Bob	{Bob, He_2}	135
Dealership	{the dealership, it_2}	57.5

Fig. 9.11 The updated discourse model after processing the third sentence

9.2 Reasoning Techniques in Text Coherence

If you have collected some well-formed text fragments that can be interpreted independently, for example, by selecting one sentence randomly from each chapter of *A Dream of Red Mansions* (《红楼梦》, /Hong Lou Meng/; one of the "Four Great Classical Novels" of Chinese Literature) and put them together, can you understand them as a meaningful whole? Almost for sure, they are incomprehensible. The reason lies in the fact that no coherence exists among the sentences.

In machine translation, research on textual coherence is of great importance. Consider the following example:

Little Johnny was very upset. He had lost his toy train. Then he found it. It was in his pen.

The example above is very similar to the one taken by Bar-Hillel when machine translation was in its early development. If machine translation programs cannot make sense of the coherence relation between the word *pen* and its preceding sentences, it is difficult to ascertain that the meaning of *pen* here should be a small piece of land surrounded by a fence where a game is played. As a result, a correct translation is impossible.

In Chinese-English machine translation, textual coherence should also be investigated. Take the following two Chinese utterances for example:

小王是医生。今天他做了手术。
(/Xiao Wang shi yi sheng。Jin tian ta zuo le shou shu。/; Xiao Wang is a doctor. He has an operation today.)
小王得了阑尾炎。今天他做了手术。
(/Xiao Wang de le lan wei yan。Jin tian ta zuo le shou shu。/; Xiao Wang suffers from appendicitis. He has an operation today.)

In the above two utterances, the subject of each first sentence is *Xiao Wang*, while that of each second sentence is *He*. By using the reference resolution methods, we can resolve *He* in the second utterance to *Xiao Wang*. However, its second sentence has two possibilities. He can either perform an operation on others (*He* is the agent) or undergo an operation performed by others (*He* is the patient). The ambiguity here can be eliminated by identifying who *He refers to*. If *He* is a doctor, it is more likely that he performs an operation on others, and thus *He* is the agent. Otherwise, he probably undergoes an operation performed by others; hence, he is the patient. To identify the referent of *He*, the coherence between the sentences of each utterance should be analyzed.

In the first utterance, as its first sentence provides Xiao Wang's identity information for the second sentence, the utterance can be reinterpreted as follows accordingly:

Xiao Wang is a doctor. Today he performs an operation.

The meaning of *Today he performs an operation* is that today he performs an operation on a patient.

In the second utterance, as its first sentence shows that Xiao Wang has been diagnosed with appendicitis, he is more likely to undergo an operation performed by others. Based on the coherence relation, this utterance can be interpreted as below.

Xiao Wang gets the appendicitis. Today he is operated by a doctor.

The sentence *Today he is operated by a doctor* means that today his appendix is removed by a doctor.

The analysis above shows that the sentence *He has an operation today* has different interpretations because of different coherence relations. Through this example, we can see how important textual coherence is for machine translation.

However, we cannot make sure that the inference above is 100% correct because real-life situations can be very complicated. As a doctor, Xiao Wang may get appendicitis and undergo an operation performed by others. On the other hand, a doctor, although suffering from appendicitis, may still carry forward the humanitarian spirit of healing the wounded and rescuing the dying and perform an operation on another patient. In either case, our interpretation is wrong. Therefore, to make sense of the textual coherence here, we need to know not only Xiao Wang's identity information but also other information such as his health status and work style. If all the information is taken into account, textual coherence becomes a very difficult and complicated issue.

Below is an interesting example of textual coherence. Readers can try to analyze the differences between utterances *a* and *b*.

(a) 张三把李四的车钥匙藏起来了。他喝醉了。
    (/Zhang San ba Li Si de che yao shi cang qi lai le。 Ta he zui le。 /; San Zhang hid Si Li's carkeys. He was drunk.)
(b) 张三把李四的车钥匙藏起来了。他喜欢菠菜。
    (/Zhang San ba Li Si de che yao shi cang qi lai le。 Ta xi huan bo cai。 /; San Zhang hid Si Li's carkeys. He liked spinach.)

Most readers may find utterance *a* to be unremarkable but utterance *b* to be weird. Why? Similar to utterance *a*, each of the two sentences in utterance *b* is well formed and readily interpretable. However, when the two sentences are juxtaposed, some problems may occur. A hearer may ask, for instance, what is the relationship between hiding someone's carkeys and liking spinach. By asking this question, the hearer wants to determine the coherence relation of the utterance. Alternatively, the hearer may offer an explanation to make the utterance coherent, for example, by conjecturing that someone gave San Zhang (张三 /Zhang San/) some spinach in exchange for Si Li (李四 /Li Si/)'s hidden carkeys. In such a context, the utterance will become easier to understand because this conjecture enables the hearer to take the fact that San Zhang (张三 /Zhang San/) liked spinach as the reason why he hid Si Li (李四 /Li Si/)'s carkeys. The cause-effect relationship explains why the two sentences are put together. The fact that hearers will try their best to recognize the connection shows that coherence construction should be a part of discourse comprehension.

All the possible connections between sentences in an utterance can be called a set of coherence relations. In the following are some common coherence relations. The symbols S_0 and S_1 represent the meanings of two related sentences (S_0 for the preceding sentence and S_1 for the subsequent sentence).

Result: The state or the event asserted by S_0 leads to or possibly leads to the state or the event asserted by S_1. For example, 张三买了一辆"奔驰"汽车。他带着他父亲到了万里长城。 (/Zhang San mai le yi liang Ben Chi qi che. Ta dai zhe ta fu qin dao le Wan Li Chang Cheng./; San Zhang bought a Benz. He brought his father to the Great Wall.)

Explanation: The state or the event asserted by S_1 leads to or possibly leads to the state or the event asserted by S_0. For example, 张三把李四的汽车钥匙藏起来。他喝醉了。 (/Zhang San ba Li Si de qi che yao shi cang qi lai. Ta he zui le./; San Zhang hid Si Li's carkeys. He was drunk.)

Parallel: a_i in p $(a_1, a_2, \ldots)$ asserted by S_0 is similar to b_i in p $(b_1, b_2, \ldots)$ asserted by S_1, for all i. For instance, 张三买了一辆"奔驰"汽车。李四买了一辆"宝马"汽车。 (/Zhang San mai le yi liang Ben Chi qi che. Li Si mai le yi liang Bao Ma qi che./; San Zhang bought a Benz. Si Li bought a BMW.)

Elaboration: S_0 and S_1 assert the same proposition. For instance, 张三在这个周末买了一辆"奔驰"汽车。他星期六下午在李四的经销店用五十万元购买了这辆非常漂亮的新的"奔驰"汽车。 (/Zhang San zai zhe ge zhou mo mai le yi liang Ben Chi qi che. Ta xing qi liu xia wu zai Li Si de jing xiao dian yong wu shi wan yuan gou mai le zhe liang fei chang piao liang de xin de Ben Chi qi che. /; San Zhang bought a Benz this weekend. On Saturday afternoon, he bought a beautiful new Benz for 500,000 Yuan at Si Li's dealership.)

Occasion: A change in state can be inferred from the assertion of S_0, the final state of which can be inferred from S_1, or a change in state can be inferred from the assertion of S_1, the initial state of which can be inferred from S_0. For example, 张三买了一辆奔驰汽车。他驾着车到了十三陵。 (/Zhang San mai le yi liang Ben Chi qi che. Ta jia zhe che dao le Shi San Ling./; San Zhang bought a Benz. He drove to Ming Tombs.)

Each of the coherence relations mentioned above is related to one or more constraints, which should be satisfied to maintain coherence. Then, how do these constraints work? To answer this question, an approach to inference is needed.

The most familiar kind of inference is deduction. Its central rule is modus ponens,[1] which can be specified as follows:

$$\alpha \Rightarrow \beta$$
$$\frac{\alpha}{\beta}$$

An example of modus ponens is given below:

所有的"奔驰"汽车都很快。(/Suo you de Ben Chi qi che dou hen kuai。/; All the Benzs drive fast.)
张三的汽车是"奔驰"。(/Zhang San de qi che shi Ben Chi。/; San Zhang's car is a Benz.)

张三的汽车很快。(/Zhang San de qi che hen kuai。/San Zhang's car drives fast.)

Deduction is a kind of sound inference. If the premises are true, the conclusion must be true. However, many natural language understanding systems rely on unsound inference. While unsound inference can generate a wide range of inferences, it can also incur false explanations and misunderstandings. One method for unsound inference is called abduction, whose central rule is given below.

$$\alpha \Rightarrow \beta$$
$$\frac{\beta}{\alpha}$$

Deduction infers an implication relation forward, reasoning from a cause to an effect. In contrast, abduction infers the implication relation backward, reasoning from an effect to a potential cause. An example of abduction is given below:

所有的"奔驰"汽车都很快。(/Suo you de Ben Chi qi che dou hen kuai。 /;All the Benzs are fast.)
张三的汽车很快。(/Zhang San de qi che hen kuai。 /; San Zhang's car is fast.)
张三的汽车是"奔驰"。(/Zhang San de qi che shi Ben Chi。 /; San Zhang's car is a Benz.)

Obviously, the reasoning is unlikely to be correct. San Zhang's car is fast, but it does not necessarily mean that his car is a Benz. It is entirely possible that the car is made by another manufacturer but is still fast.

In general, a given effect β may have many potential causes α_i. We usually do not reason from a fact to only one possible explanation but try to find out the most plausible explanation. To achieve this, we need to compare the quality of these

---

[1] As for the mechanism of modus ponens, please refer to page 9, Feng & Hu (2012) *Mathematical Linguistics*, The Commercial Press.

abductive proofs. A variety of strategies are available for doing this. One of them is to adopt a probabilistic model. However, when the strategy is employed, some problems may arise in selecting the appropriate space over which the probabilities are calculated and in finding out how to acquire the probabilities without a corpus of events. Another approach is to use a completely heuristic strategy, such as preferring the explanation with the fewest assumptions or choosing the explanation with detailed characteristics of the input. Although it is easy to implement this kind of heuristic strategies, they usually turn out to be brittle and limited. Therefore, a more general cost-based strategy can be adopted to combine the features (both positive and negative) of the probabilistic and the heuristic strategies. Such a strategy can be exemplified by the abductive interpretation below. However, to simplify our discussion, we ignore the cost part of the system to a large extent.

Here, we focus on how to make use of world and domain knowledge to determine the most reasonable coherence relation in an utterance. Again, we take utterance a for example.

张三把李四的车钥匙藏起来了。他喝醉了。(/Zhang San ba Li Si de che yao shi cang qi lai le。 Ta he zui le。 /; San Zhang hid Si Li's carkeys. He was drunk.)

Now, let us analyze the utterance step by step to determine its coherence relation.

First, we need an axiom about coherence relations themselves. The following axiom shows that a possible coherence relation is the explanation relation:

$$\forall e_i, e_j \, \text{Explanation}(e_i, e_j) \Rightarrow \text{CoherenceRe}(e_i, e_j)$$

The variables e_i and e_j stand for the events (or states) indicated by two sentences. In this axiom and the following ones, quantifiers always extend their scopes over everything to their right. The axiom tells us that if we need to establish a coherence relation between two events, a possible method is using abduction to assume that the relation is explanation.

The explanation relation requires that the second sentence denote a cause of the effect expressed by the first sentence. We can state this as the following axiom:

$$\forall e_i, e_j \, \text{cause}(e_j, e_i) \Rightarrow \text{Explanation}(e_i, e_j)$$

This axiom denotes that for events e_i and e_j, e_j can explain e_i if e_j causes e_i.

Apart from the two axioms, we also need axioms that can represent world knowledge.

The first axiom concerning world knowledge is that if someone is drunk, others will not let him drive and that the former is the reason of the latter (for simplification, we use the *diswant* predicate to denote the state of not wanting).

$$\forall x, y, e_i \, \mathrm{drunk}(e_i, x) \Rightarrow$$
$$\exists e_j, e_k \, \mathrm{diswant}(e_j, y, e_k) \wedge \mathrm{drive}(e_k, x) \wedge \mathrm{cause}(e_i, e_j)$$

Here, x and y stand for two persons. The predicates *drunk, diswant,* and *drive* mean the states of being drunk, not wanting, and driving, respectively. They are represented by e_i, e_j, and e_k. The predicate *cause* indicates making something happen. In this axiom, e_i is the cause of e_j.

Here, two points should be made clear.

First, in the first axiom about world knowledge, universal quantifiers are used to bind some of the variables. It shows that in all cases in which someone is drunk, no one wants the person to drive. Although this is the usual case, the statement is too absolute. To deal with the issue, some systems include another relation called an *etc* predicate in the antecedent of such axioms. An *etc* predicate stands for all the other attributes that must be true in order to apply the axioms but are too vague to state clearly. Therefore, these predicates cannot be proved but can only be assumed at a certain cost. As rules with lower assumption costs take priority over rules with higher assumption costs, the probability that such a rule applies can be calculated according to its cost. Nevertheless, to simplify our discussion here, we consider neither the costs nor the use of *etc* predicates.

Second, each predicate in the first argument position includes a seemingly redundant variable. For example, the predicate *drive* includes two variables instead of one. The redundant variable can reify the relation indicated by the predicate so that the argument positions of other predicates can refer to the variable. An instance is the treatment that the variable e_k reifies the predicate *drive* allows us to express "not wanting someone to drive" by referring to it in the last argument position of the predicate *diswant*.

The second axiom about world knowledge is that if someone does not want a person to drive a car, he or she does not want the person to have the carkeys because with the keys the person can drive the car.

$$\forall x, y, e_j e_k \mathrm{diswant}(e_j, y, e_k) \wedge \mathrm{drive}(e_k, x) \Rightarrow$$
$$\exists z, e_l, e_m \, \mathrm{diswant}(e_l, y, e_m) \wedge \mathrm{have}(e_m, x, z) \wedge \mathrm{carkeys}(z, x) \wedge \mathrm{cause}(e_j, e_l)$$

In the axiom above, z stands for carkeys. It is noticed that some new predicates are used. The predicate *have* means possessing something, represented by e_m. The predicate *carkeys* indicates having carkeys. The predicate *cause* involves two events, e_j (not wanting someone to drive) and e_l (not wanting someone to have carkeys).

The third axiom about world knowledge says that if someone does not want others to possess something, he may hide it.

$$\forall x, y, z, e_i, e_j \, \mathrm{diswant}(e_l, y, e_m) \wedge \mathrm{have}(e_m, x, z) \Rightarrow$$
$$\exists e_n \, \mathrm{hide}(e_n, y, x, z) \wedge \mathrm{cause}(e_l, e_n)$$

Here, the new predicate *hide*, denoted by e_n, means putting something in a place where it cannot be found.

The fourth axiom simply says that causality is transitive. Specifically, if e_i causes e_j which in turn causes e_k, then e_i causes e_k.

$$\forall e_i, e_j, e_k \; \mathrm{cause} \left(e_i, e_j\right) \wedge \mathrm{cause} \left(e_j, e_k\right) \Rightarrow \mathrm{cause}\left(e_i, e_k\right)$$

Now, we can make use of these axioms to process utterance a, which is restated below:

张三把李四的车钥匙藏起来了。他喝醉了。(/Zhang San ba Li Si de che yao shi cang qi lai le。 Ta he zui le。 /; San Zhang hid Si Li's carkeys. He was drunk.)

The first sentence can be formalized as follows.

$$\mathrm{hide}\,(e_l, \mathrm{San\ Zhang}, \mathrm{Si\ Li}, \mathrm{carkeys}) \wedge \mathrm{carkeys}\,(\mathrm{carkeys}, \mathrm{Li\ Si})$$

Here, the predicate *carkeys* means having carkeys.

We can use the free variable *he* to represent a pronoun, so the event that someone is drunk can be written as follows.

$$\mathrm{drunk}\,(e_2, he)$$

Now, we can see how the content of the sentences cooperates with the previous axioms to establish the coherence of utterance a under the explanation relation.

Figure 9.12 illustrates how the inference is made. The sentence interpretations are given in square brackets. We start from an assumption that there is a coherence

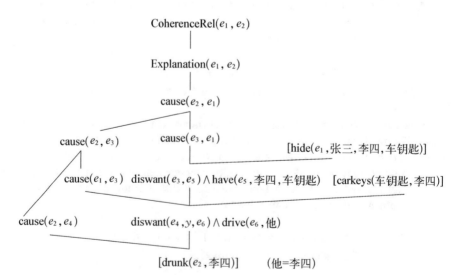

Fig. 9.12 The process to establish coherence in utterance a

relation and then use the axiom ($\forall e_i, e_j$ Explanation(e_i, e_j) $\Rightarrow$ CoherenceRe(e_i, e_j)) to infer that the relation is explanation.

$$\text{Explanation}(e_1, e_2)$$

By using the axiom ($\forall e_i, e_j$ cause(e_j, e_i) $\Rightarrow$ Explanation(e_i, e_j)), we infer that

$$\text{cause } (e_2, e_1)$$

holds. With the help of the axiom that causes are transitive ($\forall e_i, e_j, e_k$ cause (e_i, e_j) $\wedge$ cause (e_j, e_k) $\Rightarrow$ cause (e_i, e_k)), we can infer that there is an intermediate cause e_3,

$$\text{cause } (e_2, e_3) \wedge \text{cause } (e_3, e_1).$$

We repeat the axiom and expand the first conjunct of the above expression to include an intermediate cause e_4:

$$\text{cause } (e_2, e_4) \wedge \text{cause } (e_4, e_3)$$

From the sentence 张三把李四的车钥匙藏起来了 (/Zhang San ba Li Si de che yao shi cang qi lai le/; San Zhang hid Si Li's carkeys), we obtain the predicate *hide*. Then, according to the second predicate *cause* in *cause (e_2, e_3)* $\wedge$ *cause (e_3, e_1)* and the third world knowledge axiom (if someone does not want others to own something, then he may hide it), we can infer that San Zhang did not want Si Li to get his carkeys.

$$\text{diswant}(e_3, \text{San Zhang}, e_5) \wedge \text{have } (e_5, \text{Si Li, carkeys})$$

According to the above expression, the predicate *carkeys* in *carkeys (carkeys, Si Li)* and the second *cause* predicate in *cause(e_2, e_4)* $\wedge$ *cause(e_4, e_3)*, we can now use the second world knowledge axiom (if someone does not want a person to drive a car, then he or she does not want the person to have the carkeys because with the keys the person can drive) and infer that San Zhang did not want Si Li to drive:

$$\text{diswant } (e_4, \text{San Zhang}, e_6) \wedge \text{drive } (e_6, \text{Si Li})$$

According to the above expression, the first world knowledge axiom (if someone is drunk, others will not let him drive) and the second *cause* predicate in *cause(e_2, e_4)* $\wedge$ *cause(e_4, e_3)*, we can infer that Si Li was drunk:

$$\text{drunk } (e_2, \text{Si Li})$$

It can be seen that we can prove the fact on the basis of the interpretation of the second sentence if we simply resolve the free variable *he* to Si Li. Therefore, when we identify the reasoning chain between the sentence interpretations, coherence is established between the sentences. The reasoning chain in this example includes some unprovable assumptions concerning axiom selection and pronoun assignment and generates the expression *cause* (e_2, e_1), which is necessary for establishing the explanation relation.

Now, we use Fig. 9.12 to illustrate the reasoning process above. For ease of reading, please bear in your mind that the utterance for processing is 张三把李四的车钥匙藏起来了。他喝醉了。(/Zhang San ba Li Si de che yao shi cang qi lai le。Ta he zui le。/; San Zhang hid Si Li's carkeys. He was drunk.)

In Fig. 9.12, *San Zhang* is written as 张三, *Si Li* is written as 李四, and carkeys are written as 车钥匙(/che yao shi/) in Chinese.

The inference demonstrates a powerful feature of coherence construction, that is, the ability to lead the listener to infer unsaid information in the speaker's utterance. In this example, the inference is built on the assumption that San Zhang hid Si Li's carkeys because San Zhang did not want Si Li to drive the car (probably because of the fear of having a car accident or being stopped by a policeman). Other causes are not considered, such as playing pranks on Si Li. The real cause is not mentioned in any part of the utterance; it results merely from the hearer's inference, which is needed to establish coherence.

The above example shows that the meaning of an utterance is more than the sum of the meanings of its components. In other words, an utterance usually conveys far more information than the information contained in the individual sentences that constitute the utterance.

Now, we return to utterance *b* and recode it as utterance *d*. One of its distinctive features is that it lacks the coherence displayed by utterance *a*, which is now recoded as utterance *c*:

(c) 张三把李四的车钥匙藏起来了。他喝醉了。(/Zhang San ba Li Si de che yao shi cang qi lai le。Ta he zui le。/; San Zhang hid Si Li's carkeys. He was drunk.)

(d) 张三把李四的车钥匙藏起来了。他喜欢菠菜。(/Zhang San ba Li Si de che yao shi cang qi lai le。Ta xi huan bo cai。/; San Zhang hid Si Li's carkeys. He liked spinach.)

We may find that utterance *d* is somewhat weird because there is no reasoning chain that can analogously connect the two sentence representations. Particularly, there is no causal axiom similar to the axiom that if someone is drunk others will not let him drive, so we cannot infer that liking spinach may render someone unable to drive. Without additional information that can support a reasoning chain (such as the abovementioned situation that someone promised Zhang San spinach in exchange for Si Li's hidden carkeys), the coherence of the utterance cannot be constructed.

Abduction is a type of unreliable inference, so it is possible to subsequently cancel the assumptions made in the process of abduction. In other words, abductive inferences are defeasible. For example, if utterance *c* is followed by the sentence below:

李四的汽车不在这儿,张三只是想给他开个玩笑。 (/Li Si de qi che bu zai zhe er, Zhang San zhi shi xiang gei ta kai ge wan xiao。 /; Si Li's car is not here; San Zhang just wanted to play a joke on him.)

the system would have to cancel the original reasoning chain that connects the two sentences in utterance c, replace it with another one making use of the fact that the event of hiding keys is part of a joke, and begin to re-infer.

To establish a more comprehensive knowledge base capable of supporting a broader range of inferences, we need axioms that are more general than those used to construct the coherence in utterance c. For instance, consider the axiom that if you do not want someone to drive, then you do not want the person to have carkeys. A more general form of the axiom is that if you do not want someone to perform an act and an object enables the person to perform the act, you will not want the person to get the object. Accordingly, the fact that with carkeys someone can drive a car is included in the axiom. In practice, the generalized axiom may apply to other similar facts. This is a strategy of managing resources. Similarly, for the axiom that if someone is drunk, we do not want the person to drive, we can generalize it to an axiom that if someone does not want an event to occur, that person does not want a potential cause of the event to occur. This is a strategy of managing causes. Again, the fact that people do not want others to get into car accidents and the fact that drunk driving leads to car accidents are included in the generalized axiom.

Although it is important to design computational models capable of accounting for how to establish coherence, this and other similar approaches can hardly be applied to a wide range of fields. Such models are almost impractical because they require a huge number of axioms to encode all the necessary world knowledge and they lack a robust mechanism that can make use of a large set of axioms to restrict reasoning. This problem is informally called AI-complete, that is, Artificial-Intelligence-complete, an analogous term to NP-complete in computer science. An AI-complete problem is a problem about all the knowledge possessed by human beings and the ability to use the knowledge. Of course, such a problem is so difficult that it is far from being solved at present.

It should be noted that the proof that utterance c is coherent has another interesting feature: although the pronoun *he* is initially a free variable, it is limited to Li Si during the process of reasoning. In fact, no other processes are needed to resolve the pronoun because it is resolved alongside the establishment of coherence. In 1978, Hobbs proposed the mechanism of establishing coherence as another approach to pronoun resolution.[2] This approach can explain why the most reasonable referent of the pronoun *he* in utterances c and e is Si Li and San Zhang, respectively.

(e) 张三把李四的汽车钥匙丢失了。他喝醉了。 (/Zhang San ba Li Si de qi che yao shi diu shi le。 Ta he zui le。 /; San Zhang lost Si Li's carkeys. He was drunk.)

---

[2] J. R. Hobbs, Coherence and coreference, *Cognitive Science*, 3, 67-90, 1979.

To establish the coherence of utterance *e* under the explanation relation, we need an axiom that getting drunk could lead someone to lose something. As this axiom stipulates that a drunk person would lose something, the free variable *He* can only be San Zhang. The lexico-syntactic difference between utterances *c* and *e* lies in the verb of the first sentence (*hid* in *c* and *lost* in *e*). Syntactically, the pronoun and its possible antecedent noun phrases occupy the same positions in the two examples, so syntax-based preferences cannot help make a distinction between the two.

Sometimes, a speaker may add a special cue called a discourse connective, and use it to restrict the set of coherence relations holding between two or more sentences. For example, the connective *because* in utterance *f* can clearly indicate the explanation relation.

(f) 张三把李四的汽车钥匙藏起来了,因为他喝醉了。(/Zhang San ba Li Si de qi che yao shi cang qi lai le。 Yin wei ta he zui le。 /; San Zhang hid Si Li's carkeys because he was drunk.)

The meaning of *because* can be represented as *cause* (e_2, e_1). The role *because* plays in the proof is similar to the *cause* predicate, which is introduced into abductive reasoning through the axiom

$$\forall e_i, e_j \, \text{cause} \left(e_j, e_i\right) \Rightarrow \text{Explanation} \left(e_i, e_j\right).$$

Although connectives can be used in coherence resolution to restrict the range of possible coherence relations between a pair of sentences, the connectives themselves do not create coherence. Any coherence relation suggested by a connective must still be established through reasoning. Therefore, adding a connective *because* to utterance *d* does not make it coherent.

(g) 张三把李四的汽车钥匙藏起来了,因为他喜欢菠菜。(/Zhang San ba Li Si de che yao shi cang qi lai le。 Yin wei ta xi huan bo cai。 /; San Zhang hid Si Li's carkeys because he liked spinach.)

We fail to establish the coherence relation in utterance *g* for the same reason as in utterance *b*, i.e. due to the lack of the causal knowledge relating the fact that someone likes spinach to the fact that someone hides carkeys. To date, we have discussed how to establish a coherence relation between two sentences. Next, we will try to determine coherence relations for a longer discourse. Does it suffice to establish the coherence relations between adjacent sentences? The answer is definitely no. Just as a sentence has its own structure (the syntactic structure), so does a discourse. Let's look at utterance *h*.

(h) 张三去银行兑取他的薪水。(S_1)
    然后他乘火车去李四开办的汽车经销店。(S_2)
    他需要买一辆汽车。(S_3)
    他工作的那个公司附近现在还没有任何的公共交通。(S_4)
    他也想跟李四谈一谈关于他们的孩子今年考大学的事情。(S_5)

[/Zhang San qu yin hang dui qu ta de xin shui. (S1)
Ran hou ta cheng huo che qu Li Si kai ban de qi che jing xiao dian. (S2)
Ta xu yao mai yi liang qi che. (S3)
Ta gong zuo de na ge gong si fu jin xian zai hai mei you ren he de gong gong jiao tong. (S4)
Ta ye xiang gen Li Si tan yi tan guan yu ta men de hai zi jin nian kao da xue de shi qing. (S5)/;
San Zhang went to a bank to withdraw money from his salary account. (S_1)
Then he took a train to Si Li's car dealership. (S_2)
He needed to buy a car. (S_3)
There was no public transportation near the company he worked for. (S_4)
He also wanted to talk to Si Li about their children's admission to college. (S_5)]

Intuitively, discourse h is not characterized by a linear structure. The whole discourse seems to be about the sequence of events described in S_1 and S_2. S_2 is most related to S_3 and S_5, and S_3 is most related to S_4. The coherence relations between the sentences form the discourse structure in Fig. 9.13.

In the tree diagram below, each node stands for a set of locally coherent sentences, called a discourse segment. Roughly, discourse segments in an utterance are analogous to constituents of a sentence. By expanding the previous axioms used for discourse interpretation, we can establish coherence relations in longer and hierarchical discourses such as discourse h. The identification of discourse segments and discourse structures is a by-product of the process of establishing coherence relations.

First, we include the following axiom that a sentence is a discourse segment. Here, w is a string composed of words in the sentence, and e represents an event described by w.

$$\forall w, e \text{ sentence}(w, e) \Rightarrow \text{Segment}(w, e)$$

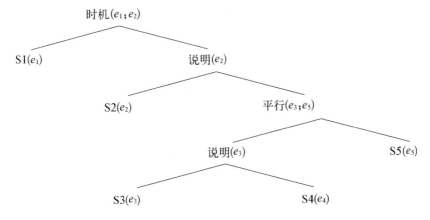

Fig. 9.13 The discourse structure of discourse h

Next, we include another axiom as follows. It states that if a coherence relation can be established between two smaller segments, they can constitute a larger segment.

$$\forall w_1, w_2, e_1, e_2, e \ \text{Segment}(w_1, e_1) \wedge \text{Segment}(w_2, e_2)$$

$$\wedge \text{CoherenceRel}(e_1, e_2, e) \Rightarrow \text{Segment}(w_1 w_2, e)$$

When using the axiom to process a longer discourse, we need to add a third argument to the *CoherenceRel(e)* predicate. Its value is a combination of the information denoted by e_1 and e_2. The variable represents the main content of the resulting segment. Here, we assume that a subordinating relation, such as the explanation relation, is correlated to only one argument (in discourse *h*, it is the effect indicated by the first sentence), whereas a coordinating relation, like the parallel or occasion relation, is related to the combination of two arguments. In Fig. 9.13, these arguments are put in the parentheses next to the relations.

Now, let us explain a coherent discourse *W*. First, we should simply prove that *W* is a segment as is shown in the following:

$$\exists e \ \text{Segment}(W, e)$$

For a discourse, these rules will lead to any possible binary branching structure of segments, as long as the structure can agree with the process of establishing coherence relations between the segments. Here, differences exist between computing syntactic structure and deriving discourse structure. Grammar at the sentence level tends to be very complicated, as it involves many syntactic problems, such as how constituents (noun phrases, verb phrases, and so on) can modify each other and what is the order of the modification. In contrast, the aforementioned discourse grammar is much simpler because it only uses two rules, i.e. a rule to rewrite a segment into two smaller segments and a rule to identify a sentence as a segment. What discourse structure should be assigned relies on how to construct coherence in the discourse.

Research on discourse structure is very useful for pronoun resolution. Pronouns often exhibit a preference for recency, which means that they tend to refer to the referents nearby. In fact, we can define recency in terms of the linear or hierarchical structure of a discourse. If we resolve a given pronoun according to the recency of the hierarchical discourse structure, its effect will be much better than relying on the linear discourse structure.

In this section, we have reviewed some studies regarding how computers can process textual coherence. Nevertheless, our discussion is limited to monologues, addressing no complicated issues such as interpersonal dialogues and human-computer interactions.

From the description above, it can be found that the information conveyed by a discourse is usually far more than the sum of the information conveyed by the sentences making up the discourse. Uncovering the additional information is another important new task in NLP.

9.3   Mann and Thompson's Rhetorical Structure Theory

In 1987, Mann and Thompson proposed Rhetorical Structure Theory in *Rhetorical Structure Theory: A Theory of Text Organization*. Based on the relations between parts of texts, Rhetorical Structure Theory (RST) is a discourse analysis theory that describes text organization. Consider the following two texts:

(a) I love to collect classic automobiles. My favorite car is my 1899 Duryea.
(b) I love to collect classic automobiles. My favorite car is my 2019 Toyota.

Text *a* makes sense because the fact that the speaker likes 1899 Duryea naturally follows from the fact that he loves to collect classic automobiles. However, text *b* is problematic. The problem resides in neither sentence, as each sentence in text *b* works perfectly well in isolation. The problem lies in their combination because 2019 Toyota obviously is not a classic automobile. However, the fact that the two sentences are arranged in sequence implies that some coherence relation exists between them and text *b* has a different coherence relation from text *a*. Specifically, the relation in text *a* is elaboration, while the relation in text *b* may be contrast. Therefore, text *b* should be phrased more appropriately as:

I love to collect classic automobiles. However, my favorite car is my 2019 Toyota.

Here, the word *however* overtly signals a contrast relation to readers so that the text becomes more coherent.

Since starting to construct RST, Mann and Thompson have articulated the following fundamental ideas about the features of language use and the way to interpret the features:

1. Discourses are used for communication purposes, so if a discourse needs to be explained, it is necessary to explicitly interpret speakers' and hearers' participation.
2. Compared with other devices, the structure of a discourse can better reflect the speaker's goal and intention, which is universally hierarchical.
3. Attention and intention are regarded as independent and interactive aspects of a text.
4. Language form, language function, and discourse structure are related to each other in a loosely inter-restrictive manner rather than a way similar to a one-to-one mapping. Therefore, there is no such a specific word or grammatical form that can uniquely indicate a certain discourse structure.

The core of RST is the concept of rhetorical relations, which are the relations existing between two mutually nonoverlapping text spans (with some exceptions of course), i.e., nucleus and satellite. The distinction comes from empirical observation. For example, in text *a*, the segment *I love to collect classic automobiles* is the nucleus, while the segment *My favorite car is my 1899 Duryea* is the satellite. This implies that many rhetorical relations are asymmetric. Here, the second segment is interpreted based on the first segment, but not vice versa. In the following, we can see that not all rhetorical relations are asymmetric. RST relations are defined according to the constraints that they exercise on the nucleus, the satellite, and the combination of the two.

Mann and Thompson, the founders of RST, have made the following assumptions on discourse structure:

Organization: A discourse is composed of segments with explicit functions.

Unity and coherence: A speaker should create a unified main idea in his utterance, each segment of which serves the main idea.

Functions derived from unity and coherence: The reason why a text or an utterance is characterized by unity and coherence is that all its segments serve the speaker's purpose.

Hierarchy: Some basic segments form a large segment, which in turn combines with other large segments into a larger one, until the whole text is created.

Homogeneity of hierarchy: Between the segments at each level of a text exists a set of high-frequency and reoccurring relations that can be used repeatedly to connect segments into a larger segment until the whole text is created. The organization of these relations does not vary with the size of the segments, but the frequency of the relations differs when genre and other factors vary.

Relational composition: The primary structural model of a multi-sentence text is relational, which means that a limited number of reoccurring relations can establish the hierarchical structure between segments of a text, namely, the rhetorical structure of a text.

Asymmetry of relations: Most of the relations in the structure of a text are asymmetric because in two segments between which a relation holds, one segment tends to be comparatively more important than the other. Of course, other structural relations may also be found between text segments, each of which is equally important.

To facilitate automated processing, RST is designed with unique features, including definitions of relations, the fundamental principles, its emphasis on recursion, ways of formalization, and so on.

Based on the analyses of large quantities of authentic texts, Mann and Thompson recognized 25 rhetorical relations, which fell into nucleus-satellite (N-S) relations and multi-nucleus (N-N(...N)) relations.

There are 21 types of nucleus-satellite relations:

Evidence, justification, antithesis, concession, circumstance, solution, elaboration, background, enablement, condition, otherwise, interpretation, evaluation, restatement, conclusion, motivation, volitional cause, non-volitional cause, volitional result, non-volitional result, and purpose

There are four types of multi-nucleus relations:

Sequence, contrast, joint, and list

In many of their papers, Mann and Thompson emphasized repeatedly that the rhetorical relations they set out were not a closed set. The nucleus-satellite relations listed above were discovered in most of the English monologue texts they had analyzed.

In RST, textual coherence is derived from a set of constraints imposed on the nucleus, its satellites, and their combinations and from the general effect created by associating one relation with each of the other relations.

To describe the structure of a text, RST identifies three main types of structure, that is, overall structure, relational structure, and syntactic structure. The second one is what the theory focuses on. RST has provided a general method to describe the structural relations between different constituent elements of a text, regardless of whether the relations are grammatical or lexical. Therefore, RST is a useful framework to connect the various senses of linking words, the grammar about clause combination and the unmarked parallel structure. Meanwhile, RST has offered a framework for investigating propositional relations, that is, unstated but inferred propositions arising from the text structure in the process of text interpretation. As the coherence of a text partially relies on these propositional relations, RST is helpful for the research on textual coherence. Additionally, RST has also been used to study inter-clause relations, linking works, implied communication, clause combination, stylistics, genre, and so on.

The 25 rhetorical relations set out in RST suffice to describe the rhetorical structure of various types of texts. In practice, researchers tend to select from these relations a subset suitable for their own application fields.

In the following, some common RST relations are defined.

Elaboration: The satellite presents some additional details concerning the subject matter of the nucleus. The details may take the form of:

A member of a given set
An instance of a given abstract class
A part of a given whole
A step of a given process
An attribute of a given object
A specific instance of a given generalization

Contrast: The nuclei present things that, though similar in some aspects, are different in some important ways. This relation is multinuclear as it does not differentiate between a nucleus and a satellite.

Condition: Some event presented in the satellite must occur prior to the situation presented in the nucleus.

Purpose: The satellite presents the goal of the behavior described in the nucleus.

Sequence: This relation is also multinuclear. The set of nuclei is realized in a successive manner.

Typically, RST relations can be depicted by a figure (Fig. 9.14):

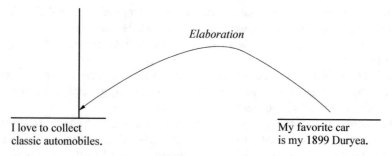

Fig. 9.14   An example of the elaboration relation

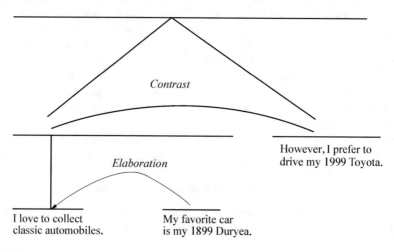

Fig. 9.15   An instance of RST structure in a paragraph

Figure 9.14 is a graphical representation of the rhetorical relation in text *a*. The two text segments are ordered sequentially along the bottom of the figure, with the elaboration relation built above them. An individual text segment is usually a clause.

Rhetorical structure analysis is performed in a hierarchical manner, so a pair of related clauses can serve as a satellite or nucleus in another higher-level relation. Consider the following paragraph:

I love to collect classic automobiles. My favorite car is my 1899 Duryea. However, I prefer to drive my 1999 Toyota.

The RST structure of the paragraph is given above (Fig. 9.15).

The figure shows that the first two clauses are related to one another through the elaboration relation and then are related, as a whole, to the third clause via the contrast relation. The process illustrates how to describe a multinuclear contrast relation. Such a recursive structure allows RST to build an analysis tree for an extended text.

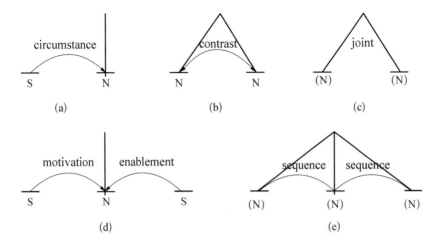

Fig. 9.16 The five schema types of RST

RST proposes the tree structure model of texts, using a tree as a formalized language to describe the structure of a given text and represent its belief, intention, communicative behavior, and so on.

According to the definition of the tree structure, each tree includes the following four elements.

Leaf node: It is a textual unit that is nonoverlapping but contiguous with other textual units in a text.

Internal node: It refers to two or more contiguous textual units connected with rhetorical relations.

Directed arc between nodes: It indicates the rhetorical relation between the nucleus and the satellite, using the arrow to mark the more important textual unit (the nucleus) and the tail to signal the unit (the satellite) that conveys the supporting or background information.

Root node: It must subsume the whole contiguous text.

In other words, each node in the rhetorical structural tree is depicted through a rhetorical relation shown by a directed arc between two or more nonoverlapping textual units.

The RST tree structure model should satisfy three conditions, that is, completeness, connectedness, and uniqueness. Starting from the root node, the tree diagram can represent the structure of all the rhetorical relations in a text.

To formalize its description and implement automated processing, RST researchers classified rhetorical relations into five schema types. Additionally, Marcu and other scholars improved the representations of the symbols due to engineering reasons. In the five schema types and the relations shown in Fig. 9.16[3], each arc labelled with a relation connects the segments where a rhetorical

---

[3] Marcu, D., *The Rhetorical Parsing, Summarization and Generation of Natural Texts*, Phd thesis, University of Taranto, 1997.

relation holds with an arrow pointing to the nucleus. The horizontal lines represent text spans, while the vertical and oblique lines represent the recognized nuclei. In SEQUENCE and JOINT relations, only nuclei exist as there is no satellite.

Mann and Thompson believe that a typical analysis of a text is applying a set of schemata such that the following constraints hold:

1. **Completeness**: The root node can subsume the whole text.
2. **Connectedness**: Except for the root node, each text span in the analysis is either a minimal unit or a constituent of another schema application.
3. **Uniqueness**: Each schema application involves a different set of text spans.
4. **Adjacency**: Each schema is applied to adjacent text spans.

Completeness, connectedness, and uniqueness work together to render an RST analysis take the form of a tree graph, which can be used to represent the RST structure of the analyzed text. In the tree graph, each vertical line descends from a text span decomposed by applying a schema down to the nucleus of the span. Numbers represent the undecomposed units of the structure.

For example, "李玲拉他去唱卡拉OK(A2), 王梅却约他一起去看电影(B2)。左右为难让他都快疯了(C2)。" [/Li Ling la ta qu chang Ka La OK (A2), Wang Mei que yue ta yi qi qu kan dian ying (B2)。 Zuo you wei nan rang ta dou kuai feng le (C2)。 /; Ling Li invited him to sing karaoke (A2), while Mei Wang asked him out to watch a movie (B2). Making a choice drove him crazy (C2).]

The RST structure of the text can be represented by Fig. 9.17.

Mann and Thompson believe that the rhetorical structure of any text can be represented by such a tree graph, whose daughter nodes stand for nonoverlapping but adjacent text spans. A text span is a text segment characterized by functional integrity from the perspective of textual organization. A relation holds between two nonoverlapping text spans and is determined according to the definitions of relations. The concept of text structure is defined by the network relations among incrementally larger text spans.

A bottom-up parsing is usually taken to perform an RST analysis on a given text: First, divide the text into various units; then, determine the spans and their relations and eliminate the non-well-formed trees; finally, disambiguate and interpret the multiple analyses that may coexist.

Fig. 9.17 A tree graph of RST structure

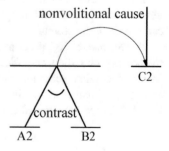

The details of the steps are given as follows:

- Divide the text into various units. Mann and Thompson point out that in RST, the size of a unit is arbitrary, ranging from a lexical entry to a whole paragraph or something even larger. In RST research, units are theory-neutral and function-integral. In their RST analyses, units are generally clauses, with the exception that clausal subjects, clausal objects, and restrictive relative clauses (RRCs) are regarded as being parts of their host clause units instead of serving as separate units.
- Determine the spans and their relations. The analyzer can describe text spans accurately in a top-down fashion, aggregate text spans at each level in a bottom-up manner, or combine the two approaches. When determining the relation between two text spans, the analyzer needs to decide whether the text author's writing purpose can fit the relation definition.
- Eliminate the non-well-formed trees. The four criteria to check the well-formedness of an RST tree are completeness, connectedness, uniqueness, and adjacency.
- Disambiguate the parsing. In accordance with the definitions given in RST, it can be predicted that a text may have more than one analysis. Therefore, disambiguation is needed to interpret the coexisting analyses.

Mann and Thompson believe that it is very common to develop different RST trees for the same text and that the multiplicity is consistent with human beings' linguistic experience. Multiple RST analyses are generated for the following reasons:

(a) Different decisions on boundary
(b) Ambiguity of text structure
(c) The coexistence of multiple analyses for the same structure
(d) Analyzers' different understandings
(e) Wrong analysis

For an experienced analyzer, the diversity of analysis primarily results from coexisting analyses and ambiguity of text structure. As the analyzer can reasonably reject weird analyses out of his experience and the specific role that he plays, ambiguities in practice are much fewer than predicted by formal grammatical analysis.

As a formalized linguistic theory, RST provides a method to investigate the connectivity and integrity of a written monologue text and how the text serves its writer's purpose. The theory is deeply influenced by Halliday's systemic functional grammar, since it is rooted in pragmatic functionalism.

Due to the achievements made by RST in NLP research, the theory has also exerted profound influence on studies concerning discourse analysis and language ontology. Examples are the use of RST to analyze the features of news broadcasts, the finding that choices between pronouns and complete noun phrases in English expositions can be made in accordance with the organizational structure revealed by RST analyses, and a study regarding Japanese and Spanish speakers' interlingua, which shows that RST is helpful for describing the grammar and rhetorical characteristics of the speakers' narratives.

Mann and Thompson have also elaborated on the relationship between RST and other studies, especially those that have influenced the development of RST.

After the theory was proposed, Mann and Thompson made some revisions to the set of RST relations. In addition, other researchers tagged corpora with RST labels. For misunderstandings and criticisms caused by researchers' different interpretations of RST, Mann and Thompson refuted two incorrect views on RST, restressing the principles of the theory.[4]

In NLP, many researchers made some formalized modifications on the basis of the RST tree graph that Mann and Thompson had put forward.

To date, only a few discourse parsers have been developed using RST. Some well-known developers include Marcu, Corston-Oliver, and, more recently, Reitter. In his doctoral dissertation, Marcu proposed the first completely definite formal model of text structure. He used 13 axioms to describe various constraints on the operation of his system and employed numerals and operators of predicate logic to compute the structure formed by 4 types of information in each text span and to derive all the possible rhetorical-intentional trees of a text.

The universality of this kind of text structure that Marcu derived suffices to ensure the applicability of RST in nonrestricted natural texts and facilitates the design of easy-to-process algorithms that can analyze the structure of texts.

First, Marcu proved that the distinction between important linguistic/nonlinguistic units (usually called nucleus and abbreviated as N) and less important units (usually called satellites and abbreviated as S) was the basis of the compositionality criterion that could help to form a valid text structure. The criterion shows that if a relation holds between two nodes in the tree graph of a text, the relation also exists between the units (linguistic and nonlinguistic) that are related to the most important parts of the nodes. Given the processing ability of NLP and artificial intelligence at that time, Marcu devised the "strong compositionality criterion," which could be easily formalized. It stated that if a relation held between two text spans of the tree structure of a text, then it also held between the most important textual units of the constituent spans. Marcu formalized the strong compositionality criterion and other textual features with first-order predicate logic so that they could apply universally to classification systems of the rhetorical relations that they could rely upon.

By applying different RST relations recursively, the rhetorical relations holding between text spans from clausal units to the whole text can be combined into a rhetorical structural tree. If the concept of salience is applied repeatedly over all the nodes of a rhetorical structure, a partial order can be induced that can indicate the importance of the units in a text. Marcu proposed an algorithm that could obtain the rhetorical structure of unrestricted texts and generate summaries by using nuclearity and discourse structures.

---

[4]Mann, W. C. and Sandra A. Thompson. Two Views of Rhetorical Structure Theory. 2000.

For the purpose of parsing texts automatically, Marcu, according to his previous research results, created a list of cue phrases (abbreviated as CP) capable of indicating rhetorical relations explicitly. Then, for each CP, he extracted from the corpus some text fragments containing the CP and analyzed the text fragments manually. After that, based on the corpus data and his intuition developed during the analysis, he connected each CP with the following information:

(a) The information that could be automatically recognized in texts
(b) The information that could help to determine the boundary between the elementary textual units near the CP
(c) The information that could help to assume the rhetorical relations holding between the textual units near the CP

Based on the corpus, Marcu proposed a series of algorithms, established the connection between corpus analysis in the context of discourse analysis and the algorithms for structural analysis of unrestricted texts, and achieved effective text planning in the context of natural language generation.

Marcu's constraint-based symbolic system was a breakthrough in automatic text parsing at the time when it was put forward. However, it appears that the model can merely make somewhat coarse-grained analyses of texts, as it relies overly on CPs and uses a simple matching model to determine CPs and elementary textual units for analysis. Before Marcu, Ono and his colleagues at Toshiba studied automatic summarization on the basis of rhetorical structures in the early 1990s. They reduced the rhetorical relations in Japanese texts to 34 types, including example, cause, conclusion, and so on. First, they derived a rhetorical structure tree similar to syntactic trees according to linking words. Then, they cut out some nodes from the rhetorical structure tree and connected the remaining parts into a coherent summary according to their rhetorical relations.

After Marcu, Corston-Oliver, by integrating CPs, anaphora, indicators, and reference coherence, improved Microsoft Encarta, a text annotation system, with RASTA, a program developed by himself. Reitter made use of support vector machine, a machine learning algorithm, for rhetorical analysis. His system employed classifiers to identify nuclei and the rhetorical relations between text fragments. Based on the classifiers, he proposed a parsing algorithm and devised a quantitative test for some surface features used in rhetorical analyses. Besides, Reitter built a German RST corpus.

Due to the text structure revealed by RST and its remarkable effect on automatic summarization, the theory has captured widespread attention in NLP and traditional linguistic research, become one of the most widely used theories concerning discourse analysis and text processing, and gained popularity in automatic pragmatic analysis in machine translation.

On the Internet, some websites and discussion groups are established for RST research (http://www.sil.org/~mannb/rst). Annotated corpora and links to the literature on RST are also available. Readers can download for free RSTTOOL (http://www.wagsoft.com/RSTTool/), a piece of software that O'Connell developed for RST analysis.

RST is usually described in the language of English, and sample sentences also tend to be English sentences, but Mann and Thompson point out that the rhetorical relations in RST are not a closed set. In addition, the frequency of the relations may vary with genres (such as narrative and expositive texts). Types of rhetorical relations may also differ in discourses of different languages.

An open list of rhetorical relations has facilitated the use of RST to study other languages and laid a foundation for research on comparative rhetoric. Now, the application of RST is expanded, as many scholars have made use of the theory to investigate their native languages, including Arabic, French, Hebrew, Spanish, German, Chinese, and so on. Papers employing RST to process Japanese, Korean, and Thai texts can often be found. Nevertheless, regarding the cross-language transferability of RST, Mann and Thompson stress that

"There is a widely shared impression that direct use of existing definitions is effective. Beyond such an impression, nothing has been established. The potential for surprises is very large, and no firm claims of significant transferability can be made."[5]

From the perspective of cultural linguistics, the view above is likely to be correct. Researchers in RST and developers of NLP practical systems should bear it in their minds.

Although RST has become one of the most popular theories regarding discourse studies in the last three decades, Mann and Thompson still hold that RST is merely a stage in the process of developing communication theories.

The strengths of RST include that it provides a complete analysis instead of a selective interpretation, that it can apply to different kinds of texts and describe in the same manner the structures of the texts without the necessity to consider genres, and that it can help to differentiate the features specific to a certain genre from the features that are, comparatively speaking, more independent of the genre.

However, as a theory still in its development, RST also has some weaknesses:

1. RST has not provided a systematic description of how various relations are realized. This description should be broader than any research on linking words and take into account examples without annotations.
2. RST has not connected itself with other theories about textual characteristics, such as information flow, thematic structure, and lexical structure.

Currently, criticisms of RST focus on some unresolved problems, such as the knowledge system to classify relations, the mapping between rhetorical relations and speech acts, the mapping between intentionality and informativeness, and its inability to interpret discontinuity in discourses.

In addition, Corston-Oliver states that although RST supporters believe the relations in RST can help to describe text structures, several questions remain:

---

[5]Mann, W. C. and Sandra A. Thompson. *Two Views of Rhetorical Structure Theory*. 2000.

1. How many types of rhetorical relations are there on earth?
2. How can a specific set of relations be reasonably explained?
3. How are the relations organized?

Especially in terms of formalization and computer processing, Corston-Oliver holds that although Marcu's algorithm to construct RST representations of texts marks a huge progress, the algorithm has its own problems. For example, Marcu asserts that the average recall of his program to identify clauses is 81.3% (his program can identify 81.3% of the clauses that are recognized by human beings) and admits that it is very difficult to distinguish sentential and non-sentential uses of the conjunction AND. Although the neglected discursive uses of AND tend to correspond to sequence and joint relations in Marcu's data and have little influence on analyses of texts, a coarse-grained RST analysis will be generated.

According to Corston-Oliver, these problems arise from the algorithm's overreliance on CPs and the use of only one matching pattern to identify CPs and terminal nodes.

Chinese is a language closely related to pragmatics, so pragmatic concepts need to be introduced into the interpretation of grammatical phenomena. Perceiving RST as a theory based on pragmatic functionalism, Mann and Thompson, since its early development, have repeatedly quoted a master thesis that had analyzed Mandarin and English papers to prove the possible universal existence of RST relations in various languages. Therefore, research on RST's transferability in Chinese has a very special background.

In 2002, Webster at City University of Hong Kong used RST to perform an in-depth case analysis. RST relations were applied to his semantic analysis of an aligned English-Chinese corpus. T'sou and his colleagues, also working at City University of Hong Kong, published *Enhancement of a Chinese Discourse Marker Tagger with C4.5* in ACL 2000 and reported the improvement made in an automated annotation system that had employed machine learning to recognize and classify discourse markers in Chinese texts. As part of another study on the use of rhetorical structures in text summarization, their work yielded encouraging results. In their report, the following tagging scheme for the SIFAS corpus was designed to tag discourse markers: Each real discourse marker in the corpus was encoded with a hepta-tuple; each apparent discourse marker that seemed to be a real discourse marker but actually not was encoded with a tri-tuple. They extracted 306 discourse markers from editorials in newspapers in Hong Kong, Chinese mainland, Taiwan, and Singapore and put these discourse markers and a NULL marker into a DMP-RR table (where DMP stands for discourse marker pairs and RR represents rhetorical relations). These markers constituted 480 distinct discontinuous pairs corresponding to 25 rhetorical relations. However, in actual use, some discourse marker pairs could imply multiple rhetorical relations, and some pairs could indicate both intra-sentence and inter-sentence relations. Therefore, the correspondence between discourse marker pairs and rhetorical relations was not single-valued. To tag the SIFAS corpus, T'sou and his colleagues adopted in their tagging algorithm the principles of greediness, locality, explicitness, superiority, and back-marker preference to resolve ambiguity in the process of matching discontinuous discourse markers. As the original naïve tagger merely partially solved the CDM identification and NULL marker location problems, a few rules based on previous statistics were added to solve the problems more effectively [22]. Specifically, they extracted some additional rules from statistics of the error analysis to guide the classification and matching of the discourse markers. Another solution is identifying syntactic/semantic information through machine learning. In sum, they presented in their research some processing principles, the SIFAS system's engineering objective, the distribution of discourse markers that helped to recognize intra-sentence and inter-sentence relations, and some sample sentences where errors could be removed through the given rules in the tagging process. They were optimistic about the system's tagging accuracy in the future. The system developed by T'sou and his colleagues recognized discourse relations through a relatively shallow analysis and typically used simple pattern matching techniques to identify cue phrases. Meanwhile, the system assumed various kinds of discourse relations on the basis of the form of a text without referring to an additional model of world knowledge. Of course, to recognize cue phrases, the system not only used some simple pattern matching techniques but also the results of word segmentation and part of speech tagging performed by the SIFAS system and some characteristics of the Chinese language such as positions of punctuation marks. However, T'sou et al. merely directly made use of Mann and Thompson's research results in 1988 and their classification of rhetorical relations. They did not localize the 25 rhetorical relations extracted from English or test the transferability of these RST relations to Chinese. Neither did they clarify the distribution of various relations in their corpus, the approach to extracting markers from the corpus, or the linguistic reasons for adding NULL markers.

Many Chinese mainland researchers have taken part in the RST studies conducted by institutions in Hong Kong, but generally, Chinese mainland's research on the use of RST to process Chinese texts mainly focuses on writing introductory papers instead of localizing and applying the theory. The reason for this may reside in the huge efforts needed in discourse analysis and a high requirement for researchers' related abilities. To analyze Chinese texts, much remains to be done in developing RST. Although many cue-phrase studies have been performed in research fields such as Chinese syntax (linking words), complex sentences, sentence groups, and discourse analysis, these experiential studies could not provide adequate data to account for how cue phrases could be used to determine the elementary textual units surrounding them and assume rhetorical relations between the units.

Bibliography

1. Brennan, S.E. 1995. Centering Attention in Discourse. *Language and Cognitive Processes* 10: 137–167.
2. Corston-Oliver, S.H. 1998. *Computing Representation of the Structure of Written Discourse.* Technical Report, MSR-TR-98-15.
3. Grosz, B.J., A.K. Joshi, and S. Weinstein. 1995. Centering: A Framework for Modeling the Local Coherence of Discourse. *Computational Linguistics* 21 (2): 203–225.

4. Hobbs, J.R. 1977. Resolution Pronoun Reference. *Lingua* 44: 311–348.
5. ———. 1979. Coherence and Coreference. *Cognitive Science* 3: 67–90.
6. Hovy, E. 1993. Automated Discourse Generation Using Discourse Structure Relations. *Artificial Intelligence* 63: 341–385.
7. Lappin, S., and H. Leass. 1994. An Algorithm for Pronominal Anaphora Resolution. *Computational Linguistics* 20 (4): 535–561.
8. Mann, W., C. Mattiessen, and S. Thompson. 1989. *Rhetorical Structure Theory and Text Analysis*. Los Angeles: ISI: Information Sciences Institute of University of Southern California. ISI/RS-89-242.
9. Mann, W., and Sandra A. Thompson. 1983. *Relational Propositions in Discourse*, 1–28. Los Angeles: ISI: Information Sciences Institute of University of Southern California. ISI/RR-83-115.
10. ———. 1987. *Rhetorical Structure Theory: A Theory of Text Organization*. ISI Reprint Series.
11. ———. 1987. Rhetorical Structure Theory: A Framework for the Analysis of Texts. *IPRA Papers in Pragmatics* 1: 1–21.
12. ———. 1988. Rhetorical Structure Theory: Toward a Functional Theory of Text Organization. *Text* 8 (3): 243–281.
13. ———. 2000. *Two Views of Rhetorical Structure Theory*. Lyon: Society for Text and Discourse.
14. Marcu, D. 1997. *The Rhetorical Parsing, Summarization and Generation of Natural Texts*. PhD thesis. University of Taranto.
15. ———. 1995. Discourse Trees Are Good Indicators of Importance in Text. In *Advances in Automatic Text Summarization*, ed. I. Mani and M.T. Maybury, 123–136. Cambridge: MIT Press.
16. ———. 2000. The Rhetorical Parsing of Unrestricted Texts: A Surface-Based Approach. *Computational Linguistics* 26 (3): 395–448.
17. Matthiessen, Christian, and Sandra Thompson. 1987. *The Structure of Discourse and "Subordination"*. Reprinted from Clause Combining in Discourse Grammar. ISI/RS-87-183.
18. Ming, Yue. 2019. *An Investigation into Markers of Textual Cohesion Based on RST Treebank*. Guangzhou: World Publishing Corporation.
19. Ming, Yue, and Zhiwei Feng. 2004. A review on the development of RST and its application in engineering. In *Proceedings of the Second Students' Workshop on Computational Linguistics (SWCL)*.
20. Moore, Johanna D., and Cecile L. Paris. 1993. Planning Text for Advisory Dialogues: Capturing Intentional and Rhetorical Information. *Computational Linguistics* 19 (4): 651–695.
21. Ono, K., K. Sumita, and S. Miike. 1994. Abstract Generation Based on Rhetorical Structure Extraction. In *Proceedings of International Conference on Computational Linguistics*, Japan, 344–348.
22. T'sou, B.K., T.B.Y. Lai, S.W.K. Chan, W. Gao, and X. Zhan. 1995. Enhancement of a Chinese Discourse Marker Tagger with C4.5. In *ACL 2000*.
23. Walker, M.A. 1989. Evaluating Discourse Processing Algorithm. In *ACL-89*, Vancouver, Canada, 251–260.
24. Webster, J. 1994. A Functional Semantic Processor for Chinese and English Texts. In *Proceedings of the 1994 International Conference on Computer Processing of Oriental Languages*, 269–273.
25. ———. 2000. *Discourse Linguistics. Text Linguistics* (trans: Xu Jiujiu). Beijing: China Social Sciences Press.
26. Zhiwei, Feng. 2004. Reference Resolution and Computer Processing of Textual Coherence. In *Collected Papers of Linguistic Research, the Second Volume*. Harbin: Heilongjiang Education Press.
27. ———. 2006. On Common-Sense Inference in Textual Coherence. In *Chinese Information Processing: Exploration and Practice—Proceedings of the Third Conference on HNC and Linguistic Research*, ed. Zhu Xiaojian et al. Beijing: Beijing Normal University Press.

Chapter 10
Formal Models of Probabilistic Grammar

To enable computers to process natural languages, Chomsky's context-free grammar is often used for rule-based syntactic parsing. Based on context-free grammar, researchers have designed effective parsing techniques, such as the top-down parsing method, the bottom-up parsing method, the left-corner parsing method, the CYK algorithm, the Earley algorithm, and the chart parsing method. However, these methods can hardly deal with ambiguities in natural languages. In recent years, improvement in context-free grammar has been made primarily in two aspects. First, probabilistic context-free grammar has been proposed so that rules in context-free grammar can be assigned different probabilities. Second, probabilistic lexicalized context-free grammar has been proposed to take into account not only the probabilities of the rules but also the influence of head words on these probabilities. These methods combine the rule-based rationalist approach and the statistical empiricist approach in a skillful way and reflect a new trend in NLP. This chapter introduces probabilistic grammar, including probabilistic context-free grammar for syntactic ambiguity, the fundamentals of probabilistic context-free grammar, three hypotheses regarding probabilistic context-free grammar, and probabilistic lexicalized context-free grammar.

10.1 Context-Free Grammar and Sentence Ambiguity

Context-free grammar (abbreviated as CFG) G can be defined as a four-tuple $G = \{N, \Sigma, P, S\}$, in which

1. N is a set of nonterminal symbols;
2. Σ represents a set of terminal symbols;
3. S is a start symbol; and
4. P stands for rewrite rules in the form of $A \rightarrow \beta$, where A is a nonterminal symbol and β is a string of terminal and/or nonterminal symbols.

© Springer Nature Singapore Pte Ltd. 2023
Z. Feng, *Formal Analysis for Natural Language Processing: A Handbook*,
https://doi.org/10.1007/978-981-16-5172-4_10

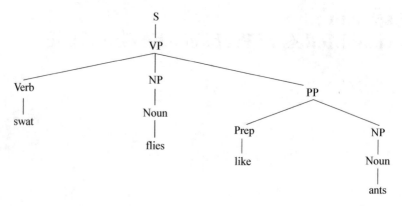

Fig. 10.1 The parse tree T_1 for *swat flies like ants*

Take the following context-free grammar $\{N, \Sigma, P, S\}$ as an example:

$N = \{S, NP, VP, PP, Prep, Verb, Noun\}$
$\Sigma = \{like, swat, flies, ants\}$
$S = \{S\}$
P:
$S \rightarrow NP\ VP$
$S \rightarrow VP$
$NP \rightarrow Noun$
$NP \rightarrow Noun\ PP$
$NP \rightarrow Noun\ NP$
$VP \rightarrow Verb$
$VP \rightarrow Verb\ NP$
$VP \rightarrow Verb\ PP$
$VP \rightarrow Verb\ NP\ PP$
$PP \rightarrow Prep\ NP$
$Prep \rightarrow like$
$Verb \rightarrow swat$
$Verb \rightarrow flies$
$Verb \rightarrow likes$
$Noun \rightarrow swat$
$Noun \rightarrow flies$
$Noun \rightarrow ants$

where both *swat* and *flies* can be either a verb or a proper noun, and *like* can serve as a verb or a preposition.

Three parse trees (Figs. 10.1, 10.2, and 10.3) can be obtained for *swat flies like ants*, if a parsing technique based on context-free grammar (such as the chart parsing method or the Earley algorithm) is used.

The string of *swat flies like ants* with the structure T_1 means someone is told to swat flies as he/she swats ants (Fig. 10.1).

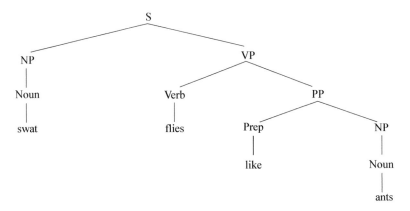

Fig. 10.2 The parse tree T_2 for *swat flies like ants*

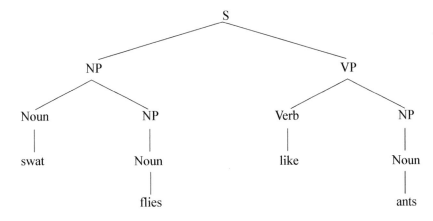

Fig. 10.3 The parse tree T_3 for *swat flies like ants*

The sentence *swat flies like ants* with the structure T_2 means swat flies as ants do (Fig. 10.2).

The string of *swat flies like ants* with the structure T_3 means that some flies called swat have a liking for ants (Fig. 10.3).

As the English expression above can be analyzed in three ways, we have little idea about how to determine its structure and meaning.

Currently, many rule-based disambiguation approaches have been proposed based on selectional restrictions, dictionaries, and so on. But these approaches are not very effective. Therefore, researchers have made efforts to improve context-free grammar by using statistical approaches to calculate the probabilities of rewrite rules. The dispute over rule-based approaches and statistical approaches in NLP in fact reflects the confrontation between rationalism and empiricism. Some researchers tend to hold extreme views, refuting either statistical approaches or rule-based approaches. In contrast, more researchers look at the issue with a peaceful mind and endeavor to explore how to combine the two approaches. Their research mainly involves two aspects: probabilistic context-free grammar and probabilistic lexicalized context-free grammar. The two types of probabilistic grammar will be introduced in the following sections.

10.2 Fundamentals of Probabilistic Context-Free Grammar

Probabilistic context-free grammar (abbreviated as PCFG), also called stochastic context-free grammar (abbreviated as SCFG), was proposed by Booth in 1969.

Context-free grammar can be defined as a four-tuple, while PCFG adds a conditional probability p to each rewrite rule $A \rightarrow \beta$.

$$A \rightarrow \beta[p]$$

Therefore, context-free grammar can be extended into a five-tuple $G = \{N, \Sigma, P, S, D\}$, where D is a function that assigns a probability p to each rewrite rule. Specifically, the function D denotes the probability p that a non-terminal symbol A is rewritten into a string β. It can be represented as

$$P(A \rightarrow \beta) \text{ or as } P(A \rightarrow \beta|A)$$

Of note, all the possible rewrite rules of a non-terminal A should be considered so that the sum of their probabilities is equal to 1.

For example, according to the probabilities of the rewrite rules occurring in a corpus, each rule of context-free grammar in Sect. 10.1 can be assigned a probability. In this manner, context-free grammar can be transformed to include probabilistic rules as follows.

$S \rightarrow$ NP VP	[0.8]
$S \rightarrow$ VP	[0.2]
NP $\rightarrow$ Noun	[0.4]
NP $\rightarrow$ Noun PP	[0.4]
NP $\rightarrow$ Noun NP	[0.2]
VP $\rightarrow$ Verb	[0.3]
VP $\rightarrow$ Verb NP	[0.3]
VP $\rightarrow$ Verb PP	[0.2]
VP $\rightarrow$ Verb NP PP	[0.2]
PP $\rightarrow$ Prep NP	[1.0]
Prep $\rightarrow$ like	[1.0]
Verb $\rightarrow$ swat	[0.2]
Verb $\rightarrow$ flies	[0.4]
Verb $\rightarrow$ likes	[0.4]

(continued)

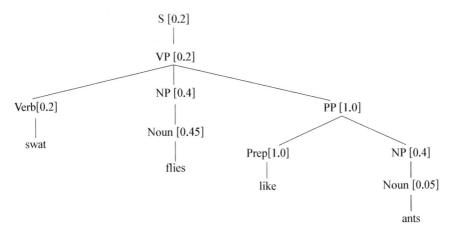

Fig. 10.4 The parse tree T_1 with probabilities added to non-terminal nodes

Noun → swat	[0.05]
Noun → flies	[0.45]
Noun → ants	[0.05]

Note that the probabilities of all the rewrite rules of the same non-terminal symbol sum to 1, except for the rules with a noun as their left part, because only a small number of nouns are listed here. These data are quoted from *Statistical Language Learning* by Eugene Charniak.[1] More accurate data should be acquired from treebanks.

If a sentence is ambiguous, PCFG can assign a probability to each parse tree of the sentence. The probability of a parse tree T is the product of the probabilities of all the rewrite rules r used to expand each non-terminal node n in the parse tree.

$$P(T) = \prod_{n \in T} p(r(n))$$

In the equation above, n denotes a non-terminal node; r stands for a rule that can expand the non-terminal node n; the lower-case p represents the probability of r; T means a parse tree; and the upper-case P is the probability of the parse tree T. With this equation, a sentence can be disambiguated by calculating the probabilities of all its possible parse trees.

Take the previous sentence *swat flies like ants* as an example. The probabilities of rewrite rules can be added to the non-terminal nodes in the three parse trees.

When assigned probabilities, the parse tree T_1 is changed into the tree in Fig. 10.4.

By multiplying the probabilities of the non-terminal nodes, the probability of T_1 can be obtained.

---

[1] Eugene Charniak, Statistical Language Learning, The MIT Press, 1993.

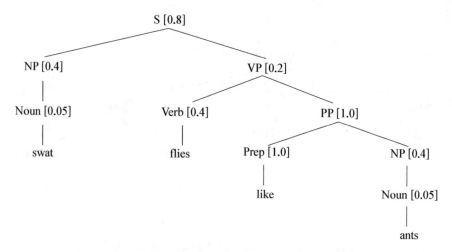

Fig. 10.5 The parse tree T_2 with probabilities added to non-terminal nodes

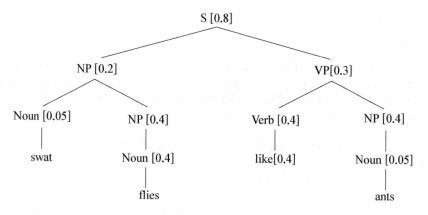

Fig. 10.6 The parse tree T_3 with probabilities added to non-terminal nodes

$$P(T_1) = 0.2 \times 0.2 \times 0.2 \times 0.4 \times 0.45 \times 1.0 \times 1.0 \times 0.4 \times 0.05$$
$$= 2.88 \times 10^{-5}$$

When assigned probabilities, the parse tree T_2 is changed into the tree in Fig. 10.5. By multiplying the probabilities of the non-terminal nodes, the probability of T_2 can be calculated as follows.

$$P(T_2) = 0.8 \times 0.4 \times 0.05 \times 0.2 \times 0.4 \times 1.0 \times 1.0 \times 0.4 \times 0.05$$
$$= 2.56 \times 10^{-5}$$

When assigned probabilities, the parse tree T_3 becomes the tree in Fig. 10.6.

By multiplying the probabilities of the non-terminal nodes, the probability of T_3 can be computed.

$$P(T_3) = 0.8 \times 0.2 \times 0.05 \times 0.4 \times 0.4 \times 0.3 \times 0.4 \times 0.4 \times 0.4 \times 0.05$$
$$= 1.2288 \times 10^{-6}$$

A comparison of the three probabilities shows that

$$P(T_1) > P(T_2) > P(T_3)$$

According to the probabilities, the most likely structure of the sentence *swat flies like ants* turns out to be T_1, which means someone is told to swat flies as he/she swats ants. That the result agrees with human beings' intuition shows that this approach does work. Therefore, disambiguation can be made by comparing the probabilities of different parse trees of the same sentence and selecting the tree with the highest probability.

Essentially, the disambiguation algorithm selects the best tree (denoted as T) from the potential parse trees for S (denoted as $\tau(S)$) as the correct analysis.

Formally, if $T \in \tau(S)$, then the parse tree with the highest probability $T(S)$ is equal to argmax $P(T)$:

$$T(S) = \arg\max P(T)$$

If argmax $P(T)$ can be determined, the parse tree with the highest probability can be obtained. Therefore, PCFG is a powerful tool for disambiguation.

As a bottom-up dynamic programming parser, the CYK algorithm (Cocke–Younger–Kasami algorithm), when augmented with PCFG, can calculate the probability of a parse tree of a sentence. The improved algorithm is called the probabilistic CYK algorithm.

First, assume that PCFG is in Chomsky Normal Form, which means that each rewrite rule in PCFG takes the form of $A \to BC$ or $A \to a$. The CYK algorithm assumes the following input, output, and data structures.

- Input

  - A Chomsky Normal Form PCFG $G = (N, \Sigma, P, S, D)$. Assume that the $|N|$ non-terminal symbols have indices $1, 2, \ldots, |N|$ and that the initial symbol has index 1.
  - n words $w_1 \ldots w_n$

- Data structures. A dynamic programming array $\pi[i, j, a]$ indicates the maximum probability for a constituent that spans words from i to j and carries a non-terminal index a. Backpointers in the area are used to store the links between constituents in a parse tree.

- Output. The maximum probability parse will be $\pi[1, n, 1]$: the parse tree takes S as its root and spans the entire string composed of $w_1 \ldots w_n$.

Like other dynamic programming algorithms, the CYK algorithm fills out the probability array by induction, starting from the base case and using induction recursively. To facilitate the description of the algorithm, w_{ij} is used to denote the string spanning words from w_i to w_j.

- Base case: Consider input strings composed of only one word (i.e., individual words w_i). In Chomsky normal form, the probability of expanding a given non-terminal symbol A into a single word w_i can only derive from the rule $A \rightarrow w_i$ (because $A \Rightarrow w_i$ holds if and only if $A \rightarrow w_i$ is a rewrite rule.)
- Recursive case: For word strings composed of more than one word, $A \Rightarrow w_i$ if and only if there exists at least a rule $A \rightarrow BC$ and some k, $1 \le k < j$, such that B derives the first k symbols of w_{ij} and C derives the remaining $j-k$ symbols of w_{ij}. As each of the two word strings is shorter than the original string w_{ij}, their probabilities will be stored in the matrix π. The probability of w_{ij} can be calculated by multiplying the probabilities of the two word strings. Of course, there may be multiple parses of w_{ij}, so the one with the highest probability (when all the possible values of k and all the possible rules are considered) should be selected.

In the same vein, we can also devise the probabilistic Earley algorithm, the probabilistic chart parsing method, and so on.

But how can we obtain the probabilities of PCFG? There are two ways to assign probabilities to grammar. The simpler one is to use a corpus in which sentences have already been parsed. This kind of corpus is called a treebank.

If we process and build a treebank, in which all the sentences have already been parsed into tree diagrams, as each terminal node and the subtree composed of the strings that the terminal node governs correspond to a rewrite rule in PCFG, we can compute the probabilities of the rewrite rules in all the tree diagrams of the treebank and obtain PCFG. The higher the quality of the treebank is, the better PCFG performs.

For example, Penn Treebank[2] released by Linguistic Data Consortium includes the parse trees of Brown Corpus and reports a size of one million words, with some of its texts collected from *Wall Street Journal* and some from Switchboard Corpus. Given a treebank, the probability of each expansion of a non-terminal node can be calculated by counting how many times the expansion occurs. After normalization, PCFG can be obtained.

However, it is very difficult to process and build a treebank. With the development of corpus linguistics, a more feasible approach is to use a large-scale raw corpus to automatically learn grammatical rules automatically. This kind of automatic learning is called grammar induction.

For ordinary context-free grammar, grammar induction requires two types of materials, i.e. positive and negative training instances. The former refers to the sentences or other types of strings that truly belong to the language in question. Obviously, positive training instances can be provided by a corpus. The so-called

[2] Marcus, M. P. Santoni, B. and Marcinkiewicz, M. A. Building a large annotated corpus of English: The Penn treebank. *Computational Linguistics*, 1993, 19(2): 313–330.

negative training instances are strings that do not belong to the language in question. Automated induction of context-free grammar is impossible if either type of training instance is unavailable. However, as there is no effective approach to obtaining negative training instances, grammar induction is difficult for ordinary context-free grammar.

For PCFG, grammar induction is essentially how to acquire a grammar with probabilities through automated learning so that each sentence in positive training instances can achieve the maximum probability. In this process, no negative training instance is needed. Therefore, grammar induction is easier for PCFG than ordinary context-free grammar.

When a treebank is unavailable, the inside-outside algorithm can be used to learn rules and probabilities and then obtain PCFG. If sentences are unambiguous, it will be an easy task: parse the corpus, add a counter for each rule in the parsing process, and then normalize to obtain probabilities. However, as most sentences are ambiguous, a separate count should be kept for each parse tree of a sentence and each partial count should be weighted according to the probability of the parse tree. The inside-outside algorithm was proposed by Baker[3] in 1979. A full description of the algorithm can be found in *Foundations of Statistical Natural Language Processing* by Manning and Schütze[4] in 1999.

Usually, context-free grammar does not consider the probability issue. Once a rule is formulated, it holds without any exception. However, as language is creative, no matter how large the corpus used for automated learning is, it is difficult to guarantee that the obtained grammatical rules have no exception. In fact, there are always some grammatical phenomena that cannot be accounted for within the existing grammatical system. If PCFG is adopted, then a rule does not necessarily hold but carries a probability. As long as the sample size is large enough, the accuracy of the probability can be ensured. For exceptional grammatical phenomena in context-free grammar, PCFG regards them as legal by assigning them low probabilities. In this manner, PCFG can properly deal with the so-called exceptional grammatical phenomena.

When context-free grammar in its usual sense is used to parse a sentence, the parsing result can only be "legal" or "illegal." Legal sentences will be accepted, while illegal sentences will be denied. However, this dichotomous approach can hardly help to analyze a corpus composed of authentic texts because it is difficult to determine the legality of many sentences in the corpus. This can often place an NLP system in a dilemma and the system can hardly serve for a practical purpose. With PCFG, legal sentences will be assigned higher probabilities, whereas illegal sentences will be assigned lower probabilities. Then PCFG can process both legal and illegal sentences, solve the dilemma of "being either legal or illegal," and carry

---

[3]Baker, J. K. Trainable grammars for speech recognition. Klatt, D. H. and Wolf, J. J. *Speech Communication Papers for the 97th Meeting of the Acoustical Society of America.* 1979, 547–550.

[4]Manning, C. D. and Schütze, H. *Foundations of Statistical Natural Language Processing*, Cambridge: MIT Press, 1999.

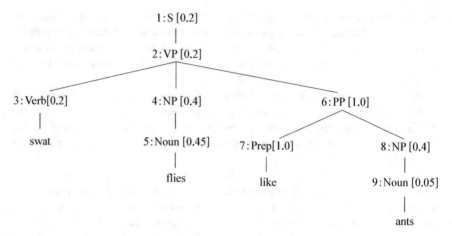

Fig. 10.7 The parse tree T_1 with nodes numbered

the flexible characteristic of "considering both legality and illegality." PCFG enables grammatical systems to be equipped with fault-tolerant ability, which is very important for improving the usefulness of NLP systems.

10.3   Three Assumptions of Probabilistic Context-Free Grammar

To perform syntactic parsing by using rules with probabilities, PCFG requires three assumptions.

Assumption 1—position invariance: the probability of a daughter node is irrelevant to the position of the string that the node dominates.

    To facilitate our description, in the parse tree T_1 where non-terminal nodes are assigned probabilities, each non-terminal node is numbered as follows.

    In Fig. 10.7, in positions No. 4 and No. 8, a rule NP → Noun exists. Although the two NP nodes are in different positions, they are assigned the same probability (0.4), as the strings governed by the two nodes are nouns. In other words, the probability of either NP node is only relevant to the noun string that it dominates, having nothing to do with the position of the noun string in the sentence.

Assumption 2—context-free: the probability of a daughter node is independent of other strings that are not dominated by the node.

    For example, in Fig. 10.7, if *swat* is changed into *kill*, only the probability of the verb node in position No. 3 will change. The probabilities of the nodes that are not dominated by the verb node are kept. This means that the change has no impact on the probabilities of the other nodes in the parse tree, such as the two NP nodes (with a probability of 0.4) and the PP node (with a probability of 1.0). The example shows that a change in a word cannot influence the probabilities of the non-terminal nodes in a parse tree except for the one that dominates the word. This assumption accounts for the fact that, in PCFG, not only the rewrite rules but also the probabilities of the rules are context-free.

Assumption 3—ancestor-free: the probability of a daughter node is independent of all the ancestor nodes that dominate the node.

For instance, in Fig. 10.7, NP nodes No. 4 and No. 8 have the same probability because the strings they dominate are both nouns. Nevertheless, the ancestor nodes of NP node No. 4 are VP node No. 2 (with a probability of 0.2) and S node No. 1 (with a probability of 0.2), whereas the ancestor node of NP node No. 8 is PP node No. 6 (with a probability of 1.0). The probabilities of the ancestor nodes do not impact the probabilities of NP nodes No. 4 and No. 8.

Due to the three assumptions, PCFG not only inherits the context-free feature of context-free grammar but also enables the probabilities of the rules to be independent of context. Therefore, PCFG can also be used for syntactic parsing. First, a common parsing algorithm for context-free grammar is used to parse a sentence and obtain a parse tree. After that, each non-terminal node in the parse tree is assigned a probability, which, under the three assumptions, is the probability of the rule for rewriting the node. Next, a parse tree with a probability is obtained. If the sentence is ambiguous, different parse trees with probabilities can be acquired. Finally, by comparing the probabilities of the trees and selecting the tree with the highest probability as the parse result, sentence meaning disambiguation can be made.

However, PCFG is not perfect, as they have problems such as structural dependencies and lexical dependencies, which will be explained in the following.

According to the above three assumptions concerning PCFG, rewriting the non-terminal symbol in the left part of a rule is independent of other non-terminal symbols. This is because each PCFG rule is independent of the other rules and the rule probabilities can be multiplied. However, in English, how a node expands is dependent on the location of the node in the parse tree. For instance, the syntactic subject of an English sentence tends to be a pronoun because the subject usually is the topic or old information. Pronouns can be used to quote old information, while nonpronominal nouns often help to introduce new information. According to the survey by Francis (1999), of the 31,021 subjects of declarative sentences in Switchboard Corpus, 91% are pronouns, and only 9% are assumed by words from other word classes. In contrast, out of the 7498 objects, only 34% are pronouns and 66% are words from other word classes.

Subject: **She** is able to take her baby to work with her. [pronouns make up 91% of the subjects]

  My wife worked until we had a family. [nonpronouns only account for 9% of the subjects]

  Most of the subjects are pronouns.

Object: Some laws absolutely prohibit **it**. [34% of the objects are pronouns]

  All the people signed **applications**. [66% of the objects are nonpronouns]

  Most of the objects are nonpronouns.

The linguistic fact poses a serious challenge to the three assumptions of PCFG, because the assumptions cannot help PCFG to handle the language phenomenon.

Then let's look at the lexical dependencies.

1. PP attachment: PP attachment refers to the problem of whether a PP is attached to a VP or an NP in an English sentence, because the PP can serve as the adverbial of the VP or the modifier of the NP. PP attachment is related to words.

   In *Washington sent more than 10,000 soldiers into Afghanistan*, the PP *into Afghanistan* is either attached to the NP *more than 10,000 soldiers* or the VP *sent* (a single verb can also be regarded as a VP). This is an instance of PP attachment.

   In PCFG, to resolve the PP attachment problem, selection needs to be made between the two rules below.

   NP → NP PP (the PP is attached to an NP)

   and VP → VP PP (the PP is attached to a VP)

   The probabilities of the two rules depend on the training corpus. Their distribution in two corpora is given as follows.

   Table 10.1 shows that PP attachment to NP has a higher probability in both corpora. Accordingly, PP attachment to NP is preferred. This means that in the example sentence, the PP *into Afghanistan* is likely to be attached to the NP *more than 10,000 soldiers*. However, the correct choice should be the VP *sent* because *sent* usually requires a destination and the PP *into Afghanistan* satisfies the requirement exactly. Obviously, PCFG cannot deal with lexical dependencies like this one.

2. Coordination ambiguities.

   The sentence *dogs in houses and cats* is ambiguous due to different parses (Fig. 10.8).

   Although the left parse tree may be intuitively seen as correct, both trees make use of the same rules as follows.

   NP → NP Conj NP

   NP → NP PP

   NP → Noun

   PP → Prep NP

   Noun → dogs

   Noun → house

   Noun → cats

   Prep → in

   Conj → and

According to the three assumptions about independence, as both trees involve the same set of rules, the probabilities of the two trees calculated by multiplying the probabilities of the rules are also the same. Therefore, PCFG will assign the same probability to the two parse trees. In other words, PCFG cannot solve the ambiguity problem.

Table 10.1 The probabilities of PP attachment to NP and PP attachment to VP

Corpus	PP attachment to NP	PP attachment to NP
AP Newswire (13 million words)	67%	33%
Wall Street Journal and IBM manuals	52%	48%

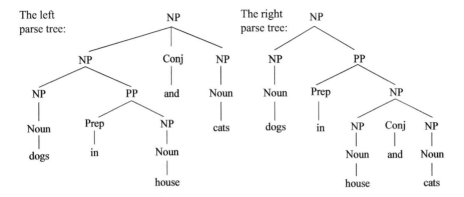

Fig. 10.8 Coordination ambiguities

The above analyses reveal that PCFG can hardly deal with lexical dependencies and structural dependencies. Accordingly, other approaches should be explored to improve context-free grammar. One of them is to introduce lexical information into PCFG by using the probabilistic representation of lexical heads and augment PCFG to probabilistic lexicalized context-free grammar.

10.4   Probabilistic Lexicalized Context-Free Grammar

In 1997, Charniak (Fig. 10.9) proposed the probabilistic representation of lexical heads. As a kind of lexical grammar, the representation is also called probabilistic lexicalized context-free grammar.

In Charniak's probabilistic representation, each node in a parse tree is annotated with its head. For example, the sentence *workers dumped sacks into a bin* can be parsed as follows (Fig. 10.10).

Probabilistic lexicalized context-free grammar has far more rules than PCFG. Take the following rules for instance. Each of these rules includes both a probability and lexical information.

VP(dumped) → VBD(dumped) NP(sacks) PP(into)	$[3 \times 10^{-10}]$
VP(dumped) → VBD(dumped) NP(cats) PP(into)	$[8 \times 10^{-11}]$
VP(dumped) → VBD(dumped) NP(hats) PP(into)	$[4 \times 10^{-10}]$
VP(dumped) → VBD(dumped) NP(sacks) PP(above)	$[1 \times 10^{-12}]$

This sentence can also be parsed into another tree, which is incorrect though (Fig. 10.11).

Fig. 10.9 Charniak

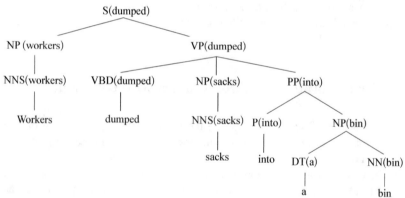

Fig. 10.10 A lexicalized parse tree

If the VP (dumped) is rewritten into VBD NP PP, the correct parse tree can be obtained. In contrast, if the VP (dumped) is rewritten into VBD NP, then the incorrect parse tree above results.

The probabilities of such lexicalized rules can be calculated according to the Brown Corpus in Penn Tree bank.

The probability of the first lexicalized rule VP(dumped) → VBD NP PP is

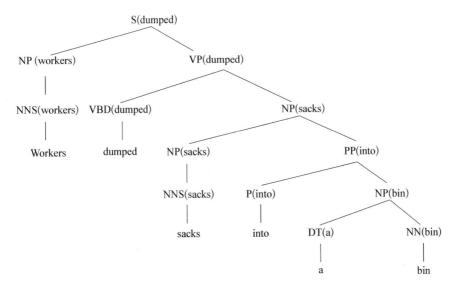

Fig. 10.11 An incorrect parse tree

$$P(\text{VP} \rightarrow \text{VBD NP PP}|\text{VP, dumped}) = \frac{C(\text{VP(dumped)} \rightarrow \text{VBD NP PP})}{\sum_{\beta} C(\text{VP(dumped)} \rightarrow \beta)}$$

$$= 6/9 \approx 0.67$$

The second lexicalized rule VP(dumped) $\rightarrow$ VBD NP is never found in the Brown Corpus, because the verb *dump* requires the location which the action points to be given explicitly. As a result, it makes no sense if the verb is not followed by any prepositional phrase.

$$P(\text{VP} \rightarrow \text{VBD NP}|\text{VP, dumped}) = \frac{C(\text{VP(dumped)} \rightarrow \text{VBD NP})}{\sum_{\beta} C(\text{VP(dumped)} \rightarrow \beta)} .$$

$$= 0/9 = 0$$

In practice, the problem of zero probability is usually solved by a smoothing algorithm. To simplify the discussion here, no smoothing is considered.

As the probability of the second lexicalized rule is zero, the corresponding parse tree is thus incorrect.

The same approach can be used to calculate the probabilities of head words.

The mother node (X) of PP is the head word *dumped* in the correct parse tree and the head word *sacks* in the incorrect tree.

According to Brown Corpus in Penn Tree bank, their probabilities are

$$P(\text{into}|\text{PP}, \text{dumped}) = \frac{C(X(\text{dumped}) \rightarrow \text{PP}(\text{into}))}{\sum_{\beta} C(X(\text{dumped}) \rightarrow \text{PP})}$$

$$= 2/9 \approx 0.22$$

$$P(\text{into}|\text{PP}, \text{sacks}) = \frac{C(X(\text{sacks}) \rightarrow \text{PP}(\text{into}))}{\sum_{\beta} C(X(\text{sacks}) \rightarrow \text{PP})}$$

$$= 0/0 = ?$$

Obviously, calculating the probabilities of PP's potential mother nodes can also help to reveal that *dumped* is more likely than *sacks* to be modified by PP (into).

Of course, a single example does not suffice to prove that one approach out-performs another. Furthermore, the probabilistic lexicalized grammar mentioned above is merely a simplified version of Charniak's actual algorithm. He adds additional conditioning factors (such as the rule-expansion probability of the syn-tactic category of a node's grandparent) and puts forward various backoff and smoothing algorithms, because the existing corpora are too small to acquire these statistics. Other statistical parsers include more factors, such as making a distinction between argument and adjuncts and assigning more weight to lexical dependencies that are closer in a parse tree than to those further away (Collins 1999),[5] taking into account the three left-most word classes in a given constituent (Magerman and Marcus 1991),[6] considering general structural dependencies (such as the preference for right-branching structures in English) (Briscoe and Carroll 1993),[7] and so on. Due to space constraints, these special approaches will not be elaborated on in this book. Readers who would like to know more about them can refer to the literature listed in the footnote of this section.

Having made fruitful explorations into combining rule-based approaches and statistical approaches, PCFG and probabilistic lexicalized context-free grammar greatly strengthen the ability of context-free grammar to resolve ambiguity. As a formal model for NLP, this kind of probabilistic grammar should be paid enough attention to.

---

[5]Collins, M. J. Head-driven Statistical Models for Natural Language Parsing. Ph.D. Thesis. Philadelphia: University of Pennsylvania, 1999.

[6]Magerman, D. M. and Marcus, M. P. Pearl: A probabilistic chart parser. *Proceedings of the 6th Conference of the European Chapter of the ACL*. Berlin, 1991.

[7]Briscoe, T. and Carrol, J. Generalized Probabilistic LR parsing of natural language (corpora) with unification-based grammars. *Computational Linguistics*, 1993, 19(1): 25–59.

Bibliography

1. Charniak, E. 1993. *Statistical Language Learning*. MIT Press.
2. ———. 1997. Statistical Parsing with a Context-Free Grammar and Word Statistics. In *AAAI-97*, 598–603. Menlo Park: AAAI Press.
3. Chengqing, Zong. 2008. *Statistical Natural Language Processing*. Beijing: Tsinghua University Press.
4. Jurafsky, D., and J. Martin. 2009. *Speech and Language Processing*. 2nd ed. London: Pearson Education, Inc.
5. Manning, C.D., and H. Schütze. 1999. *Foundations of Statistical Natural Language Processing*. Cambridge, MA: MIT Press.
6. Zhiwei, Feng. 2005. Probabilistic Grammars for Natural Language Processing. *Contemporary Linguistics* 2: 166–179.

Chapter 11
Formal Models of Neural Network and Deep Learning

Having been widely used in NLP in recent years, neural networks and deep learning have gradually become the mainstream technology in NLP research. Therefore, this chapter will present some details about models based on neural networks and deep learning, including the evolution of neural networks, neural networks of our brain, artificial neural networks, machine learning, deep learning, word vectors, word embedding, dense word vectors, perceptrons, feedforward neural networks, convolutional neural networks, recurrent neural networks, attention mechanisms, external memory, and pretrained models (such as Transformer and BERT).

11.1 Development of Neural Network

The evolution of neural networks can be basically divided into five stages.

The first stage (the emergent stage): This stage (from 1943 to 1969) marked the first fast development of neural networks. During this stage, scientists put forward many neuron models. In 1943, Warren McCulloch, a psychologist, and Walter Pitts, a mathematician, described an idealized artificial neural network and built a computation mechanism based on simple logical calculations. Their neural network model, which was called the MP model, served as the prelude to studies on neural networks. In 1948, Allen Turing depicted a Turing machine in one of his papers. After that, researchers endeavored to apply Hebb's thought of networks to Turing machines. In 1951, McCulloch and Pitts' student Marvin Minsky built the first machine, SNARC, to simulate neural networks. In 1958, Rosenblatt proposed a neural network model, called a perceptron, to simulate human beings' perception and devised a learning algorithm close to human beings' learning process. However, as the structure of a single perceptron was oversimplified, it could not solve any linearly inseparable problem. During this stage, neural networks made remarkable achievements when applied to some fields, such as automatic control and pattern

© Springer Nature Singapore Pte Ltd. 2023
Z. Feng, *Formal Analysis for Natural Language Processing: A Handbook*,
https://doi.org/10.1007/978-981-16-5172-4_11

recognition, because of their special structures and approaches to information processing.

The second stage (the stagnation stage): In this period (from 1969 to 1983), neural networks hit rock bottom for the first time, and relevant research slid into long-term stagnation. In 1969, Minsky and Seymour Papert pointed out in their book *Perceptron* the fact that computers at that time could not provide the computing power that large-scale neural networks required. This assertion directly rendered the neural networks represented by perceptrons fall out of favor with researchers so that research on neural networks entered a stagnant period lasting for more than 10 years. In 1974, Paul Webos at Harvard University proposed the backpropagation algorithm (BP), but it received inadequate attention. In 1980, enlightened by the receptive field of simple and complex cells in animals' primary visual cortex, Fukushima proposed Neocognitron, which is a multilayer neural network with convolutions and pooling. However, as Neocognitron used unsupervised machine learning instead of the BP algorithm for training, it did not receive enough attention either.

The third stage (the resurgence period): This stage (1983–1995) witnessed the resurgence of research on neural networks because the BP algorithm re-sparked researchers' interest in neural networks in this period. In 1983, John Hopfield, a physicist at the California Institute of Technology, devised the Hopfield Network, which was a neural network used for associative memory and optimization of computation. When the Hopfield Network was applied to the Traveling Salesman Problem, it achieved the best result at that time and caused a sensation. In 1984, Geoffrey Hinton designed a Boltzmann machine, which was a randomized Hopfield network. The use of the BP algorithm led to the resurgence of research on neural networks. In 1986, David Rumelhart and James McClelland conducted a thorough investigation into the application of connectionism in computer simulations of neural activities and improved the BP algorithm. After Geoffrey Hinton and his colleagues introduced the BP algorithm into multilayer perceptrons, artificial networks began to win researchers' attention again and became a new hot issue. Later, LeCun and his fellow researchers made use of the BP algorithm in convolutional neural networks and achieved huge success in recognizing handwritten digits.

The fourth stage (the slump years): During this stage (1995–2006), support vector machines and other more simplified algorithms (such as linear classifiers) have gradually gained more popularity than neural networks in machine learning. Although layers and neurons could be easily added to a neural network to build a more complicated network, the computational complexity also increased exponentially. Computers and data available at that time were not able to help train a large-scale neural network. In the mid-1990s, statistical learning theories and machine learning models represented by support vector machines began to spring up. These algorithms amplified the weaknesses of neural networks, such as no clear theoretical basis, difficulties in optimization, and weak interpretability. Therefore, research on neural networks hit rock bottom for the second time.

The fifth stage (the rising period): In 2006, Hinton and Salakhutdinov discovered that feed-forward neural networks, when pretrained layer by layer and then finely tuned with the help of the BP algorithm, could achieve good machine learning results. Due to the great success of deep neural networks in speech recognition, image classification, NLP, and other fields, deep learning, an algorithm based on neural networks, gained instant fame. In recent years, with the widespread application of massively parallel computing and GPUs, computers' computing power has been substantially improved. In addition, the size of data available for machine learning has become increasingly larger. These factors made it possible to train large-scale artificial neural networks. As a result, giant technology companies have made a huge investment in deep learning, and research on neural networks has undergone rapid development for the third time.

11.2 Brain Neural Network and Artificial Neural Network

All human beings' intelligent behavior is related to brain activities. As the organ of consciousness, thought, and emotion, the human brain controls the neurological system. Enlightened by the neurological structure of the brain, scientists constructed a mathematical model that could imitate the structure, called an artificial neural network or a neural network for short. In machine learning, a neural network refers to a network model that is composed of artificial neurons, the connectivity between which can be learned by computers.

The brain, the most complicated organ in our body, is composed of neurons, neuroglial cells, neural stem cells, and blood vessels. As the elementary units of the brain, neurons, also called nerve cells, are cells that carry and transmit information. The human brain includes nearly 86 billion neurons, each of which has thousands of synapses connected to other neurons. These neurons and the connections among them form a large-scale complex network. The total length of these connections can amount to thousands of kilometers. Compared with the neural network of the brain, artificial complex networks are much more simplified.

As early as 1904, biologists uncovered the structure of neurons. A typical neuron consists of a cell body or soma, dendrites, and an axon.

A cell body is primarily composed of a cell nucleus and a cell membrane. The cell membrane has various channels for receptors and ions. When different neurotransmitters act on the corresponding receptors, changes can be generated in terms of ion permeability and potential differences inside and outside the cell membrane. As a result, a physiological activity, either activation or inhibition, is stimulated. A neurite, including an axon and dendrites, is a long and thin structure extended from a cell body. Each neuron has only one axon and one or multiple dendrites. Dendrites can receive stimuli and transmit impulses to the cell body, while axons can transmit impulses from the cell body to other neurons or tissues through the axon terminal. Figure 11.1 shows the typical structure of a neuron in the brain.

A neuron can both receive information from and send information to other neurons. Between neurons exists a gap of 20 nm, called a synapse. Neurons transmit information to each other through synapses and form a neural network. In other words, a synapse can transmit the state of one neuron to another, so it can be

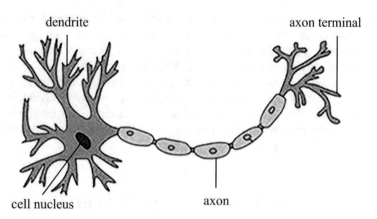

Fig. 11.1   The typical structure of a neuron in the brain

perceived as access to neurons. Each neuron is a cell that can only be activated or inhibited. Which state a neuron is in depends on the amount of information the neuron receives from other neurons and the strength with which a synapse is activated or inhibited. When the total amount of information exceeds a certain threshold value, the cell body will be activated and generate an electric impulse. The electric impulse will be transmitted along the axon and then through synapses to other neurons.

A person's intelligence is not completely genetically determined. Instead, much of it is acquired through continuous learning from life experience. Accordingly, neural networks in the brain are in fact a system capable of learning.

Then, a question arises as to how neural networks learn in the brain. In such neural networks, it is not the neurons but the connections between them that are important. The connectivity between neurons boasts plasticity, as it can be changed through learning (training). Different connections form different memory traces.

In 1949, Donald Hebb (1904–1985), a Canadian psychologist, proposed synaptic plasticity in *The Organization of Behavior*. He held that if two neurons were always activated together, their synaptic strength would be increased. This means that when the axon of a neuron A is so close to another neuron B that A can participate in the activation of B continuously and repeatedly, then growth or some metabolic change will be stimulated on either or both of them, resulting in a stronger effect of A on the activation of B. This principle is named the Hebb rule. Hebb believed that human beings had two types of memory, i.e. long-term memory and short-term memory. Short-term memory cannot last for more than one minute. If some experience is repeated an adequate number of times, the experience can be stored in long-term memory. The process by which short-term memory is converted to long-term memory is called consolidation. The hippocampus of the brain is the core region where consolidation takes place.

As a data or computational model, artificial neural networks are designed to simulate the structure, mechanism, and functions of neural networks in the human brain.

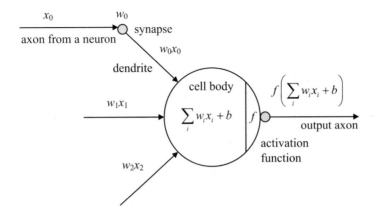

Fig. 11.2 Artificial neural networks

In Fig. 11.2, when information x_0 delivered by an axon from a neuron is sent to the synapse, it will be assigned a weight w_0 and sent with a value of w_0x_0 to a dendrite of the current neuron and then to the cell body. In the same vein, other information, such as x_1 and x_2, will be sent to the cell body with a value of w_1x_1 and w_2x_2.

In the cell body, there is an activation function f, which controls w_ix_i. When w_ix_i is larger than a threshold value, the output of the function is 1, and otherwise 0. In this way, an output axon controlled by the activation function f can be obtained.

$$f\left(\sum_i w_ix_i + b\right)$$

In the expression above, w_i is the weight of information x_i, while b stands for a bias.

Artificial neural networks can basically simulate how neural networks work in the brain. Artificial neural networks consist of multiple artificial neurons that are connected to each other so that the complex interrelationships among data can be modeled. The connections among artificial neurons are assigned different weights, each of which means how much one artificial neuron can influence another. For artificial neurons, each one of them stands for an activation function, taking weighted information from other neurons as inputs and producing an activation value to represent activation or inhibition.

From a systematic point of view, an artificial neural network is a self-adaptive nonlinear dynamic system consisting of a large number of neurons that are densely connected to each other.

Although it is not difficult to build an artificial neural network, how to enable it to learn is no easy task.

Artificial neural networks could not learn in their early days. The first artificial neural network capable of learning was the Hebb network, which made use of unsupervised machine learning based on Hebb rules. Perceptrons were the earliest neural networks that could perform machine learning by themselves, but their learning method could not be extended to multilayer neural networks. Around 1980, the BP algorithm effectively solved the learning issue of multilayer neural networks and became the most popular machine-learning algorithm to train neural networks.

In their early development, artificial neural networks were not used to solve machine learning problems. However, since a two-layer neural network can approximate any function, artificial neural networks can be perceived as a universal function approximator and used for machine learning purposes. Theoretically, if sufficient training data and neurons are available, artificial neural networks can learn many complex functions. An artificial neural network's ability to approximate any function is called network capacity, which is related to the complexity and the amount of information stored in the network.

11.3   Machine Learning and Deep Learning

As deep learning (DL) is a subproblem of machine learning (ML), machine learning is discussed first in the following.

Machine learning refers to the methods that computers rely on to learn rules from a limited amount of observational data and apply the rules to new samples.

Traditionally, machine learning focuses on how to learn a prediction model. First, data usually need to be represented as a group of features, which can take the form of continuous numbers, discrete symbols, or others. After that, a prediction model takes these features as inputs and then produces a prediction outcome. This type of machine learning can be regarded as shallow learning.

An important characteristic of shallow learning is that it does not learn features but extracts features according to researchers' experience or feature transformation. When machine learning is used to solve a practical problem, the data involved may take various forms, such as sounds, images, texts, and so on. For data such as images, pixel color values can be naturally represented as a vector consisting of continuous variables. Text data are composed of discrete symbols. The symbols are meaningless codes, so it is difficult to represent them in a proper way. Generally, machine learning models in practice tend to include the following steps.

1. Data pretreatment: Data pretreatment is a process including denoising. An instance is stop word removal in text classification.

2. Feature representation: Some features of raw data are represented in a certain manner. For example, in image classification tasks, features can include edge features, scale-invariant feature transform (SIFT), and so on.
3. Feature transformation: Features are processed at this stage, such as dimensionality reduction, which usually can be realized by feature extraction or feature selection. The commonly used feature transformation approaches are principal components analysis (PCA) and linear discriminant analysis. Many feature transformation methods are also machine learning algorithms.
4. Prediction: Computers learn a prediction function, which is the most important part of machine learning.

In the above steps, feature processing and prediction are usually conducted separately. Traditional machine learning models focus on the last step, i.e., building a prediction function. However, in practice, these models do not differ much in their performance, whereas feature processing plays a critical role in determining the prediction accuracy of a system.

Feature processing requires manual intervention, which means that human beings' experience is needed to select good features and improve the performance of machine learning systems. Therefore, many pattern recognition problems are feature engineering problems. Much of the work in the development of a machine learning system is about data pretreatment, feature representation, and feature transformation. In this sense, feature engineering is an arduous task.

To improve the accuracy of a machine learning system, the input data should be transformed into useful features, or more generally called representations. If an algorithm can learn useful features automatically and finally improve the performance of the system, this kind of learning is called representation learning.

The key to representation learning is to solve the semantic gap problem, which refers to the incongruence between low-level formal features of input data and high-level semantic information indicated by the data. For example, images of vehicles may differ greatly in terms of pixel representations (low-level features) because the vehicles have different colors and shapes. However, human beings construe these images as vehicles, which are a high-level semantic concept. If a prediction model is directly based on low-level features, it is difficult for the model to achieve good prediction performance. If a good representation is available that can reflect high-level semantic features of data to some extent, we can build a machine learning model more easily.

Representation learning has two core problems. One is "what is a good representation," and the other is "how to learn a good representation."

The so-called good representation is a very subjective concept that is hard to define with explicit criteria, but a good representation generally demonstrates the following characteristics.

- A good representation should have a strong representation ability, which means that it can represent more information than another vector of the same size.
- A good representation should facilitate the learning task, which means that the representation should carry high-level semantic information.

- A good representation should be generalized so that it can be independent of any task or field. Although most representation-learning algorithms are designed to accomplish a specific task, the representations automatically learned are expected to be able to transfer to other tasks somewhat easily.

In traditional machine learning tasks, features are often represented in two ways: local representation and distributed representation.

Take color representation for example. Many words can be used to describe colors in Chinese. In addition to basic words, such as 红 (/hong/; red) 蓝 (/lan/; blue) 绿 (/lü/; green), 白 (/bai/; white), and 黑 (/hei/; black), some color words exist that are named after regions or objects, like 中国红 (/zhong guo hong/; Chinese red), 天蓝色 (/tian lan se/; sky blue), 咖啡色 (/ka fei se/; coffee), and 琥珀色 (/hu po se/; amber).

According to incomplete statistics, there are more than 1300 color words.

The way that colors are represented by different names is called local representation, discrete representation, or symbolic representation.

Local representation usually takes the form of a one-hot vector. Suppose the names of all the colors constitute a word list V and the size of V can be denoted as $|V|$, then each color can be represented by a one-hot vector of $|V|$ dimensions, where the value of its ith dimension is 1, while the other dimensions are assigned 0.

Local representation has two problems.

1. The dimensionality of a one-hot vector can be very high and cannot be expanded. If a new color is created, one more dimension should be added to the vector.
2. The similarity between colors is 0. It cannot be shown that 红(/hong/; red) has a higher degree of similarity to 中国红(/zhong guo hong/; Chinese red) than to 黑(/hei/; black).

The other way to represent colors is to use RGB values (red–green–blue values). Different colors correspond to a point in a three-dimensional RGB color space. This is called distributed representation, which implies that the meaning of a color is decomposed into basis vectors in semantic space.

Compared with local representation, distributed representation is characterized by stronger representation ability and lower dimensionality. A three-dimensional RGB dense vector suffices to represent all the colors, including those newly created ones. Additionally, the similarity between colors can be easily calculated.

Local representation and distributed representation of four colors are listed in the following.

Color	Local representation	Distributed representation
琥珀色 (/hu po se/; Amber)	[1, 0, 0, 0]	[1.00, 0.75, 0.00]
天蓝色 (/tian lan se/; Sky blue)	[0, 1, 0, 0]	[0.00, 0.5, 1.00]
中国红 (/zhong guo hong/; Chinese red)	[0, 0, 1, 0]	[0.67, 0.22, 0.12]
咖啡色 (/ka fei se/; Coffee)	[0, 0, 0, 1]	[0.44, 0.31, 0.22]

Neural networks can be used to map a high-dimensional local representation space $R^{|V|}$ into a low-dimensional distributed representation space R^d, where $d \ll |V|$. In the low-dimensional space, each feature is not a point just lying on a coordinate axis but a vector distributed in the whole space. In machine learning, this process is

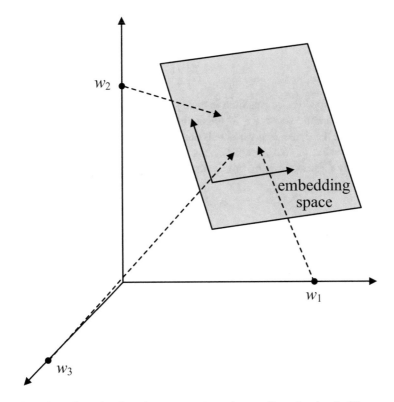

Fig. 11.3 A three-dimensional one-hot vector space and a two-dimensional embedding space

called embedding, which means that some objects are mapped from a high-dimensional metric space to a lower-dimensional metric space with their topological relations maintained as much as possible.

The distributed representation of words in the natural language is often called word embedding.

The above figure illustrates the difference between a three-dimensional one-hot vector space and a two-dimensional embedding space (Fig. 11.3). In the one-hot vector space, each feature is situated on a coordinate axis, and on each coordinate axis, a feature is located. Their similarity cannot be calculated because the similarity between any two of these features is 0. In contrast, none of the features is on a coordinate axis in the two-dimensional embedding space, so their similarity can be computed.

In the following, a simple model (linear regression) is employed to help readers know more about the general process of machine learning and the relationship between different learning criteria (empirical risk minimization, structural risk minimization, maximum likelihood estimate, and maximum a posterior estimate).

As the most widely used model in machine learning, linear regression models the relationship between independent variables and dependent variables. When only one independent variable is involved, the model is called simple regression. When there is more than one independent variable, the model becomes multivariate regression.

Fig. 11.4 A BoW
representation of unigrams

	我	喜欢	讨厌	读书
v1 = [	1	1	0	1],
v2 = [	1	0	1	1].

From the perspective of machine learning, independent variables constitute the target samples' feature vector $x \in R^d$ (each dimension corresponds to an independent variable), while the dependent variable is denoted as y, where $y \in R$ and y is assigned a continuous value (a real number or a consecutive integer). Suppose a space is represented by a linear function with parameters as follows:

$$f(x, w, b) = w^T x + b$$

and the weight vector w and the bias b are learnable parameters, the function can be called a linear model.

In text classification tasks, the sample x is a natural language text, while $y \in (+1, -1)$ represents an affirmative or negative decision whether the text belongs to a certain class or not. To transform x from a text to a vector, a simple way is to use the bag-of-words (BoW) model.

If all the words in the training set come from a word list V with its size denoted as $|V|$, then each sample text can be represented as a $|V|$-dimensional vector x, each dimension of which means whether the ith word in V appears in the sample text or not. If the word is found, x_i is 1. Otherwise, x_i is assigned 0.

For example, in two short Chinese texts 我喜欢读书 (/Wo xi huan du shu/; I like reading) and 我讨厌读书 (/Wo tao yan du shu/; I hate reading), there are altogether four words 我 (/wo/; I), 喜欢 (/xi huan/; like), 讨厌 (/tao yan/; hate), and 读书 (/du shu/; reading). Their BoW representations are given in Fig. 11.4.

The figure above is a BoW representation of unigrams, which is in fact a one-hot vector.

The BoW model perceives a text merely as a collection of words and leaves out word sequence information, so it cannot fully represent the information contained in the text.

An improved approach is to use n-gram features, taking every n adjacent word as a unit and representing the unit according to the BoW model. An instance is bigram representation (a combination of two adjacent words). In the above two texts, there are six bigrams: "$我" (/$ wo/; $ I), "我喜欢" (/wo xi huan/; I like), "我讨厌" (/wo tao yan/; I hate), "喜欢读书" (/xi huan du shu/; like reading), "讨厌读书" (/tao yan du shu/; hate reading), and "读书#" (/du shu #/; reading #). The symbols $ and # denote the beginning and the end of a text, respectively.

Their BoW representations of bigrams take the form of the following vectors.

Figure 11.5 exemplifies BoW representations of bigrams.

As n increases, the number of n-gram features will increase exponentially, with an upper limit of $|V|^n$. Therefore, hundreds of thousands of or even millions of textual features are usually involved in practice.

	\$ 我	我喜欢	我讨厌	喜欢读书	讨厌读书	读书#	
v1 = [	1	1	0	1	0	1	],
v2 = [	1	0	1	0	1	1	].

Fig. 11.5 A BoW representation of bigrams

In text classification tasks that aim to distinguish English and German texts, letter frequency can serve as a good feature. An example is the frequency of letter bigrams. The 26 alphabets, whitespace, and one special character (such as a numeral, a punctuation mark, a currency symbol, and so on) make up a total of 28 characters so that a text can be regarded as a vector of 784 (28×28) dimensions.

$$x \in R^{784}$$

Each component of the vector x, denoted as x_i, is the number of an alphabet combination normalized according to the length of a given text. For instance, the component x_{ab} corresponds to the letter bigram ab,

$$x_{ab} = \frac{\#_{ab}}{|D|}$$

where $\#_{ab}$ is the frequency of the letter bigram ab in a text, while $|D|$ is the total number of letter bigrams in the text, i.e., the length of the text.

Figure 11.6 presents frequency histograms of some letter bigrams in German and English texts. The left part of the figure shows the frequency distribution of letter bigrams in different English texts. These histograms are basically the same. For example, th has a higher frequency, while the frequency of ie is relatively lower. Such features reflect how letter bigrams are distributed in English texts. The right side of the figure shows the frequency distribution of letter bigrams in German texts. These histograms of the same language are similar to each other. Examples are th and en in German. The frequency of the former is very low, whereas the latter occurs much more frequently. These features reflect how letter bigrams are distributed in German texts.

Now, we have a new text whose frequency histograms of letter bigrams are given in Fig. 11.7.

It is likely to be a German text, as the histogram in Fig. 11.7 is close to the histograms in the right part of Fig. 11.6.

In addition to English (En) and German (Ge), if French (Fr), Italian (It), Spanish (Sp), and one other language (Other, abbreviated as O) are also considered, then a matrix W can be trained

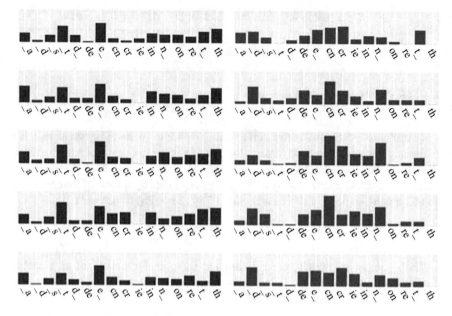

Fig. 11.6 Frequency histograms of letter bigrams in English (the left side) and German (the right side) texts, with the underline representing whitespace

Fig. 11.7 The frequency distribution histogram of letter bigrams in a new text

$$W \in R^{784 \times 6}$$

to represent the frequency distribution of letter bigrams of the six languages, as shown in Fig. 11.8.

W can be analyzed from its rows and columns. Each column in W corresponds to and serves as a representation of one of the six languages in the form of a 784-dimensional vector for the frequency distribution of letter bigrams. The similarity among the vectors can help to group the six languages into different clusters. In the same vein, each row in W corresponds to a letter bigram and acts as a six-dimensional vector for the frequency distribution of the bigram, with each component obtained by analyzing texts of the corresponding language.

In Fig. 11.8a, the six columns correspond to English (En), French (Fr), German (Gr), Italian (It), Spanish (Sp), and one other language (O), while each row in Fig. 11.8b is about the frequency distribution of one of the 784 letter bigrams, which range from aa to zz. Representation is a core concept of deep learning, as its primary task is to learn a good representation. Through the approach mentioned above, each dimension of the vector representation can be assigned a meaningful interpretation.

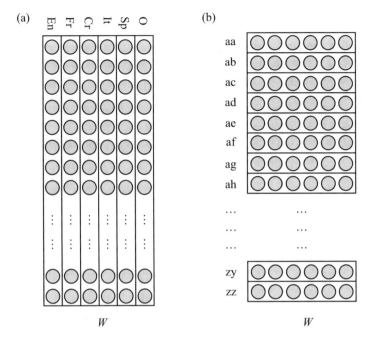

Fig. 11.8 (**a, b**) Two ways to analyze the matrix *W*. (This figure is quoted from Goldberg 2017, to whom acknowledgment is made hereby)

After feature selection or feature extraction, the number of features and feature dimensions will be reduced. Therefore, feature selection and feature extraction are often called dimension reduction.

If representation learning directly employs raw features of data, the machine learning models involved need to be equipped with strong predictive power. These raw features may have the following deficiencies.

1. the features are simple, and only when features are combined in a nonlinear fashion can they work;
2. the features have a relatively high redundancy rate;
3. not all the features are useful for prediction;
4. many features do not have stable effects;
5. noise usually exists in the features.

To improve the performance of machine learning algorithms, effective and stable features should be extracted. Traditional feature extraction is performed manually, demanding a large quantity of manual work and expert knowledge. To build a successful machine learning system, a huge number of features usually need to be tested. This process is called feature engineering.

To learn a good representation, a model with a certain depth should be constructed, which can automatically learn good feature representations (from lower-level features to intermediate-level features and then to higher-level features) through a learning algorithm and finally improve the system's prediction accuracy. The so-called depth refers to how many times raw data undergo nonlinear transformations. If a representation learning system is perceived as a directed graph, depth can then be regarded as the maximum path length from an input node to the output node.

In other words, a learning algorithm is needed to learn from data a model with depth. This is called deep learning (DL for short).

As a subproblem of machine learning, deep learning primarily aims to automatically learn from data effective feature representations. Through multiple feature transformations, raw data become higher-level and more abstract representations, which can replace manually selected features so that the arduous feature engineering task can be circumvented.

Deep learning is a process in which raw features of data, through multiple feature transformations, are converted into other representations, which in turn serve as inputs of a prediction function generating the final output. Different from shallow learning, deep learning needs to solve a critical problem called the credit assignment problem (CAP). Specifically, it denotes to what degree a system's components or their parameters can contribute to or impact the final output of the system.

Take go games for example. Every round of go games ends with a win-or-lose decision. Chess players may think about what steps lead to the decision. How to evaluate the contribution made by each step is the de facto CAP, a thorny issue. In some sense, deep learning can be regarded as reinforcement learning, each component of which receives supervision not in a direct way but from the whole model and with some delay.

Currently, deep learning models are primarily based on neural networks. The main reason is that neural networks can make use of back propagation of errors so that the CAP can be solved to a large extent. The CAP can be found in any neural network that contains more than one layer of nodes, so a more-than-one-layer neural network can be called a deep-learning model. With the rapid development of deep learning, deep-learning models have evolved from 5 to 10 layers of nodes in their early days to hundreds of layers at present. As the number of layers increases, the models' ability to represent features becomes stronger, and the follow-up prediction becomes easier.

In some complex tasks, traditional machine learning methods require a manual division of the process between receiving inputs and generating outputs into multiple submodels (or stages), in each of which learning is performed independently. For instance, a natural language understanding task is usually divided into stages including word segmentation, morphological analysis, syntactic parsing, semantic analysis, semantic reasoning, and so on. This kind of learning has two problems. One is that each model needs a separate optimization, the goal of which does not necessarily agree with the overall goal of the task. The other problem is cumulative errors, which means that errors in the preceding stage may cause a substantial impact on the following learning models. This problem makes it more difficult to apply machine learning methods in practice.

End-to-end learning, also called end-to-end training, means that the overall goal of the task is optimized directly without dividing the whole learning process into several submodels or stages. In end-to-end learning, it is not necessary to clearly define the function of each submodel or stage. Nor is human intervention needed. The training data in end-to-end learning takes the form of input-output pairs, whereas additional information is not required. Therefore, both end-to-end learning and deep learning need to solve CAP. Currently, most deep-learning models using neural networks can also be viewed as end-to-end learning models.

11.4   Word Vector and Word Embedding (CBOW, Skip-Gram)

In recent years, word vectors have become a critical scientific concept in NLP, as they have been widely used in deep learning and have drawn wide attention from researchers in linguistics.

As illustrated in Fig. 11.9, neural machine translation (NMT), by using deep-learning technology, can map discrete word symbols in the natural language into continuous word vectors in an n-dimensional space.

In Fig. 11.10, discrete word symbols including *David*, *John*, *Mary*, *play*, *loves*, and *like* are mapped into different word vectors in a vector space.

In Fig. 11.11, word vectors in an n-dimensional space consist of real numbers.

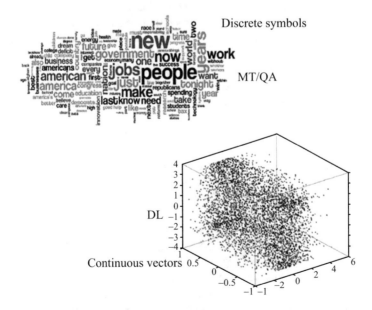

Fig. 11.9 Mapping discrete word symbols into continuous word vectors

Fig. 11.10 Discrete words mapped to an *n*-dimensional space

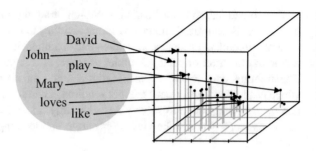

Fig. 11.11 Word vectors represented as groups of real numbers in an *n*-dimensional space

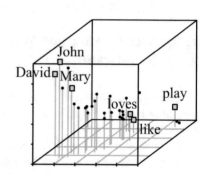

NMT does not compute linguistic symbols but transforms these symbols into word vectors that are embedded and then computed in a vector space. Therefore, NMT computation is performed on real values instead of linguistic symbols. In contrast, phrase-structure-rule-based machine translation and statistical machine translation need to compute with linguistic symbols and their feature representations. It is a tough feature engineering task. In NMT, as word symbols are mapped into word vectors in a vector space, neither large-scale language feature engineering nor manually designed language features are needed. Computers can automatically acquire and compute language features from bilingual corpora. This marks great progress of machine translation research in knowledge acquisition.

Representing words as vectors is called word embedding. Word embedding maps every word in the natural language into a word vector in a vector space and defines in a formal manner the relations between words in the vector space.

Word embedding can be implemented in two ways.

One is Continuous-Bag-of-Word (abbreviated as CBOW). As shown in the left part of Fig. 11.12, CBOW predicts the head word w_i by using the sum of the words w_{i-2}, w_{i-1}, w_{i+1}, and w_{i+2} in its context window.

The other is continuous skip-gram (skip-gram), which uses the head word w_i to predict the words w_{i-2}, w_{i-1}, w_{i+1}, and w_{i+2} in its context window. It can be illustrated by the rights side of Fig. 11.12.

In NMT, word vectors can represent the contextual information in source and target language sentences. The higher the dimension of vector space, the greater the similarity between source and target language sentences. Word vectors guarantee

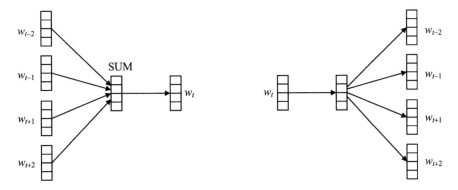

Fig. 11.12   Word embedding: CBOW (left) and Skip-gram (right)

that source language sentences at the input end can be effectively translated into target language sentences at the output end and that the fluency and fidelity of machine translation are improved.

The concept of word embedding derives from value and distribution in linguistics.

As early as 1916, De Saussure, in *Cours de Linguistique Générale*, pointed out that language symbols had values.

He believes that language symbols are not only language facts but also constituent elements of a system representing a language. The functions of symbols in the system are determined by the interrelationships among the member elements of the system. A language is a system, all the elements of which form a whole. Just as chess can be regarded as a game about the combination of chessmen's positions, language is a system grounded only on the opposition of its elements.

He comments that[1]

"A state of the set of chessmen corresponds closely to a state of language. The respective value of the pieces depends on their position on the chessboard just as each linguistic term derives its value from its opposition to all the other terms.

The system is always momentary; it varies from one position to the next. It is also true that values depend above all else on an unchangeable convention, the set of rules that exists before a game begins and persists after each move. Rules that are agreed upon once and for all exist in language too; they are the constant principles of semiology."

Furthermore, Saussure explains value with chess (ibid.).

"Take a knight, for instance. By itself is it an element in the game? Certainly not, for by its material make-up-outside its square and the other conditions of the game-it means nothing to the player; it becomes a real, concrete element only when endowed with value and wedded to it. Suppose that the piece happens to be destroyed or lost during a game. Can it he replaced by an equivalent piece? Certainly. Not only another knight but even a figure shorn of any resemblance to a knight can he declared identical provided the same value is attributed to

---

[1]Saussure De Ferdinand, 1959. *Course in General Linguistics.* Translated by Wade Baskin. New York.

it. We see then that in semiological systems such as language, where elements hold each other in equilibrium in accordance with fixed rules, the notion of identity blends with that of value and vice versa."

A word denotes one sense, but more importantly, it has a function because it is part of a language system. For example, *mouton* in French and *sheep* in English differ in their values, although they may have the same sense. Especially when English speakers refer to a hunk of cooked sheep meat that is served on table, they use *mutton* instead of *sheep*. This can be attributed to several reasons. One of them is that English includes not only *sheep* but also *mutton*, but French does not. In other words, the position of *mouton* in the French lexical system is different from that of *sheep* in the English lexical system.

The example shows that the value of a word is determined by its relations with other words and its position in that language instead of the objective entity it denotes. Value, also called the function of a system, concerns the meanings of language facts in the corresponding language system.

Therefore, Saussure draws his conclusion that language is not a substance but a form.

Value is a basic concept in Saussure's linguistics theory. As one of the concepts deriving from the notion of system, value is intertwined with other concepts that Saussure proposes to analyze language systems. For instance, identity blends with value and vice versa. Another example is his belief that value encompasses concepts such as unit, concrete entity, and reality.

As value determines the functions of symbols, it is not only one of the core concepts in Saussure's linguistics theory but also an important linguistic foundation of word vectors in NLP.

Another important linguistic foundation of word vectors is distribution, which is a term with a special meaning in American descriptive linguistics.

In 1934, M. Swadesh, in his paper *The Phonemic Principle*, used *distribution* as a term for the first time. He believed that the word could be used in the same way as in *geographical distribution*. He commented that "If it is true of two similar types of sounds that only one of them normally occurs in certain phonetic surroundings and that only the other normally occurs in certain other phonetic surroundings, the two may be sub-types of the same phoneme. ... an example is the *p* of English speech whose distribution is complementary to that of the voiced labial *b* as well as to that of the voiceless labial stop sounds of *peak, keep, happen*, but goes with the latter rather than the former because of the phonetic similarity."[2]

Accordingly, if the surroundings where two linguistic phenomena occur happen to be exclusive, the two phenomena complement each other so that they form one unit.

In 1950, M. Joo pointed out that "the linguistic meaning of a morpheme ... can be defined by possibilities and impossibilities of combination among the units of that

---

[2] Swadesh M., 1934. The phonemic principle, *Language*, 10, p. 117.

level."[3] His words suggest that the meaning of a morpheme can be determined by the conditional probabilities with which the morpheme goes together with other morphemes in its context.

In 1951, Z. Harris, in *Methods in structural linguistics*, defined distribution as "(t)he distribution of an element is the total of all environments in which it occurs, i.e. the sum of all the (different) positions (or occurrences) of an element relative to the occurrence of other elements."[4]

According to Harris's definition, linguistic units with the same distribution belong to one class. For example, by distribution analysis, Harris identified some morphemes in Hebrew as belonging to the same category, as illustrated by the following fragments.

xašav**ti**kax	(I thought like this)
xašav**ta**kax	(You thought like this)
xašav**nu**kax	(We thought like this)
xašav**tem**kax	(You all thought like this)
xašav**u**kax	(They thought like this)
xašav**a**kax	(She thought like this)
xašavkax	(He thought like this)

Morphemes such as *-ti-, -ta-, -nu-, -tem-, -u-, -a-*, and the null form ϕ all occur in the same linguistic environment, *xašav-kax*. Because of the same distribution, Harris perceived them as one class, i.e., the pronoun class.

Similarly, Hocket, also by distribution analysis, saw a set of linguistic forms with similar surroundings in larger linguistic forms as a class, called the form-class. For instance, *she, he, it, I, we, they,* and *the men across the street* belong to the same form-class, as they all can occur before *can, can go,* and *can go there*.

These examples show that distribution analysis is in fact a classification approach based on the same environment.

In Harris's definition of distribution, the word "position" also entails environment. As Bloch and Trager commented, "Sameness of position means not only sameness of location with respect to the beginning and end of forms (initial, medial, final) but also sameness of environment as determined by preceding or following sounds, by junctural conditions, and by accent."[5]

Harris also defined the "environment" of distribution as "(t)he environment of position of as element consist of the neighborhood ... 'Neighborhood' refers to the position of elements before, after, and simultaneous with the element in question."[6]

Therefore, distribution analysis is the most important approach for American descriptive linguistics. Harris even believed that it was the only approach for

---

[3] Joos M., 1950. Description of Language design, *JASA*, 22. p. 701–708.

[4] Harris Z., 1951. Methods in Structural Linguistics, p. 15.

[5] Bloch B., G. L. Trager, 1942. Outline of Linguistic Analysis, p. 42, Baltimore.

[6] Harris Z., 1951. Methods in Structural Linguistics, p. 15.

descriptive linguistics. In his *Structural Linguistics*, he argued that "(t)he main research of descriptive linguistics, and the only relation which will be accepted as relevant in the present survey, is the distribution or arrangement within the flow of speech of some parts or features relatively to others."[7] For this reason, American descriptive linguists are sometimes called distributionists.

In 1954, Harris (ibid.) pointed out that "*oculist* and *eye-doctor* . . . occur in almost the same environments." Accordingly, he made a generalization that "(i)f A and B have almost identical environments . . ., we say they are synonyms". In other words, words with similar environments tend to have a similar sense.

In 1957, J. R. Firth stated clearly that "you shall know a word by the company it keeps!"[8] This statement has been widely known as one of Firth's famous sayings.

In 1975, Nida pointed out that the sense of a word was related to the environment of the word. Suppose we have never seen a word like *tesgüino*, but, based on the following four sentences, i.e.

A bottle of tesgüino is on the table.
Everybody likes tesgüino.
Tesgüino makes you drunk.
We make tesgüino out of corn.

we can guess that *tesgüino* is a fermented alcoholic beverage, which, like beer, is brewed out of grain. We can easily obtain this intuition by examining the words in the environment of *tesgüino*, such as *bottle* and *drunk*. These words and other similar contextual words may also occur in the environment of *beer* and *liquor*. This fact can help us to recognize the similarity among *tesgüino*, *beer*, and *liquor*. A closer investigation can also be made into the contextual and syntactic features of *tesgüino*. For example, the word occurs before *drunk* and after *bottle*, serving as the direct object of *likes*. These messages can help to describe the syntactic and semantic properties of *tesgüino*.

Of note, viewpoints similar to "distribution" in linguistics can also be found in psychology. In 1957, the psychologist Osgood and his colleagues proposed that the sense of a word could be modeled as a point in a Euclidean space, while the sense similarity between two words could be modeled as the distance between two points in a Euclidean space.

Therefore, the sense of a word can be represented by the distribution of its surrounding words. The notion of distribution is the other important linguistic basis of word vectors in NLP.

In traditional linguistics, although value is an inspiring notion and the distribution of words in texts can be described in a formal way, neither of them can be computed. However, in NLP, as computers are used to process natural languages, words in texts must be computable. It becomes a necessity that the notion of vectors in mathematics

---

[7] Harris Z., 1963. Structural Linguistics, p. 5.
[8] Firth J. R., 1957. A Synopsis of linguistic theory 1930–1955.

Sugar, a slicedlemon, a tablespoonful of **apricot**   preserve or jam, a pinch each of,

Their enjoyment, Cautiously she sampled her first **pineapple**   and fruit whose taste she likened

Well suited to programming on the **digital**   computer. In finding the optimal R-stage policy from

For the purpose of gathering data **information** necessary for the study authorized in the

Fig. 11.13 Concordances in the Brown Corpus

be employed to accomplish the computational task. As a result, the notion of word vectors is created.

The meaning of a word can be roughly determined according to the frequency of words in its neighborhoods. The frequency can be represented by a vector, called a word vector. Nevertheless, such an approach can lead to long, high-dimensional, and sparse word vectors. Moreover, for a given word, as most of the other words never occur in its surroundings, many zero word vectors are generated.

Intuitively, the so-called vector space model is a model that embeds a word into a vector space. For this reason, representing a word as a word vector is usually called word embedding. Word embedding can help to describe the meaning of a word by using multiple reference words. The discipline is called vector semantics that aims to study semantic representations of word vectors.

Generally, distribution models of words or senses are based on co-occurrence matrices. Here, co-occurrence matrices are $|V| \times |V|$-dimensional term-context matrices. Each cell represents the occurrence of the word (the target word) in the corresponding column, while the words found in the context window of the target word in the training corpus are recorded in rows. Most of the time, a small context window is used. For example, in some training corpora, the context window is set to include four words on the left side and four words on the right side. In this case, each cell indicates the occurrence of the target word in a ± 4-word context window.

Figure 11.13 is an example, which shows ± 7-word context windows of four words, i.e. *apricot, pineapple, digital*, and *information*, in the Brown Corpus (only one instance is given for each word).

With the context window defined, we can then calculate for each target word the frequencies of its surrounding words.

Figure 11.14 is a term-context matrix made for *apricot, pineapple, digital*, and *information* according to the Brown Corpus.

Figure 11.14 lists merely six surrounding words: *aardvark, computer, data, pinch, result*, and *sugar*. The box is the word vector of *digital* (0, 2, 1, 0, 1, 0). Notably, a real word vector has much higher dimensions, so the data will be sparser.

Figure 11.14 also shows that compared with *digital, apricot* is more similar to *pineapple* (as surrounding words such as *pinch* and *sugar* tend to occur in their window contexts). In contrast, *digital* is more similar to *information* than to *apricot*.

Figure 11.15 visualizes the similarity between *digital* and *information*.

The vectors in Fig. 11.15 consist of two dimensions, as *digital* and *information* are correlated with *data* and *result*. In a real corpus, $|V|$ is the length of word vectors,

	aardvark	...	computer	data	pinch	result	sugar	...
apricot	0	...	0	0	1	0	1	
pineapple	0	...	0	0	1	0	1	
digital	0	...	2	1	1	1	0	
information	0	...	1	6	1	4	0	

Fig. 11.14 A term-context matrix made according to Brown Corpus

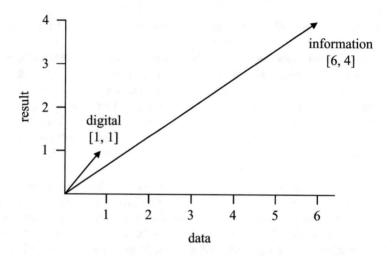

Fig. 11.15 The word vectors of *digital* and *information* are visualized in a term-context matrix

which usually refers to the vocabulary size, ranging from 10,000 words to 50,000 words (generally speaking, 50,000 high-frequency words are used in a training corpus, and a larger vocabulary size may offer little help). Of course, as most of the counts are zero, data sparsity is incurred. To tackle this issue, effective algorithms have been designed for storage and computation based on sparse matrices.

The size of a context window may vary with representation purposes. In practice, the size is set to one to eight words on both sides of the target word, so the full length of the context string amounts to three to 17 words. Generally, the smaller the window is, the more syntactic information is represented, as syntactic information tends to be carried by nearby words. In contrast, the larger the window is, the more semantic information is conveyed.

Figure 11.16 demonstrates the cosine distance between the word vectors of *Sweden* and other countries, or in other words, the cosine values between these word vectors. The cosine distance between *Sweden* and other northern European countries, such as *Norway* and *Denmark*, is more than 0.7, which means that the two countries are highly similar and thus close to *Sweden*, whereas the cosine distance between *Sweden* and the other countries is below 0.7, which means that they exhibit

Word	Cosine distance
norway	0.760124
denmark	0.715460
finland	0.620022
switzerland	0.588132
belgium	0.585835
netherlands	0.574631
iceland	0.562368
estonia	0.547621
slovenia	0.531408

Fig. 11.16 The cosine distance between the word vectors of *Sweden* and other countries

relatively low similarity to *Sweden* and thus seem distant from it. Such results agree with our language intuition. Therefore, it is believed that word vectors can represent human beings' language intuition.

In 2006, Rohde and his colleagues, using the hierarchical clustering method and word embedding classified nouns into four classes automatically and then visualized them. The four classes included the body class (wrists, ankles, feet, etc.), the animal class (such as dogs, cats, and bulls), the city class (such as Chicago, Atlanta, and Tokyo), and the country/region class (China, Russia, Africa, and so on). To represent these word vectors, they set the window size to ± 4, created a 14,000-dimensional space, and deleted 157 closed class words. Visualization was realized through hierarchical clustering. The clustered words showed great similarity to each other, for example, wrist and ankle, hand and foot, dog and cat, lion and bull, Chicago and Atlanta, China and Russia, Africa, and Asia.

With the help of hierarchical clustering, Fig. 11.17 displays the similarities among the words and the similarities agree with our language intuition.

In 2013, T. Mikolov and his colleagues employed the skip-gram algorithm for word embedding to cluster words that were similar to each other. For instance, for a target word Redmond,[9] the algorithm could put Redmond Wash., Redmond Washington, Microsoft, and other words or expressions in the same cluster; for another target word capitulate, clustering could be made for such words as capitulation, capitulated, and capitulating. These clustering results fit our language intuition.

Figure 11.18 is part of their clustering results.

Additionally, in 2013, T. Mikolov and his colleagues discovered in their machine learning research that semantic offsets existed in words that were related to each other. An instance was that the word vector of *Man* could be obtained in the case of the word vector of *King* minus that of *Queen* and then plus the vector of *Woman*.

---

[9] Situated in the State of Washington, west of U.S.A, Redmond is the place where the headquarters of Microsoft are located.

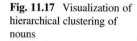

Fig. 11.17 Visualization of hierarchical clustering of nouns

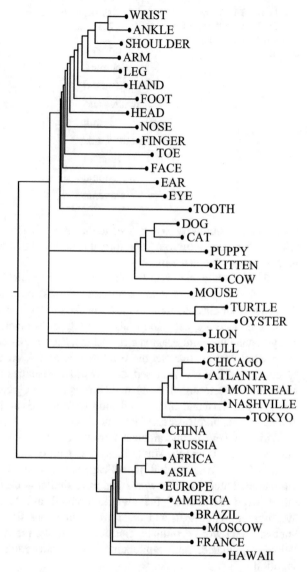

Similarly, the word vector of *Berlin* resulted if the word vector of *France* was subtracted from that of *Paris* and then added to the vector of *Germany*. These computational results coincided with our intuition about the semantic offset relationships among these words. Figure 11.19 is an illustration.

According to the word vectors' values, Mikolov and his colleagues, in the vector space created by word embedding, discovered some interesting word pairings, as shown in Fig. 11.20.

target:	Redmond	Havel	ninjutsu	graffiti	capitulate
	Redmond Wash.	VaclavHavel	minja	spray paint	capitulation
	Redmond Washington	president Vaclav Havel	martial arts	graffiti	capitulated
	Microsoft	Velvet Revolution	swordsmanship	taggers	capitulating

Fig. 11.18 Word clustering based on the skip-gram algorithm

$$V_{King} - V_{Queen} + V_{Women} = V_{Man}$$

$$V_{Paris} - V_{France} + V_{German} = V_{Berlin}$$

Fig. 11.19 The results of computation performed on word vectors agree with our language intuition

Relationship	Example 1	Example 2	Example 3
France-paris	Italy: Rome	Japan: Tokyo	Florida: Tallahassee
big-bigger	small: larger	cold: colder	quick: quidker
Miami-Florida	Baltimore: Maryland	Dallas: Texas	Kona: Hawaii
Einstein-scientist	Messi: midfielder	Mozart: violinist	Pieasso: painter
Sarkozy-France	Berlusconi: Italy	Merkel: Germany	Koizumi: Japan
copper-Cu	zinc: Zn	gold: Au	uranium: plutonium
Berlusconi-Silvio	Sarkozy: Nicolas	Putin: Medvedev	Obama: Barack
Microsoft-Windows	Google: Android	IBM: Linux	Apple: iPhone
Microsoft-Ballmer	Google: yahoo	IBM: McNealy	Apple: Jobs
Japan-sushi	Germany: bratwurst	France: tapas	USA: pizza

Fig. 11.20 Word pairings revealed by the vector space created by word embedding

It is not difficult to see that word pairs, including *France: Paris, Italy: Rome, Japan: Tokyo,* and *Florida: Tallahassee,* indicate the relationship between a region and its capital. Word pairs that consist of *big: bigger, small: larger, cold: colder, quick: quicker* are about the relationship between an adjective and its comparative degree.[10] Despite some minor errors, the figure also shows that word vectors accord with our language intuition.

The computations performed on word vectors vividly reveal that word vectors are closely related to language meaning. It is inspiring and encouraging that the computational results obtained by means of mathematics agree with our intuition. Moreover, as word vectors derive from linguistics, the computational results

---

[10]The word pair *small: larger* is wrong, as it should be *small: smaller*. However, both small and larger are adjectives that describe the volume of space and are thus semantically related to each other. Therefore, this is merely a minor clustering error.

demonstrate that word vectors are a good way to describe the mathematical properties of natural languages.

As the distribution of words in context is represented as word vectors, computation can be facilitated.

In the following, two methods for computation of word vectors will be detailed:
point-wise mutual information (PMI) and cosine values of the angles between word
vectors.

PMI can help to describe the closeness of a target word to its surrounding words,
and thus reveal their semantic relations, while cosine values of the angles between
word vectors can describe the similarity between any two words in a text, and thus
uncover the semantic connections between words in that text. Both are important
mathematical indicators in vector semantics research.

In the term-context co-occurrence matrix shown in Fig. 11.13, each cell in a row
represents the co-occurrence frequency of two words. However, such a frequency is
not the best measurement of the correlations between words, as the frequency may
do little to differentiate one word from another. If we want to determine what kind of
context *apricot* and *pineapple* share but *digital* and *information* do not, a good
distinction cannot be made only on the basis of those high-frequency words such as
the, *it* or *they*, as these words often occur in the surroundings of other words and
cannot help to distinguish them.

Therefore, we prefer to use the surrounding words that boast stronger discriminative ability. The best weight or measurement of correlations between words not
only shows whether they co-occur or not but also displays their co-occurrence
frequency. If such an indicator is found, semantic correlations can be revealed
between the target word and its surrounding words that have discriminative ability.

A typical measurement is point-wise mutual information (PMI), which was
proposed by Church and Hanks based on the notion of mutual information.

The mutual information of two random variables X and Y is

$$I(X, Y) = \sum_x \sum_y p(x, y) \log_2 \frac{p(x, y)}{p(x)p(y)}$$

Point-wise mutual information measures whether two events x and y often occur.
If they are independent of each other, $I(x, y)$ can be calculated according to the
following formula.

$$I(x, y) = \log_2 \frac{p(x, y)}{p(x)p(y)}$$

Accordingly, we represent the PMI between a target word w and one of its
surrounding words c as

$$\text{PMI}(w, c) = \log_2 \frac{p(w, c)}{p(w)p(c)}$$

In the above PMI formula, the numerator $p(w, c)$ stands for the co-occurrence probability calculated according to the observed co-occurrences of the two words. The denominator $p(w)p(c)$, a product of w's and c's occurring probability, stands for the expected co-occurring probability of the two words if the two words are independent of each other. Therefore, PMI(w, c), the ratio of the numerator and the denominator, can help to estimate how frequently the target word and a context word co-occur.

PMI can range from negative infinity to positive infinity. Nevertheless, a negative PMI means that the co-occurrence of the two words is even less frequent than their estimated co-occurrence in the case of an independence assumption. Negative PMIs are unreliable unless the corpus is very large. For example, to show whether two words, each of which occurs individually with a probability of 10^{-6}, co-occur more frequently than they do when an independent relationship is assumed between the two, their co-occurring probability cannot be smaller than 10^{-12}, which requires the corpus to consist of a huge number of words. Therefore, positive-point-wise-mutual information (PPMI) is usually used to replace all negative PMIs with zero.

$$\text{PPMI}(w, c) = \max \left(\log_2 \frac{p(w, c)}{p(w)p(c)}, 0 \right)$$

More formally, assuming there is a term-context co-occurrence matrix F with w rows (each row representing a target word) and c columns (each column standing for a word in context), f_{ij} can then represent the occurrence frequency of the word w_i with the word c_j in its context. As a result, F can be transformed into a PPMI matrix, each cell of which, PPMI$_{ij}$, gives the PPMI value of w_i with c_j in its context.

$$p_{ij} = \frac{f_{ij}}{\sum_{i=1}^{w} \sum_{j=1}^{c} f_{ij}} \qquad p_{i*} = \frac{\sum_{j=1}^{c} f_{ij}}{\sum_{i=1}^{w} \sum_{j=1}^{c} f_{ij}} \qquad p_{*j} = \frac{\sum_{i=1}^{w} f_{ij}}{\sum_{i=1}^{w} \sum_{j=1}^{c} f_{ij}}$$

$$\text{PPMI}_{ij} = \max \left(\log_2 \frac{p_{ij}}{p_{i*}p_{*j}}, 0 \right)$$

With these formulae, PPMI values ($w = information$, $c = data$) can be illustrated with examples. According to Fig. 11.13, the calculation can be made as follows.

In the term-context co-occurrence matrix shown in Fig. 11.13, the sum of all the words' frequencies is

$$\sum_{i=1}^{w} \sum_{j=1}^{c} f_{ij} = 2 + 1 + 1 + 6 + 1 + 1 + 1 + 4 + 1 + 1 = 19$$

The frequency of *information* with *data* in its context is

$$f_{ij} = 6$$

The frequency of *information* in all contexts is

$$\sum_{i=1}^{w} f_{ij} = 1 + 6 + 4 = 11$$

The total frequency of *data* in the contexts of all target words is

$$\sum_{j=1}^{c} f_{ij} = 1 + 6 = 7$$

Therefore, it can be calculated that

$P_{ij} = P(w = information, c = data) = 6/19 \approx 0.316$
$P_{i*} = P(w = information) = 11/19 \approx 0.576$
$P_{*j} = P(c = data) = 7/19 \approx 0.368$
$\mathrm{PPMI}_{ij}(information, \quad data) \quad = \quad \log_2(0.316/(0.576 \quad \times \quad 0.368)) \quad = \quad \log_2$
$1.48306676 \approx 0.568$

As the PPMI value of *information* with *data* in its context is 0.568, the correlation between the two is relatively strong. In other words, for the target word *information*, the context word *data* is found to have a high discriminatory power. In real language use, *information* and *data* indeed often co-occur. Accordingly, the PPMI value agrees with our language intuition.

What follows is an introduction of how to calculate the cosine values between word vectors.

To measure the similarity between two target words v and w, it is necessary to calculate the similarity between their vectors. To date, the most widely used approach in NLP is to calculate the cosine values of the angles between word vectors. Such cosine values are usually based on the notion of dot products in linear algebra.

$$\text{dot-product} \left(\vec{v} \cdot \vec{w} \right) = \vec{v} \cdot \vec{w} = \sum_{i=1}^{N} v_i w_i = v_1 w_1 + v_2 w_2 + \cdots + v_N w_N$$

In most cases, the similarity between two word vectors is measured by their dot product. The reason is that the dot product will be large if the two vectors have high value along the same dimension. However, the dot product will be zero when they have zero values in different dimensions. The zero dot product value means no similarity between the word vectors.

However, when used to compute similarities, this kind of raw dot product has a problem of preference for long word vectors. The length of a word vector can be defined as

$$|\vec{v}| = \sqrt{\sum_{i=1}^{N} v_i^2}$$

The longer a word vector is, the larger its dot product will be and so will be its value along each dimension. Vectors of high-frequency words are usually longer than those of low-frequency words, as the former tends to co-occur with more words and thus have more co-occurrences. Therefore, the raw dot product of a high-frequency word is relatively large. Nevertheless, it is hoped that the similarity value can reveal how similar the two words are to each other, regardless of how frequently they occur in the corpus.

To improve the dot product representation, the easiest way is to normalize the length of word vectors. Specifically, by dividing the dot product of two word vectors by their length, the normalized dot product can be obtained, which happens to be the cosine value of the angle between the two vectors. According to the definition of the dot product, the dot product of two word vectors $\vec{a}$ and $\vec{b}$ is

$$\vec{a} \cdot \vec{b} = |\vec{a}||\vec{b}| \cos\theta$$

$$\frac{\vec{a} \cdot \vec{b}}{|\vec{a}||\vec{b}|} = \cos\theta$$

As a result, the cosine value of the angle between two word vectors $\vec{v}$ and $\vec{w}$ can be calculated by the following formula.

$$\cos\left(\vec{v}, \vec{w}\right) = \frac{\vec{v} \cdot \vec{w}}{|\vec{v}||\vec{w}|} = \frac{\sum_{i=1}^{N} v_i w_i}{\sqrt{\sum_{i=1}^{N} v_i^2}\sqrt{\sum_{i=1}^{N} w_i^2}}$$

In some cases, word vectors need to be normalized in advance by transforming them into unit vectors. To achieve this, the word vector $\vec{a}$ can be divided by its length $|\vec{a}|$. One benefit of the treatment is that the cosine values of the angles between word vectors remain unchanged.

Fig. 11.21 A term-context occurrence matrix

	large	data	computer
apricot	2	0	0
digital	0	1	2
information	1	6	1

In theory, cosine values can range from 1 (word vectors in the same direction) to 0 (orthogonal word vectors) to -1 (word vectors in the opposite direction). However, as the raw frequency of words is always non-negative, the corresponding cosine values merely range from 0 to 1.

Now, we can explore how similar *apricot* and *digital* are to *information* by using the raw frequencies given in the term-context co-occurrence matrix in Fig. 11.21 and calculating their cosine values.

For *apricot* and *information*, the following data can be obtained.

$$\sum_{i=1}^{N} v_i w_i = 2 \times 1 + 0 \times 6 + 0 \times 1 = 2 + 0 + 0$$

$$\sqrt{\sum_{i=1}^{N} v_i^2} \sqrt{\sum_{i=1}^{N} w_i^2} = \sqrt{2^2 + 0^2 + 0^2} \sqrt{1^2 + 6^2 + 1^2} = \sqrt{4 + 0 + 0} \sqrt{1 + 36 + 1}$$

For *digital* and *information*, the data involved are as follows.

$$\sum_{i=1}^{N} v_i w_i = 0 \times 1 + 1 \times 6 + 2 \times 1 = 0 + 6 + 2$$

$$\sqrt{\sum_{i=1}^{N} v_i^2} \sqrt{\sum_{i=1}^{N} w_i^2} = \sqrt{0^2 + 1^2 + 2^2} \sqrt{1^2 + 6^2 + 1^2} = \sqrt{0 + 1 + 4} \sqrt{1 + 36 + 1}$$

Therefore, their cosine values can be calculated.

$$\cos(\text{apricot}, \text{information}) = \frac{2 + 0 + 0}{\sqrt{4 + 0 + 0}\sqrt{1 + 36 + 1}} = \frac{2}{2\sqrt{38}} = .16$$

$$\cos(\text{digital}, \text{information}) = \frac{0 + 6 + 2}{\sqrt{0 + 1 + 4}\sqrt{1 + 36 + 1}} = \frac{8}{\sqrt{38}\sqrt{5}} = .58$$

As 0.58 is larger than 0.16, the cosine values show that *information* is closer to *digital* than to *apricot*. Figure 11.22 is the visualization of the results.

Figure 11.22 shows that for the vectors of *apricot*, *digital*, and *information* in the two-dimensional space defined by two context words, *data* and *large*, the angle between the vector of *digital* and that of *information* is smaller than the angle

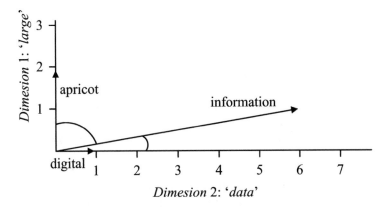

Fig. 11.22 Visualization of the semantic similarity between *information* and the other two words, i.e., *apricot* and *digital*

between the vector of *apricot* and that of *information*. The result demonstrates that compared with *apricot*, *digital* is closer to *information*. In real language use, *information* often co-occurs with *digital* but seldom with *apricot*. Therefore, cosine values of the angles between word vectors also agree with our language intuition.

Generally, the more similar two word vectors are to each other, the smaller the angle between them is and thus the larger the corresponding cosine value turns out to be. When the angle between them reaches its minimum (0°), the cosine value is the largest (1). For other angles, their cosine values are smaller than 1.

The approach of word vectors has been used in NLP for more than 50 years. It is used to represent words in tasks such as named entity recognition, automatic parsing, and annotation of semantic roles. It is the most commonly used approach to measure the similarity between two words, sentences or texts. It also serves as an important tool in information retrieval, neural machine translation, question answer systems, text summarization, automatic essay grading, and so on. In other words, word vectors have received extensive publicity and wide use in NLP.

11.5   Dense Word Vector (Word2vec)

The previous section demonstrates how to represent a word as a sparse word vector, each component of which is the frequency at which the target word co-occurs with the corresponding surrounding word. However, the word vector is usually long and sparse. It is long because the vocabulary size, $|V|$, may amount to 20,000 to 50,000. It is sparse, as most components of the word vector are zero.

To overcome these weaknesses, another method will be used to represent words in this section. With this method, word vectors can be short and dense, because all their dimensions involve merely 50 to 100 words and most components are nonzero values.

Short and dense word vectors may have the following strengths.

First, such word vectors can easily serve as features in machine learning. For example, if 100-dimensional word embedding is used for feature representation, classifiers merely need to learn 100 weights to represent the meaning of a word instead of learning thousands of weights from long and sparse word vectors. As short and dense word vectors include much fewer parameters than long and sparse word vectors, they can be generalized more easily so that they can help to avoid overfitting in machine learning.

Second, compared with long and sparse word vectors, short and dense word vectors can capture synonyms better. For instance, car and automobile are synonyms, but if they are represented as long and sparse vectors, their components will be quite different, and their relations cannot be modeled easily. The reason is that long and sparse word vectors usually cannot capture the similarity between a surrounding word of car and a surrounding word of automobile.

To generate short and dense word vectors, the following three approaches are available.

1. Dimensionality reduction techniques such as singular value decomposition (including principal component analysis and factor analysis);
2. Neural network approaches like skip-gram or CBOW; and
3. A special approach, Brown clustering, based on adjacent words.

The three approaches will be explained individually.

- **Using singular value decomposition to generate short and dense word vectors**

  Singular value decomposition (SVD) is a classical approach to generating short and dense word vectors. In 1988, Deerwester and his colleagues employed the approach for the first time to generate word embeddings based on term-document matrices. The model they used was called latent semantic indexing (LSI) or latent semantic analysis (LSA).

  Through dimensionality reduction, SVD endeavors to seek the most important dimensions of a data set, along which the data vary the most. SVD can be applied to any matrix that takes the form of a rectangle. As a method to use as few dimensions as possible to approximately represent an n-dimensional dataset, SVD includes approaches such as Principal Component Analysis (PCA) and Factor Analysis.

  Generally, dimensionality reduction techniques will first rotate the axis of the raw dataset to a new space. The new space enables the highest-order dimension to capture the largest variance of the raw dataset, renders the second-to-the-highest-order dimension to capture the second largest variance, and so on. Figure 11.23 is the visualization of PCA. Dots in the two dimensions are rotated so that the new

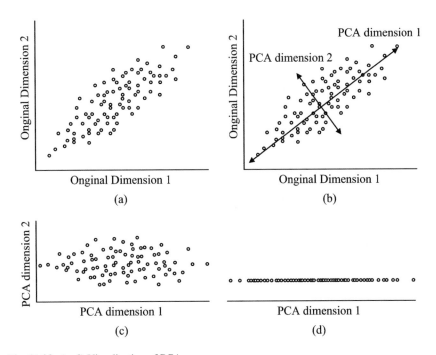

Fig. 11.23 (**a–d**) Visualization of PCA

dimensions can capture the largest variance of the raw dataset. In the new space, a minimal number of dimensions can be used to represent data (for instance, two dimensions can be replaced with one dimension) and capture much of the variance in the raw data set. In Fig. 11.23, given the raw dataset (a), a rotation method (b) renders the first dimension capture the largest variance, and the second dimension, which is orthogonal to the first dimension, captures the second largest variance. Through PCA, the new space (c) can be obtained, and each dot can find its representation in one dimension (d) of the new space. As a result, some dimensions concerning the relationships among the raw dots will disappear, while the remaining dimensions can keep the raw information as much as possible.

Meanings of words can be represented using a high-dimensional sparse vector space, whose dimensionality can be reduced through SVD. Applied to information retrieval first, this approach was called latent semantic indexing (LSI), but later, it was more commonly known as latent semantic analysis (LSA).

LSA applies SVD to process a $|V| \times c$ term-document matrix X, where $|V|$ represents the number of word types and c stands for the number of documents or the size of the window in which the target word type occurs. SVD decomposes the $|V| \times c$ matrix X into the product of three matrices: W, Σ, and C^T. In W, which is a $|V| \times m$ matrix, each row still stands for a word type, but each column is one of the m dimensions in the latent space. The m column vectors, which are orthogonal to each other, are arranged according to the variances in the raw dataset in descending order. The number of column vectors, m, is the rank of X (the rank of a matrix is the number of linearly independent columns). Σ is an $m \times m$ orthogonal matrix, where its singular values on the diagonal represent the important part of each dimension. In C^T, the $m \times c$ matrix, each column still denotes a document or a window, but each row is a new and latent dimension. In addition, the m row vectors are orthogonal to each other.

If the first k dimensions are used to represent all the m dimensions in the three matrices, i.e., W, Σ, and C^T, their product will be a least-square approximation to the raw matrix X. As the first dimension encodes the largest variance, a method to perform such structural transformation is modeling the most important information in the raw dataset.

When SVD is applied to the co-occurrence matrix X, the result is as follows (Fig. 11.24).

The following figure shows the application of SVD to the co-occurrence matrix X when the first k ($k \leq m$) dimensions are extracted (Fig. 11.25).

The $|V| \times k$ matrix W_k enables each word type to be represented by a k-dimensional row vector, which can be used for word embedding. More specifically, as only the first k dimensions are extracted (correspondingly, the most important k singular values are kept), a lower-dimensional $|V| \times k$ matrix W_k can be obtained so that each word type has a k-dimensional row vector. Therefore, the row vectors can serve as dense k-dimensional vectors (embeddings) to represent the word types and replace those high-dimensional row vectors in the original matrix X.

For word embeddings obtained by LSA, k is usually set to 300, shorter than dense vectors created by other approaches.

LSA does not use such methods as PPMI or tf-idf to weight the original term-document matrix but employs a commonly used approach to locally and globally weight each co-occurrence cell (i, j), where i represents a term and j the corresponding document, and multiply the two weights. The local weight of the term i is its logarithmic frequency:

$$X_{|V| \times c} = W_{|V| \times m} \begin{bmatrix} \sigma_1 & 0 & 0 & \cdots & 0 \\ 0 & \sigma_2 & 0 & \cdots & 0 \\ 0 & 0 & \sigma_3 & \cdots & 0 \\ \vdots & \vdots & \vdots & \ddots & \vdots \\ 0 & 0 & 0 & 0 & \sigma_m \end{bmatrix}_{m \times m} C_{m \times c}$$

Fig. 11.24 SVD for factor analysis decomposes the matrix X into the product of three matrices, i.e. W, Σ, and C^T

$$X = W_k \begin{bmatrix} \sigma_1 & 0 & 0 & \cdots & 0 \\ 0 & \sigma_2 & 0 & \cdots & 0 \\ 0 & 0 & \sigma_3 & \cdots & 0 \\ \vdots & \vdots & \vdots & \ddots & \vdots \\ 0 & 0 & 0 & 0 & \sigma_k \end{bmatrix}_{k \times k} \begin{bmatrix} C \end{bmatrix}_{k \times c}$$

$|V| \times c \qquad |V| \times k$

Fig. 11.25 SVD for factor analysis when the first k dimensions are extracted

$$\log f(i + j) + 1$$

The global weight of the term is a kind of entropy:

$$1 + \frac{\sum_j p(i,j) \log p(i,j)}{\log D}$$

where D is the number of documents.

LSA is widely used in NLP as a cognitive model.

SVD has received widespread use in processing term-document, term-term, and term-context matrices, where the context is represented by words. The mathematical rationales involved are the same as those described in Fig. 11.23. SVD decomposes a term-context matrix X into three matrices, i.e. W, Σ, and C^T. The only difference is that the original matrix X is no longer a term-document but a term-term matrix weighted by PPMI.

For each word, the first k dimensions are kept (corresponding to the k most important singular values), leading to a reduced $|V| \times k$ matrix W_k, with each k-dimensional row vector representing a word. Similar to SLA, each row is a dense k-dimensional vector (embedding) that can represent the word.[11] The other two matrices (Σ and C^T) are simply discarded.

The extraction of the first k dimensions, whether from term-document matrices in SLA or from term-term matrices, is called truncated SVD. The parameter k in truncated SVD stands for the number of dimensions of each word, typically ranging from 500 to 5000. Accordingly, SVD run on term-context matrices uses more dimensions than the 300-dimensional embeddings produced by SLA. It is likely that the difference has something to do with the difference in granularity. When LSA is used to calculate the co-occurrences in an entire document,

---

[11] Originally, some systems weighted W_k with singular values and used the product of $\Sigma_k \cdot W_k$ instead of just the matrix W_k as an embedding. However, such weighting could lead to bad embeddings. Therefore, it is basically no longer in use.

word counts are coarse-grained, while in term-context PPMI matrices, word counts are limited to a small window. Generally, the dimensions that need to be retained are the highest-ranking dimensions, although for some tasks, it helps to discard a small number of the highest-ranking dimensions, such as the first dimension or even the first 50 dimensions.

Figure 11.26 is a sketch of the entire SVD process.

The first step: SVD. SVD can decompose a term-term PPMI matrix into three matrices: W, Σ, and C^T.

The second step: truncation. Two matrices, Σ and C^T, are thrown out, while the remaining matrix W is truncated.

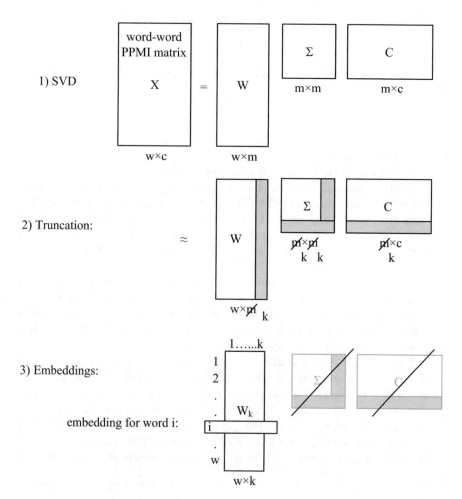

Fig. 11.26 The use of SVD to generate a k-dimensional dense embedding from a c-dimensional sparse PPMI matrix

The third step: embedding. Each word can be represented by a k-dimensional embedding vector.

Dense embeddings created by SVD sometimes perform better than raw PPMI matrices on semantic tasks such as calculating lexical similarity. Usually, dimensionality reduction can contribute to improving the performance of systems. If low-ranking dimensions represent unimportant information, then truncation of SVD can serve for denoising purposes. By removing parameters, the truncation can also help to generalize the models to unseen data. When vectors are used in NLP tasks, a small number of dimensions can make it easier for machine learning classifiers to properly weight the dimensions involved in the task.

However, if the co-occurrence matrix is very large, the computational cost of SVD will be sky high, and the system's performance is not definitely better than using sparse PPMI word vectors. As a result, sparse word vectors should also be considered in some applications.

The neural network models in the following also provide a popular and effective approach to generating dense embeddings.

- **Generating short and dense word vectors by using neural network models such as skip-gram and CBOW**

The second approach to generating dense embeddings derives from the neural network models used for language modeling. Given a word, neural network language models can predict its contextual words. The prediction process can also be used to learn embeddings for a target word. The underlying intuition is that when words with similar meanings occur in a text, they are usually near each other. Therefore, neural network models can learn embeddings by starting with any word vector and then moving its embedding to the embeddings of more similar adjacent words. Additionally, non-adjacent words are moved to the embeddings of less similar words.

Although the architecture gains insight from word prediction, the process to learn the neural network embeddings is in effect strongly correlated with PMI co-occurrence matrices, SVD factorization, and dot-product similarity matrices.

After software packages were developed to generate dense embeddings by using the skip-gram model and CBOW, the most widely used approach is the word2vec model proposed by Mikolov and his colleagues.

Similar to neural language models, the word2vec model learns embeddings by training a neural network to predict neighboring words. However, in this scenario, prediction is not the primary goal. As words that are semantically similar often occur as neighbors in texts, embeddings that are good at predicting neighboring words must also excel in representing lexical similarity. The strength of the word2vec method is its fast speed, good training results, and convenience for coding online and pretraining embeddings.

In the following, the skip-gram model will be detailed. Similar to SVD models, for each word w, the skip-gram model also needs to learn two different embeddings: the word embedding v and the context embedding c. The two embeddings are encoded into a word matrix W and a context matrix C. Each row of W, i, is a

$1 \times d$ vector, which is the word embedding v_i of the word i. Each column of C, denoted c_i, is a $d \times 1$ vector, which serves as the context embedding of the word i. In principle, the word matrix and the context matrix can use different vocabularies V_w and V_c. To simplify our discussion here, it is assumed that the two matrices share the same vocabulary called V.

Now let's focus on the prediction task. A corpus with length T should be traversed, and the current pointer points to the i_{th} word $w^{(i)}$, which is indexed as j in the vocabulary and thus denoted as w_j ($1 < j < |V|$). The skip-gram model is used to predict for the current word its neighboring words in a context window of $2L$ words. Therefore, when L is equal to 2, the context can be represented as $[w^{j-2}, w^{j-1}, w^{j+1}, w^{j+2}]$, and each word in the window can be predicted based on the word w_j. However, here, we predict only one of the $2L$ words, such as w^{j+1}, whose index in the vocabulary is k ($1 < k < |V|$). Accordingly, our task now is to compute $P(w_k|w_j)$.

For the skip-gram model to compute $P(w_k|w_j)$, the most important step is to calculate the dot product between the vectors w_k (the context vector) and w_j (the target vector). For simplicity, the dot product is represented as $c_k \cdot v_j$ (a more accurate representation is $c_k^{T} v_j$), where c_k is the context vector of the word k and v_j is the target vector of the word j. The higher the dot product between the two vectors is, the more similar they are to each other (intuitively a cosine value is used to measure similarity, as it is a normalized dot product). Figure 11.26 illustrates the intuition that the similarity function $similarity(j, k)$ selects a target vector v_j from the target embeddings W and a context vector c_k from the context embeddings C (Fig. 11.27).

Obviously, the dot product is not a probability but a number within the range of $-\infty$ to $+\infty$. However, the dot product can be normalized into a probability by using a denominator that is obtained by calculating the dot products between the target word w_i and all the other words w in the vocabulary:

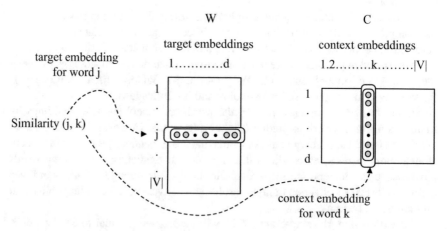

Fig. 11.27 The similarity function $similarity(j, k)$

$$p(w_k|w_j) = \frac{\exp(c_k \cdot v_j)}{\sum\limits_{i \in |V|} \exp(c_k \cdot v_j)}$$

In other words, when the skip-gram model is used to calculate the probability, it utilizes the dot product between the word vector of $j(v_j)$ and the context vector of k (c_k) and turns the dot product into a probability.

However, the algorithm has a problem that too much time is needed to compute the denominator. For each word w_i, the denominator requires computing its dot products with all the other words. Hence, computing the denominator is time consuming. Nevertheless, the problem can be solved by using an approximation of the denominator.

The CBOW model is roughly the mirror image of the skip-gram model. Similar to the skip-gram model, the CBOW model serves for the purpose of prediction. However, it aims to predict the current word w_i according to the context window of 2L words. For instance, when L is equal to 2, the context window is $[w_{i-2}, w_{i-1}, w_{i+1}, w_{i+2}]$.

The CBOW model and the skip-gram model show striking similarities and produce similar embeddings, so they are often interchangeable. But they do have some slight differences. One may turn out to be a better choice than the other for a particular task.

For word embeddings, one semantic property that may be of practical use is their ability to capture relational meanings. Mikolov and his colleagues in 2013 showed that some relations between words could be captured by offsets, which referred to the addition–subtraction relations between word vectors. For example, the result of subtracting the vector of *man* from and then adding the vector of *woman* to the vector of *king* is a vector close to *queen*. Similarly, subtracting the vector of *France* and then adding the vector of *Italy* to the vector of *Paris* results in a vector that is very close to *Rome*.

In the left part of Fig. 11.28, offsets such as king → queen, uncle → aunt, and man → woman seem to have captured the gender property of these words. On the right side of Fig. 11.28, the offsets, which include king → kings and queen → queens, seem to have captured the number category in grammar.

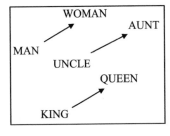 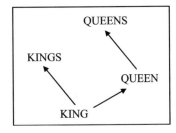

Fig. 11.28 The use of PCA to map vectors into two dimensions, where offsets can demonstrate the relations between vectors

- **Brown clustering**

    Brown clustering was proposed by Brown and his colleagues in 1992. It is an agglomerative clustering algorithm that can derive the vector representations of words according to the relations between the clustered words and their preceding or following words.

    The algorithm adopts a class-based language model. In this language model, each word $w \in V$ is assigned to a class $c \in C$ according to the conditional probability $P(w|c)$. A class-based language model assigns a probability to the word pair w_{i-1} and w_i by modeling the transition between classes instead of words.

    $$P(w_i|w_{i-1}) = P(c_i|c_{i-1})P(w_i|c_i)$$

    The class-based language model can be used to assign a probability to the whole corpus given a particular cluster C.

    $$P(\text{corpus}|C) = \prod_{i-1}^{n} P(c_i|c_{i-1})P(w_i|c_i)$$

    Usually, the class-based language model cannot be applied to tasks such as machine translation or speech recognition, as the model does not perform as well as n-gram models or neural language models. However, the language model is an integral part of Brown clustering.

    Brown clustering is a multilayered clustering algorithm. A simplified version of it is described as follows.

    - Initially, each word is assigned to its own cluster.
    - Each clustered word pair is merged with another. According to the class-based language model, word pairs are merged if the merging results in the slightest reduction of the likelihood of the corpus.
    - The merging process does not stop until all the words are in one large cluster.

    If two words share similar probabilities in terms of their preceding and following words, then the two words can be assigned to the same cluster. In this way, a more coherent cluster can be generated. One result for the treatment is that if two words have similar contexts, they will be automatically merged.

    If a model can trace the order in which clusters are merged, the model can build a binary tree in a bottom-up manner. In this tree, each leaf represents a word in the vocabulary, while each node stands for the cluster that is formed by merging all its daughter nodes. Figure 11.29 is part of such a tree. Each word in the figure is represented by a binary string, while each binary prefix denotes the class to which the word belongs. Therefore, the binary string can serve as the vector representing the word.

Fig. 11.29 A binary tree created by Brown clustering

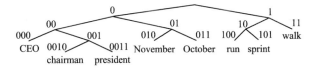

After clustering, a word can be represented by a binary string, which denotes a path starting from the root node. For each node in a binary tree, the left branch is marked 0, while its right branch is labeled 1. Taking the binary tree in Fig. 11.29 as an example, *chairman* and *October* are vectorized as 0010 and 011, respectively. As Brown clustering is a hard clustering algorithm, each word can only be represented as a bit string composed of 0 and 1.

Some useful features can be extracted from the binary prefixes that consist of bit strings represented by 0 and 1. Each prefix denotes a cluster to which the word belongs. For instance, in Fig. 11.29, the bit string 01 stands for the cluster of month names (November, October); the bit string 001 represents nouns for leaders of groups (chairman, president); 1 means a verb (run, sprint, walk); and 0 indicates a noun. These prefixes can serve as vector representations of words. The shorter the prefix, the more abstract the cluster. Therefore, the length of a vector representation can be adjusted according to the needs of a particular task.

In 2008, Koo et al. used multiple features to improve syntactic parsing, with 4-6-bit prefixes capturing part-of-speech information and full bit strings representing words. In 2011, Spitkovsky et al. found that vectors formed by the first 8 or 9 bits of Brown clustering performed well in grammatical induction.

As the clusters are based on immediately neighboring words, they are commonly used to represent syntactic properties of words, and thus are usually used as features for syntactic parsing.

In addition, the clusters can also represent some semantic properties. Figure 11.30 gives some examples from Brown et al.'s work in 1992. The clustering was based on 260,741 words obtained by training dynamic texts with a total size of 365 million words.

In the clusters shown in Fig. 11.30, words such as *Friday, Monday, Thursday, Wednesday, Tuesday, Saturday, Sunday,* and *weekends* are automatically identified as one group, as they are all day names; words such as *June, March, July, April, January, December, October, November, September,* and *August* are automatically regarded as belonging to the same category because all of them are month names.

The simplified version of the Brown clustering algorithm described above is not efficient, as its computational complexity is $O(n^5)$. For each of the n iterations, the algorithm takes into account n^3 rounds of merging, while for each round, the clustering probability will be computed over n^2 words because the algorithm must consider all the possible word pairs for merging purposes. In practice, a more efficient $O(n^3)$ algorithm is adopted, which uses a table to precompute the clustering probability.

Friday Monday Thursday Wednesday Tuesday Saturday Sunday weekends Sundays Saturdays
June March July April January December October November September August
pressure temperature permeability density porosity stress velocity viscosity gravity tension
anyone someone anybody somebody
had hadn't hath would've could've should've must've might've
asking telling wondering instructing informing kidding reminding bothering thanking deposing
mother wife father son husband brother daughter sister boss uncle
great big vast sudden mere sheer gigantic lifelong scant colossal
down backwards ashore sideways southward northward overboard aloft downwards adrift

Fig. 11.30 Some examples of Brown clustering. Note that these clusters have both semantic and syntactic properties

11.6 Perceptron

Artificial neural networks (ANNs) refer to a series of mathematical models that have gained insight from biology and neurology. Enlightened by the networks of neurons in the human brain, these models can help to build artificial neurons and establish connections between them by following topological structures to simulate biological neural networks.

In artificial intelligence, artificial neural networks are often called neural networks (NNs) or neural models.

In their early days, neural networks served as an important connectionist model. Especially in the late 1980s, the most popular connectionist model was the parallel distributed processing (PDP) model.

The three main features of PDP networks are as follows.

1. Information in PDP networks is in the form of distributed representations;
2. Memory and knowledge in PDP networks are stored in the connections between nodes;
3. PDP networks learn new knowledge by gradually changing the strength of the connections between nodes.

Connectionist networks include a multitude of network architectures and learning algorithms. Although biological plausibility was emphasized in early connectionist models, more attention was later paid to simulating some cognitive ability, such as object recognition and language understanding. Especially when back propagation of errors was introduced to improve the learning ability of neural models, neural networks have been increasingly used in various pattern recognition tasks. With more training data and stronger (parallel) computational power, neural networks have displayed their outstanding learning ability in pattern recognition tasks such as speech or image signal processing.

Compared with linear models for machine learning, neural networks can be generally regarded as highly nonlinear models, whose basic constituents are large quantities of interconnected neurons with nonlinear activation functions. The connection weights between neurons, which are parameters to be learned, can be obtained by using the gradient descent algorithm.

In 1957, Frank Rosenblatt, a psychologist at the laboratory for astronautics at Cornell University, proposed the mathematical model of perceptrons according to the mechanism of neurons and the Hebb rule.

Perceptrons are the simplest artificial neural network, because they have only one neuron.

As a simplified mathematical model, perceptrons can explain how neurons work in our brain. A perceptron receives a set of inputs x_1, x_2, x_3, ..., x_n from neurons nearby and multiplies each input by a continuous-value weight (the synaptic strength of each nearby neuron) w_1, w_2, w_3, ..., w_n, as expressed by the following formula.

$$\sum_{i=0}^{n} w_i x_i$$

Each perceptron should have a threshold value θ. If the weighted sum of all the inputs is greater than θ, the perceptron will output 1 (denoted as $y = 1$), and the neuron will be activated. Otherwise, the output will be 0, and the neuron will be inhibited (Fig. 11.31).

With such a neuron, a perceptron can accomplish a classification task. Therefore, perceptrons can be regarded as a linear classification model.

The discussion above shows that, as an artificial neural network with only one neuron, a perceptron is a simplified mathematical simulation of neurons in our brain. Specifically, a perceptron has components that behave like different parts of a neuron. The weight w_i is similar to a synapse, while the threshold θ, serving as the control mechanism of a perceptron, performs basically the same function as a cell body of neural networks in our brain. Such a perceptron has learning ability.

By adjusting the weights of inputs, a perceptron provides a very simple and intuitive learning approach. Given a training set with input and output instances, a perceptron can "learn" an activation function f by increasing its weights if its output is much lower than the desired output and by decreasing its weights otherwise. The details of the algorithm are as follows.

Fig. 11.31 The neuron of a perceptron

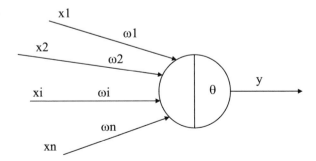

1. A perceptron can start from a training set and random weights.
2. For inputs $x_1, x_2, x_3, \ldots, x_n$ of an instance in the training set, y_1, the output of the perceptron can be computed.
3. If the output of the perceptron differs from the expected output, the weights involved can be adjusted. To be more specific, if the output should be 0 but turns out to be 1, decrease the weights of the inputs that are equal to 1. If the output should be 1 but turns out to be 0, increase the weights of the inputs that are 1.
4. Repeat steps 2–4 for the next instance in the training set until no error is made.

The mechanism of a perceptron is illustrated in Fig. 11.32.

In Fig. 11.32, the inputs x_1, x_2, x_3, x_4, controlled by the activation function f of the perceptron's neuron, generate the output y_1.

According to the mathematical model of perceptrons, Rosenblatt made a piece of hardware to implement perceptrons. Figure 11.33 shows the Mark I Perceptron developed by the laboratory for astronautics at Cornell University.

Using customized hardware, Rosenblatt made a perceptron that could classify images of simple shapes (20 × 20 pixels). The perceptron hardware could learn an approximate function from the given input–output pairs, so it was the first computer that could perform machine learning in the world. Although it merely learned a function as simple as a knickknack, it was not hard to predict its broad usefulness.

Rosenblatt first proposed two types of algorithms to implement perceptrons and then proposed perceptrons' convergence theorem. However, due to the discrete outputs of perceptrons and the simplicity of machine learning algorithms, the application of perceptrons was limited. In 1969, Minsky and Seymour Papert, in

Fig. 11.32 The mechanism of a perceptron

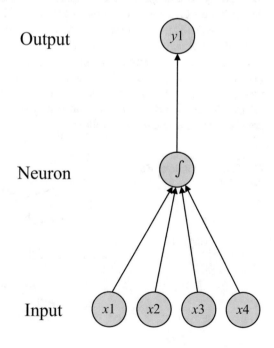

Fig. 11.33 The first piece of hardware to implement perceptrons

their *Perceptrons: An Introduction to Computational Geometry*, analyzed the limitations of perceptrons and pointed out two crucial weaknesses.

First, perceptrons could not solve the linearly inseparable problem in classification tasks, although the problem was common in practice.

Second, training a perceptron-based neural network would consume large amounts of computational resources. However, computers could not perform the task because of technological constraints.

Minsky and Papert's book exerted such a seriously negative impact on research into perceptrons and artificial intelligence that academia and the public believed that neural network approaches were of no value. It was not until the 1980s, when Geoffrey Hinton, Yann LuCun, and other researchers replaced discrete outputs with continuous outputs and introduced the backpropagation algorithm into multi-layer perceptrons that artificial neural networks began to draw public attention once again. Minsky also changed his opinion on neural network approaches.

On the other hand, perceptrons were also in development. In 1999, Freund and Schapire improved perceptrons' learning ability with kernel functions and designed the voted-perceptron algorithm to enhance perceptrons' generalization ability. In 2002, Collins applied perceptrons to structured learning, presented convergence proof, and proposed a more effective and practical strategy to average parameters. In 2010, McDonald improved the averaged perceptron algorithm and rendered perceptrons capable of parallel computing in a distributed computing environment so that perceptrons could be used for large-scale machine learning.

11.7   Feed-Forward Neural Network (FNN)

The functions of a single neurological cell are relatively simple, but artificial neurons are simpler, as they are merely a simplified version of neurological cells. A perceptron has only one artificial neuron, so it is far from capable of simulating the human brain. To accomplish a complicated task, coordination is required among a large number of neurons. The neurons that can coordinate with each other in a way to build connections and transfer information can be regarded as a network, which is also called a neural network.

To date, researchers have created neural networks with different architectures. In this section, feed-forward neural networks (FNN) are explained.

In an FNN, neurons can fall into different sets according to the order they receive information. Each set can be perceived as a neural layer, which receives the output from the previous layer and sends its own output to the next layer. As information in each layer is sent to the following layer in a forward manner without any feedback, a directed acyclic graph (DAG) is thus formed.

Given a set of neurons, a network can be established by taking each neuron as a node. Different neural networks have different topological structures to connect nodes. A not-so-complex topological structure is called a feed-forward network, which is the earliest artificial neural network.

In an FNN, neurons belong to different layers. Each layer of neurons can receive input information from the previous layer and send its output information to the next layer. The initial layer and the last layer are called the input layer and the output layer, respectively, while the middle layers are named the hidden layers. No feedback is generated in the whole network, as information is sent from the input layer to the output layer in one direction. The mechanism behind the process can be represented by a directed acyclic graph (DAG). FNNs are also often called multilayer perceptrons (MLPs). The structure of an FNN is illustrated in Fig. 11.34.

We use the following signs to describe an FNN.

- l: the number of layers in a neural network;
- $m^{(l)}$: the number of neurons in the lth layer;
- $f_l(\cdot)$: the activation function of neurons in the lth layer;
- $W^{(l)} \in \mathbf{R}^{m(l) \times m(l-1)}$: the weight matrix from the $l-1$th layer to the lth layer;
- $b^{(l)} \in \mathbf{R}^{ml}$: the biases from the $l-1$th layer to the lth layer;
- $z^{(l)} \in \mathbf{R}^{ml}$: the inputs of neurons in the lth layer;
- $a^{(l)} \in \mathbf{R}^{ml}$: the outputs of neurons in the lth layer.

Information is propagated in an FNN with the help of the following formulae.

$$z^l = W^{(l)} \cdot a^{(l-1)} + b^{(l)}$$

$$a^{(l)} = f_l\left(z^{(l)}\right)$$

Fig. 11.34 An FNN

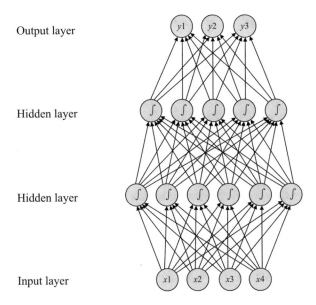

Output layer

Hidden layer

Hidden layer

Input layer

The first formula means that the inputs of neurons in the lth layer are the sum of the products between the weight matrix from the $l − 1$th layer to the lth layer and the outputs of neurons in the $l − 1$th layer and the biases from the $l − 1$th layer to the lth layer.

The second formula shows that the outputs of neurons in the lth layer are the outputs of the activation function in the lth layer on the inputs of neurons in the lth layer.

The two formulae can be integrated as

$$z^{(l)} = W^{(l)} \cdot f_{l-1}\left(z^{(l-1)}\right) + b^{(l)}$$

or

$$a^{(l)} = f_l\left(W^{(l)} \cdot a^{(l-1)} + b^{(l)}\right)$$

Accordingly, an FNN can send information in a layer-by-layer manner and generate the final output $a^{(l)}$. The whole network can be regarded as a composite function $\phi(x; W, b)$, which sees the vector x as the inputs of the first layer $a^{(0)}$ and takes the outputs of the lth layer $a^{(l)}$ as the outputs of the function. The whole process is as follows,

$$x = a^{(0)} \rightarrow z^{(1)} \rightarrow a^{(1)} \rightarrow z^{(2)} \rightarrow \cdots \rightarrow a^{(l-1)} \rightarrow z^{(l)} \rightarrow a^{(l)} = \varphi(x; W, b)$$

where W and b represent all the weights and biases in the network, respectively.

In this sense, an FNN is a composite function that performs a complex mapping from the input space to the output space by using a simple nonlinear function layer by layer. The simple network structure facilitates the implementation of an FNN.

In an FNN, the neurons in neighboring layers are fully connected, so it is also called a fully connected neural network (FCNN).

As a very powerful nonlinear model, FNNs were widely used in the late 1980s, but most of them were two-layer networks (one hidden layer and one output layer). Although parameter learning was still a difficult problem for FNNs at that time, they were a typical connectionist model, marking the transfer of artificial intelligence from a period of highly symbolic knowledge representation to a period of learning with few symbols. This is an important turning point of artificial intelligence research.

In FNNs, each neuron consists of two parts, i.e., one using the linear weighted sum method, called the linear layer, and the other using the activation function, called the nonlinear layer due to the definition of the activation function as a nonlinear one. Although an activation function can also be used in a single-layer perceptron, the function is usually unimportant, as it has nothing to do with the perceptron's classification performance. However, for a multilayer perceptron, activation functions play a critical role in the neural network's performance. If linear activation functions are used, the whole network is on par with one linear function, regardless of how many layers it may contain. From a mathematical point of view, the network differs little from a single-layer perceptron. Accordingly, nonlinear activation functions have greatly improved FNNs' performance.

Theoretically, given a continuous function, there always exists a neural network of limited size that contains at least one hidden layer and can approximate the continuous function with any exactitude if the activation function meets a set of specific lenient conditions. This feature of FNNs is called the universal approximation theorem.

In the following are some commonly used activation functions.

1. Sigmoid functions

Sigmoid functions are those that take the form of an S-shaped curve, with both ends saturated.

Usually, two types of sigmoid functions are used: the logistic function and the tanh function.

(a) The logistic function

The logistic function is defined as

$$\sigma(x) = \frac{1}{1 + \exp(-x)}$$

The logistic function can be regarded as a "squeezing" function, as the function can "squeeze" an input from the real number domain into the range from 0 to 1. When the input value is around 0, the logistic function is approximate to a linear function. When the input value is near either end of the real number domain, the output value will be compressed. The smaller the input is, the closer the output is to 0. In contrast, the larger the input is, the closer the output is to 1. The property of the logistic function is similar to that of a biological neuron, which can be activated by some inputs (with an output of 1) and inhibited by other inputs (with an output of 0).

The feature above enables an artificial neuron equipped with the logistic function to have two properties. First, its output can be directly seen as a probability distribution so that neural networks can better integrate with statistical learning methods. Second, it can also be perceived as a soft gate controlling the amount of other neurons' output information.

(b) The Tanh function

Also called the hyperbolic tangent function, the tanh function is another type of sigmoid function.

The Tanh function is defined as follows.

$$\tanh(x) = \frac{\exp(x) - \exp(-x)}{\exp(x) + \exp(-x)}$$

The tanh function can be perceived as an augmented and translated logistic function, whose range becomes $(-1, 1)$.

Figure 11.35 describes the shapes of the logistic function and the Tanh function. The output of the Tanh function is zero-centered, while that of the logistic function is constantly larger than 0. Nonzero-centered outputs can cause a bias shift for the inputs of neurons in the next layer so that the convergence of gradient descent becomes slower.

2. The ReLU function

As the abbreviation of the rectified linear unit, the ReLU function is the most commonly used activation function. The ReLU function is in fact a ramp function, which is defined as follows.

$$\text{ReLU}(x) = x, \quad \text{if } x \geq 0$$
$$\text{ReLU}(x) = 0, \quad \text{if } x < 0$$

Simple as the ReLU function is, it can help models to learn and converge fast in practice.

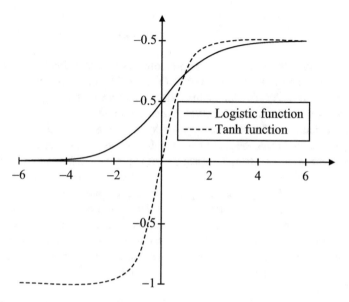

Fig. 11.35 The logistic function and the Tanh function

For a simple neural network such as a two-layer perceptron, the gradient analysis expression for the loss function can be computed manually to obtain each network parameter. However, as the composite functions in a multilayer feed-forward neural network (i.e., a multilayer perceptron) are usually very complicated, calculating gradients manually is almost an impossible task. To solve this difficult problem, Hinton proposed the back-propagation algorithm (the BP algorithm) in 1986 and experimentally proved the effectiveness of the algorithm for updating weights in hidden layers.

The training process of the BP algorithm consists of two stages, i.e., the stage of activation and error propagation and the stage of updating weights.

The stage of activation and error propagation can also be divided into two steps.

The first step is forward propagation, where the network is provided with inputs, and the outputs at each layer are computed and saved.

The second step is back propagation. In this step, the gradients of the output layer are calculated by using the error between the predicted value and the actual value. After that, in the order opposite to forward propagation, errors and the gradients of all the network parameters are computed layer by layer until the input layer.

Regardless of how complicated a composite function is, as long as each subfunction within the composite function is derivable, the partial derivatives of the composite function to any variable and to any subfunction can be obtained automatically with the help of a computer algorithm. The BP algorithm lays a theoretical foundation for the design and implementation of highly complex neural networks.

The BP algorithm enables computers to automatically calculate the gradients of any complex neural network without manual intervention. Therefore, it is believed that the BP algorithm provides systemized and effective schemes to train and apply multilayer neural networks.

11.8   Convolutional Neural Network (CNN)

Convolutional neural networks (CNNs) are deep feed-forward neural networks characterized by local linking and weight sharing.

Originally, CNNs were mainly used to process image information, as FNNs had two problems when dealing with the task.

1. Too many parameters: If the size of an input image was $100 \times 100 \times 3$ (the height and width of the image were both 100 pixels, with three color channels being red, green, and blue), each neuron in the first hidden layer of a fully connected FNN would have $100 \times 100 \times 3 = 30,000$ mutually independent connections with the input layer, with each connection corresponding to one weight. As more neurons in hidden layers could lead to a sharp increase in the number of parameters, training the whole neural network would be a task far from being efficient, and overfitting could also be easily incurred.

2. Local invariant features: Objects in images had local invariant features. For example, when an image was scaled, translated, or rotated, its semantic information would not be undermined. However, fully connected feed-forward neural networks could hardly capture these features. To improve the performance of fully connected feed-forward neural networks, usually more data should be provided.

CNNs are inspired by receptive field mechanisms in biology.

A receptive field refers to the phenomenon that some neurons in the visual or auditory nervous system receive signals only from the region they dominate. In the visual nervous system, the outputs of neurons in the visual cortex depend on photoreceptors in the retina. When photoreceptors are activated by external stimuli, nerve impulses will be transmitted to the visual cortex. However, not all neurons in the visual cortex can receive signals. The receptive field of a visual neuron is a special region in the retina. Only stimuli in that region can activate the neuron.

Currently, CNNs usually take the form of FNNs consisting of convolutional layers, pooling layers, and fully connected layers and are trained with the help of the BP algorithm.

In terms of its structure, a CNN has three features, i.e., local linking, weight sharing, and pooling. These features enable the CNN to translate, scale, and rotate an image invariantly to some extent. Compared with FNNs, CNNs have fewer parameters.

CNNs are mainly used in tasks of analyzing images and videos, such as image classification, face recognition, object recognition, and image segmentation, with much higher accuracy than other neural network models. In recent years, CNNs have also been widely used in NLP.

In fully connected FNNs, if there are n^l neurons in the lth layer and $n^{(l-1)}$ neurons in the $l-1$th layer, there will be $n^l \times n^{(l-1)}$ connections. In other words, the weight matrix has $n^l \times n^{(l-1)}$ parameters. When n is quite large, the weight matrix has so many parameters that training neural networks will be far from being efficient.

If convolutions are used to replace full connections, the input of the lth layer, $z^{(l)}$, is the convolution between the activation of the $l-1$th layer, $a^{(l-1)}$, and the convolutional kernel $w^{(l)} \in Rm$, as shown by the following formula.

$$z^{(l)} = w^{(l)} \bigotimes a^{(l-1)} + b^{(l)}$$

In the formula above, the sign $\bigotimes$ denotes the convolution operation; the convolutional kernel $w^{(l)}$ is the weight vector that needs to be learned; and $b^{(l)} \in R^{nl-1}$ represents the bias that needs to be learned.

Convolutional layers are characterized by local linking and weight sharing. The two features are explained separately as follows.

- **Local linking**: Each neuron in the lth convolutional layer is connected only with neurons in a local window of the preceding layer (the $l-1$th layer), thus forming a locally connected network. As illustrated in Fig. 11.36, much fewer connections are established in the convolutional layer than in the fully connected layer. Specifically, the original $n^l \times n^{(l-1)}$ connections are reduced to $n^l \times m$ connections, where m stands for the number of local linking established for one neuron by the convolutional kernel in a window. In the fully connected layer, there are $n^l \times n^{l-1} = 5 \times 7 = 35$ connections, while in the convolutional layer, there are only $n^l \times m = 5 \times 3 = 15$ connections, as the convolutional kernel establishes three connections for each neuron in the lth layer. Therefore, connections in the convolutional layer are much fewer than those in the fully connected layer (Fig. 11.36).
- **Weight sharing**: The above formula also shows that the convolutional kernel $w^{(l)}$ applies to all the neurons in the lth layer; in other words, the weights are shared by all the neurons in the lth layer.

In NLP tasks, CNNs show higher training efficiency.

For example, as illustrated in Fig. 11.37, if a CNN receives an input, which takes the form of a seven-word English sentence *the actual service was not very good*, the input, after the convolution operation, turns out to be a series of bigrams with 12 connections, which are *the actual, actual service, service was, was not, not very*, and *very good*. Then a group of trigrams with ten connections are formed, which are *the actual service, actual service was, service was not, was not very*, and *not very good*. The reduction of connections can help train the CNN more efficiently.

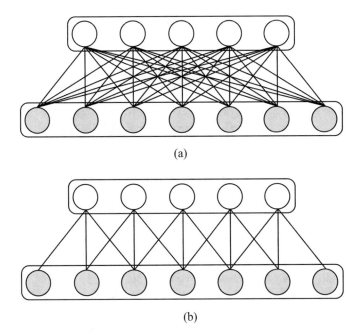

(a)

(b)

Fig. 11.36 A comparison between a fully connected layer and a convolutional layer

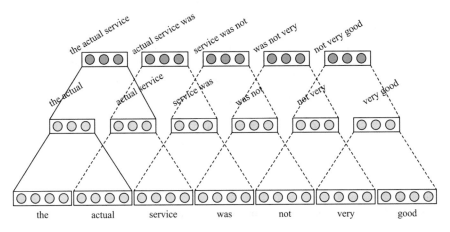

Fig. 11.37 The layer-by-layer reduction of connections in a CNN. (This figure is quoted from Goldberg 2017, to whom acknowledgment is made hereby)

As demonstrated in Fig. 11.38, when the number of layers increases in a CNN, the number of connections decreases layer by layer. In the first layer, there are 14 connections. The number is reduced to 6 in the second layer. For the third layer, only two connections are established. More layers lead to fewer connections.

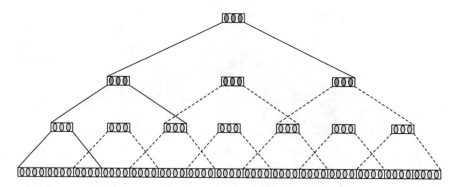

Fig. 11.38 An increase in the number of layers results in a decrease in the number of connections in a CNN. (This figure is quoted from Goldberg 2017, to whom acknowledgment is made hereby)

Therefore, the training efficiency of CNNs is much higher than that of fully connected FNNs.

Additionally, a CNN includes a pooling layer, also called a subsampling layer. A pooling layer can help to select and reduce features, thus leading to fewer parameters. Although the convolutional layer can significantly reduce connections in a network, the number of neurons in feature mapping does not decrease significantly. If a classifier immediately follows the convolutional layer, the dimensionality of its input will still be high, and overfitting can easily result. If a pooling layer can be added after the convolutional layer, the dimensionality of input features will be reduced, and overfitting can be avoided.

Currently, CNNs tend to employ smaller convolutional kernels and deeper architectures. In addition, as the increasing flexibility of the convolution operation leads to a less important role of the pooling layer, pooling layers are less used in currently popular CNNs. Fully convolutional networks have gradually become the mainstream of CNNs.

The widespread use of CNNs can be seen in various NLP tasks.

For the sentiment analysis in NLP, the sentiment of a sentence needs to be identified as positive, negative, or neutral. Take the following sentences for example.

Part of the charm of Satin Rouge is that it avoids the obvious with humor and lightness.
Still, this flick is fun and host to some truly excellent sequences.

Some words (such as *charm*, *fun*, and *excellent*) can express sentiments, while others (such as *still*, *host*, *flick*, *lightness*, *obvious*, and *avoids*) can hardly achieve that. The former group can be used as cue words for sentiment analysis. As the sentiments conveyed by the cue words have nothing to do with their positions in sentences, CBOW can be employed to input all these words into fully connected neural networks.

However, in other cases, word positions do make a difference. Consider the following two sentences.

It was not good, it was actually quite bad.
It was not bad, it was actually quite good.

If word positions are not taken into account, CBOW will lead neural networks to generate the same representation for the two sentences. In contrast, if n-grams are used, word positions in sentences will be considered. The words *not* and *quite* precede *good* and *bad*, respectively, in the first sentence, while in the second sentence, they stand before *bad* and *good*. Therefore, the use of n-grams will improve the accuracy of sentiment analysis to a large extent.

CNNs can be used to analyze word positions in sentences. As CNNs are characterized by local connections and weight sharing, the convolutional structure can be expanded into hierarchical convolutional layers, each of which can make effective use of n-grams. The architecture of CNNs can help to analyze word positions in sentences and capture the local features that may facilitate the current prediction task.

11.9 Recurrent Neural Network (RNN)

In FNNs, information is transmitted in only one direction. This constraint enables FNNs to learn more easily, but to some extent, their learning ability is undermined. In contrast, the connections among neurons are much more complicated in biological neural networks. FNNs can be perceived as a complex function receiving inputs which are independent of each other and generating outputs based on the current inputs alone. However, in real tasks, network inputs are not only related to the current inputs but also to previous outputs. Take a finite-state automaton (FSA) for example. Its output is correlated with both the current input and the previous output.

Additionally, it is difficult for FNNs to process time series data, such as videos, voice messages, and texts. The reason is that time series data usually do not have a fixed length, while FNNs require the dimensions of inputs and outputs to be invariable. Therefore, when dealing with time series data, a more powerful model is needed.

Recurrent neural networks (RNNs) refer to a type of neural network that boasts short-term memory. In RNNs, as neurons can receive signals not only from other neurons but also from itself, a loop structure is formed. Compared with FNNs, RNNs are more similar to biological neural networks. Currently, RNNs have been widely used in tasks such as speech recognition, language modeling, and natural language generation.

By using self-feedback neurons, RNNs can process time series data of any length. Given an input sequence $x_{1:T} = (x_1, x_2, \ldots, x_t, \ldots, x_T)$, an input layer, and a hidden layer, an RNN can use a delay device to update with the following formula the activation value h_t in the hidden layer carrying a feedback edge.

Fig. 11.39 An example
of RNNs

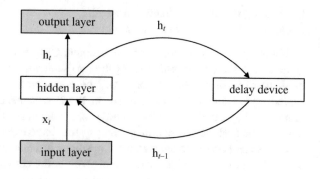

$$h_t = f(h_{t-1}, x_t).$$

In the above formula, $h_0 = 0$, while $f(\cdot)$ can be a nonlinear function or a feed-forward network.

Through recurrent processing, h_t is the output in the output layer.

Figure 11.39 is an example of an RNN.

Mathematically, the above formula can be perceived as a dynamical system, whose state may vary with time by following some rule. Specifically, a dynamical system uses a function to describe how all the points vary with time in a given space (such as the state space of a physical system). Therefore, the activation value h_t in the hidden layer is also called a state or a hidden state. Theoretically, an RNN is close to any nonlinear dynamical system.

A simple recurrent network (SRN) is a neural network with only one hidden layer connected to itself. In contrast, in a two-layer FNN, connections are established between adjacent layers, while nodes in one hidden layer are not connected with each other.

Assume that at the time step t, the network receives an input, x_t, while the state of the hidden layer (the activation value of the neuron in the hidden layer), h_t, is related to not only the current input x_t but also the state of the hidden layer at the previous time step $t - 1$, i.e., h_{t-1}. The relationship can be represented by the following formula.

$$z_t = Uh_{t-1} + Wx_t + b$$

$$h_t = f(z_t)$$

The symbol z_t is the input of the hidden layer, while $f(\cdot)$ is a nonlinear activation function. The symbol U represents a state–state weight matrix. W and b stand for the weight and the bias, respectively. The formula above can also be rewritten as follows.

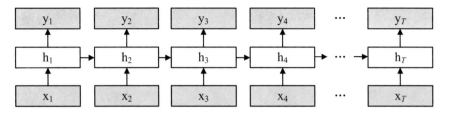

Fig. 11.40 An RNN expanded in chronological order

$$h_t = f(Uh_{t-1} + Wx_t + b)$$

If the state at each time step is perceived as a layer in an FNN, then an RNN is a weight-sharing neural network in the time dimension. Figure 11.40 illustrates an RNN expanded in chronological order.

Figure 11.40 shows that in this RNN, the following feedback connection is established between hidden layers.

$$h_1 \rightarrow h_2 \rightarrow h_3 \rightarrow h_4 \rightarrow \ldots \rightarrow h_T$$

RNNs can be applied to various machine learning tasks. According to their features, these tasks can be divided into three models, i.e., the sequence-to-class model, the synchronous sequence-to-sequence model, and the asynchronous sequence-to-sequence model.

The three models will be detailed in the following.

1. The sequence-to-class model

The sequence-to-class model is mainly used to classify sequence data. It takes a sequence as its input, while its output is a class. For example, in text classification, the input data are a sequence of words, while the output is the class of the text. Assume a sample $x_{1:T} = (x_1, \ldots, x_T)$ is a sequence with a length of T, and its output belongs to the class y, where $y \in \{1, \ldots, C\}$. The sample x can be inputted into an RNN at different time steps, so different hidden states, $h_1, \ldots, h_r$, can be obtained at these time steps. The state h_r can be regarded as the final representation (feature) of the whole sequence and be inputted into the classifier $g(\cdot)$. The value of $\widehat{y}$ can be calculated using the following formula.

$$\widehat{y} = g(h_T)$$

The function $g(\cdot)$ is either a simple linear classifier or a complicated classifier. This is a commonly used model (as shown in Fig. 11.41a).

In addition, we can average all the states of the sequence, i.e., $h_1, \ldots, h_r$ and use the average hidden state h to represent the whole sequence. In this case, the value of $\widehat{y}$ can be calculated with the formula below.

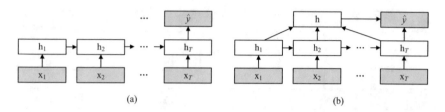

Fig. 11.41   The sequence-to-class model. (a) The commonly used model and (b) average sampling by time

$$\widehat{y} = g\left(\frac{1}{T}\sum_{t-1}^{T} h_t\right)$$

This is called average sampling by time (as demonstrated in Fig. 11.41b).

In NLP tasks, the sequence-to-class model can be used to classify documents. For example, if some documents need to be classified into four categories, such as sport, policy, gossip, and economy, we can employ the sequence-to-class model and hundreds of instances that have been manually classified and then conduct machine learning according to their patterns of lexical use to implement automated document classification.

2. The synchronous sequence-to-sequence model

Mainly used for sequence labeling tasks, the synchronous sequence-to-sequence model means that there is an input and an output of the same length at each time step. An instance of the model is part-of-speech (POS) tagging.

In the synchronous sequence-to-sequence model, the input takes the form of a sequence with the length T, $x_{1:T} = (x_1, \ldots, x_T)$, while the output is a sequence $y_{1:T} = (y_1, \ldots, y_T)$. When the sample x is inputted into an RNN at different time steps, the corresponding hidden states $h_1, \ldots, h_T$ can be obtained. The hidden state h_t at each time step includes both the current and previous information, serves as the input of the classifier $g(\cdot)$, and helps generate the current label $\widehat{y}_T$.

$$\widehat{y} = g(h_t), \quad \forall t \in [1, T]$$

The whole process can be illustrated with Fig. 11.42.

A more specific example is the following English POS tag set, which is adopted in the Penn Tree Bank developed by Pennsylvania State University (Fig. 11.43).

The synchronous sequence-to-sequence model can be used to perform POS tagging for an English sentence *The grand jury commented on a number of other topics* with the following result.

The/DT grand/JJ jury/NN commented/VBD on/IN a/DT number/NN of/IN other/JJ topics/NNS./.

Fig. 11.42 The synchronous sequence-to-sequence model

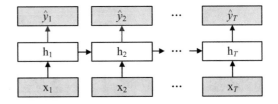

Fig. 11.43 The English POS tag set

Tag	Description	Example	Tag	Description	Example
CC	Coordin. conjunction	*and, but, or*	SYM	symbol	*+, %, &*
DD	Cardinal number	*one, two, three*	TO	"to"	*to*
DT	Determiner	*a, the*	UH	Interjection	*ah, oops*
EX	Expistential 'there'	*there*	VB	Verb, base form	*eat*
FW	Foreign word	*mea culpa*	VBD	Verb, past tense	*ate*
IN	Preposition/sub-conj	*of, in, by*	VBG	Verb, gerund	*eating*
JJ	Adjective	*yellow*	VBN	Verb, past participle	*eaten*
JJR	Adj.,comparative	*bigger*	VBP	Verb, non-3sg pres	*eat*
JJS	Adj.,superlative	*wildest*	VBZ	Verb, 3sg pres	*eats*
LS	List item marker	*1, 2, One*	WDT	Wh-determiner	*which, that*
MD	Modal	*can, should*	WP	Whpronoun	*what, who*
MN	Noun, sing. or mass	*llama*	WPS	Possessive wh-	*whose*
NNS	Noun, plural	*llamas*	WRB	Wh-adverb	*how, where*
NNP	Proper noun, singular	*IBM*	S	Dollar sign	*$*
NNPS	Proper noun, plural	*Carolinas*	#	Pound sign	*#*
PDT	Predeterminer	*all, both*	"	Left quote	*('or")*
POS	Possessive ending	*'s*	"	Right quote	*('or")*
PP	Personal pronoun	*I, you, he*	(	Left parenthesis	*([, (, {, <)*
PPS	Possessive pronoun	*your, one's*	)	Right parenthesis	*(],), }, >)*
RB	Adverb	*quickly, never*	,	Comma	*,*
RBR	Adverb, comparative	*faster*	.	Sentence-final punc	*(. ! ?)*
RBS	Adverb, superlative	*fastest*	:	Mid-sentence punc	*(: ; … – -)*
RP	Particle	*up, off*			

This is an extended-ASCII file whose word sequence and label sequence are synchronously processed. Each word is followed by a label, with a dash between the two. Of course, the labels can also be marked in other ways.

3. The asynchronous sequence-to-sequence model

The asynchronous sequence-to-sequence model, also called the encoder-decoder model, does not require the input sequence and the output sequence have a strict correspondence to each other or have the same length. For example, in machine translation, the input and the output are a sequence of words in the source language and target language, respectively. The two sequences neither exactly correspond to each other nor necessarily have the same length.

The asynchronous sequence-to-sequence model receives as the input a sequence with a length of T, $x_{1:T} = (x_1, \ldots, x_T)$ and outputs another sequence

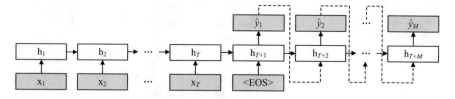

Fig. 11.44 The asynchronous sequence-to-sequence mode

with a length of M, $y_{1:M} = (y_1, \ldots, y_M)$. The whole process is usually implemented in a manner of encoding first and then decoding. The sample x is first inputted into an RNN (the encoder) at various time steps and encoded as h_T. After that, another RNN (the decoder) is used to generate an output sequence $\widehat{y}_{1:M}$. To establish the interdependence between output sequences, nonlinear self-regression models are usually employed in the decoder.

$$h_t = f_1(h_{t-1}, x_t), \quad \forall t \in [1, T]$$
$$h_{T+t} = f_2(h_{T+t-1}, \widehat{y}_{t-1}), \quad \forall t \in [1, M]$$
$$\widehat{y}_t = g(h_{T+t}), \quad \forall t \in [1, M]$$

In the above formula, $f_1(\cdot)$ and $f_2(\cdot)$ are RNNs that serve as the encoder and the decoder, respectively. The function $g(\cdot)$ is the classifier and $\widehat{y}_t$ is the vector representation of the predicted output. As shown in Fig. 11.44, <EOS> means the end of a sentence.

The asynchronous sequence-to-sequence model can be used in machine learning. Figure 11.45 is an example of English-to-French machine translation. An English sentence *I am a student* is inputted into an encoder, while <s> means the end of the sentence. After the input is processed by attention weight, context vector, and attention vector, the French sentence *Je suis étudiant* is generated at the decoder, with </s> as the end of the French sentence. The French sequence and the English sequence do not exactly correspond to each other. The two also differ in their length, with four words in the English sentence and three words in the French sentence. This is an example of the asynchronous sequence-to-sequence model.

However, a simple recurrent network (SRN) can incur the gradient exploding problem or the gradient vanishing problem.

Hochreiter and Schmidhuber proposed a variant of RNNs, the long short-term memory (LSTM) networks, which could effectively solve SRN's gradient exploding problem or gradient vanishing problem.

The improvements made by LSTM networks are in the following two aspects.

First, an internal state is used. An LSTM network makes use of an internal state c_t to transfer information recurrently in a linear manner and generate information as an external state h_t in a nonlinear manner for its hidden layer.

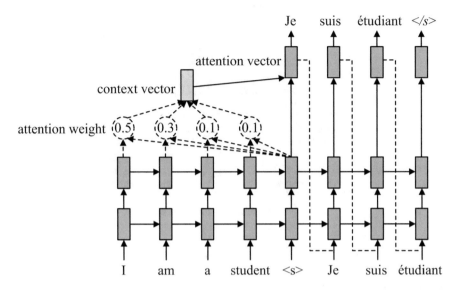

Fig. 11.45 An asynchronous sequence-to-sequence model in English–French machine translation

$$c_t = f_t \odot c_{t-1} + i_t \odot \bar{c}_t$$
$$h_t = o_t \odot \tanh(c_t)$$

In the above two formulae, f_t, i_t, and o_t are three gates to control the information transfer route, while $\odot$ and $\bar{c}_t$ represent the dot product of vectors and the candidate state, respectively.

Second, a gating mechanism is designed. LSTM networks utilize the gating mechanism to control the information transfer route. There exist altogether three gates: the forget gate f_t, the input gate i_t, and the output gate o_t. In digital circuits, the gate is a variable that can be logic 0 or 1. Logic 0 means the off state, allowing no transfer of information, while logic 1 represents the on state, where all the information can be transferred. Different from digital circuits, LSTM networks use soft gates, which can be any number within the range of 0 to 1 and denotes that the corresponding proportion of information can be transferred.

Details of the three gates in LSTM networks are given below.

The forget gate f_t controls how much information of the internal state c_{t-1} developed at the previous time step needs to be forgotten.

The input gate i_t controls how much information of the current candidate state $\bar{c}_t$ needs to be saved.

The output gate o_t controls how much information of the current internal state c_t needs to be transferred to the external state h_t.

When f_t is 0 and i_t is 1, previous information will be removed from the current memory unit, which the candidate state vector $\bar{c}_t$ is then written into. However, the current memory unit c_t is still related to the information generated at the previous time step.

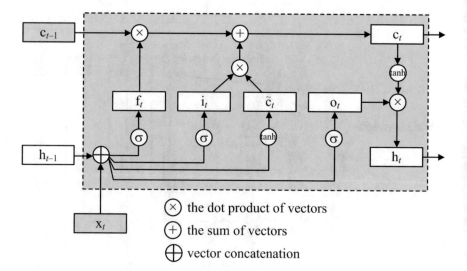

Fig. 11.46 A recurrent unit of LSTM networks

When f_t is 1 and i_t is 0, the current memory unit will copy the information generated at the previous time step and reject any new information.

Figure 11.46 is a recurrent unit of LSTM networks.

What follows is the computation in the three gates.

1. By using the external state h_{t-1} at the previous time step and the current input x_t, the three gates and the candidate state are calculated;
2. The forget gate f_t and the input gate i_t can help to update the memory unit c_t;
3. The internal state information is transferred to the external state h_t with the help of the output gate o_t.

Through the recurrent units of LSTM networks, long-distance sequential dependencies can be established for the whole network.

In RNNs, the previous-time-step information, which can be perceived as a kind of memory, is stored in the hidden state h. In SRNs, as h at each time step can be updated, it can be regarded as short-term memory. In neural networks, long-term memory can serve as another network parameter, which contains information obtained from the training data and is updated far more slowly than short-term memory. In contrast, memory units in LSTM networks can keep only for a period of time some critical information captured at a certain time step. The life span of the information is longer than short-term memory but much shorter than long-term memory. Therefore, the information is called long short-term memory.

As the most successful type of RNN, LSTM networks have been widely used in NLP tasks such as speech recognition, machine translation, speech modeling, and text generation. LSTM networks alleviate the problem of long-distance dependency by using linear connections. Despite the huge success, researchers have been trying to restructure LSTM networks to improve their performance.

f=(La, croissance, économique, s'est, ralentie, ces, dernières, années,.)

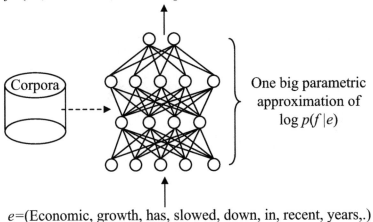

One big parametric
approximation of
$\log p(f \mid e)$

e=(Economic, growth, has, slowed, down, in, recent, years,.)

Fig. 11.47 The mechanism of neural machine translation

In NLP, LSTM networks can be used to capture the long-distance dependencies between words. For example, when analyzing an English sentence "*I wish you a happy college –*", ordinary RNNs and LSTM networks can correctly predict that the word following *college* can be *life*. However, for another English sentence, "*I grew up in America, but I can speak fluent –*", although an RNN can predict that the next word is probably the name of a language, it cannot make use of long-distance contextual information (i.e., the word *America*) and infer which language should be filled in due to the limitations of the algorithm. In contrast, an LSTM network can establish long-distance sequential dependencies, which can help to memorize the information provided by the long-distance word *America* so that the word following *fluent* is predicted to be *English*.

In recent years, the use of neural networks has made remarkable achievements in NLP tasks, especially in machine translation. Therefore, neural machine translation will be specified in the following.

Machine translation (MT) is a very important domain of NLP. Early MT was based on phrase structural rules, so it was called phrase-based machine translation (PBMT). Later, MT began to use statistics as its basis, called statistical machine translation (SMT). Since 2006, SMT has evolved into NMT, which is also based on large-scale bilingual or multilingual parallel corpora. From the perspective of the methodology, both SMT and NMT make use of an empirical approach grounded on language data, while PBMT utilizes a language-rule-based rationalist approach.

The mechanism of Google Neural Machine Translation (GNMT) developed by Google is demonstrated in Fig. 11.47.

In Fig. 11.47, e stands for English, the source language, while f represents French, the target language. The linguistic sequence e is translated into the other linguistic sequence f through a multilayer neural network, which obtains knowledge from

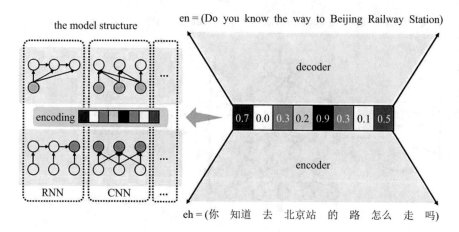

Fig. 11.48 End-to-end neural machine translation

parallel corpora. As shown by the example in Fig. 11.46, an English sequence *Economic growth has slowed down in recent years* is translated into a French sequence *La croissance économique s'est ralentie ces dernières années*. When the translation is made by a computer, large-scale parallel corpora are needed to facilitate deep learning so that language features can be automatically obtained from the corpora. Large-scale parallel corpora can be regarded as a form of big data, so GNMT is in fact a neural machine translation system based on big data. In this multilayer neural network, there exist a large number of connection weights, or in other words, the parameters to be trained and learned by relying on large-scale corpora. After training, the neural network can receive an English (the source language) input *e* and generate a French (the target language) output *f*. In Fig. 11.47, log $p(f|e)$ is the logarithm of the conditional probability of *f* given *e*. The larger the conditional probability is, the better the performance of the neural machine translation system. The aim of the algorithm is to obtain as good a parametric approximation of log $p(f|e)$ as possible. This is the language model of GNMT.

As an end-to-end language model, GNMT encodes a source language input in an encoder composed of an RNN or a CNN and then outputs the translation in a decoder (as shown in Fig. 11.48).

In Fig. 11.48, the Chinese input "你知道去北京站的路怎么走吗?" (/Ni zhi dao qu Bei Jing Zhan de lu zen me zou ma? /; Do you know the way to Beijing railway station?) is encoded by an encoder first, then processed by an RNN or a CNN, and finally decoded by a decoder into the English equivalent "Do you know the way to Beijing railway station?" As few steps are involved in this process, cumulative errors are reduced in information transmission. In this way, end-to-end machine translation is realized.

Compared with traditional machine translation, NMT possesses the following characteristics.

1. A large-scale multilayer neural network should be designed in NMT, while such a kind of neural network is not needed in traditional machine translation.
2. Linguistic symbols are not computed in NMT. They are transformed into word vectors and then embedded into vector space so that computation is performed on real values. However, in traditional machine translation, linguistic symbols and their feature representations need to be described and computed.
3. Word alignment is not needed in NMT but necessary in traditional machine translation. Although the attention mechanism in NMT can help to discover differences between the source language and the target language, this is not alignment in its real sense but a kind of soft alignment.
4. Phrase tables, rule tables, or man-made language feature rules are not necessary in NMT. In contrast, traditional machine translation should be supported by manually or semi-automatically made phrase tables or rule tables. The tables or features require arduous language-feature engineering.
5. NMT does not need an n-gram model of the target language, while such a model is necessary in traditional machine translation (especially statistical machine translation) so that the fluency of the target language output can be guaranteed.
6. NMT does not require a translation model, but the model is needed in traditional machine translation to ensure the fidelity of the target text.

The above features show that NMT, no longer in need of arduous language-feature engineering, can implement fully automatic machine translation by relying on bilingual parallel corpora only. With large-scale authentic corpora, NMT can be developed successfully, even if no language rules are available. Moreover, NMT's performance is much better than that of PBMT and SMT. NMT turns into reality the idea of fully automatic and high-quality machine translation (FAHQMT), which was proposed years ago by Bar-Hillel, the famous forerunner of machine translation.

The following figure compares translation quality of GNMT and PBMT.

Figure 11.49 demonstrates that GNMT performs much better than PBMT. In particular, GNMT is close to human translation in language pairs such as English–Spanish, English–French, Spanish–English, and French–Spanish, although it cannot be called perfect translation. GNMT's use of large-scale parallel corpora to obtain language knowledge greatly improves the performance of machine translation and makes machine translation more practical and commercialized. Both NMT and SMT are based on empiricism and large-scale language data, but compared with SMT, NMT can be more easily influenced by the size of corpora, as it needs to be supported by more corpus data.

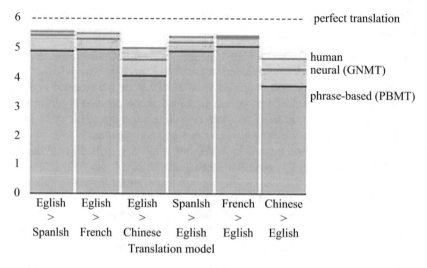

Fig. 11.49 Comparison of translation quality of GNMT and PBMT

11.10   Attention Mechanism

As an empiricist approach to NLP requires a large amount of language data, information overload can be easily incurred. If computational power is limited, one resource distribution strategy to solve information overload is the attention mechanism, which can allocate more computing resources to more important tasks.

Attention, as a necessity for human beings, refers to the complicated cognitive ability that a person can ignore some information while he is focusing on other information. In our daily life, although we receive large quantities of sensory inputs through our visual, auditory, tactile, and other sense organs, our brain can process external information in a well-ordered manner. The reason is that human beings' brain can consciously or unconsciously select and process a fraction of the information and ignore other unrelated information. The ability of the human brain to select information is called attention, which can apply to external stimuli (hearing, sight, taste, and so on) and internal consciousness (thought, memory, and others).

Attention usually falls into two types. One is top-down conscious attention, called focus attention. It refers to a kind of task-dependent attention consciously paid to an object with a predefined goal. The other is bottom-up unconscious attention, called saliency-based attention. Driven by external stimuli, this type of attention neither requires active interference nor pertains to a specific task. If the stimulus provided by an object is different from surrounding information, an unconscious winner-take-all or gating mechanism can help to direct attention to the object. Regardless of whether attention is conscious, most people need to rely on attention so that they can remember, read, or think.

An example related to attention is the cocktail party effect. When a man attends a cocktail party and chats with his friends in a noisy room, he can hear his friends' talk and filter out other peoples' voice despite background noise. It is the focus attention that is taking effect. However, if he finds that there exist some words related to him in the background noise (for instance, he overhears his name), he will become alert immediately and capture the important words due to the saliency-based attention. Therefore, for the cocktail party effect, both focus attention and saliency-based attention can be found.

Focus attention may select different information when different environments, situations, or tasks are involved. For example, when looking for a person from a crowd of people, we will pay attention to everyone's face. In contrast, while counting the number of the group of people, we just need to focus on everyone's silhouette.

Neural networks, when processing large amounts of input information, may gain some insights from the attention mechanism of the human brain by selecting some important information to improve their efficiency. In current neural network models, mechanisms such as max pooling and gating can be regarded as an approximation to bottom-up saliency-based attention. Additionally, top-down focus attention is also an effective way to select information.

Take reading comprehension tasks for example. Given a passage long enough, readers can raise several questions, each of which is probably related to only one or two sentences in a paragraph. To lighten the computational burden of the system, only those relevant segments instead of the whole passage need to be inputted into the subsequent neural networks.

More generally, for N input messages denoted as $X = [x_1, \ldots, x_N]$, if the attention mechanism is adopted, a neural network model does not have to take as input all the N messages but merely those related to a given task.

Computation based on the attention mechanism consists of two steps. The first is to calculate the distribution of attention for all the input messages, while the second is to calculate the weighted average value of input messages according to the distribution.

For the first step, given a task-related query vector q, the attention variable $z \in [1, N]$ can be defined, where $z = i$ means the i_{th} input message is selected. The index of the selected message can be determined using a dynamic generation approach. For convenience, the index can also take the form of a learnable parameter.

When a variable-length vector sequence is inputted into neural network models, it can be encoded by a CNN or an RNN to generate an output vector sequence of the same length, as shown in Fig. 11.50.

Sequence encoding based on a CNN or an RNN can be perceived as local encoding, which aims to build mathematical models only for local dependencies in input sequences. Although theoretically RNNs can help to establish long-distance dependencies, only short-distance dependencies can be found due to the limited volume of information transfer and the vanishing gradient problem.

To establish long-distance dependencies in an input sequence, the following two approaches are available. One is to increase the number of layers to build a deep network and implement long-distance information interaction. The other is to use

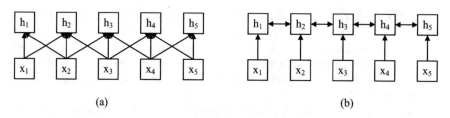

Fig. 11.50 Encoding a dynamic sequence based on (**a**) a CNN or (**b**) a bidirectional RNN

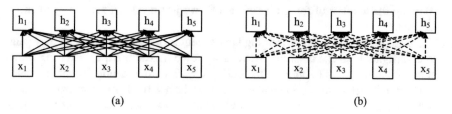

Fig. 11.51 (**a**) A fully connected model and (**b**) a self-attention model

fully-connected networks. Fully connected networks can help to build models directly for long-distance dependencies but cannot process variable-length input sequences. As the input length varies, the connection weights also differ. To solve this problem, the attention mechanism can be employed to generate different connection weights in a dynamic manner. This kind of model is called the self-attention model.

Figure 11.51 presents a comparison between a fully connected model and a self-attention model. The solid lines represent learnable weights, while the dotted lines represent the weights generated dynamically. As the weights of the self-attention model are dynamic, the model can process variable–length sequences.

The attention mechanism in NMT was put forward by Bengio and his colleagues in 2014. In recent years, it has drawn growing attention from machine learning researchers and has become a research focus.

The attention mechanism is characterized by the fact that the decoder can selectively acquire coded messages, or in other words, word vectors with different weights in NLP tasks. In essence, this is a self-regression mechanism, i.e., soft alignment. Simply speaking, when predicting the next word, the attention mechanism will traverse all the information in the hidden layers, predict the attention weight of each word, and select an output most likely related to the current word so that computers can generate a self-perception output.

Figure 11.52 demonstrates the process of soft alignment in machine translation based on the attention mechanism.

Figure 11.52 displays the following soft alignment between English and German.

economic grows → Das Wirtschaftswachstum
has → hat
slowed down → verlangsamt

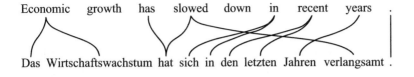

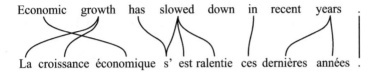

Fig. 11.52 Soft alignment based on the attention mechanism

In → sich in
recent → den letzten
year → Jahren

In Fig. 11.52 exists the following soft alignment between English and French.

economic → économique
growth → La croissance
has → s'
slowed down → est ratentie
in → ces
recent years → dernières années

It is not difficult to see that the soft alignment above is basically correct.

Although manual alignment is usually used in conventional machine translation, human beings can hardly cope with such an arduous alignment task. The attention mechanism helps to realize automatic alignment between a source language word or phrase and its equivalent in target language, bringing a historic breakthrough to machine translation.

11.11   External Memory

To increase network capacity, memory-aiding devices can be used so that information can be stored and retrieved if needed. The memory-aiding devices are usually called external memory, which differs from internal memory (i.e., the hidden states) of RNNs.

In biological neural networks, memory refers to the mechanism that determines how external information is stored in the human brain. Undoubtedly, memory is preserved with the help of biological neural networks. Although details about memory are unclear, memory is intuitively related to the connections of neural networks and to neurons' behavior. Physiologists have uncovered that information is stored in the brain as a collective effect. When different parts of the cerebral cortex are damaged, differences in the resulting behavior seem to rely on the degree rather than the location of the damage. Therefore, it appears that each part of the brain carries some information capable of leading to similar behavior. In other words, memory is stored not in a localized area of our brain but in the whole cerebral cortex in a distributional manner.

Memory in the human brain is periodic and associative.

Although how memory is stored in the human brain is unclear, it is almost certain that different parts of the brain are involved in different stages of memory formation.

Memory usually falls into long-term memory and short-term memory. Long-term memory, also called structured memory or knowledge, takes the form of connections between neurons and is updated rather slowly. Short-term memory, lasting from a few seconds to several minutes, is in the form of neuron activities and is updated more quickly. Short-term memory strengthens the connection between neurons only temporarily. When short-term memory is consolidated repeatedly, it can develop into long-term memory. The dynamic process is called evolution.

In addition to long-term and short-term memory, buffer memory, also called working memory, exists in the human brain. When some cognitive behavior (such as memorizing a telephone number or performing arithmetic operations) is made, working memory, which lasts for a few seconds, guarantees that information can be stored temporarily and processed. Although working memory is similar to short-term memory in the matter of time, the two are different. Short-term memory is about how external inputs are represented and stored temporarily in the brain, showing little concern for the use of the inputs, while working memory is related to tasks, being able to temporarily store short-term memory specific to a certain task and other relevant information. Generally, the capacity of working memory is small.

A not-so-exact analogy can be taken to storage devices in modern computers. According to the differences in memory cycle time, storage devices include registers, internal memory, and external memory.

Another characteristic of human beings' memory is the use of associations to retrieve information.

Associative memory is the ability to learn and memorize the relationships between different objects. For example, when we see a person, we think of his or her name. Another instance is that chili often reminds us of its spicy flavor. As associative memory can help to search for the address of information through content matching, it is also called content-addressable memory (CAM).

Analogously, information is stored in modern computers according to its address. This kind of information storage is called random access memory (RAM). External memory can accommodate more information, participate indirectly in computation, and work through read/write access. In contrast, memory units in LSTM have to fulfill two functions, i.e., information storage and computation, so they cannot store much information. As a result, memory units in LSTM are analogous to registers in computers, while external memory plays the same role as other storage devices (such as memory banks, magnetic tapes, and hard disks).

With the insight gained from working memory in the brain, an external memory unit can be introduced into neural network models to increase the network capacity.

Memory duration	Computer	Human brain	Neural network
Short-term	Register	Short-term memory	State (neuron activation)
Medium-term	Memory	Working memory	External memory
Long-term	External storage	Long-term memory	Learnable parameters
Storage manner	Random addressing	Content-addressing	Basically content-addressing

Fig. 11.53 A not-so-exact analogy for memory models in different fields

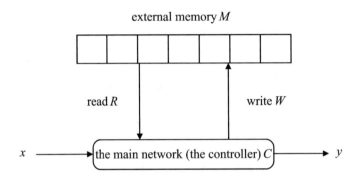

Fig. 11.54 The structure of a memory network

Two approaches are available to realize external memory. One is structured memory, which behaves like information storage in computers by segmenting memory into pieces and storing them according to a certain structure. The other is associative memory based on neurodynamics. The latter approach can obtain better biological interpretability.

A not-so-exact analogy for memory models in different fields is given in Fig. 11.53.

A simple way to increase network capacity is to use a structured memory model, preserve in it the short-term memory related to a certain task, and read the information when necessary. A neural network equipped with external memory is also called a memory network (MN) or a memory augmented neural network (MANN).

Figure 11.54 shows the structure of a memory network usually consisting of the following modules.

1. The main network C, also called the controller, serves to process information, receive an input x from outside, and generate an output y. The main network can also interact with the external memory through the read-write module.
2. The external memory unit M, where information is stored, usually consists of numerous memory segments organized according to a certain structure. As memory segments are often represented as vectors, the external memory unit can be represented as a vector $m_{1:N} = [m_1, \ldots, m_N]$. Most of the information is stored in the external memory unit, so it does not have to participate in the computation of the main network all the time.

3. The read module R, according to the query vector q_r generated by the main network, reads information $r = R(m_{1:N}, q_r)$ from the external memory unit.
4. The write module W, according to the query vector q_w generated by the main network and the information a that is about to be written, updates the external memory $m_{1:N} = W(m_{1:N}, q_w, a)$.

Each memory segment can be read from or written into the external memory in accordance with its address. To simulate associative memory in the human brain, it is necessary to locate information in a content-addressable manner and read or write it. This can be achieved by making use of the attention mechanism. To be more specific, the attention mechanism can help to implement soft addressing, i.e., calculating the distribution of the target information in all the memory segments rather than finding an absolute address.

By taking an analogy to computers' read operation in storage devices, calculating the distribution of attention is similar to the addressing process, and computing the weighted average of information is analogous to computers' reading process. Therefore, structured external memory is also a kind of associative memory, yet its structure and read-write operations are similar to the computer architecture.

The use of external memory "separates" parameters of neural networks from memory capacity, so with a slight increase in network parameters, network capacity can be augmented to a large extent. Accordingly, external memory is very important for processing large amounts of data in NLP tasks.

11.12   Pretrained Models (Transformer and BERT)

Conventional machine learning assumes that the training data and the testing data have the same distribution. If the assumption is unmet, the model learned from the training set will perform awkwardly on the test set. However, in practice, the cost of annotating data is so high that it is impossible to provide a target task with adequate training data following the same distribution. Therefore, if large amounts of training data have already been prepared for a relevant task, it can be assumed that due to the large data size, pretraining may produce some generalized knowledge helpful for the target task, though the training data and the data for the target task have different distributions. How to transfer generalizable knowledge obtained from the training data in relevant tasks to the target task is what transfer learning aims to find out.

To be more specific, assume a machine learning task T has a sample space $X \times Y$, where X and Y are the input space and the output space, respectively, and the probability density function of X and Y is $p(x, y)$. To put it simply, it can be assumed that X is a subset of a d-dimensional real number space $p(x, y) = P(X = x, Y = y)$, while Y is a discrete set. A sample space and its distribution can be called a domain: $D = (X, Y, p(x, y))$. Given two domains, if they differ in input space, output space, or probability distribution, they are perceived as different domains. From the perspective of statistical learning, a machine learning task T can be defined as how to calculate the conditional probability $p(y|x)$ in the domain D. Transfer learning refers to the process of knowledge transfer between two domains, i.e., how knowledge learned from source domains (SD) can be utilized to facilitate a learning task in a target domain (TD). Generally, the sample size of the training set in SD is much larger than the sample size in TD.

Transfer learning can fall into inductive transfer learning and transductive transfer learning, which correspond to two paradigms of machine learning, i.e., inductive learning and transductive learning. Conventional machine learning makes use of the inductive approach, which aims to learn a model with the smallest error probability from a training set. In contrast, transductive learning endeavors to learn a model with the smallest error probability from a given test set.

In inductive transfer learning, a general rule is learned from tasks in source domains and then is transferred to tasks in target domains. However, transductive transfer learning, a kind of sample-to-sample transfer learning, directly utilizes samples in both source domains and target domains.

- Inductive transfer learning. For inductive transfer learning, source domains and target domains share the same input space but not necessarily the same output space. Source tasks and target tasks are often different. Inductive transfer learning usually requires that source domains and target domains be relevant to each other and that source domains contain a large volume of annotated or unannotated training data.

  - When source domains contain unannotated data only, source tasks turn out to be unsupervised learning tasks. Through these unsupervised tasks, a representation can be learned and then transferred to target tasks. This kind of learning is close to self-taught learning and semisupervised learning. For example, due to the high cost of annotation, many NLP tasks are deficient in annotated data. As a result of the limited training sample size, deep-learning models cannot be made full use of. However, given that a large number of unannotated natural language texts can be obtained at a very low cost, one reasonable way to implement transfer learning is to transfer to a new task the knowledge learned in an unsupervised way from a large-scale text set. Pretrained vector representations, which may range from the word to the sentence level, can facilitate the accomplishment of NLP tasks.
  - When a large amount of annotated data can be found in source domains, the models trained on source domains can then be transferred to target domains. For example, in computer vision research, as many pretrained image classification models can be found in ImageNet, a large image dataset, the pretrained models can be transferred to target tasks.

For inductive transfer learning, due to the large size of the training data in source domains, the pretrained models can usually be generalized to target tasks.

Inductive transfer learning involves two types of transfer.

- The feature-based approach. The output generated by the pretrained models or by the hidden layers can be directly used as features and added to the learning models in target tasks. The learning models can be a shallow classifier or another neural network.
- The fine-tuning approach. Target tasks reuse part of the pretrained models, whose parameters can be fine-tuned.

If a pretrained model is a deep neural network, its transferability differs in different layers. Usually, the lower layers of a neural network can learn some shallow features for general use; the middle or higher layers can learn some advanced and abstract semantic features; and the last few layers can learn some features specific to a certain task. Therefore, based on the features of a target task and its pertinence to the source task, different layers of the pretrained model can be selected and transferred to the target task.

Generally, transferring a pretrained language model to the target task is usually better than learning from scratch. The reasons are as follows.

- The pretrained model often performs better than a randomly initialized model;
- During the training process, the pretrained model has a faster learning rate and a better convergence property than a model built from scratch;
- The pretrained model shows better final performance and greater generalizability.

- Transductive transfer learning.

    Transductive transfer learning is a sample-to-sample transfer learning approach that directly uses samples in source domains and target domains to implement transfer learning. Transductive transfer learning is usually based on the assumption that there are large amounts of annotated data in source domains, while target domains have no or few annotated data but contain plenty of unannotated data available at the training stage.

In NMT research, the deficiency of language data is a very serious issue, as an NMT system for commercial use generally requires a training corpus consisting of tens of millions of sentences. Without sufficient language data, the translation quality of NMT cannot be guaranteed. To solve this issue, researchers have made efforts to investigate the feasibility of NMT under the constraint of small-scale language data resources and have in recent years put forward a new NMT paradigm called pretrained language models (as shown in Fig. 11.55).

The new paradigm utilizes a large-scale corpus for pretraining purposes, builds pretrained language models, applies the models to small-scale task datasets, fine-tunes using inductive transfer learning, and develops models for downstream tasks.

The new paradigm enables researchers to focus on a specific task. In addition, pretrained language models generalizable to various tasks reduce the

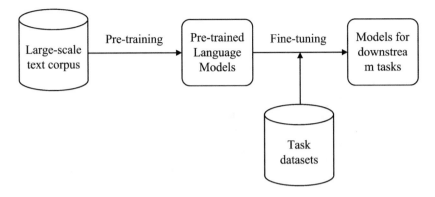

Fig. 11.55 A new NMT paradigm: a pretrained language model

difficulty of developing NMT systems and quicken the pace of innovation in NMT research.

Recently, Google researchers have compared the representations of different multilingual models. They have found that multilingual models can learn without external constraints shared representations of languages close to each other and that these representations are effective for cross-language transfer in downstream tasks.

Figure 11.56 shows that a multilingual model can learn without external constraints shared representations of similar languages. For example, without any external representation, the multilingual model can learn that Russia (ru), Byelorussian (be), Ukrainian (uk), Bulgarian (bg), Polish (pl), Croatian (hr), and Slovenian (sl) share the same language representation. The finding from machine learning agrees with human beings' linguistic knowledge that all these languages belong to Slavic languages.

In 2009, Google, based on language resources consisting of over 25 billion sentence pairs from 103 languages and more than 50 billion parameters, trained an NMT model breaking the limit in the field of multilingual NMT research.[12] The model was called the Massively Multilingual Massive Neural Machine Translation Model (the M4 model for short), which could improve translation quality to a large extent in both low-resource and high-resource languages, adapt easily to a different domain or language, and exhibit high efficiency in cross-language downstream transfer tasks. What exciting improvement it was!

In China, a company called NiuTrans, as it states on its website, can implement machine translation on more than 100 languages.

The languages include the official languages of UN members and countries and regions along the "Belt and Road." To date, no translation engine can translate more languages than the one provided by NiuTrans (Fig. 11.57).

---

[12] https://arxiv.org/pdf/1907.05019.pdf.

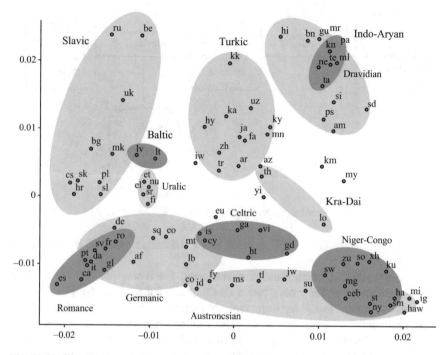

Fig. 11.56 Visualization of representation clustering of 103 languages

Although NLP is so complicated that it is still an arduous task to implement fully automated high-quality machine translation, initial success has already been achieved.

In June 2017, Google, in *Attention is All You Need*, proposed a pretrained language model called Transformer, which was completely built on the basis of the attention mechanism. Transformer abandoned RNNs or CNNs kept in the other models using the attention mechanism. Due to its excellent performance in various tasks, it became a very important baseline model in natural language understanding and machine translation.

Prior to the development of Transformer, most NMT systems were based on RNNs.

RNNs utilize the asynchronous sequence-to-sequence model. For example, in English–Chinese machine translation, an RNN encoder can encode an input sentence *I have a pen*, produce attention scores, assign attention weights, obtain the attention output through attention distribution, and finally decode the information with the help of an RNN decoder into a Chinese sentence "我有一支钢笔" (/Wo you yi zhi gang bi/; I have a pen.) (Fig. 11.58).

Information contained in a hidden layer of RNNs derives from the current input layer and the preceding stage. In other words, information generated in the preceding stage serves as an input into the current input layer. Although RNNs have a powerful capacity to build models for sequences, training the asynchronous sequence-to-

Supporting Live Translation of Minority Languages in China and Other 110-odd Languages

A B C D	E F G H I	J K L M N	P Q R S	T U V W X Y Z
Afrikannas	English	Japanese	Papiamento	Tahitian
Albanian	Esperanto	Javanese	Pashto	Tajik
Amharic	Estonian	Kannada	Perisan	Tamil
Arabic	Fijian	Kazakh	Polish	Tatar
Armenian	Filipino	Kazakh(Cyrillic)	Portuguese	Telugu
Azerbaijani	Finnish	Khmer	Punjabi	Tjao
Bashkir	French	Korean	Queretaro Otomi	Tibetic
Basque	Frisian	Kurdish	Romanian	Tongan
Belarusian	Galician	Kyrgyz	Russian	Turkish
Bengali	Georgian	Lao	Samoan	Udmurt
Bosnian	German	Latin	Scottish Gaelic	Ukrainian
Bulgarian	Greek	Latvian	Serbian	Urdu
Burmese	Gujarati	Lithuanian	Sesotho	Uyghur
Cantonese	Haitian Creole	Luxembourgish	Shona	Uzbek
Catalan	Hausa	Macedonian	Sindhi	Vietnamese
Cebuano	Hawaiian	Malagasy	Sinhalese	Welsh
Chewa	Hebrew	Malay	Slovak	Xhosa
Chinese(Simplified)	Hill Mari	Malayalam	Slovenian	Yiddish
Chinese(Traditional)	Hindi	Maltese	Somali	Yoruba
Corisican	Hmong	Maori	Spanish	Yucatec Maya
Croatian	Hungarian	Marathi	Sundanese	Zulu
Czech	Icelandic	Mari	Swahili	
Danish	Igbo	Mongolian(Cyrillic)	Swedish	
Dutch	Indonesian	Nepali		
	Irish	Norwegian		
	Italian			

Fig. 11.57 Languages NiuTrans can handle to implement machine translation

sequence model takes too much time. If the input is a long sentence, more processing steps are needed. In addition, the complex recurrent structure also makes it difficult to train a machine translation model. As a result, the performance of RNNs is less satisfying.

Compared with RNNs, Transformer does not require recursion but processes all the words or symbols in a parallel manner and, at the same time, uses the attention mechanism to associate context with some long-distance words. By processing all the words in a parallel manner and enabling each word to pay attention in multiple steps to the other words in the same sentence, Transformer can be trained at a faster speed and with a better performance than RNNs. The structure of Transformer is shown in Fig. 11.59.

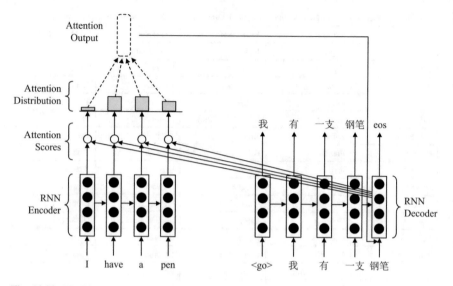

Fig. 11.58 Machine translation based on the RNN model

In Fig. 11.59, the left part is the encoder, while the right part represents the decoder.

The encoder consists of six identical layers ($N = 6$), each of which in turn is composed of two sublayers (Fig. 11.60). The first sublayer includes a multi-head attention layer, and the second sublayer includes a fully connected feed forward layer. Both sublayers include the operations of addition (abbreviated as Add) and normalization (Norm for short).

When machine translation is performed, a source sentence, after being inputted into the encoder, will first enter the multi-head attention layer, which can help the encoder encode each word in the source sentence and distribute attention to the remaining words. The output of the multi-head attention layer can be sent to a feed forward neural network shared by each word in the source sentence.

As in most NLP systems, each input word in neural machine translation will be transformed with the help of a word embedding algorithm into a word vector. In *Attention Is All You Need*, each source word was embedded into a 512-dimensional vector. Therefore, in our discussion here, each word is also embedded into a 512-dimensional vector. Although word embedding takes place only in the lowest-layer encoder, all the encoders need to receive a vector list, each vector of which has 512 dimensions. The lowest-layer encoder takes word vectors as input, while encoders in other layers take as input the output (i.e., the vector list) generated by the encoder in the immediately preceding layer. The size of the vector list is a parameter usually set to be the length of the longest sentence in the training set.

After word embedding is performed on the input sequence, each source word will pass the multi-head attention layers and the feed forward layers in the encoder.

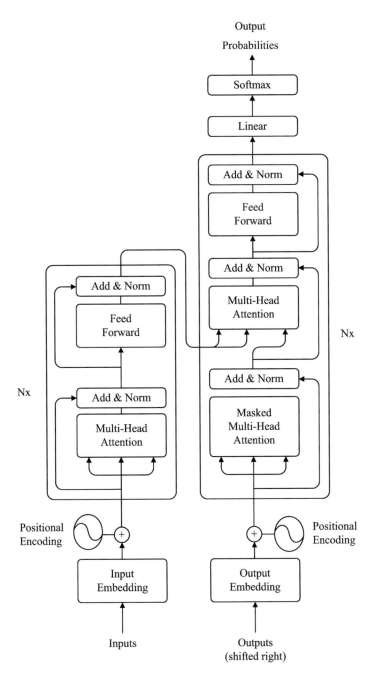

Fig. 11.59 The structure of Transformer

Fig. 11.60 The encoder in Transformer ($N = 6$)

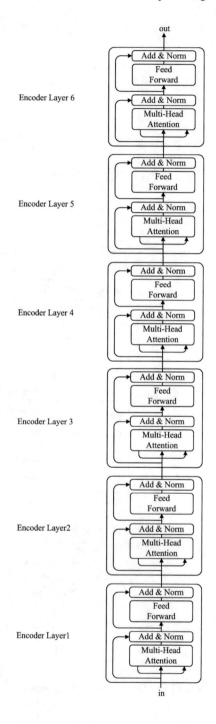

The multi-head attention layers employ the self-attention mechanism so that the close relationships among words can be represented.

For example, for an English sentence "The law will never be perfect, but its application should be just – this is what we are missing, in my opinion," the self-attention mechanism can help to establish the following lexical connections.

Figure 11.61 demonstrates that *Law*, *application*, *missing*, and *opinion* are most closely related to the other words in this sentence.

As the multi-head attention layers can also combine related words with the word that is currently processed, the machine translation model is more capable of paying attention to different positions in a sentence.

For instance, assume that an input English sentence is "*The animal didn't cross the street because it was too tired.*" What does *it* refer to? Does *it* refer to the *animal* or the *street*? Human beings can easily resolve *it* to the *animal*, because only animals can feel tired. However, this poses a big problem for algorithms. As Transformer is equipped with multi-head attention layers, when the word *it* is processed, the layers can combine *it* with all the related words so that a much closer relation can be established between *it* and *animal*.

In Fig. 11.62, the self-attention mechanism can help to establish the connections between *it* and other related words. When Encoder Layer 5 (#5) encodes *it*, the self-attention mechanism will focus on *the animal* and encode part of the representation of *the animal* into that of *it*. It can be easily found in Fig. 11.62 that *the animal* is most closely related to *it*.

In the self-attention mechanism, the intensity of the attention is calculated according to three vectors: the Query vector (Q for short), the Key vector (K for short), and the Value vector (V for short). The formula involved is as follows.

$$\text{Attention}\,(Q, K, V) = \text{soft max}\left(\frac{QK^T}{\sqrt{d_k}}\right)V$$

In this formula, Q, K, and V represent the query vector, the key vector, and the value vector, respectively, and d is the dimension of Transformer.

The decoder also consists of six ($N = 6$) identical layers, but they differ from the layers of the encoder. Each layer of the decoder includes three sublayers, i.e., a multi-head self-attention layer, a fully connected feed forward layer, and a masked multi-head attention layer.

The reason why the last layer is called a masked layer is that words generated later should not be used when the machine translation model is trained. When processing the current word in the training stage, the model cannot make use of the words generated later, so these words should be masked. The masked multi-head attention layer keeps the decoder from using subsequent information. In other words, for a sequence at the time step t, the output of the decoder can only rely on the output generated before t.

As Transformer utilizes no RNN, whose greatest strength lies in its capability to represent time series data and attach importance to the position of the object being

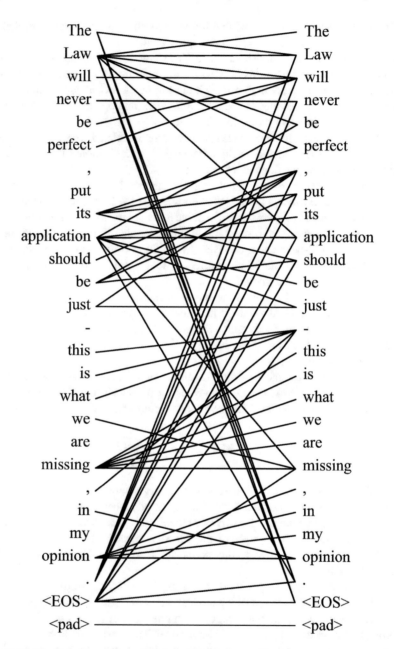

Fig. 11.61 The lexical connections built by a self-attention mechanism

processed, positional encoding (PE for short) is added to the input embedding during encoding and to the output embedding during decoding. Positions can be calculated by using the following formula.

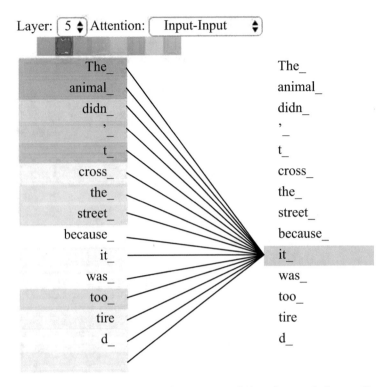

Fig. 11.62 The connections established between *it* and the other words by a self-attention mechanism

$$PE_{(pos,2i)} = sin(pos/10000^{2i/d_{model}})$$
$$PE_{(pos,2i+1)} = cos(pos/10000^{2i/d_{model}})$$

In the formula above, *sin* and *cos* are two trigonometric functions, while *pos*, *i*, PE, and d_{model} represent word position, the current dimension, position, and dimension of the model, respectively. When positional encodings are conducted, the two functions can be transformed into each other with the help of linear transformation.

When machine translation is implemented, the input data about the source language are processed by the encoder and the decoder, and then subsequently normalized by the linear transformation layer (the linear layer for short) and the softmax layer. After that, the output probabilities of target language expressions can be obtained (Fig. 11.63).

The linear layer is a simple fully connected neural network that can project the vector generated by the decoder into another vector called logits. Suppose the model learns 10,000 different English words from the training set, the logits vector will contain 10,000 elements, each of which corresponds to the score of an English word.

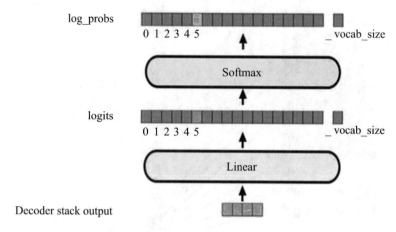

Fig. 11.63 The linear transformation layer and the softmax layer

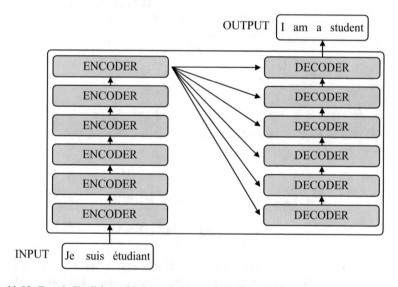

Fig. 11.64 French–English machine translation made by Transformer

After that, the softmax layer can transform the scores of the words into different probabilities. Finally, the element that carries the highest probability will be selected, and the corresponding word will serve as the output at the current time step.

The collaboration between the six-layer encoder and the six-layer decoder in Transformer is presented in Fig. 11.64. For instance, for French–English machine translation, a French sentence "Je suit étudiant," after being processed by Transformer, can be transformed into its English equivalent "I am a student" at the output end.

In July 2018, Google, in a paper entitled *Universal Transformer*, elaborated on how its researchers improved Transformer and enhanced the speed of machine translation. The improved version of Transformer could run faster than RNNs and show superior performance to the original version.

In 2019, Google built Bidirectional Encoder Representations from Transformers (BERT), which exhibited the best performance in 11 NLP tests and brought a landmark change to NLP. BERT marked the latest greatest achievement in the field of NLP.

Based on the structure of Transformer, BERT is a bidirectional Transformer encoder that aims to pretrain deep bidirectional representations from unannotated texts by joint calculation of left and right context. Accordingly, BERT, after pretraining and with only one additional output layer, can conduct fine-tuning to generate the latest models for various NLP tasks. BERT is pretrained using English Wikipedia (2.5 billion words) and BooksCorpus (800 million words). As a deep bidirectional model, BERT utilizes information on both left and right context in pretraining.

BERT's most salient feature is bidirectionality, which can be exemplified by the following two sentences.

We went to the river **bank**.
I need to go to **bank** to make a deposit.

The word *bank* can denote either an organization providing financial services or one side of a river.

The left context of *bank* in the above two sentences, i.e.

We went to the river _____
I need to go to _____

may allow readers to predict that the first *bank* means one side of a river because the first sentence contains a word *river*. However, it will be wrong if readers guess that the second *bank* carries the same meaning as *bank* in the first sentence. Therefore, the left context alone cannot help readers to make a correct prediction.

If only the right context of *bank* in the two sentences is investigated, i.e.

.
to make a deposit.

the word *bank* in the second sentence is predicted to denote a financial organization, because the sentence includes *deposit*. However, it is wrong if the word *bank* in the first sentence is also inferred to mean a financial organization. Accordingly, the right context alone cannot help readers to make a correct prediction either.

The architecture of BERT is given in Fig. 11.65.

In Fig. 11.65, E, Trm, and T represent embedding, transformer block, and token, respectively. It is not difficult to see that bidirectional encoder representations are used in BERT.

BERT provides a simple model ($BERT_{base}$) and a complex model ($BERT_{large}$) with the following hyperparameters.

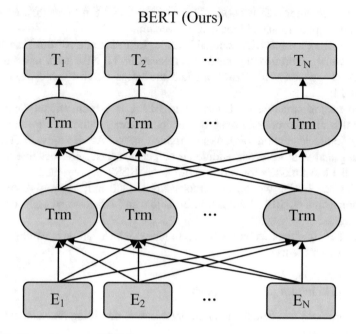

Fig. 11.65 The architecture of BERT

- $\text{BERT}_{\text{base}}$: $L = 12$, $H = 768$, $A = 12$, the total number of parameters amounts to 110 M;
- $\text{BERT}_{\text{large}}$: $L = 24$, $H = 1024$, $A = 16$, the total number of parameters amounts to 340 M;

For the hyperparameters listed above, L, A, and H represent the number of layers (i.e. the number of Transformer blocks, which are abbreviated as Trm), the number of self-attention heads in multi-head attention, and the number of hidden layers.

The structure of the two models can be illustrated with Fig. 11.66.

Each input embedding E consists of three embeddings:

1. Position embeddings: BERT learns and uses position embeddings to indicate the position of a word in a sentence, such as E_1, E_2, and E_3.
2. Segment embeddings: BERT can use sentence pairs as input for question answering tasks. After learning the embeddings of the first and second sentences, BERT can help question answering models to distinguish the two, such as E_A, and E_B.
3. Token embeddings: BERT can learn the embeddings of some special tokens from WordPiece.

As shown in Fig. 11.67, the input representations of BERT are the sum of the position embeddings, the segment embeddings, and the token embeddings.

These steps make BERT more generalizable. A slight modification of the model during the pretraining stage enables BERT to handle various NLP tasks.

Fig. 11.66 BERT$_{base}$ and
BERT$_{large}$

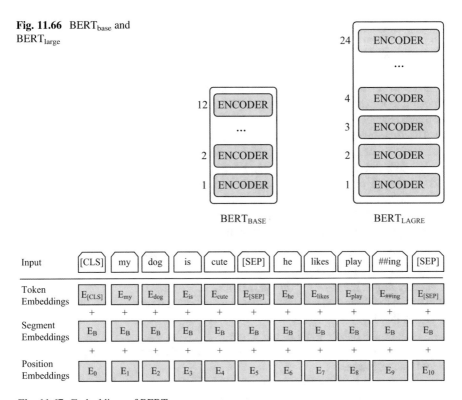

Fig. 11.67 Embeddings of BERT

BERT can support Chinese and more than 100 languages used in Wikipedia.

When running BERT, users should first implement embedding with WordPiece and a 30,000 token vocabulary and employ the symbol ## to denote participles. After that, positional embeddings are obtained, which can support sequences with a maximum length of 512 tokens. The first token of each sequence (sentence pairs are packed into one sequence) is a special classification embedding (denoted as [CLS]). Two methods are utilized to differentiate sentences. First, sentences are separated with a special token ([SEP]). Second, "E_A" (referring to sentence A) and "E_B" (referring to sentence B) are embedded in each token in the first and second sentences, respectively. If the input is a single sentence, only "sentence A" is added. In Fig. 11.67, the input is as follows.

[CLS] my dog is cute [SEP] he likes play ##ing [SEP]

Pretraining BERT also makes use of the masked language model (MLM).

To train a deep bidirectional representation, BERT uses a simple method to randomly mask some of the input tokens and then predict those masked tokens only. The whole process is called MLM or Cloze.

During the pretraining stage, the final hidden vectors corresponding to masked tokens are inputted into a softmax layer built on the vocabulary, as in a standard language model. In all experiments over BERT, 15% of WordPiece tokens in each sequence are masked at random and denoted as [MASK]. Therefore, only those masked words instead of the entire input need to be predicted.

Although masked tokens can help BERT to perform bidirectional pretraining, this approach has two problems.

The first problem is the mismatch between pretraining and fine-tuning because the mask tokens ([MASK]) are invisible during fine-tuning. To solve this issue, BERT does not always replace masked words with the [MASK] token. The training data generator chooses 15% of the tokens randomly. For example, in an English sentence "my dog is hairy," the token used to mask words may be "hairy."

However, BERT does not always replace the selected word "hairy" with the [MASK] token but carries out the following steps through the data generator.

1. 80% of the time: replacing the selected word with the [MASK] token, as shown by the following example.

   my dog is hairy → my dog is [MASK]
2. 10% of the time: replacing the selected word with a random word, like "apple" in the following.

   my dog is hairy → my dog is apple
3. 10% of the time: keeping the selected word unchanged, as exemplified by the following instance.

   my dog is hairy → my dog is hairy

   The purpose of this treatment is to render the representation more likely to be the observed word "hairy."

Transformer's encoder knows neither which words need to be predicted nor which words have been replaced with random words, so it has to rely on the distributional contextual representation of each input token. In addition, as random replacement occurs in only 1.5% (10% of 15%) of all tokens, the tiny proportion seems to have little influence on the language understanding ability of BERT.

The second problem is that more pretraining steps are possibly required for BERT to converge, as prediction is made by MLM only on 15% of all the tokens in each round of pretraining. Experiments show that BERT's MLM does converge more slowly than the model that predicts each token in a left-to-right manner. However, generally speaking, the improvements made by MLM far exceed the increased pretraining cost.

BERT can also predict the next sentence. Many downstream tasks in NLP, such as question answering (QA) and natural language inference (NLI), require an understanding of the relationship between two sentences.

To understand the relationship between two sentences, a binarized next-sentence-prediction task can be pretrained on the basis of a monolingual corpus.

To be more specific, when sentence A and sentence B are used as pretraining samples, the next sentence following sentence A can be sentence B with a probability of 50% or a sentence randomly extracted from the corpus with a probability of 50%.

Take the following sentence pairs for example.

Input = [CLS] the man went to [MASK] store [SEP]
he bought a gallon [MASK] milk [SEP]

As the former sentence "[CLS] the man went to [MASK] store [SEP]" is probably semantically related to the latter sentence "he bought a gallon [MASK] milk [SEP]", the latter one can be labeled with "IsNext", which means that the latter is probably the Next of the former.

Another instance is the following sentence pair.

Input = [CLS] the man [MASK] to the store [SEP]
penguin [MASK] are flight ##less birds [SEP]

Having no semantic relationship with the former sentence "Input = [CLS] the man [MASK] to the store [SEP]", the latter sentence "penguin [MASK] are flight ##less birds [SEP]" can be labeled with "NotNext", which means that the latter one is unlikely to be the Next of the former one.

BERT can select NotNext sentences at random. Finally, the pretrained model can achieve an accuracy of 97–98% in this downstream task.

The combination of these pretraining steps equips BERT with greater generalizability so that BERT can be easily applied to many NLP downstream tasks without any significant change in its structure.

In recent years, BERT has made astonishing achievements in SQuAD1.1, the top reading comprehension test for machines. It outperforms human beings in all indicators. In addition, BERT scores the highest on 11 NLP tests, improving the baseline of GLUE to 80.4% (with an absolute increase of 7.6%) and increasing the accuracy of MultiNLI to 86.7% (with an absolute increase of 5.6%). How exciting the achievements are!

As mentioned previously, BERT is pretrained on the basis of big data, which consists of English Wikipedia (2.5 billion words) and BooksCorpus (800 million words). Only when such large-scale data are available can the functions of BERT be performed to the full extent.

A complete set of techniques has been developed in NLP in the last 2 years, including word embedding, encoder-decoder end-to-end language models, the attention mechanism, Transformer, and the pretraining of BERT. These techniques have achieved better performance in important NLP tasks, such as information retrieval, reading comprehension, machine translation, text classification, question answering, human computer dialogue, chatbot, information extraction, text summarization, text generation, and so on. The improvement suggests that NLP has entered a period of large-scale industrialization.

Reviewing the development of NLP reveals that its paradigm, namely, the working pattern of NLP systems, has undergone three shifts and is now experiencing the fourth one.

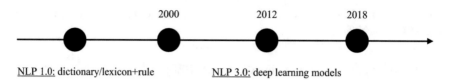

Fig. 11.68 The paradigm shifts of NLP

The first shift is the "dictionary/lexicon + rule" paradigm, which took place before the 1990s.

The second shift is the "data driven + statistical machine learning" paradigm (called statistical models for short) from the 1990s to 2012.

The third shift started in 2012, when the "end-to-end neural network deep learning" paradigm (called deep learning models for short) gained popularity.

Around 2018, researchers began to focus on the "pretraining + fine-tuning" paradigm. In this paradigm, the knowledge obtained through pretraining (similar to teachers) can be fine-tuned for downstream tasks (similar to students). Therefore, this paradigm is also called the "teacher–student learning" paradigm. As the fourth NLP paradigm, it represents the future development of NLP (Fig. 11.68).

The principle of the current mainstream NLP paradigm, i.e., the "pretraining + fine-tuning" paradigm represented by BERT, is dividing the training of a large and deep end-to-end neural network into two steps. First, most parameters are pretrained on large-scale text data through unsupervised (self-supervised) learning. After that, fine-tuning is performed for a specific NLP task by including task-related neural networks, whose parameters are much fewer than the parameters in pretraining and can be adjusted based on the annotated data for the downstream task. Therefore, the fourth paradigm can also be called pretraining models.

In this manner, the language knowledge obtained through pretraining from large-scale text data can be transferred to downstream natural language processing and understanding tasks. Pretrained models have shown outstanding performance in nearly all NLP downstream tasks, including both natural language understanding (NLU) and natural language generation (NLG) tasks. Additionally, pretrained models have expanded from monolingual to multilingual and multimodal pretrained models, demonstrating excellent performance in related downstream tasks and proving the great effectiveness of the fourth paradigm.

Since BERT and GPT were developed in 2019, pretrained models have flourished. New pretrained models are released almost every month and have exerted a powerful impact on research and application.

Generally, pretrained models exhibit the following trends.

First, pretrained models become increasingly large, containing an increasing number of parameters. An instance is that the number of parameters has grown from 93 M in EMLo to 340 M in BERT to 1.5 B in GPT-2 (OpemAI) and to 11 B in T5 (Google).

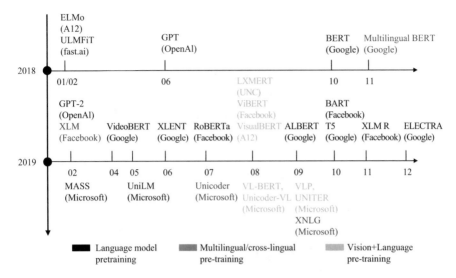

Fig. 11.69 The development history of pretraining

Second, increasing amounts of text data are used in pretraining. BERT (Google) uses merely 16 GB of text data, while the data employed in RoBERTa (Facebook) increase to 160 GB. However, the two systems are dwarfed by T5 (Google), which makes use of 750 GB of text data.

Third, pretraining is applied to a growing number of tasks. Pretraining models were initially used in NLU tasks and later in NLG tasks. The latest pretrained models, such as UniLM (Microsoft), T5 (Google), and BART (Facebook), can simultaneously support NLU and NLG tasks.

Due to the increasingly large size of pretrained models, these models can hardly meet the demand of high concurrency and low response speed in real engineering programs and reap limited economic benefits. Therefore, model compression or knowledge distillation are needed in real tasks to build small-scale models that can run fast as well as effectively. Such a small-scale model can also be built during training. This is currently an important and heated topic in NLP research.

In 2018, pretrained models sprang up one after another, including ELMo, ULMFiT, GPT (OpneAI), BERT (Google), Multilingual BERT (Google). In 2019, some other pretrained models were devised, such as GPT-2 (OpneAI), VideoBERT (Google), XLNet (Google), RoBERTa (Facebook), BART (Facebook), T5 (Google), and XLM R (Facebook). The development of pretraining is shown in Fig. 11.69.

In May 2019, MSRA (Microsoft Research Asia) released the latest pretrained language model, called Unified Language Model pretrained (UniLM). This model was characterized by two key innovations. One was the unified pretraining framework, which enabled one model to simultaneously support NLU and NLG tasks. In contrast, previous pretrained models mostly aimed at NLU tasks. The other innovation was its pretraining approach, which used partially self-regressive models. This

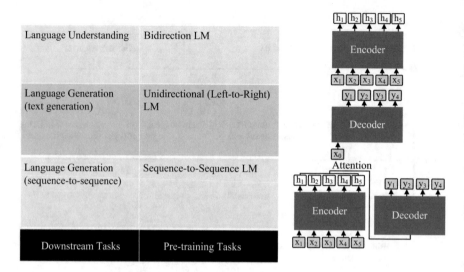

Downstream Tasks	Pre-training Tasks
Language Understanding	Bidirection LM
Language Generation (text generation)	Unidirectional (Left-to-Right) LM
Language Generation (sequence-to-sequence)	Sequence-to-Sequence LM

Fig. 11.70 Downstream tasks in NLP

rendered the construction of a better natural language pretrained model more efficient.

The unified language modeling mechanism of UniLM enables one model to simultaneously support different downstream tasks and pretraining tasks. Generally, these downstream tasks are of three types.

1. NLU tasks, such as text classification, question-answering, and named entity recognition;
2. Long text generation tasks, such as news or story generation tasks;
3. Sequence-to-sequence generation tasks include summarization, retelling, dialogue generation, machine translation, and so on.

UniLM can pretrain models specific to a downstream task. Examples are bidirectional language models for NLU downstream tasks, unidirectional language models for long text generation tasks, and sequence-to-sequence language models for sequence-to-sequence language generation tasks.

These different downstream tasks and pretraining tasks correspond to different neural network architectures. For instance, as illustrated in Fig. 11.70, the bidirectional language model for NLU corresponds to the bidirectional encoder for NLU; the unidirectional language model for long text generation tasks corresponds to the unidirectional decoder for long text generation; and the sequence-to-sequence language model corresponds to the sequence-to-sequence bidirectional encoder, the unidirectional decoder, and the related attention mechanism.

UniLM uses Transformer's multilayered network architecture, which is currently widely used in NLP and pretraining. The core of the architecture is to control the context of each word in a text through self-attention masks so that one model can

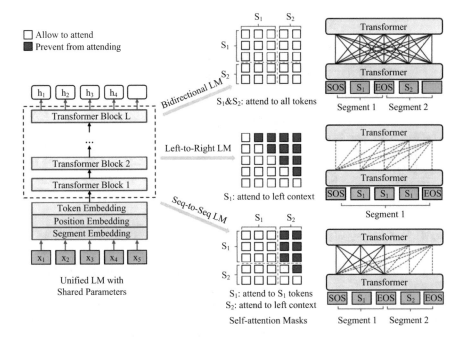

Fig. 11.71 The network structure of UniLM

simultaneously support the pretraining of bidirectional LM, left-to-right LM, and sequence-to-sequence LM. Therefore, the same self-attention masks can be applied to various tasks. In addition, NLU and NLG downstream tasks can also be supported simultaneously through fine-tuning. Before training, UniLM keeps its parameters unchanged, so the parameters can be shared and the text representations that are learned can be generalized to various tasks. Additionally, overfitting can be avoided in single tasks.

The network structure of UniLM is demonstrated in Fig. 11.71.

Compared with other models, UniLM has achieved the best performance in a series of NLU and NLG tasks. In October 2019, MSRA's UniLM and machine reading comprehension technology won the Award of World Leading Internet Scientific and Technological Achievements at the Sixth World Internet Conference.

The other feature of the fourth paradigm of NLP is the construction of cross-language pretrained models.

Apart from the lack of cross-task resources, cross-language resource insufficiency can also be remedied with the help of pretrained models. Specifically, due to limited project demands and expensive annotated data, adequate annotated data can only be found for very few languages (such as English) in NLP research, while no or few annotated data are available for other languages. This leads to the problem of cross-language resource insufficiency. How to make use of the models that are built on the annotated data in a specific language and transfer the knowledge learned

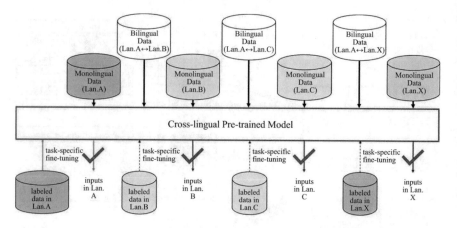

Fig. 11.72 Cross-lingual pretraining models

to other languages is a difficult problem that needs to be addressed in pretraining research.

Cross-language pretraining is an effective way to alleviate the issue of insufficient language resources. Given monolingual corpora in multiple languages and bilingual corpora composed of sentence pairs from different languages, cross-language pretraining can help to learn the correspondence between different languages so that vectors representing the same meaning in different languages can be stored in the same semantic space. In that way, fine-tuning can be implemented for a specific downstream task on pretrained models that have been built using a large volume of annotated data in some language. The fine-tuned models can then directly receive data in another language as input. If a small amount of annotated data is available in that language in the downstream task, fine-tuning can be implemented again to improve system performance.

Figure 11.72 shows that, based on monolingual and bilingual data, task-specific fine-tuning can be implemented on cross-lingual pretrained models so that annotated data in various languages can be obtained.

Additionally, MSRA proposed a joint encoding model called Unicoder, which demonstrated a powerful ability to perform cross-language understanding tasks by introducing five cross-language tasks into pretraining.

The first pretraining task, based on the shared model parameters and multilingual glossaries, aims to perform the task of masked language models on input sequences from different languages. This task can map vectors representing the same meaning in different languages to the same semantic space.

The second pretraining task endeavors to combine a bilingual sentence pair into a new input sequence and perform the task of masked language models on the new sequence. By explicitly using bilingual aligned information as supervision signals, the cross-lingual pretrained model, Unicoder, can learn better the correspondence between different languages and develop more powerful cross-language understanding ability.

Text	Judgments	Hypothesis
A man inspects the uniform of a figure in some East Asian County.	Contradiction CCCCC	The man is sleeping
An older and younger man smiling.	Neutral NNENN	Two men are smiling and laughing at the cats playing on the floor.
A black race car starts up in front of a crowd of people.	Contradiction CCCCC	A man is driving down a lonely road.
A soccer game with multiple males playing.	Entailment EEEEE	Some men are playing a sport.
A smiling costumed woman is holding an umbrella.	Neutral NNECN	A happy woman in a fairy costume holds and umbrella.

Fig. 11.73   Natural language inference

The next pretraining task also receives a bilingual sentence pair as input. This task first calculates the attention score for every target-source word pair in a bilingual sentence pair. After that, each source word is represented as the weighted sum of vectors of all the target words to generate a vector representation of the source sentence. Finally, according to the newly generated vector representation, the original source sentence sequence is restored.

The fourth pretraining task receives two sentences from various languages as input and tries to determine whether the two sentences are translations of each other. Through this task, Unicoder can learn the correspondence between different languages at the sentence level.

The input of the fifth pretraining task is a paragraph consisting of sentences from multiple languages. Based on this task, the task of masked language models is performed.

Grounded on the five cross-language pretraining tasks, Unicoder can learn the semantic correspondence between different languages to dilute the differences and blur the distinctions among these languages. As a result, Unicoder is able to train models for cross-language downstream tasks.

The effectiveness of Unicoder has been confirmed in experiments related to cross-lingual natural language inference (XNLI) tasks.

Natural language inference (NLI) tasks aim to identify the relationship between two input sentences. The output of such tasks can be entailment (E), contradiction (C), and neutral (N).

Figure 11.73 shows that the meaning of "A man inspects the uniform of a figure in some East country" contradicts that of "The man is sleeping" and that the five scores are CCCCC. Therefore, the relationship between the two sentences is judged to be C (contradiction). Take another sentence, "Some men are playing a sport," for example. It entails the sentence "A soccer game with multiple males playing." As the five scores are EEEEE, their relationship is identified as E (entailment). A third example is that the semantic relationship between the sentence "Two men are smiling and laughing at the cats playing on the floor" and the sentence "An older

Language	Premise/Hypothesis	Genre	
English	You don't have to stay there. You can leave.	Face-To-Face	Entailment
French	La figure 4 montrel la courbed'offre des services de partage de travaux. Les services de partage de travaux on tune offer variable.	Government	Entailment
Spanish	Y se estremeció con el recuerdo. El pensamientosobre el acontecimientohizosuestremecimiento.	Fiction	Entailment
German	Während der Depression war es die ärmsteGegend, kurzvor dem Hungertod. Die Weltwirtschaftskrisedauertemehralszehn Jahre an.	Travel	Neutral
Swahili	Ni silahayaplastikiyaplastikiyamojakwamojainayopigarisasi. Inadumu Zaidi kulikosilahayachuma.	Telephone	Neutral
Russian	И мызанимаемсязтимуженаиротяжении 85 лет. Мытольконачализтимзаниматься.	Letters	Contradiction
Chese	让我告诉你，美国人最终如何看待你作为独立顾问的表现。 美国人完全不知道您是独立律师。	Slate	Contradiction
Arabic	نحناج الوكالات لأن تكون قادرة على قياس مستويات النجاح. لا يمكنالللوكانات أ اتعرف ما إذا كانت ناجحة أم لا	Nine-Eleven	Contradiction

Fig. 11.74 Cross-lingual natural language inference

and younger man smiling" is found to be NNENN. As there are four Ns (neutral) and one E (entailment), the relationship is judged to be N (neutral).

XNLI can implement natural language inference tasks in multiple languages. Specifically, in XNLI, the English language has a training set, while other languages only have a validation set and a test set. The purpose of the design is to determine whether the knowledge learned from the English training set can be transferred to other languages. The experimental results are shown in Fig. 11.74.

In Fig. 11.74, the four columns are Language, Premise/Hypothesis, Genre, and Label. In the English training set, the relationship between the sentence "You don't have to stay here" and the sentence "You can leave" is labeled Entailment. When the knowledge learned from the English training set is transferred to the validation set and the test set of other languages, inference can then be made for these languages (including French, Spanish, German, Swahili, Russian, Chinese, and Arabic).

By using more multilingual pretraining tasks, the performance of Unicoder is much better than that of Multilingual BERT and XLM. The experiment results are given in Fig. 11.75.

Figure 11.75 shows that Unicoder outperforms Multilingual BERT and XLM in terms of TRANSLATE-TRAIN, TRANSLATE-TEST, Cross-lingual TEST, and Multilanguage Fine-tuning.

As a new paradigm of NLP research in the deep-learning era, the "pretraining + fine-tuning" paradigm not only brings the performance of NLP models to a new level but also promotes to a large extent the application of the models to real tasks.

	en	fr	es	de	el	bg	ru	tr	ar	vi	th	zh	hi	sw	ur	average
Machine translate at training (TRANSLATE-TRAIN)																
Conneau et al. (2018)	73.7	68.3	68.8	66.5	66.4	67.4	66.5	64.5	65.8	66.0	62.8	67.0	621.	58.2	56.6	65.4
Multilingual BERT (Devlin et al., 2018)	81.9	-	77.8	75.9	-	-	-	-	70.7	-	-	76.6	-	-	61.6	-
Multilingual BERT from Wu and Dredze 2019	82.1	76.9	78.5	74.8	72.1	75.4	74.3	70.6	70.8	67.8	63.2	76.2	65.3	65.3	60.6	71.6
XLM (Lample and Conneau, 2019)	85.0	80.2	80.8	80.3	78.1	79.3	78.1	74.7	76.5	76.6	75.5	78.6	72.3	70.9	63.2	76.7
Unicoder	85.1	80.0	81.1	79.9	77.7	80.2	77.9	75.3	76.7	76.4	75.2	79.4	71.8	71.8	64.5	76.9
Machine translate at test (TRANSLATE-TEST)																
Conneau et al. (2018)	73.7	70.4	70.7	68.7	69.1	70.4	67.8	66.3	66.8	66.5	64.4	68.3	64.2	61.8	59.3	67.2
Multilingual BERT (Devlin et al., 2018)	81.4	-	74.9	74.4	-	-	-	-	70.1	-	-	70.1	-	-	62.1	-
XLM (Lample and Conneau, 2019)	85.0	79.0	79.5	78.1	77.8	77.6	75.5	73.7	73.7	70.8	70.4	73.6	69.0	64.7	65.1	74.2
Unicoder	85.1	80.1	80.3	78.2	77.5	78.0	76.2	73.3	73.9	72.8	71.6	74.1	70.3	65.2	66.3	74.9
Evaluation of cross lingual sentence encoders (Cross-lingual TEST)																
Conneau et al. (2018)	73.7	67.7	68.7	67.7	68.9	67.9	65.4	64.2	64.8	66.4	64.1	65.8	64.1	55.7	58.4	65.6
Multilingual BERT (Devlin et al., 2018)	81.4	-	74.3	70.5	-	-	-	-	62.1	-	-	63.8	-	-	58.3	-
Multilingual BERT from Wu and Dredze 2019	82.1	73.8	74.3	71.1	66.4	68.9	79	61.6	64.9	69.5	55.8	69.3	60.0	50.4	58.0	66.3
Artetxe and Schwenk (2018)	73.9	71.9	72.9	72.6	73.1	74.2	71.5	69.7	71.4	72.0	69.2	71.4	65.5	62.2	61.0	70.2
XLM (Lample and Conneau, 2019)	85.0	78.7	78.9	77.8	76.6	77.4	75.3	72.5	73.1	76.1	73.2	76.5	69.6	68.4	67.3	75.1
Unicoder	85.1	79.0	79.4	77.8	77.2	77.2	76.3	72.8	73.5	76.4	73.6	76.2	69.4	69.7	66.7	75.4
Multi-language Fine-tuning																
XLM (Lample and Conneau, 2019)	85.0	80.8	81.3	80.3	79.1	80.9	78.3	75.6	77.6	78.5	76.0	79.5	72.9	72.8	68.5	77.8
Unicoder w/o Word Recovery	85.2	80.5	81.8	80.9	79.7	81.1	79.3	76.2	78.2	78.5	76.4	79.7	73.4	73.6	68.8	78.2
Unicoder w/o Paraphrase Classification	85.5	81.1	82.0	81.1	80.0	81.3	79.6	76.6	78.2	78.2	75.9	79.9	73.7	74.2	69.3	78.4
Unicoder w/o Cross-lingual Language Model	85.5	81.9	81.8	80.5	80.5	81.0	79.3	76.4	78.1	78.3	76.3	79.6	72.9	73.0	68.7	78.3
Unicoder	**85.6**	**81.1**	**82.3**	**80.9**	**79.5**	**81.4**	**79.7**	**76.8**	**78.2**	**77.9**	**77.1**	**80.5**	**73.4**	**73.8**	**69.6**	**78.5**

Fig. 11.75 Experimental results of running Unicoder on the XNLI dataset

Currently, NLP researchers are making efforts to design more models and methods through pretraining, such as pretrained models based on the natural language and structured language, pretrained models based on the natural language and videos, pretrained models based on the natural language and speech, and how to speed up, compress and interpret pretrained models. The development of pretrained models will take NLP research and related interdisciplinary research to a higher level.

Currently, lack of language resources is still a thorny problem in NLP. As corpus is the source of knowledge in NMT (neural machine translation), corpus size has a direct impact on the performance of NMT.

In Fig. 11.76, the abscissa axis represents corpus size, i.e., the number of English words in the corpus, while the ordinate axis indicates the BLEU (Bi-Lingual Evaluation Understudy) score, a metric for automatic machine translation evaluation. Figure 11.76 demonstrates that for the phrase-based statistical machine translation system, its BLEU score is 18.1 when the corpus size amounts to 10^6 words. The score rises steadily to 23.5 and 26.9 when the corpus size reaches 10^7 and 10^8 words, respectively. For the phrase-based-with-big-LM statistical machine translation system, its BLEU score is 23.4 when the corpus includes 10^6 words. The score ascends steadily to 27.9 and 29.6 when the corpus contains 10^7 and 10^8 words, respectively. It is not difficult to see that with the gradual increase in corpus size, the quality of statistical machine translation improves progressively. In contrast, for the NMT system, the BLEU score is merely 7.2 when the corpus size is 10^6 words, but the score leaps to 22.4 and 29.2 when the corpus size is 10^7 and 10^8 words, respectively. With the growth of the corpus size, the quality of neural machine translation is enhanced more dramatically than that of statistical machine translation. This demonstrates that corpus size has a much greater impact on neural machine

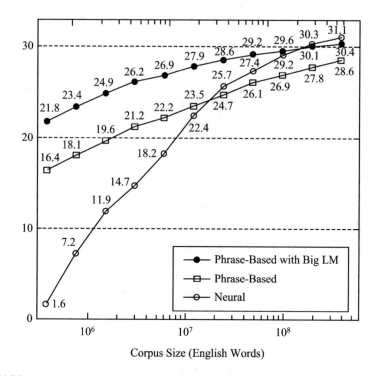

Fig. 11.76 A comparison between the performance of SMT and NMT

translation systems than on statistical machine translation systems. If the corpus consists of fewer than 10^7 words, neural machine translation is worse than statistical machine translation. When the corpus size is 10^8 words, the two types of machine translation systems display similar translation quality. Only when the corpus is composed of more than 10^9 words can neural machine translation probably outperform statistical machine translation.

There are approximately 7000 languages in the world, but only very few of them (dominant languages such as English, Chinese, Spanish, French, German, and Russian) boast rich data resources. As a result, NMT systems designed for these dominant languages achieve favorable performance. In WMT17, NMT systems for news translation were evaluated in terms of direct assessment (DA) scores. The results showed that NMT systems scored higher in translation between dominant languages. For example, both the Chinese–English and English–Chinese NMT systems obtained the same DA score of 73%. The German–English NMT system achieved a DA score of 78%, and the English–German NMT system scored 73%. The DA score of the Russian–English NMT system was 82%, and that of the English–Russian NMT system was 75%. As NMT systems between French, Spanish, and English were pretty mature, these systems were not evaluated. Obviously, NMT between dominant languages in the world has made satisfying progress. However, it is very difficult to implement NMT for nondominant languages due to

Language pairs	Medline training		Medline test		Terminology test
	Documents	Sentences	Documents	Sentences	Terms
de/en	3,669	40,398	50	589	-
en/de			50	719	-
es/en	8,626	100,257	50	526	-
en/es			50	599	6,624
fr/en	6,540	75,049	50	486	
en/fr			50	493	-
pt/en	4,185	49,918	50	491	-
en/pt			50	589	-
zh/en	-	-	50	283	-
en/zh			50	351	-

Fig. 11.77 Biomedical data resources in WMT19

the lack of sufficient language data resources. In WMT17, the DA scores of all the NMT systems designed for nondominant languages (such as Finnish, Turkish, Latvian, and Czech) were far from satisfactory. The NMT systems translating texts from English to Finnish, Turkish, and Latvian scored below 60%, and the English–Czech NMT system merely yielded a DA score of 62%. Without rich language data resources, NMT cannot be implemented for most languages in the world. Therefore, the poverty of language data resources has already become a serious issue in NMT development. In China, there are 56 ethnic groups and 80-odd minority languages (only 30 of them are written languages). Except for Chinese, the other languages used by minority ethnic groups (such as Uygur, Kazak, Tibetan, and Yi ethnic groups) do not have sufficient language data resources. As a result, it is still quite difficult to implement NMT for these languages.

In terms of specialized translation, the poverty of language data resources is even more serious. Take biomedical translation tasks for instance. WMT19 witnessed a gross inadequacy of data resources for training biomedical NMT systems. The de/en: en/de MT system made use of only 3669 documents consisting of 40,398 sentences. The es/en:en/es MT system had merely 8626 documents, which consisted of 100,257 sentences. For the fr/en:en/fr and pt/en:en/pt MT systems, they included only 5640 and 4185 documents (composed of 75,049 and 49,918 sentences, respectively). Moreover, almost no biomedical data resources could be found for the zh/en: en/zh MT system. Additionally, to test the biomedical NMT systems, only 50 documents were used, each document made up of 283 to 719 sentences. For biomedical terminology, only the es/en:en/es MT system included 6624 terms, and no terminology database was available for other languages. In other words, the size of the training corpus for each language pair in WMT19 was far smaller than 10^8 words, so NMT was of poor quality (Fig. 11.77).

As the most important resource in NMT, language data are also the source of language knowledge. Accordingly, researchers should pay more attention to the acquisition of and research on language data in NMT.

The discussion above shows that the latest NLP paradigm, the "pretraining + fine-tuning" paradigm, will help to alleviate the poverty of language data resources.

Bibliography

1. Ashish, V., S. Noam, P. Niki, U. Jakob, J. Llion, N.G. Aidan, K. Lukasz, P. Illia, et al. 2017. Attention Is All You Need. *ArXiv*. https://arxiv.org/abs/1706.03762.
2. Goldberg, J. 2017. *Neural Network Methods for Natural Language Processing*. San Rafael, CA: Morgan & Claypool Publishers, Inc.
3. Jurafsky, D., and J.H. Martin. 2009. *Speech and Language Processing, An Introduction to Natural Language Processing, Computational Linguistics, and Speech Recognition*. 2nd ed. Upper Saddle River, NJ: Prentice Hall.
4. Mostafa, D., G. Stephan, V. Oriol, U. Jakob, et al. 2018. Universal Transformers. *ArXiv*. https://arxiv.org/abs/1807.03819.
5. Mu, Li, Shujie Liu, Dongdong Zhang, and Ming Zhou. 2018. *Machine Translation*. Beijing: Higher Education Press.
6. Nan, Duan, and Ming Zhou. 2018. *Question Answering*. Beijing: Higher Education Press.
7. Pater, J. 2019. Generative Linguistics and Neural Networks at 60: Foundation, Friction, and Fusion. *Language* 95 (1).
8. Xipeng, Qiu. 2019. *Neural Networks and Deep Learning*. http://nndl.github.io.
9. Zhiwei, Feng. 2012. Artificial Neural Network, Deep Learning and Natural Language Processing. *Journal of Shanghai Normal University* 2: 110–122.
10. ———. 2019. Word Vectors and Their Application in NLP. *Technology Enhanced Foreign Language Education* 1: 3–11.
11. ———. 2021. Pre-training Paradigm in Natural Language Processing. *Foreign Languages Research* 1: 1–14.
12. ———. 2021. Three Approaches for Generation of Word Vectors. *Technology Enhanced Foreign Language Education* 1: 18–26.
13. ———. 2021. Two-Wheel Driven Natural Language Understanding. *Frontiers in Corpus Studies* 1: 149–176.

Chapter 12
Knowledge Graphs

Knowledge graphs are a large-scale knowledge base designed by Google for intelligent search. Having become an important knowledge source in NLP research, knowledge graphs are now used by many internet companies to organize knowledge stored in the Semantic Web.

For the purpose of applying knowledge graphs to NLP, this chapter addresses issues such as types of knowledge graphs, knowledge representation, knowledge merging, named entity recognition, disambiguation, relation extraction, event extraction, and knowledge storage.

12.1 Types of Knowledge Graphs

Since the Dartmouth Artificial Intelligence Conference in 1956, the whole world has witnessed a rapid development of artificial intelligence. Researchers have designed various automated reasoning models for problem solving and have proposed a series of theories for knowledge description, such as the Semantic Web, frames, and scripts. Based on these theories, domain experts began to manually collect data and build knowledge bases. Their efforts have attained success in some restricted domains.

After the appearance of the internet, human beings have generated a huge amount of data in their interaction with the world. In the era of big data, data can take the form of different modalities, including texts, images, and audio and video files. It has become one of the core objectives of next-generation information services to explore how computers can identify, read, analyze, and understand big data to obtain valuable information and provide customized information services. In 2001, Tim Berners Lee proposed the notion of the Semantic Web by defining a conceptualized way to describe the objective world and annotate content on the internet with detailed semantic labels. With this notion, World Wide Web could be transformed into the Semantic Web, which stressed content interconnections. Due to the impact

© Springer Nature Singapore Pte Ltd. 2023
Z. Feng, *Formal Analysis for Natural Language Processing: A Handbook*,
https://doi.org/10.1007/978-981-16-5172-4_12

of the Semantic Web, billions of netizens have co-constructed Wikipedia, which promoted the rapid increase of knowledge resources and reached an unprecedented level in terms of knowledge type, knowledge domain, and data size.

In May 2012, Google proposed the concept of knowledge graphs by building a large-scale knowledge graph, which led to a dramatic upsurge of research on knowledge graphs.

In a knowledge graph, each vertex is a semantic symbol, while each edge stands for the semantic relation between two symbols. Therefore, knowledge graphs are a generalized framework for describing how to formalize semantic knowledge. In computers, such vertices and edges can represent objects in the physical and cognitive worlds through symbol grounding and thus facilitate individuals' description and interaction between information and knowledge in the cognitive world. As knowledge graphs' unified framework for knowledge description is convenient for sharing and learning knowledge, knowledge graphs have gained widespread popularity in NLP research.

Since Google built the first knowledge graph, many other internet companies have followed suit and constructed their own knowledge graphs. Examples include Probase by Microsoft, Zhixin by Baidu, and Zhi Lifang by Sougou. In addition, domain-specific knowledge graphs have greatly promoted the application of artificial intelligence in industries such as finance, medicine, law, education, and publishing. Researchers have begun to attach importance to the theories and methods of knowledge graph construction.

Knowledge graph technology has a long history. It originated from artificial intelligence research concerning semantic representations of the natural language, underwent a series of changes to meet the ever-growing demand for internet information service, and has now become the core instrument in internet knowledge service.

Additionally, the development of knowledge graphs has also been promoted by theoretical research on knowledge representation (represented by the Semantic Web), the practice of intelligent processing of internet information, and the initiative to construct knowledge resources through network collaboration (represented by Wikipedia).

Figure 12.1 is a knowledge graph of the German physicist Max Planck.

The knowledge graph above describes the famous German physicist Max Planck by using triples recording his nationality, year of birth, prize he won, job, and so on.

Each triple in a knowledge graph is represented as (h, r, t), where h, r, and t stand for head, relation, and tail, respectively. Examples of triples are given below.

(Max Planck, nationality, German)
(Max Planck, place of birth, Kiel, Denmark)
(Max Planck, prize, Nobel Prize)
(Max Planck, job, physicist)

For the triple of (Max Planck, nationality, German), h = Max Planck, r = nationality, and t = German. With these triples, we can obtain a relatively comprehensive understanding of Max Planck.

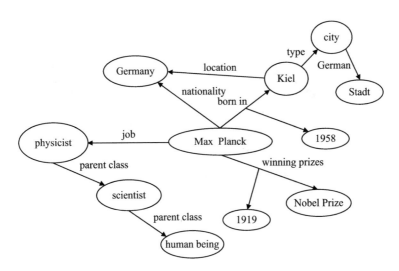

Fig. 12.1 A knowledge graph of Max Planck

Obviously, such a knowledge graph is a convenient and clear way to describe knowledge. The knowledge graph can inform us of the fact that Max Planck is a German physicist born in Kiel, Denmark (now Holstein, Germany), and he won the Nobel Prize.

By relying on these data and connecting them with other structured data about Max Planck, we can know more about him.

For example, through "Kiel, Denmark," we can learn that "Kiel" is a "city," which in turn can be connected to its German counterpart "Stadt."

Through the parent node of "physicist," we can learn that the parent class attribute of the word is "scientist," and the parent class attribute of "scientist" is "person."

When "year of birth" is added to the birth information as an additional resource, we can learn that "Max Planck was born in Kiel, Denmark, in 1858."

When "the year when he won the prize" is added to the prize-winning information as an additional resource, we can learn that "Max Planck won the Nobel Prize in 1919."

The knowledge described above is very useful.

It is not difficult to see that a knowledge graph can fully describe knowledge if data can be presented in a structured manner according to a given framework and connected to the existing structured data.

In practice, it is usually required that the framework of a knowledge graph be mapped to a framework supported by some database. If necessary, the database can be extended. In this way, knowledge graphs become more powerful.

In knowledge graphs, knowledge refers to human beings' understanding of the world; graphs are the carrier of knowledge; databases enable computers to process the knowledge data. In other words, a knowledge graph is a system that can represent

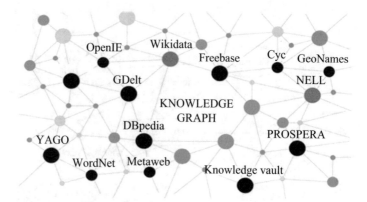

Fig. 12.2 Some well-known large-scale knowledge graphs

human beings' knowledge in a database by using a graph as an abstract way to carry information.

Currently, some well-known large-scale knowledge graphs (shown in Fig. 12.2) are Wikipedia, DBpedia, YAGO, Freebase, Wikidata, NELL, Knowledge Vault, and so on. With their powerful semantic representation ability and flexible structure, these knowledge graphs can effectively represent and carry information and knowledge in both cognitive and physical worlds.

Details concerning some important large-scale knowledge graphs are given below.

- Wikipedia. In 2001, Wikipedia was developed through global collaboration as a multilingual encyclopedia, aiming to provide people across the world with an encyclopedia for free use. Within just a few years, hundreds of thousands of entries were compiled in Wikipedia due to the concerted efforts made by users from the whole world. To date, Wikipedia has become a large-scale knowledge graph including millions of entries. Wikipedia has promoted the construction of many structured knowledge bases based on encyclopedias.
- DBpedia: In 2006, Tim Berners Lee called on internet users to publicize their data on the internet by following a certain principle and then put forward the notion of linked data. The purpose of creating linked data was not only to release data to the Semantic Web but also to establish the links between data to form a huge network. The most representative linked data network is DBpedia, which started to run in 2007. It is the first known large-scale network for open-domain linked data. DBpedia was developed by researchers at Free University of Berlin and University of Leipzig with the aim of solving some problems the Semantic Web faced at that time. In 2007, DBpedia released its first open dataset and allowed users to access it under a free license. Developers of DBpedia believed that the traditional top-down approach to design ontologies without relying on data was not practical in the context of large-scale web information and that data and their meta-data should be updated as information increases. Adding and updating data

could be accomplished through cooperation between community members. Therefore, ontologies should be based on data and designed in a bottom-up manner. However, this approach had many problems, such as data inconsistency, data uncertainty, and lack of a unified representation of implicit knowledge. They held that the most effective way to solve these problems was to provide a pluralist corpus, which could promote the development of technologies such as knowledge reasoning and data uncertainty management and help to design Semantic-Web-oriented operation management systems.

Based on the notion of linked data, DBpedia constructs a large-scale network of linked data by using the Semantic Web and the resource description frame (RDF) and establishing links with knowledge bases such as WordNet and Cyc. Figure 12.3 is an illustration of DBpedia.

DBpedia constructs a large-scale knowledge base by extracting structured information from Wikipedia with standard templates, which are defined and provided by community members. In addition, ontologies in DBpedia are also constructed through cooperation between community members.

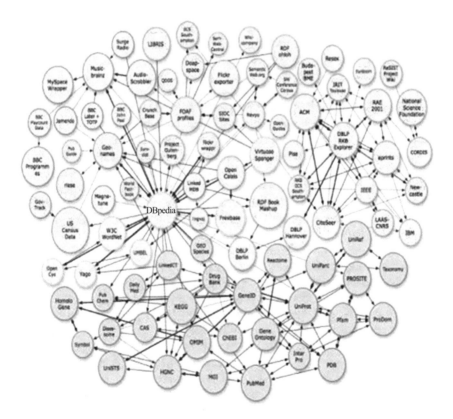

Fig. 12.3 A linked data network based on DBpedia

However, as information in Wikipedia is provided by community members, knowledge can hardly be represented in a unified way. To overcome this weakness, DBpedia employs mapping technology and extraction templates to give a unified description of knowledge.

In addition, DBpediaLive was developed to update data in DBpedia with Wikipedia. In its 2016 version, DBpedia included more than six million entities. In these entities, 5.2 million of them contained summary information; 1.53 million of them carried geological information; and 1.6 million of them were provided with descriptive information. Apart from that, ontologies could be connected to the 5.2 million entities, including 1.5 million pieces of person's information, 0.81 million pieces of place information, 0.49 million pieces of work information, 0.275 million pieces of organization information, 0.301 million pieces of species information, and 5000 pieces of disease information.

DBpedia can also support 127 languages and describe 17.31 million entities. DBpedia extracts from Wikipedia 9.5 billion triples in total. Regarding the triples, 1.3 billion of them come from the English version of Wikipedia, and another 5 billion of them derive from other versions of Wikipedia. Therefore, DBpedia is equipped with a large amount of cross-language knowledge.

- YAGO: The system was a project launched by the Max Planck Institute in Germany in 2007. To overcome the weakness that only mono-source background knowledge was used for knowledge graphs at that time, YAGO built a knowledge base based on multiple-source background knowledge. WordNet was an ontology knowledge graph with an extremely high accuracy, but the knowledge therein was only about some common concepts or entities in daily life. For Wikipedia, although it included more entity knowledge than WordNet, its hierarchical structure of concepts, which was similar to a label structure and thus not accurate, was not suitable for constructing ontology directly. YAGO combined the strengths of WordNet and Wikipedia and made up for their weaknesses. By adding ontology knowledge in WordNet to hypernyms of the entities in Wikipedia, YAGO built a large-scale, high-quality, and broad-coverage knowledge base. To date, YAGO has included 120 million pieces of factual knowledge about more than ten million entities. Additionally, it is also linked to other knowledge bases.
- Freebase: Based on Wikipedia and a swarm intelligence method called crowdsourcing, Freebase is a structured knowledge resource and a large-scale openly accessible knowledge graph, including 58.13 million entities and 3.2 billion triples. Freebase was acquired by Google on July 16, 2010 and then incorporated into Google's knowledge graph. In 2015, Google closed Freebase and transferred the data in Freebase into Wikipedia.
- NELL: With its full form being "Never-Ending Language Learning," NELL is a machine-learning system developed by Carnegie Mellon University on the basis of the "Read the Web" program. Each day, it keeps carrying out two tasks, i.e. reading and learning. The reading task is obtaining knowledge from texts on web pages and adding it to NELL's knowledge base. The learning task uses machine learning algorithms to acquire new knowledge and consolidate and

NELL knowledge fragment

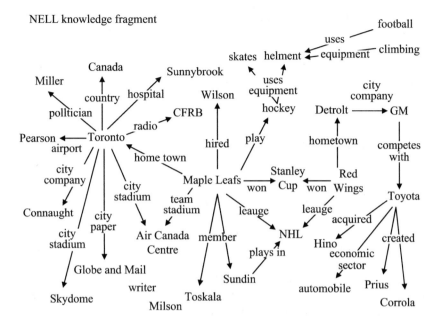

Fig. 12.4 A knowledge segment extracted by NELL

extend NELL's understanding of the knowledge. NELL can extract a large number of triples, annotate them with the number of iterations, time, and the confidence level for the extraction, and allow manual validation. NELL started to learn from 2010. After half a year, it extracted 350,000 triples about the relations between entities. With manual annotation and validation, it could extract more facts. The accuracy of knowledge extraction could amount to 87%.

Figure 12.4 is a knowledge segment of the hockey team "Maple Leafs" extracted by NELL. The figure shows that a very complicated knowledge system is constructed around the notion of the hockey team "Maple Leafs."

- Knowledge Vault: This system is a large-scale knowledge graph developed by Google in 2014. Compared with Freebase, Knowledge Vault was no longer built through crowdsourcing. Instead, with the help of algorithms, it could automatically search for information on the web, use machine learning methods to integrate the existing structured data (such as the structured data in YAGO or Freebase), and transform the data into accessible knowledge. To date, Knowledge Vault has collected 1.6 billion pieces of factual data, 271 million of which boast a high confidence level with an accuracy of 90%.

The knowledge graphs above are based on data in English. However, even for multilingual knowledge graphs, English is still the dominant language, and data in other languages are obtained through cross-language knowledge linking.

In recent years, many knowledge graphs with Chinese being the dominant language have been built in China by using structured knowledge in BaiduBaike and Wikipedia. Examples are zhishi.me by Shanghai Jiao Tong University, XLore by Tsinghua University, and CN-pedia by Fudan University. In 2017, several Chinese universities launched the cnSchema.org program, aiming to maintain the criteria of Schema, an open-domain knowledge graph, with the help of community members.

12.2   Knowledge Representation

Knowledge representation poses some difficulties for knowledge reasoning, which in turn creates some difficulties for knowledge use.

Knowledge graphs always employ the criteria and knowledge systems of the Semantic Web. In this section, the approaches to knowledge representation in the Semantic Web will be introduced first. After that, how knowledge is represented in knowledge graphs will be discussed.

To expand the functions of the World Wide Web and enhance its smartness, Tim Berners Lee, the creator of the World Wide Web, put forward the notion of the Semantic Web. Therefore, the Semantic Web is also called Web 3.0.

The knowledge representation system in the Semantic Web includes three levels: XML, RDF, and OWL.

1. XML: The full form of XML is Extensible Markup Language.

    The content of XML is recorded using tagged elements (such as people, organizations, events and so on). These tags, which can be texts, numbers, time, or null, must be composed of letters, underlines, or colons.

    Elements in XML can take the form of a nested structure, the depth of which is not restricted.

    For example, the following XML structure presents some basic information about a person.

    <person>
        <name> Max Planck <name>
        <nationality> Germany <nationality>
        <job> a physicist <job>
        ...
    <person>

    In the example above, the <person> element is in the form of a nested structure, which describes the person's name, nationality, job, and other information. In contrast, the <name> element includes only one piece of textual information and cannot be nested further.

    XML presents a tree structure that can start from a root node and reach any element or attribute through a certain path. Therefore, XML is called XML path language (XPath), its function being to help XML parsers implement structural parsing.

2. RDF: The full form of RDF is the resource description frame.

RDF assumes that any complex meaning can be represented by a combination of (h, r, t) triples. In each (h, r, t) triple, h (head) indicates "entity" or "subject"; r (relation) refers to "attribute" or "predicate"; t (tail) stands for "value" or "object". Accordingly, a head-relation-tail triple can be instantiated as an entity-attribute-value or subject-predicate-object triple. This explains why a (h, r, t) triple can also be written as (S, P, O), where S, P, and O represent Subject, Predicate, and Object, respectively. In this section, the form of (h, r, t) is adopted.

Any public or universal resource needs to be added with an identifiable universal resource identifier (URI).

What follows demonstrates how DPpedia describes the attributes of Max Planck by using RDF.

<http://dbpedia.org/resource/Max_Planck>
<http://xmlns.com/foaf/0.1/name>"Max Planck"@en
and
<http://dbpedia.org/resource/Max_Planck>
<http://xmlns.com/foaf/0.1/surname>"Planck"@en

The examples above describe Planck's name and surname. The URI "http://dbpedia.org/resource/Max_Planck" directly points to Max_Planck, while the URIs "http://xmlns.com/foaf/0.1/name" and "http://xmlns.com/foaf/0.1/surname" show that the name of the person is Max and his surname is Planck. These attributes are recognized and shared on the internet.

Therefore, some basic information about Max Planck can be represented as entity-attribute-value triples. Take the triple <Max Planck, nationality, Germany> for example. Max Planck is the entity; nationality is the attribute; Germany is the value of the attribute.

In addition, we can use the following triples to describe other attributes of Max Planck.

<Max Planck, job, physicist>
<physicist, parent class, scientist>
<scientist, parent class, human being>
<Kiel Denmark, location, Germany>
<Kiel Denmark, type, city>

Sometimes more than two attributes need to be represented, but triples alone can hardly achieve that. One solution is to define a predicate verb as an additional resource taking two attribute-value arguments, and to create a new triple to describe the complex situation.

For instance, if we need to describe the fact that Max Planck was born in Kiel Denmark in 1858, as more than two attributes, including birth place and year of birth, are involved, an additional resource, denoted as "birth information 135," is introduced within RDF first. After that, a two-argument predicate about "people, time, place" is used to describe "birth information 135." The description takes the form of the following triples.

<birth information 135, person, Max Planck>
<birth information 135, time, 1858>
<birth information 135, place, Kiel Denmark>

If we also need to describe the fact that Max Planck won the Nobel Prize in 1919, we can introduce another additional resource, "prizewinning information 87" and employ two-argument predicates about person, time, and prize name to describe "prizewinning information 87." The descriptions are as follows.

<prizewinning information 87, person, Max Planck>

<prizewinning information 87, time, 1919>

<prizewinning information 87, prize name, the Nobel Prize>

Obviously, this method increases the complexity of knowledge representation. As the newly introduced resources, such as "birth information 135" and "prizewinning information 87," cannot be directly linked to other arguments, subsequent processing will become more difficult. The new problem brought by additional resources awaits further research.

Apart from the additional resources, RDF also uses RDF schema (abbreviated as RDFs) to define domain-specific knowledge. An example is that we can define rdfs:Class to represent the subclass-superclass relation between physicists and scientists, i.e., scientists are the parent class of physicists. More details about the definition are given below.

<Physicist, rdf:type, rdfs:Class>

<Physicist, rdfs:subClassOf, scientist>

3. OWL: The full form of OWL is Ontology Web Language.

Based on RDF and RDFs, researchers have defined OWL-specific grammar as including the head and body.

Head: To describe an ontology using OWL, a series of namespace needs to be defined in advance, such as xmlns:owl, xmlns:rdf, xmlns:rdfs, xmlns:xsd, and so on. In addition, labels predefined in the namespace make up the head part of the ontology.

For example, the head of "the physicist ontology" is as follows.

<owl:Ontology rdf:about="">

<rdfs:comment>an instance of ontology</rdfs:comment>

<rdfs:label>the physicist ontology</rdfs:label>

<owl:Ontology>

<owl:Ontology rdf:about=""> means the head part above describes the current ontology.

Body: The body part of OWL describes the connections among classes, instances, and properties of an ontology. It is the core of OWL.

For instance, the body part of "the physicist ontology" is:

<owl:Classrdf:ID = "physicist">

    <rdfs:subClassOf rdf:resource= "scientist">

    <rdfs:labelxml:lang= "en">physicist</rdfs:label>

    <rdfs:labelxml:lang = "zh">物理学家(/wu li xue jia/)</rdfs: label>

    . . .

</owl:Class>

<owl:ObjectProperty rdf:ID = "nationality">

    <rdfs:domain rdf:resource = "person">

    <rdfs:range rdf:resource="xsd:string">

. . . . . .

</owl:ObjectProperty>

In the example above, the body part of OWL includes Class and Object Property. Class is what the current ontology belongs to, i.e. the parent class of physicists is scientists. Object Property describes the domain and range of the "nationality" property as person and string, respectively.

In addition, OWL also provides functional labels, which define some restrictive properties of classes, such as Transitive Property, Symmetric Property, Functional Property, Inverse Property, and Restriction Property.

Through semantic grounding, the Semantic Web can assign a unique identifier to each notion. The uniqueness makes it possible to share knowledge in a larger domain.

Knowledge graphs use the same knowledge representation methods as the Semantic Web and represent with structured triples the relations between entities in the real world. In the first section, it has already been mentioned that, as knowledge graphs use the same methods as the Semantic Web, triples in knowledge graphs also consist of head, tail, and the relation between head and tail.

An example is a triple that describes people in Freebase.

People/person/nationality (Jorge Amado, Brazil)

The triple above shows that the nationality of the person named Jorge Amado is Brazil. Jorge Amado, which represents "person," is head, while Brazil, representing "nationality," is tail.

Representing knowledge with this kind of triple is the same with the triples about Max Planck in the first section.

To represent multiple relations, Freebase represents knowledge with triples a virtual node structure called compound value type (CVT).

For instance, population information in different periods needs to be recorded when a population census is conducted. Additionally, other information related to the population census, such as time and name, should also be documented. In this case, triples can hardly carry the required information alone. As such, Freebase uses CVT to represent the information as the following set of triples.

<China, population information, e_1>

    <e_1, population, 1,332,810,869@int>

    <e_1, time, "2010"@Date>

    <e_1, name, "The Sixth National Population Census of China">

<China, population information, e_2>

    <e_2, population, 1,242,610,000@int>

    <e_2, time, "2000"@Date>

    <e_2, name, "The Fifth National Population Census of China">

The example above demonstrates that CVT can represent more information than triples.

In addition, with the development of neural networks and deep learning, numerical approaches to knowledge representation have also been explored in research concerning knowledge graphs.

12.3   Knowledge Merging

As all institutions or individuals can freely build knowledge graphs to satisfy their own demands, quite a number of knowledge graphs are created with different qualities and in different domains. In addition, these different knowledge graphs are also characterized by different structures. Therefore, it is necessary to implement knowledge merging by aligning, connecting, and merging these knowledge graphs so that they can form an organic whole and provide more comprehensive knowledge sharing.

As stated in the following, knowledge merging mainly includes frame matching, entity alignment, and conflict detection and resolution.

1. Frame matching: Frame matching can fall into two types, i.e. element matching and structure matching.

   (a) Element matching: Frame elements in knowledge graphs are represented by symbols capable of indicating meaning. Therefore, methods based on string matching can be employed for frame matching at the element level.

   The more similar strings two words share, the more likely that the two words carry the same meaning. Strings can be matched according to prefix distance, suffix distance, edit distance, and n-gram distance.

   Due to polysemy and synonymy in language, strings that are similar to each other in terms of spelling do not necessarily indicate the same meaning. Therefore, matching can also be conducted using constraint-based methods, which take into consideration the context of the target strings.

   In addition, neutral networks and deep learning can be employed to transform lexical symbols into word vectors. As each word is represented as a point in a vector space, the similarity between words can be computed by making use of the distance between points in the vector space. This is a better approach to frame matching due to word vectors' more powerful ability to capture the semantic similarity between words.

   (b) Structure matching: If two or more concepts are similar, similarity can also be found in their conceptual structure. Accordingly, structure matching can be conducted on the basis of conceptual structure.

   Structure matching can be performed with three methods: graph-based, classification-system-based, and statistic-based methods.

   When the graph-based method is used, knowledge graphs to be matched are treated as annotated graph structures. For vertices in two knowledge graphs, if their neighboring vertices are similar, they are close to each other and vice versa. This matching approach perceives a knowledge graph as a multi-relational graph, whose vertices and edges stand for entities and relations between the entities, respectively. Similar elements can be discovered by investigating isomorphism in graphs.

The classification-system-based approach assumes that if an "is-a" relation or SubClassOf relation is found between two words or phrases, they and their neighboring vertices should be similar to each other.

To perform frame matching, the statistic-based approach requires using statistical analysis such as correlation analysis and frequency analysis and classifying the concepts, attributes, instances, and relations in knowledge graphs into categories.

2. Entity alignment: The purpose of frame matching is to connect heterogeneous knowledge bases, build a large and unified knowledge base from the top level, and help computers understand the underlying data. Entity alignment is also called entity matching, the goal of which is to identify whether two entities represent the same object. Examples are the entity "Liu Yang (Astronaut)" in Hudong Baike and the entity "Liu Yang (the first female astronaut in China)" in Baidu Baike. The entity alignment task aims to decide whether the two persons named "Liu Yang" refer to the same entity. Entity alignment plays an important role in knowledge merging.

   Entity alignment is of two types: paired entity alignment and collective entity alignment.

   By matching the attributes of two entities, paired entity alignment can determine their degree of alignment and identify whether the two entities correspond to the same physical object. Collective entity alignment aims to coordinate the matched features of different objects and obtain globally optimal alignment.

   In addition, deep learning can also be utilized to represent multiple knowledge bases in the same semantic vector space and treat the alignment of entities in different knowledge bases as a calculation of the similarity between entities. Through computing semantic vectors based on knowledge resources, correspondence between entities in different knowledge bases can be obtained, and thus the entity alignment task is accomplished.

3. Conflict detection and resolution: Based on frame matching and entity alignment, knowledge merging endeavors to solve the conflicts between different instances.

   For example, as the height of the entity "Yao Ming" (a famous basketball player in China) differs in different knowledge graphs, conflict detection and resolution is necessary.

   To address conflicts, three approaches are available: conflict ignorance, conflict avoidance, and conflict resolution.

   Conflict ignorance means that systems choose to ignore the conflicts that have been detected and let users themselves discard or edit some instances according to their demands.

   Conflict avoidance makes use of rules or constraints to filter out some sources of data. For instance, setting limits on a person's age range and assigning priority levels to different knowledge sources can help to avoid conflicts.

   Conflict resolution uses the frames of knowledge graphs and the features of instances to resolve conflicts.

A typical example of knowledge merging is YAGO. It relates the category labels in Wikipedia to their synonyms in WordNet, mounts Wikipedia entries under the framework of WordNet, and merges the knowledge in Wikipedia and WordNet.

12.4   Entity Recognition and Disambiguation

An entity is the basic unit in knowledge graphs.

Entity recognition is closely related to entity mention. Therefore, entity mention is discussed first in the following.

There are three types of entity mentions in natural language texts: named entity mentions, nominal mentions, and pronoun mentions. For example, in the sentence "中国乒乓球男队主教练刘国梁出席了会议，他布置了备战世乒赛的具体安排" (/Zhong Guo ping pang qiu nan dui zhu jiao lian Liu Guo Liang chu xi le hui yi, ta bu zhi le bei zhan shi ping sai de ju ti an pai。/; Guoliang Liu, the head coach of China men's national table tennis team, attended the meeting and made detailed arrangements for World Table Tennis Championships.), "中国乒乓球男队主教练" (/Zhong Guo ping pang qiu nan dui zhu jiao lian/; the head coach of China men's national table tennis team), "刘国梁" (/Liu Guo Liang/; Guoliang Liu), and "他" (/ta/; he) belong to nominal mentions, named entity mentions, and pronoun mentions, respectively.

Of all the three types of entity mentions, named entity mentions are our focus in this section.

A typical instance of named entity mentions is named entity recognition. The task aims to automatically extract named entities from natural language texts.

Generally, named entity recognition endeavors to enable computers to recognize three classes and seven subclasses of named entities in texts.

The three classes of named entities include the entity class, the time class, and the number class, and the seven subclasses are the name of a person, the name of an institution, the name of a place, time, date, currency, and percentage. It is relatively easy to recognize time, date, currency, and percentage because language expressions about these entities are made up by using a limited number of rules. In contrast, the other three subclasses of named entities are much more difficult to recognize due to their various possible forms. Therefore, named entity recognition usually refers to recognizing the name of a person, an institution, or a place.

Named entity recognition usually includes two steps. The first step is to recognize the boundary of a named entity. The second one is to determine its type, that is, to determine whether the named entity is the name of a person, an institution, or a place.

In English, named entities are usually marked out in language form. Each word making up the name of a person, institution, or place begins with a capitalized letter, so the boundary of a named entity can be recognized without many difficulties. The main problem is to determine the type to which the named entity belongs.

However, in Chinese, the following difficulties are identified in named entity recognition.

First, named entities can take various forms. The inner structure of named entities is very complicated, especially in Chinese. Details of the complexity are given below.

The name of a person: The name of a Chinese is usually composed of a family name (consisting of one or two Chinese characters) and a given name (consisting of one or more Chinese characters). Although family names are limited to a set of characters, given names have a wider range of possibilities. In China, a person can be referred to by using his/her given name, courtesy name, literary name, or surname with a prefix, suffix, or his/her position. For example, "杜甫(/Du Fu/; Fu Du), 杜子美(/Du Zi Mei/; Zimei Du), 子美(/Zi Mei/; Zimei), 杜工部(/Du Gong Bu/; Gongbu Du)" all refer to the same person, that is, the great poet 杜甫(/Du Fu/; Fu Du)in Tang Dynasty.

The name of a place: The name of a place in China usually consists of several Chinese characters, sometimes including key characters as a suffix, or even an alternative name may be used. For instance, "广州" (/Guang Zhou/; Guangzhou), "广州市" (/Guang Zhou Shi/; the city of Guangzhou), and "羊城" (/Yang Cheng/; literally the sheep city, which is an alternative name of Guangzhou) have the same reference. In addition to the complete names, short names can also represent a place. An example is that "湖北" (/Hu Bei/; Hubei), "湖北省" (/Hu Bei Sheng/; Huibei province), and "鄂" (/E/; the short name of Hubei province) all refer to the same place.

The name of an organization: The name of a Chinese organization tends to include a named constituent, a modificatory constituent, a place constituent, and a key word. For example, for a company called "北京百富勤投资咨询公司(/Bei Jing Bai Fu Qin Tou Zi Zi Xun Gong Si/; Beijing Baifuqin Investment Consulting Company)", "北京" (/Bei Jing/; Beijing) is a place constituent; "百富勤" (/Bai Fu Qin/) is a named constituent; "投资咨询(/tou zi zi xun/; Investment Consulting)" is a modificatory constituent; "公司(/gong si/; Company)" is a key word. The name of an organization can also be embedded into the name of its affiliate. For instance, "北京大学(/Bei Jing Da Xue/; Peking University)" is embedded into "北京大学附属小学 (/Bei Jing Da Xue Fu Shu Xiao Xue/; Peking University Elementary School)". In addition, many organizations have short names too. Examples are "中国奥委会" (/Zhong Guo Ao Wei Hui/; the short name of "中国奥林匹克委员会"/Zhong Guo Ao Lin Pi Ke Wei Yuan Hui/, which stands for Chinese Olympic Committee) and "北师大二附小" (/Bei Shi Da Er Fu Xiao/; the short name of "北京师范大学第二 附属小学"/Bei Jing Shi Fan Da Xue Di Er Fu Shu Xiao Xue/, which represents The Second Elementary School Attached to Beijing Normal University).

Second, the linguistic contexts of named entities are very complicated. As named entities are common in every language, they may appear in various kinds of linguistic contexts. In different contexts, the same sequence of Chinese characters may refer to different entities or even something that is not an entity.

For instance,

the name of a person: "彩霞" (/cai xia/; literally rosy clouds) may refer to a person or a natural phenomenon;

the name of a person: "河南" (/He Nan/; literally river south) may mean a province in China or the south of a river;

the name of an organization: "新世界" (/xin shi jie/; literally new world) can stand for an organization or is just a word group meaning the new world.

Compared with English, Chinese named entity recognition is much more difficult for the following two reasons.

1. Different from English texts, Chinese texts contain no mark that can explicitly indicate word boundaries. Therefore, automatic word segmentation is necessary. However, the accuracy of automatic word segmentation is interdependent on the accuracy of named entity recognition.
2. English named entities often begin with a capitalized letter. An instance is that "Liu Changle is the founder of Phoenix TV", where the initial letters of the family name and the given name are capitalized. In contrast, such marks cannot be found in its Chinese equivalent, as "刘常乐" (/Liu Chang Le/; Changle Liu) is mixed with other Chinese characters in "凤凰卫视的创始人是刘常乐" (/Feng Huang Wei Shi de chuang shi ren shi Liu Chang Le/; Changle Liu is the founder of Phoenix TV.).

In natural language texts, named entities are important linguistic units conveying information. Accordingly, named entity recognition is an important task in research on knowledge graphs.

To implement named entity recognition, two methods are usually used. One is the rule-based method, while the other is based on machine learning.

The most representative rule-based method is based on dictionaries of named entities. This method uses complete or partial matching between strings and endeavors to identify words or phrases that can best match the words or phrases in dictionaries.

Machine learning-based methods make use of an annotated corpus to train a model that can learn the probability of a given string as a constituent of a named entity and then estimate the probability of a candidate string as a named entity. If the latter probability is larger than a threshold value, then the string is regarded as a named entity.

Specifically, machine learning-based methods can fall into two groups, that is, the feature-based methods and the neural-network-based methods. The former makes use of traditional machine learning models and manual feature engineering to recognize named entities, while the latter uses neural networks to automatically obtain features and then identify named entities.

Currently, techniques for named entity recognition are far from meeting the requirements of large authentic tasks. In terms of research methodology, research on named entity recognition should be oriented toward a large volume of web data characterized by redundancy, diversity, and noise.

The same entity may be referred to by different linguistic expressions. For example, Michael Jordan, the famous American basketball player, is also called Air Jordan or MJ. On the other hand, the same linguistic expression can refer to different entities in different contexts. For instance, Michael Jordan can refer to a famous American basketball player, a British soccer player, a statesman in Ireland, or a student at the University of California, Berkeley. Another example is Yao Ming, which may refer to a famous basketball player in China, deputy director of the Salt Administrative Bureau of Chenggu County Shaanxi Province, or deputy consultant at a court in the city of Anqing city. Such a problem is called Name Ambiguity.

Therefore, entity disambiguation is necessary for named entity recognition so that the exact reference of a linguistic expression can be determined.

Entity disambiguation, denoted as M, can be defined through the following sextuple.

$$M = (N, E, D, O, K, \delta)$$

For the sextuple above, N is the set of named entities to be disambiguated, denoted as $N = n_1, n_2, \ldots, n_t$. Examples are "Michael Jordan" and "Yao Ming".

$E = e_1, e_2, \ldots, e_k$. E is the list of target entities that named entities can refer to. Examples include Michael Jordan (a famous American basketball player), Michael Jordan (a British soccer player), Michael Jordan (a statesman in Ireland), Yao Ming (a famous American basketball player), Yao Ming (deputy director of the Salt Administrative Bureau of Chenggu County Shaanxi Province), and Yao Ming (deputy consultant at a court in the city of Anqing city). In practice, the list of target entities can be obtained by resorting to knowledge bases, such as Wikipedia and Freebase.

$D = d_1, d_2, \ldots, d_n$. D is the set of documents that include the named entities to be disambiguated. For example, D can be the set of the first resulting 100 webpages when "Michael Jordan" is searched for on Google.

$O = o_1, o_2, \ldots, o_m$. O stands for the set of entity reference items that take the form of named entities and need to be disambiguated in D. Take the sentence "Michael Jordan is the greatest NBA star" in document D as an example. "Michael Jordan" is an entity reference item to be disambiguated.

K is the background knowledge used for named entity disambiguation. As information carried in an entity does not suffice to differentiate itself from others, much background knowledge is needed. The most commonly used background knowledge is a textual description of the target entity. Examples are Wikipedia's descriptions of Michael Jordan as follows.

Description 1: Michael Jordan (an NBA star): Michael Jeffrey Jordan (born on February 17, 1963), a retired basketball player at the National Basketball Association (NBA), is regarded as the greatest basketball player of all time. He is 6 ft 6 in. (1.98 m) tall, and he plays shooting guard with number 23. He is now the principal owner and chairman of the Charlotte Hornets.

Description 2: Michael Jordan (a soccer player): Michael Jordan (born in Enfield on April 7, 1986) is an English professional soccer goalkeeper. He used to be a player at Arsenal. Currently he is the goalkeeper of Chesterfield.

Obviously, such background knowledge is very useful for entity disambiguation.

δ represents an entity disambiguation function $O \times K \rightarrow E$, which maps entity reference items in O and K into E (the list of target entities) or performs clustering to identify the target entities.

Two approaches can be used for entity disambiguation. One is based on clustering, while the other is based on linking. The two approaches are detailed in the following.

1. Clustering-based entity disambiguation: Given a set of entity reference items $O = o_1, o_2, \ldots, o_m$, clustering can be performed for the purpose of disambiguation through the following steps.

   (a) Extract the features of each entity reference item o and represent the features as a feature vector $O = w_1, w_2, \ldots, w_m$.
   (b) Compute the similarity between entity reference items according to their surface features, expanded features, or social network features.
   (c) Perform clustering on entity reference items by using clustering algorithms so that each cluster can correspond to a target entity.

      Take Michael Jordan for example. Its entity reference items are obtained as follows (Fig. 12.5).

      By using entity features and clustering algorithms, entity disambiguation can be achieved. For the example above, the first and third entity reference items belong to one cluster, as they refer to an American basketball player. The second item refers to another cluster, a student at the University of California, Berkeley. The fourth item is about a third cluster, which refers to a goalkeeper in Britain.

2. Linking-based entity disambiguation: Entity linking means that entity reference items are linked to a certain entity in a knowledge base.

   The input of entity linking includes the following two parts.

   (a) A knowledge base of target entities: The most commonly used knowledge base is Wikipedia. Usually, a knowledge base includes a list of entities, their textual descriptions, structured information, categories, and so on.
   (b) Entity reference items to be disambiguated and their contextual information.

   An entity linking task consists of two steps.

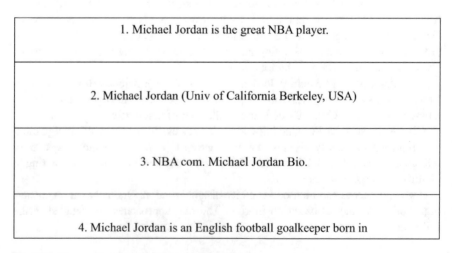

Fig. 12.5 Four entity reference items of Michael Jordan

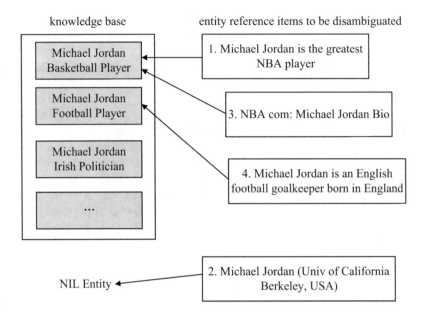

Fig. 12.6 Linking-based entity disambiguation

(a) Blocking: As an entity base usually includes millions of entities, it is impossible to calculate the probability that an entity reference item is linked to each of them. Therefore, the entities that the entity reference item cannot refer to should be filtered out first so that only a limited number of candidate entities are kept.

(b) Linking: An entity reference item is finally linked to a target entity.

In Fig. 12.6, entity reference items No. 1, 2, 3, and 4, which need to be disambiguated, are inputted into the knowledge base. The items are disambiguated when items No. 1 and 3 are linked to "Michael Jordan Basketball Player" and item No. 4 is linked to "Michael Jordan Football Player." However, item No. 2 cannot be linked to any entity in the knowledge base, so it is linked to NIL Entity.

The core issue of clustering-based and linking-based entity disambiguation is to compute the similarity between an entity reference item to be disambiguated and a candidate entity. In recent years, dominant methods for similarity computation have been based on neural networks. Such methods are widely used because they require no manually designed features, boast good scalability, and capture deep semantic relations easily.

12.5   Relation Extraction

The relations between entities are integral to a knowledge graph. How to extract the relations between entities from texts is one of the core tasks in knowledge graph construction.

Relations in knowledge graphs refer to the connections between two or more entities. Relation extraction is a task that aims to automatically extract the semantic relations between entities. As the basis of relation extraction, the binary relation between any two entities can be defined as a triple (arg1, relation, arg2), where arg1 and arg2 stand for two entities (arguments) and relation is the semantic connection between them.

For example, given two entities, "China" and "Beijing", their semantic relation is "capital." Therefore, a triple (China, capital, Beijing) can be extracted. Similarly, a triple (Liu Xiang, place of birth, Shanghai) can be extracted from the sentence "刘翔, 1983年7月13日出生于上海" (/Liu Xiang, yi jiu ba san nian qi yue shi san ri chu sheng yu Shang Hai/; Xiang Liu was born in Shanghai on June 13, 1983). Also, a triple (Zhang Yimou, director, Ju Dou) can be extracted from the sentence "张艺谋在1990年与杨凤良合作导演影片《菊豆》" (/Zhang Yi Mou zai yi jiu jiu ling nian yu Yang Feng Liang he zuo dao yan ying pian Ju Dou/; Yimou Zhang co-directed the movie *Ju Dou* with Fengliang Yang). Again, a triple (Steve Jobs, founder, Apple Inc.) can be extracted from the sentence that "苹果公司的董事会主席、联合创始人史蒂夫•乔布斯周三辞世, 享年56岁" (/Ping Guo gong si de dong shi hui zhu xi、lian he chuang shi ren Shi Di Fu Qiao Bu Si zhou san ci shi, xiang nian wu shi liu sui/; Steve Jobs, cofounder and chairman of Apple Inc., passed away on Wednesday at the age of 56).

Compared with entity recognition and entity disambiguation, relation extraction is more complicated for the following reasons.

1. The results of relation extraction may vary because the same relation can be expressed by different words. Examples are "姚明出生于上海" (/Yao Ming chu sheng yu Shang Hai/; Ming Yao was born in Shanghai) and "姚明的出生地是上海" (/Yao Ming de chu sheng di shi Shang Hai/; Ming Yao's place of birth is Shanghai). Both sentences can indicate that between Ming Yao and Shanghai exists a relation, place of birth.
2. The same word or phrase may denote different relations. For instance, the word "姑娘" (/gu niang/) in "王璐璐是我的姑娘" (/Wang Lu Lu shi wo de gu niang/) can mean "daughter" (Lulu Wang is my daughter) or "girlfriend" (Lulu Wang is my girlfriend). The word "姑娘" (/gu niang/; daughter or girlfriend) may represent different relations in different contexts.
3. More than one relation may be found between the same pair of entities. For example, in "姚明的出生地是上海" (/Yao Ming de chu sheng di shi Shang Hai/; Ming Yao's place of birth is Shanghai) and "姚明的居住地也是上海" (/Yao Ming de ju zhu di ye shi Shang Hai/; Ming Yao's place of residence is also Shanghai), the extracted triples are (Ming Yao, place of birth, Shanghai) and (Ming Yao, place of residence, Shanghai). Accordingly, more than one relation exists between Ming Yao and Shanghai.
4. Relation extraction involves not only two or more entities but also their contexts, so the extraction task can be very complex. For example, "三国时期的蜀国有多位能征善战的将军:关羽、张飞、赵云、黄忠" (/San Guo shi qi de Shu Guo you duo wei neng zheng shan zhan de jiang jun：Guan Yu、Zhang Fei、Zhao Yun、Huang Zhong/; in China's Three Kingdoms Period, many generals skillful in war could be found in Shu State, such as Yu Guan, Fei Zhang, Yun Zhao, and Zhong Huang).

5. Sometimes, relations between entities are not explicit but implicit in texts. For instance, in the sentence that "库克与中国移动董事长会面商谈合作事宜，透露出他将带领苹果公司进一步开拓中国市场的讯号" (/Ku Ke yu Zhong Guo Yi Dong dong shi zhang hui mian shang tan he zuo shi yi, tou lu chu ta jiang dai ling Ping Guo gong si jin yi bu kai tuo Zhong Guo shi chang de xun hao/; The fact that Cook met with chairman of China Mobile Limited to discuss cooperation revealed that he would lead Apple to tap Chinese markets further), the relation between Cook and Apple is not described, but, from the expression "他将带领苹果公司" (/Ta jiang dai ling Ping Guo gong si/; he would lead Apple), it can be inferred that he is CEO of Apple and a triple (Cook, position, CEO of Apple) can be obtained.

When all these factors are taken into account, relation extraction turns out to be very difficult.

According to the domain in which relation extraction is implemented, relation extraction can fall into two types: restricted-domain relation extraction and open-domain relation extraction.

1. Restricted-domain relation extraction

This type of relation extraction aims to determine within one or several given domains the semantic relations between entities in texts. The method of restricted-domain relation extraction is as follows.

(a) Template-based relation extraction: Relation extraction is performed on the basis of templates created manually or obtained through machine learning. For instance, if X and Y stand for two types of companies and the following templates exist in texts

X is acquired by Y

X is purchased by Y

X is bought by Y

then an acquisition relation can be established between X and Y. Their relation can take the form of a triple (X, ACQUISITION, Y).

(b) Machine learning-based relation extraction: Template-based relation extraction is of limited use due to the quality and coverage of templates. Machine learning-based relation extraction regards relation extraction as a classification task and fulfills the task by using machine learning algorithms. This type of relation extraction makes use of the following two approaches.

• The feature-engineering-based approach: relation instances are transformed into feature vectors that classifiers can make use of. Specifically, this approach consists of three steps.

First, feature extraction. Lexical, syntactic, and semantic features are extracted from texts and then integrated as local or global features that can describe relation instances.

Second, model training. Classification models are trained using the extracted features.

Third, relation extraction. Texts are classified according to the models that have been trained so that the relation extraction task can be accomplished.

- The neural-network-based approach: CNNs or RNNs are employed to automatically learn the features of texts and perform the relation extraction task. This approach includes four steps.

  First, feature representation. Features composed of textual symbols are transformed into distributed representations such as word vectors.

  Second, building neural networks. A neural network is built to transform distributed representations into high-level features.

  Third, model training. Classification models are trained by using annotated data and optimizing network parameters.

  Fourth, classification. New samples are classified according to the neural-network models that have been trained. In this way, the relation extraction task can be accomplished.

2. Open-domain relation extraction

   This type of relation extraction does not require a set of predefined relations but automatically performs the relation extraction task by using the descriptions of some words in open-domain corpora.

   An example of an open-domain relation extraction system is TextRunner, which was developed by Washington University on the basis of the notion of open information extraction (Open IE for short). By automatically extracting positive and negative samples of entity-relation triples from Penn Tree-Bank through some heuristic rules and making use of their shallow syntactic features, TextRunner could first train a classifier to identify whether any semantic relation exists between two entities. After that, TextRunner could treat web texts as candidate sentences, extract their shallow syntactic features, and use the classifier to estimate whether the extracted triples are reliable. Finally, redundant information in web data was used to reevaluate those triples identified as reliable in the previous step. Through the three steps, the relation extraction task was fulfilled.

   In addition to TextRunner, other open-domain relation extraction systems include Kylin, WOE, ReVerb, and so on.

12.6 Event Extraction

An event refers to a thing or a change in a state. It occurs in some place at some time, involves one or several participants, and consists of one or more actions.

The most important factors in an event are time, place, participants, actions or changes in states.

For example, "出生" (/chu sheng/; birth) and "死亡" (/si wang/; death) are different events. So are "就职" (/jiu zhi/; taking office) and "辞职" (/ci zhi/; resigning).

Research on event extraction aims to determine how to extract from texts the event information that users are interested in and present the information in a structured manner.

The following three texts describe different types of events.

A. "成龙和林凤娇于1982年12月1日在美国洛杉矶举行婚礼。"

(/Cheng Long he Lin Feng Jiao yu yi jiu ba er nian shi er yue yi ri zai Mei Guo Luo Shan Ji ju xing hun li。/; Long Cheng and Fengjiao Lin held their wedding ceremony in Los Angelis on December 1, 1982.)

B. "2017年1月20日中午, 特朗普在美国首都华盛顿就任美国第45任总统。"

(/Er ling yi qi nian yi yue er shi ri zhong wu, Te Lang Pu zai Mei Guo shou du Hua Sheng Dun jiu ren Mei Guo di si shi wu ren zong tong。/; Trump was sworn in as the 45th president of the United States in Washington, the capital of America, at noon on January 20, 2017.)

C. "2015年11月24日, 俄罗斯一架苏24战机在土耳其与叙利亚边境被土耳其F16军机击落。"

(/Er ling yi wu nian shi yi yue er shi si ri, E Luo Si yi jia Su er si zhan ji zai Tu Er Qi yu Xu Li Ya bian jing bei Tu Er Qi F shi liu jun ji ji luo。/; A Su-24 fighter jet from Russia was shot down by a Turkish F-16 fighter jet at the border between Turkey and Syria on November 24, 2015.)

The three sentences above describe three different events.

Sentence A describes a marriage event. People who got married were Cheng Long and Lin Fengjiao. Its time and place were December 1, 1982 and Los Angelis, respectively. Therefore, the event extraction task endeavors to identify that sentence A describes a marriage event and to extract arguments such as the couple, time, and place of the wedding ceremony.

Similarly, sentence B describes an inaugural event, so the purpose of event extraction is to identify elements related to the inauguration. Sentence C describes an attack, so the aim of event extraction is to determine elements about the attack.

Event extraction involves the following concepts.

1. Event mention: An event mention, usually taking the form of a sentence or a sentence group, refers to a natural language description of an actual event. The same event mention may be found in different parts of a text or even in different texts.

2. Event trigger: As an important clue to identify the class to which an event belongs, event triggers are words that best represent the event. "婚礼" (/hun li/; Wedding), "就任" (/jiu ren/; sworn in), and "击落" (/ji luo/; shot down) in the above examples are event triggers.

3. Event argument: As the core component of an event, event arguments refer to participants in an event. Event arguments and event triggers make up the framework of an event. Examples are "成龙" (/Cheng Long/; Long Cheng), "林凤娇" (/Lin Feng Jiao/; Fengjiao Lin), "1982年12月1日" (/yi jiu ba er nian shi er yue yi ri/; December 1, 1982), and "洛杉矶" (/Luo Shan Ji/; Los Angeles) in sentence A. In sentence B, "特朗普" (/Te Lang Pu/; Trump), "美国首都华盛顿" (/Mei Guo shou du Hua Sheng Dun/; Washington, the capital of America), and "美国第45任总统" (/Mei Guo di si shi wu ren zong tong/; the 45th president of the United States) are event arguments. Regarding sentence C, event arguments encompass "俄罗斯一架苏24战机" (/E Luo Si yi jia Su er si zhan ji/; a Su-24 fighter jet from Russia), "土耳其F16军机" (/Tu Er Qi F shi liu jun ji/; a Turkish F-16 fighter jet), and "土耳其与叙利亚边境" (/Tu Er Qi yu Xu Li Ya bian jing/; the border

between Turkey and Syria). Event arguments consist of words or phrases indicating entities, time, and attributes.

4. Argument role: An argument role is the role that an event argument plays in an event. An argument role represents the semantic relation between an event argument and an event. For example, "成龙" (/Cheng Long/; Long Cheng) and "林凤娇" (/Lin Feng Jiao/; Fengjiao Lin) assume the roles of "husband" and "wife", respectively, in sentence A. In sentence B, "特朗普" (/Te Lang Pu/; Trump) takes on the role of "the parties concerned", and "俄罗斯一架苏24战机" (/E Luo Si yi jia Su er si zhan ji/; a Su-24 fighter jet from Russia) plays the role of "target" in sentence C. Argument roles, event arguments, and event triggers constitute the framework of an event.

5. Event type: An event type means the type to which an event belongs. Event types can be identified using event arguments and event triggers. An event type can include several sub-types. For example, the event type of sentence A is "life", with "marriage" being the subtype. Sentence B belongs to the type of "start-position," which is a subtype of "personnel." Sentence C can be attributed to the type of "attack," which in turn serves as a subtype of "conflict."

According to the domain in which event extraction is conducted, event extraction can fall into restricted-domain event extraction, open-domain event extraction, and event relation extraction.

- Restricted-domain event extraction

    Before this type of event extraction is conducted, types and structures of target events should be predefined, such as business events, conflict events, and transaction events.

    Methods of such event extraction are as follows.

    – Pattern-matching-based event extraction. This method includes three steps.

        First, manual annotation of corpora. A large-scale manually annotated corpus can serve as the source of knowledge for pattern matching.

        Second, pattern learning. Patterns of event extraction are learned from a large-scale corpus.

        Third, pattern matching. The event extraction task is accomplished by matching patterns that have been learned to the candidate texts.

        Pattern-matching-based event extraction systems include AutoSlog and AutoSlog-TS. AutoSlog requires entities and events in sentences be manually annotated, while AutoSlog-TS, by merely annotating sentences with whether target events are mentioned, can learn to automatically extract patterns of events according to pre-classified data and then complete the event extraction task.

    – Neural-network-based event extraction. Since 2015, neural-network-based methods have been used for event extraction. Such methods usually consist of four steps.

        First, feature representation. Symbolic information in texts is transformed into distributed vector representations of words.

        Second, neural networks are constructed and high-level learning is performed. CNNs are constructed to represent sentence-level features. After that, dynamic pooling is used to automatically capture high-level features and event information in sentences according to event triggers and candidate arguments.

Third, model training. Annotated data are employed to optimize the parameters of neural networks and train neural network models.

Fourth, classification. The trained model is utilized to classify new samples and fulfill the event extraction task.

- Open-domain event extraction

  The types of target events are not limited in open-domain event extraction. In other words, the types and structures of events are unknown before event extraction.

  Methods of open-domain event extraction are primarily based on the distribution hypothesis, which assumes that two words have similar meanings if they share the same context and usage. In event extraction, if the event triggers or event arguments of candidate events occur in similar contexts, then the event triggers and the corresponding event arguments tend to indicate the same type of events. According to the distribution hypothesis, the context of candidate words serves as an important feature to represent event meanings in open-domain event extraction.

- Event relation extraction

  Events are not isolated from but interrelated to each other in the real world. Therefore, event relation extraction is also necessary. This extraction task aims to extract co-reference relations, cause–effect relations, temporal relations, or sub-event relations.

  - Extraction of co-reference relations between events: If two events refer to the same target event in the real world, then a co-reference relation exists between the two events. For example,

    The event that "2014年10月，联想集团正式完成了对摩托罗拉移动的收购" (/Er ling yi si nian shi yue, Lian Xiang Ji Tuan zheng shi wan cheng le dui Mo Tuo Luo La Yi Dong de shou gou/; Lenovo finished the acquisition of Motorola Mobility in October 2014) and the event that "联想集团以29.1亿美元的价格收购了摩托罗拉移动" (/Lian Xiang Ji Tuan yi er shi jiu dian yi yi mei yuan de jia ge shou gou le Mo Tuo Luo La Yi Dong/; Lenovo acquired Motorola Mobility for $ 2.91 billion) describe the same event. Therefore, the two have a co-reference relation.

    Co-reference relations between two events are extracted according to their similarities, primarily in terms of texts, event types, and event arguments.

  - Extraction of cause–effect relations between events: Cause–effect relations can help decision makers to better understand the development of events and provide them with a basis for decision making, so extraction of cause–effect relations is important for a deeper semantic interpretation of texts.

    Background knowledge is often needed to infer cause–effect relations between events. For example, a cause–effect relation can hardly be established between the sentence that "今日国家公布消息称在未来五年将加大对于新能源汽车行业的扶持力量" (/Jin ri guo jia gong bu xiao xi cheng zai wei lai wu nian jiang jia da dui yu xin neng yuan qi che hang ye de fu chi li liang/;

According to the news released by China today, more aid will be given to the new energy vehicle industry in the following 5 years) and the sentence that "今天比亚迪汽车的股价开盘10分钟就停涨了" (/Jin tian Bi Ya Di qi che de gu jia kai pan shi fen zhong jiu zhang ting le/; The stock price of BYD Auto reached its ceiling just 10 min after the stock market opened today). However, if we can learn from a knowledge graph that "比亚迪是一家中国新能源汽车制造厂家" (/Bi Ya Di shi yi jia Zhong Guo xin neng yuan qi che zhi zao chang jia/; BYD Auto is a new energy vehicle manufacturer in China), we can infer that a cause–effect relation exists between the two events.

- Extraction of temporal relations between events: Temporal relations between events describe the chronological order of events. A corpus often used in research on temporal relations is "TimeBank," which classifies the chronological order into Before, After, Includes, Is Included, Simultaneous, and so on. Entities in events that have temporal relations with each other partially overlap. An event chain can be formed if, in the same text, temporal relations are found between instances of events that involve the same event arguments. Therefore, the extraction of temporal relations from texts can help to understand the cause–effect relations between events.

- Extraction of sub-event relations: Sub-event relations reflect the inclusion relations between events. For example, an earthquake event usually includes sub-events such as "injuries and deaths," "rescue," "donation," and "rebuilding." Automatic extraction of sub-event relations from news texts can help users to better understand the events in question.

Currently, many knowledge graphs only include knowledge about and relations between entities. If event knowledge can be added to knowledge graphs, their ability to represent knowledge will be improved.

12.7   Knowledge Storage

As an increasing amount of data is currently stored in knowledge graphs, how to store and retrieve data more efficiently has become an important issue in knowledge graph research.

As mentioned in Sect. 12.1, knowledge graphs take the form of a directed graph structure, which can help to describe entities, events, and their relations in the real world. Each vertex represents an entity or event, and each edge stands for the relation between two vertices.

Figure 12.7 is a knowledge graph of Enrico Fermi, an American physicist.

The knowledge graph shows Fermi's nationality, date of birth, main achievements, job, and birth place. In addition, it includes information about Fermi's mentor, Max Born, such as his nationality, date of birth, main achievements, and job. Additionally, some information about Fermi's research partner, Julius Robert Oppenheimer, is presented, including his nationality, date of birth, main achievements, job, and the university he graduated from. Moreover, the knowledge graph also displays the size, average elevation above sea level, and postcode of Rome, the

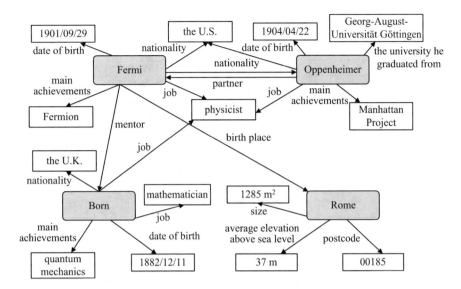

Fig. 12.7 A knowledge graph about Enrico Fermi

city where Fermi was born. Through the knowledge graph, a comprehensive understanding of Fermi can be gained.

Knowledge in knowledge graphs is represented using the RDF structure of the Semantic Web. Its basic element is a fact. Each fact can be represented as a triple (S, P, O) consisting of S, P, and O.

The triple corresponds to the triple (h, r, t) in knowledge graphs. Regarding the triple (S, P, O), S, P, and O stand for subject, predicate, and object, respectively. The value of each argument in the triple can be entities, events, concepts, strings, numerals, and so on.

It is not difficult to see that the RDF structure of the Semantic Web is also a triple, which corresponds to the triple (h, r, t) in Sect. 12.1.

For example, the knowledge graph in Fig. 12.7 can be represented by the following list of triples.

<S,	P,	O>
<Fermi,	main achievements,	Fermion[1]>
<Fermi,	date of birth,	1901/09/29>
<Fermi,	nationality,	the U.S.A.>
<Fermi,	job,	physicist>
<Fermi,	birth place,	Rome>
<Fermi,	mentor,	Born>

(continued)

---

[1] In 1926, Fermi discovered that Fermi-Dirac statistics is applicable to all particles that follow Pauli's principle of incompatibility. These particles are called Fermion.

<S,	P,	O>
<Fermi,	research partner,	Oppenheimer>
<Born,	main achievements,	quantum mechanics>
<Born,	date of birth,	1882/12/11>
<Born,	nationality,	the U.K.[2]>
<Born,	main achievements,	quantum mechanics>
<Born,	job,	mathematician>
<Born,	job,	physicist>
<Oppenheimer,	main achievements,	Manhattan Project>
<Oppenheimer,	date of birth,	1904/04/22>
<Oppenheimer,	nationality,	the U.S.A.>
<Oppenheimer,	job,	physicist>
<Oppenheimer,	graduated from,	the University of Göttingen[3]>
<Oppenheimer,	academic partner,	Fermi>
<Rome,	size,	1285 m^2>
<Rome,	average elevation,	37 m>
<Rome,	post code,	00185>

The example above shows that rich information can be stored in knowledge graphs. To extend the applicability of knowledge graphs, an important issue is finding an easy way to store information in knowledge graphs.

In practice, storage of information in knowledge graphs can fall into table-based storage and graph-based storage according to how the storage task is accomplished.

1. Table-based storage

For this type of information storage, two-dimensional tables are used to store information in knowledge graphs. Knowledge graphs can have different table structures due to their different design principles.

(a) Tables of triples: Facts in knowledge graphs can be represented by a series of triples, so a table of triples can be used to store the factual information. Table 12.1, in which information about Fermi and Born is stored, is an example.

   Such a table of triples can be easily understood. However, if all the information in a knowledge graph is stored in only one table, the list will be excessively large. As a result, operations such as queries, insertions, edits, and deletions will consume too much memory. In addition, as a table of triples includes only three fields, query efficiency will be compromised. For instance, if users want to search for Fermi's nationality, main achievements, and date of birth, the task will be divided into three queries, i.e. Fermi's

---

[2] Born in Germany, Born, a Jew, was the leader of the Göttingen school of physics. He made a significant contribution to quantum mechanics. He moved to England in 1933 and obtained British nationality.

[3] Born in the United States, Oppenheimer graduated from Harvard University as an honorary student in 1925, then transferred to the University of Göttingen, Germany, in 1926, and finally received a doctorate from the University of Göttingen in 1927.

Table 12.1 A table of triples for knowledge storage

S	P	O
Fermi	Main achievements	Fermion
Fermi	Date of birth	1919/09/29
Fermi	Job	Physicist
Fermi	Nationality	The U.S.
Fermi	Birth place	Rome
Fermi	Mentor	Born
Born	Main achievements	Quantum mechanics
Born	Job	Physicist
Born	Job	Mathematician
...	...	...

Table 12.2 Two tables of classes to store information in knowledge graphs

A table of cities

Subject	Size	Average elevation above sea level	Postcode	
Rome	1285 m^2	37 m	00185	

A table of figures

Subject	Main achievements	Nationality	Date of birth	Birth place
Fermi	Fermion	The U.S.	1901/09/29	Rome
Oppenheimer	Manhattan Project	The U.S.	1904/04/22	
Born	Quantum mechanics	The U.K.	1882/12/11	

nationality, Fermi's main achievements, and Fermi's data of birth. How time-consuming it is!

(b) Tables of classes:

Storing information in knowledge graphs by using tables of classes means that a table needs to be created for each class of information. Information that belongs to the same class should be stored in the same table. Each column of such a table represents an attribute of the entities belonging to that class, while each row stands for an instance of the entity class. For example, as shown in Table 12.2, a table of cities and a table of figures can be used to store information about cities and figures, respectively.

However, if different classes share one or more attributes, repeated storage and data redundancy will be brought about. For instance, Born is both a physicist and a mathematician. As shown in Table 12.3, if his information is stored in the table of physicists and the table of mathematicians, duplicate data in the two tables will lead to data redundancy.

In Table 12.3, the information about Born such as "subject," "main achievements," "nationality," and "date of birth" is stored in both tables.

A solution to this problem is tiered storage, which aims to store the attributes shared by different entity classes in an upper-layer table so that

Table 12.3 An example of data redundancy in tables of classes

A table of physicists

Subject	Size	Nationality	Date of birth
Born	Quantum mechanics	The U.K.	1882/12/11
Fermi	Fermion	The U.S.	1901/09/29
Oppenheimer	Manhattan Project	The U.S.	1904/04/22

A table of mathematicians

Subject	Size	Nationality	Date of birth
Born	Quantum mechanics	The U.K.	1882/12/11

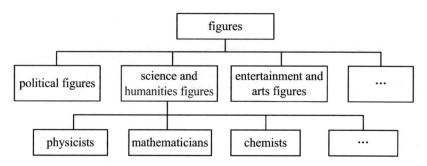

Fig. 12.8 A hierarchical table of classes of figures

the attributes can be inherited by lower-layer tables. An example is the following hierarchical table of classes.

Figure 12.8 is a hierarchical table of classes of figures. The top layer is "figure"; the middle layer includes "political figures," "science and humanities figures," "entertainment and arts figures," and so on; the bottom layer consists of more specific classes of figures. For example, science and humanities figures include physicists, mathematicians, chemists, and so on.

Accordingly, we can avoid data redundancy by storing Born's attributes such as subject, gender, date of birth, and nationality in a table of figures, the subject attribute in a table of science and humanities figures, and attributes such as subject and main achievements in a table of physicists and a table of mathematicians (see Fig. 12.9).

In Fig. 12.9, tiered storage enables users to obtain information about an entity in a hierarchical manner.

However, when a query involves different types of entities, this type of structure will require linking between multiple tables and thus occupy much memory. Therefore, it is difficult for the table structure to cope with complex queries.

(c) Relational databases:

Knowledge in knowledge graphs can also be stored in relational databases.

Relational databases describe things in the real world on the basis of their attributes. The potential values of each attribute constitute a set called the field

a table of figures

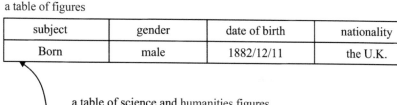

subject	gender	date of birth	nationality
Born	male	1882/12/11	the U.K.

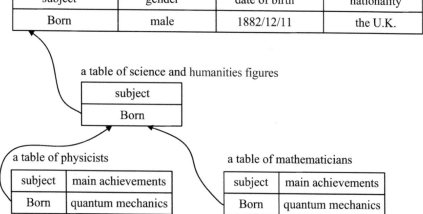

a table of science and humanities figures

subject
Born

a table of physicists

subject	main achievements
Born	quantum mechanics

a table of mathematicians

subject	main achievements
Born	quantum mechanics

Fig. 12.9 A hierarchical table of classes

of the attribute. The field can only include atomic data, such as integers and strings, which cannot be broken down further.

Data are organized and stored in relational databases in the form of two-dimensional tables. Each column of a two-dimensional table represents an attribute, while each row stands for an instance. The number of attributes is not limited in the table, so the two-dimensional table is strongly capable of representing knowledge.

What follows are keys to represent attributes of data in relational databases.

(i) Candidate keys: A candidate key refers to the minimal set of attributes that can uniquely identify an instance in a table. In other words, for a given instance, its candidate key has a unique value in one table, so different instances cannot be characterized by the same candidate key value. In addition, the attributes of a candidate key should be minimal, that is, all the attributes involved are necessary. If any attribute is deleted, the remaining attributes cannot constitute a candidate key.

(ii) Primary keys: If a table includes multiple candidate keys, one of them can serve as the primary key. In practice, a candidate key with only one attribute is often selected as the primary key.

(iii) Foreign keys: If an attribute or a set of attributes in one table is the candidate key in another table, the attribute or the set of attributes is called the foreign key of the current table. Foreign keys can guarantee data consistency between different tables.

If an attribute is included in a candidate key, it is called a primary attribute. Otherwise, it is called a non-primary attribute.

Through structure query language (SQL), relational databases provide users with a series of operational accesses. The core functions of SQL include insertions, edits, deletions, and queries. If relational databases are used to

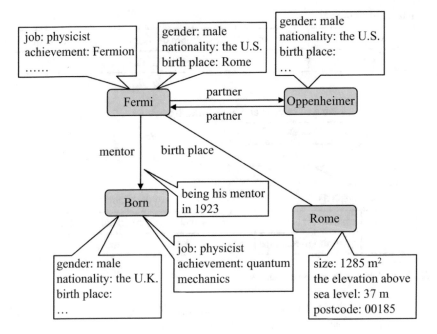

Fig. 12.10 An instance of graph-based storage

store information in knowledge graphs, all the operations should conform to the conventions of SQL.

2. Graph-based storage

If entities and their relations are perceived as vertices and edges in a graph, then the way to organize data in knowledge graphs can be regarded as a graph structure. Graph-based storage is directly based on the inner structure of knowledge graphs, so it can facilitate information retrieval from knowledge graphs. Fig. 12.10 exemplifies graph-based storage.

When the graph-based storage approach is adopted, different tables can be used to define the different attributes of the entities represented by the vertices. For graph-based storage, entities are organized in a way different from table-based storage. For example, for the vertex Fermi in Fig. 12.10, a table can be created to define Fermi's job (physicist) and main achievements (Fermion). Another table can be utilized to define Fermi's gender (male), nationality (the U.S.A.), and birth place (Rome). In addition, tables can also help to define the attributes of the edges. For instance, Born is Fermi's mentor. The relation is not only defined by the edge marked with "mentor" but also detailed by a table that shows Born became Fermi's mentor in 1923.

Data in knowledge graphs are organized in a graph structure, so graph-based storage can directly help to store and represent knowledge in knowledge graphs.

The mathematical foundation of graph structure is graph theory. According to graph theory, a graph G can be defined as a bi-tuple (V, E), where V and E stand for a set of vertices and edges respectively.

$$G = (V, E)$$

A graph query task endeavors to find the query graph from the given graph data. In mathematics, the task is a problem of identifying whether the query graph is a sub-graph within a set of graph data. The problem is called sub-graph mapping.

Sub-graph mapping can be defined as follows.

Given a query graph Q and a set of target graphs D, sub-graph mapping aims to determine in D all the sub-graphs that are isomorphic to Q.

However, sub-graph mapping has been proven an NP complete problem. In other words, no algorithm with polynomial time complexity can help to solve the problem at present. As a result, researchers try to circumvent the difficulty in practice. Instead, they tend to make use of the rich data in knowledge graphs to reduce algorithm complexity and accomplish a not-so-complicated sub-graph mapping task.

Bibliography

1. Jun, Zhao, Kang Liu, Shizhu He, and Yubo Chen. 2019. *Knowledge Graphs*. Beijing: Higher Education Press.
2. Lee, Tim Berners, James Hendler, and Ora Lassila. 2001. The Semantic Web. *Scientific American* 284 (5): 28–37.
3. Xianpei, Han, and Jun Zhao. 2010. Structural Semantic Relatedness: A Knowledge-Based Method to Named Entity Disambiguation. In *Proceedings of the 48th Annual Meeting of the Association for Computational Linguistics*, 50–59. Association for Computational Linguistics.
4. Zhiwei, Feng. 2021. Knowledge Graph – An Important Resource in NLP. *Journal of Foreign Languages* 5: 1–6.

Chapter 13
Concluding Remarks

The development of the Internet has led us into the era of big data, which has amazingly accelerated statistics-based research on NLP.

To a large extent, such accelerated development has been driven by the following three synergistic trends.

The first trend has been the building of tagged corpora. Currently, large-scale and massive spoken and written corpora of languages are available to NLP researchers due to support from the Linguistic Data Consortium (LDC) and other relevant organizations. Importantly, among them have been labeled corpora such as Penn Treebank, Prague Dependency Tree Bank, PropBank, Penn Discourse Treebank, RST-Bank, and TimeBank. These corpora with different levels of markers, such as syntax, semantics, and pragmatics, are standard text language resources containing a wealth of linguistic knowledge. These marked language resources greatly promote the use of supervised machine learning to handle the traditionally very complex problems of automatic syntactic analysis and automatic semantic analysis. These language resources also promote the establishment of competitive evaluation, mainly including automatic parsing, information extraction, word sense disambiguation, Q-A systems, and automatic abstracting.

The second trend is statistical machine learning. In the era of big data, a growing emphasis on machine learning has prompted more frequent dialogues between researchers of NLP and those of statistical machine learning. Topics such as support vector machine technology, maximum entropy technology and their formally equivalent multinomial logistic regression, schema Bayesian model, DL, and other technologies have become important issues within NLP.

The third one is the development of high-performance computer systems. Today, the wide application of a high-performance computer system provides favorable conditions for large-scale training and performance of machine learning, which was absolutely beyond our imagination in the last century.

Recently, large-scale unsupervised machine learning has gained renewed attention. The progress of statistical methods in machine translation and text theme simulation suggests that we can also train an effective machine learning system

© Springer Nature Singapore Pte Ltd. 2023   787
Z. Feng, *Formal Analysis for Natural Language Processing: A Handbook*,
https://doi.org/10.1007/978-981-16-5172-4_13

using a completely unlabeled corpus in addition to using annotated ones. However, difficulty and high cost in building reliable tagged corpora have limited the use of supervised machine learning in many cases. As a result, more unsupervised machine learning methods will be adopted, reducing the cost of building annotated corpora.

Accordingly, current research on NLP follows the prevailing empirical approach based on linguistic data rather than the rationalist approach based on linguistic rules.

However, most NLP researchers are not complacent about the brilliant achievements of linguistic-data-based empirical methods.

Lori Levin, a computational linguist, put forward a thought-provoking proposal at the Symposium on Linguistics and Computational Linguistics organized by European Association of Computational Linguistics (EACL) in 2009, calling for attention paid to the basic research on linguistics and setting up of a special linguistic committee in the Association of Computational Linguistics (ACL). Levin pointed out that linguistics has been essentially placed in a very secondary position in current NLP engineering and that almost all practitioners are engaged either in program technology or algorithms, leaving behind the linguistic issues hidden behind NLP engineering. Consequently, NLP has actually become a discipline without linguistic support, indicating that linguistics is completely out of its proper place in the study of NLP.

In 2009, Shuly Wintner, a senior lecturer in the Department of Computer Science, Haifa University, Israel, published an article entitled "What Science Underlies Natural Language Engineering" in the *Journal of Computational Linguistics* (Vol. 35, No. 4), in which she strongly calls for linguistics returning to computational linguistics.[1]

Shuly Wintner pointed out that in the big data environment, we have completed the overall paradigm transformation of NLP. The previously rule-based paradigm could no longer meet the needs of handling large-scale authentic texts. The failure to apply linguistic rules to the extended data in the real world and the dominant role that the theory of formal linguistics plays prompt a shift toward the use of corpora and toward the use of language itself as our potential knowledge resources. In line with this shift, subtle changes in the goal of NLP have begun to emerge. Twenty years ago, NLP researchers were interested in developing application systems and in basic research such as the formalization of linguistic processes and automatic reasoning. Currently, they are only interested in developing the application system and indifferent to basic research, such as the formalization of linguistic processes and automatic reasoning. Most papers presented at important conferences in the field are about engineering solutions to practical problems, whereas few papers are devoted to an investigation into basic linguistic issues. Alas, NLP engineers do not study linguistics after all.

---

[1] S. Wintner, What Science Underlies Natural Language Engineering? *Computational Linguistics*, 35(4), 2009.

We wonder what science actually supports NLP engineering. What is the theoretical basis for its application? Definitely, it should be linguistics. Matter-of-factly, all NLP engineers should study linguistics.

Anyone interested in issues concerning NLP applications, such as machine translation, part-of-speech tagging, lexical ambiguity resolution, random parsing, text classification, automatic Q-A systems, semantic role tagging, speech recognition, and knowledge ontology development, should ask himself what kind of science NLP is based on, which theory supports it, and where its theoretical fulcrum lies. Obviously, the answer to all of these questions lies in linguistics.

Therefore, Wintner concludes that no application of NLP systems without linguistic knowledge as the basis can go far. NLP is certainly not a branch of applied statistics. If so, NLP systems would be indistinguishable from nonverbal processing systems such as DNA sequences, musical scores, and board games. There must be something unique in the NLP system that deals with linguistic strings, something that can be generalized theoretically and that can be studied in a scientific sense. I believe that is the natural language, whose defining feature makes an NLP system special. Therefore, the only science that guides NLP practitioners is linguistics. In fact, the more new things there are in the linguistic world, the more NLP can benefit from them.

Wintner is an NLP expert with knowledge of computer science. Her far-sighted advice is much appreciated.

In 2011, Kenneth Church, an American computational linguist, published an article entitled "A Pendulum Swung Too Far" in *Linguistic Issues in Language Technology* (Vol. 6, No. 5, 2011), which deserves our close attention.[2]

In this article, Church recalls why he and his younger colleagues organized a "Special Interest Group for Data" (SIGDAT) in the Association of Computational Linguistics (ACL) in the 1990s. "At that time, out of practical considerations, we set up a special interest group to study data in a way separate from the rationalist approach," he says. "Because data is now easily obtainable, we can take it and use it. It is better to push the boat down the river with the current and do something approachable by picking the readily available fruits on the low branches of the big tree instead of aiming unreasonably high." The approach they followed is an empirical one based on linguistic data.

At that time, those youngsters were just trying to gain a foothold among the numerous interest groups in ACL without much bigger ambitions. A few years later, however, the empirical approach based on linguistic data in NLP not only revived but also achieved great success due to the use of big data, finally becoming the mainstream method of NLP. As a result, statistical research on linguistic data has become increasingly important. Church and SIGDAT's young colleagues take the lead in picking the readily available fruits on the low branches of large trees and have achieved encouraging achievements by using statistical methods based on linguistic

---

[2] K. Church, A Pendulum Swung Too Far, *Linguistic Issues in Language Technology*, 6(5), 2011.

data. What they have achieved shows they did have a foresight when they established SIGDAT.

If Church and his colleagues had followed their teachers closely and had been confined themselves to the narrow world of rationalistic methods based on language rules, they would not have had such brilliant achievements as today.

However, they were not carried away by their achievements. Instead, Church is clearly aware of the fact that the pendulum of this linguistic-data-based empirical approach has swung too far. He was wondering who will pick the fruits on the top of the tree and how people could pick them if all the low-hanging fruits have been picked up. He believes that to pick the fruits on the top of the tree, people should rely on structural linguistic knowledge.

In his article, Church suggested that his students should earnestly study the knowledge of linguistics and various rules in linguistics. They should integrate linguistic rules into statistical methods. Only when linguistic-data-based empirical methods are combined effectively with linguistic-rule-based rationalist methods can it be possible to pick off the fruits on the tall branches.

Apparently, the introduction of linguistic rules to linguistic-data-based empirical methods can counterbalance the limitations of statistical methods, making empirical methods even more powerful. Therefore, in the big data environment, the key to the NLP development is to closely integrate empirical methods with rationalistic ones.

In June 2012, the Google Brain Project was released by *the New York Times*. This project trains a machine learning model based on "deep neural networks" (DNNs) using a parallel computing platform with 16,000 CPU cores. DNNs have achieved great success in speech recognition and image recognition.

In November 2012, Microsoft publicized a fully automatic simultaneously interpreting system at an event in Tianjin, China. This system completed, smoothly, English speech recognition, English-Chinese translation, and Chinese speech synthesis simultaneously when a speech was delivered in English at that event. The speaker later revealed that the key technology behind this is also DNN, a deep learning (DL) model.

On September 16, 2014, Jiangsu TV's Program, "Raid the Gate," welcomed a "nonhuman" challenger, an intelligent robot called "Xiaodu." He interacted with the host and answered all 40 questions ranging from music, film, television to history and literature in fluent Mandarin. His excellent performance won the audience a lot of applause. From time to time, the room burst out cheerful laughter. Robot Xiaodu is a product developed and promoted by Baidu's Natural Language Processing Department. To develop this intelligent robot, the researchers also trained computers to interpret the meaning of the natural language through DL methods and to formulate answers to questions raised from massive web data, conducting an "in-depth Q-A." Currently, this DL model has also been applied to intelligent search by Baidu, having completed technological upgrades and breakthroughs in more complex grammatical structures and semantic relations in Chinese.

This shows that in the era of big data, to build a relatively complex DL model, knowledge of linguistics, mathematics, and computer science should be

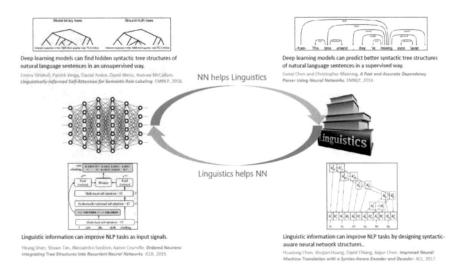

Deep learning models can find hidden syntactic tree structures of natural language sentences in an unsupervised way.

Emma Strubell, Patrick Verga, Daniel Andor, David Weiss, Andrew McCallum. *Linguistically-Informed Self-Attention for Semantic Role Labeling.* EMNLP, 2018.

Deep learning models can predict better syntactic tree structures of natural language sentences in a supervised way.

Danqi Chen and Christopher Manning. *A Fast and Accurate Dependency Parser Using Neural Networks.* EMNLP, 2014.

NN helps Linguistics

Linguistics helps NN

Linguistic information can improve NLP tasks as input signals.

Yikang Shen, Shawn Tan, Alessandro Sordoni, Aaron Courville. *Ordered Neurons: Integrating Tree Structures into Recurrent Neural Networks.* ICLR, 2019.

Linguistic information can improve NLP tasks by designing syntactic-aware neural network structures.

Huadong Chen, Shujian Huang, David Chiang, Jiajun Chen. *Improved Neural Machine Translation with a Syntax-Aware Encoder and Decoder.* ACL, 2017.

Fig. 13.1 Linguistics and deep learning boost each other

comprehensively combined to fully explore the rich information contained in the massive amount of language data, moving NLP research onto a brand-new stage. And NLP has an encouraging glorious prospect.

Over the past few years, with the development of DL, neural networks (NNs) have played an increasingly important role in NLP. As a result, some people even think that linguistic knowledge is useless for NLP. However, I don't think this view holds water.

In fact, linguistics is instrumental in DL (NNs) only if linguistic knowledge can be formalized. Only formalized linguistic knowledge can be integrated into DL (NN) and can be used by computer.

Formalized linguistic knowledge as an input signal can be used either to enhance the effect of DL (NN) or to improve the performance of the NLP system by assigning syntactic-aware NN structures, thereby advancing the research on DL (NN).

Conversely, DL (NN) can be of great help to linguistics. DL (NN) models help explore hidden syntactic tree structures behind the superficial strings of the natural language by using unsupervised learning methods. Similarly, these models attempt to predict better syntactic tree structures in the natural languages by using supervised learning methods.

Therefore, linguistics and DL (NNs) boost each other, as is clearly illustrated in Fig. 13.1. The upper part of the figure shows that DL (NN) can help linguistics, and vice versa, as shown in the lower part of the figure.

At present, we have made remarkable achievements in big-data-driven DL, but we have just started research on linguistic-knowledge-driven DL. We must continue to work at it as "the road ahead is rough and long."

F. Bacon (1561–1626, Fig. 13.2), British empiricist, opposes both rationalism and narrow empiricism. He pointed out that different views held by rationalists and

Fig. 13.2 Bacon

empiricists stand adversely in the way of the healthy development of scientific knowledge. To improve the situation, he put forward a collaborating principle that both rationalists and empiricists should follow. He said, "I thought I had, permanently, established a truly legal marriage between empiricism and rationalism. However, a lack of harmony and the unhappy divorce between the two had left all affairs of the human family in chaos."[3] He said vividly and profoundly, "Historically, those who have dealt with science have been either experimentalists or dogmatists." Experimenters, like ants, only collect data and use them, whereas rationalists are like spiders that weave a web of their own materials. Bees, unlike experimenters and rationalists, gather materials from flowers in gardens and fields and digest them with their own power. This is what the true mission of philosophy is. It is neither completely nor mainly dependent on the mental ability, nor is it just to keep the materials obtained from nature, history, and mechanical experiments intact and to store them by rote memory. Instead, the original materials should be retained after they have been interpreted and digested. There is, then, much to be hoped for if rationalism and narrow empiricism can be combined more closely and more tenuously than what has been done so far.[4]

As a well-known philosopher, Bacon's ideas are worth pondering. In the study of NLP, we can neither take rationalist methods such as spiders, relying solely on language rules, nor empirical methods such as ants, relying solely on statistics of data. Instead, both rationalist methods based on linguistic rules and empirical methods based on linguistic data should be combined closely and functionally, such as bees, to promote the development of NLP.

In 2019, an article entitled "Generative linguistics and neural network at 60: Foundation, friction and fusion" by Peter was published in *Language* (95(1) 2019), an internationally renowned linguistic magazine. Together with six response essays to this article on the same issue, the authors all focus on DL and linguistics research

---

[3] History of Foreign Philosophy, Department of Philosophy, Peking University, *Philosophy of Western European Countries in the 16th to 18th Centuries*, p. 8, the Commercial Press.

[4] Bacon, *New Tools*, p.75, the Commercial Press.

through connectionist methods, especially on friction and fusion of generative linguistics.

In his article, Peter calls for more dialogues between NNs and linguistics. He believes that generative linguistics will not be able to fulfill its commitment to the interpretation of language learning mechanisms if it continues to remain detached away from NNs and statistical learning.

In this regard, Berent and Marcus (2019) believe that connectionism and generative linguistics are fundamentally different. The solution to the issue is either to adhere to the parallel distributed representation of connectionism to make major adjustments to generative grammar theory or to replace both theories by another one. There will be no fusion between the two without a structured representation of the language after all.[5]

Dunbar (2019) believes that the fusion of DL and linguistics is now only a wonderful wish because the internal NN fails to explain the grammatical structure it learns and because the learnt grammatical structure does not correspond to generative grammar theory. Fusion is possible only when the implementational mapping problem between the two is resolved theoretically.[6]

Linzen (2019) expands on the above topics, believing that linguistics and DL can contribute to each other. Linguists can describe the language learning capabilities of NN models in detail and verify them through experiments; in return, NNs can simulate the process of human language processing, helping linguists to study the necessity of its internal constraints.[7]

Personally, I am in complete agreement with the ideas proposed by Pater and Linzen. To promote the further development of NLP, DL researchers and linguists should work together using both empirical methods and rationalistic methods, resulting in their mutual improvement and bringing out their best.

Scholars, in the golden age of linguistic-data-based empiricism, can readily pick off the fruits on the low branches using empirical methods in DL (NN), leaving behind the most challenging ones on the high branches for the coming generation. Therefore, we are indebted to inform scholars of the next generation that they should be aware of the limitation of the currently prevailing empirical methods and that they should not remain indifferent to now sidelined rationalist ones. At the same time, we should prepare them for innovation, advancing NLP research by tenuously integrating the empirical method with the rationalistic method.

Recently, an increasing interest in DL (NN) has added fuel to empirical methods based on language data. This enthusiasm will continue to dominate the field of NLP for many years, which may delay our scheduled return to a rationalist approach

---

[5]I. Berent, G. F. Marcus, No integration without structural representations: Response to Pater, *Language*, 95(1), 2019.

[6]E. Dunbar, Generative grammar, neural networks, and the implementational mapping problem: Response to Pater, *Language*, 95(1), 2019.

[7]T. Linzen, What can linguistics and deep learning contribute each other? Response to Pater, *Language*, 95(1), 2019.

based on linguistic rules. However, we always believe that in the study of NLP, the pace of the revival of rationalist methods will not change and that the fusion of empirical methods with rationalist ones leads its way to its brighter future.

In the *Formal Analysis for Natural Language Processing: A Handbook*, we introduce both linguistic rule-based rationalist methods and empirical methods based on linguistic data. It is hoped that readers will combine these two methods to further promote the NLP development.

Epilogue

It has been over 2 years and a half since the University of Science and Technology of China Press telephoned me to ask if I would like to publish the English version of my book *Theory and Method for Formal Analysis of Natural Language by Computer* (《自然语言计算机形式分析的理论与方法》). And now the English version of this book will be published in July this year. I am very delighted for its upcoming publication.

Since the object of natural language processing is the natural language, linguists consider it as a branch of linguistics; since natural language processing uses advanced computer science and technology to study and process the natural language, computer scientists consider it as a branch of computer science; since natural language processing has to study the formal structure of the natural language and algorithms of natural language processing, mathematicians consider it as a branch of applied mathematics. This clearly shows that natural language processing is not a pure scientific subject, but an interdisciplinary scientific one.

Approaches to formal analysis of the natural language have been constantly evolving, from rule-based approaches to statistics-based approaches, and further to neural network-based and deep learning-based approaches. This book provides a comprehensive and systematic introduction to these approaches to help readers learn and understand the full aspects of formal analysis approaches of the natural language and to combine these different approaches to advance natural language processing.

The publication of this book is a joint effort made collaboratively by many friends of mine.

The book was translated by three Chinese scholars, Prof. Lan Sun (孙蓝), Dr. Bo Sun (孙波), and Prof. Xiaowei He (何晓炜). Prof. Lan Sun was responsible for the translation of Preface, Concluding Remarks, and Chaps. 1, 2, 7, and 8. Dr. Bo Sun translated Chaps. 6, 9–12. Prof. Xiaowei He undertook the task of translating Chaps. 3–5. I would like to extend my sincere thanks to them.

My thanks also go to the project leader of the USTCP Xiumei Yu (于秀梅), and editors of the USTCP Panfeng Li (李攀峰), Xiangbing Xiao (肖向兵), Shuo Yao (姚硕), and Xinqi Yang (杨昕琦), for their conscientious work and ready help. They

© Springer Nature Singapore Pte Ltd. 2023 795
Z. Feng, *Formal Analysis for Natural Language Processing: A Handbook*,
https://doi.org/10.1007/978-981-16-5172-4

have coordinated the necessary tasks to make the publication of this book possible among three parties, the author, the translators, and Springer Nature. I am also indebted to Jingjing Hu (胡婧静), a Chinese teacher working at the Middle School Attached to University of Science and Technology of China, for her phonetic annotation of Chinese characters and Qianqian Zhang (张茜茜), a student pursuing a master's degree at the University of Science and Technology of China, for her help with the typesetting and proofreading of all the phonetic annotation of Chinese characters in this book.

I am grateful to Arul Vani, project manager at Springer Nature. During the translation of this book, she did a careful and meticulous editing to ensure the quality of the book.

The book is jointly published by Springer Nature and the University of Science and Technology of China Press.

As the author of the Chinese version of this book, I would like to express my sincere thanks to them all.

冯志伟

Zhiwei Feng
2022-04-15

Printed in the United States
by Baker & Taylor Publisher Services